Nation and Novel

begon 27 Mar 2011

Nation & Novel

The English Novel from its Origins to the Present Day

PATRICK PARRINDER

OXFORD
UNIVERSITY PRESS

OXFORD

UNIVERSITY PRESS

Great Clarendon Street, Oxford OX2 6DP

Oxford University Press is a department of the University of Oxford.
It furthers the University's objective of excellence in research, scholarship,
and education by publishing worldwide in

Oxford New York

Auckland Cape Town Dar es Salaam Hong Kong Karachi
Kuala Lumpur Madrid Melbourne Mexico City Nairobi
New Delhi Shanghai Taipei Toronto

With offices in

Argentina Austria Brazil Chile Czech Republic France Greece
Guatemala Hungary Italy Japan Poland Portugal Singapore
South Korea Switzerland Thailand Turkey Ukraine Vietnam

Oxford is a registered trade mark of Oxford University Press
in the UK and in certain other countries

Published in the United States
by Oxford University Press Inc., New York

British Library Cataloguing in Publication Data

Data available

Library of Congress Cataloging in Publication Data

Data available

Typeset by Newgen Imaging Systems (P) Ltd., Chennai, India
Printed in Great Britain
on acid-free paper by
Clays Ltd, St Ives plc

ISBN 0–19–926484–8   978–0–19–926484–1

For Anna and Monika, and for Mia and Eve

Preface and Acknowledgements

Nation and Novel is a literary history of the English novel and its distinctive, often subversive contribution to ideas of nationhood. In it I have concentrated for the most part on the major novelists, those whose writings have been most influential and have attracted a lasting and international readership. I have engaged in more detailed textual interpretation than is usual in literary history, pursuing the approach to the nature of the novel form and its relationship to English national identity that I outline in Chapter 1. My primary intellectual debt in writing this book has been to the small army of literary critics and cultural historians who have transformed the study of English fiction of the seventeenth, eighteenth, nineteenth, and twentieth centuries in recent decades. This book could not have been written without their labours of historical research, textual editing, cultural theorizing, and reinterpretation. Few of the scholars on whom I have drawn are explicitly named in the chapters that follow—the alternative would have been to have put their names, which can be distracting for the non-specialist reader, on every page—but my appreciation of their work is no less heartfelt for that. All citations in the text are identified in the notes, and it is there and in the Further Reading that my indebtedness can be traced.

Nation and Novel has taken me many years to write—I am embarrassed to say how many—and there have been a number of false starts. At every stage I have benefited from the encouragement, criticism, and support of more friends and colleagues than I can possibly name. Above all, I would thank the University of Reading for institutional and technical support and for research leave, and my students with whom I have discussed so many of the novels that feature in these pages. I am profoundly indebted to the Leverhulme Trust for granting me a Major Research Fellowship (2001–4), without which this book might never have been completed. I have received invaluable detailed comments from those friends who have been willing to read and criticize draft chapters or sections, including Eric Homberger (a comrade of almost forty years), Andrzej Gasiorek, David Gervais, David Smith, Zohreh Sullivan, and Jim Hurt. Earlier versions of some of this material have been given as seminar or conference papers and, in some cases, published in journals: in this respect I would particularly thank David Blewett, Regenia Gagnier and Angelique Richardson, Annette Gomis, Susana Onega, Max Saunders,

Joseph Wiesenfarth, Lawrence Phillips, Catherine Hall, and Stefan Kohl. Parts of Chapters 6, 9, 12, and 14 have appeared in a different form in *Eighteenth-Century Fiction*, *Victorian Literature and Culture*, and *International Ford Madox Ford Studies*, respectively. Others to whom I am deeply grateful for their encouragement, support, and intellectual stimulus include Coral Howells (the best of colleagues), Michael Foot (who sent me back to Disraeli and Hazlitt), Ron Knowles (who presented me with a complete set of Scott's novels), Robert Baldock, Christine Berberich, Maria Teresa Chialant, Christie Davies, Loraine Fletcher, John Lucas, Cora Kaplan, Hermione Lee, Michelle Reid, John Pilling, Sue Roe, Sita Schutt, Mohammad Shaheen, John Spiers, John Stotesbury, John Sutherland, Darko Suvin, Charles Swann, Marina Warner, Frances Wilson, and Michael Wood. In earlier years I learned much from two peerless critics of the novel, Tony Tanner and Raymond Williams. Some friends and colleagues have helped me most through a single conversation which set me on a track I might not have found for myself: I think particularly of Michèle Barrett, Andrew Gurr, Athena Leoussi, Giulio Lepschy, Brian Vickers, and others. For unfailing technical support (and so much else) I am indebted to Carole Robb, Jan Cox, and my daughter Monika. Special thanks are due to my editors at Oxford University Press, Sophie Goldsworthy, Andrew McNeillie, and Tom Perridge, and to my copy-editor, Mary Worthington, whose guidance and expertise have contributed immeasurably to this book in its final form.

My greatest debt is to Jenny Bourne Taylor, who has spurred me to keep writing, helped me to shape this work in more ways than she perhaps knows, and put up with the burden of living with its author with a love, cheerfulness, and forbearance that have never failed. Of Jenny's scholarship, intellectual curiosity, and deep knowledge of eighteenth- and nineteenth-century literature and history, all I can say is that they deserve a better book than this one.

P. P.

Contents

Introduction

NGLISH novels—like French, Russian, and American novels—are
read all over the world, and the fact that they express and help to
define a particular nationality is part of their appeal. Fictional
narrative gives us an inside view of a society or nation, just as it gives
access to personal experiences very different from our own. There are few
more enjoyable ways of increasing our knowledge and satisfying our
curiosity than reading a novel that we cannot put down. But the ideas and
information that we derive from reading fiction are not always easy to
single out. The Frenchness of a French novel, or the Russianness of a
Russian novel, is a thing that most readers (whether native or foreign)
only vaguely sense. Often it resides in impressions that are wholly or
largely subconscious as well as in those that are crudely obvious. The
same is true of English novels, with the added complication that English
identity has itself come to be seen as notoriously elusive and idiosyncratic.

We must begin, then, with a brief preliminary account of what the
historian E. P. Thompson once called 'the peculiarities of the English'.[1]
There is no written constitution and no readily available national ideology, as in the United States. There is no generally agreed name for
the Anglo-British state (England? Great Britain? The United Kingdom?
The UK?) except in a formal or ceremonial context. To the extent that the
state is held together by time-worn institutions such as the monarchy, the
House of Lords, and the national system of patronage and titles, it wins at
best a grudging allegiance from many English—and Scottish, Welsh, and
Northern Irish—people. But the British mainland with its three separate
nationalities has learned to live fairly easily with political and cultural
divisions. The necessity of division is enshrined in such typically English
social forms as the adversarial system of justice and the two-party system
(Government and Opposition) in Parliament.

What, then, is the novel's representation of Englishness? Does it reflect
what seems to be the national characteristic of unity-in-division? If the
answer to this question is far from being simple and straightforward, it is
not only because of the multiplicity of English novels themselves. The

novel is not patriotic propaganda, nor is it dispassionate analysis, and there is much truth in the observation that the truest fictional plots are the most deviant.[2] What Kipling called 'Just So Stories' are for children, not for adults. Moreover, many respected novelists and critics have described nationality as, ultimately, a trivial and accidental aspect of the novelist's art. Even the English novel's warmest admirers sometimes think of it as being 'English' in the way that Pimm's fruit cup or Stilton cheese are English.[3] Henry James, one of the greatest champions of the novel as an art form, hoped his readers would be unable to tell whether he was an American writing about England or an Englishman writing about America. More recently, Milan Kundera, the Czech novelist who became a French citizen, reminded us that a novel's aesthetic value cannot be judged in a narrowly national context.[4] But it is also true that much of the knowledge we acquire in reading novels is local knowledge, and that considering them solely in relation to an imaginary museum of world art can impoverish as well as enrich our experience. James Joyce is reported to have said that literature is national before it is international, and that 'If you are sufficiently national you will be international'.[5]

Joyce's great work was written at a time of Irish political and cultural revival from which he felt detached, and towards which he was often bitterly critical. Cultural historians often assume that there is a direct relationship between the state of literary art and the state of the nation, so that literary change becomes a metaphor for national resurgence or national decline.[6] There is no inevitability about such a relationship, although it is not merely coincidental that the English novel rose to prominence in the eighteenth century when Britain was fast becoming the centre of a world empire. The classic novelists from Defoe onwards speak from within the imperial nation even though they themselves were often indifferent, and in some cases hostile, to empire.

In the twentieth century the British world empire fell apart. The philosopher Bertrand Russell wrote in a personal memorandum dated 1931 that 'As a patriot I am depressed by the downfall of England, as yet only partial, but likely to be far more complete before long'.[7] His prognostication was correct so far as Britain's status as a world superpower was concerned, and the cultural climate after the Second World War was profoundly affected by a (possibly exaggerated) sense of national decline. As Margaret Drabble's narrator observes in *The Ice Age* (1977), there was 'no rational explanation for the sense of alarm, panic, and despondency' in the atmosphere of post-imperial England.[8] The same irrationality was found in many of the stimulants to a revived English patriotism in the years that followed. Imperial decline, however, may be a setting for national cultural revival as well as for cultural decline.[9] Whether and in what form this has taken place in the novel is a question I shall address at the end of this book.

An English novel as usually understood today is (i) written in the English language, and (ii) by an author of English nationality, descent, or domicile: English, that is, as opposed to American, Irish, Scottish, Welsh, or other forms of English-speaking national identity. Until the middle of the twentieth century the term was customarily used to denote all English-language fiction, but the different national traditions of anglophone literature are now routinely treated as separate from one another. Literary history of the kind exemplified by Richard Chase's *The American Novel and its Tradition* (1957) and Leslie Fiedler's bravura account of *Love and Death in the American Novel* (1960) identifies the novel as a vehicle for national myth and as the principal artistic expression of postcolonial nationhood. For critics like Chase and Fiedler, what is most significant about the American novel is its divergence from the supposed norm of the English novel. 'English novels', however, are not invariably written by authors who are English in the terms set out above; and one cannot enquire into the Englishness of the English novel without calling into question the central and normative status accorded to English fiction by a previous generation of critics. That status was, in any case, confined to anglophone fiction, since critics have always been aware that the English novel differed from, and was in some ways inferior to, its European counterparts. English novels were about adolescence and courtship where the great European novels were about adults committing adultery; and the humour, sentiment, and fantasy of the English narrator or storyteller was made to look self-indulgent and naive by continental doctrines of realism, aesthetic form, and artistic impersonality. These peculiarities of the English novel have left their mark on a very wide range of English-language fiction.

To distinguish English from other forms of anglophone fiction it is not enough to rely on an author's nationality, descent, or domicile. Domicile is frequently irrelevant in literary terms: nobody has ever called James Joyce an Austrian, Swiss, or French writer because he spent his writing life in Trieste, Zurich, and Paris. Someone of English descent, like the American Pilgrim Fathers, may cease to be English, while people of non-English descent are constantly becoming English. Whatever may be true of other nationalities, the term 'English novel' needs to allow for the autonomy of the imagination and the continual flux and reflux of migration and settlement in the modern world. We may best do this by invoking a third, surprisingly neglected, way of defining an English novel—a definition not by language or authorial nationality but by subject matter. According to this definition, a novel wholly or partly set within a fictionalized version of English society would qualify as an English novel. As it happens, some works that have hugely influenced the idea of English identity were written by non-English authors: Walter Scott's *Ivanhoe* with its portrayal of medieval England torn apart by bitter resentments between Saxons and Normans is perhaps the prime example. Scott is a Scottish novelist and poet whose life's work includes a series of novels with English settings. Other authors who qualify as 'English' under this definition include Tobias Smollett, Maria Edgeworth, Washington Irving, Henry James, V. S. Naipaul, and Samuel Selvon, although the degree of 'English' content in their works varies considerably. Boundaries must be drawn somewhere, so that I have excluded a novel such as Tayeb Salih's *Season of Migration to the North* (1966) from consideration despite its partly English subject matter, since it was originally written in Arabic. (There is, of course, a vast literature on England as seen by the non-English, including such a novel as J.-K. Huysmans's *A Rebours* (Against Nature) in which the Parisian hero, supposedly bound for London, never gets beyond the Gare du Nord, but this is material for a quite different study.)[10] An English novel for my purposes is an English-language work which may be considered 'English' in terms either of authorship, or subject matter, or both. I would add that a growing number of novels, including Rudyard Kipling's *Kim* which I discuss at length, may be seen to possess and to rejoice in dual nationality.

The role that subject matter can play in establishing the national status of fiction suggests the predominant reading method that will be used in this book. Not only is it what Peter Brooks calls 'reading for the plot', but it pays more attention to the ostensive signification and cultural coding of plot elements than to the rhetorical and formalist aspects that a critic such as Brooks would emphasize. However, I agree with Brooks that plot is the 'logic and dynamic of narrative', and that narrative is 'a form of understanding and explanation'.[11] Brooks opens his study of *Reading for the Plot: Design and Intention in Narrative* with an intricate analysis of Sir Arthur Conan Doyle's short story 'The Musgrave Ritual' (1894), which he describes as an 'allegory of plot'.[12] It would be equally plausible to call the story a national allegory (a term that I shall discuss in Chapter 1); but the truth is that once we have commented on the 'Englishness' of the relationship between Sherlock Holmes and Dr Watson, and analysed the mixture of Arthurian legend and aristocratic Royalist sentiment in the case that Holmes unravels, there is little more to be said. The story concerns the theft by the passionate Welshwoman Rachel Howells of the ancient crown of the Stuart kings from its ancestral resting-place with the Musgrave family, and the discovery that it has been thrown into a nearby lake. 'The Musgrave Ritual' resembles a great deal of modern popular fiction in that, far from offering any very original or startling view of national identity, it is largely content to reiterate the national stereotypes already exploited by earlier novelists. (The Holmes–Watson pairing is undoubtedly original, but the Musgraves and their hangers-on are stereotypical to the core.) It is for this reason that in the present book I have restricted myself to what is now called the 'literary' novel, as opposed to popular subgenres such as romantic fiction, the spy novel, the detective novel, fantasy, science fiction, and children's literature, not to mention film and television adaptations of all kinds of fiction. It is the classic English novelists, particularly those who have been the most widely read over the longest period, whose explicit or implicit conceptions of English identity were the most innovative in their own time, and who remain most influential or potentially influential today. Their novels, thanks in part to their inclusion on student syllabuses, the frequency of translations and media adaptations, and their widespread availability in inexpensive editions, retain an extraordinary currency in today's world.

We may assume that for fiction before 1950 the work of canonization has largely been done, although novelists such as Aphra Behn, William Godwin, Charlotte Smith, and Ford Madox Ford have only come back into favour quite recently. With English fiction of the middle and later twentieth century it is a different matter. My treatment here has been rigorously (some may say rigidly) selective, and I cannot deny that many good novelists have been excluded, or all but excluded, from the four chapters devoted to the twentieth century. Some of my choices arise naturally from my view of the earlier English fictional tradition; for example, throughout this book I have aimed to trace the novel's adaptations and transformations of central English myths such as the stories of Dick Whittington and King Arthur. In all cases, the novelists I have selected seem to me to express and explore national identity in challenging new ways. Their views and definitions of national identity are present, whether or not they are acknowledged, in the current, often agonized debates on the topic. To this extent, my decision to highlight the achievements of novelists such as Evelyn Waugh, V. S. Naipaul, Hanif Kureishi, and Meera Syal has a social and political bearing whether or not I agree with their expressed politics.

What, then, can a study of the English novel add to the topic of English and British identity as investigated by recent historians, social scientists, cultural commentators, and political journalists? First of all, the nature of national identity and of its now rather unfashionable counterpart 'national character' has been consistently debated by English novelists across the centuries. Secondly, novels are the source of some of our most influential ideas and expressions of national identity. Works of art which are enjoyed and appreciated by subsequent generations play a key part in the transmission and dissemination of national images, memories, and myths. Thirdly, the fictional tradition adds a largely untapped body of evidence to historical enquiry into the origins and development of our inherited ideas about England and the English.

At one extreme, this identity is traced back to the Anglo-Saxon foundations of English common law; at the other, it has been claimed that the English lacked a sense of common nationhood until the late nineteenth century.[13] Antony Easthope, a literary scholar, has described the period 1650–1700 which saw the fall of the Stuarts as 'the great foundational moment for Englishness'.[14] England, that is, is neither a revolutionary republic like France nor an absolute monarchy; it is a constitutional monarchy, the product of a failed revolution, a Restoration, and a historic compromise to establish the Protestant ascendancy and the ability of Parliament and the legal system to control the actions of the monarch. The same period saw the rise of British naval power, without which the nation's constitution would have been a matter of purely local interest; the growth of Dissent and the hard-won achievement of religious freedom; and the foundation of the Royal Society which symbolizes England's growing pre-eminence in empirical philosophy and natural science. But in literary and popular culture reaction to these foundational seventeenth-century events was somewhat delayed, so that English national pride was not fully developed—as the work of historians such as Linda Colley and Gerald Newman, among others, has shown—until the next century.[15] The new sense of Englishness found expression in journalism and satire and then in the novel, which was less in thrall to the state and more a vehicle for popular feeling than either poetry or drama. A number of the major novelists were also polemicists and historians concerned with English identity and English history. Critics of eighteenth-century English fiction such as Hazlitt and Scott were, perhaps, the first to identify and describe the 'cast of nationality' in the English novel. The development of the form from the earliest times to the twenty-first century has been intimately linked to changes in national consciousness in successive epochs. At the

same time, fiction is, at best, a distorting mirror of the society that produces it, since it is subject to varieties of class, caste, racial, gender, and
other kinds of bias that are, no doubt, the blindnesses contingent upon its
insights. Both blindness and insight are part of the historical record, but
the fictional canon will continue to change as new works come to join it,
familiar texts are reinterpreted, and novels either fall into or are rescued
from literary obscurity. A study of national identity in the English novel
cannot be more than a frozen snapshot of a moving object.

∼ I ∼

The Novel and the Nation

NOVELS are stories of ordinary people, not kings and princes. They are written in prose not verse, and are intended for silent reading, not recitation in public. A few novelists such as Dickens have given public readings of their work, but the fact that novels are not written for performance has profound implications for their relationship to the state and civic authority. Novels can be and are subject to censorship, but the reading of prose fiction is a private act. There are no court novelists or prose writers laureate, and patronage has played very little part in the history of fiction. Famous novelists are rewarded by their popularity, not by any kind of official status, and they have often depicted the apparatus of government from a satirical or subversive standpoint. They may speak to the nation but rarely, if ever, do they see it as their task to 'speak for the nation'. Novels exert a powerful influence on our perceptions of society and of our individual selves precisely because they lack any official sanction. Their authority comes from their readers and not from the cultural apparatus of the state.

The novel is a latecomer among literary forms. Unlike epic poetry, myths, drama, folk tales, and ballads it was not present at the origins of recorded history or the birth of the idea of nationhood. While there is a dispute over when the novel began—since some scholars extend the term to include all forms of prose narrative including romances and written folk tales[1]—it is clear that it could only come to prominence in an age of widespread literacy. The novel superseded both epic verse narrative and popular oral or semi-oral forms such as the ballad, but, unlike them, it was a medium of individual and not of communal expression—the product of a single author or narrator addressed not to an audience but to separate and isolated readers.

The distinction between the novel and forms of verbal expression which depend on performance for their full effect is a fundamental distinction in literary history and genre theory. The long-standing but never uncontroversial distinction between the novel and the romance is a secondary distinction, resting on the authority of individual writers and critics and

endlessly debatable, as experience shows. What is important in the present
context is the way in which the distinction between the novel and the
romance has shaped European literary and cultural history, for it was this
belief that brought 'the novel' into being. Without it, whether or not there
were individual novels, the novel as an institution could not exist. In
England the distinction was first formulated in the late seventeenth century.
William Congreve, the dramatist and occasional author of prose fiction,
wrote in his preface to *Incognita* (1692) that romances are 'generally
composed of the constant loves and invincible courage of heroes, heroines,
kings and queens, mortals of the first rank, and so forth'; they are
characterized by 'lofty language, miraculous contingencies, and impossible
performances'. Novels, by contrast, are of a 'more familiar nature'.[2] One
hundred and thirty years later Walter Scott distinguished between romance
plots, with their 'marvelous and uncommon incidents', and the novel
which is 'accommodated to the ordinary train of human events, and the
modern state of society'.[3] The distinction is not as clear-cut as these critics
have wished to suggest, since virtually all novels contain romance elements
such as coincidence, extremes of good and bad fortune, and a manifest
moral significance in events. The keyword of Scott's definition is, in fact,
'modern'; all attempts to separate the novel from folk tales and romances
depend on the novel's identification with rationality and modernity. To
anyone who is troubled by the restrictiveness of Congreve's and Scott's
definitions, we should simply say: for 'novel' read 'modern novel'.

Modernity is implied in the very word 'novel', which means, literally,
'news'. (The term was derived from Latin and first used in the seventeenth
century; in other European languages such as French and Italian it was
originally a plural form used of collections of short stories.) Folk-tale and
fairy-tale heroes are always the same, no matter how often their stories
are told, but a novel must be novel just as today's newspaper (also a
seventeenth-century innovation) must differ from yesterday's. Characters
in novels 'live and die once—in *their* novel'.[4] The story that each novel
tells is a new one, however neatly it fits an established pattern. Ian Watt,
who identified Defoe and Richardson as the first English novelists, called
them with pardonable exaggeration 'possibly the first great writers in
literature who did not take their plots from mythology, history, legend, or
previous literature'.[5]

Since poetry and drama must appeal to the ear, their use of traditional
plot material is (among other things) an aid to the listener's memory.
Novels must be decoded by the eye, forcing their readers to concentrate on
the printed page for long periods. The rise of the novel coincided with the

relegation of folk tales to an audience largely consisting of the preliterate, the subliterate, and the illiterate, and to forms such as the children's story, the pantomime, and the puppet show. Take, for example, the story of Dick Whittington and his cat, which since the late sixteenth century has been the principal folk tale associated with London. The story of Dick being summoned by Bow Bells to become the Lord Mayor was told in a play of 1604, in a printed ballad, and then in a prose narrative of 1636/7—*The Famous and Remarkable History of Sir Richard Whittington*, attributed to the dramatist Thomas Heywood. In 1668 the Whittington story was dramatized as a puppet show at Southwark Fair, where it was seen by the diarist Samuel Pepys. It was, wrote Pepys, an 'idle thing', but 'pretty to see'; he felt unaccountably moved by it.[6] As it happens, the Whittington story models one of the classic themes of later English fiction, as we shall see in Chapter 9; but no character in a novel, unless for the purposes of humour or satire, is likely to be named after Whittington. Pepys's diary, which reveals his minute-to-minute private experience and stamps his personality on everything he records, is far closer to the modern novel than are either the *Famous and Remarkable History* or the anonymous puppet show.

Pepys's diary was written between 1660 and 1669 in cipher—effectively, a secret language—and remained unpublished for some 200 years. In the printed form in which modern readers encounter it, it exemplifies many of the features that distinguish the novel from poetry, drama, or the folk tale: intimacy, unpredictability, private observation and confidential communication, and a certain aloofness from staged ceremonial and public performance. This aloofness or apartness of observation which is typical of the novel applies both to popular spectacles such as the puppet show and to the rituals of the court and the political world, the '*theatrical show of society*' which, as the Victorian essayist Walter Bagehot observed, enables the ruling class to impose its will on a nation.[7] Novels typically show individual characters, who are more or less outsiders, getting caught up in the public world that they first experience as distanced spectators. The peculiarity of the novel in this respect is closely matched by its social history as a narrative form.

The Novel and its Readers

The culture of aristocratic display finds a natural reflection in the poetry and drama of the court, but not in prose fiction, which can only serve the purposes of private entertainment, whether in court circles or in society at large. Some sixteenth-century narratives such as Sir Philip Sidney's *Arcadia* (to be discussed in Chapter 2) have a strongly aristocratic bias, but between Sidney's death in 1586 and Fanny Burney's appointment as a lady-in-waiting 200 years later there was no significant writer of prose fiction who would have been found personally acceptable at the English court. Novels, lacking the ceremonial value of poetry and drama, appealed to booksellers who stood to make money out of them rather than to aristocratic patrons. With a few exceptions, such as Scott's dedication of the Waverley novels to George IV, novelists have not addressed their works to a muse, patron, ruler, or other exalted personage. Jane Austen was deeply embarrassed when after the success of *Pride and Prejudice* and *Mansfield Park* she was commanded to dedicate her next novel to the Prince Regent.

The novelist as literary newcomer can easily be seen as a social intruder. The novel is famously a product of the commercial middle classes, describing the pomp and privilege of office for satirical effect but glorying in its protagonists' ability to stand on their own feet and rise on their merits. The poets of the late eighteenth and early nineteenth centuries lamented their marginality and their sense of exclusion from the social world; but novelists, who had always been marginalized, began at this time to supplant the poets in the public eye. The earliest English novelists tended to portray the experiences of criminals, rogues, prostitutes, orphans, and other displaced persons, as well as of women and children. It was Virginia Woolf who observed that 'the later works of successful novelists show, if anything, a slight rise in the social scale';[8] this is even more true of the history of the novel as a form. The upward mobility of the middle classes led to a society in which, while the monarchy and aristocracy still took nominal precedence, actual power and wealth increasingly belonged to the mercantile caste and their descendants. The novel, as we shall see, faithfully reflects this idea of the nation as what Bagehot called a 'disguised republic'.[9] As fiction began to dominate the literary marketplace, all authors came to be seen as tradesmen or entrepreneurs rather than as courtiers offering servility and literary flattery in exchange for aristocratic favours.

The novel, like any consumer product, is shaped by its readers' demands and capacities. Virginia Woolf summed up the reader's attributes in a posthumous essay:

He can pause; he can ponder; he can compare … He can gratify many different moods. He can read directly what is on the page, or, drawing aside, can read what is not written. There is a long drawn continuity in the book that the play has not. It gives a different pace to the mind. We are in a world where nothing is concluded.[10]

Woolf is of her time in referring to the reader as 'he' even though novel readers are so often female. Oral poetry and drama appealed to public audiences observing the social codes of male-dominated society. The novel, by contrast, inserts itself into the interludes of domestic life and finds its readers there. Its status as private reading-matter gives it its unstable and potentially subversive function in relation to the family and the community at large. Novels, in highly regulated societies, are treasured by the young because what they teach is intimate, immediate, and not to be found on any approved syllabus. They can only be read in periods of leisure, but the leisure is often stolen from time meant to be spent working, studying, in religious observance, or in some form of service to the community. (The novelist J. B. Priestley recalled that, during nearly five years in the army, he devoured books 'as if they were hot buttered tea-cakes'.)[11] The 'long drawn continuity' of fictional narrative encourages daydreaming, self-dramatization, and imaginative identification with the hero or heroine, all of which can take place outside the leisure hours specifically allotted to reading.

We must beware of associating daydreaming, imaginative identification, and other extended pleasures of reading solely with novels, since Robert Louis Stevenson, for one, claimed that they belong more exclusively to the romance.[12] (The classic English novels, in any case, have long been canonized and put on syllabuses, so that the book read by torchlight under the bedclothes is more likely to be a teenage novel or a work of contemporary popular fiction.) The revival of traditional romance from the late eighteenth century onwards had a huge impact on the novel, spawning subgenres explicitly mixing the characteristics of novel and romance such as the Gothic, the sensation novel, the thriller, the crime novel, science fiction, children's fiction, and modern fantasy. Frequently theorists of the novel praise the idea of romance with one hand while censuring it with the other; it is as if the intense, secret pleasures of reading should not be too freely indulged. William Hazlitt—perhaps the greatest early critic of English prose fiction—is exemplary in this respect. Hazlitt's essay 'Standard Novels and Romances' (1814; later revised in *Lectures on the English Comic Writers*, 1819) outlines a series of flexible, subtle, and occasionally puzzling contrasts between the novel and the romance.

Without romance, Hazlitt asserts, we should have no ideas of beauty, no hope, no belief in social progress. Romance is inextricable from desire, since it involves a 'longing after something more than we possess'.[13] But writers who pander too readily to our desires are condemned as 'wild and chimerical', 'romantic and impracticable' (23); their narratives blatantly falsify reality. The novel's task, according to Hazlitt, is to teach 'a knowledge of the world, through the airy medium of romance'.[14] The novelist should take us out of ourselves, while never forgetting 'the mortifying standard of reality' (6).

This 'standard of reality' applies not to a representation of our shared, public world based on documents that could in principle be verified (as in history and biography), but to fictional stories about it. The novelist draws us into a fictional community, often described as the novel's 'society' or 'world', which is knowable precisely because it is invisible and intangible. To read a novel is to be invited to share the private, unspoken thoughts of fictional characters—characters who are seen to act and behave like real people whose silent thoughts we could never know. The novel's reality, therefore, is something overseen, overheard; it has an intimacy that takes us beyond the limitations of personal experience. George Eliot, for one, believed that the novelist's task was to enlarge her readers' understanding of their community and their society: 'The greatest benefit we owe to the artist, whether painter, poet, or novelist, is the extension of our sympathies.'[15]

The communities represented in fiction are, necessarily, imagined communities; but if a novel is a representation of an imagined community then so, as many recent writers have argued, are our ideas of nationhood.[16] The nation, that is, is not a material entity like a country or a state. It is an invisible and (at least partly) theoretical construction which elicits powerful emotional and imaginative identifications. Patriotism or love of country, according to this argument, may imply an attachment to real things, but nationalism is loyalty to an idea. The 'nation-state' like the novel is a characteristically modern institution, a fact which leads the critic Franco Moretti, echoing a widespread consensus, to describe the novel as 'the symbolic form of the nation-state'.[17] But such generalizations should be treated with caution. The notion of a symbolic form is, in this context, hopelessly vague—are not Shakespeare's history plays, to be discussed in the next section, a symbolic form of the nation-state?— while the concept of the nation-state itself is much debated and cannot be taken for granted. To put the two ideas together is as epigrammatic as it is ultimately mystifying. What can be said at this stage is that novels have been influential sources of ideas of nationhood and national belonging, and that numerous English novelists from Defoe to Peter Ackroyd have doubled as commentators on England's history and national identity. There is, as we shall see, a direct link between the peculiarities of the novel as a literary genre and the part played by novelists in the definition of Englishness.

The Nation and National Literature

The idea of a national literature is inseparable from the phenomenon of national languages. In the transition from medieval to modern Europe, national literatures written in the vernacular took the place of the unified canon of ancient Greek and Latin authors. National literatures are therefore plural and exist in relation to one another; translation and cross-cultural adaptations have always been commonplace, and literary genres do not respect linguistic boundaries. The prose of fictional narrative is more readily translatable than poetry or verse drama. At the same time, novels typically draw upon a variety of dialects and registers, echoing the divisions of class, region, age, and occupation within each linguistic area. Novelists have frequently used the authority of the narrating voice to set up a hierarchy of discourses, paralleling the social hierarchy and privileging the written, the more elaborate, and the more educated linguistic registers over the spoken, the familiar, and the parochial. In fiction this hierarchy is usually manifested in the interplay between narration and dialogue. But the novel's presentation of narration and dialogue was influenced by earlier forms of writing, and particularly by writing for the stage where they are not formally distinguished from one another. In drama a hierarchy of discourses can only be established through stage rhetoric and the spoken voice, and Shakespeare is the great master of this practice in English. The variety of his dramatic language is in sharp contrast to the regularity and evenness of, for example, French neoclassical verse tragedy.

In Shakespeare there is verse drama with its 'mighty line' which has the effect of uniting the nation—or, at least, the national territory—with the power of the state, even as it calls the state to account; it speaks for and to the nation at the same time. John of Gaunt's dying speech is a famous example:

> This royal throne of kings, this scept'red isle,
> This earth of majesty, this seat of Mars,
> This other Eden, demi-paradise,
>
> .   .   .   .
>
> Is now leas'd out—I die pronouncing it—
> Like to a tenement or pelting farm.
>
> (*Richard II*, II. i. 40–60)

But Shakespeare sometimes uses narrative prose at moments of high dramatic emotion, as in the Hostess's account of the death of Falstaff:

'a parted ev'n just between twelve and one, ev'n at the turning o' th' tide; for after I saw him fumble with the sheets, and play with flowers, and smile upon his fingers' end, I knew there was but one way; for his nose was as sharp as a pen, and 'a babbl'd of green fields. 'How now, Sir John!' quoth I 'What, man! be o' good cheer'...So 'a bade me lay more clothes on his feet; I put my hand into the bed and felt them, and they were as cold as any stone; then I felt to his knees, and so upward and upward, and all was as cold as any stone.

(*Henry V*, II. iii. 11–24)

Falstaff and John of Gaunt die thinking of England, of the land and its neglected agriculture. For John of Gaunt it has become like a 'pelting' (paltry) tenant-farm, while Falstaff babbling of green fields must be remembering his neglected estate; when all is said and done, the roistering Knight of Eastcheap is a country squire who has left his substance behind. John of Gaunt's speech is a deathbed oration, a piece of public theatre theatrically represented, while the Hostess's account of Falstaff's death is familiar storytelling expressing deep feeling in the plainest and most colloquial terms. The difference between the two passages has little to do with the presence or absence of rhetoric—since the Hostess's narrative is full of figures of speech—but it very clearly relies upon a difference of social register, setting the polysyllabic Latinate vocabulary of the court against a series of plain Anglo-Saxon monosyllables which in the Hostess's speech become a kind of wild poetry. Put side by side, these passages from Shakespeare's historical cycle exemplify a deep split in the English language and English society.

Both extracts help to define the idea of a national literature. They do so, first, by virtue of their explicit or implicit subject matter—the land of England—although (as Paul Gilbert has written in a wide-ranging examination of this topic) something more than a certain kind of content is needed to typify a national literature. For Gilbert, 'the treatment of the subject matter must express an *insider's* view of it', but beyond that there are no intrinsic properties which belong to one literary nationality rather than another: 'What is exemplary of a national literature is something chosen to be so, without any grounding in properties that make it so.'[18] In other words, Falstaff's green fields are English by habitual association, not because the fields in other countries or literatures—the fields of Ireland, for instance—are necessarily less green. Within Shakespeare's own writing we can see, through abundant examples, how the associations of Englishness are built up. Gaunt's notion of England as Eden, a walled island-garden, connects not only to Falstaff's green fields but to some of the other details recalled by the Hostess: the time as marked by the turning of the tide, reminding us of London's situation as the capital and chief port of an island nation; and Falstaff's toying with the flowers, and his feet 'as cold as any stone', where the stone or rock is not just dead, inorganic matter but uncultivated ground. The potential of a national literature is present in these passages from Shakespeare, in ways that could never be forgotten so long as his plays continued to be performed and read. Moreover, the Shakespearian revival in the eighteenth century coincided with, and thus helped to shape, the rise of the English novel as a new branch of national literature.

With the rise of the novel came a shift in the literary idea of nationhood. In *The Making of English National Identity* (2003) Krishan Kumar adopts the distinction, first put forward in 1907 by Friedrich Meinecke, between the 'political' and the 'cultural' nation. The political nation is the nation as defined by John of Gaunt. It is, in Kumar's words, 'the "state-nation", rather than, strictly speaking, the "nation-state". It is a nation formed, in many cases, "from the top down", as in France, Spain and Britain where centralizing monarchies accomplished the main work of nation-building as the necessary complement to their state-making.' The cultural nation is, according to Kumar, the 'nation-state proper'; it is a concept in which the state arises from the nation rather than vice versa.[19] It is the idea of the cultural nation, not the political nation, that inspires cultural nationalism and popular independence movements. The political nation is monarchical and autocratic; the cultural nation is democratic, at least in the sense that the people, not God, are the ultimate source of political authority. Falstaff's Englishness belongs to the cultural, not the political nation, while Prince Hal, Falstaff's friend and adversary, mixes with the common people and later succeeds—as Henry V at the Battle of Agincourt—in enlisting the cultural nation in the service of the political nation.

But the novel's affiliations are with the cultural nation and not the political nation. In England, between the age of Shakespeare and the age of Defoe and Fielding there had come the revolutionary upheavals of the seventeenth century which brought the period of absolute monarchy to an end. Whether the immediate outcome was the transformation of 'state-nation' into 'nation-state', or simply a reformulation of the 'state-nation' in the interests of a new kind of oligarchy, is a question for historians, although the oligarchical nature of the eighteenth-century Whig Ascendancy is implicitly alleged in Fielding's *Amelia* (1752); later it would be fully charted in Disraeli's novels. What is important is that, with few exceptions, English novelists have not sought to balance the political and the cultural nation—the nation as seen from the top down and from the bottom up—in the way that Shakespearian drama does. Novels typically speak to us from outside the ruling elite but from inside the nation.

This book will ask how the novel has represented the cultural nation of England, not the political nation officially known as the United Kingdom of Great Britain and Northern Ireland. But the English outlook—like that of France and Spain, Kumar's other examples of 'centralizing monarchies'—has long been imperious and expansionist, leading to the formation both of an internal empire within the British Isles and to a global, seafaring empire. The result, according to Kumar, is a kind of nationalism stressing not ethnic identity but the nation's 'political, cultural or religious mission'.[20] But, while missionary activity is directed outwards, much of the power and magnetism of empires comes from their ability to draw people in and to bring them to the centre. Thus it goes without saying that many 'English' writers are of Welsh, Scottish, Irish, or more distant origin. It is in relation to the home population, not just the imperial diaspora, that 'Englishness' has long ceased to have any connection with ethnic purity. Strictly speaking, there never was such a connection, since all accounts of England's early formation agree that the nation was constituted by successive waves of immigrants—Romans, Angles, Saxons, Danes, Vikings, Normans, and others—so that ethnic mixing and miscegenation are at the root of Englishness. And, though England is an old country, the immigration and mixing continues. No definition of the national identity can ignore it.

It is due to the missionary nationalism of the internal empire that 'England' and 'Britain' have been so often confused as to become virtual synonyms in many contexts. Until very recently, Great Britain and the United Kingdom were customarily referred to as England. The distinction between Great Britain as the political nation and England as the cultural nation is neatly, if teasingly, summed up when Swift's Lemuel Gulliver speaks of the 'kingdom of Tribnia by the natives called Langden, where I had long sojourned'.[21] Gulliver, like the Anglo-Irish Jonathan Swift, was descended from an old English county family and normally describes his native country as England, but his use of the verb 'sojourned' begs the question of what kind of difference there is between a native and a long-term 'sojourner' or temporary resident. Can English identity be acquired voluntarily and through a process of naturalization like the issue of a British passport, or does it only belong to those who have resided long enough to develop, or inherit, what is known as the 'English character'? These questions have been intensely debated both by the earliest and the most recent English novelists.

In present-day arguments about immigration, but also in the work of novelists and commentators going back to Defoe, we can distinguish between radical and conservative definitions of Englishness. The radical definition is fluid, hospitable, and welcoming to immigrants while the conservative definition is static, defensive, and xenophobic to a greater or lesser extent. As we shall see in Chapter 3, Defoe's satire 'The True-Born Englishman' (1702) is one of the greatest sources of the radical definition of Englishness. A century later, it was enthusiastically endorsed by William Hazlitt; most recently, it has been quoted by the novelist Caryl Phillips at the start of his anthology of immigrant literature, *Extravagant Strangers* (1997).[22] Hazlitt described 'The True-Born Englishman' as

> a satire which, if written in doggerel verse... is a masterpiece of good sense and just reflection, and shows a thorough knowledge both of English history and of the English character. It is indeed a complete and unanswerable exposure of the pretence set up to a purer and loftier origin than all the rest of the world, instead of our being a mixed race from all parts of Europe, settling down into one common name and people.[23]

There are some underlying problems in this passage, since the idea of the 'English character'—relatively new in Hazlitt's day, as we shall see— could seem to be inherently biased in favour of the native and against the immigrant. Moreover, if the English have settled down into 'one common name and people', when did the settlement take place? According to the great conservative theorist Edmund Burke, England is an 'old establishment' with an '*antient* constitution of government' deriving from Magna Carta. Burke's 'firm ground of the British constitution' is a foundation likely to be radically disturbed by new waves of immigrants.[24] Popular hostility towards new arrivals and 'asylum seekers' is not likely, therefore, to be assuaged by simple appeals to national history. In conservative thought, however, the idea of the 'true-born Englishman' was taken at face value and Defoe's irony was soon forgotten. Walter Scott, for example, described Defoe's hero Robinson Crusoe (the English-born son of a German immigrant father), 'with his rough good sense, his prejudices, and his obstinate determination not to sink under evils which can be surpassed by exertion', as 'no bad specimen of the true-born Englishman'.[25] Crusoe has not merely acquired the 'English character'; he exemplifies it. Not only has Scott apparently forgotten that Crusoe was the son of an immigrant, but he uses the adjective 'true-born' in precisely the glib, journalistic sense that was the target of Defoe's mockery.

The division between the native and the immigrant is one between being and becoming English, or what Edward W. Said has called filiation and affiliation. Filiation is something we are born into, whereas affiliation involves a deliberate and self-conscious choice of allegiance. Said's account of modern culture speaks of the failure of filial relationships held together by 'natural bonds and natural forms of authority', and their replacement by affiliative links belonging 'exclusively to culture and society'.[26] But it can equally be argued that there is a constant reversion from 'cultural' to 'natural' bonds and from the affiliative to the filiative. In the tradition of the novel, for example, as well as in some of the classics of political thought, the nation is often implicitly or explicitly seen as a kind of extended family. This has the advantage of presenting national allegiance as a natural and filiative condition rather than an external discipline imposed by the power of the state. In families, however, survival and growth depend upon the readiness to welcome and absorb new members through marriage, since ingrown and unfertilized families wither and die. The process of intergenerational continuity in families transforms affiliation into filiation and incomers into natives. The 'national family' is an empty metaphor if one has to be born into the nation in order to belong to it.

National Character and National Identity

The philosopher David Hume argued in his essay 'Of National Characters' (1748) that 'each nation has a peculiar set of manners', and that 'some particular qualities are more frequently to be met with among one people than among their neighbours'.[27] National character, it was felt, arose from the process of imitation and mutual conformity natural to a settled population. Founded in historical continuity, it was threatened with disappearance in times of cosmopolitanism and mass migration. The idea of national character dominated discussion of cultural nationality during the eighteenth and nineteenth centuries, and it can still be met with today. Yet in the twentieth century, as Perry Anderson has noted, 'the discourse of national difference...shifted from character to identity', two terms which are by no means synonymous.[28] There is a continuing demand for quasi-biographical studies of nations and national cultures such as J. B. Priestley's *The English* (1973) and Jeremy Paxman's *The*

English: A Portrait of a People (1998), but the last serious academic study of national character, Ernest Barker's *National Character and the Factors in its Formation*, was published in 1927.

The emergence of the idea of national character has itself been linked to the rise of the novel, since fiction and biography are the literary genres most typically associated with character portrayal and character analysis.[29] The concept of character, in Anderson's words, is a comprehensive and self-sufficient principle, 'covering all the traits of an individual or a group'.[30] 'Character' like 'identity' may be invoked in purely external and summary fashion—in the sense that employers require character references and the police hold identity parades—but in the literary context, as George Eliot wrote, 'character...is a process and an unfolding'.[31] Moreover, character is not subjective; an individual cannot truly know his or her own character. It is for this reason that first-person narrators and autobiographers are notoriously unreliable, since readers are likely to arrive at a judgement of their character which differs to a greater or lesser extent from the narrator's declared self-perception. Conscious attempts to live up to our ideas of our own character introduce a histrionic, self-dramatizing element into behaviour, which may in the end lead—as, most famously, in Conrad's *Lord Jim* (1900)—to complete self-deception. To enquire into one's own character is to ask the, at best, very imperfectly answerable question 'What am I?', whereas enquiry into identity involves the much more negotiable question 'Who am I?'

The idea of character, then, presupposes an objective standpoint from which character can be observed in action or behaviour. The idea of character in fiction and biography also presupposes a degree of subtlety and complexity in human behaviour, since the literary presentation of character is typically an accumulation of apparently conflicting traits which cannot be understood without prolonged observation. (Even the most absorbing and memorable fictional characters, such as Robert Lovelace or Emma Woodhouse, can in principle be analysed as structures of oxymorons or self-contradictions.) Popular ideas of national character are very much simpler than the idea of character conveyed in fiction. Character in the novel, however, is fixed, since the actions through which it is revealed are circumscribed and there are no traits left to be exhibited once the novel is over. Biographies similarly end with the death of the individual subject, while national character is perpetually open to change. It is, then, hardly surprising that nearly all accounts of an achieved and settled national character are marked either by the fear of loss or by an unconcealed idealization and nostalgia. Early twentieth-century novelists' accounts of the English national character, like E. M. Forster's 'Notes on the English Character' (1936) and George Orwell's *The Lion and the Unicorn* (1941), can now be seen to present a more or less transient set of traits as essential and permanent. More recently the portrayal of national character has become a favourite medium for conservative elegies for the English nation, as in Peter Vansittart's *In Memory of England: A Novelist's View of History* (1998) and Roger Scruton's *England: An Elegy* (2001).

Some of the earliest accounts of the English 'national character' argued that the notion was a contradiction in terms and that it was the essence of Englishness—as opposed to Irishness, Scottishness, or Welshness—to lack a distinct character. For Defoe, the Englishman was a 'man akin to all the universe', a harbinger of the coming globalization of culture.[32] For Hume, England's perceived complexity and diversity meant that its sole national characteristics were those of internal difference and individual eccentricity:

> We may often remark a wonderful mixture of manners and characters in the same nation, speaking the same language, and subject to the same government: And in this particular the ENGLISH are the most remarkable of any people, that perhaps ever were in the world. . . . the ENGLISH government is a mixture of monarchy, aristocracy, and democracy. All sects of religion are to be found among them. And the great liberty and independency, which every man enjoys, allows him to display the manners peculiar to him. Hence the ENGLISH, of any people in the universe, have the least of a national character; unless this very singularity may pass for such.[33]

The term 'eccentricity' did not come into use until a generation after Hume. It is, Paul Langford has remarked, a more benign idea than Hume's 'peculiarity' and 'singularity', since it provides 'an engaging diversity without threatening conformity'. Eccentricity implies a common 'centricity' from which it deviates.[34] If this is very much in the spirit of Hume's passage, it is because the shift from character to identity as a basis for nationality is already implied in it. In fact, an underlying tension between character and identity runs through the whole tradition of thought about cultural nationality.

Identity, in Anderson's words, 'always possesses a reflexive or subjective dimension', involving self-awareness and self-identification.[35] The plot of many novels hinges on the external verification of an identity that the protagonist has all along embodied and seemed to take for granted—Tom Jones, for instance, behaves like a well-born young gentleman long before he is proved to be one—and first-person narratives typically describe the progressive construction or discovery of identity. There are conflicting models of identity, since the term refers both to an unchanging inward core of the self and to the sociological and psychological roles that individuals adopt. The modern view of identity leans heavily towards the provisional and performative, in which, as Anthony D. Smith explains, 'the self is composed of multiple identities and roles—familial, territorial, class, religious, ethnic and gender'. Similarly, the modern idea of national identity reflects the political ideology of nationhood.[36] National identity became an explicit concern in the late nineteenth and early twentieth centuries at a time of the construction of new nation-states, the persecution and mass migration of peoples, the collapse of established empires, and the compulsory introduction of passports for travel between states. Modern national identity always exists in relation to (though it is far from being identical with) the bureaucratic registration of nationality that governments impose.

Anderson adds that 'the preoccupations of national identity are a product of the material erosion of much of what was once associated with national character'.[37] National character, we may say, emphasizes the separateness of peoples, while identity comes to the fore in a world where nationalities are easily confused. The debate between national character and national identity can be observed in two of the principal Victorian theorists of nationality, Walter Bagehot and John Stuart Mill. Mill's liberalism leads him to emphasize the voluntary character of national communities, while Bagehot stresses the conservative inheritance of national character. According to Mill's definition in *Representative Government* (1861),

[a] portion of mankind may be said to constitute a Nationality if they are united among themselves by common sympathies which do not exist between them and any others—which make them co-operate with each other more willingly than with other people, desire to be under the same government, and desire that it should be government by themselves or a portion of themselves exclusively.

The emphasis here is on 'desire', the will to cooperate, and common sympathies. Mill admits the strength of the 'feeling of nationality', which is based on 'identity of political antecedents; the possession of a national history, and consequent community of recollections; collective pride and humiliation, pleasure and regret, connected with the same incidents in the past'. But he also discusses how small nations, including the Welsh and the Scots, are capable of blending into larger ones, and he believes that globalization and world government are in the long-term interest of the human race.[38] The advantage of separate nationhood is that for the time being it makes possible a cohesive and responsive political democracy. Mill's liberal definition of nationhood relies on voluntary affiliation, not unconscious filiation, and it implies that national loyalties have a pragmatic and temporary basis.

Walter Bagehot, by contrast, argues in *Physics and Politics* (1872) that nations have been formed and held together by the largely instinctual processes of 'unconscious imitation', including the 'imitation of preferred characters' and the 'elimination of detested characters', which took place during the ages of authoritarian discipline which preceded modern liberal democracy.[39] Bagehot defined a nation as 'a *like* body of men, because of that likeness capable of acting together, and because of that likeness inclined to obey similar rules'; their sense of common identity is the direct outcome of a long period of uninterrupted settlement during which the nation's character was formed.[40] Bagehot's Darwinian reasoning led him to question the ability of settled national characters such as the English (which he believed to be virtually unchanged since the age of Chaucer) to adapt to the changing conditions of the nineteenth century. Implicitly, Bagehot portrayed the form of the nation as what Victorian anthropologists and social theorists called a 'survival', a product of the archaic conditions of a previous era which could function only as a conservative symbol in the modern world. Modern democratic nations, he suggested, relied on the 'myth' of national character while repudiating the authoritarian and oppressive conditions that gave rise to it. Bagehot, however, believed that a 'real nation' like England, fortified by 'long ages of transmitted discipline', could survive the pressures of modern cosmopolitanism and globalization.[41]

Bagehot, then, is the theorist of national character where Mill is the theorist of identity. National character is an unconscious inheritance, while national identity for Mill is a matter of choice; but it seems that no sooner do we become conscious of national character than its existence is threatened. So far as fiction is concerned, there is a long history in which English novels have been read as expressing the English national character, but the novel itself has increasingly foregrounded questions of identity rather than character.

Character and Identity in the Novel

Henry Fielding, the most theoretically minded of the great early English novelists, was a strict neoclassicist who believed that all valid literature was derived from the ancient Greek and Roman literary forms. He could not, therefore, regard the novel as strictly novel. It must be a variation on something that already existed: hence his famous definition, in the preface to *The Adventures of Joseph Andrews* (1741), of the novel as a 'comic epic poem in prose'. His characters, likewise, were not intended as eccentric individual portraits but as representatives of immemorial human types such as the lawyer or the soldier.[42] Later eighteenth-century critics, however, saw Fielding, together with Defoe, Richardson, and Sterne, as 'novelists'— the precursors, that is, of a new and rapidly growing class of authors— rather than as writers in the comic epic mode. At the same time, they came to value Fielding's characters not (or not only) as universal and timeless portraits but for their local and historical authenticity. Criticism of the novel almost invariably entailed an awareness of the role of nationality in fiction. Fielding's novels were read as embodiments of Englishness, not of universal nature, and the novel in general came to be widely regarded as the principal source for a 'History of National Manners'.[43]

The new mode of criticism of fiction is exemplified in a passage from Walter Scott's *Lives of the Novelists* (1824):

Of all the works of imagination, to which English genius has given origin, the writings of Henry Fielding are, perhaps, most decidedly and exclusively her own. They are not only altogether beyond the reach of translation, in the proper sense and spirit of the word, but we even question whether they can be fully understood, or relished to the highest extent, by such natives of Scotland and Ireland as are not habitually and intimately acquainted with the characters and manners of Old England. Parson Adams, Towwouse, Partridge, above all, Squire Western, are personages as peculiar to England as they are unknown to other countries. Nay, the actors, whose characters are of a more general cast, as Allworthy, Mrs Miller, Tom Jones himself, and almost all the subordinate agents in the narrative, have the same cast of nationality, which adds not a little to the verisimilitude of the tale. The persons of the story live in England, travel in England, quarrel and fight in England; and scarce an incident occurs, without its being marked by something which could not well have happened in any other country.[44]

For all his no doubt sincere admiration, Scott is suggesting that Fielding's 'verisimilitude' has been bought at the cost of insularity, untranslatability, and obsolescence: in other words, it runs directly counter to the novelist's own neoclassical principles. Even the somewhat jocular reference to 'Old England' plays its part in reminding Scott's readers that the England of two generations earlier reflected in Fielding's novels now only survives in the imagination. Fielding was not, apparently, even aware that his personages were 'peculiar to England' and that they offered a true representation of the national character. It takes a cosmopolitan reader such as Scott—a reader thoroughly acquainted both with the English and with other nationalities—to see this, or so Scott implies. He does not define what he calls the English 'cast of nationality'—he rather assumes that those 'in the know' will know it when they see it—but he clearly thinks that the novelist should be a conscious analyst of national character, as he himself was. The Scottish novelist is gently patronizing the English one.

Scott's essay on Fielding has the effect of making space for a new kind of novel, the so-called 'national tale' by which he himself had been decisively influenced. The national tale originated in Irish fiction, in novels such as Maria Edgeworth's *Castle Rackrent* (1800) and Lady Morgan (Sydney Owenson)'s *The Wild Irish Girl* (1806) and *O'Donnel: A National Tale* (1814), where Anglo-Irish colonists were juxtaposed with typical specimens of 'native' Irish people. Scott's own Waverley novels often follow a young English gentleman on an expedition of discovery through lowland and highland Scotland. The term 'national allegory' has been applied to this kind of fiction, which sets English wealth and power against a defeated but potentially resurgent Celtic nationalism.[45] An earlier kind of national allegory, however, was of English, not Scottish or Irish, origin; this was the body of Augustan essay-writing and prose satire based around such obvious national caricatures as Joseph Addison's Tory squire Sir Roger de Coverly and John Arbuthnot's robust English tradesman John Bull. *The History of John Bull* (1712) has a cast of characters representing the contending nations in the War of Spanish Succession, but the satire is purely ephemeral and Bull's fame owes everything to the eighteenth-century cartoonists who turned him into the epitome of the truculent English bully.

If John Bull is the eighteenth century's most famous characterization of the typical Englishman, his nearest rival (as we shall see in Chapter 3) is Defoe's Robinson Crusoe. It is no accident, perhaps, that the novel in which he appears is for most of its length more sparsely populated than almost any other work of world literature. Novelists have usually been concerned with contrasts and differences of character, so that Fielding's reflection of Englishness in a novel such as *Tom Jones* is spread across several characters rather than being concentrated into a single one. Where, as often, these differences of character serve to dramatize the nation's internal divisions we have a form of national allegory which may be covert or hidden, rather than foregrounded as in the 'national tale'. An acute critical reader will often detect national allegory as a level of submerged meaning in the work of a novelist with apparently very different intentions. In the words of one recent literary historian, a novel may '*contain* the nation within its form, its structure, its silences'—above all, through the interplay of its characters.[46]

The strength of characterization in English fiction up to the time of Dickens is due partly to the novel's effectiveness as national allegory and partly to the perceived link between English character and eccentricity. The novelists delight in the foibles and peculiarities of individual temperaments. Hazlitt, for example, explains in 'Standard Novels and Romances' that the achievement of Fielding, Richardson, Smollett, and Sterne belongs to the age of the early Hanoverian kings in which the English character was 'more truly English than perhaps at any other period—that is, more tenacious of its own opinions and purposes'. It was an 'age of hobby-horses' (19–20). The 'hobby-horse' here alludes to Sterne's Walter Shandy and Uncle Toby; the latter is a disabled army veteran living out his days in tranquil retirement, and Hazlitt strongly implies that the English novel's genial view of character could not survive the domestic repression and the devastating wars of the revolutionary epoch that succeeded the 'age of hobby-horses'.

What gradually overshadowed the prominence of individual eccentricity in the novel was not, however, an awareness of war and political revolutions but rather the growing consciousness of society as a monolithic institution or organization containing and dwarfing the individual. This sociological awareness begins with the idea of the social machine first expounded in Thomas Carlyle's early essays such as 'Signs of the Times' (1829). The social machine was figured as an interconnected system or grid, holding its members in narrowly confined positions and reducing them, ultimately, to animated puppets. The efflorescence of individual character which had fascinated earlier novelists now came to seem something of a charade. For H. G. Wells's narrator at the beginning of *Tono-Bungay* (1909), for example, the social system is a complex arrangement of 'character parts':

Most people in this world seem to live 'in character'; they have a beginning, a middle and an end, and the three are congruous one with another and true to the rules of their type. You can speak of them as being of this sort of people or that. They are, as theatrical people say, no more (and no less) than 'character actors'. They have a class, they have a place, they know what is becoming in them and what is due to them, and their proper size of tombstone tells at last how properly they have played the part.[47]

In a rather similar passage in her essay 'The Niece of an Earl' (1932), Virginia Woolf described society as seen by the English novelist as a 'nest of glass boxes one separate from another, each housing a group with special habits and qualities of its own'.[48]

Once character and a fixed place in the social organization are seen to go together, the emphasis naturally falls on those who have somehow lost their place and no longer know 'what is becoming in them and what is due to them'—who no longer know who they are. Novelists beginning with Charlotte Brontë in *Jane Eyre* (1847) had described protagonists who feel themselves to be aliens and misfits, and who, like Rudyard Kipling's Kim, repeatedly have to ask themselves 'Who am I?' By the early twentieth century the search for identity had become open-ended and exploratory; in a novel such as D. H. Lawrence's *Women in Love* (1920), it almost entirely supersedes the depiction of individual character as traditionally understood. The following exchange takes place between two of Lawrence's protagonists, Rupert Birkin and Gerald Crich, as they travel by train from Nottinghamshire to London:

'What do you think is the aim and object of your life, Gerald?' [Birkin] asked. . . . 'Wherein does life centre, for you?'

'I don't know—that's what I want somebody to tell me. As far as I can make out, it doesn't centre at all. It is artificially held together by the social mechanism.'[49]

What Gerald is describing here is an emptiness of identity: the need for a centre. The 'character' he presents to the world as an industrialist and former army officer is purely artificial, he thinks. Lawrence's novel portrays a series of actions by his protagonists in which they effectively choose their identities. The choice is not merely individual, however, since choice of identity in fiction can almost invariably be linked to national allegory. Jane Eyre, who as a child thought of herself as an alien, ends her narrative in apparent contentment living in fortress-like privacy in the English countryside. Not only is Charlotte Brontë one of the greatest English courtship novelists, but her fiction presents courtship as, overwhelmingly, a means of forging identity as well as a test of character. In early twentieth-century fiction Kim must decide whether, and in what senses, he is English, Indian, and/or Irish, while Wells's narrator and the principal characters of *Women in Love* are all shown as voluntarily or involuntarily leaving England. The choice of identity is emphatically present in these novels, and in the novels of immigration (to be discussed in Chapter 15) which have succeeded them; but it has been an undercurrent in English fiction from the beginning.

Forms of English Fiction

The history of the English novel reveals both a changing sense of what it is to be English and a gathering awareness of the weight of fictional tradition, whether as a source of veneration or an object to be parodied. Within that tradition particular forms of narrative have come to the fore, dominating fiction for a time and then, it may be, receding or being absorbed into others. The last section of this chapter offers a preliminary sketch of three of these forms: the journey novel and male *Bildungsroman*, the novel of courtship, and the family saga and extended novel-sequence.

In the background to the novel are the romances of knight-errantry. Cervantes's Don Quixote set out, in Hazlitt's words, to 'revive the example of past ages, and once more "witch the world with noble horsemanship"',[50] but the Don's pretensions were mocked by his shabby, ill-conditioned horse and by Sancho Panza, the servant and man of the people, who rode behind him on a donkey. Noble horsemanship is a theme for traditional epic, romance, and the modern historical costume drama beginning with Scott's *Ivanhoe*. *Don Quixote* is the great masterpiece of the early European novel because it debunks the pretensions of horsemanship, preferring the comedy of the low horse and the donkey or carnival horse. After Cervantes the novel's aspiring male heroes would go on foot, or would keep horses they could not afford. The difference between those who could manage to keep a stable of horses and the pedestrian majority is one of the oldest marks of class division.[51]

The European novel's debt to the chivalric romances can be measured by the prominence, from its earliest beginnings down to Fielding and Dickens, of the journey trope or 'romance of the road'. Don Quixote and Sancho Panza ride across the plains of La Mancha; the giant Gargantua is given a hobby-horse as a child, and then sent to Paris on a huge mare; and Guzman de Alfarache sets out from Seville on foot to mend his 'miserable Estate', and celebrates the good company to be found on the road which 'makes horse-men, of footmen'.[52] These works by Cervantes, Rabelais, and Aléman were translated into English in the early seventeenth century, some decades before Bunyan's Pilgrim took to the road with his backpack and staff. English readers were already familiar with Chaucer's pilgrims, with the early highwayman legends, and with the Elizabethan 'road fiction' of Thomas Deloney and Thomas Nashe. The journey as narrative framework immediately distinguished prose fiction from drama, since the theatre with its static stage sets is ill-equipped to portray continuous movement from place to place. Such a journey is typically undertaken on foot, even if (as in Fielding's *Joseph Andrews* and *Tom Jones*) the characters originally intended to travel on horseback or in a stagecoach. The male hero of the journey novel is always (in the words of Nashe's most famous title) an unfortunate traveller.

Unfortunate, but—if he is an English protagonist—not irredeemably so. The Spanish picaresque novel beginning with the anonymous *Lazarillo de Tormes* (1553) provided a model for Nashe and for several of Defoe's narratives, but the *picaro*'s autobiography is that of an orphan and a social outcast. His life's journey is constantly interrupted by violent and sensational episodes, and the only way in which he ever can be said to rejoin his society is through his success as an autobiographer and story-teller.[53] The novels of Fielding and his successors are 'anti-picaresque' in the sense that they move towards an achieved settlement and a reconciliation with the social order.[54]

The outcast, in English mythology and English fiction, is only temporarily dispossessed. In the end his society will recognize him and save him from destitution. Robin Hood, the highwayman and thief, is the rightful Earl of Huntingdon, a faithful follower of the king whose authority has been usurped by an unlawful tyrant; Dick Whittington's flight from London comes to a quick end when the bells reveal that he is the future Lord Mayor. These mythic happy endings foreshadow the fate of the characters of the English *Bildungsroman* or 'novel of development', in which the orphan or foundling is the true heir to an estate and the same person may be both robber and benefactor. The despised servant or apprentice marries his master's daughter, or (in Samuel Richardson's female variant) the maidservant marries her former mistress's son. But in Richardson the journey novel, with its international origins, gives place to the English domestic fiction of courtship.

The courtship novel offers at least a diluted journey narrative, since it traces the protagonist's path from provincial innocence to broadening experience. The subtitle of Frances Burney's *Evelina* (1778)—*The History of a Young Lady's Entrance into the World*—suggests the social topography of these narratives of coming of age and the approach to marriage. The second part of Richardson's *Pamela* (1741), showing the heroine's life once the drama of her courtship and marriage is complete, found few imitators, though in the late eighteenth century a new kind of novel emerged to portray the sufferings of restless, unhappily married women. For many critics, however, the story of courtship portraying a young girl's awakening has remained the typically English form of the novel, since it is

sharply opposed to the dangerously adulterous liaisons of classic
European fiction. English domestic novels endorsed family values and were,
therefore, addressed to all levels of society, not merely to connoisseurs of
the *demi-monde* or gentlemen in the privacy of their libraries. The fiction
of courtship appealed to the curiosity of young readers, since it offered
both instruction in the social proprieties and the indulgence of (licit or
illicit) desire.[55]

Sexual desire in English fiction is famously muted, even in the case of
Richardson's *Clarissa* (1748) where the climactic event is the rape of the
heroine. But the gratification of social desires, and above all of individual
ambition, is one of the perennial attractions of reading fiction. Walter
Bagehot wrote in *The English Constitution* that 'Courts and aristocracies
have the great quality which rules the multitude, though philosophers can
see nothing in it—visibility'.[56] Today the cult of celebrity centres on
singers, film stars, sports personalities, and politicians rather than the
traditional aristocracy, but it still enforces a sharp separation between the
visible elite and the invisible multitude. The novel's great task was to
make its middle-class heroes and heroines visible by representing them as
newcomers eligible for admission into the charmed spectacle of upper-
class society. The eighteenth-century novel of courtship led almost
inevitably to the early nineteenth-century 'silver-fork school' of popular
novels of fashionable life, and even today the proportion of peers and
persons of title in contemporary English fiction greatly exceeds that in the
population at large. Jane Austen is by no means a 'silver-fork' novelist in
the vulgar sense, yet the heroine of *Pride and Prejudice* marries one of
England's greatest landowners, while in *Mansfield Park* Susan, Fanny
Price's younger sister, sits in the coach on her first journey to her rich
uncle's estate 'meditating much upon silver forks, napkins, and finger
glasses'.[57] Austen (herself a clergyman's daughter) clearly expects us to
sympathize with Susan's anxieties as she prepares to enter the great house
where Fanny, the novel's heroine, has made her first timid appearance
forty-six chapters earlier.

The pretence to intimate knowledge of the lives of people higher in the
social scale than either the authors or their readers can be found
throughout English fiction. As one of Richardson's twentieth-century
critics observed, 'It is remarkable, on cool reflection, how much of their
talents good middle-class radicals of the great middle-class age, like
Thackeray and Dickens and Meredith, devoted to narrations of lords,
baronets, knights and their hangers-on.'[58] The novel of courtship is much
more than a vehicle for the romance of social climbing and upward

mobility, however. The form's potential for national allegory resides in
the so-called 'national marriage plot',[59] in which an alliance between
families bears a weight of political symbolism implying the resolution of
contraries and the reconciliation of national differences.

Pride and Prejudice, with its union between the Tory gentry and the
Whig aristocracy, is a story of courtship with political repercussions of
which most modern readers are blissfully unaware. In Richardson's
Pamela, where the heroine's Puritan virtue triumphs over the Cavalier
immorality of her high-born suitor, the resulting marriage has the effect of
healing the religious and social divisions which had torn the nation apart
a century earlier. In the great novels of courtship the twists and turns of
the romantic intrigue are so engrossing that readers can accept a degree of
political symbolism without even thinking about it. The courtship
romance has the effect of removing the spectacle of social reunification
beyond the reach of political controversy. The power of national allegory
in these novels may be in reverse proportion to its obviousness.

In Victorian and later fiction the novel of courtship merges into the
more elaborate form of the family saga, which projects an idea of
the nation as a network of extended families; this is an extension of the
traditional political analogy between family and state in which the
monarch is father of his people. George Orwell, who once planned to
write such a saga, described England as a 'family with the wrong members
in control': 'It is a family in which the young are generally thwarted and
most of the power is in the hands of irresponsible uncles and bedridden
aunts.'[60] Whatever we make of this as political analysis, it is a novelist's-eye
view in which the paternal figure is either sidelined or altogether absent;
novels rarely uphold a father's authority.

At the head of the English state 'family' is still the so-called 'royal
family', a dynasty that is sharply criticized whenever it fails to display
traditional family virtues. But the monarchy seldom if ever appears in
English fiction. It may be argued that this is due to a desire to avoid
mentioning actual historical personages, to a natural deference, or to the
novelists' fear of possible censorship. 'What does a King feel? What does a
Duke think? We cannot say,' observed Virginia Woolf.[61] 'Royalty must be
worth knowing, and very great fun,' confides the narrator of Wells's
Tono-Bungay (4–5), but he does not get to know them. A century and a
half after Bagehot's description of the English political system as one in
which 'A Republic has insinuated itself beneath the folds of a Monarchy',[62]
it is still often asserted that England is essentially monarchical and that the
national identity is held together by patriotic investment in the royal family.

This is arguably true of the United Kingdom as a whole, since Unionism's political force depends heavily on the monarchy as overarching symbol, and in England the popular press, the educational system, and the political class remain at least ostensibly loyal to the monarchy. In contrast to such professions of loyalty, we do not meet with or (usually) even hear of members of the royal family in mainstream English fiction. Royalty is confined to historical romances set in much earlier centuries. Traditional epic poetry and drama introduced kings and queens as a matter of course, but if any character in a novel has intimate relations with a 'royal person-age', that personage (as in Defoe's *Roxana*) is likely to be masked under a pseudonym and heavily disguised. The England of the novelists, however status-conscious, is implicitly republican.

The courtship novel explores relationships between two or more families, which may or may not be brought together. But novelists are notably economical with the number of families which might in principle be involved in the ups and down of courtship. Fictional marriages are quite often endogamous—that is, conducted within an extended family, as for example between cousins—rather than exogamous. The pattern of *Mansfield Park*, in which a brother and sister form relationships with a sister, a brother, and a female cousin—but the two cousins end up marrying one another—is an extreme example of the courtship novel's customary simplification of family structures and intermarriage.

'The usual plan is to take two couples and develop their relationships,' said D. H. Lawrence of his first novel; 'Most of George Eliot's are on that plan.'[63] In *The Rainbow* (1915) and *Women in Love* (1920), however, Lawrence turned to a family saga extending over two volumes and three generations. *The Rainbow* is one of innumerable English novels that might usefully contain a family tree as a guide for their readers, and many *agree* stories of mysterious foundlings (like *Tom Jones* and *Oliver Twist*) would contain rather little mystery if an explicit family tree had been printed at the beginning. Family genealogies in the English novel are often loaded with cultural meaning, conveying a hint—and sometimes far more than a hint—of national allegory through their links to the Civil War and other traumatic episodes of English history. This sense of dynastic succession, from *Tristram Shandy* through to Ian McEwan's *Atonement* (2001), forms a background to the trials and divisions of the novel's protagonists. In general, the more prominently the genealogy is stated at the outset, the more clearly is family identity linked to national identity.

The novel-sequence, as pioneered by the great French novelist Balzac, may be seen as a development of the family saga. The sequence replicates the idea of a social network by introducing recurring characters in novel after novel, so that the protagonist of one novel is likely to feature as a peripheral figure in others. Disraeli, Thackeray, and Trollope introduced this technique into English fiction, using it to evoke a continuous and overlapping social world. In the twentieth-century novel-sequences by Ford Madox Ford, Evelyn Waugh, and Anthony Powell there is a curious return to the novel's origins in a parody of chivalric romance, both in the thwarted 'knight-errantry' of particular characters and in the presentation of the novel's world as a 'round table' or charmed circle of initiates. If, as seems possible, the family saga and novel-sequence are now at least temporarily exhausted, the novel of immigration (to be discussed in Chapter 15) can bring new energy to these old forms. Where the conflicts and continuities in the family saga point to an assessment of the nation's present and future, novels of immigration openly question the idea of national identity.

And not, perhaps, before time. The tradition of journey novels ending in settlement, national marriage plots, and sagas of family reunion and family conflict suggests an overwhelmingly domestic agenda, which has been summed up by the critic Martin Green as 'the story of caste psychology and intercaste conflict, of manners taken seriously and marriage taken solemnly, with which we are all familiar because it has been central to our literary culture'.[64] But in every generation of English fiction there have been novelists who broke away from the domestic sphere to examine the often shocking conditions of the 'greater England' of the empire, or to contrast life at home with life abroad. The English novel, like other national literatures, will in future have to depend upon national identity for its life support if it is to survive as a distinctive form. National identity, for its part, will continue to draw strength from the concern with identity in the nation's fictions.

Royal Academy of Arts

Modern British Sculpture

Exhibition Preservation Partner
American Express Foundation

Friday 25-March-2011 6:00 pm

£10.00 *Senior*

Inc. Includes £2.50 for a printed gallery guide
www.royalacademy.org.uk

26472

Royal Academy of Arts, Piccadilly, London W1J 0BD

Admit One

Friends receive:
Free admission to every exhibition with a family adult guest, no queuing, quarterly RA magazine & use of Friends Rooms.

Ask at the Friends Desk for details.

Eating, Drinking and Shopping
The RA Shop, Restaurant and Café are open daily, plus late on Fridays.
Shop online for exhibition catalogues, books and gifts at www.royalacademy.org.uk/shop

Friday Nights
The RA is open until 10pm every Friday with free live music

www.royalacademy.org.uk

Royal Academy of Arts

Cavaliers, Puritans, and Rogues: English Prose Fiction from 1485 to 1700

ENGLISH prose fiction was a comparatively late arrival in European literature. Before *The Pilgrim's Progress* in the late seventeenth century there is no popular masterpiece comparable to Giovanni Boccaccio's story cycle *The Decameron* (1349–51) or François Rabelais's *Gargantua* and *Pantagruel* (1532–4), let alone to Miguel de Cervantes's *Don Quixote de la Mancha*, which is the greatest of all early novels. Until the Elizabethan period English prose fiction consisted of romance narratives translated or adapted from Latin and French, together with a few original short stories.[1] The two prose works that survive as literary classics are Sir Thomas More's *Utopia*, published in Latin in 1516 and not translated into English until 1551, and Sir Thomas Malory's translation of the Arthurian romances from French and Welsh originals. It is small wonder that the conventional history of the English novel begins with Defoe and fails to acknowledge the novel's prehistory.

But English fiction before Defoe outlines many of the national themes that were to become familiar in the later tradition. Sixteenth-century prose narratives provided stories and plots for Elizabethan and Jacobean drama, a mode of expression that matured so much faster that it comprehensively outclassed the early novel. The comparative failure of Elizabethan fiction reveals, above all, the futility of the idea of the novel as a 'book of the Courtier', a sophisticated, learned, and highly elaborate art intended, like much of the poetry of the time, to win royal patronage and the praise of the aristocracy. John Lyly, Sir Philip Sidney, and other writers of Elizabethan courtly prose were thwarted by the novel's adaptation to private reading and its inability to engage with the public and performative role of the arts in the life of the court.

Nor did prose fiction have any roots in, or much apparent connection with, English popular culture. The surviving early accounts of folk heroes

such as Robin Hood are verse ballads or dramatic interludes, not
fictional narratives. There is a fourteenth-century prose romance, *Fouke
Fitzwarine*, the story of an earl who rebels against King John and leads a
band of outlaws in the greenwood; its basis is an Anglo-Norman poem,
and some of its motifs later reappear in the Robin Hood ballads.[2]
Malory's *Le Morte d'Arthur* (1485) was a work of reclamation, avowedly
based on a 'French boke' and annexing the stories about the 'matter of
Britain' which had been passed down in languages other than English.
One of the best-known early sources of Arthurian legend is the Latin of
Geoffrey of Monmouth's *Historia Regum Britanniae* (*c*.1136), which
identifies Arthur as a Celtic king of Britain who set out to unite the whole
island and to 'harry the Saxons'.[3] The Warwickshire knight Sir Thomas
Malory not only translated the Arthurian romances into English prose but
asserted that the 'matter of Britain' was really the matter of England—
that Arthur was the first great English king. In Geoffrey of Monmouth's
version, the Last Battle against Mordred takes place near Tintagel in
Cornwall, and Arthur's defeat leaves the Saxons in control of Loegria
(Malory's Logres), the Welsh name for England. *Le Morte d'Arthur*
installs the Round Table at Winchester (Camelot) and later at Westminster,
the political heart of the English nation.

According to his most famous twentieth-century editor, Sir Thomas
Malory was the founder of the modern English novel.[4] But Malory's
claim owes everything to William Caxton, the Westminster printer and
courtier who brought out the Arthurian romances in the year in which the
young Welshman Henry Tudor became King of England after defeating
Richard III at Bosworth Field. It was Caxton who divided the romances
into twenty-one books and no less than 507 chapters, each with a
descriptive chapter-heading in a style that would be imitated by innumerable later novelists. Caxton dedicated his edition—produced, he
claimed, at the urgent request of a group of English noblemen—'unto all
noble princes, lords and ladies, gentlemen or gentlewomen, that desire to
read or hear read of the noble and joyous history of the great conqueror
and excellent king, King Arthur, some time king of this noble realm, then
called Britain'.[5] The wording makes it clear that the noble realm 'then
called Britain' is now the kingdom of England and Wales. Caxton also
promises that his book will teach young noblemen the arts of chivalry,
and that 'for to pass the time [it] shall be pleasant to read' (i. 3). But this
raises the spectre that would later trouble Jane Austen's young lady, the
suspicion that *Le Morte d'Arthur* is 'only a novel'—that it is no more than
a trivial, perhaps childish, entertainment.[6]

As a publisher of serious historical and devotional works, Caxton was anxious to refute the charge that the Arthurian romances were 'but feigned and fables' (i. 2). His preface to *Le Morte d'Arthur* sets out Arthur's credentials as an authentic national hero, whose relics are to be found all over England. He would, Caxton writes, have been more widely acclaimed 'save only it accordeth to the Word of God, which saith that no man is accept for a prophet in his own country' (i. 2). It is a matter of national pride, therefore, that the 'French boke' should be turned into an English book. Malory's text describes friendly tournaments in which Arthur and his knights take on the combined forces of Celtic and Viking Britain, led by the kings of North Wales, Scotland, Ireland, and Northumbria. It ends with the civil war between Arthur and Mordred splitting England in two, and with the most Saxon-dominated parts of the country (the South-East and East Anglia) providing the bulk of Mordred's supporters. Some modern commentators have seen *Le Morte d'Arthur* as an allegory of the Wars of the Roses, and at one point the narrator intervenes in the text—'Lo ye all Englishmen, see ye what a mischief here was'—to denounce the fickleness of the English people who have deserted Arthur (ii. 384). The national epic culminates in an overwhelming tragedy redeemed only by the Grail knights' example of Christian chivalry and by the promise that Arthur, *Rex quondam Rex que futurus*, will come again. England for Malory and Caxton is also Logres, the magical realm overseen by Arthur and Merlin. This idea would be revived by Victorian poets and painters, but it lay dormant, so far as the novel was concerned, until the twentieth century.

After Malory and Caxton there is, except for the *Utopia* written in Latin, no English prose fiction of any note for nearly a hundred years. Even in the late sixteenth century, when there was an efflorescence of prose romance, most of the fiction was either actually based on classical or Italian sources, or pretended to be so. George Gascoigne's *The Adventures of Master F.J.* (1573) is a story of adultery set in a dissolute Italian country mansion, possibly a tale of the English aristocracy in disguise. The prose tale serves as the frame for a sequence of love poems, sonnets and songs, as in Sir Philip Sidney's much more famous *Arcadia* (1580; partly revised in 1590), dedicated to his sister the Countess of Pembroke. Divided into five acts with verse interludes, *Arcadia* with its themes of disguise, cross-dressing, senile adultery, and teenage passion— not to mention a dead king belatedly coming back to life—manifestly foreshadows Shakespearian pastoral comedy and romance. At first Sidney's melodrama suggests the performance of an aristocratic court playing at being shepherds and shepherdesses. Later the plot darkens, as a series of debates about the king's supposed murder dramatizes the issues of justice and mercy. But Sidney is so steeped in his classical and Renaissance sources that it would be hard, if not impossible, to read his pastoral Arcadia as a representation of dilemmas of state in contemporary England.[7]

In the same year as the first version of *Arcadia*, John Lyly produced *Euphues and His England*, the sequel to his highly successful *Euphues: The Anatomy of Wit* (1578) and, perhaps, the first deliberate celebration of the English nation in prose fiction. The story of the visit of Euphues, a young Athenian, and his friend Philautus to Queen Elizabeth's court is a piece of unashamed nationalist propaganda, dedicated to the Earl of Oxford and evidently intended to advance its author's own standing at court.[8] Euphuism, as Lyly's famously high-flown style became known, is a flattering mirror for the court, appealing to its members' learning, refinement, and literate sensitivity.[9] The actual narrative of Euphues's travels is of little or no interest, but the book offers a series of exemplary dialogues, love stories, and letters culminating in 'Euphues Glasse for Europe', where England, its women, and its Queen are held up as a model for rival nations.

Both Sidney and Lyly reflect the tensions between masculinity and femininity in Elizabethan court life. Euphues's description of England as a second Paradise and a 'new *Israel*'[10] contributes to the ideology of the Protestant nation presided over by a Virgin Queen, although he portrays Elizabeth not as a warrior monarch but as an aristocratic *grande dame* surrounded by chaste and pious ladies-in-waiting who spend their mornings in prayer and the rest of the day listening to learned discourses of courtly love. They take greater pleasure 'to heare of love, th[a]n to be in love' (445), but the category of 'learned discourses' seems meant to exclude a light-minded romance such as the *Arcadia*. Sidney, however, described his sister as his first reader, claiming that much of the *Arcadia* was written in her presence at Wilton, her country seat. His character Musidorus speaks of love as a passion that 'doth...womanize a man...making reason give place to sense, and man to woman' (18), and it is love that brings Musidorus and his friend Pyrocles into mortal danger in their Arcadian retreat. Sidney's feminine romance—so unlike the masculine world of *Le Morte d'Arthur*—was written for the Countess's aristocratic circle, but it anticipates the emergence a century later of romantic prose fiction as a commercial literary genre concerned, overwhelmingly, with matters of love, and mostly read by women. The

Arcadia remained popular in England throughout the seventeenth century until it was supplanted by the romances of women authors such as Delarivier Manley and Eliza Haywood.

But the Elizabethan novels that remain attractive to readers today are not the fiction of the country house and the feminized court. Instead, they are strongly masculine texts in which violence, sexual promiscuity, trickery, and roguery take the place of amorous passion. Moreover, they are historical novels set in past reigns and making no allusion, therefore, to the cult of the Virgin Queen. Thomas Nashe's *The Unfortunate Traveller* (1594), dedicated to the Earl of Southampton, is a bastard offshoot of Elizabethan courtly fiction employing a racy first-person narrative voice rather than the distanced storytelling of the romance tradition. Nashe's narrator, the swaggering, unscrupulous Jack Wilton, presents himself as one of the underlings of court society, a page; he is, he boasts, the 'King of pages'.[11] After serving as a soldier in Henry VIII's army, he leaves the English court, following what he calls the 'vocation of my cavaliership' (291) through Germany and Italy. Eventually he returns to the King's service. His story is one of an interlude or sabbatical in his career at court, the devious wanderings of an errant page. Not only is Nashe concerned to entertain a Protestant public with the corruption and skulduggery of Catholic Europe, but he specializes in a kind of pornography of violence, with torture and execution scenes too disgusting, and too mechanically ingenious, for theatrical representation. *The Unfortunate Traveller* is fiction for fiction's sake, the story without the moral discourse, the poetic interludes, and the court flattery, but nevertheless aimed at an aristocratic or sub-aristocratic readership. Jack Wilton himself is a self-proclaimed cavalier and rogue, and both terms call for some amplification.

A *cavalier* in the strict sense in which Nashe uses the term is a gentleman trained to arms, the successor of the medieval knight; the word, taken into English from Spanish and Italian, is closely linked to cavalry and horsemanship. But a cavalier was also a gallant and, by extension, a roistering, devil-may-care kind of gentleman. From 1642 the Royalist supporters of Charles I were known as Cavaliers, and by the following century the adjective *cavalier* had come to mean haughty, supercilious, and careless in manner. (Still later, the noun came to mean no more than a lady's escort or dancing partner.) Jack Wilton's willingness to trust his luck in what he calls the 'lottery of travel' is evidence of a purely secular outlook, the reverse of the Christian chivalry that lay behind the courtly ideal. Jack may be forced by circumstances into the roles of manservant, page, thief, and so on, but he is born a gentleman and manifestly thinks himself the equal of any Englishman alive. For some time he travels in the service of Henry Howard, Earl of Surrey, but when Surrey wishes to pass incognito in order to pursue his career of gallantry, he and Jack Wilton exchange places. (Predictably this leads to a farcical mix-up in which both men claim to be the real Earl of Surrey.) Wilton's narrative is itself a cavalier act of defiance on the part of Thomas Nashe, a penniless university graduate who was manifestly not a blue-blooded aristocrat like the Earl of Surrey or Sir Philip Sidney.

Rogue is the conventional English translation of the Spanish *pícaro*, whose fictional career began with the anonymous *Lazarillo de Tormes*, first translated into English in 1586. *The Unfortunate Traveller* is a picaresque novel in all but the strictest sense of the term. Unlike the protagonists of the Spanish picaresque, Jack Wilton has an accepted, if subordinate, place in the English gentry, and it is his desire for adventure, rather than poverty and hunger, that sets him wandering across Europe. But his story, like the *pícaro*'s, consists of a long series of lurid episodes involving hair's-breadth escapes from prison, from the gallows, and (in Jack's case) from being disembowelled by the Pope's physician in the course of an anatomy lesson. His instinctive individualism draws intellectual justification from his meeting at Rotterdam with the most revered of English humanists, 'Quick-witted Sir *Thomas More*'. In More's opinion, we are told, 'principalities were nothing but great piracies which, gotten by violence and murther, were maintained by private undermining and bloodshed...in the chiefest flourishing kingdoms there was...a manifest conspiracy of rich men against poor men' (240). More's response to this is to 'lay down a perfect plot of a commonwealth or government which he would entitle his *Utopia*'; but for the cynical Jack Wilton, such a diagnosis of existing society confirms the absolute necessity of living by his wits. Only at the end does he elect to go straight, marrying his mistress or 'courtesan' and hastening back to France to rejoin the King's army.

Where Lyly had portrayed the English court as a virtuous model for Europe to emulate, Nashe wallows in the vicious excitements awaiting an English traveller abroad. Once he has left the ordered society and (somewhat lax) military discipline of the court, Wilton enters the no-holds-barred world that would be described half a century later in Thomas Hobbes's *Leviathan*:

To this warre of every man against every man, this also is consequent; that nothing can be Unjust. The notions of Right and Wrong, Justice and Injustice have there no place. Where there is no common Power, there is no Law: where no Law, no Injustice. Force, and Fraud, are in warre the two Cardinall vertues.[12]

Here life is 'solitary, poore, nasty, brutish, and short', and it is 'thought no dishonour to be a Pyrate, or a High-way Theefe' (156–7). Hobbes adds that, where there is no writ of society higher than the family, men live by the 'Lawes of Honour' (224). Jack Wilton's adventures culminate in the nauseating spectacle of the execution of Cutwolfe, a murderer who makes a defiant last speech to the crowd before his body is broken on the wheel and left out for the vultures. Cutwolfe, who claims to speak for '[a]ll true Italians', maintains that 'Revenge is the glorie of armes, and the highest performance of [valour]' (355). He has, in his own eyes, lived by the principle of honour, while the state's retribution, brutally performed by the executioner or 'hackster', is simply another kind of vendetta. At Rome, Jack Wilton has earlier met with a banished English earl, who self-righteously holds Italy responsible for teaching young English visitors 'the art of atheisme, the art of epicurising, the art of whoring, the art of poysoning, the art of Sodomitrie' (336). These words, 'worse than an upbraiding lesson after a britching' (337), could sum up the lessons of *The Unfortunate Traveller*, although Jack's scorn for the banished earl is also part of the story. Nashe's novel seems in retrospect like an early pre-emptive strike against the Puritan ideology that was to transform English society in the coming century. Together with Lyly and others, Nashe had written in defence of the Anglican bishops against the Presbyterians in the Marprelate controversy of 1588–9, and it is part of Jack Wilton's 'cava-liership' that Puritans are to be despised as poisonous, malicious toads. Since life and art are worthless without a 'lyttle spice of wantonnesse' (310), the Puritan, in Jack's eyes, is inevitably a hypocrite. Fifty years before the outbreak of the Civil War, the conflict between Puritan and Cavalier values in English fiction had already begun.

The Genteel Tradesman

Nashe's Cavalier fiction was no match for the popularity of Thomas Deloney, a silk-weaver of unknown origins who, after a ribald youth, is said to have become a fervent Puritan.[13] Deloney's novels are grounded in civic responsibility and the Protestant ethic, although his plot material, which has its sources in folk tales and jest books,[14] resembles Nashe's in its devotion to roguery and trickery. But Deloney's heroes are (with certain exceptions) fortunate travellers, whose adventures open up possibilities of social advancement leading to civic honours and recognition at court. The merry young apprentice turns into a proud merchant or a substantial alderman. These stories of men of business celebrate the independence of the mercantile middle classes, reflecting the status of the City of London as a self-governing corporation, subject only to its fealty to the king. Like Dick Whittington, Deloney's bourgeois heroes may be aided by predestination, quick wits, or magical good fortune, but they inhabit a broadly republican ethos and owe nothing to the official apparatus of Church and State. They are free citizens of civil society rather than the subjects of the absolute monarchy to which, formally, their allegiance is pledged. Their relationship with the king is a commercial one, since it is their own power and wealth, rather than the royal prerogative of dignified patronage, which forces him to deal favourably with them. They do business with the court rather than simply seeking preferment.

Deloney's novels are in themselves neither courtly nor Puritanical, but they constitute a series of foundation legends of the English merchant caste which would soon become Puritanism's political base.[15] These lively, down-to-earth narratives are invariably cast in the mode of historical romance, since their object is to show the origins of the national prosperity enjoyed by Deloney's Elizabethan contemporaries. One of the signs of national prosperity is what we would now call gentrification. Deloney, like Nashe, employs the conventional address to the 'Gentle Reader', but he also refers to shoemaking as a 'gentle craft', implying that such a skilled luxury trade paradoxically confers genteel status on those who get rich by it. *The Gentle Craft* (1597) is subtitled 'A Discourse Containing many matters of Delight, very pleasant to be read', suggesting that Deloney, like Nashe, aims to provide casual, light-minded entertainment for people of leisure.

In his guise as a historian of the middle classes, Deloney was often content to recycle very traditional material. In *Jack of Newbury* (1597) the apprentice Jack Winchcomb is lured into marriage by his master's widow, whose time-honoured seduction technique has been traced back to a twelfth-century Latin tale.[16] After her death Jack inherits her fortune, becoming a gentleman and favourite at court. He refuses the King's personal offer of a knighthood, preferring to remain a broadcloth manufacturer rather than waste his substance supporting the 'vain titles of gentility'.[17] The 'greene king' of the second part of *The Gentle Craft* (1598) is a 'jolly Shoemaker' and a carnival figure who clothes his men in green when they put on a performance before King Henry I. Simon Eyre, the hero of the first part of *The Gentle Craft* who is also celebrated in Thomas Dekker's play *The Shoemaker's Holiday*, was a shoemaker's apprentice from the North of England who rose to become Lord Mayor of London in the fifteenth century. The Eyre of *The Gentle Craft* owes his legendary good fortune not to a fairy-tale sequence of events like Dick Whittington's, but to a smart confidence trick in which the penniless apprentice persuades the captain of a newly arrived merchant ship to sell him his whole cargo on credit. Deloney's novel displays a kind of social realism that is absent from the Whittington legend. Eyre's ability to inspire confidence and to return a profit to the person who invests in him, while keeping a handsome percentage for reinvestment in his next venture, is the way in which City fortunes have been made from his day to ours. By the end, he has become in reality the rich alderman he had earlier pretended to be. But there is no breath of satire in Deloney's revelation of capitalism's dependence on the creation of illusory confidence and the calculated exploitation of risk. Eyre's trickery ends in triumph as he becomes one of the City's founding fathers, building Leadenhall and keeping his promise to feast his fellow apprentices once he has become Lord Mayor. (The Lord Mayor's Banquet continues to this day, though it has long ceased to be for the benefit of City apprentices.)

If *The Gentle Craft* reveals the foundation of London's wealth as a centre of world trade, *Thomas of Reading* (*c*.1600) celebrates the growth of provincial manufacturing industry. Its characters are rich clothing manufacturers from the West of England who journey to and from London on business in the early twelfth century. They are large employers, so much so that half the population of England, including children as young as 6, are said to earn their livelihood through the clothing trade. Textiles are 'the greatest merchandise, by which our Countrey became famous through all Nations', or so Deloney alleges,[18] and he shows how this was achieved by strict regulation of the home market, including the grant of a royal monopoly and the introduction of a standard yard, regular coinage, and capital punishment for stealers of cloth. The very remote historical setting of *Thomas of Reading* is puzzling, since there were no merchant princes like Deloney's clothiers in the reign of Henry I.[19] But the story illustrates both the power of the middle-class merchants and their fear of an anarchic, Hobbesian social state in which they could be cheated or robbed at will. The mood of civic self-congratulation that Deloney creates is brutally interrupted by the murder of the Reading clothier Thomas Cole at the Crane Inn at Colnbrook on the western edge of Hounslow Heath (later to become one of the classic locations of highwayman biography). The merchants regularly put up here on their return from London even though the host and hostess of the Crane Inn are, as Deloney reveals, serial killers who have devised a mechanism with a hidden trapdoor for killing their sleeping guests and disposing of the bodies. At their trial they confess to some sixty murders. Once they have been found guilty and hanged, the river where Cole's body was found is named after him (giving the origin of the name Colnbrook), and the inn is burnt to the ground. Cole's widow uses his wealth to endow a monastery. The story is a curious mixture of folk legend, fanciful historical reconstruction (it concludes with Henry I's burial at Reading Abbey), and bloodcurdling invention.

Deloney, who was almost an exact contemporary of Shakespeare, is a direct ancestor of some of the major English novelists although his work remains deservedly obscure. He is an author of historical romances, but with none of the aristocratic and chivalric values traditionally associated with romance. He might be called the inventor of the 'romance of commerce'. Like Defoe, he was a London novelist, a propagandist for capitalism, and a writer capable of linking individual destinies to a sense of national history. Yet his novels have little emotional depth or spiritual power, and almost no insight into character. Their author's reported conversion to Puritanism was not allied to any capacity to tap the resources of biblical language, or to anticipate Bunyan's use of Puritan allegory. In so far as his achievement was to give crude fictional shape to the rise of the middle classes and to the economic processes that were transforming Elizabethan England from a small kingdom to the heart of a great empire, then Deloney should be remembered as the first English writer to make his career as a novelist. But the novel in his hands was a small affair, and there were no successors before Defoe to build on his work.

The English Rogue

Apart from the works of two major writers at the end of the century, neither of whom can be unambiguously classed as a novelist—Aphra Behn and John Bunyan—the seventeenth century is largely a missing chapter in the history of the English novel. This remains true despite the success of recent scholars in bringing to light a number of forgotten works. Most seventeenth-century fiction remains obstinately unavailable except in scarce original editions or in unmodernized, facsimile reprints.

It has never become part of the English literary canon. One reason for this is that, of the 450 new works of prose fiction published in England during the century, 213 were translations.[20] Another is that some of the liveliest seventeenth-century fiction is underground literature, scandalous, immoral, and unashamedly popular. Highly derivative, if not openly plagiarized, it has been contemptuously dismissed by literary historians who would like to believe that the English novel had more respectable antecedents.

The great political contention of the seventeenth century was that embodied in the Civil War between King and Parliament. There are few memorable depictions of the Civil War and the Commonwealth in the fiction of the time or, indeed, in English novels of any period. At most the novel would mirror the experience of civil war indirectly, leaving the task of providing straightforward narrative accounts of the most traumatic episode in modern English history to historians from the Earl of Clarendon onwards. There is, however, one contemporary fictive version of the Civil War that has recently been rediscovered: Percy Herbert's *The Princess Cloria: or, The Royal Romance*, a turgid, long-winded allegory. The first two volumes, published in 1653 as *Cloria and Narcissus*, take the story up to the defeat of King Euarchus of Lydia (Charles I) and his imprisonment by his senate. The full five volumes appeared in 1661, immediately after the Restoration, with a prefatory address to the reader setting out the work's Royalist credentials. Here the author explained that the Princess Cloria was an allegorical conception who was 'not only to be taken for the Kings Daughter, but also sometimes for his National Honour'. The allegorical form had been adopted to escape the censorship of Cromwell's 'Tyrannical Government', but also because readers would find it more instructive and entertaining than an unvarnished historical account.[21] (For example, Euarchus's speech on receiving the death sentence is set out at length, although Charles I had been prevented from making any such speech.)

Beneath the historical struggle between the King and Parliament was the contest between anarchy and the rule of law, which was central to the political philosophy of the age. At his trial in Westminster Hall, Charles I demanded to know 'by what authority, I mean lawful', he was accused of being a '*tyrant, traytor, murtherer* and *publique enemy of the Commonwealth*'. The King repudiated the prosecutor's claim to speak for the people of England, retorting to his 'pretended judges' that there were 'many unlawful authorities in the world, thieves and robbers by the highways'.[22] Parliament, he was asserting, had brought England back to what Hobbes would soon call an anarchic state of nature. Later in the century John Locke, in answer to the Royalist Sir Robert Filmer, set out to justify the impeachment of a tyrant by a properly constituted tribunal. If there were no circumstances in which the king's authority could be overruled, then there must be open war between the 'Rulers Insolence' and the 'Peoples Wantonness', according to Locke.[23] The popularity of criminal biography and crime fiction (two genres that are often barely distinguishable) after the Restoration may be seen partly as a response to Charles II's relaxation of censorship, but partly, also, as reflecting the widespread sense of a suspension or usurpation of lawful authority in the preceding decades. Once the Puritan judges and regicides had been silenced, there was a feeling that thieves and highway robbers might be allowed to put their case and try to justify their actions, at least through the medium of fiction. In particular, the rogue narratives drew attention to crucial changes in seventeenth-century England which had passed almost unnoticed while the nation was obsessed by the conflict between King and Parliament. England was fast becoming a major European power, its national and international trade was growing steadily, and it was beginning to acquire a global empire.

The prototype of seventeenth-century rogue fiction was not the courtier Jack Wilton but the Spanish 'Guzman' or *picaro* whom society regards as no better than a common thief. James Mabbe's translation of *The Rogue, or the Life of Guzman de Alfarache* was published in 1623 with a dedicatory poem by Ben Jonson, who claimed that its hero was already a byword at home and abroad:

> For though Spaine gave him his first ayre and Vogue,
> He would be call'd, henceforth, the English-Rogue.[24]

Guzman leaves his home in Seville after his father's death to seek out his 'Noble Kindred and Alliance' in Italy.[25] Fortune always eludes him, and he is by turns a kitchen scullion, a beggar, a page, and a thief. He spends periods in the service of a cardinal and an ambassador, and twice marries in the hope of gain, but all to no purpose; at the end, after four volumes, he suffers the ultimate degradation of being sentenced to the galleys. By the middle of the century Guzman was such a proverbial figure that a biography of the Royalist highwayman James Hind was published in 1652 as *The English Gusman*. Thirty years later, the Essex-born Thomas Dangerfield adopted the name of Don Tomazo when he set out on the road to become a 'young Gusman'.[26] The story of Dangerfield's supposed adventures is a tiresome rodomontade, but his book is full of memorable asides about 'gusmans' and 'gusmanry'. Far from being a helpless victim of society, the English rogue is 'Lawless as an Irish Tory' (a species of highwayman), 'as impatient as Ajax and as choleric as Hector' (374). Tomazo goes rampaging round the Mediterranean, deals in counterfeit money in several European countries, fits out a pirate ship, and runs a network of spies for Prince William of Orange. 'He delights in large-scale operations', as one critic has commented.[27] Dangerfield contrasts his greedy, imperious hero with the poor-spirited Spanish *pícaro*: 'See here the difference between a Spanish and an English gusman: the one pursuing a poor, hungry plot upon his penurious master's bread and cheese, the other designing to grasp the riches of a fourth part of the world by the ruin of a national commerce' (390). London is the 'grand receptacle of all the most refined virtuosos in gusmanry' (389), making the English rogue a symbol of the fall of the Spanish and the rise of the British empires.

There is a notable female 'English rogue' biography, *The Case of Madam Mary Carleton* (1663), revised ten years later as *The Counterfeit Lady Unveiled* by Francis Kirkman. Carleton, a thief who defends herself in court against a charge of bigamy, has been identified as the prototype of Defoe's Moll Flanders.[28] The most famous and popular of the rogue novels, however, was Richard Head's *The English Rogue* (1665), to which three further volumes were appended (with or without Head's collaboration) by Francis Kirkman. *The English Rogue* spawned a series of imitations, all by English writers: *The French Rogue* (1672), *The Dutch Rogue* (1683), *The Irish Rogue* (1690), and *The Scotch Rogue* (1706).[29] Head's rogue Meriton Latroon (roughly translatable as the Virtuous Highwayman) is a Royalist who, unlike his martyred King, narrowly escapes execution in the year 1650. He sits out the rest of the Commonwealth years in exile in Siam and the East Indies. The three later volumes consist largely of the life histories of various members of the English trading fleet whom Meriton, now a substantial local businessman, entertains when they arrive at Java.

Don Tomazo and *The English Rogue* are narratives of empire, celebrating an unscrupulous lawlessness that was felt to be a powerful weapon of the English abroad even if it was frowned upon at home. Significantly, both Tomazo and Meriton Latroon initially set out as self-styled knights-errant intent upon winning their spurs. They are travelling in the footsteps not only of the Arthurian knights but of the hero of *Don Quixote*, which had been translated into English by Thomas Shelton immediately after its first publication in 1605–15. Meriton's first stopping-place is a barn rather than an 'enchanted castle', while

Tomazo's is a Scottish peasant hovel shared by the family and their livestock. Criminal biographies drew upon Cervantes's mode of satirical anti-romance in the act of creating a kind of underworld romance. Meriton's attempt at 'knight-errantry' leads inevitably to his later adventures on the 'High Pad' with a gang of 'knights of the road', or highwaymen.[30] His first-person narrative is embellished with thieves' cant and highwayman lore, much of it plagiarized from earlier sources, and some of which would reappear in Head's later criminal biography *Jackson's Recantation* (1674).

Among other things, the engagingly frank eroticism of *The English Rogue* must have won it many readers. As a child, Meriton begins 'night practices' with the maid, 'being so young my mother did not in the least suspect me; but my too forward lechery would not let me lie quiet, putting her frequently to the squeak' (15). For all his expertise Meriton is not sexually insatiable, complaining that 'there is no slavery greater than that of the smock' and abandoning one of his sexual partners because 'the more I endeavoured to satisfy her, the further I was from it' (204–5). His adventure with three amorous highwaywomen ends in disappointment since, as he confides, 'my strength could not cope with such excesses' (166). Having turned transvestite in order to penetrate a girls' boarding school, he tells us that 'In the very height of these my jollities, I could not forebear thinking sometimes on my eternal condition' (82). Another aspect of sexual disillusionment found in *The English Rogue* is that Meriton's partners are constantly getting pregnant, forcing him either to get rid of them or to make himself scarce.

Having sired at least nine illegitimate children, and cuckolded and ruined the merchant to whom he was apprenticed, our hero gets married—an unwise move that leads him to report that 'Now began our domestic Civil Wars' (115). He flees to Ireland, returns to find that his wife has resorted to prostitution, and sets her up in a brothel with two other young whores. When they are committed to Bridewell he goes to watch them being 'well lashed, I hoped' (210). He himself is imprisoned again in Newgate, and then transported to the East, where he commits some of his bloodiest acts. Later three of his former mistresses turn up in Java and tell their stories. Meriton excuses his multiple infidelities with the claim that people like himself are 'like such who are upon a trading voyage, it is not one port but a great many that makes up their market' (632). The morality of the rogue's life is also the logic of mercantile capitalism. But the rogue is by definition an unsuccessful capitalist, since if he were conventionally successful he would have won the respect of his fellow citizens and no longer be called a rogue. His tale of wickedness (leading in the end to a perfunctory repentance) is told for the benefit of respectable male readers who can, presumably, reflect that there but for God's grace go they. Kirkman and Head's compilation was frequently reprinted in bulky complete editions which, according to one modern scholar, 'would have been available only to more prosperous members of the commercial and trading classes'.[31] Doubtless they were kept well locked away from the apprentices, servants, and women of the household.

However well-off he may claim to be at the end of his tale, the rogue's success is never secure and it is certainly not providentially ordained. In a prefatory 'Epistle to the Reader' Head claims to be presenting 'an original in your own mother-tongue', though he immediately admits that the work is also a 'translation' drawn 'from the black copy of men's wicked actions' (1); a good deal of it, as it happens, is simply plagiarized. The rogue's autobiography is simply another expedient, the latest temporary venture in a life spent on the make. As the critic Paul Salzman argues, he 'slips from one disguise to another in a world of surfaces'.[32] Head and Kirkman's company of criminal storytellers in exile on the other side of the globe, at a safe distance both from the lawful authorities and from their intended readers, invites comparison with the defeated Cavaliers in exile from the Commonwealth during the same years. The Cavaliers, however, were exiles, not colonists, and had a home country to which they would eventually return in order to reclaim their estates. The rogue, as would be seen in Defoe's *Colonel Jack* and *Captain Singleton*, could only return in disguise. Like other colonists since his time, his necessary field of operations is outside England, the home country he has left involuntarily and in disgrace. It should be added that Meriton Latroon, like Richard Head, was born in Ireland, where he tells us that his father, a Protestant preacher, was murdered by Catholic rebels (although the date of his birth, 1637, cannot be reconciled with his transportation in 1650). At the end of the four volumes he is an Anglo-Irish settler in the East Indies, married to a local woman, and likely to stay there for good, yet he is still the self-proclaimed 'English Rogue'.

The Cavalier: Aphra Behn

There is a conscious affinity between rogue fiction and Royalism, as already suggested: the Puritan Commonwealth turned both criminals and followers of the defeated King into footloose adventurers. Charles II's

Restoration was widely welcomed in the novels of the period, so much so that Meriton Latroon, in retirement in Java, writes a poem to celebrate it. Under the surface, the hatreds engendered by the Civil War continued to fester, and Puritan and Cavalier became cultural stereotypes that were used to stir up class and religious dissensions throughout the remaining years of the Stuart dynasty. Aphra Behn, the dramatist, Restoration wit, and outspoken Royalist, satirizes the Puritan preacher Ananias Gogle in her play *The Round-heads* (1681). Gogle mistakes Puritan London for 'the Holy City, which the Saints have prepared for the Elect, the Chosen ones', and for his pains is beaten up by the soldiers and the London mob at the time of the Restoration. A Royalist gallant accuses Ananias of being a spiritual highwayman or 'Padder', who robs 'on the High-way i' th' Pulpit'.[33] John Bunyan was in some respects a real-life Ananias Gogle. In 1660, when literature and the theatre were enjoying their new-found freedom from censorship, Bunyan was arrested for preaching without a licence and imprisoned in Bedford Jail. Among his books are *The Holy City, or the New Jerusalem* (1665) and an allegorical novel, *The Holy War* (1682), in which the city of Mansoul is captured after prolonged fighting and pacified by the ruthless lawgiver Prince Emanuel. One of those sentenced to crucifixion is Mr Lustings, a stereotypical Cavalier nobleman who pleads before the court that 'I am a man of high birth, and have been used to the pleasures and pastimes of greatness, I have not been wont to be snub'd for my doings, but have been left to follow my will as if it were Law'.[34] Bunyan takes a grim pleasure in bringing those who consider themselves above the law to summary justice in his imaginary English Commonwealth. In the early 1680s the Civil War of forty years earlier was still being fought at the level of literary propaganda, with two major writers of English fiction ranged on opposite sides.

Aphra Behn turned to prose fiction in 1683, when her income as a popular dramatist had dried up and she had been imprisoned for insulting the Duke of Monmouth in a stage performance. Not surprisingly, her novels are less politically outspoken than her plays, though everything she wrote bears the stamp of a dedicated Royalist. The Cavalier and Roundhead stereotypes who romp through Behn's drama are not found in her fiction. *The Round-Heads* pillories actual members of the Puritan government and shows Lady Lambert, formerly Oliver Cromwell's mistress, starting an intrigue with Loveless, a Royalist gallant. Behn's most widely known novel, however, is *Oroonoko, or The Royal Slave* (1688), which will be discussed in Chapter 4. Although in some respects a Royalist allegory, *Oroonoko* is set in tribal Africa and the former English colony of Surinam, 'an obscure world, that afforded only a female pen to celebrate [the hero's] fame'.[35] Another novel, *Love-Letters Between a Nobleman and His Sister* (1684–7), ostensibly a saga of amorous intrigues in France and the Low Countries during the sixteenth-century Huguenot wars, contains a thinly veiled allegory of events leading up to the Monmouth rebellion of 1685.

Behn's fiction offers fantasies of aristocracy and gallantry; Bunyan offers allegorical fantasies of virtue and justice. The English courtship novel of the eighteenth century would later combine these two sorts of fantasy in a decorously romantic fable with a moral calculated to appeal to the respectable middle classes. Some of Behn's novellas, such as 'The Unfortunate Happy Lady' in which the libertine Sir William Wilding is eventually reclaimed by his virtuous sister, end in a triumph of innocence just as the courtship novel generally does. But her most memorable characters are aristocratic rebels living by a code of 'honour' and ruthlessly intent on following their desires. Retribution follows, sometimes in the gruesome style of Cutwolfe's execution in *The Unfortunate Traveller*.

For the novel to function as a fantasy of aristocracy, the middle-class professional novelist must either impersonate an upper-class narrator or, at least, claim to reveal the inner feelings and secrets of a higher social class. Aphra Behn's fiction has all the marks of social aspiration: its subject matter consists of upper-class scandals and the intimate histories of wealthy families, told in a sometimes gossipy, sometimes high-flown and declarative style, and introduced by witty dedications to people of fashion whom Behn addresses as friends—possibly lovers—and political allies. In *The Fair Jilt* (1688) and *Oroonoko* she appears as an eyewitness narrator who was on the periphery of the events she relates. *The Fair Jilt* is supposedly a true story of crimes committed in Antwerp in 1666, the year in which Behn had visited the city as a Royalist spy, and biographers have deduced from *Oroonoko* that the author must have lived in Surinam at some point in her earlier life. *Love-Letters* is one of the first epistolary novels in English. The novel in letters was a particularly appropriate forum for portraying the intimate lives of persons of 'quality', who were presumed to have more time on their hands, a higher standard of literacy, freer access to writing materials, more to write about, and more reliable means of sending clandestine letters than their social inferiors.

The epistolary novel has two apparently contradictory purposes. It reveals the scandalous secrets of the aristocracy at the same time as providing its readers with information on the modes of conducting love affairs, engaging in polite discourse, and corresponding with friends of either sex. Epistolary novels might be presented, in the jargon of the age, as 'true secret histories', but they exemplify a kind of narrative language that is informal, gossipy, full of emotion—both true and pretended—and unashamedly subjective. Although not an easy form for the writer to negotiate, the novel in letters soon became one of the most influential models of fictional narration. Readers were quick to identify with an aristocratic or genteel protagonist who was a keen letter writer, and often the letter writers were also represented as readers of novels. For all the rigid stratifications of rank in the societies they depict, the works of Behn and her successors and imitators tend to promote solidarity and cultural homogeneity between the upper and middle classes. They express a fantasy of social assimilation, and function as a guide to the socially aspiring.

Love-Letters is to some extent based on a French epistolary novel, Gabriel de Bremond's *Hattigé*, which reflected the love affairs of Charles II.[36] But Behn's protagonists, Philander and Sylvia, allude to the Duke of Monmouth's associate Lord Grey of Werke and his sister-in-law Lady Henrietta Berkeley, whom he abducted in 1682. Philander and Sylvia are supporters of the Prince of Condé, who died in the Huguenot wars in 1569, but the two lovers live in exile in the Low Countries, to which Monmouth and his closest supporters had fled in 1683. The topicality of *Love-Letters* must be approached through an intricate series of masks, one of which is the mask of the *chronique scandaleuse* or novel of adultery. The defeat of the Huguenots at the end of the third volume (echoing Monmouth's defeat at Sedgemoor in 1685) is introduced with the proviso that 'it is not the business of this little history to treat of war, but altogether love; leaving those rougher relations to the chronicles and historiographers of those times' (447). 'Little history' here refers to the scandalous and fashionable genre of *petites histoires*, such as the 'little *French* novels' (300) that Behn's characters use to while away the odd brief interlude between episodes of sexual dalliance.

The characters of *Love-Letters* are so besotted with sex that they tend to disregard politics even when political allegiance has put their lives in danger. Philander frequently ignores the Prince's summonses; the Prince only with the greatest reluctance tears himself away from erotic dalliance to lead an ill-prepared and half-hearted rebellion. At least one recent commentator has read *Love-Letters* as a 'cautionary romance' warning against the immorality of Lord Grey and his fellow Whigs, though its moral atmosphere closely resembles that of Behn's well-known comedy *The Rover, or The Banished Cavaliers* (1677), where Willmore, the 'Rover of Fortune', suggests the future Charles II living in exile during the

Commonwealth.[37] For the banished cavaliers of *Love-Letters*, love is the supreme form of military campaign, its aim being to exercise a tyrannical rule over captured territory. Defeat and erotic enslavement, however, can also be enjoyed to the full. Taking possession of a woman is a matter of storming the 'loose and silken counterscarps that [fence] the sacred fort' (50). The maid Antonet, asked by Sylvia ' "[W]hat sort of man would soonest incline you to a yielding" ', replies that the man to ' "villainously incline" ' her would, first, be one who would make her fortune, and, secondly, one who would give pleasure. What if both were combined in the same person? ' "Why then most certainly, madam," ' Antonet replies, ' "I should yield him my honour, after a reasonable siege" ' (205–6). Sylvia, like Behn's other female libertines, often appears in night attire with her clothes disarranged and her bosom temptingly half-exposed. She shows pornography's customary disregard for the mundane inconveniences which tend to damp down sexual activity, and both the fury of her own desires, and the ardour with which she is being pursued, persist unabated when she is heavily and visibly pregnant. During her pregnancy she dons male disguise, keeping it up for longer than the plot strictly requires since she is 'pleased with the cavalier in herself' (117).

Love-Letters deals in two kinds of honour, women's 'honour' and aristocratic honour. For the Cavalier novelist chastity, the first kind of honour, has no intrinsic value and is worth only a token defence. Sixty years later, both Richardson's *Pamela* and Fielding's *Joseph Andrews* were to portray lower-class protagonists who firmly reject the advances of wealthy libertines and yet succeed in rising in society. Their sense of rectitude, however much it might appeal to the respectable middle classes, appears laughable in terms of the Cavalier ethic. In *Love-Letters* the chief representative of middle-class Puritanism is Sebastian, a member of the Dutch States-General and a consummate hypocrite in sexual and other matters. Sebastian accuses his nephew Octavio of immorality with Sylvia—' "A little fornication in a civil way might have been allowed" ', he pontificates, but ' "this is flat adultery" ' (286)—but, like Octavio, he too discovers that he would rather be a slave at Sylvia's feet than a 'monarch over all the nasty provinces' (286–7). The Puritan legislator is capable of any degree of crime or treachery against his nephew. Sebastian's main function in the novel is to show the corruption and imposture of official justice, which appears irrevocably tarnished beside the personal honour of the aristocratic Cavalier ready at all times to stake his life on his sword.

Philander, as befits a gentleman and a libertine, fights several skirmishes and duels with his rivals; each fight is a trial of strength which invariably produces a just outcome. By contrast, his former servant Brilliard is a cowardly bourgeois who does his best to get out of the duel to which he is challenged. Only a true Cavalier can live or die by the aristocratic code. In this code the language of duelling overlaps with the language of gallantry, so that swordplay suggests loveplay and the sword the phallus. A gentleman's performance with either weapon is a matter of 'honour'. Each instance of duelling and hand-to-hand fighting in Behn's novel is referred to as a 'rencounter', but the same term is sometimes used to denote the sexual act, substituting for the more frequent 'encounter'.[38] When Sylvia allows herself to be seduced by Octavio, for example, the occasion is described as 'this soft rencounter' (284–5). The whole intricate plot of *Love-Letters* can be reduced to a sequence of encounters and rencounters between male and female libertines, ending with defeat on the battlefield and the Prince's beheading. Philander survives the debacle, and he and Sylvia carry on much as before. Philander's sense of honour had made him turn out with the rebels, but he is also suspected of betraying them. He is eventually pardoned by the King and returns to court 'in as much splendour as ever, being very well understood by all good men' (461); his honour is not lost, though possibly a little tarnished. Aphra Behn died in 1689, an unrepentant Cavalier who never had to trim her sails or seek a pardon from the new Whig regime after the final banishment of the Stuarts. 'Scandalously but rather appropriately', in Virginia Woolf's words, this first professional author of prose fiction to live by the female pen was buried in Westminster Abbey.[39]

The Puritan: John Bunyan

Aphra Behn's fiction with its Cavalier eroticism went out of favour once the middle-class novel had been instituted by Richardson, Fielding, Fanny Burney, and their contemporaries. Her works came to be excluded from serial reprints of the 'British Novelists', and fell into near-oblivion for almost two centuries. John Bunyan, by contrast, remained securely installed in the literary canon, and *The Pilgrim's Progress* (1678–84) has long been recognized as a great classic of English prose fiction. Bunyan is the leading devotional writer in the Nonconformist tradition, but his relationship to the modern novel remains a fascinating and puzzling problem. He was not, in the fullest sense, a novelist—partly because he would not allow himself to become one—but his work has profoundly influenced the English novel's language and structure.

We may begin by considering *The Life and Death of Mr Badman* (1680), an allegorical fable which clearly alludes to the genre of criminal biography and has been called a 'Puritan rogue novel'.[40] Just as criminal biographies could only be written and published once the individual concerned had been sentenced to hang or had gone through some form of repentance, so, in Bunyan's scheme, Mr Badman's death is even more noteworthy than his life. Both are recounted by his fellow townsman Mr Wiseman, an obituarist whose motto seems to be *de mortuis nihil nisi malum* (speak nothing but ill of the dead). Bunyan's difficulty is that he can do no more than hint at the sensational aspects of his protagonist's career in crime, since the reader must be edified and not (or not overtly) entertained by his story. Wiseman's racy, demotic account thus engages in a kind of narrative striptease, constantly insinuating what it will not perform. For example, he tells us that Badman was still able to get money 'by hatfulls and pocketfulls' even though he had squandered his wife's dowry and ruined his own business by neglect. Wiseman's interlocutor Mr Attentive understandably wants to hear more:

Why I trow he was no Highway man, was he?

Wise[man]. I will be sparing in my speech as to that, though some have muttered as if he could ride out now and then, about no body but himself knew what, over night, and come home all dirty and weary next morning. But that is not the thing I aim at.[41]

Earlier we have been told that Badman courted his future wife 'under a Vizzard of Religion, as if he had been for Honesty and Godliness, one of the most sincere and upright-hearted in England' (66). The situation would reappear in countless English courtship novels, and we cannot help being curious as to how this devout and intelligent woman was so thoroughly deceived. But, once again, this is not the thing Bunyan aims at.[42]

A vizard is literally a face mask, and Bunyan's allegorical method could be described as a sustained masquerade. His characters' 'true' identities, which are so clear to the reader, are often mysterious to one another. The names by which we know them are nicknames or given names rather than patronymics.[43] (It is true that Badman is one of a large family of 'Badmans', 'both Brothers and Sisters', yet they are the 'Children of a godly Parent' (16), whose name can hardly have been Badman as well. Nor, it would seem, is Badman's wife Mrs Badman, since she admonishes her husband on her deathbed that she is going 'where no bad man shall come' (142).) Characters in Bunyan's other narratives occasionally hide under false names, and Badman himself is in danger of becoming a good man if he does not act badly enough. The task of showing what a bad man he was is tiresomely repetitive, though Bunyan imparts humour and variety by allowing Attentive to become, from time to time, a little impatient with Wiseman's narrative. At one point Wiseman wonders aloud why it is necessary to enumerate all the 'particular actions' of his subject, given that 'his whole life and all his actions, went as it were to the making up of one massie body of sin' (126–7). Such a detailed indictment is perhaps needed because Mr Badman stands for a tide of wickedness which, Bunyan feared, was 'like to drown our English world' (7). 'Mr. *Badman* and his Friends', he announced in a prologue, had practically brought the nation to its knees (2).

The use of allegorical names is part of the novel's inheritance from earlier literature. In drama and poetic narrative, characters' names were either derived from existing historical and legendary sources, or they were inflected with meaning to a greater or lesser extent. The name invariably helped to characterize the character who bore it. What is surprising in modern fiction is not that names often bear an allegorical inflection but that characters' names increasingly tend to be neutral and uninflected. This innovation is part of the novel's commitment to everyday realism, but it appeared relatively late in the history of fiction. Jack Wilton and Robinson Crusoe, for example, though relatively col-ourless, are not wholly uninflected names.[44] They lack the pronounced moral insinuation conveyed by innumerable characters' names in later fiction, such as Lovelace (pronounced, but not spelt, like Loveless in *The Round-Heads*), Allworthy, Random, Willoughby, Knightley, Eyre, and Snowe. It was not until the realistic and naturalistic fiction of the late nineteenth century that it became commonplace to encounter characters with completely ordinary 'telephone book' names devoid of social or moral significance. Even in the twentieth century this innova-tion was often discarded. This penchant for allegorical naming lends some support to those critics who have accused English novelists of a fairy-tale simplicity of moral outlook;[45] but in both drama and the novel the gap between characters' behaviour and their inflected names is regularly exploited as a source of suspense and dramatic irony. Mr Allworthy does not seem to be all-worthy, nor is Mr Knightley particularly knightly. This tension ought to be suppressed in Bunyan's moral allegories, since we are never meant to think of Mr Badman as being anything but bad. In practice, however, the tension is often intriguing and sometimes disturbing.

At a simple level, Bunyan's plain language and sharpness of observation are huge assets for fictional characterization. Consider Great-heart's account in *The Pilgrim's Progress* of 'Madam Bubble, or this vain world':

She is a great gossiper, she is always, both she and her daughters, at one pilgrim's heels or other, now commending, and then preferring the excellencies of this life. She is a bold and impudent slut; she will talk with any man. She always laugheth poor pilgrims to scorn, but highly commends the rich. If there be one cunning to get money in a place, she will speak well of him, from house to house. She loveth banqueting, and feasting mainly well; she is always at one full table or another.[46]

Great-heart warns his listeners not to surrender to Madam Bubble's charms—'whoever doth lay their head down in her lap, had as good lay it down upon that block over which the axe doth hang'—but he goes further than this, declaring that 'whoever lay their eyes upon her beauty are counted the enemies of God' (362). By this standard, of course, the reader is condemned; anybody who enjoys and responds to Bunyan's prose is condemned. Behind this delightful description, the setting of an impossible standard suggests both Puritan hypocrisy and the threat of a Puritan tyranny. The author of Puritan fiction would force us to look upon beauty and then consign us to eternal damnation for finding it beautiful; he would trick us by his lies, and then denounce us for believing in lies.

Puritan tyranny at its starkest is depicted in Bunyan's *The Holy War*. Here a military tribunal passes sentence on numerous characters who are seen as agents of Prince Diabolus, the enemy commander whose forces have been routed from the City of Mansoul. Diabolus has a fifth column within the city, many of whom go under false names. In terms of Bunyan's allegorical naming conventions this is undoubtedly disturbing; it is as if Mr Badman had suddenly decided to call himself Goodman. Mr Good-deed in *The Holy War* is 'A man that bare only the name, but had nothing of the nature of the thing' (98). Lord Covetousness passes as Prudent-thrifty, and Lasciviousness as Harmless-mirth, and both are brutally punished for their deception. The ruler of the city who decrees these righteous punishments is Prince Emanuel's deputy, Lord Wilbewill—itself a curiously ambiguous name, denoting the Lord's Will that will be done but also suggesting high-born self-will.[47] Wilbewill crucifies Harmless-mirth's two sons, Jolley and Griggish, with his own hands. Any-thing and Loosefoot are clapped in irons and held ready to be crucified publicly at the time when 'twould be for the best to the Corporation, and most for the discouragement of the camp of the enemies' (199). Meanwhile three other petty malefactors, Fooling, Letgoodslip, and Clip-promise, are hanged in the streets. This is truly a bloody assize, the more so since Bunyan's narrator is aware that some of the characters' punishments do not seem to fit either their names or their crimes. Clip-promise, for example, is guilty of reneging on a commercial contract, but, we are told, his hanging is in no sense unduly harsh: 'truly my judgment is that all those of his name and life should be served even as he' (243). The 'holy war' turns into a holocaust carried out in the name of godliness and good business.

During his long imprisonment, John Bunyan himself seems to have been treated punctiliously according to the law, and in many ways leniently. What should we make of his allegory of the soul as a well-run town or city where godless miscreants are judicially murdered in an orgy of legal vengeance? *The Holy War* draws on Bunyan's knowledge of actual Civil War sieges, and its immediate stimulus was Charles II's political campaign to take back control of the English cities and boroughs from the Dissenters by 'remodelling' their corporations and issuing new charters. In Bunyan's home town of Bedford this led to the granting of a new charter in 1684.[48] It seems, to say the least, a slender basis for a long and bloodthirsty fiction of military history. The crucial point, no doubt, is that *The Holy War* is an allegory of the individual soul in which, as one scholar has put it, 'the battles of the interior self are conflated with the battles of saints against sinners and of Roundheads against Cavaliers'.[49] The ruthlessness with which a Puritan ought to suppress a rebellion within his own soul does not translate very happily into methods of civic government.

If the City of Mansoul itself were seen as Bunyan's protagonist, then *The Holy War* could be understood as a distorted version of the traditional tale of suffering, of which the most distinguished example is the Book of Job. The lesson of Job—perhaps the most influential of all devotional texts in seventeenth and eighteenth-century English culture— was that the true Christian must have the patience to withstand suffering, however harsh and unjust it might seem. Mansoul is fought over by Diabolus and King Shaddai (the Hebrew name for God used in Job and Revelation) and his son Prince Emanuel. Like Job, the rulers of Mansoul cry out to Shaddai and Emanuel for help, but receive no response. On one occasion when the Lord Mayor is sent away empty-handed, 'he smote upon his breast and returned weeping, all the way bewailing the lamentable state of *Mansoul*' (160), a very Job-like reaction. It is only when Shaddai judges that the people of Mansoul are '*heart and soul* in the matter' (208)—that is, that they are at their last extremity—that he sends Prince Emanuel to relieve them and to accomplish the ethical and spiritual cleansing of their city.

Bunyan had produced a much more palatable rewriting of the Book of Job in his spiritual autobiography *Grace Abounding* (1666). Here the narrator uses his reading of the Bible, including the Book of Job, to help him resist temptation. Eventually Bunyan is thrown into prison, parted from his wife and children, and threatened with hanging. Earlier he has reported the malicious rumours that were spread against his ministry, 'that I was a Witch, a Jesuit, a Highway-man, and the like'.[50] Moreover, he knows that 'when *Job* had passed thorow his captivity, *he had twice as much as he had before*' (78). In prison, he prays for comfort, 'yet no comfort appeared' until he remembers Satan's challenge: 'Doth *Job serve God for naught?*' (100–1). He must be content to 'serve God for nothing' (101) and then, para-doxically, God will give him everything—hence the work's full title, *Grace Abounding to the Chief of Sinners*. This structure of deprivation, impri-sonment, and spiritual abandonment leading to a final reward is found again and again in the plots of English eighteenth- and nineteenth-century fiction, as we shall see in Chapter 5. It testifies to the novel's indebtedness to Puritan spiritual autobiography and also to criminal biography. Clarissa, Tom Jones, Humphrey Clinker, the Vicar of Wakefield, Caleb Williams, and several of Dickens's heroes all suffer imprisonment. Their imprison-ment is usually unjust in human terms, yet it is also part of the framework of poetical justice with which the novelist represents God's plan for the world. It follows the pattern not only of the story of Job, but of the great moral lesson that was commonly drawn from the Civil War and the Commonwealth—that of the expropriation, banishment, and eventual restoration of the English monarchy. Everything must be taken away from the protagonist in order that, by God's grace, everything may be restored.

There is a spiritual grimness in all the texts by Bunyan considered so far. *The Pilgrim's Progress*, by contrast, became one of the best-loved books in English. Underlying it, nevertheless, is a contest between a rightful and a usurping king, in which no compromise is possible. The Celestial City which is the pilgrims' ultimate goal is the site of a judicial regime potentially as harsh as that presided over by Lord Wilbewill. Justice for Bunyan means the revenge of the righteous, not the ideal of an impartial civil justice that was emerging in his lifetime. In the Celestial City the pilgrims are expected to sit beside the King of Glory on the Throne of Judgement, so that 'when he shall pass sentence upon all the workers of iniquity, let them be angels or men, you also shall have a voice in that judgement, because they were his and your enemies' (201). Bunyan promises his Christian readers an eternity in Heaven spent not just playing the harp, but paying off old scores.

And yet to write a denunciation of *The Pilgrim's Progress* from the standpoint of our supposedly more enlightened and secular age would be grotesquely unfair and small-minded. Bunyan's other fictional works share a sense of spatial and spiritual claustrophobia, of confinement within a town, a besieged city, a prison, a beleaguered soul, or an unredeemed life of sin. *The Pilgrim's Progress* breaks out of these confines, taking us on the open road with a lively company of travellers. Bunyan's pilgrims reach back to Chaucer's Canterbury pilgrims, and also to the knights-errant of courtly romance. They are constantly meeting with spiritual challenges and life-threatening obstacles on a quest which could be compared with the Arthurian knights' quest for the Holy Grail, except that they journey on foot. The landscape through which they pass (which overlaps very slightly with the landscape of *The Holy War*)[51] is a synthetic, allegorical creation composed of at least three elements: the biblical Holy Land, the land of folk tales and medieval romance, and modern England.

At the scriptural level, the landmarks passed on the journey include the River Jordan and the monument to Lot's wife overlooking the Cities of the Plain. The pilgrims are heading for the New Jerusalem and carrying Mediterranean-style provisions such as wine, raisins, figs, and pomegranates. Their language is the 'language of Canaan' (126). They pass through the Delectable Mountains where there are both vineyards and shepherds. On the other hand, they only have to cross the wrong stile to come upon Doubting-Castle, the home of Giant Despair and the last resting-place of innumerable victims whose skeletons litter the castle yard. Christian has already overcome the dragon Apollyon, and later his family will be threatened by the giant Grim. Despair and Grim have been interpreted as modern English landlords erecting 'Keep Out' and 'Trespassers will be prosecuted' signs,[52] but they are primarily fairy-tale figures.

Nevertheless, the King's highway from the City of Destruction to the Celestial City traversing such obstacles as the Slough of Despond (where the King's surveyors are unable to mend the road) and the Hill Difficulty is recognizably an English main road. Vanity Fair is a modern market town in which produce from Britain, France, Germany, Italy, and Spain is bought and exchanged. There is the Valley of Humiliation where 'many labouring men...have got good estates' (289) and there is 'no rattling with coaches, nor rumbling with wheels' (291)—not merely an Earthly Paradise, but an England in which the landowning classes are no longer allowed to oppress the poor. Bunyan's 'good companions' are spiritual 'footmen' (170), in sharp contrast not only with the Arthurian knights but with the rogues, gentlefolk, and haughty Cavaliers of other seventeenth-century fiction. The only legitimate rider in *The Pilgrim's Progress* is Faithful, the martyr of Vanity Fair who is taken direct to the Celestial City in a heavenly chariot.

Bunyan's pilgrims stop at roadside inns and other resting-places such as the Delectable Mountains and the House Beautiful. They must also keep a perpetual lookout for highwaymen and robbers. Christian's advice to travellers on the road combines both spiritual and practical good sense: they should go armed (with the shield of faith), and in a convoy with other pilgrims. Preferably they should be accompanied by an experienced guide such as Great-heart, who kills the robber captain Slay-good, or Valiant-for-Truth whose bloody face and drawn sword reveal that he has just dispatched three highwaymen. The pilgrim who has his purse snatched is called Little-faith, a name suggesting he is too ill-equipped to travel safely.

If Christian is both pedestrian knight-errant and fortunate traveller, he is also a young man in search of his destiny. Thanks to the parchment roll given to him by Evangelist, he goes to 'seek an inheritance' (42). This inheritance lies in the city of the *'righteous nation'* (203), a city whose streets are paved with gold. Here the New Jerusalem of the biblical Apocalypse, in which 'the street of the city was pure gold' (Revelation 21: 21), joins hands with Dick Whittington's London even though the profanity of the folk tale would have appalled Bunyan. But neither Christian nor the other pilgrims are shown actually entering the Celestial City. Instead, they wait by the riverside on the opposite bank while the Shining Ones, emissaries from the city, move among them. And far from portraying Christian's life inside the City of Gold, the second part of *The Pilgrim's Progress* accomplishes a remarkable doubling-back by showing the women Christiana and Mercy undergoing the same journey that Christian has already made.

To write a narrative sequel in which the protagonist's steps are literally retraced by new characters would be unthinkable in a modern novel. It is one of the features that most clearly reveals the uniqueness of Bunyan's allegory. A novel cannot appropriately describe the same journey twice, and even a reverse journey (such as the return up or down a river in late nineteenth-century romances like *Huckleberry Finn* and *Heart of Darkness*) is normally got over as quickly as possible. A novel, whether or not it is a tale of travel and adventure, relies on vivid, unexpected, and unique events, while Bunyan's allegory openly valorizes repetition and recapitulation just as a fairy tale does. It is possible that part one of

The Pilgrim's Progress was too much like a novel or a modern fantasy narrative for Bunyan's austere purposes. In the second part the landscape and adventures become less vivid, and as the itinerary is repeated the allegory is foregrounded. The physical journey that seemed to take Christian a matter of days or perhaps weeks now takes several years, becoming a pilgrimage of life during which Christiana ages, her sons grow up, and Mercy marries and has children. But the journey is also a textual one in which the pilgrims in part two find that their predecessors' journey has already been narrated, being inscribed on stone monuments along the King's highway that they have to follow. This narrative self-consciousness is a profoundly novelistic touch, reminding us, for example, of the second part of *Don Quixote* where the knight-errant's fame is already established because the characters have read and laughed over his adventures in the first part.

John Bunyan died in 1688, the year before Aphra Behn, and is buried with his fellow Dissenters, including Daniel Defoe, in London's Bunhill Fields. Bunyan and Behn belong to the period immediately before the so-called Glorious Revolution of 1688–9, when England took a turn towards national unity and reconciliation to which neither the Puritan saint nor the libertine novelist ever had to accommodate themselves. Neither author would have been at ease (though Behn, doubtless, was more adaptable) with a nation broadly at peace with itself, or with a civil society whose greatest conflicts were not between contending spiritual and temporal powers, but simply between political parties. Bunyan's *The Holy War* with its tyrannical vision of justice was soon forgotten by a new England anxious to bury its memories of religious division and civil war. *The Pilgrim's Progress*, on the other hand, found its readership not only among the tiny minority of Nonconformists but throughout a decidedly unrighteous nation.[53]

Cross-Grained Crusoe: Defoe and the Contradictions of Englishness

F EW writers have been as insistent about their nationality as Daniel Defoe. He was a prolific journalist and author of histories, travel books, handbooks, and advice books, whose titles include *A Tour through the Whole Island of Great Britain* (1724–6), *The Complete English Tradesman* (1726), and *A Plan of the English Commerce* (1728). Not only is he the principal claimant for the title of father of the English novel, but his non-fictional writings amount to a kind of ramshackle encyclopedia, a comprehensive compendium of facts and opinions about the English nation. His greatest contribution to world literature was his creation of Robinson Crusoe, a fictional character who has long been regarded as an archetypal Englishman. Yet Defoe and his fictional creations have a more complex relationship to national identity than appears at first sight.

The historian Linda Colley argues that the construction of the sense of British national identity began with the union of England and Scotland in 1707, more than a century after the two countries were first brought together under the Stuart monarchy.[1] The early eighteenth century was a time when nationalities were forcefully asserted and new national symbols invented. However, it is Englishness, not Britishness, that is stressed in Defoe's works and in the literary characterizations of his contemporaries such as Addison's Sir Roger de Coverly (the prototypical country squire) and Arbuthnot's John Bull. Sir Roger and his friends are old-timers who reflect the Whig belief in the healing of national differences and the mellowing of the English nation two generations after the Civil War. John Bull is a symbol of outwardly turned national aggression, an expression of England's growing readiness to challenge France, Holland, and Spain for dominance on the world stage.

In Joseph Addison's *Spectator* essays of 1711–12, the Tory country squire is shown on his visits to London attending the Club frequented by Mr Spectator, Will Honeycomb, and the City merchant Sir Andrew

Freeport. Sir Roger de Coverly's great-grandfather was supposedly the inventor of the well-known country dance, but his name is manifestly allegorical and can be taken to suggest a former Cavalier who has gone to earth in the country—a shy fox who rarely emerges from his covert. In his youth Sir Roger fought a duel and mixed with the Restoration rakes Etherege and Rochester, but he has mellowed into a state of benevolent patriotism and is the embodiment of his own belief that country squires are the 'Ornaments of the *English* Nation'.[2] Sir Roger's natural opponent is the Puritan tradesman Sir Andrew Freeport, an ardent republican who (as Will Honeycomb reports on one occasion) 'is grown Cock of the Club since [Sir Roger] left us, and if he does not return quickly, will make every Mother's Son of us Commonwealths Men' (95–6). Freeport, far from exuding benevolence, is full of cheeseparing maxims; but eventually he saves enough money to retire from business and devote himself to religious contemplation in the country. The Club (which is brought to an end by Sir Roger's death and Sir Andrew's retirement) is, therefore, a literary forum bringing together Tories and Whigs, country gentlemen and city merchants, and ageing Cavaliers and ageing Roundheads. Fifty years have passed since Charles II's Restoration and, however challenging they may once have been, Sir Andrew's Cromwellian doctrines are now no more than debating society opinions. Civil war has given place to a friendly dispute among a group of mildly ridiculous turkey-cocks long past their prime. The *Spectator* essays are highly effective as national allegory precisely because the allegory is so understated.

Nobody could accuse the John Bull pamphlets of understatement. John Arbuthnot's satire on the War of Spanish Succession takes the form of a 'property romance' in which two tradesmen, John Bull and the Dutchman Nicholas Frog, take legal action against the French king Lewis Baboon to recover the estate of the late Lord Strutt (Charles II of Spain). Soon they all become hopelessly bogged down in litigation. Bull, the representative of the 'English People',[3] is no Puritan. The boozing, corpulent, cudgel-wielding figure looks like a plebeian, but makes his money by trade and spends it like a lord:

For the better understanding of the following History, the Reader ought to know, that *Bull*, in the main, was an honest plain-dealing Fellow, Cholerick, Bold, and of a very unconstant Temper . . . he was very apt to quarrel with his best Friends, especially if they pretended to govern him: If you flatter'd him, you might lead him like a Child. *John*'s Temper depended very much upon the Air; his Spirits rose and fell with the Weather-glass. *John* was quick, and understood his business very well, but no Man alive was more careless, in looking into his Accounts, or more cheated by Partners, Apprentices, and Servants: This was occasioned by his being a Boon-Companion, loving his Bottle and his Diversion; for to say Truth, no Man kept a better *House* than *John*, nor spent his Money more generously.[4]

Bull may be a laughing stock, but he soon became the eighteenth-century cartoonists' standby, a homely and likeable substitute for the more heraldic and mythological representatives of the English nation.[5] He personifies the first four of the 'British beatitudes' recited at a drunken moment two centuries later in James Joyce's *Ulysses* (beer, beef, business, bulldogs, Bibles, battleships, buggery, and bishops).[6] For the best part of these two centuries he remained instantly recognizable abroad, and—though Arbuthnot's ephemeral satire scarcely deserves the title of a novel—he is an appropriate national symbol for a novel-reading age.

There could be no starker contrast than that between Bull and Defoe's fictional protagonists. The latter may be rogues but they are also Puritans, notoriously addicted to bookkeeping and the balancing of material and spiritual accounts. Their national identity is frequently uncertain. For the most part they are wanderers of no fixed abode, unpredictably changing their manner of life and even their names—the 'half-outsiders' without national ties who are the typical heroes of picaresque fiction.[7] Their hunger for independence, wealth, and adventure constantly draws them away from England. Crusoe, whose name is a corruption of Kreutznaer, is born at York of a German father. He leaves England as soon as he can, and spends a total of forty-five years overseas. Finally he returns to England at the age of 72 for a life of spiritual reflection in preparation for 'a longer journey than all these'.[8] Whether or not the nickname Moll Flanders hints that Defoe's heroine is part-Flemish, she is born in Newgate and spends much of her life in America before returning to England in old age. Colonel Jack grows up in the streets of London but later joins an Irish regiment in the French Army, changes his name to Jacques, and lives for some time as a Frenchman at Canterbury. Captain Bob Singleton poses as a retired Greek merchant speaking no English when he finally returns to settle in England after decades of piracy on the high seas. These characters are not without jingoistic feelings and pre-judices—Captain Bob, for example, loathes the Portuguese because 'it is natural to an Englishman to hate a coward'[9]—but their patriotism is for the most part muted and undemonstrative. Roxana, born in Poitiers of French Huguenot stock, calls herself an Englishwoman even though Paris is the scene of many of her triumphs. She is known as Mademoiselle de Beleau and the Countess de Wintelsheim, but prefers to be remembered by the Turkish nickname acquired when she was mistress of the English king. Eventually she marries a Dutch merchant and settles in Holland. The anonymous narrator of *Memoirs of a Cavalier* is a Shropshire landowner's son who gains his military experience in the Swedish Army before fighting for Charles I in the Civil War. He is a remarkably dispassionate observer who turns Royalist for partly mercenary reasons, without, as he puts it, troubling himself to examine sides: 'I was glad to hear the Drums beat for Soldiers; as if I had been a meer *Swiss*, that had not car'd which Side went up or down, so I had my Pay'. It is true that he later feels some remorse over his lack of concern for his country's 'approaching Ruin', but nationality and allegiance are often no more than flags of convenience for Defoe's protagonists.[10] Their cosmopolitanism and capacity for switching identities is still more remarkable when set beside Defoe's lifelong output as a journalist and commentator on national themes, beginning with his *Essay upon Projects* (1697) with its pioneering futurological vision of a reconstructed and modernized England.

Defoe served as a government agent and as a commentator on English politics in the *Review* (1704–12), and by the time of his death in 1731 he had published more or less comprehensive accounts of English commerce, geography, politics, history, religion, sex, and family life. His urge to demonstrate mastery of such a disparate catalogue of knowledge reminds us of Crusoe laboriously teaching himself all the trades necessary for his island existence. His novels written in the early 1720s were followed by *A Tour through the Whole Island of Great Britain* and by his series of advice books culminating in the unfinished *Complete English Gentleman*. It could be said that his slowly maturing ambition had made him a kind of English Walt Whitman whose large, all-embracing song of himself was also a song of the nation. His fiction is centrifugal, his non-fiction centripetal, with London always as the centre. Moreover, his vision of the national life projects the nation as a kind of body in which the blood courses back and forth from centre to circumference, from nucleus to periphery. This is most plainly announced in his descriptions of the circulation of trade, where London is the heart, the main roads are the arteries, and commerce is the instrument of national prosperity joining together the remotest parts of the kingdom.[11] In terms of the volume of home trade and foreign trade, England, as Defoe asserted 'without the least partiality to our own country', was the 'greatest trading country in the world'.[12] His schemes in the *Essay upon Projects* for a national banking system, for the improvement of main roads, and for better education for men and women would all tend to promote the circulation of trade.

Defoe observes in *The Complete English Tradesman* that 'trade increases people, and people increase Trade' (226). A healthy economy implies a constantly moving and circulating population, with plentiful immigration and emigration. The more pluralistic the nation, the better its prospects. Thus the narrator of *The Consolidator* (1705)—Defoe's strange and tedious politico-religious satire cast in the form of a moon voyage—lives in a country which 'had been peopled from all parts, and had in it some of the blood of all the nations in the moon'. Its people are 'the weakest, strongest, richest, poorest, most generous, covetous, bold, cowardly, false, faithful, sober, dissolute, surly, civil, slothful, diligent, peacable, quarrelling, loyal, seditious nation that ever was known'.[13] That *The Consolidator* was a national allegory about the English nation would have been immediately evident to readers of *The True-Born Englishman* (1700), Defoe's witty, impassioned verses prompted by a pamphlet attacking King William for his foreign birth. Defoe's England is the world's melting-pot, its population the bastard fruit of 'spurious generation' from 'all the nations under Heav'n':

> A True-Born Englishman's a contradiction,
> In speech an irony, in fact a fiction.
> A banter made to be a test of fools,
> Which those that use it justly ridicules.[14]

Multicultural and multi-ethnic England stands in stark contrast to its weaker and ethnically purer neighbours, Ireland, Scotland, and Wales, 'three nations . . . as clear from mixtures of blood as any in the world'.[15] But if the Englishman is a 'man akin to all the universe' (36), he is also indefinable, and verging on the invisible and unmentionable—'Europe's sink, the jakes where she | Voids all her offal out-cast progeny' (32). Thus Defoe confounds the popular Tory idea of the national breed, since the 'true-born' Englishman is a mongrel rather than a thoroughbred, a pariah and not a pedigree bulldog. Far from being the heir to a unique national past, he represents the coming age of global commerce in which all nations will gradually become miscegenated and pluralistic. The English may be tempted to despise foreigners, but 'what they are to-day we were yesterday, and to-morrow they will be like us'.[16]

It may be said that in this poem Defoe had discovered that one of the best ways of flattering the English is to insult them. Any straightforward enumeration of national virtues is likely to sound embarrassing and tasteless in English ears. Defoe was not invariably a good judge of his readers' responses, and soon after *The True-Born Englishman* a badly aimed satire would have him sent to the pillory; but here, speaking in the voice of 'Satire' (with a brief interlude of Britannia's song eulogizing King William),[17] his sense of tone is almost unerring, and he can get away with lampooning the English as a 'vile degenerate race' (58) who have nothing to boast of but their bastardy. This does not mean that the poem is free of self-contradiction—far from it. As an ardent Williamite, Defoe dismisses the growing opposition to the Dutch Protestant King on the grounds that the English are a 'discontented nation' of hot-headed rebels, 'Easily set together by the ears' and 'Harder to rule in times of peace than war' (44). But English truculence and discontent must have their uses, since without them William would never have come to the throne; so Defoe in his role as people's tribune asserts that

> Whate're the dialect of courts may tell,
> He that his right demands, can ne're rebel. (48)

Elsewhere in the poem his fulsome praise of 'great Nassau' (King William), who was Charles I's grandson, is hard to square with a rollicking populist attack on the worship of heredity and rank. Radical as he may have been in his statement of the people's rights, Defoe was by no means a modern democrat.

Who exactly are 'the people of England'? In *The True-Born Englishman* they appear as a promiscuous, unruly, crime-ridden multitude, but a later tract addressed to the King, *The Original Power of the Collective Body of the People of England, Examined and Asserted* (1702), puts forward a much more restricted and legalistic definition of the English people. Here Defoe maintains that the public good, the commonwealth, the English constitution, and the laws and 'liberties of England' are all reducible to 'that great term, the People of England', but the latter consist only of freeholders and property owners.[18] The others have 'no right to live there but upon sufferance'. Only the property owners qualify as full citizens, or rather as free subjects under the King, the 'universal landlord' (102). For Defoe in this tract submission to constitutional monarchy is part of the national character—'The genius of this nation has always appeared to tend to a monarchy, a legal limited monarchy' (96)—while property-owning Englishmen enjoy 'more freedom in our regal, than any people in the world can do in a popular, government' (97).

On examination, then, Defoe's radical Englishness contains as many self-contradictions as the xenophobic notions he set out to attack. He was a notable contributor to the myth of English freedom, but he restricted that freedom to members of the upper and middle classes, the 'tradesmen' and 'gentlemen' at whom his advice books would later be aimed. If the laws and liberties of England are reduced to the People, the People to the freeholders, and the freeholders to tenants of a royal landlord, the great majority of the nation's inhabitants do not even enjoy squatter's rights. But whatever his political affiliations may have led him to embrace, Defoe's novels reveal his imaginative identification with outlaws who have no rights and who, by and large, become property owners only on false pretences, and in fear of being found out. Crusoe pretending to govern his island, Moll Flanders posing as a penitent, and Captain Singleton living disguised as a Greek are at once manifest impostors and narrators with an irresistible urge to confess their imposture. They want to be both visible and invisible, both present and absent. If their narratives speak for the English people it can only be through the medium of the 'irony', 'fiction', 'metaphor', and 'contradiction' that Defoe had under-lined in *The True-Born Englishman*.

Crusoe and the Naked Quaker

Defoe's identification with his exiled and outlawed protagonists is made possible by the fact that theirs is, from one point of view, a common tale of original sin leading to suffering, calamity, and eventual deliverance. Crusoe in his volume of *Serious Reflections* asserts that 'The fable is always made for the moral, not the moral for the fable',[19] and numerous modern critics have concurred that the sometimes perfunctorily stated morals at the end of Defoe's fictions ought to be taken seriously. At some point in their careers, even the most unregenerate of Defoe's protagonists will come to feel that they have been deservedly condemned to the terrors of hell. Later, often much later, they will seek divine forgiveness. Moll Flanders experiences Newgate as an 'emblem of hell itself';[20] Bob Singleton is so tormented by guilt over his successful life of crime that his Quaker friend William has to dissuade him from suicide; and Roxana compares her fear of divine vengeance to a 'Dart struck into the Liver . . . a secret Hell within, even all the while, when [my] Joy was at the highest'.[21] Both Crusoe and Colonel Jack identify with the biblical Job. Jack, sur-veying his twenty-four years of 'levity and profligate wickedness', plans, he says, to 'with a just detestation, learn, as Job says, to abhor myself in dust and ashes'.[22] And yet, far from wallowing in Job-like despair and self-hatred, Defoe's characters find comfort, first in the life of action, and later, when their time for repentance has officially come, in reliving and retelling the exploits of their wicked lives in narrative.

Robinson Crusoe freely confesses to the 'original sin' of filial disobedience, and critics have suggested that his self-dramatization as a Job-like figure is spurious, since he is the author of his own tribulations.[23] His shipwreck on the island is, he thinks, a manifest sign of God's displeasure. He has 'Reasons . . . to expect particular Misfortunes to my self', and he cannot believe that God has singled him out without cause.[24] He tries to eliminate the word 'accident' from his vocabulary, since nothing in his world is accidental. Experience is full of 'secret Hints and Notices' which may be put down to a 'Converse of Spirits', and which ought to guide the conduct of the wise man (128, 180). The need to pay due regard to these 'providences' is the chief spiritual lesson of his life on the island.

Crusoe's superstitions, and above all his belief that 'there was a strange Concurrence of Days in the various Providences which befel me' (97), are faithfully repeated throughout Defoe's works. As we read in the *Serious Reflections*, 'a man killed by accident is a man whom God has delivered up . . . to be killed in that manner, perhaps vindictively, perhaps not' (204). Defoe's God is frequently a jealous and vindictive God. Not even Crusoe's twenty-eight years of punishment and repentance on the island are enough to satisfy Him, since in the *Farther Adventures* Crusoe again suffers bewildering reversals of fortune exhibiting the 'justice of Providence' (185). But, in an eloquent passage from the *Serious Reflections*, Crusoe claims to support his afflictions with the proverbial patience of Job:

I, Robinson Crusoe, grown old in affliction, borne down by calumny and reproach, but supported from within, boldly prescribe this remedy against universal clamours and contempt of mankind: patience, a steady life of virtue and sobriety, and a comforting dependence on the justice of Providence, will first or last restore the patient to the opinion of his friends, and justify him in the face of his enemies; and in the meantime, will support him comfortably in despising those who want manners and charity, and leave them to be cursed from heaven with their own passions and rage. (225)

At this point, a later novelist such as Samuel Richardson would surely have observed that Job's sufferings had to be borne patiently since they were, by all merely human reckoning, arbitrary and unjust. There is a world of difference between Clarissa Harlowe's tragedy and Crusoe's display of spiritual smugness. The biblical Job was exhorted by his wife to 'curse God, and die' (Job 2: 9), but Crusoe, vindictive for all his protestations of stoicism, is calmly waiting to see God curse his enemies. He seems oblivious to the doctrine of 'future remuneration' which holds that injustices in this life will only be compensated for in the next. There is something 'stage-managed' about his devotionalism.[25]

The plots of many of Defoe's novels can be seen as devices for isolating the individual from society and getting him alone with his God. Historically, however, the belief that God's vengeance was manifested on Earth, and not merely in the afterlife, was more often associated with nations than with individuals. It is the rationale of Bunyan's *The Holy War* as well as of countless ancient and modern wars. Defeat in war has invariably been regarded as a token of divine displeasure, although the individual soldier killed on the losing side may well be in a state of grace. The interpretation of wars as the instruments of God's chosen vengeance, so powerful during the English Civil War and its aftermath, was doubtless fading by the time that Defoe wrote *Robinson Crusoe*.[26] Nevertheless, Crusoe discusses the idea of God's national vengeance, and Defoe explores it at length in *A Journal of the Plague Year* (1722).

Why did God choose to visit a great plague on London in 1665, five years after the Restoration? H.F., the eyewitness narrator of Defoe's *Journal*, reports the explanations put forward by prophets and enthusiasts at the time with considerable scepticism, yet he himself is in his quiet way as superstitious as they are. The wildest of the prophets of doom is Solomon Eagle, the 'naked Quaker' who 'though not infected at all but in his head, went about denouncing of judgement upon the city in a frightful manner, sometimes quite naked, and with a pan of burning charcoal on his head'.[27] Before, during, and after the plague Defoe's narrator largely concurs with Eagle's diagnosis of his times, even if he stops short of proclaiming it in the streets and rending his clothes. For example, the narrator confronts a bunch of mocking atheists in a tavern, who laugh at him for 'calling the plague the hand of God' (84). Retiring from the scene somewhat crest-fallen, he reflects that the atheists' time of triumph will be short, since God 'had, as it were, His sword drawn in His hand on purpose to take vengeance not on them only, but on the whole nation' (87). But, though the whole nation may be laid low, H.F. himself has received a divine token that he enjoys the Lord's special protection. Opening the Bible at random, he has read in Psalm 91 that 'A thousand shall fall at thy side, and ten thousand at thy right hand; but it shall not come nigh thee. Only with thine eyes shalt thou behold and see the reward of the wicked' (34).

The fact that 1665 is to be a time of God's anger is announced by numerous portents. In the heavens there are two comets, and on Earth people 'were more addicted to prophecies and astrological conjurations, dreams, and old wives' tales than ever they were before or since' (41–2). This popular addiction is a sign of impending calamity, yet it is also a reason for it, being part of the 'error of the times' which God is concerned to punish (41). In *A Journal of the Plague Year* God's anger is never ascribed to political causes, yet it will have been in Defoe's and his readers' minds that it was the events of the Civil War, the Commonwealth, and the Restoration which called for the punishment of one or other of the contending parties. Are the people of London being scourged for their waywardness in Cromwell's time, or for the explosion of licentiousness and wickedness that supposedly accompanied the Restoration? Defoe's narrator will not say. Though fully convinced that the plague is God's vengeance, he is extremely vague about what might have provoked it. Solomon Eagle may have been more specific, but the words of his frightful denunciations of judgement on the city are never directly recorded.

If Eagle the 'naked Quaker' is, in some sense, H.F.'s alter ego, two of Defoe's other protagonists are closely associated with Quaker companions. Captain Bob Singleton's partner in crime is the Quaker William, while Roxana becomes so intimate with her Quaker landlady that she herself is taken for a Quaker.[28] The English Quakers notoriously changed within Defoe's lifetime from a cruelly persecuted sect of militant enthusiasts to a congregation of quiet, sober, high-minded people who were extremely successful in banking and other businesses. We could well see Robinson Crusoe on his island, as—at least by his own account—a type of the new Quaker. At first he loudly protests against his fate, crying out '*Why has God done this to me? What have I done to be thus us'd?*' But, he adds, 'My Conscience presently check'd me in that Enquiry, as if I had blasphem'd', and, moreover, his conscience rebukes him 'like a Voice' (68). Once Crusoe has thus been moved by the Spirit (in Quaker parlance), he does not waste time in lamentations but buries himself in work. Where Job did little more than sit down and complain under his afflictions, Crusoe builds and cultivates until his island is fit for its 'King and Lord', as he describes himself (73). In *A Journal of the Plague Year* Solomon Eagle and the narrator, the prophet and the practical man, are supposed to be quite distinct, and in *Robinson Crusoe* it might at first appear that we see a practical man on his own. But Crusoe, for all his understatement, is also a prophet.

Admittedly, to begin with he has not a nation's evils to denounce, but his own. Is his filial disobedience—without which we should have very few novels or adventure stories—really such a heinous sin that it deserves to be punished with twenty-eight years' imprisonment on an island? Defoe gets around this dilemma by emphasizing not his castaway's afflictions but his good fortune or, to use Crusoe's own term, his deliverance. But Crusoe's stress on the cheerful and providential aspects of his shipwreck is made very much easier by a process of erasure and retrospective editing. For example, there is the unwritten diary entry in which he informs us that on his first day ashore he ran around wringing his hands and beating his head and face, exclaiming at his misery, and crying out that he was undone. This is one of the 'dull things' he would have written on the day of his shipwreck (30 September 1659) if he had not been in 'too much Hurry' and 'too much Discomposure of Mind'— always supposing he had found a pen and dry paper—but his actual, retrospective entry for 30 September speaks merely of his 'afflicting my self at the dismal Circumstances I was brought to' (51–2). But Crusoe continues his habit of Job-like lamentation, as we learn not from his own relatively tight-lipped account—for he only ever mentions his bouts of grief and despair when they are over—but from the cries of his parrot. The parrot, a true witness of its master's demeanour on the island, repeats the words he must have heard most often: '*Poor* Robin Crusoe... *How came you here?*' (104).

A wet, hungry mariner cast ashore on a desolate island would worry first of all about finding food and building a fire. Crusoe mentions that when he is first washed ashore he has a knife, pipe, and tobacco in his pockets, but there is no sign of his having even the means of lighting his pipe. Among Defoe's sources, Captain Woodes Rogers's account of his rescue of Alexander Selkirk lays emphasis on the building of fires and shows Selkirk, in a classic boy-scout scene, rubbing two sticks together when his powder has run out. Crusoe is remarkably evasive about where and how he laid his fires. More than twenty years have passed in his narrative before he reveals that he has made a tinderbox from 'the Lock of one of the Muskets' (129) that he salvaged from the cornucopia of the ship's stores two days after he was washed up on the island. How long did this take? And how many working days did he lose as a result of the sudden storms of grief to which he confesses? How did he deal with the temptations of idleness and suicide, not to mention the store of rum which he faithfully husbands for twenty-eight years (despite taking a stiff dram at the first opportunity while he is searching the wreck)? These are some of the things that Crusoe's narrative omits: details which might have spoilt his insistence on his happiness in his 'beloved Island' (102), and might have compromised his ability to speak airily of 'my Reign, or my Captivity, which you please' (100).

Not surprisingly, Crusoe has struck many readers and critics as the inhabitant of a one-man utopia—a 'bourgeois utopia' or a 'utopia of the Protestant ethic'[29]—rather than as a national or religious prophet. His repentance is but a step on his road from relative discomfort to full, self-satisfied enjoyment of his possessions. But matters change with the arrival of the cannibals. Between his discovery of a footprint in the sand and his capture of Friday he spends much of his time terrified of intruders, lurking in his cave or going out armed to the teeth. Does he have a 'higher' responsibility, however—a white man's burden to take up? At first he settles for inaction; he cannot be the instrument of God's vengeance towards the savage nations:

As to the Crimes they were guilty of towards one another, I had nothing to do with them; they were National, and I ought to leave them to the Justice of God, who is the Governor of Nations, and knows how by National Punishments to make a just retribution for National Offences; and to bring publick Judgments upon those who offend in a publick Manner, by such ways as best pleases Him. (125)

The difficulty for Crusoe is that if he obeys his belligerent instincts and launches an attack on the cannibals, he may be guilty of murder. Yet not to act in a case where conscience required him to act would clearly be sinful. As time goes on and his firepower is increased by the addition of Friday, it becomes increasingly obvious that, like any leader anxious to go to war, he is looking for a lawful *casus belli*. He finds it, needless to say, when he realizes that there is a captive European about to go into the cannibals' cooking-pot. Now at last the moment has come when, as he has foreseen, God 'would take the Cause into his own Hands, and by national Vengeance punish them as a people for national Crimes' (168). Armed at last with prophetic certainty, Crusoe and Friday open fire. Three pages later, our narrator offers a meticulous body count of one wounded and seventeen dead.

Is this an isolated moment of bloodthirsty action in an otherwise peaceful story? Taking *Robinson Crusoe* on its own, this is arguably the case, notwithstanding Crusoe's earlier fight with Moorish pirates. But adding in the *Farther Adventures* and *Serious Reflections* gives a very different picture. At Madagascar, in the *Farther Adventures*, Crusoe witnesses the sacking of a village and the massacre of its men, women, and children by the crew of his ship in revenge for the killing of one of their number. He condemns this at the time, and later says he grew 'sick of killing such poor savage wretches' (231); but then he advocates massacring the inhabitants of a Tartar village whom he accuses of devil-worship, citing 'the story of our men at Madagascar' as a moral precedent (285). (Although his partner dissuades him from spilling blood, they manage to set off a full-scale war by stealing the Tartars' wooden idol and burning it.) Crusoe's hypocrisy about European imperialism is further evidenced in his *Serious Reflections*. Where in *Robinson Crusoe* he had condemned the Spaniards' slaughter of the Aztecs in Mexico as 'meer Butchery' (125), he now compares them to Joshua and Moses casting out the heathen in the name of 'God in his Providence' (215). The newly militant Crusoe disclaims any belief in planting religion by the sword (217), but this again is pious humbug. What is needed, he asserts, is 'an universal war against paganism and devil-worship' (224), a Holy War to be launched by the Christian princes: 'This is my crusado; and it would be a war as justifiable on many accounts as any that was ever undertaken in the world, a war that would bring eternal honour to the conquerors and an eternal blessing to the people conquered' (232). This 'crusado' is assured of certain victory, thanks to the 'concurrence of Heaven' (227). 'Crusoe' is supposedly a corruption of 'Kreutznaer', but it seems he is also a true-born Crusader.

Not content with his trumpet call to the Christian princes, the author of the *Serious Reflections* is also a visionary and mystic who claims special insight into the ways of Providence. The *Reflections* culminate in a 'Vision of the Angelic World', in which Crusoe affirms the 'reality of spirits, and of the intelligence between us and them'. His argument for the 'superintendency of divine Providence in the minutest affairs of this world' relies on the evidence of dreams, voices, impulses, hints, apprehensions, and other phenomena which the unreflecting would be likely to dismiss as merely accidental. It is, to say the least, hard to reconcile the soothsayer convinced of the 'manifest existence of the invisible world' (314) with the hard-headed, pragmatic colonist intent on building a rational and civilized life on his desert island. It would be tempting to argue that the *Serious Reflections* is not a true sequel and that there is no continuity between its narrator and the Crusoe of the original story. (In fact, the later book has rarely been reprinted, and most admirers of *Robinson Crusoe* are unaware of its existence.) Crusoe's preface to the *Reflections* invites us to consider his life as a 'parable or allegoric history' written for the purpose of moral and religious improvement (p. xii). If this is, after all, to be taken seriously then we must conclude that, at some point in his island solitude, he became as wild and half-crazed as the Quaker prophet Solomon Eagle.

Crusoe as Universal Englishman

Taking *Robinson Crusoe* together with the *Farther Adventures* and *Serious Reflections*, Crusoe's story is that of a victim of divine vengeance who comes increasingly to think of himself as God's appointed agent. His greatest achievement and greatest happiness is to live in peace on his island, yet he is also a missionary advocating a holy war engulfing the world. We have seen how Crusoe becomes an instrument of 'national Vengeance' in his attacks on the savages. Can it be that in his 'Reign' or 'Captivity' on the island he is also a kind of scapegoat whose suffering and expiation is for national as well as personal crimes?

The rough coincidence between the dates of his exile (1659–87) and the period of the Restoration and Charles II's reign has often been noted.[30] Since in Defoe's view coincidence of dates is always providential, Crusoe's punishment can easily be seen as a displaced equivalent to the Great Plague. The England that he leaves behind, cheerfully disobeying his father, is one that has just lost its Lord Protector (Oliver Cromwell died on 3 September 1658); the England to which he returns is on the verge of becoming what Defoe clearly saw as the redeemed nation of William III—an England no longer torn apart by national divisions and national crimes, and ready for domestic reconstruction and foreign wars. Crusoe's 'deliverance' from shipwreck and his survival during these years may be read as a form of national allegory, since, as Paul J. Korshin argues, 'the most obvious type of deliverance is that of the Jews from Egypt'. Puritans under the Restoration were accustomed to regard their position in England as a kind of Egyptian or Babylonian captivity.[31] The difficulty with such a typological reading of Defoe's novel (a reading which remained hidden from Defoe's time until the late twentieth century) lies in Crusoe's ignorance and insouciance about English politics. Political emotions and forebodings play no part in his decision to rebel against his father and leave the country, nor does he feel any need to register any political changes in the England to which he returns nearly thirty years later, 'as perfect a Stranger to all the World, as if I had never been known there' (200). But the portrait of a religious prophet, ideological crusader, and potential national scapegoat emerging from between the lines of *Robinson Crusoe* subverts the patriotic stereotypes that crop up time and again in conventional accounts of Defoe's protagonist.

The myth of Crusoe as a definitive study in national character began with his conversion into a pantomime hero not long after Defoe's death. On the stage, and to some extent in the national and international imagination, his name rivals those of legendary figures such as Whittington and Robin Hood. The mythical Crusoe is an English pragmatist and a universal man; it is his achievements as a settler, colonist, and mentor of Friday that are remembered, not his religious visions or his destiny as a wanderer dreaming of an imperial crusade. Among Defoe's influential critics, Walter Scott's opinion that Crusoe's 'rough good sense, his prejudices, and his obstinate determination not to sink under evils which can be surpassed by exertion, forms no bad specimen of the True-Born Englishman' has already been quoted in Chapter 1. The same idea was taken up by Victorian critics such as Leslie Stephen and Walter Raleigh. For Raleigh, Crusoe manifested the 'spirit of the Anglo-Saxon race' as seen in the conquest of India and North America—a view that was subsequently repeated by James Joyce.[32] Leslie Stephen's account of Defoe's protagonist as the 'typical Englishman of his time' deserves to be quoted at length:

He is the broad-shouldered, beef-eating John Bull, who has been shouldering his way through the world ever since. Drop him in a desert island, and he is just as sturdy and self-composed as if he were in Cheapside. Instead of shrieking or writing poetry, becoming a wild hunter or a religious hermit, he calmly sets about building a house and making pottery and laying out a farm. . . . Cannibals come to make a meal of him, and he calmly stamps them out with the means provided by civilisation. Long years of solitude produce no sort of effect upon him morally or mentally. He comes home as he went out, a solid keen tradesman, having, somehow or other, plenty of money in his pockets, and ready to undertake similar risks in the hope of making a little more. He has taken his own atmosphere with him to the remotest quarters. Wherever he has set down his solid foot, he has taken permanent possession of the country.[33]

Here Stephen is so carried away that he has evidently forgotten Crusoe's religious conversion, his expressions of penitence, and the fact that he is neither attacked nor threatened by the cannibals whom he so ruthlessly stamps out. The comparison of the goat-eating Crusoe with beefeating John Bull is totally misleading. If Crusoe had been no more than a 'solid keen tradesman' he would never have gone to Brazil, let alone have embarked on his disastrous slave-hunting voyage, and if Bull had been marooned on an island nothing more would have been heard of him once he had exhausted his rum ration. Stephen explicitly identifies Crusoe with the stereotypical British imperialist, 'eating roast beef and plum-pudding; drinking rum in the tropics; singing "God Save the King" and intoning

Watts's hymns',[34] but the portrait is wildly inaccurate. Above all, Crusoe fails to display any ambition to take 'permanent possession of the country'. Instead, he cannot wait to leave it.

Robinson Crusoe's global popularity suggests that its hero cannot simply be identified with any one nationality, and another school of criticism suggests that he is not a second John Bull but, as Defoe had said of the 'true-born Englishman',

> A metaphor invented to express
> A man akin to all the universe.[35]

Crusoe's universality was largely a discovery of the Romantic critics, especially Rousseau and Coleridge: for Coleridge he is the 'universal representative, the person for whom every reader could substitute himself'.[36] The idea that Defoe's novel expresses universal sentiments is common to later critics in the Romantic tradition such as Walter de la Mare,[37] as well as to some recent writers aware of deconstructive and postcolonialist onslaughts on the notion of literary universality. Louis James, for example, finds that Crusoe's contradictions are 'basic to the human predicament' for Western and non-Western readers alike.[38] Samar Attar, a specialist in Arabic literature, traces Arabic echoes in *Robinson Crusoe* and asserts with reference to James Joyce's view of the book that 'Audacity, prudence, courage, sexual apathy, well-balanced piety, self-confidence and tenacity are all human traits which do not have any specific affinity to one race more than the other'.[39] A compromise view is that of James Sutherland: 'Crusoe may be all Mankind in difficulties, but he is first of all an Englishman of the lower middle class making the best of things.'[40] But this has its own kind of carelessness, since Crusoe's upbringing as the third son of a 'good Family', 'and not bred to any Trade' (4) raises him above Defoe's own class position. It is remarkable how often the characterizations of Crusoe (whether in terms of nationality or universality) imitate their subject in resorting to the technique of listing or making an inventory. This is parodied by the American critic Harvey Swados when he cites Alphonse Daudet's estimate of Crusoe as 'the typical Englishman par excellence, with his adventuresomeness, his taste for travel, his love of the sea, his piety, his commercial and practical instincts, and so on and so on'.[41] Constructing lists of national or universal import, the critics take possession of Crusoe and reduce him to order just as Crusoe does with his life and his island.

In fact, the inventories of Crusoe's character conceal sharp differences of interpretation which have come to the fore in some recent criticism. For example, is Crusoe or is he not a born ruler and colonist? According to Manuel Schonhorn, his fortification of the island and his ascendancy over Friday reflect Defoe's adulation of the warrior-king ideal personified by William III and Gustavus Adolphus of Sweden. Crusoe evidently prefers absolute monarchy to parliamentary government.[42] David Trotter, however, maintains that Crusoe was 'never meant to be a colonist' and is manifestly unfit for positions of authority.[43] In part, this disagreement results from Defoe's own inconsistencies, since the image of authoritarian kingship that can be drawn from *Robinson Crusoe* is wholly discredited by the *Farther Adventures*.[44] The high point of Crusoe's enjoyment of authoritarian kingship occurs when he is in total solitude, reigning over a parrot, a dog, and two cats; he becomes embroiled in unwanted complications from the moment that Friday, his first human subject, appears. When his island becomes an organized colony in communication with the outside world, Crusoe loses all interest in it except in so far as it ministers to his vanity.

It is true that Crusoe tells us, of his time with Friday, that the 'three Years which we liv'd there together [were] perfectly and compleatly happy' (159). But Friday is often homesick, bewildered, and terrified, and Crusoe helps him to subdue his unhappiness in Christian piety and a frenzy of unnecessary work.[45] Friday would like Crusoe to accompany him back to his nation and become a missionary there, while Crusoe's thoughts are turning to war against the cannibals. Both of them, anticipating the later heroes of the eighteenth-century European *contes philosophiques* such as Candide and Rasselas, are looking for the first route out of the Happy Valley. Their society is briefly and precariously expanded with the rescue of a Spaniard and of Friday's father, but then comes a party of English mutineers, and Crusoe can no longer act the absolute monarch. His island is reconstituted as a colony with himself as governor, but no sooner has he been installed than he begins his voyage back to England.

In the *Farther Adventures* Crusoe returns for a single ceremonial visit of twenty-five days, exercising his legislative function and dispensing justice, but his efforts to reconcile the Spanish settlers with the English mutineers come to nothing. The Englishmen, led by Will Atkins who prefers staying on the island to being 'carry'd to *England* to be hang'd' (199), need much firmer government than Crusoe provides. He could easily have turned the island into a proper colony and have 'carried over cannon and ammunition, servants and people, to plant, and taking possession of the place, fortified and strengthened it in the name of England, and increased it with people', but he prefers not to, omitting even to name the island, and leaving it 'belonging to no man'. He will neither govern it properly nor relinquish the governorship to one of the other settlers. Not surprisingly, the plantation fails to prosper, being racked by wars within and without. Crusoe, 'possessed with a wandering spirit', is content to play at being an 'old patriarchal monarch' over this no man's land, leaving it as a refuge of outlaws and accidental castaways, a fallen utopia not marked on any map (184). The 'truth' about the place that he hears many years later—that 'they went on but poorly; were malcontent with their long stay there' (184–5)—is offset by his remarkable capacity to idealize and senti- mentalize the island once he has abandoned it. It is his idealization, not the supposed reality, that is remembered. The whole narrative of *Robinson Crusoe* is testimony to this idealization, which teeters over into absurdity at the end of the *Farther Adventures* when he finds himself stranded in Siberia, the polar opposite of his tropical island. Here Crusoe boasts to his companion, a Russian political exile, that his power over his dominions exceeded the 'Czar of Muscovy': 'never tyrant, for such I acknowledged myself to be, was ever so universally beloved, and yet so horribly feared, by his subjects' (300). For Crusoe his colony has now become a mere fantasy, with no more substance than the island over which Sancho Panza was governor.

Crusoe, despite his dreams of imperialist wars, is far from being the practical empire-builder envisaged by Walter Raleigh, James Joyce, and others. In Defoe's own allegory (as stated in the *Serious Reflections*) Crusoe is meant to embody the examined life; ironically, though, he is most English in his unexamined inconsistencies. His life and thought are cross-grained and self-contradictory, exemplifying both miracle and muddle. For all his successful self-projection as a calm, efficient, practical Englishman, he is perpetually homeless, wandering, and lost, a prey to superstition and religious mania. The defeated, quixotic fantasist pondering obsessively over his lost greatness and his unhappy destiny is also a magnificent storyteller. He is a representative of the European adventurer, but his loyalty is entirely to himself and not to an English king; his island is less a one-man colony than a one-man nation. Nevertheless, his Puritan origins cannot be concealed, and they come out most tellingly in moments of pretended abstinence, self-denial, and down-to-earth bluntness. When he loots the second (Spanish) wreck on the island he helps himself to rich clothes, liquor, cordials, sweetmeats, and bags of doubloons and pieces of eight. He lugs the money home to his cave, adding it to what he has already stowed there, and dreams of coming back from England one day to fetch it. But, as his feet are itching, he stoutly protests that 'I would have given it all for three or four pairs of *English* Shoes and Stockings' (140). Here is Defoe's contradictory Englishman made flesh. To Crusoe the colonist, Crusoe the religious fanatic, and Crusoe the wanderer must be added Crusoe the whingeing Pom and home-grown humbug.

4

Histories of Rebellion: From 1688 to 1793

Once, when Mr Crawley asked what the young people were reading, the governess replied 'Smollett.' 'Oh, Smollett,' said Mr Crawley, quite satisfied. 'His history is more dull, but by no means so dangerous as that of Mr Hume. It is history you are reading?' 'Yes,' said Miss Rose; without, however, adding that it was the history of Mr Humphry Clinker.

(Thackeray, *Vanity Fair*)

I N this anecdote from Becky Sharp's life as a governess, Thackeray has managed to pick one of the few mid-eighteenth-century novels that did not contain the word 'history' in its title. Eighty years before *The Expedition of Humphry Clinker* (1771), Aphra Behn's *Oroonoko, or the Royal Slave* had been subtitled 'A True History'. The popular novels of Delarivier Manley (1670–1724) and Eliza Haywood (?1693–1756) were presented to the public as 'true histories', 'secret histories', or even 'true secret histories'. Richardson's *Pamela, or Virtue Rewarded* (1740–1) was followed by *Clarissa: or the History of a Young Lady* (1748–9) and *The History of Sir Charles Grandison* (1754), while Fielding's masterpiece was *The History of Tom Jones, a Foundling* (1749). Fielding repeatedly plays on the various meanings of 'history' in his novels. In *The History of the Adventures of Joseph Andrews* (1742) he ridicules 'those romance writers who entitle their books, "The History of England, the History of France, of Spain, & c." '.[1] In *The Journal of a Voyage to Lisbon* (1755) he calls romance the 'confounder and corrupter of true history'.[2] The narrator of *Tom Jones* pours scorn on 'some pages, which certain droll authors have been facetiously pleased to call *The History of England*'.[3] Here Fielding's target was the Jacobite historian Thomas Carte, and Fielding's writings in the anti-Jacobite cause included a brief pamphlet on *The History of the Present Rebellion in Scotland* (1745). His successors among the eighteenth-century novelists include Smollett, Oliver Goldsmith, and

William Godwin, each of whom was also a historian in something like the modern professional sense of the term. In November 1791 the 16-year-old Jane Austen made her own crisp comment on English history-writing with 'The History of England from the Reign of Henry the 4th to the Death of Charles the 1st, by a Partial, Prejudiced, and Ignorant Historian'.[4]

Histories of England, like English dictionaries, lives of the poets, and editions of Shakespeare, bear witness to the systematic construction of a 'republic of letters' or national literary culture in eighteenth-century Britain. For the first time, the modern nations of Western Europe could be identified by their possession of a separate syllabus of knowledge, a codified language, and a distinctive literary canon and library of books. The demand for patriotic reference works and textbooks was exploited to the full by the commercial booksellers, who competed fiercely to fill the vacant shelves of this putative national library. Beginning with White Kennett's *Complete History of England* (1706) there are over twenty separate works carrying the general title *History of England* during this period, often in multiple volumes, and with the title prefixed by adjectives such as *Chronological, Critical, General,* and *Impartial,* as well as *Complete*.[5] At a lower level than the encyclopedic histories were works for the schoolroom, from John Lockman's *History of England, by way of Question and Answer* (1735) to works by the novelists Oliver Goldsmith and Charlotte Smith. Goldsmith's *History of England, from the Earliest Times to the Death of George II* (1771) was confessedly an abridgement compiled from the works of Rapin, Carte, Smollett, and Hume. His choice of rival historians suggests an attempt at fair-mindedness, but Goldsmith was aware of the impossibility of pleasing all parties.[6] As Mr Crawley's comparison of Smollett and Hume implies, most eighteenth-century historiography was, and was seen to be, intensely partisan. The historians of the time are easily divisible into Whigs and Tories, Hanoverians and Jacobites, Anglicans and Dissenters, and Royalists and republicans. David Hume's *History of Great Britain* (1754–7) is condemned as dangerous by the Whiggish Mr Crawley even though its claim to be above party has stood the test of time better than any of its rivals.[7]

For history to be partisan, it must have something to be partisan about. Eighteenth- and nineteenth-century Whigs and Tories traced their ancestry back to the contending sides in the English Civil War, and the same is true of numerous fictional heroes beginning with Tristram Shandy and Goldsmith's *Vicar of Wakefield*. Two hundred and fifty years after Charles I had raised his standard at Nottingham, William Lecky could write in *The Political Value of History* (1892) that 'We are Cavaliers or

Roundheads before we are Conservatives or Liberals'.[8] For historians and novelists alike, the Civil War and its aftermath was the pivotal moment in the emergence of modern England. The Jacobite rebellions of 1715 and 1745 and the American and French revolutions confirmed the pressing topical relevance of the great historical issues of the previous century. The first volume of Hume's history ends with Charles I's execution in 1649, while Jane Austen's playful historical essay terminates with a vindication of Charles I against the 'misconduct and Cruelty of his Parliament' and especially the 'leaders of the Gang', Cromwell, Fairfax, Hampden and Pym.[9]

The essentials of the Tory and Royalist creed had been magisterially set out in the Earl of Clarendon's *History of the Rebellion*, completed immediately before his death in 1674 but not published until 1702–4. White Kennett's Whig history celebrated the defeat of popery and absolutism in the Glorious Revolution of 1688, though the legacy of Stuart tyranny lived on in the Tories and the High Church party.[10] Fielding's *bête noire*, the Jacobite historian Thomas Carte, not only described the Civil War as the great calamity of modern history but viewed Whigs and Dissenters, like their Puritan and Parliamentary forebears, as secret republicans and regicides.[11] Oliver Goldsmith in his *History of England, in a Series of Letters from a Nobleman to his Son* (1764) divides the nation's history into three periods, with the middle period running from the Norman Conquest to 1649. William Godwin in an unpublished essay described the Stuart period as 'the only portion of our history interesting to the heart of man', though its noblest virtues were 'obscured with the vile jargon of fanaticism and hypocrisy'.[12] Towards the end of his life Godwin wrote the first full-length history of the Interregnum, the *History of the Commonwealth of England* (1824–8). The obsession with the Civil War continued into the Victorian period, when, as John Burrow has noted, no less than four leading Whig politicians—Fox, Macaulay, Russell, and Sir James Mackintosh—wrote histories of seventeenth-century England, while the Conservative Benjamin Disraeli undertook a 'rehabilitation of the policies of Charles I, of whose reign his father had written a sympathetic history'.[13]

The contending parties in the Civil War themselves appealed to versions of the national past to justify their actions; thus the Civil War and its outcome came to be viewed as the culmination of earlier historical themes such as the Norman Conquest, Magna Carta, and the authority of Parliament, all of which remained highly controversial.[14] Eighteenth-century historians tended to believe that the relationship between the crown and the people had been settled, for better or worse, by the sequence of rebellion, restoration, and deposition in the previous century. Hume's *History of Great Britain* keeps this firmly in view throughout his narrative of the reigns of the four Stuart kings. Parliaments, he observes, invariably arose from the 'consent of monarchs', but monarchies owed their existence to the 'voluntary submission of the people'.[15] The Civil War stemmed from Charles I's decision to treat the nation like a conquered province (278). The Parliamentary victory, however, destroyed the balance of powers necessary to a stable society:

No sooner had they subdued their sovereign, than their own servants rose up against them, and tumbled them from their slippery throne. The sacred boundaries of the laws being once violated, nothing remained to confine the wild projects of zeal and ambition. And every successive revolution became a precedent for that which followed it. (626)

Hume's use of the term 'revolution' here is closer to its modern sense than that of earlier political theorists such as Hobbes and Locke; but his vertiginous picture of successive revolutions consuming one another has only one likely end, which is eventual restoration—the wheel turning full circle, having accomplished a revolution in the old sense.[16] The effect of the 1688 constitutional settlement was to stop these imploding forces and, in the words of an anonymous writer of 1760, to turn political conflict into a 'transient dispute among friends, not an implacable feud that admits of no reconciliation'.[17] (It may be noted that in Parliament under the two-party system the bitterest opponents have to address each other as 'my honourable friend'.)

In the self-congratulatory vein that was to become known as the Whig interpretation of history, the English Civil War became a necessary bloodletting prior to an age of prosperity, political civility, and overseas expansion. Oliver Goldsmith wrote that the miseries of the Civil War were 'ultimately productive of domestic happiness and security; the laws became more precise, the monarchy's privileges better ascertained, and the subject's duty better delineated; all became more peacable, as if a previous fermentation in the constitution was necessary for its subsequent refinement'.[18] The metaphor of fermentation combines the idea of popular turbulence with the settling and maturation necessary to produce a superior vintage. This quotation from Goldsmith's professedly monarchist history suggests how the nation could be seen to have undergone its period of rebellion and restoration like a stormy adolescent on the verge of adulthood. At such moments, the underlying patterns of English historiography and the patterns established by eighteenth-century fictional narrative can be seen to coalesce. Both historians and novelists were depicting a national rite of passage.

Goldsmith seeks to understand history as a natural process, and identifies the conflict between monarchy and republicanism as the central issue for an English historian (i, p. vi). Godwin, as a republican, condemned the post-1688 history of constitutional monarchy as a history of 'negotiations and tricks', 'revenues and debts', and 'corruption and profligacy'.[19] But he also condemned the 'vile jargon of fanaticism and hypocrisy' with which the seventeenth century sought to dress up its conflicts of natural appetite and rational principle. Both thinkers, in other words, were Enlightenment historians who would find it absurd to search for signs of supernatural intervention or guidance in the affairs of the nation, as Defoe and his Puritan forebears had done.[20] In 'Of History and Romance', Godwin argues that fiction, or 'romance', should be written from the same naturalistic standpoint as history. The writer of romance is 'to be considered as the writer of real history', and 'True history consists in a delineation of consistent, human character, in a display of the manner in which such a character acts under successive circumstances'.[21] As novelists, though, Goldsmith and Godwin do not confine themselves to naturalistic principles in constructing their plots. Like *Joseph Andrews* and *Tom Jones*, *The Vicar of Wakefield* relies flagrantly on coincidence and poetical justice, while Godwin altered the conclusion to *Caleb Williams* to bring about a final, providential reversal of fortunes.

If the novel according to eighteenth-century theorists should be a kind of history, history sometimes came disguised in the form of fiction. The origins of the historical novel and historical romance are complex, but one crucial factor is the resort to fictional allegory and to distant times and places in order to avoid possible censorship. This is seen in works such as *The Princess Cloria: or, The Royal Romance* and Behn's *Love-Letters*, both discussed in Chapter 2. Herbert's preface to the enlarged (1661) edition of *The Princess Cloria*, his Royalist allegory of the Civil War, explained that he had added 'several sorts of Invention and Fancies' to his historical narrative, partly for aesthetic reasons, and partly in the interests of historical completeness. There was a history of private, unrecorded passions as well as of public acts; moreover, 'the common Occurrances of the World, do not arrive alwayes at a pitch high enough for example, or to stir up the appetite of the Reader, which things feigned may do under the notion of a *Romance*'.[22] Romances could serve the interests of political propaganda, moral example, entertainment, and historical instruction all at once. The ostensible *roman à clef*, reporting 'secret' histories under the guise of fiction, became an increasingly popular mode of writing.

By the early eighteenth century, the 'true' or 'secret history' was normally a sensational love story drawing on the material of the gossip column and the crime report. Eliza Haywood's 'The Double Marriage' (1726), for example, is the 'True Secret History' of a bigamous liaison set in the merchant community of Plymouth. The principal characters' identity is hidden under such obviously made-up names as Bellcour, Alathia, and Mirtamene.[23] Whether or not the novel's events culminating in a double suicide actually took place at Plymouth (or elsewhere) hardly matters. Readers were expected to believe in them, and the borders between fiction and journalism have remained highly permeable from Haywood's day to ours.

If *The Princess Cloria* represents political allegory, and 'The Double Marriage' the sensational *roman à clef*, Aphra Behn's *Oroonoko, or the Royal Slave* (1688) is a more puzzling case. Beginning with a description of the native inhabitants of Surinam and an account of the slave trade, *Oroonoko* appears to be an eyewitness history of a slave rebellion in the former British colony which had subsequently been lost to the Dutch. (There are also episodes of a kind later to become familiar in colonial adventure fiction, such as the 'tiger' hunt and the fishing expedition to catch an electric eel.) Behn uses the colonial setting as pretext for some sensationally violent scenes, such as Oroonoko's murder of his wife and his attempt to disembowel himself (he is captured in the act and stitched up again by a doctor). Later, with the narrator's mother and sister looking on, he is mutilated, quartered, and burnt at the stake by British plantation owners.

According to Behn's narrator, this execution is illegal, since it took place in a kind of interregnum when Oroonoko's owner, who was also the governor of the colony, was absent. Before his transportation to Surinam Oroonoko had been a prince of Coramantien in West Africa, and his regal status and dignity were recognized both by his fellow slaves and by some of the white planters. He was given the slave-name of Caesar. Although he was the ringleader of the rebellion, his killing could be seen as an act of regicide. The narrator's friend Colonel Martin swears that 'he had rather see the quarters of [the prosecutors], than those of Caesar, on his plantations'.[24] This recalls the fate of the surviving English regicides who were tried and executed after the Restoration in 1660.

In general terms *Oroonoko* is unmistakably a Royalist allegory. Coramantien is represented as a pastoral and Orientalized version of a European court, and, and, thanks to his princely education there, Oroonoko 'had heard of the late Civil Wars in England, and the deplorable death of our great monarch, and would discourse of it with all the sense, and abhorrence of the injustice imaginable' (80). Recent scholars have also suggested that *Oroonoko* parallels the events of 1688, the year of its publication, as well as 1649 to which the hero's execution provides an explicit pointer. Thus Oroonoko's position as a 'royal slave' might suggest James II's dilemma as the Roman Catholic monarch of a Protestant country, while the fall of Surinam to the Dutch might anticipate the imminent fall of the Stuart kingdom to the Dutchman William of Orange.[25] But *Oroonoko* remains continuous with Behn's plays which insist on the moral, social, and sexual superiority of the 'Banished Cavaliers', and the cowardly tyranny and hypocrisy of the usurping Roundheads.[26]

What remains mysterious, however, is whether Behn herself visited the 'obscure world' of Surinam in the 1660s, and whether a slave rebellion actually took place there. Does *Oroonoko* combine elements of the 'true history' of imperial tyranny with a domestic political moral, or is the moral tacked onto a bloodcurdling exotic romance? And does this matter anyway? The story of *Oroonoko*'s narrator, who fails to prevent the hero's condemnation and punishment, is a crucial sub-theme in the story. Partly because of her status as a powerless female, she is torn between the rebellious Royal Martyr and his avenging enemies, but at least she can use her pen to tell Oroonoko's story. Behn's political romance offers a suggestive precedent for the innumerable eighteenth- and early nineteenth-century novels which would use the language of slavery and rebellion to describe the position of young women within the domestic household. If Behn's 'obscure world' was that of the colonies, Richardson, Fielding, and their successors would turn their attention to the obscure worlds of well-to-do families.

In the terms of Congreve's preface to *Incognita* (1692), *Oroonoko* is plainly a romance and not a novel. It tells of the 'constant love' and 'invincible courage' of a royal hero engaged in 'wholly unusual' and 'unprecedented' events; it lacks the 'more familiar nature' of modern fiction.[27] The first English historical novels according to Congreve's definition would seem to be Defoe's eyewitness narratives of the Civil War and the Restoration, *Memoirs of a Cavalier* and *A Journal of the Plague Year*. The *Memoirs*, which went through seven editions before 1800, were at first assumed to be an authentic contemporary document, sometimes attributed to Colonel Andrew Newport of Shropshire. Defoe's name first appeared as editor in 1784, but was later dropped. The book was not fully admitted to the Defoe canon until the twentieth century.[28] The narrator begins with a preface claiming to correct some errors in Clarendon's *History of the Rebellion*, a book from which Defoe had in fact freely plagiarized. In the text the Cavalier claims hitherto secret knowledge of such matters as the arguments in the Royalist camp before the Battle of Marston Moor, and Charles I's regrets after the defeat at Naseby. He includes an appendix of superstitious 'Remarks and Observations', advancing the theory that nemesis overtakes a king or statesman on the 'very same Day of the same Month' on which he committed his greatest crime (272), and revealing the conspicuous providential justice of the war and its outcome. As with *The Princess Cloria*, the narrative concludes with the Restoration, which puts an end to the ceaseless feuding on the Parliamentary side, so that 'the same party that began the war ended it' (279).

The texture of *Memoirs of a Cavalier*, and still more of *A Journal of the Plague Year*, is that of meticulously detailed documentary and eyewitness reporting. One text anticipates modern autobiography, the other modern journalism. Yet, unobtrusive as is Defoe's fictional shaping of these narratives, its purpose is to reveal the hand of Providence behind seemingly contingent events. His Cavalier memoir, therefore, paradoxically belongs to the Puritan tradition of narrative drawing on popular superstition and apocalyptic fantasy in order to testify to an order of divine justice hidden in the events of everyday life. This would eventually be transmuted into the 'poetical justice' of the classical English novel with its providential plot resolutions. It has its sublime counterpart in John Milton's post-Restoration verse epics, which transfer the pattern of a political rebellion succeeded by a restoration from Earth to Heaven. *Memoirs of a Cavalier* seems to argue that, regardless of political rights and wrongs, God will punish those whose actions on Earth amount to rebellion against the divine order. But what exactly does constitute a rebellion against the divine order? How far does God underwrite the authority of the monarch over his subjects, or of the patriarch over his family? These questions, hotly debated in political and moral philosophy, also stand behind the classic literary theme (which extends from ancient drama to the modern novel) of youthful rebellion against arbitrary authority.

Fathers and Children

Mikhail Bakhtin describes the world of the traditional epic as a 'heroic national past ... a world of "beginnings" and "peak times" in the national history, a world of fathers and of founders of families'.[29] In contrast, the world of the eighteenth-century novel as exemplified by Fielding and Richardson is a world of sons and daughters who may or may not know their own fathers. Its characters are typically born with a dynastic identity, which is sometimes correct and sometimes mistaken; even Tom Jones gains such an identity by virtue of being found in Squire Allworthy's bed. Growing up in filial subordination, the protagonists are pulled in two directions by the need to rebel and the urge to conform—they must differ from their 'parents' and yet, in some sense, repeat what those parents have stood for. A remarkably high proportion of classical English novels centre on the crisis of generational change and the transfer of property by inheritance or marriage. In *Pamela* and *Joseph Andrews*, Richardson and Fielding pioneered the novel that ends with the settlement of a new generation, just as traditional history centres on the succession of kings and queens. Their protagonists are mostly still young and relatively innocent at the end of the narrative, mirroring the relationship between novel and epic which is also somewhat filial. Tom Jones's departure from his childhood home of Paradise-hall deliberately recalls the Fall of Man, yet to the end of his adventures Tom remains a child in experience compared with Milton's Adam.

Thanks to its quasi-filial relationship with the epic world, the English novel after Richardson and Fielding does not need to apologize for being domestic, provincial, and (to use George Eliot's term at the end of *Middlemarch*) 'unhistoric' in scope. The founders of nations and the great military heroes such as Caesar and Alexander belong to the distant past; the modern novel's virtue is its contemporaneity, so that its events usually take place at a specific, and very recent, date. If at the end the young hero and heroine have only just succeeded to an inheritance, they are free to make of it as much, or much more, than their predecessors did. Thus the novel shows its characters' early development and potential for mature action, rather than their maturity itself. There is no danger of our being invited to judge whether or not Tom Jones, for example, will come up to expectation in fulfilling what one critic has called his 'responsible place in the fabric of English national life'; the novel simply leaves him in the place he has won as the dynastic successor to Allworthy and Western.[30] The same quality of prematurity characterizes the relationship between family and state implied in the novels of Fielding, Richardson, and their successors. Family and state in traditional political theory are linked by the patriarchal analogy, exemplified by the quotation from Bakhtin above. The family both constitutes the origin of the state and provides a model of the state in miniature. Similarly, the family-oriented, domestic world of the English novel mirrors the larger political world and contains the essence out of which states are constructed. The fictional family represents the state both in miniature and in embryo.

When Thomas Hobbes in *Leviathan* (1651) described the family as a 'little Monarchy',[31] he was repeating a conception that can be traced back to Plato and Aristotle. Cicero, for example saw the family as 'the foundation of civil government, the nursery, as it were, of the state'.[32] Where some thinkers including Hobbes sought to distinguish between the governance of the state and the family, the seventeenth-century defence of absolutism came to derive political obligation from the father's authority over his family: if the family was in its nature an absolute monarchy, the same must be true of the state. James I at the end of the sixteenth century used the patriarchal analogy to assert that subjects could not legally rebel against their rulers. Fifty years later Sir Robert Filmer based his justification of absolutism on the obedience that all men supposedly owed to their father and first ancestor Adam.[33] Locke's *Two Treatises of Government* ridiculed Filmer's patriarchalist ideas while continuing to argue from the supposed origins of society in the 'voluntary Compact between Man and Woman' exemplified by Adam and Eve, the joint rulers of the first family.[34] Where Filmer held that the power of the father over his offspring was potentially lifelong, Locke and the Whig historian James Tyrrell asserted that children were only subject to their parents' absolute dominion during the period of 'nonage' which lasted, according to Tyrrell, to the age of 25 at most. By such means the patriarchal defence of absolute monarchy had been intellectually discredited by the end of the seventeenth century, but it had also been rendered largely irrelevant in England by the fall of the Stuarts.[35] After 1688, Locke's declaration that absolute monarchy was 'inconsistent with Civil Society' (369) could be regarded as a basis for national pride and as evidence of England's superiority over France and other European nations.

Walter Shandy, Tristram's father, is one of Sir Robert Filmer's last disciples and a believer in absolute monarchy both in the state and the home. Mrs Shandy is the victim of Walter's tyranny—she must stay at home to knit her husband a pair of breeches, for example, while the rest of the family go on the Grand Tour—but, so far as Tristram is concerned, Walter's authority is so feeble that his son has no need and no impulse to rebel. *The Life and Opinions of Tristram Shandy* (1759–67) undermines Walter's patriarchalism as surely as it stages the castration of Tristram and Uncle Toby. The result is a comprehensive defeat for the *jus paternum*, or Law of the Father, and an ironic victory for the idea of the novel as cock-and-bull narrative and scapegrace offspring of the ancient epic.

At the level of political debate the Law of the Father came under attack from writers such as the feminist Mary Astell, who discussed the scandal of women's subjection to 'private Tyranny' in marriage.[36] But the pious abstractions of political thought about the family had been subverted in literature, and especially in stage comedy, from the beginning. Aristophanes shows wives rebelling against their husbands, and Greek and Roman New Comedy pits the healthy desires of the young against the obstructive instincts of authoritarian fathers who refuse to accept that the period of nonage is over and the parental writ no longer runs. The conflict between wise children and foolish parents is a source of tragedy, as in *Romeo and Juliet* and *King Lear*, but it more often leads to farce as senile domestic tyrants struggle to lock up their daughters. The image of the family presented in traditional stage comedy is one of disorder, rebellion, and anarchy rather than the tidy monarchy envisaged by the political theorists. Wives, children, and household servants win the audience's support by challenging or simply ignoring patriarchal authority. At best, wives and husbands, or children and parents, may hope to be reconciled by the end of the play, with the aid of the servants whose interest lies in promoting a stable and prosperous household. The domestic conflicts in Fielding, Richardson, and their successors draw on the traditions of youthful rebellion on the stage and in popular culture, as well as on philosophical debates about the limits of patriarchal authority.

There is a direct line of descent from Greek and Roman New Comedy to Restoration comedy, which is full of metaphors of tyranny, slavery, rebellion, and liberty.[37] Like the institution of carnival, the notoriously licentious Restoration theatre can be regarded as a political safety valve simultaneously subverting and consolidating the restored Stuart monarchy. Modern scholars are apt to read the frivolous hedonism of late seventeenth-century drama as a cloak for national allegory.[38] The theatre's self-consciously aristocratic and anti-Puritan ethos brings into focus two different ideas of liberty which are at war both in the drama and in the fiction of seduction and courtship. On the one hand, there is the right of freedom from parental oppression traditionally demanded by young lovers who have passed the age of puberty and claim to have outgrown their nonage; but this is opposed by the unbounded aristocratic 'liberty' of libertines and Cavaliers, which—whatever it may mean in practice—in theory requires total submission to the tyranny of erotic desire which is freedom's logical opposite. Philander in Behn's *Love-Letters Between a Nobleman and His*

Sister imagines Cupid as a rebel leader who, after a 'thousand conflicts' with the 'tyrant' honour, now reigns 'absolute monarch' in his soul.[39] Mrs Marwood in Congreve's *The Way of the World* describes love as the 'lawful tyrant' who will 'resume his empire in our breasts'.[40] Libertine love combines its egotistical assertion of freedom with a debased form of power worship: the supposed slave to love is actually planning to enslave others. The conflict between orthodox liberty (or freedom from oppression) and coercive libertinism was a source of comedy both on the Restoration stage and, later, in Fielding's fiction—as in Lady Booby's attempted dalliance with Joseph Andrews. But the same conflict is tragically and exhaustively dwelt upon in Richardson's *Clarissa*, where Lovelace plans to liberate Clarissa from her oppressive family only to subject her to a still more brutal and imperious regime.

Samuel Richardson: Virtue and Rebellion

After thirty years of a business career which had taken him to the top of the London printing trade, Samuel Richardson claimed to have become a novelist by chance.[41] Born in 1689, he was a middle-class opponent of the aristocratic libertine ethos exemplified by the novels of Behn, Manley, and Haywood. At the age of 50, and with four surviving daughters, he wrote *Pamela* in order to 'cultivate the Principles of VIRTUE and RELIGION' in the minds of the young, and to provide an alternative to the 'pernicious novels, and idle romances' which he regarded as the 'poison of female minds'.[42] In the sequel that he produced in response to pressing public demand, the heroine recalls that as a young girl her reading was censored by her mistress, whose chief fear was that adolescent minds would be exposed to 'heightened and inflaming' descriptions.[43] Pamela and her author share the Puritan belief that all fiction should have the effect of a parable and pass the test of moral instruction; hence the novel's alternative title *Virtue Rewarded*. But Richardson went far beyond the limits of the Puritanical moral fable, developing an intensely melodramatic, emotionally charged mode of fiction whose domesticity was in sharp contrast to the '*marvellous* and *improbable*' settings of romance. His novels might be full of '*love and intrigue*' (P2 462), but they would not, like *The Princess Cloria* or the anonymous *Clorana* (1739) which has the words *Virtue Triumphant* in its subtitle, deal with complicated love affairs among the princes of fictitious countries.[44]

Richardson's protagonists are born with, or aspire to, inherited property or landed estates. Pamela's success in holding Mr B to his promise of marriage raises her into the gentry. Mr and Mrs Harlowe are a 'gentleman born and educated' and a viscount's daughter,[45] and their son James hopes to join the peerage. In Richardson's last novel Harriet Byron rises from the gentry to the aristocracy when she succeeds in marrying the hereditary baronet Sir Charles Grandison despite the latter's romantic involvement with Clementina Porretta, the 'noblest young lady in Italy'.[46] It could be argued that Richardson's concern with the upper classes is essential to his project of moral reformation and his polemic against libertinism. In *Pamela*, for example, he exposes the abuses of power which enable the rich to treat the poor as they please, and he satirizes upper-class boorishness in his portrayal of the drinking, whoring, 'hunting, racing, cock-fighting, and . . . swearing and cursing' of his spendthrift heirs and aristocratic rakes (*P2* 203). At the same time, the popularity of fictional romance suggested that it was the aristocracy and gentry that people wanted to read about, and Richardson was happy to go along with them. His ladies and gentlemen are, for better or worse, the backbone of the fictional nation—the only class whose breadth of knowledge and experience entitles them to speak for it.

One particular catchphrase, which bears his signature even though it is also frequently found in Fielding and Jane Austen, conveys Richardson's sense of the ruling class's right and duty to dictate the nation's values. When Pamela is a servant girl, she is reputed to be only the 'greatest beauty in the county'.[47] Wider geographical comparisons cannot be meaningfully offered in respect of a person of such subordinate status. But her employer Mr B, although the least socially elevated of Richardson's three male protagonists, is a Member of Parliament with estates in three counties, so that his standard of comparison is national not local. Once he takes a serious interest in Pamela she is entered, so to speak, in a nationwide rather than a county-wide beauty competition; she is running not for Miss Bedfordshire but for Miss England. Accordingly she becomes 'the loveliest maiden in England' (321) and, after her wedding, 'the finest lady in England' (*P2* 165); her humble parents are 'one of the happiest and honestest couple in England' (482) and she makes her husband 'the happiest man in England' (427). These careless hyperboles have the aristocratic ring of phrases accustomed to strut the national stage and to boast without fear of contradiction. Their (usually male) utterer, in flattering somebody else, also flatters himself. Richardson is remarkably fond of treacly superlatives of the 'loveliest woman in England' type, which tend to proliferate at points in his novels where his plots are sagging and his characters' rhetoric is at its most expostulatory. The implicit chauvinism of these phrases should not be overlooked. While Miss Bedfordshire must defer to Miss England, the 'loveliest woman in England' is, as *Sir Charles Grandison* shows, a far more fitting match for the hero than the beauties of other nations.[48]

Pamela's virtue is rewarded and her beauty validated by marriage to a landowner and Member of Parliament; but her virtue, as one critic has said, is in large measure the virtue of rebellion.[49] Her rebellion is that of a servant against a tyrannical master who claims the right of absolute government over her person. For her to withhold her sexual favours from him, Mr B claims at one point, is an act of theft. Pamela retorts that, as a Justice of the Peace, he has the right to send her to jail (91)—a sinister reminder of the extent to which Mr B and his like in eighteenth-century England might genuinely consider themselves to be above the law. But B understandably prefers to keep their conflict within the bounds of the family rather than invoking the corrupted powers of the state. He holds her under house arrest at his property in Lincolnshire, where her jailer, Mrs Jewkes, is a family retainer who loyally affirms her master's droit de seigneur: ' "And pray," said I . . . "how came I to be his property? What right has he in me, but such as a thief may plead to stolen goods?" "Was ever the like heard!" says [Mrs Jewkes]. "This is downright rebellion, I protest!" '(163). Pamela is a 'rebel' in the terms of the libertine's code, but, though Mr B claims the prerogative of an absolute ruler, he has no title to his claim, and he knows it. He is no 'professed debauchee' (165) but an inexperienced opportunist. Fairly soon he will forgive Pamela's 'treasonable resistance' (265) and agree to marry her. In retrospect his accusations of treason and rebellion become part of the game of love in which Pamela, knowingly or not, so successfully plays her part. But, if her honour is to be saved in more than name, her conduct has to be judged by the standards of spiritual integrity as well as of amorous politics.

In refusing to comply with her oppressor's demands Pamela may act like a political rebel, but—since she believes that her suffering is sent to try her virtue and is, to that extent, divinely ordained—she cannot be seen to rebel against the fact of suffering. Instead, Richardson's focus on his female protagonist's ordeal allows him to portray a state of passive (but supremely articulate) victimhood. Pamela can do nothing apart from patiently and steadfastly resisting her oppressor's demands, but she can record everything. When she does act, as in her abortive escape attempt when she is tempted to commit suicide by drowning herself, she is in grave spiritual peril. On more than one occasion she is saved from Mr B's advances by 'Providence' in the shape of a timely fainting fit. Pamela's most successful and positive actions are those by which she is able to maintain her stores of ink and paper and, as she thinks, to conceal the minute-by-minute account of her ordeal that she is incessantly writing. Literature becomes her salvation as Mr B, the would-be rapist, becomes seduced in his turn by the power of her storytelling.

The novelist as Christian reformer may approve of political rebellion in the domestic sphere (in so far as resistance to a lawless tyrant is properly described as 'rebellion'), but will always condemn spiritual rebellion. This means that Richardson judges the question of rebellion from two opposing points of view, the temporal and the eternal, the one using political and military, and the other biblical, terms and analogies. Pamela emphatically places her suffering in a biblical context when she adapts Psalm 137 to fit the circumstances of her own imprisonment in Lincolnshire, thus putting herself in the position of the Jewish nation in Babylonian captivity.[50] The contradictory imperatives of political and spiritual rebellion are much more sharply juxtaposed in *Clarissa*, where the language of government and war is systematically ransacked for analogies to the heroine's domestic ordeal.

How far should we read Pamela's rebellion as a political allegory? Thomas Keymer, one of the novel's modern editors, has pointed out that, before becoming a respectable government printer under the Walpole ministry, Richardson had narrowly escaped charges of sedition for printing Jacobite propaganda in the 1720s. Mr B thus 'seems very much the embodiment of Walpole's oligarchy'.[51] At the same time, Pamela's implicit comparison of herself to the Jewish nation is one of many details which identify her predicament with that of seventeenth-century Pur-itanism. Her moral and sexual scruples, her filial and religious piety, and her humble social station are in sharp contrast to Mr B's Cavalier habits of careless generosity, sexual indiscretion, and haughty family pride. Mr B speaks of randy young squires such as himself as 'keen fox-hunters' (269) and boasts of being 'without disparagement to any man, the best fox-hunter in England' (342) once he has secured Pamela. What makes her such a challenging quarry is her beauty, her displays of piety—'thou art a perfect nun, I think' (117), he sneers on one occasion—and what, as an avid reader of her letters and journal, he comes to think of as her romanticism. The symbolism of clothes expresses the gulf between them. Mr B gives her a suit of her late mistress's fine silk, and then (to Pamela's great embarrassment) some stockings; but she retaliates by buying a length of cloth and making her own 'home-spun gown and petticoat' (43) worn with plain leather shoes, a Quakerish uniform that she steadfastly continues to wear until the eve of her marriage. Her plain clothes are the sign of a Puritanical renunciation of worldly display, yet, by a paradox that is entirely typical of the courtship novel, they also serve as a mark of coquetry. Her mentor Mrs Jervis tells her that ' "I never saw you look more lovely in my life than in that new dress of yours" ' (43).

Pamela for her part avows her interest in the state of Mr B's soul, regardless of his mockery of her 'unfashionable jargon' of piety (101). The more he persecutes her, the more her sexual awareness of him grows. This has led many readers to accept B's characterization of her as a Puritanical hypocrite, though it may also be viewed as the emotional transference of a kidnap victim. In the end, however, the sexual attraction of opposites prevails and the civil war between the two lovers subsides into a highly charged courtship. But their reconciliation cannot be staged without a grand religious conversion, as B renounces the errors of his past and agrees to marry his bride in the hastily refurbished chapel of his Lincolnshire retreat. (Pamela, meanwhile, has rejected the advances of the plain and virtuous Mr Williams, the clergyman who later performs her wedding ceremony.) As Pamela becomes a fine lady, not omitting to thank God for his mercies, Mr B has to undergo the indignity of his sister Lady Davers's ridicule: ' "Egregious preacher!" said she: "my brother already turned puritan!" ' (443). The opposing values for which the lovers once stood will continue to spice their relationship, as in the masquerade scene in *Pamela: II* where Pamela goes appropriately dressed as a Quaker, while Mr B is a Spanish Don or 'caballero'. (Things threaten to get out of hand when he is all but seduced by a masked Nun, offering an impious parody of the Cavalier–Puritan courtship which sustained the earlier volume.)

Reluctant Redcoats (i): Tom Jones

In *Pamela* a national allegory of rebellion leading to moral reformation is played out entirely at the level of the family. The heroine's imprisonment remains a private affair, and—though the eventual Cavalier–Puritan marriage is a public event—national politics and an awareness of historical events are conspicuously absent. By contrast, Fielding's sense of the novel's epic ancestry meant that he could never remain content with a simple fiction of courtship. His immediate response to Richardson's achievement was to ridicule it in the brief parody of *Shamela* (1741). *Tom*

Jones is the story of a foundling who, expelled from his family and forced to live by his wits, prepares to become a soldier. Not only was the army a respectable profession for younger sons of the gentry, but the portrayal of a military campaign was an easy way to bring the processes of history into fiction. Billy Booth, the male protagonist of Fielding's *Amelia* (1752), is also an army officer, though neither Jones nor Booth sees active service. In Tom's case, the supposed rebel against his family is put in a situation where he might have helped to put down the state rebellion of 1745—but, despite his professions of loyalty to the King, he chooses not to do so. Andrew Marvell's 'Horatian Ode', written a century earlier under the Commonwealth, had celebrated the 'forward youth' who in times of rebellion eagerly turns to 'adventurous war'. Tom Jones, we are told, 'has some heroic ingredients in his composition' (336), and in *Clarissa* Robert Lovelace boasts to his friend Belford that 'Had I been a military hero, I should have made gunpowder useless' (ii. 55). Yet, when it comes to marching to the colours, Tom, Lovelace, and most other male protagonists in eighteenth-century English fiction turn out to be remarkably backward youths.

Henry Fielding had made his literary debut at the age of 20 with odes on the coronation and the King's birthday. Later he wrote the original lyrics for 'The Roast Beef of Old England', a song in the *Grub-Street Opera* (1731). His fiercest writings as a political journalist date from the period of the Jacobite rebellion, when he edited *The True Patriot*, to be followed in 1747 by the ironically titled *Jacobite's Journal*. His 'Serious Address to the People of Great Britain' (1745) seeks to rouse his countrymen against invasion by 'a Banditti, a Rabble of Thieves or Outlaws' intent upon replacing English liberty with French slavery and the tortures of the Spanish Inquisition.[52] The 'Serious Address' calls on every able-bodied man to do 'his Duty in the defence of his Country' against the Jacobites (31), a call repeated in the *True Patriot* and the *History of the Present Rebellion in Scotland*. For a short time Tom Jones acts as if inspired by his author's political journalism, only to abandon the defence of his country at the first opportunity.

Both *Tom Jones* and *Sir Charles Grandison* offer contemporary accounts of England during and just after the 1745 rebellion. Grandison, however, is in Italy when the 'troubles, now so happily appeased' break out in Scotland (ii. 124). Tom, disgraced and penniless, is on the road in England. His initial intention is to seek his fortune at sea, but no sooner does he encounter a company of soldiers than he decides to join them as a gentleman volunteer. Fielding now confides, as a 'circumstance which we have not thought necessary to communicate before'—it is already book seven of the novel—that the Jacobite rebellion is at its height and that Tom is a 'hearty well-wisher to the glorious cause of liberty' and the Protestant monarchy (336). Tom's Hanoverian loyalties may come as a surprise to the reader, since we have seen him as the crony and drinking companion of the Tory Squire Western, a self-styled 'true Englishman' (308) given to drinking to the exiled 'King over the Water' and to patriotic outbursts against 'Roundheads and Hannover rats' (297). Western's ineffectual Jacobite bluster is counterbalanced by the testimony of the Man of the Hill, a recluse who has remained ignorant of public affairs since the Monmouth rebellion (in which he fought for the Protestant cause and narrowly escaped with his life) sixty years earlier. Strengthened by this encounter with a veteran of 1685, Tom's purpose of fighting in defence of the Protestant monarchy apparently remains firm despite the brutality and dishonesty of his brother officers, and despite the Jacobitism of his companion Partridge.[53] When Tom reaches Upton he is still on the road northwards to join the Duke of Cumberland, whose campaign would eventually culminate in the Battle of Culloden, and it is in the Upton episode—though the novelist's primary concern is with farcical battles 'of the amorous kind' (452)—that Fielding offers his principal representation of a country at war.

The inn at Upton seems to be full of rebels. We have earlier heard that 'the banditti were now marched into England' (336), and news arrives that they have given Cumberland's army the slip and advanced a day's march nearer London. A Jacobite squire comes to spread the rumour that the French have landed in Suffolk. Sophia and Mrs Honour are mistaken for Jacobite ladies travelling incognito. The landlady becomes 'in a moment a staunch Jacobite' (517), but the loyally Hanoverian Mrs Honour is outraged that her mistress should be taken for Jenny Cameron, 'that nasty, stinking wh–re . . . that runs about the country with the Pretender' (538). The joke, of course, is that Sophia's flight to Upton results from her rebellion against her father's tyranny. Her escape from his imprisonment has been handled in the tradition of stage comedy, but her aunt's protests that 'we are not to be locked up like the Spanish and Italian wives' (296), and that 'English women are not to be treated like Circassian slaves' (496), underline its political meaning.

Next morning the principal characters all leave the inn, with Jones (who believes he has terminally offended Sophia) determined to pursue the course of glory: 'Come on, my brave lad, now for the army' (558). Instead, he encounters a beggar at a crossroads, whom he finds to be in possession of Sophia's pocket-book. He proceeds irresolutely in a north-easterly direction, losing his way between Upton and Coventry, and failing to find any horses for hire—which, at this moment of national crisis, is perhaps not surprising. When he and Partridge do get horses it becomes obvious that Tom has forgotten about the rebels, and is riding headlong to London in pursuit of Sophia. Once he has arrived there we see that the life of the aristocracy and their hangers-on goes on as normal. Tom gets into a fight and finds himself in prison and under threat of execution, but neither his military desertion nor the Pretender's retreat to Scotland are ever mentioned. *Tom Jones*, in effect, is an anti-historical novel in which the hero casually throws up his chance of becoming a contributor or at least an eyewitness to historical events, preferring to follow the circuitous road of his private fortunes in an instinctive gesture that no reader regrets, and few critics have questioned or even paused over. Fielding's chronological scheme implies that Tom and Sophia are eventually married in December 1745, well before the rebels' final defeat at Culloden.[54]

Nevertheless, *Tom Jones* is not without certain hints as to the relationship between family and state. Between Upton and Coventry, Tom and Partridge encounter a band of gipsies, self-confessed thieves or 'banditti' who seem to be living unobserved like wild beasts in a forest. But they are also a well-ordered society, 'subject to a formal government and laws of their own' (593), and Tom admires their king's political wisdom and skill as a magistrate. The gipsy camp is portrayed as an ideal commonwealth in subjection to an absolute monarch. This alludes to the legends of medieval outlaws living in the greenwood, but it also suggests the Stuart prince and his encampment not very much farther north. Fielding's narrator rather anxiously intervenes towards the end of the episode to warn against the dangers of absolute monarchy.[55]

At the level of the family, Squire Western attempts to play the role of absolute monarch. Squire Allworthy is shown as a wise and liberal magistrate, but his constitutional monarchy is no more successful than his neighbour's absolutism. Fielding, though hostile to political rebellion, is on the side of family rebellion, making us fully aware of Allworthy's folly and injustice in taking the advice of his 'ministers' (Blifil, Thwackum, and Square) and banishing Tom. When, finally, Allworthy begins to think better of his ward, Fielding writes that 'As a conquered rebellion strengthens a government...danger, when removed, gives new life to affection' (829). This simile is the novel's sole hint as to the outcome of the '45. It also suggests the happy outcomes of Tom's exile and Sophia's rebellion, even though the analogy between the governance of family and state is less than exact. The novel ends with a form of restoration as both Tom and Sophia resubmit to parental authority. Western's motives for approving his daughter's marriage to Tom are in a sense dynastic (if not merely greedy); earlier he had favoured Blifil's suit when Blifil was Allworthy's heir. Allworthy seems indifferent to the union of their two estates, viewing it as a mere property transaction rather than as a symbolic reunification of Hanoverian and sentimentally Jacobite—or Whig and Tory—England.[56]

In old age, we are told, Western is distinguished for drunkenness and jollity, and Allworthy for 'discretion and prudence' (874). Tom and Sophia and their children, we must believe, will somehow combine these eternally conflicting qualities. Fielding's ecumenical poise—which involves consolidating the squirearchy rather than overturning its values—would have been difficult, if not impossible, to maintain had Tom played an active part in defeating the '45 rebellion. The plot of *Tom Jones* turns on danger and division which are on the point of tearing apart both family and state, but the conclusion—with its happy reunion of parents and children and, somewhere in the background, the retreat of the Jacobite rebels back to Scotland—reaffirms the sturdy, pluralistic, and basically benevolent nature of Fielding's England.

Reluctant Redcoats (ii); From 'Roderick Random' to 'The Old Manor House'

In 1746, before he became a novelist, Tobias Smollett had written a moving elegy for the Jacobites defeated at Culloden.[57] *The Adventures of Roderick Random* (1748), published the year before *Tom Jones*, traces the fortunes of a disinherited young Scot who joins the French Army, fighting against the English and Hanoverian forces at Dettingen in 1743. Roderick, however, is a soldier of fortune, not a political rebel. He bears no grudge for the racist insults to which he was subjected after arriving penniless in London. His service under the French King is as incidental as his other employments as a servant, an apprentice, a naval rating, a ship's surgeon, and a slave trader. Roderick is, in fact, a Unionist who astonishes his French comrades-in-arms by his advocacy of English freedom and independence. Smollett's next hero, the would-be knight-errant of *The Adventures of Peregrine Pickle* (1751), becomes involved in a pitched battle with French porters the moment he lands on the quayside at Calais.

Peregrine is careful to avoid a military career even though his patron
Hawser Trunnion is a retired naval officer and his best friend Godfrey
Gauntlet is an army lieutenant. He prefers to turn civil society into his
battlefield.

There could be no greater contrast between Peregrine Pickle's truculent
aggression and mindless roistering, and Laurence Sterne's gentle, retired
army captain. Sterne, a soldier's son born in Ireland, had first-hand
experience of life in barracks, but the only recognizable aspect of military
discipline in *Tristram Shandy* is Uncle Toby's relationship with the loyal
and ever-resourceful Corporal Trim. Quixotically, Toby and Trim have
turned the bowling green in the neighbourhood of Shandy Hall into a toy
battlefield. They fight through the Duke of Marlborough's campaigns
in chronological sequence until they reach the Treaty of Utrecht and the
long hobby-horse ride is over. Once the harbour and fortifications on
the bowling green have been demolished in accordance with the terms
of the treaty, Toby must awake from his dream: 'having done that,
corporal,' he says, 'we'll embark for England—We are there, quoth the
corporal, recollecting himself—Very true, said my uncle Toby—looking
at the church.'[58]

'O England! England! thou land of liberty, and climate of good sense,
thou tenderest of mothers—and gentlest of nurses,' exclaims Tristram
Shandy (501). What is the relationship between Tristram's nurturing,
village-green view of Englishness and his family's experience of past
wars? Is gentleness simply synonymous with rural retirement, redund-
ancy, and impotence, as in the story of the bull which Walter Shandy
keeps in vain 'for the service of the parish' (614)? Toby's instinctive
benevolence in releasing the fly he has caught in his hand, exclaiming that
'This world surely is wide enough to hold both thee and me' (131), must
be reconciled with his war-gaming obsession and his devotion to the
memory of the Protestant King William. His ancestor Sir Roger Shandy
fought, presumably in the Royalist cause, at the Battle of Marston Moor
in 1644. Then there are Tristram's embarrassed hints as to the destiny of
Mr Hammond Shandy, 'a little man—but of high fancy' who 'rushed into
the Duke of Monmouth's affair' in 1685 and was, apparently, hanged
during the period of the Bloody Assize shortly before the overthrow of the
Stuarts (180). Hammond Shandy's disastrous part in the Monmouth
rebellion and his allegiance to the Protestant cause cast an ironic shadow
over the peace and ecumenicalism of Shandy Hall, where the family's
spiritual and physical needs are respectively looked after by the Anglican
parson Yorick and the Catholic 'man-midwife' Dr Slop.[59]

It is to Yorick that Uncle Toby makes his apology for the military life:

For what is war? what is it, Yorick, when fought as ours has been, upon principles of *liberty*, and upon principles of *honour*—what is it, but the getting together of quiet and harmless people, with their swords in their hands, to keep the ambitious and the turbulent within bounds? (444)

Toby's idealized English militia has no bureaucratic structure or military chain of command. It is a spontaneous coming together of ordinary citizens and their neighbours, and in English history it resembles nothing so much as the legends of Monmouth's doomed campaign. Toby has been a regular soldier taking the King's shilling in a foreign war, but his ideal army is one that could only have been formed by free citizens upon their native soil. His reverence for the principles of liberty and honour links him to the rebel and martyr Hammond Shandy; but such reverence is comically undermined by the sentimental whimsy and unconscious hypocrisy of his pacifistic apology for militarism. Samuel Johnson, who celebrated 'The Bravery of the English Common Soldiers', wrote that 'their insolence in peace is bravery in war'.[60] Smollett—as if to justify the quarrelling and fighting of which his novels are full—observed in his *History of England* that there was an 'ingredient of savage ferocity mingled in the national character'.[61] If there is one generalization upon which all eighteenth-century observers agree, it is that the English are not a 'quiet and harmless people' when they have swords in their hands.

It is curious that *Tristram Shandy*, of all novels, should inaugurate the role of dynastic history and Civil War genealogies in English fiction down to the twentieth century. Goldsmith's *The Vicar of Wakefield*, contemporary with the later volumes of Sterne's masterpiece, reveals, as a passing detail, that the Vicar's father died with Lord Falkland at the Battle of Newbury. Harley, the hero of Henry Mackenzie's *The Man of Feeling* (1771), has the Royal Oak in his family crest, commemorating an ancestor who was a Royalist captain at the Battle of Worcester.[62] There is a still more extensive use of the Civil War as a picturesque background to family history in the works of Charlotte Smith, the radical novelist and poet who sympathized with the American War of Independence and the French Revolution; Smith, in turn, influenced Walter Scott's deployment of the same technique in *Waverley* and elsewhere. *The Old Manor House* (1793) centres around Rayland Hall, a house whose historical identity goes back to the Wars of the Roses. In the seventeenth century the Raylands were 'famous cavaliers in the great rebellion' and the Hall became the hiding-place for some of the King's followers after the Battle of

Edgehill, when it was besieged by Fairfax's army.[63] The protagonist of
Smith's *Marchmont* (1796) has a Cavalier great-grandfather who was
knighted in the field by Charles I, and who sheltered the future Charles II
during his flight after Naseby. He was a friend of Falkland and the
Cavalier poet Richard Lovelace. His country house was, once again,
besieged by the Parliamentary army, and one of his sons was killed;
meanwhile, a daughter loved the son of a neighbouring family who sided
with Cromwell. One room in the old family house is haunted by the spirits
of the defeated Cavaliers. *The Old Manor House*, too, uses Civil War
history to create an English domestic version of the Gothic novel's French
and Italian castles and fortresses. Rayland Hall is full of hidden doors,
cellars, staircases, and secret passages, the architectural embodiments of
its tortuous past.

Richardson in *Pamela* had introduced the protagonist as domestic
rebel; *Tom Jones* had shown the foundling at odds with his family but
willing (in principle at least) to take up arms against a political rebellion.
Charlotte Smith in *The Old Manor House* locates domestic and national
rebellion in the context of a 'great house' and its dynasty, anticipating
nineteenth-century fiction such as Dickens's *Bleak House*. This 'political
house' is a microcosm of an English nation torn between Royalist and
republican values.[64] Republicanism, which Addison had tried to bury
with his gentle mockery of Sir Andrew Freeport, was once more an issue
following the American and French revolutions. In America the British
Army had lost its first foreign war since the Treaty of Ryswick eighty
years earlier. Orlando Somerive, the protagonist of *The Old Manor
House*, is shipped to America in 1776 as an unwilling volunteer in the
King's cause.

Orlando is both the heir presumptive of his distant relative Mrs Rayland
and the clandestine lover of her ward Monimia, an orphan who is virtually
imprisoned at Rayland Hall. During the daytime, Orlando pays his
respects to the formidable owner of the Hall and dutifully does her bidding;
at night he secretly returns to the Hall by the back stairs for his trysts
with Monimia. He is at once the legitimate heir of Rayland and the chief
subverter of its Royalist, ruling-class values. Eventually his friend General
Tracy procures him an army commission to stop him hanging around the
heiress and her ward, and the novel's focus shifts from the 'politics of
Rayland Hall' (230) to British imperial politics.

The Somerives are not a military family, and Orlando and his friends
assume that he will not actually have to serve abroad. But they have
reckoned without the American colonists, and without Mrs Rayland who

regards the colonists as 'the descendants of the Regicides, against whom her ancestors drew their swords' (136). To conquer these 'rebels and round heads' is 'not only a national cause, but one in which her family were particularly bound to engage' (329). The country gentry are unanimous that 'the rebellious colonists ought to be extirpated' (147), and General Tracy thinks it will be all over by Christmas. Orlando struggles to believe in the justice of the British cause until a conversation with an American prisoner of war arouses his pity and respect for the rebels. The War of Independence, he now sees, is an English civil war by proxy—a product of 'national pride' (246) and imperial arrogance. But, though he sympathizes with the King's enemies, Smith cannot allow him to join them. Instead he is captured by the Iroquois, and then freed in Canada only to be recaptured by the French. He returns to England penniless to find that Mrs Rayland is dead and he, apparently, has been disinherited. Predictably, after his hardships he is finally reunited with Monimia and—since Mrs Rayland has never suspected their liaison—he becomes master of Rayland Hall as well.

By this time, however, the focus of *The Old Manor House* has moved away from the allegory of national and family rebellion to other concerns. The novel is a 'property romance' which ends with Orlando frantically searching Rayland Hall for his patron's lost will.[65] It also turns on Monimia's unjust deprivation and prolonged suffering, and on Orlando's similar experiences on the run in America and England following the rout of the British Army. He is one of numerous eighteenth-century protagonists who has to lose everything and to share the fate of the victimized outlaw in order to gain his inheritance. Like many other English novels, *The Old Manor House* involves an experience of suffering and a pilgrimage towards grace modelled, in part, on the biblical story of Job.

~5~

The Novel of Suffering: Richardson, Fielding, and Goldsmith

I N his *History of England from the Revolution to the Death of George the Second*, Tobias Smollett digressed from the royal, political and diplomatic events of the year 1753 to give a surprisingly circumstantial report of an episode which, he says, 'could not deserve a place in a general history, if it did not serve to convey a characteristick idea of the English nation'.[1] The story he tells bears a close parallel to one of the greatest of eighteenth-century novels, Richardson's *Clarissa* published four year earlier; and it also bears all the hallmarks of tabloid journalism.

Elizabeth Canning, an 'obscure damsel of low degree', claimed to have been abducted by two men outside Bedlam hospital and taken to the house of a Mrs Wells at Enfield Wash, where she was robbed of her stays and kept on bread and water in a small cell because she refused to turn prostitute. After a month's imprisonment she escaped and 'ran home to her mother's house, almost naked' (iii. 357). Later she testified before the novelist and magistrate Henry Fielding, who was strongly convinced by her story and wrote a pamphlet in her defence. But her allegations were not sustained in court. Mrs Wells's maidservant, Virtue Hall, retracted evidence she had earlier given on Canning's behalf, while other witnesses were shown to have been intimidated by Canning's supporters. Mrs Squires, the 'old gipsey-woman' charged with removing Canning's stays, produced an alibi and eventually secured a royal pardon. Despite intense popular agitation on her behalf, Canning was eventually found guilty of perjury and transported.

Could Elizabeth Canning have been a reader of *Clarissa*? Her story was either a true deposition or, more likely, a fabricated or semi-fabricated account of an absence from home that she felt otherwise unable to explain. Its most intimate moment, the removal of her stays by the old gipsy woman, is either a criminal violation of her bodily integrity or the symbol of some kind of release of imprisoned libido. Canning is either a victim of kidnapping and the 'white slave' trade, or she is a fantasist describing a moment of intolerable freedom from the norms of respectable society. The story might have ended with her running home to her mother's house, but it did not end there because either she or her family were determined to obtain legal retribution for her unauthorized absence. Canning's sojourn in Enfield Wash represents a rebellion against or usurpation of domestic authority, with her return home as a kind of restoration. Mrs Wells's alleged tyranny took an oppressively parental form. Canning's punishment for refusing to submit to the loss of her virginity involved the loss of her stays and restrictions on her movement and diet, reducing her to the helpless status of a small child. Her escape and restoration to her family were only temporary, however, and in the end the legal process she had initiated tore her away from the maternal home and into exile.

For Smollett, the interest of the Canning case lay not in the commonplace details of teenage abduction or truancy, but in the intense popular agitation and partisanship surrounding her appearances in court. Her supporters refused to accept the verdict and sentence and, as Smollett reports, they 'supplied her with necessaries of all sorts, paid for her transportation in a private ship, where she enjoyed all the comforts and conveniences that could be afforded in that situation, and furnished her with such recommendations as secured to her a very agreeable reception in New-England' (iii. 359). Smollett saw these events as illustrating the inherent turbulence and restlessness of the English nation. Similarly, Oliver Goldsmith's Chinese philosopher in *The Citizen of the World* (1762) lists 'superior pride', 'impatience', and 'ferocity' among the characteristics of the 'vulgar English': their 'untameable spirit', he says, is such that English prisons have to be the most strongly built in the world.[2] Canning's supporters may have formed what historians of eighteenth-century England customarily refer to as a 'mob', but she also seems to have had wealthy and influential patrons. What is most significant about this episode is that the determination and depth of public feeling it aroused would not, in any previous age, have been attached to the criminal trial of an obscure young girl. It is as if the people's latent political passions, which a century earlier had been involved in the great issues of the Civil War and the fall of the Stuarts, had been excited by a story that belongs more in a novel than in the annals of national history. At the heart of this story was an experience of female imprisonment and sexual harassment.

In *Pamela* and *Clarissa*, Samuel Richardson had introduced a lurid, somewhat sadomasochistic element into English courtship fiction.

Clarissa's antecedents lie in the theatre rather than the novel: they include Charles Johnson's *Caelia* (1732), where the innocent heroine is seduced by a villain called Wronglove and imprisoned in Mrs Lupine's whore-house.[3] But the novel, unlike eighteenth-century drama, could invest a heroine's sufferings with spiritual dignity as well as prurient melodrama, heightening the reader's emotional identification to such an extent that it was said that all Europe cried over the death of Clarissa Harlowe. Richardson's second work of fiction set a fashion for novels wallowing in what one modern critic has called the 'unrelenting, irredeemable hope-lessness' of their heroines' histories.[4] Rejecting false comforts and con-solations, Clarissa can find true comfort only in the religious promise of heavenly rewards as compensation for earthly sufferings. Pamela comes through her relatively brief ordeal unscathed and triumphant, but the much darker-toned *Clarissa* leads inexorably to the heroine's passage from this world to the next. As Clarissa's meditations show, there was in English Protestant culture a recognized scriptural model for the course taken by the heroine's suffering, in the Old Testament story of Job. The Book of Job was the subject of intense theological debate in the very decades in which Richardson, Fielding, Goldsmith, and others found themselves rewriting aspects of the Job story.[5] By telling stories of female suffering within this biblical framework, Richardson was able to achieve his aim of 'enlisting the passions on the side of Virtue'.[6] Other novelists, however, entertained less high-minded notions of virtue. As the Gothic villain Montoni says to Emily St Aubert in Ann Radcliffe's *The Mysteries of Udolpho* (1794), ' "You speak like a heroine... we shall see whether you can suffer like one." '[7]

Clarissa's Rebellion

The novel of modern courtship with a background of national allegory is Richardson's hallmark. The events of *Pamela* lead to the reconciliation of the Puritan and the Cavalier under the sign of moral reformation and middle-class family propriety. In *Sir Charles Grandison*, the well-travelled English aristocrat elects to marry a home-grown Protestant rather than an Italian Catholic bride. Clementina, his Italian lover, displays a refined spirituality which at last finds its appropriate home in a convent. In *Clarissa*, however, an outbreak of civil war between two families becomes an irreconcilable split, with tragic consequences for the female victim.

   Clarissa's tragedy begins with her family's determination to make an arranged, political marriage for her; political in the sense of furthering the family's, rather than her own, material interests. Christopher Hill has explained the complicated reasons why the Harlowes prefer an alliance with Roger Solmes to one with Robert Lovelace, whose connections are likely to get Clarissa raised to the peerage.[8] The Harlowes' determination to marry her to a man who 'knows nothing but the value of estates and how to improve them' is the cause of Clarissa's suffering.[9] Her Aunt Hervey had thought that Clarissa and Lovelace were destined to become the 'finest couple in England' (i. 9), but it is not to be.

Solmes's father was Sir Oliver, recalling Oliver Cromwell, while Lovelace is named after England's most famous Cavalier poet. Richardson's later hero Sir Charles Grandison takes his family name from a leading seventeenth-century Royalist aristocrat and his first name from the Stuart kings.[10] The presence of a political subtext in the names of Richardson's characters was not lost on subsequent English novelists, including Jane Austen, as we shall see. Solmes, however, makes very few direct appearances and we are forced to reconstruct his mean and malicious nature from Clarissa's instinctive loathing. She finds him morally repugnant, just as her family's objections to Lovelace are invariably couched in moral terms. The civil war between the Harlowes and Lovelace begins with the so-called 'rencounter' in which hot-tempered James Harlowe draws his sword against his sister's suitor without provocation and without apology, apparently with the mistaken idea of defending his sister's honour. Jealous Arabella Harlowe is convinced that Lovelace is a 'roving' type, a rake with 'half a score [of] mistresses' (i. 11), and of course she is right. Their mother expostulates with Clarissa that 'a young creature of your virtuous and *pious* turn ... cannot surely love a profligate' (i. 72), an assertion that Richardson's previous novel had disproved and that must seem absurd to romance readers everywhere.

Apart from his name, Lovelace is not given a political dynastic history of the kind that would become commonplace in English fiction one or two generations later. But there is no need for his Royalist antecedents to be specified, since he embodies the conception of absolute monarchy in his own person. He has no intention of going into Parliament, 'though nobody knows the interests of princes and courts better than he is said to do' (i. 50). He has learnt his manners at the French court, the model of absolute monarchy throughout Europe. As his fevered imagination turns his pursuit of Clarissa into a full-scale military campaign, he uses the terms 'king', 'emperor', 'tyrant', 'monarch', and 'conqueror' to describe himself, and models himself on Alexander, Hannibal, and Julius Caesar. After he has raped her he will be 'the greatest conqueror in the world', he thinks (ii. 250). His three passions, 'all imperial ones', are 'love, revenge, ambition, or a desire of conquest' (ii. 495). He is tireless in self-justifications and those who oppose his will are accused of rebellion, enmity, and high treason. At times his military vocabulary of love seems half-demented. Metaphors of world domination are used to justify a series of ultimately trivial pranks and escapades; his imperial ambitions become the excuse for a kind of permanent stag party. He represents a degenerate aristocracy whose hunger for power has been transmuted into a love of sport, with Clarissa as his quarry.

Lovelace's resort to physical violence to defend himself against James Harlowe is over almost before the novel has begun. Both here and in *Sir Charles Grandison* the Richardson hero demonstrates his physical prowess with occasional, highly effective, and very quickly stifled outbreaks of swordplay, but the hero's real game lies elsewhere. How serious, in the end, are Lovelace's crimes? The exaggerated rhetoric to which he is prone is easily turned against him, so that he can be viewed as a criminal psychopath and devil incarnate. One recent critic has described him as the 'archetypal enemy of society', which aligns him with the worst torturers and mass murderers of history.[11] It can, however, be said that his vampirish fastening onto Clarissa and the mental tortures he inflicts upon her are manifestations of a game that has gone wrong. He did not expect Clarissa and her family to resist him so fiercely, and his decision to drug and rape her since he cannot preside over a willing surrender is in fact a humiliating defeat. Beneath the mask of the Cavalier, Lovelace will stoop to anything rather than admit that his game is lost.

But for Lovelace as well as the Harlowes, patriarchy, or what Clarissa calls the 'prerogative of manhood' (i. 61), is more than a game. His will to dominate is confronted by her belief in sexual equality. Harriet Byron in *Sir Charles Grandison* protests to her abductor Sir Hargrave Pollexfen (a pale shadow of Lovelace) that she is a 'free person'.[12] Clarissa, too, demands the freedom which is her 'birthright as an English subject' (iii. 267). It is her fate, however, to be torn between the tyranny of her family and the tyranny of libertinism. Her civil rights and her rights within her own family should have been assured by the fact that she is an independent property owner, having been left a small estate by her grandfather. She owns a house that she is never allowed to occupy. Her financial independence has earned her the hatred of her brother and sister and her uncle Antony, despite the filial piety that has led her to place control of her estate in her father's hands. This voluntary renunciation of power marks the distance between Clarissa and Lovelace, and also between Clarissa and the rest of the Harlowes.

In volume one, Clarissa refuses to submit to her family's tyranny while insisting that she would be prepared to submit to an authority that is lawful. By definition, the Harlowes' determination to marry her off means that (in the Lockeian terms discussed in the previous chapter) she must have outgrown the period of nonage during which she owed unquestioning obedience to her parents. But her family defines her as a rebel and uses a rich vocabulary of terms such as 'opposition', 'defiance', 'sullenness', 'perverseness', 'obstinacy', and 'pervicacity' to condemn her resistance to an arranged marriage. Clarissa asserts her 'liberty of *refusal*' (i. 226), and resents all attempts to treat her as a 'child' or a 'slave'. 'My brother is not my sovereign', she asserts (i. 227), although she does acknowledge her father as legitimate sovereign. Mr Harlowe weakly delegates his authority to his other children, James and Arabella, but Clarissa refuses to accept such a delegated authority, complaining that her brother and sister are pursuing their own selfish interests and are not, therefore, entitled to obedience. During her month-long imprisonment at home (which takes up some 400 pages of Richardson's narrative) the novelist exercises extreme ingenuity in keeping Clarissa and her father physically apart, often with only a door between them. In this petty monarchy the headstrong and vindictive James takes on the role of day-to-day governor and prime minister, with communications flying back and forth via an endless series of deputies and intermediaries. Having failed to command her 'absolute obedience' (i. 36), Mr Harlowe eventually orders that 'the rebel' should be expelled from under his roof (i. 390). But she still refuses to define herself as a rebel, and it is James, not her father, whom she defies outright: 'If you govern everybody else, you shall not govern me,' she asserts (i. 381).

Clarissa tries for as long as she can to justify her behaviour as that of a loyal parliamentary opposition, attacking her father through his 'ministers' such as James.[13] Slowly we realize that she is more deeply involved in acts of rebellion than Pamela was. Although the novel is made up almost entirely of secret letters, nearly all her letters to Lovelace are edited out of the narrative. Were we allowed to see her perseverance in writing to him repeatedly once her family has forbidden it, we might take a different view of Clarissa, as Lovelace himself does. Her rebellion is inseparable from her pen, which 'roves' (i. 61) in ways that neither the reader nor her faithful correspondent Arabella Howe are always privy to. Her elopement with Lovelace towards the end of volume one is, of course, voluntary despite Lovelace's trickery as to its likely consequences. Once she is with him, she can no longer be forced to marry Solmes. She has thought herself capable of loving her abductor, and only gradually comes to see their mutual incompatibility. Having rebelled against her family, she must now become what Lovelace calls a 'rebel to love' (ii. 328).

A contemporary reviewer called Lovelace 'the Cromwell of women'.[14] Once he has become what the language of gallantry calls Clarissa's 'protector', he has usurped Mr Harlowe's legitimate rule and may therefore be described as Cromwellian. His government of Clarissa is icily logical, being based on ruthless cunning and brute force rather than on headstrong but divinely sanctioned paternal rage. Lovelace's vindictive and illegal tyranny anticipates the 'reign of terror' theme in Godwin's *Caleb Williams* and in English Gothic fiction. Clarissa's path, by contrast, lies in passive submission to her abductor, as the theme of her rebellion gradually subsides. He is a demonic outlaw and 'fallen angel' (iii. 41), while she becomes less an apostle of self-determination than a Christian martyr. Lovelace and Clarissa stand at the head of all subsequent English novels—*Wuthering Heights, Tess of the d'Urbervilles,* and even *Frankenstein*—featuring a demonic and angelic pair of lovers whose conflict can only lead to mutual destruction. Clarissa alone, however, can turn death and defeat into a spiritual triumph.

In opposition to Lovelace's tyranny, Clarissa ceases to appear as the rebellious slave she had been at home and becomes, instead, both a queen and a saint. Lovelace compares her to Mary Queen of Scots at the mercy of Elizabeth I (iv. 31). Her 'renunciation' of Lovelace's passion is at once an act of imperious banishment and a Last Judgement sending him to damnation: ' "I renounce thee for ever, Lovelace! Abhorred of my soul! for ever I renounce thee! Seek thy fortunes wheresoever thou wilt!" ' (iii. 232). She renounces her father, too. When at the end she states that she is 'setting out with all diligence for my father's house' (iv. 157), the father she means to return to is God himself. Not only has she refused to allow Mr Harlowe to delegate his patriarchal authority to James, but she is no longer willing to recognize delegation from a heavenly to an earthly father. Clarissa's final 'coming of age', which is marked by her decision to devote herself to God alone, is the means of her victory over Lovelace, since the more she is beatified the more he is criminalized. Clarissa believes that his actions are 'really of a *capital nature*' (iii. 374) and merit hanging, though he will not be tried in a civil court. Dr Lewen tries to persuade her to testify against him, but she refuses on the grounds that a woman cannot get justice in a rape case (iv. 184–5, 189). This is why

Colonel Morden, her kinsman and eventual champion, is brought to the fore as Clarissa's life begins to ebb away. Lovelace and Morden are both aristocrats living by the code of honour. The former is 'one who knows how to defend his own cause as well as any man in England', while the latter, according to Mowbray who knows both of them, has 'a superiority which I know not how to allow to the best man in Europe' (iv. 226, 229). After Clarissa's death—and despite her posthumous instruction to Morden that duelling is both an 'insult upon magistracy and good government' and a 'usurpation of the Divine prerogative' (iv. 462)—the scene is set for Morden's challenge and the ensuing duel, which decorously takes place outside England. Lovelace expires gracefully with a compliment to his opponent: 'I fall by a man of honour' (iv. 529).

It is enormously gratifying for Richardson's unscrupulous Cavalier that he is allowed to perish by the aristocratic code, in a fight with a social equal rather than an upstart like James. But why should Colonel Morden have had to stake his life in somebody else's cause? Clarissa's final declaration to Morden is unexceptionable both in civil and religious terms—justice, she says, 'ought not to depend upon a private sword' (iv. 462)—and these were certainly Richardson's views. Yet, as a novelist, he must have realized that he could not possibly give Lovelace a fair trial in front of a British judge and jury. If Clarissa were still alive and virtually friendless, judge and jury would have been exposed to the various means of persuasion open to the defendant; but once she is dead, her evidence dies with her. And any verdict of legal acquittal would have amounted to an indictment of the whole governing class, which Richardson is clearly anxious to avoid. Every instance of aristocratic vice in his novels is matched by a parallel instance of virtue or virtuous potential. His resort in *Clarissa* to aristocratic trial by combat suggests that, however deep are the social divisions implied by the novel's plot, the ruling class is capable of applying its own remedies and that these can be reconciled with divine or providential justice. Colonel Morden's usurpation of the divine prerogative helps to assure us that there is such a prerogative, and that Clarissa's pious endurance of suffering will not, in the larger scheme of things, go unrewarded.[15]

Clarissa's Patience

Clarissa has been called 'the eighteenth century's ultimate example of a religious novel'.[16] After her abduction and rape, the heroine gradually changes from a rebellious defender of her rights to a resigned and contemplative victim, whose favourite reading is the Book of Job. 'Patience' and 'comfort' (or 'comforter') are the keywords of the English novel's allusions to Job. Richardson's readers may have been alerted to Job as early as the opening sentence of *Pamela*, where the heroine tells her parents that 'I have great trouble, and some comfort, to acquaint you with'.[17] In *Clarissa* Lovelace is the Satan of the Job story, determined to break down the virtue of an antagonist who like Job is 'perfect and . . . upright', 'one that feareth God, and escheweth evil' (Job 1: 8). And so long as Clarissa continues to express her opposition to him in terms of rebellious impatience—'I have no patience, said she, to find myself a slave, a prisoner, in this vile house' (iii. 267)—we know that her spiritual development is still incomplete.

The Book of Job in eighteenth-century England was generally acknowledged as the greatest and most ancient of poems.[18] Job's story poses in the starkest terms the problems of divine justice (or injustice) and the morality of rebellion against spiritual authority. Christian exegesis has always struggled to reconcile the prose prologue and epilogue, regarded by modern commentators as a folk tale, with the poetic core of the Book of Job. That the book must have had at least two authors is a commonplace of biblical criticism. As one analyst has put it, 'The Job of the poem is as bitterly in revolt as the Job of the tale is unquestioningly supine and superlatively submissive. It is hard to imagine greater contrast.'[19] Clarissa's meditations are all based on extracts from the poem, not the surrounding folk tale, but the theological orthodoxy to which she adheres sought a unified interpretation of the text in terms of submission and patience rather than revolt. Nevertheless, in any reading of Job the arguments of the 'Tempter' must be strong ones, and the challenge to God's justice powerful and perplexing.

In the prologue in Heaven, God boasts of Job's virtue and steadfastness and challenges Satan to undermine it if he can. When Satan has destroyed his victim's possessions and killed his sons, God can still boast that Job 'holdeth fast his integrity' (2: 3). Satan is now permitted to attack Job's person, sparing only his life, and so he is smitten with boils from head to foot. At this point Job sits down 'among the ashes', while his wife exhorts him to rebellion: 'Dost thou still retain thine integrity? Curse God, and die' (2: 9). The comforters arrive and join Job in the ashpit, and after a week of silent mourning their dialogue begins with Job 'cursing his day'.

Job at the beginning is a rich farmer and patriarch, master of a large household, 'the greatest of all the men of the east' (1: 3). He is deposed from his position of power, but finally restored. Because he never curses God in his heart, God accepts his repentance. Modern biblical scholarship acknowledges that there are two versions of the Hebrew God in the poem (Jahweh and Shaddai) whose words and behaviour are inconsistent, and, moreover, the poem seems to show that Job does in fact rebel; but in any case the divine experiment concludes with Job gaining a new family and another great estate, 'So the Lord blessed the latter end of Job more than his beginning' (42: 12). Two of the 'miserable comforters', Eliphaz and Bildad, argue that God will see that Job receives his just deserts in the long run, but Job rejects their assurances, since true religious faith cannot be based on the promise of earthly rewards. This is the doctrinal issue that gripped the eighteenth century. Belief in an 'unequal Providence' asserts that it is only in the afterlife that the manifest injustices and wrongs of this world can be righted. On earth, it is part of God's plan that the virtuous should suffer and the vicious should prosper.[20] An observer like Robinson Crusoe who marked down instances of 'providential justice' in earthly affairs would, therefore, be guilty of superstition rather than showing the abject humility demanded of Job.

At this point, the dominant view of eighteenth-century theologians contrasts sharply with the ethos of eighteenth-century fiction and drama, since in literature 'poetical justice' is normally dispensed at the moment of narrative denouement rather than being reserved for a future state. Richardson's novels show the full force of the tension between earthly and heavenly justice. In *Pamela* the heroine's prudence leads to an outcome celebrated in the novel's title as *Virtue Rewarded*, whereas the final volume of *Clarissa* turns into a prolonged elegy for a heroine deprived of any possibility of earthly reward.[21]

Richardson carefully manipulates the plot to keep Clarissa in solitary confinement, perpetually separated from her correspondent Miss Howe.[22] We are told that her Bible opens naturally at the Book of Job. In her will she orders a funeral sermon to be preached on a text from Job, and another text from the same book, along with two from the Psalms, is engraved on her coffin. Before this, as her bodily presence fades, the biblical texts begin to take the place of the reams of epistolary narrative she has earlier generated. A series of 'meditations', almost all of them taken from the words of her 'admired exclaimer' (iii. 578), fill up the space of her letters. Readers' interest in these meditations was so great that Richardson subsequently extracted them from the novel, added to them, and published them separately as *Meditations Collected from the Sacred Books* (1750).[23] The fact that Clarissa's meditations begin with Job's curses—so that Lovelace sees her preoccupation with Job as an 'incitement to excessive complaints'—must be reconciled with her use of the biblical story to help her to achieve spiritual restoration and eventual triumph.[24]

Richardson's friend William Warburton, one of the principal eighteenth-century Job commentators, both acknowledged that Clarissa's situation was analogous to Job's and regarded the Job story itself as a national allegory of the plight of the Jews in Babylonian captivity.[25] For a century which regarded Job as the type of 'true Christian fortitude and faith in adversity',[26] there were clearly temptations to apply the Job story to episodes in English history. Charles I had compared himself to Job, as well as to Samson and other biblical heroes;[27] Bunyan had invoked the Job story in *Grace Abounding* and *The Holy War*; and it could evidently be applied to the plight of English Puritanism after the collapse of the Commonwealth. It is as if Job's suffering became an index of national self-pity and victimization among the English. The ideology of the Protestant nation was confirmed by the fact that Job's enemy, against whom he eventually triumphed, was Satan himself. Innumerable English novels before and after *Clarissa* allude to Job's distress and final vindication, while being content to repeat the biblical story's self-contradictions.[28]

The narrative elements common to these fictional versions of Job are, first, the role either of Satan in subjecting the protagonist to excessive and unreasonable punishments, or of a hidden God who permits the punishment but finally intervenes on the side of the protagonist; and, second, the humiliations, including the loss of family, friends, and property, to which the protagonist is subjected. Among the eighteenth-century fictional characters unjustly or unluckily imprisoned are Fielding's Mr Wilson (in *Joseph Andrews*), Heartfree (in *Jonathan Wild*), and Billy Booth (in *Amelia*), as well as Tom Jones; Smollett's Roderick Random, Peregrine Pickle, and Humphry Clinker; Goldsmith's Vicar of Wakefield; Radcliffe's Emily St Aubert; Charlotte Smith's Marchmont; Godwin's Caleb Williams; and Mary Raymond, the heroine of Mary Hays's *The Victim of Prejudice* (1799). (Admittedly, not all of these protagonists submit to their imprisonment with the proverbial Jobian fortitude.) Robinson Crusoe sees his uninhabited island as a prison. The prison became an inescapable port of call in the eighteenth-century novel partly because, in the words of Moll Flanders (who was born in Newgate, and who—inevitably though not, of course, innocently—finds her way back there), it is an 'emblem of hell itself, and a kind of entrance into it'.[29] Time and again, the protagonist is an accidental or arbitrary victim to be rescued from the jaws of hell after coming into Satan's clutches.

From *Amelia* to *The Wrongs of Woman*: The Suffering Heroine and the Suffering Nation

Sir Richard Blackmore commented in 1716 on the 'Air of Contrivance' by which the Book of Job manages 'to sink a Man so suddenly from the most prosperous Condition, and to lay him under such grievous Sufferings and the very Extremity of Misery, and by a no less sudden and surprizing Revolution, in so short a space of time, to make him again the most happy Man in the World'.[30] Whether contrived or not, Blackmore had hit on the favourite fictional plot of the later eighteenth century, and one that has left a permanent impress on later English novelists. After *Clarissa* it soon became evident that the same basic plot could serve for domestic romance or Gothic melodrama, for a social-problem novel verging on political rebellion, or for a humorous pastoral. All that was certain, in the 'Age of Sensibility', was that tears would be shed during the narration by the bucketful, and that more tears—often, but not always, tears of joy— would be provoked by the sudden denouement.

Introducing the theme of his last novel *Amelia* (1753), Henry Fielding says of its protagonists that 'The distresses which they waded through were some of them so exquisite, and the incidents which produced these so extraordinary, that they seemed to require not only the utmost malice, but the utmost invention, which superstition hath ever attributed to Fortune'.[31] This is the formula for the novel of suffering. For a novelist close to Richardson in moral outlook, such a tale would teach the virtues of humility and submission to a higher power; but the same plot could be used to awaken discontent and inspire rebellion against what were seen as human and social, rather than divine, causes. *Amelia*, which has a foot in both camps, belongs halfway between the extremes marked by *Clarissa* and the feminist Jacobin novel such as Mary Wollstonecraft's *The Wrongs of Woman* (1798).

One of the earliest novels after *Clarissa* to draw its moral directly from the Book of Job was *The Adventures of David Simple* (1753) by Fielding's sister Sarah, a member of Richardson's circle. The first two volumes of *David Simple* are a kind of Pilgrim's Progress in which the hero goes to the metropolis to enquire into the 'Characters of Men', and, after numerous encounters, settles down with an idyllic group of friends. Volume three, however, is a Job story in which David, swindled out of his money by a Chancery suit, loses his family and companions and sinks into penury. Had he been an 'Infidel', we are told, 'He would have raved to

Madness, or wept himself to Death', but as a good Protestant he submits patiently, 'like *Job* ... to the temporary sufferings allotted him'.[32] Eventually a rich patron comes on the scene, too late to help David but in time, at least, to rescue his orphaned daughter.

Another novel of this kind, dedicated to the 'Author of Clarissa and Sir Charles Grandison', was Frances Sheridan's *Memoirs of Miss Sidney Bidulph* (1761), which went through numerous editions and was translated into French and German. Once again, the multiply unfortunate Miss Bidulph is summed up by her faithful friend Cecilia as a paragon of meek and submissive womanhood: 'Her natural disposition ever sweet and complying, was improved by her sufferings into a patience very rare in woman; and a resignation imbibed at first from a rigid education, was heightened by religion into an almost saint-like meekness and humility.'[33] Miss Bidulph, however, is more interesting, and her story more sensational, than this recital of Puritan virtues might suggest. The novel is one of adulterous passion culminating in bigamous marriage; the heroine, guilty in the eyes of the world, is nevertheless entirely innocent, though her innocence looks remarkably like guilt. There are grounds for suspecting Sidney Bidulph of a full-blown Puritan hypocrisy. Just a few pages before Cecilia delivers her final encomium on her friend's unblemished character, we find Sidney exclaiming against her fate in a very Job-like way: ' "Cecilia! have I been a murmurer at the decrees of providence? have I been an impious repiner when heaven has poured down its wrath upon my head? if not, why am I marked out for divine vengeance?" '(420). The novel's dedication to Richardson in 1761 (the year of his death) seems a species of opportunism, since it is unlikely that the fastidious author of *Clarissa* would have appreciated such a blatant demonstration of how to be a murmurer while claiming not to murmur. Sheridan's readers were surely meant to ask, why did God not do more to protect the innocent? And why was there so much female suffering in the world?

The same questions are addressed—not always very satisfactorily—in *Amelia*, Henry Fielding's least popular and least understood novel. Far from being the mature masterpiece that might have been expected of the author of *Tom Jones*, this is an obscure and transitional work which holds an intriguing place among the eighteenth-century rewritings of Job. Amelia's misfortunes begin in her youth, when a carriage accident leaves her with a badly broken nose—a rather grotesque fate to befall a beautiful heroine. The name of the biblical patriarch appears only once in the novel, in a reference to 'the patience of any Job in petticoats' (ii. 378), though Fielding frequently resorts to the language of patience and comfort.

Amelia suffers greatly as a result of the weakness and foolishness of her husband, Billy Booth, who finally becomes a Christian penitent; at the same time, the couple are the more or less helpless victims of legal injustice, jobbery, corruption, and a vicious and brutal aristocracy. Fielding's Dedication puts forward *Amelia* as a social-problem novel, perhaps the first in English literature, setting out to 'expose some of the most glaring evils, as well public as private, which at present infest the country'.[34] The novel begins with Booth being sent to prison (where he meets, and takes up with, a former mistress) on a trumped-up charge of assault. But Booth at the time of his arrest is already a fugitive confined within the 'verge of the court' (the area around Whitehall under the jurisdiction of the Lord High Steward) to avoid imprisonment for debt. He spends most of the novel in confinement of one sort or another.

Booth and Amelia have a somewhat fickle patron and protector, Dr Harrison, whose role resembles that of God in the Job story. Harrison, a clergyman, may be named after the regicide Thomas Harrison, since he holds that Oliver Cromwell 'carried the reputation of England higher than it ever was at any other time' (ii. 511). He embodies the Puritan virtues of piety, prudence, financial probity, and personal rectitude, while Booth, whose name suggests Sir George Booth, the Presbyterian turned Royalist general who assisted at the Restoration, is a down-at-heel Cavalier. When Booth first marries Amelia, Harrison helps him to set up as a farmer, but loses patience when he hears the follies that cause Booth to be nicknamed the 'Squire Farmer'. Booth becomes an army officer, is retired on half pay, and comes under the influence of unscrupulous comrades who lend him money that he cannot repay. Finally another false comforter persuades him to lay out his last fifty pounds in a bribe to a politician who 'received the money, not as a gudgeon doth a bait, but as a pike receives a poor gudgeon into his maw' (ii. 526). At this time Dr Harrison, whom Booth has described as ' "Of all mankind . . . the best of comforters" ' (i. 95), is absent abroad. When he comes back, he provokes the novel's crisis by having Booth rearrested for debt, causing even the loyal and passive Amelia to rebel. ' "Dr Harrison!" ' she exclaims when she finds out the identity of her husband's accuser, ' "Well, then, there is an end of all goodness in the world" ' (ii. 337). She has ' "no comfort, no hope, no friend left" ' (ii. 378). Later she denounces Booth as a 'wicked man' in front of her children and laments aloud, ' "Why did I bring these little wretches into the world?" ' (ii. 544). But by this time Harrison's benevolence and good intentions have been vindicated, and he and Booth are working together to secure the estate of which she has been unfairly disinherited. When, in fury, she abandons her children and drives to a magistrate's house only to find Booth and Harrison dining together in triumph, she is judged too confused and distraught to be told their good news at once. But soon they are complimenting her on her heroism while she readily accepts that she has passed her ordeal in the true Christian spirit: ' "If it had pleased Heaven . . . to have tried me, I think, at least I hope, I should have preserved my humility" ' (ii. 587). For much of *Amelia* Fielding's sense of humour seems to have deserted him, but the novel ends with what seems a sly joke at the expense of his Job-like heroine. Finally we are assured that Booth and his long-suffering wife will leave for the countryside to produce more children and live happily ever after, since 'Fortune seems to have made them large amends for the tricks she had played them in their youth' (ii. 593).

Shortly before this, Harrison has announced to Booth that ' "Your sufferings are all at an end, and Providence hath done you the justice at last which it will, one day or other, render to all men" ' (ii. 581). There is an air of temporizing, not to say outright casuistry, about Fielding's narrative interventions devoted to 'Fortune' and 'Providence' in *Amelia*. To what extent should a benefactor such as Harrison be expected to shoulder the burden of Providence? Booth somewhat implausibly takes advatage of his imprisonment in the bailiff's house to become a sincere Christian, studying the sermons of the seventeenth-century Royalist Isaac Barrow, which teach him to revere Harrison's benevolence and Amelia's self-sacrificing love.[35] His religious conversion makes him a fit object of Harrison's charity and the justice of Providence, a conclusion that suggests that coming to the aid of Booth and his family was a matter of less urgency while he remained a religious reprobate.

The other side of *Amelia*, barely compatible with its presentation as a religiously orthodox Job story, is Fielding's bitter onslaught on the ruling Whig aristocracy. The novel contains not just frequent references to the divinity ('Our Lord'), but no less than four peers who are not named but referred to as 'my lord'. One of these is the petty seducer, riddled with venereal disease, who attacks Amelia's chastity; the last that we hear of him is that he has 'become so rotten that he stunk above-ground' (ii. 592). Another is the nobleman whom Harrison approaches, in a chapter called 'Matters Political', to secure Booth's preferment in the army. 'My lord' is thoroughly amenable so long as Harrison promises, as a quid pro quo, to vote for his nominee in a local election. This attempted bargain, comparable (it might be suggested) to the position of a God who would only see earthly justice done for the devout, is angrily rejected by Harrison,

who delivers a long diatribe on political corruption. The lord complacently agrees that England is ' "as corrupt a nation as ever existed under
the sun" ' (ii. 509). Harrison's professions of high principle are, he says,
' "all mere Utopia . . . the chimerical system of Plato's commonwealth,
with which we amused ourselves at the university" ' (ii. 509). Harrison
laments that ' "The people sink into sloth and luxury and prostitution" '
(ii. 510), a heartfelt complaint for which the novel suggests no remedy
apart from the Christian virtues.[36] Fielding in some parts of *Amelia* voices
the hatred and suspicion of the eighteenth-century Whig oligarchy that we
shall later find in Godwin, Disraeli, and even Jane Austen. But Amelia, a
heroine who 'has great moral rectitude but little moral force',[37] cannot be
taken as an embodiment of England suffering under a corrupt regime,
whatever her individual virtues. The novel's greatest defect is that her
sufferings leave most readers cold.

One of the very few eighteenth-century repudiations of the book of
Job is to be found in a short tale and an unfinished novel by Mary
Wollstonecraft. In *Mary* (1788), Wollstonecraft undertook to display
'the mind of a woman, who has thinking powers', as opposed to such
heroines as Clarissa, Harriet Byron (in *Sir Charles Grandison*), and
Sophia Western.[38] *The Wrongs of Woman* begins with a preface recommending the 'delineation of finer sensations', as opposed to 'What are
termed great misfortunes, [which] may more forcefully impress the mind
of common readers' (74). Nevertheless, these are both tales of extreme
suffering. Mary is destined to experience 'almost every species of sorrow'
(17), while Maria in *The Wrongs of Woman* is lost in 'mazes of misery'
(92) and confined in a madhouse where, as she reflects, 'Was not the world
a vast prison, and women born slaves?' (79). Maria like Clarissa has
grown up in a cruel patriarchal family where her eldest brother acted as
'deputy-tyrant' (125). Her marriage is a trap in which she believes herself
to be 'caged for life' (144), and she escapes from the madhouse only to
suffer the loss of her baby and to be tried and found guilty of adultery.
Maria's indignation is directed not merely against her vicious husband
but against 'the laws of her country—if women have a country—[which]
afford her no protection or redress from her oppressor, unless she have
the plea of bodily fear' (159). In other words, to achieve redress she would
have to be able to prove an allegation of rape; but her husband is too
cunning for that, and has had her locked up on suspicion of insanity since
she is not meek and submissive like the standard eighteenth-century
heroine. Maria's imprisonment expresses the full power and logic of
social oppression, and her embodiment of female suffering is an index of

women's enslavement. In her passionate indignation she tries to speak for women everywhere, and, far from being a figure of national allegory, she implies that women are social and legal outcasts and, therefore, stateless. But Wollstonecraft's fiction was destined for nearly two centuries of neglect until rescued by late twentieth-century feminists, while the eighteenth century's experience of female suffering was handed down to succeeding generations in fiction of a very different kind. The suffering heroine never quite became the embodiment of a suffering nation.

From Gothic Victim to Golden Ass

Where the London of Fielding's *Amelia* is painstakingly realistic, the madhouse in *The Wrongs of Woman* is an altogether more Gothic setting, a 'huge pile of buildings', half in ruins, in which Maria contemplates the 'most terrific of ruins—that of a human soul' (77, 83). Landscape is a projection of psychic experience just as in the Gothic fiction exemplified by Radcliffe's *Mysteries of Udolpho*, where the bleak wildernesses of the Pyrenees and Apennines become a backdrop for the heroine's torments. Characteristically, Gothic novels take place in a vague and unspecified past and outside England. Horace Walpole's *The Castle of Otranto* (1764) is set in the time of the Crusades, while *The Mysteries of Udolpho* opens in the year 1584. Female virtue, in such settings, is at the mercy of ruthless medieval barons living in elaborate fortresses. Matthew Lewis's *The Monk* (1796) portrays the Spanish Inquisition, with Lucifer himself as one of the characters. The ideological gulf between Protestant and Catholic Europe had been explored much more even-handedly in Richardson's *Sir Charles Grandison*, with its highly sympathetic portrayal of an Italian Catholic nobility which Grandison, the ideal English gentleman, finds deeply attractive—though not so attractive as to be worth the sacrifice of his Protestant faith. For Richardson, England is superior to Italy not only as a Protestant stronghold but as the home of the female equality personified by Grandison's outspoken sister Charlotte. It is Charlotte who exclaims, 'How could Sir Charles, so thorough an Englishman, have been happy with an Italian wife?' (iii. 263). From her perspective Grandison's Italian lover, the long-suffering and chaste Clementina, appears slavish in her filial obedience and religious devotion. When Charlotte initiates a discussion of 'Man's usurpation and woman's natural independency', Sir Charles tactfully interrupts her with a patriotic effusion: 'O my Charlotte, said he, how I love my country! ENGLAND is the *only* spot in the world, in which this argument *can* be properly debated!' (iii. 242). The argument about female independence is a secondary matter; what is primary is the warm glow created by England's superiority. In the Gothic novel, English superiority is taken for granted and the supposed corruption, cruelty, and immorality of Catholic Europe provide lurid and thrilling entertainment. Radcliffe's and Lewis's sagas involving perverted monks and mad or debauched nuns offered their readers a satisfying definition of what could not happen in the Protestant homeland.

If the social-problem novel modelled on the Book of Job has a protagonist forcibly detained in the grim metropolis, while Gothic melodrama is usually set in an exotic southern Europe, the novel as humorous pastoral ought to begin and end in a lush English countryside. There was ample suffering in ordinary rural England, though it is recorded by late eighteenth-century poets (particularly George Crabbe) rather than in English fiction. A partial exception might be made for Oliver Goldsmith, the poet of *The Deserted Village* (1770) and author of a single classic novel, *The Vicar of Wakefield* published four years earlier. *The Vicar of Wakefield* is yet another rewriting of the Book of Job, though it also suggests another ancient literary model of the tale of suffering involving sudden and violent changes of fortune, *The Transformations of Lucius, otherwise known as the Golden Ass* by the second-century Latin writer Apuleius. In *The Golden Ass* Lord Lucius, led astray by his love for a slave girl and his interest in the black arts, is changed into a donkey and shown the underside of society through a series of horrifying but highly entertaining ordeals. Finally he prays to the Moon-Goddess and is released from his misery to become a rich and famous lawyer. Lucius looks back on his adventures as a donkey with considerable complacency, since, as he says, they have enormously enlarged his experience.[39]

In English fiction Defoe had pioneered the male adventure story with a moral loosely tacked on from the Book of Job. Goldsmith's great innovation was to centre his fiction on a clergyman and man of God who would naturally echo the Jobian sentiments, yet whose pious reflections were consistently subjected to gentle mockery. Beginning in a state of patriarchal complacency where he is 'happier...than the greatest monarchs upon earth', Dr Primrose suffers calamitous misfortunes with what might seem undaunted good spirits.[40] He shares Job's human fallibility, but his impetuous outbursts are soon stilled either as a result of his angelic temperament, his Panglossian quality as a retrospective narrator, or sheer obstinacy. He loses his fortune, his house burns down, his daughters are abducted and apparently ravished, his son is arrested, and he is evicted by his landlord and imprisoned for debt, until finally he is lifted out of adversity by a mysterious benefactor. Goldsmith mocks the readers as well as the writers of novels, burlesquing some of Richardson's most familiar scenes and reminding us, for example, that 'every reader, however beggarly himself, is fond of high-lived dialogues, with anecdotes of Lords, Ladies, and Knights of the Garter' (56).

The avatars of God and Satan in this version of the Job story are two all-powerful rural landlords, the baronet Sir William Thornhill and his villainous nephew Squire Thornhill. Sir William, 'one of the most generous yet whimsical men in the kingdom' (15), goes in disguise as the 'poor Gentleman' Mr Burchell. He becomes the Primrose family's bosom friend, entertaining them with ballads and old folk tales, until Primrose's wife and daughters conclude that he is a 'low-lived fellow' (69) and turn him away. Squire Thornhill takes Burchell's place in their home, posing 'in the character of Alexander the Great' (85)—a probable allusion to Lovelace—in a pompous portrait of the Primrose family in fancy dress. Soon afterwards, Olivia Primrose is abducted by two gentlemen in a post-chaise, and, recalling Clarissa, is later reported to have died of grief. Mr Burchell valiantly rescues Primrose's other daughter Sophia from a second forcible abduction in a post-chaise, coming to the rescue much as Sir Charles Grandison saved Harriet Byron. When Dr Primrose hears of Olivia's disappearance he turns to Job-like complaints, but is instantly rebuked by his son Moses: ' "You should be my mother's comforter, and you increase her pain" ' (97). Later when he learns of Sophia's abduction and his son George's arrest, Primrose again breaks into curses and lamentations, and this time it is George who warns him not to 'fling those curses upward that must soon descend to crush thy own grey head with destruction!' (186). But Primrose has not forgotten his holy calling. When fifty of his poor parishioners band together to save him from eviction, he quells their show of force with a stern lecture and meekly goes off to prison. Here, where all is 'riot, laughter, and profaneness' (161), he preaches a sermon from his sickbed bidding his listeners to take comfort from the heavenly consolations promised for the poor and unfortunate. Mr Burchell (Sir William Thornhill) now reveals himself as a 'disguised spectator of [Primrose's] benevolence' (199). Returning like the disguised Duke in Shakespeare's *Measure for Measure*, he reveals that he has watched everything that has happened and then dispenses justice to all the protagonists. The conclusion, while modelled on stage comedy, is also a parody or pastiche of divine judgement.

The Primrose family has a Royalist pedigree, as we saw in Chapter Four.[41] In a rather comical political discourse delivered on the road, Dr Primrose describes himself as both Leveller and monarchist: ' "I would have all men kings! I would be a king myself" ' (106). Sir William Thornhill's return and the defeat of his usurping nephew not only repeats God's role in the Job story but serves as a restoration of the absolute authority invested in the just landlord. He judges his nephew to be 'as complete a villain as ever disgraced humanity' (208), yet they remain on cordial terms, like God and Satan in the Book of Job. The outcome of Sir William's high-handed manoeuvres is that Olivia and Sophia are both happily and advantageously married and that Sir William's nephew is now also his brother-in-law.

Sir William, then, exemplifies the capriciousness of the benefactor 'whose greatest pleasure was in doing good' (216). Primrose's last words are that 'It now remained, that my gratitude in good fortune should exceed my former submission in adversity' (222). The submissive humility exemplified by the story of Job is also an abject feeling of gratitude towards his human benefactor and the arbitrary power he has exercised. Among those whom Primrose must thank are Mr Jenkinson, apparently one of Sir William Thornhill's agents, who swindled Primrose and his son while he thought they were rich, but later befriended the Vicar and shared his bedding with him in prison. In terms of the Job story which is central to *The Vicar of Wakefield*, Dr Primrose has learned patience, meekness, and acceptance of apparent injustice, while his incipient rebellion has been suppressed and turned into its opposite.[42] But there are more subversive energies at work in this apparently counter-revolutionary pastoral tale, and in English eighteenth-century fiction more generally. These may be summed up in the figure of Jenkinson, the former horse dealer, fairground prankster, and benefactor to the poor and deserving. The title *The Vicar of Wakefield* apparently alludes to the ballad of 'Robin Hood and the Pinder of Wakefield', and not merely Jenkinson but Sir William Thornhill himself, in his double role as 'poor gentleman' and rich absentee landlord, have been seen as representing the legendary outlaw.[43]

The Benevolent Robber: From Fielding to the 1790s

A T the beginning of *Tom Jones* Fielding presents Squire Allworthy in his glory, 'a human being replete with benevolence, meditating in what manner he might render himself most acceptable to his Creator, by doing most good to his creatures'.[1] The eighteenth century saw submission as the duty of the weak, and benevolence as the duty of the powerful and wealthy. Lord Shaftesbury in his *Characteristics* (1711) argued that human virtue was derived from the 'natural and good affections', following the example set by a loving and benevolent deity.[2] But benevolence has its dark side, as Bernard Mandeville pointed out in *The Fable of the Bees* (1714). For Mandeville, the 'disinterested' virtue that Shaftesbury idealized was an invitation to hypocrisy and a mask for pride. The dispute between Shaftesbury and Mandeville forms a background to the comedy of *Tom Jones*, since Allworthy's firm belief in Christian benevolence is contested on theological grounds by his brother-in-law Captain Blifil, the father of Tom's rival as Allworthy's heir. Blifil finds little to praise in acts of charity, even when they give pleasure to the benefactor, since we are 'liable to be imposed upon, and to confer our choicest favours often on the undeserving' (101). Whether or not Allworthy's benevolence is a mask for pride, it certainly proves an open invitation to the hypocrisy of the Blifils, father and son.

Shaftesbury's *Characteristics* represents a crucial moment in the emergence of the idea of the English gentleman, or, as he put it, the 'man of thorough good breeding' who is 'incapable of doing a rude or brutal action' (86). Shaftesbury was both a Whig and the grandson of a leading Royalist statesman, and his doctrine of natural goodness is arguably the old Cavalier ideal, sublimated and sanitized. He believed that '*Gravity* is of the very essence of imposture' and that the weapons of the gentleman are wit and raillery rather than the old Puritanical 'mill-stones' of pedantry and bigotry (10, 48). Social privilege, or what he calls the 'liberty of *the club*', should lead to freedom from prejudice and liberality of outlook: 'It belongs to men of slavish principles to affect a superiority over the vulgar, and to despise the multitude' (53). Shaftesbury's commitment to innate good breeding and mutual goodwill is fundamentally opposed by the conservative pessimism of Mandeville and, before him, Thomas Hobbes. For Hobbes we are all, in a sense, would-be criminals.

In Hobbes's *Leviathan*, as we saw in Chapter 2, the doctrine of human selfishness rests on the conception of a state of nature, coming before the institution of the social contract, in which justice has no place and life is a war of all against all. What every individual demands from life is the satisfaction of desires which are, in fact, insatiable, 'a perpetuall and restlesse desire of Power after power, that ceaseth onely in Death'.[3] Outside the social contract, robbery is a natural and justifiable means of satisfying one's desires—a point that Hobbes repeatedly makes—since 'where there is no Common-wealth, there is no Propriety; all men having Right to all things' (202). The institution of state power has necessarily brought an end to the licensed brigandage of feudal clans and robber barons, but still, according to Hobbes, it is a greater crime to rob a poor man than to rob a rich one (352). He must have known that English criminal justice, buttressed by the property qualification for jury service, took precisely the opposite view.[4]

For Hobbes and Mandeville, benevolence and robbery, giving and taking away, are not simple opposites. These writers are sceptical of the moral virtue of generosity and, in Mandeville's case, convinced of the social benefits of crime. Hobbes considers benevolence as a relationship between a giver and a receiver, which is as likely to end in hypocrisy and resentment as in gratitude and mutual love:

To have received from one, to whom we think our selves equall, greater benefits than there is hope to Requite, disposeth to counterfeit love; but really secret hatred; and puts a man into the estate of a desperate debtor, that in declining the sight of his creditor, tacitly wishes him there, where he might never see him more. For benefits oblige; and obligation is thraldome; and unrequitable obligation, perpetuall thraldome; which is to ones equall, hateful. But to have receivd benefit from one, whom we acknowledge for our superiour, enclines to love . . . Also to receive benefits, though from an equall, or inferiour, as long as there is hope of requitall, disposeth to love: (162–3)

To Hobbes's moral calculus Mandeville cynically adds that, in economic terms, fair exchange and robbery have very similar effects, being equally productive of prosperity and trade. Hobbes had observed that money circulates around the Commonwealth with the same nourishing effect as the circulation of blood in the body, and that monopolies and the hoarding of wealth were a 'Disease' akin to physical inflammation or pleurisy (300, 374). Mandeville praises riotous sons and spendthrift heirs for 'refunding to the public what was robbed from it'. The whole nation stands to benefit when a miser is robbed:

A highwayman having met with a considerable booty, gives a poor common harlot he fancies, ten pounds to new rig her from top to toe ... She must have shoes and stockings, gloves, the stay and mantomaker, the sempstress, the linen-draper, all must get something by her, and a hundred different tradesmen dependent on those she laid her money out with, may touch part of it before a month is at an end. The generous gentleman, in the mean time, his money being near spent, ventured again on the road, but the second day having committed a robbery near *Highgate*, he was taken with one of his accomplices, and the next Sessions both were condemned, and suffered the law. The money due on their conviction fell to three country fellows, on whom it was admirably well bestowed.[5]

Here the harlot is the first of the hundred different tradespeople to benefit from the highwayman's generosity, while the 'three country fellows' (whose circumstances Mandeville proceeds to describe) also receive a handsome reward. Mandeville's passage is not unlike one of Defoe's novels, reminding us how the novel itself, with its fluctuations of fortune, reproduces the tonic effects of circulation within the social body.

Mandeville's casual allusion to his highwayman as 'the generous gentleman' suggests the extent to which highway robbers, in the early eighteenth century, had inherited some of the glamour of the Cavalier blade and Restoration rake. The highwayman is naturally gallant towards the opposite sex, even if the object of his fancy is only a 'poor common harlot'. *The Fable of the Bees* was contemporaneous with the first edition of Captain Alexander Smith's *Complete History of the Lives and Robberies of the Most Notorious Highwaymen*, a classic compilation of criminal biographies (once wrongly attributed to Defoe) which went through several editions in the next few years. The popularity of the highwayman as a subject for criminal biography reflects the 'gentleman of the road's' position as an emblem of national character. The legendary English highwayman, in his temporary position of power over his victims, chooses to exercise that power benevolently, unlike the robbers and thugs bred by continental absolutism. Defoe's Cavalier reports that 'the Highway-Men in *France* do not always give a Traveller the Civility of bidding him Stand and Deliver his Money, but frequently Fire upon him first, and then take his Money'.[6] Oliver Goldsmith spent his first twenty-five years in Ireland, and presumably had some experience of Irish 'Tories' or bandits. Here is his Chinese philosopher, in *A Citizen of the World*, on the genteel English highwayman:

> But the greatest eulogy of this people is the generosity of their miscreants, the tenderness in general of their robbers and highwaymen. Perhaps no people can produce instances of the same kind, where the desperate mix pity with injustice; still shew that they understand a distinction in crimes, and even, in acts of violence, have still some tincture of remaining virtue. In every other country robbery and murder go almost together, here it seldom happens upon ill-judged resistance or pursuit. The banditti of other countries are unmerciful to a supreme degree, the highwayman and robber here are generous at least to the public, and pretend even to virtues in their intercourse among each other.[7]

The murderousness of Italian and French *banditti* was highlighted in Richardson's *Sir Charles Grandison*. Sir Charles's pre-eminence as an English gentleman is partly based on amazing acts of physical prowess, overcoming armed (and mostly continental) opponents without drawing his weapon.[8] The genteel highwayman and the gentleman as super-highwayman are negative and positive versions of the same image. We may never know how far the behaviour and self-image of actual criminals was influenced by the extraordinary glamour that came to be attached to English highwaymanship.

The moral effect of the literary representation of crime was hotly debated after the success of John Gay's *The Beggar's Opera* (1728), when young men, it was alleged, were rushing to imitate the robber-hero Captain Macheath.[9] Virtually every canonical novel of the eighteenth century after Fielding's *Joseph Andrews* (1742) includes episodes of actual or pretended highway robbery, and the line separating fiction and criminal biography is not always easy to draw.[10] The highwayman's destiny of imprisonment, often in Newgate, followed by a public hanging also figures largely in the fiction of the period. One of the functions of the 'benefactor' plot in novels such as *Tom Jones*, *Amelia*, *Humphry Clinker*, and *The Vicar of Wakefield* is to provide a convenient means of rescuing the innocent protagonist from the jail to which the law has unjustly confined him.

Fielding's Highwaymen

Introducing his collection of highwaymen's lives in 1734, Captain Smith's successor Captain Charles Johnson asserted that a 'universal History of Robbers' would be little less than a 'general History of all Nations'.

Caesar, Alexander the Great, and the founders of all monarchies were notorious plunderers, and even in Great Britain, 'where Property is better secur'd than anywhere else in the Universe', robbery was endemic—but only the '*little Villains*' tended to get caught.[11] A very similar message is conveyed in *The Beggar's Opera*, and later in Fielding's *Jonathan Wild* (1743). In Gay's drama one of Macheath's gang speaks of the avaricious rich as the 'robbers of mankind', whose 'superfluities' it is the 'free-hearted and generous' highwayman's task to retrench. The 'gentleman of the road' whom the 'fine gentlemen' imitate, and vice versa,[12] is, however, only one of several contemporary versions of the highwayman figure in fiction and criminal biography. The robbers' gallery in Fielding's novels provides a much more varied and realistic picture of the eighteenth-century criminal fraternity. Fielding, after all, was an experienced and influential magistrate whose non-fictional writings include *An Enquiry into the Causes of the Late Increase of Robbers* (1751), designed to 'rouse the CIVIL Power from its present lethargic state'. In a single week in 1750, Fielding was reported to have sent nearly forty highwaymen and street robbers to prison.[13]

The causes of the perceived increase in highway robbery in the period 1600–1750 include the expansion of overland trade and commerce within Great Britain, the poor state of the nation's roads, the lack of a provincial banking system which meant that merchants and tradesmen had to carry their wealth around with them, and the displacement of the population by civil and foreign wars.[14] After 1750 there was much less need for money to be transferred physically from place to place. In the later eighteenth century not only were Fielding's fears for the safety of travellers in and to the metropolis unfulfilled, but forgers rather than robbers became the most celebrated contemporary criminals. By then, however, the glamour of the masked and mounted highwayman had become a seemingly permanent part of popular culture. The nostalgic romance of high-waymanship reached its culmination in the 'Newgate novels' of the 1830s, against which Dickens was to react in *Oliver Twist*. Dick Turpin, hanged in 1739, is the hero of Harrison Ainsworth's *Rookwood* (1834), while the protagonist of Bulwer-Lytton's *Paul Clifford* (1830) is first seen as a boy reading Turpin's life and adventures. In reality, the majority of highway robberies were committed by gangs of footpads[15]—a prosaic detail that had little impact on the legends although it is faithfully reflected in *Joseph Andrews*.

Fielding's first novel begins as a satire in which the supposed brother of Richardson's Pamela Andrews virtuously rejects the amorous advances of his employer Lady Booby and her maid Mrs Slipslop. Dismissed from their service in London, Joseph is returning to his family in Somerset when, walking alone down a dark, narrow lane (not the traditional open heath), he is robbed, beaten, stripped of his clothing, and left for dead by a gang of ruffians. As an unemployed servant Joseph is barely worthy of the thieves' notice, yet he insists on fighting them although they are armed with pistols and clubs. The episode is one of violent initiation comparable to the physical force and threats of rape that Pamela had to undergo. The robbers manage to relieve Joseph of the gold keepsake given to him by his sweetheart Fanny, something that Lady Booby and Mrs Slipslop have notably failed to do. Joseph's eventual rescue by a postilion leads to a second hold-up as the highwaymen rob the stagecoach, treating the middle-class passengers far more leniently than they have treated Joseph.[16] One member of the gang is later arrested, but soon escapes as a result of bribing the constable. The robbers play no further part in the story.

Once he has been robbed and stripped naked, Joseph's prospects are transformed by his chance encounters with two benefactor figures, first the quixotic traveller Parson Adams and then the reclusive Mr Wilson. Adams is a fervent believer in charity—defining it, unlike Captain Blifil, as a 'generous disposition to relieve the distressed'—although he never has any money.[17] Wilson as a young man wasted his inheritance in the City and then languished in a debtors' prison. Now, having failed in business as a wine merchant, he lives in rural retirement until Adams and Joseph find him out. The theme of robbery re-emerges to play a romantic part in the resolution of the plot, since it turns out that both Joseph and Fanny were stolen by gipsies in their infancy. Fanny is Pamela's sister; Joseph is Mr Wilson's son, and thus a gentleman fit to be entertained at Mr Booby's country house. The introduction of Mr Booby (who is, in effect, Pamela's Mr B) at the end constitutes a curious return on Fielding's part to the sub-Richardsonian parody with which, here and in *Shamela* (1741), he had begun. For the most part, thanks to the interruption provided by the robbers, *Joseph Andrews* occupies a much wider world symbolized by the open road and the hero's unpredictable and frequently hazardous journey.

Fielding would return to the open road in *Tom Jones*, but the year after *Joseph Andrews* he published his satirical fable *The Life of Jonathan Wild the Great*, in which the hero leads a gang of robbers. Wild, whom Fielding invariably represents in capital letters as a 'GREAT MAN', is a Caesar or Alexander among thieves, an aristocrat in command of subordinates who—apart from his youthful dexterity as a pickpocket—rarely gets his hands dirty. His gang may engage in 'that noble kind of Robbery which was executed on the Highway', but Wild, nobler still, is seen creaming off their takings, courting the ladies, and playing cards with a fellow criminal known as the Count.[18] He has a distinguished genealogy, being a descendant of the legendary seventeenth-century robber James Hind and of another ancestor who 'distinguished himself on both Sides the Question in the Civil Wars' (14). His gang are divided into two parties, one called 'Cavaliers and Tory Rory Ranter Boys', the other going by the names of 'Wags, Round-Heads, Shake-Boys, Old-Nolls, and several others' (276). Jonathan Wild, like The Beggar's Opera, is in one respect a satire on the rapacious prime minister Sir Robert Walpole, illustrating the roundabout tactics of the political allegorist. Fielding takes care to have one of his characters state that 'there is a nearer Connection between high and low Life than is generally imagined, and . . . a Highwayman is entitled to more Favour with the Great than he usually meets with' (28). But, though it is a Newgate novel, Wild's story is very different from those presented in the more straightforward criminal biographies.

Where we might have expected an episodic narrative illustrating the range, scope, and ingenuity of his hero's crimes, Jonathan Wild is in effect the story of a single obsession, Wild's pursuit of the harmless small tradesman Heartfree. The root of Wild's character is not, therefore, gallantry and dash, but the ruthless, scheming hatred and hypocrisy later to be associated with Mr Blifil in Tom Jones. Like a master politician (to use Fielding's own analogy) Wild knows how to 'play with the Passions of Men, and to set them at Variance with each other, and to work his own Purposes out of those Jealousies and Apprehensions, which he was wonderfully ready at creating' (92). The reverse of Fielding's benefactor figures, Wild is a deliberate malefactor who does not hesitate to use the instruments of corrupted justice to achieve his ends. When one of his gang tells him to ' "Take your Pistols yourself, and go out on the Highway, and don't lazily think to fatten yourself with the Dangers and Pains of other People" ' (178), Wild shows no compunction in turning him over to the constable and getting him hanged. The innocent Heartfree narrowly escapes a similar fate. Wild finally overreaches himself and is led in the cart through a cheering crowd to the 'Tree of Glory' (254). His last act at Tyburn is to steal a corkscrew from the parson's pocket, so he will be well provided for in the next world. He expires with a curse, not the traditional show of repentance, and his demonic apotheosis is complete.

Fielding's sympathies lay not with the robber as 'great man', and still less with the lower-class ruffians who beat up Joseph Andrews, but with the middle-class highwayman who might be reclaimed. The *Enquiry into the Causes of the Late Increase of Robbers* singles out the case of an indigent tradesman whose motive for turning to the highway was 'to pay a Bill that was shortly to become due' (78). In *Tom Jones*, Allworthy reveals that he has often pitied a highwayman's fate and looked for mitigating circumstances (862). Tom himself, who is 'certainly born to be hanged' (123), and who carries the same name as that of a highwayman executed at Launceston in 1702,[19] shares Allworthy's and Fielding's sympathies. His encounter with highwaymanship comes when Mr Anderson, a 'genteel-looking man, but upon a very shabby horse' (602), tries to rob him as they ride together from Barnet to London. Tom (who, unknown to Anderson, possesses Sophia's pocket-book containing a hundred-pound note) overpowers his adversary, confiscates his unloaded pistol, and then listens to his tale of hard luck—it is Anderson's first attempt on the highway, and he is desperate to feed his hungry children and pregnant wife—before tipping his hitherto respectable assailant two guineas and letting him go. The episode plays a part in restoring Tom's own fortunes, since Anderson turns out to be related to Mr Allworthy's London landlady. Tom's generosity towards the highwayman is to some extent based on a recognition of spiritual kinship; moreover, it turns out that their situations are significantly parallel since Anderson has had his goods distrained as a result of standing bail for a dishonest brother. Here Fielding approaches the problem of social justice, or the lack of it, from the opposite perspective to that of the robbery in *Joseph Andrews*. The money that a middle-class apprentice highwayman such as Anderson plans to steal is money that, under a fairer and more benign dispensation, he would already possess.

There is a comparable episode in Fanny Burney's *Evelina* (1778), where the heroine saves the debt-ridden poet Macartney from committing suicide. Macartney, who turns out to be her long-lost brother, is about to shoot himself with a pistol he has bought in order to rob a stagecoach. Like the poor tradesman in Fielding's *Enquiry*, he has decided to go on the highway in order to pay the rent. The leniency that Fielding and Burney show towards these middle-class unfortunates may be contrasted with Allworthy's verdict on the irredeemably proletarian Black George, the gamekeeper turned poacher who dishonestly appropriates the £500 that he has found in Tom's carelessly discarded pocket-book. When George's actions come to light, Allworthy observes that ' "a highwayman, compared to him, is an innocent person" ' (862); but all that George has done is to hold onto a piece of money found under a hedge. Would Anderson or

Macartney have returned a banknote in these circumstances? Happily, the question is not put to the test.

The Cavalier Highwayman

In *Tom Jones* there is, besides Anderson, a gallant highwayman whose cavalier insolence is sufficiently appealing to persuade Mrs Western, Sophia's maiden aunt, to break the law by not prosecuting him. He robs her of her earrings, 'at the same time d—ning her, and saying "such handsome b—s as you, don't want jewels to set them off, and be d—ned to you"' (326). This is the only one of Fielding's highwaymen who remotely resembles the pseudo-aristocratic 'gentleman of the road', whose fondly recalled behaviour suggests a kind of collusion—cultural and also, not infrequently, sexual—between the robber and his intended victim. This is the highwayman whose memory lives on in the phrases 'Stand and deliver' and 'Your money or your life'.

The legendary highwayman is mounted, reflecting the immemorial class division between horsemen and foot passengers, and is capable of outstanding feats of horsemanship such as the ride to York which was credited to at least two earlier figures before being attributed to Turpin and Black Bess. He is a prankster and confidence trickster, an adept of masks and disguises—an association that can be traced back to the Robin Hood ballads. It would be hard to name the first of the legendary highwaymen, though in the collections of eighteenth-century criminal biographies Robin Hood and Shakespeare's Sir John Falstaff take pride of place. By the time of Gamaliel Ratsey, hanged at Bedford in 1605, the conventions were well established. Contemporary pamphlets record that Ratsey posed as a gentleman with two accomplices as servants, and that on one occasion he 'knighted' two woolmen he had robbed, dubbing them Sir Samuel Sheepskinne and Sir Walter Woolsack.[20] Such a masquerade could be played out in reverse, since it was not unknown for a traveller to pass himself off as a rival highwayman in order to avoid being robbed. Captain Alexander Smith tells that when Whitney and his gang held up a gentleman on Bagshot Heath and ordered him to stand, the reply was, '"*I was just going to say the same to you, gentlemen*"'. Whitney let the 'false' highwayman go, but ambushed him again the next day, telling him that he 'should know him for a black sheep another time'.[21]

Captain Smith and Captain Johnson, the principal early eighteenth-century criminal biographers, were both outspoken Royalists. Through their work the story of political highwaymanship in England is ineradicably linked to the memory of the Civil War. Periods of public anxiety about highway robbery normally coincided with the ends of wars, when there was popular displacement and high unemployment, and Parliament in the years 1647–9 issued a series of proclamations against burglars and robbers.[22] Charles I's tendency to pardon convicted highwaymen had already attracted controversy.[23] Under the Commonwealth certain dispossessed Royalist gentlemen such as Captain Zachary Howard returned from exile and took to the highway, and authors such as Smith and Johnson later presented them as virtual guerrilla fighters in the King's cause. At least three of them were credited with robbing the 'great villain' Cromwell in person, while Mary Frith was said to have robbed Fairfax on Hounslow Heath, and Howard raped Fairfax's wife and daughter. In his speech at the gallows (as quoted by Johnson) Howard said that, were he at liberty, ' "*he would never leave off robbing the Roundheads, so long as there were any of them left in England*" '. John Cottington similarly reassured the frightened passengers in a convoy carrying the soldier's pay for Cromwell's army that he came not for their private purses but for the Commonwealth's money.[24]

A century later, the stereotyped masked and mounted highwayman remained a recognizably Cavalier type. Richardson, Goldsmith, and Burney all play on the associations between highway robbery and libertinism which can be traced back to the time of Aphra Behn.[25] Robert Lovelace loiters in the woods near the Harlowes' estate in a 'horseman's coat', and is described by the heroine's family as a 'desperate *ruffian*' plotting to waylay her with a gang of armed men.[26] In *Sir Charles Grandison* Harriet Byron is abducted by Sir Hargrave Pollexfen only to be rescued by the saintly hero in a dexterous hold-up on Hounslow Heath, one of the classical locations of criminal biography. Sir Hargrave tells the turnpike men that he has been attacked by thieves on horseback, while a witness claims to have seen ' "two young rakes in their chariots-and-six, one robbing the other of a lady" '. Since Grandison is a paragon of virtue he has removed Harriet from moral danger, yet he cannot resist the libertine jibe that ' "Sir Hargrave ... might well give out that he was robbed" '.[27] In Burney's *Evelina*, Captain Mirvan and Sir Clement Willoughby mask themselves as highwaymen to intercept Madame Duval and the heroine on a country outing. Willoughby, who has already tried to make love to Evelina in her carriage, seizes the opportunity to do so once again. In two of these three scenes the cavalier pseudo-highwayman plays what Ruth Bernard Yeazell has called the role of the 'disagreeable suitor', but in all of them the female victim is subjected to theft and 'deliverance' like a piece of personal property.[28]

The links between robbery, theatricality, and sexual aggression in these episodes suggest that they might be considered in relation to the formal masquerade scenes in English fiction.[29] But while robberies in fiction frequently involve transgression, identity confusion, role reversal, and a manifest sexual symbolism, there are crucial differences between representations of public entertainment and violent crime. The normal range of eighteenth-century masquerade costumes does not seem to have included the dress of the 'gentlemen of the road' or even of Robin Hood and his men. (There are, however, reports of highwaymen being arrested at a London masquerade.[30]) For masqueraders to have dressed up as highwaymen, rather than vice versa, might have been uncomfortably reminiscent of the pickpockets and rogues who haunted the streets outside any public assembly.

Why, then, is the legendary highwayman masked? The obvious answer—to escape detection—is not entirely convincing, since at some point the highwayman needs to be discovered. To become famous, he must be unmasked. His masking, reminiscent of the domino and the knight's lowered visor, is as much theatrical as practical. It goes together with the rather intimate violation involved in forcing travellers to hand over their property. Unlike the clandestine thief or the ruffian armed with a cosh, the legendary highwayman openly confronts his victims, putting on a show of gallantry and striking up with them a relationship of sorts, which is why his command to 'stand and deliver' is so well remembered. If in the moment of self-revelation he ritualistically hides himself, this makes it easier for the victims to part with their money. Robbery becomes a fetishistic act, and the legendary highwayman is one 'by whom it would be delightful to have been robbed'.[31]

There is another element in the highwayman's masking, since he is asserting a double identity as 'gentleman' and thief. Wearing a mask, an unemployed tradesman might be able to convince his victims that he was a real gentleman down on his luck; or he might simply put on a deliberate travesty of genteel behaviour.[32] The highwayman's double identity was already explicit in the tales of Ratsey. So far as fictional highwaymen are concerned, the duality or duplicity that they express is a general feature of the novel's dealings with crime and its transgression of class boundaries.

'Without the appearance of the whore, the rogue, the cutpurse, the cheat, the thief, or the outsider', it has been said, 'it would be impossible to imagine the genre of the novel'.[33] This comment reveals both the middle-class reader's fascination with the criminal and the antisocial, and, more generally, the same reader's desire to live vicariously at both ends of the social scale, the high and the low. Hence the obsession with criminals posing as aristocrats and aristocrats behaving like criminals. The novel's power in eighteenth-century culture lay in its pretence of intimate knowledge of all levels of society from Newgate to the fashionable lady's boudoir. At the same time, the narrative journey involving criminal episodes almost invariably ends up in gentility. Epistolary fiction and the confessional first-person narrative gave to the novelist the means of aristocratic impersonation, while the image of the highwayman was yet another aspect of the novel's duplicity. What linked the wealthy to those who preyed upon them was, it goes without saying, the lure of property.

The historian Douglas Hay has written that the constitutional settlement of 1688–9 established the 'freedom, not of men, but of men of property'. The ruling class 'worshipped' property.[34] Recently the term 'gentrification' has been used to describe the bourgeois anxiety to acquire secured and, if possible, landed property in the eighteenth and nineteenth centuries. Notoriously, the successful middle classes tended to adopt what Martin J. Wiener has called a 'comparatively aloof and passive economic role'.[35] Whether or not gentrification is one of the peculiarities of British economic history, it is certainly commonplace in fiction. Moreover, it is opposed to the circulation of money that was championed by Defoe, Mandeville, and others. The 'aristocratic' highwayman embodies a get-rich-quick fantasy of robbing and spending while the gentrified merchant does his best to secure his capital and remove it from circulation.

The English novel's attachment to gentrification appears in the fact that the pursuit of economic individualism so often leads by accident or design to the acquisition of inherited wealth and a country estate. The fictional plot puts the protagonists and their wealth (or aspirations to wealth) into circulation, but the moment of narrative closure is the moment of genteel settlement and rural retirement. The experience of circulation usually involves a descent on the city and an episode of imprisonment in which the protagonist's identity becomes joined or confused with that of highwaymen and robbers. Moll Flanders and the other women prisoners in Newgate rush to get a sight of three 'brave topping gentlemen' arrested after a pursuit from Hounslow to Uxbridge; one of the three is Moll's Lancashire husband, and they are transported to America together. He might have preferred to face the gallows, since 'Servitude and hard Labour were things Gentlemen could never stoop to', but, once in America, Moll inherits a plantation from her mother.[36] Billy

Booth in *Amelia* is mistaken for a highwayman by the prison governor, who ' "know[s] no more genteeler Way than the road" '.[37] Smollett's Humphry Clinker, falsely charged with robbery on Blackheath, is locked up with ' "[t]wo or three as bold hearts as ever took the air upon Hounslow" ', and told to prepare to ' "make his exit like a true-born Englishman" ' at Tyburn.[38]

The convoluted plot of *Humphry Clinker* explores complex relations between gentlemen, servants, highwaymen, and the new middle classes. Clinker, an 'excellent horseman' (153), owes his release on bail from Clerkenwell Prison to the fact that he is Matthew Bramble's servant. The crime of which he is accused was actually committed by 'Mr' Martin, who later redeems himself by rescuing Bramble and his party when they are attacked by a rival gang of robbers near Hatfield. Described by the constable as 'the best qualified for business of all the gentleman of the road he had ever known', Martin is a master of disguise who is regularly seen smoking a pipe with the magistrate (148–9); but he applies successfully to be taken on as one of Bramble's servants, and is later found a place in the East India Company. Meanwhile, Humphry Clinker turns out to be Bramble's bastard son and is entrusted with the duties of a farm manager. Thus both the genteel highwayman and the falsely accused pseudo-highwayman are taken out of livery to join the lower-middle classes; Clinker's fate contrasts with the outright gentrification that was the destiny of Joseph Andrews and Tom Jones, while Martin's Cavaliership gives place to a humble clerkship. The Cavalier highwayman must choose between the glory of being hanged and the comfortable, humdrum way of life typical, perhaps, of the novelist himself, and certainly of his readers.

Robbin' the Rich

In England the 'Arch-thief'[39] and the uncanonized patron saint of footpads and highwaymen was the legendary Robin Hood. 'Free-hearted' and generous like the thieves in *The Beggar's Opera*, Robin could also claim to stand for a 'just partition of the world'.[40] Even Captain Smith, in whose history he figures as a 'Highwayman and Murderer', acknowledged that he was a benefactor who robbed the rich to feed the poor.[41] In legend (if not necessarily in fact) Robin's liberality was much imitated. Gamaliel Ratsey acknowledged a duty to 'pitie them that are poore, for the rich can helpe themselves'. When Ratsey held up a poor parson's daughter going to market to buy a new dress, he gallantly gave her the money for a petticoat as well. The ballad of 'Turpin's Appeal to the Judge' praised Dick Turpin for fulfilling the biblical commands to clothe the naked, feed the poor, and send the rich away empty.[42] Does the benevolent robber stand for 'true justice', or are his motives prudential rather than disinterested? The casuistical highwayman Luke Page, who told the Ordinary at Newgate that he thought robbing was 'no great sin' and that 'persons getting the unrighteous Mammon this way might be saved if they, out of it, be charitable to the poor', sounds more like a modern businessman than a rebel against society.[43] Some historians of eighteenth-century crime have argued that the highwayman's protest against social injustice is too self-serving to be taken seriously, while others maintain that the highwayman ballads helped to keep alive the radicalism of the Civil War and the Commonwealth.[44] Later in the century, the revival of revolutionary sentiments coincided with the scholarly editing of the Robin Hood ballads by the Jacobin supporter Joseph Ritson.

The Robin Hood of the ballads and legends is a political figure of a distinctly ambiguous kind. He is at once a fighter against tyranny and a loyal subject, a peer and a commoner, an outlaw and an upholder of the true law. Some say he was born at Locksley and is the dispossessed Earl of Huntingdon, others that he is the son of poor shepherds. The Robin Hood play acted at Nottingham on the day of Charles II's coronation in 1661 and 'alluding to the late rebellion, and the subject of the day' implied that Robin, as Earl of Huntingdon, was a direct ancestor of the banished Cavaliers and of the highwaymen who robbed the Commonwealth. To Captain Smith, however, the story of his aristocratic origins was a mere fiction.[45] As the century progressed Robin became both a hero of popular melodrama and a subject of learned discussion in Bishop Percy's *Reliques of Ancient English Poetry* (1765); meanwhile groups of urban radicals were forming Robin Hood Debating Societies, which attracted Fielding's scorn.[46] In Ritson's definitive edition of the ballads the plebeian bandit of the highwayman biographies, who stole the King's deer and robbed Richard I and his retinue on the Great North Road, became both a high-born revolutionary and the 'prince of all robbers'.[47] His legendary benevolence was now seen not as exhibiting the 'Grandeur and Hospitality' of his temperament but as a sign of innate political virtue.[48] Nevertheless, Robin Hood's political uses were always double-edged—was he Royalist or Roundhead, a champion of the people or a defender of hereditary rights?—and the more he came to be idealized and incorporated into English literature (as in the Ritson-influenced works of Scott, Peacock, Tennyson, and others), the less he resembled actual robbers.

While there was a prose narrative of Robin Hood at least as early as 1678, his first appearance as a character in English fiction was not until Scott's *Ivanhoe* (1819). Nevertheless, figures of the robber-cum-benefactor with traits reminiscent of Robin Hood can be found before *Ivanhoe*. Jenkinson and Mr Burchell in *The Vicar of Wakefield* have already been mentioned. Defoe's *History and Remarkable Life of the Truly Honourable Colonel Jack* (1722), the only canonical eighteenth-century novel which is indisputably a highwayman's tale, provides another example. Jack starts out as a highway robber, but gives up the trade when, having robbed an old nurse, he suffers acute remorse and seeks her out to give the money back. Realizing that he cannot make restitution to all his victims, he reflects that 'certainly this was not the life of a gentleman'.[49] Curiously, he has encountered the nurse on the fringes of north London near a place that he calls 'Pindar of Wakefield'—presumably the name of a public house in what is now the King's Cross area.[50] Notwithstanding Defoe's topographical realism, there is a flavour of romantic legend about Jack's kindness to the poor nurse, and the allusion to the ballad of 'Robin Hood and the Pinder of Wakefield' can hardly be accidental.

A fictional character truly modelled on Robin Hood, however, would not merely have to be a generous robber but a political outlaw and rebel. Even in the Jacobin novels of the 1790s, the ideal put before us is usually one of 'benevolent landlordism'—a more politically engaged version of Squire Allworthy and Sir Charles Grandison—rather than outright rebellion.[51] In Charlotte Smith's *The Old Manor House*, it is true, Orlando Somerive forms a secret compact in the cellars of Rayland Hall with Jonas Wilkins, a notorious smuggler. On another occasion, lurking outside the Hall at dawn, Orlando is collared as a suspected poacher, though in the end he will be vindicated as the true inheritor of the house. Only one of the Jacobin novelists went so far as to question the very institution of private property, taking up a theme that had been very little voiced in English writing since the revolutionary pamphlets of 1649. William Godwin's philosophical treatise *Political Justice* (1793) argues for a system of equal property based on need, since social inequality is the principal cause of crime. But the redistribution of wealth should be brought about by reason and benevolence, not by violence or legal expropriation, since, in Godwin's view, a law against amassing property would be incompatible with true social freedom. The paradoxes inherent in this view of justice are a minor theme in Godwin's principal contribution to English fiction, *Things as They Are or the Adventures of Caleb Williams* (1794).

Caleb's adventures hinge on his rejection and persecution by his guilty benefactor Falkland (named after the seventeenth-century Royalist general), who pursues him with unrelenting malice once Caleb has seen through his veneer of Grandison-like virtue. Falsely accused of burglary, Caleb is imprisoned on Falkland's orders. He escapes from prison only to be ambushed and beaten up by a gang of thieves, who take him to a ruined castle in the middle of a forest where he comes under the protection of Captain Raymond, their leader. Godwin had prepared himself to write *Caleb Williams* with a course of reading in the *Newgate Calendar* and also, we must suspect, in the literature surrounding Robin Hood, since his short-lived friendship with Joseph Ritson had begun the year before *Caleb Williams* was published.[52] Captain Raymond, evidently inspired by Ritson's 'prince of robbers', presents himself as a social rebel and a soldier in an unacknowledged civil war: ' "We, who are thieves without licence, are at open war with another set of men who are thieves according to law." '[53] Caleb acknowledges Raymond's 'fervent benevolence' (233), and a reader unfamiliar with the argument of *Political Justice* might expect Godwin's narrator to be a ready convert to the gang leader's Noble Robber philosophy. But Caleb rejects the outlook of this modern Robin Hood, arguing that the robbers' 'justice' is no better than vengeance, that their ends are merely selfish, and their energy is 'unassisted by liberal and enlightened views, and directed only to the most narrow and contemptible purposes' (227).

Shortly before he leaves the robber band, Caleb engages in open debate with Raymond. The robbers' purpose, Caleb maintains, is 'incompatible with the general welfare' and 'diametrically at war with the first interests of human society'. Raymond, used to 'arguments derived from religion and the sacredness of law', is taken aback by Caleb's 'missionary quixotism', though the details of the argument are left significantly vague. Caleb—rather surprisingly for a character who seems to be his author's mouthpiece—speaks of the 'necessary though atrociously exaggerated precautions of government in the matter of property' (235), implying that in a rational and peaceful society people should feel secure to enjoy their property if they want to. Godwin's opposition to the forcible redistribution of property necessarily leads him to reject the image of the highwayman as a champion of the oppressed proletariat.

Moreover, Caleb cannot respond to Captain Raymond because his hopes for genuine justice are all directed towards Falkland, his persecutor.

The intensity of the novel's central conflict and of Caleb's psychological torments is so great that the Raymond episode has generally been regarded as merely incidental. Falkland has distinguished himself in Italy like Sir Charles Grandison, and aims at the reputation of the perfect knight; his 'Ode to the Genius of Chivalry' has been read out at a public assembly (27). But Caleb, having stumbled on his secret papers, suspects him of having murdered his rival Barnabas Tyrrel, the 'true model of the English squire' (19) who has been found in the street stabbed in the back, a method of assassination associated with ruthless Italian *banditti* rather than with English criminals.[54] The struggle between Falkland and Caleb becomes one of haunted victimization and demonic pursuit, repeating the earlier relationship of Tyrrel and Falkland; but Caleb, unlike Falkland, does not ultimately revenge himself upon his tormentor. Instead, in the revised ending of the novel, Falkland's vendetta against Caleb gives way to a melodramatic recantation which suggests that he is still capable of the 'liberal and enlightened views' proper to a benefactor. But it is too late for him to resume his position as Caleb's patron; the novel concludes not with their reconciliation but with mutual remorse and self-incrimination. Nevertheless, Caleb's capacity for fanaticism and hero-worship responds far more strongly to his rich benefactor's godlike demeanour and demonic pursuit of vengeance than to the modern prince of thieves who idealizes robbery.

   In popular culture the chief successors to the eighteenth-century English highwayman tales are the frontier legends of American and Australian outlaws. The highwayman represents an England of open heaths and treacherous roads, not yet criss-crossed by McAdam's highways, though much travelled by the growing numbers of merchants and property owners, as well as by fictional protagonists. The novel, not tied to the largely posthumous viewpoint of criminal biography, offers a spectrum of pseudo-aristocratic, bourgeois, and supposedly benevolent robbers. The fictional robber raises questions of justice and the circulation and distribution of property either through his affinity with the protagonist (as in *Tom Jones* and *Evelina*), or through a suppressed and usually secret affinity with the figure of the benefactor. Sir Charles Grandison, who sweeps Harriet Byron off her feet by a rescue that is tantamount to highway robbery, is the deliberate antithesis of *Clarissa*'s aristocratic rapist and robber. Falkland, the benefactor as robber, is a much more powerful and compelling inversion of Captain Raymond, the robber as would-be benefactor. Raymond's 'civil war' is not a credible threat to society, but Falkland's tyranny and persecution clearly do pose such a threat. The hidden link between robber and benefactor is the most subversive element in the discourse about the English highwayman, which in some other respects simply placed an acceptable gloss on the century's actual experiences of plebeian violence, and on the vengeful and retributive acts constituting 'British justice'.

The legendary highwayman is a marginal and nostalgic presence in some of Scott's novels, such as *Rob Roy* (1817) and *The Heart of Mid-Lothian* (1818). Francis Osbaldistone in *Rob Roy* hears 'the names of the Golden Farmer, the Flying Highwayman, Jack Needham, and other Beggar's Opera heroes' as he travels away from London on the Great North Road. Rob Roy himself, Scott writes, 'is still remembered in his country as the Robin Hood of Scotland, the dread of the wealthy, but the friend of the poor'.[55] When Jeanie Deans travels southwards in *The Heart of Mid-Lothian*, she hears Dick Ostler at York singing a snatch of a Robin Hood ballad, while her landlady warns her against highwaymen, ' "for ye are come into a more civilized, that is to say, a more roguish country" '.[56] *Rob Roy* is set in 1715, *The Heart of Mid-Lothian* in 1736. The highwayman continued to enjoy a nineteenth-century afterlife in the novels of Lytton and Ainsworth and in Robert Louis Stevenson's unfinished romance *The Great North Road*, as well as in children's writing and popular entertainment. In *Rookwood* Harrison Ainsworth speaks of Dick Turpin as *'ultimus Romanorum*, the last of a race', but offers no explanations for the 'decline and fall of the empire of the tobymen'.[57] Not only was the theme now confined to historical fiction, but the *coup de grâce* to the 'old English highwayman'[58] was surely administered by Dickens in his preface to *Oliver Twist* (1837–8): 'Here are no canterings on moonlit heaths, no merry-makings in the snuggest of all possible caverns, none of the attractions of dress, no embroidery, no lace, no jack-boots, no crimson coats and ruffles, none of the dash and freedom with which "the road" has been time out of mind invested.'[59] But for all Dickens's powerful defence of a new, more brutal, and sordid mode of criminal realism, *Oliver Twist* raises similar issues about crime, property, and benevolence to its eighteenth-century predecessors. The cruel benevolence of the Guardians of the Poor is openly contrasted with Oliver's deceptively free-hearted and generous reception in Fagin's den. As the hapless protagonist circulates back and forth between his two 'fathers' Fagin and Brownlow, our sense of the robber shadowing the benefactor and vice versa confirms the hidden affinity between the two figures. The Artful Dodger, a would-be fine gentleman, has earlier been sent out 'on the road', though with the task of recruiting new gang members rather than robbing rich travellers.

In a parting salute to the 'empire of the tobymen', he first falls in with Oliver on the Great North Road at Barnet. Since *Oliver Twist* may be regarded as the prototype of all Dickens's fiction, it is highly significant that the author surrounds his criminal gang with the figures of the robber as benefactor and the benefactor as robber.[60]

7

Romantic Toryism: Scott, Disraeli, and Others

'IT may be asked, it has been asked, "Have we no materials for romance in England? Must we look to Scotland for a supply of whatever is original and striking in this kind?"' wrote Hazlitt in his essay on Sir Walter Scott in *The Spirit of the Age* (1825). 'Every foot of soil is with us worked up; nearly every movement of the social machine is calculable. We have no room left for violent catastrophes; for grotesque quaintnesses; for wizard spells. The last skirts of ignorance and barbarism are seen hovering (in Sir Walter's pages) over the Border.' Hazlitt might have added that, like the Gothic novels to which they succeeded, Scott's romances were set in an increasingly remote past; and that Scott's fiction beginning with *Ivanhoe* (1819) had brought historical romance back to England. Nevertheless, the 'England' of Hazlitt's essay is a nation of rational economics and agri-business. Even the gipsies, he says, 'live under clipped hedges, and repose in camp-beds'.[1] England in the early nineteenth century had been pacified and brought to order; Scotland and Ireland had not.

The contrast between romance and realism implied by Hazlitt is a contrast between violent landscapes and peaceful ones. Ann Radcliffe's Gothic romance demands the most dramatic mountain scenery, and Mary Shelley's *Frankenstein* (1818) takes us to the highest Alps and the remote Arctic ice-fields; Radcliffe's *The Mysteries of Udolpho* (1794) begins and ends, however, in a 'happy valley', the lush valley of the Garonne, which is much closer to the well-tilled landscapes of English domestic fiction. Catherine Morland, Jane Austen's avid romance reader in *Northanger Abbey*, concludes (even as she is becoming somewhat disillusioned with her favourite Gothic authors) that 'human nature' is perhaps different in mountainous regions:

Charming as were all Mrs. Radcliffe's works, and charming even as were the works of all her imitators, it was not in them perhaps that human nature, at least in the midland counties of England, was to be looked for. Of the Alps and

Pyrenees, with their pine forests and their vices, they might give a faithful delineation; and Italy, Switzerland, and the south of France, might be as fruitful in horrors as they were there represented. Catherine dared not doubt beyond her own country, and even of that, if hard pressed, would have yielded the northern and western extremities. . . . Among the Alps and Pyrenees, perhaps, there were no mixed characters. . . . But in England it was not so; among the English, she believed, in their hearts and habits, there was a general though unequal mixture of good and bad.[2]

Here the 'mixed' English character matches the temperate English land-scape. Austen paid her best-known tribute to this landscape in the view of Donwell Abbey, the home of Mr Knightley, with its river and Abbey-Mill Farm, in *Emma*: 'It was a sweet view—sweet to the eye and the mind. English verdure, English culture, English comfort, seen under a sun bright, without being oppressive.'[3] What is missing from this little vignette, though presupposed by it, is what numerous eighteenth-century landed proprietors would have cleared away out of sight in order to preserve the green view from their windows: the cottages of Mr Knightley's farm labourers.

Washington Irving, Mary Russell Mitford, and the Rural Picturesque

The English village or hamlet became a subject for narrative verse long before it was taken into the novel. Eighteenth-century fiction is largely concerned with interrelationships between the gentry, and between the gentry and domestic servants, with walk-on parts for the gamekeeper and the village clergyman and for outlaws such as gipsies and highwaymen. The novelists showed far less interest in the ordinary people who worked the land than did poets such as Goldsmith in 'The Deserted Village', Thomas Gray in the 'Elegy written in a Country Church-Yard', and George Crabbe in 'The Village' and later verse tales, not to mention the line of so-called 'peasant poets' such as Robert Bloomfield and John Clare. By and large, the poets depicted an idealized communal village life, lamenting its disappearance as the land was enclosed. Goldsmith evoked the 'loveliest village of the plain' before it was devastated by rural depopulation, while Crabbe portrayed the squalid underside of rural capitalism. Eighteenth-century agricultural history is a history of enclos-ures, emparkments, clearances, the withdrawal of villagers' traditional rights, the persecution of poachers, and the loss of common land. Out of this history, however, came the image of the tranquil and picturesque English village that was perpetuated in prose fiction from the 1820s onwards.

Walter Scott was a true-blue Tory, but he had little to do with constructing this image of what was essentially a Tory England. In an anonymous review of his own Waverley novels, he praised them for 'conveying the genuine sentiments of the Scottish peasant in the genuine language of his native land'.[4] But he felt no such responsibility towards the English peasantry: his Berkshire village in *Kenilworth* (1821), for example, is almost deserted apart from an eccentric schoolmaster and a legendary rural spirit. It was, however, Scott's friend the American novelist and essayist Washington Irving who, more than any other writer, created the image of the stereotypical English village. In *The Sketch Book of Geoffrey Crayon* (1820) Irving offered a tourist's-eye view of contemporary England as, in Malcolm Bradbury's words, a 'half-mythic land of stage coaches and ivy-covered cottages, festive Christmases and forelocked peasants, high church spires and quaint crooked byways'.[5] The *Sketch Book* was, as Hazlitt remarked in *The Spirit of the Age*, a collection of 'literary *anachronisms*' (349), but it was also hugely popular. It would become a topic of conversation in novels ranging from Disraeli's *Vivian Grey* (1826) to Elizabeth Gaskell's *North and South* (1855), and it would move George Eliot's Maggie Tulliver to tears.

For Irving, rural England with its 'charms of storied and poetical association' was a refuge from the raw and imaginatively barren landscapes of his native America.[6] But he was also aware of the spread of industrialization in England, and of the ravages of war and revolution in neighbouring Europe. His *Sketch Book* portrays the victorious nation which had just defeated Napoleon and restored Europe's old monarchies. The signs of domestic conflict and class oppression are largely ignored by his narrator Geoffrey Crayon, a 'humble lover of the picturesque' who moves from one rural scene to the next like a stroller admiring the displays in print-shop windows (745). Conveniently, the very first object of the newly arriving traveller's gaze is a village landscape rather than the port of Liverpool where he is about to disembark:

As we sailed up the Mersey I reconnoitered the shores with a telescope. My eye dwelt with delight on neat cottages with their trim shrubberies and green grass plots. I saw the mouldering ruin of an abbey over run with ivy, and the taper spire of a village church rising from the brow of a neighbouring hill—all were characteristic of England. (750)

Characteristic of England, too, are its 'little home scenes of rural repose and sheltered quiet', where the 'lower orders' in their cottages nestle down next to the nobility and gentry in their castles and palaces. All gather together on the hunting field, where 'the sound of hound and horn blends all things into harmony' (799–800). The tourist idyll reaches its apotheosis in the English Christmas, which for Irving is an unmistakably Tory Christmas. The country gentleman presiding over these deliberately archaic festivities is a direct descendant of the old Cavaliers and Royalists.

Until the *Sketch Book* appeared, English writers since the Restoration had had remarkably little to say about Christmas customs.[7] Geoffrey Crayon reminded his readers that the Christmas holiday had been banned under the Commonwealth, and that Parliament sat on 25 December from 1652 onwards. Plum puddings were denounced as 'mere popery', roast beef as anti-Christian, and there was a 'fiery persecution of poor Mince-pie throughout the land' (943). Crayon's host, Squire Bracebridge of Bracebridge Hall, belatedly sets out to revive the old customs observed 'when England was itself' before the Puritan Revolution (925). His ancestors went into exile and returned with the Restoration, and now he has created a symbol of the lost 'merry England' of Elizabethan times; his is perhaps the 'only family in England' where the full English Christmas is punctiliously observed (961). The stagecoach on Christmas Eve is loaded with hampers and returning schoolboys, while Christmas dinner is eaten in front of a crackling log fire in the great hall, with minstrels singing carols, and a mummers' performance including a Robin Hood and a Maid Marian. These festivities provided the model for Dickens's Christmas at Dingley Dell in *The Pickwick Papers* some sixteen years later.

Irving's 'worthy old Cavalier' (929) is a portent in other ways, too, since he is necessarily opposed to the changes which were becoming increasingly obvious in the English countryside. *Bracebridge Hall* (1822) describes the Squire's resentment of Mr Faddy, a retired manufacturer who has abandoned his 'steam-engines and spinning jennies' for the life of a country gentleman:

In his warmth [the Squire] inveighed against the whole race of manufacturers, who, I found, were sore disturbers of his comfort. 'Sir,' said he, with emotion, 'it makes my heart bleed to see all our fine streams dammed up and bestrode by cotton mills; our villages smoking with steam-engines, and the din of the hammer and the loom scaring away all our rural delights. What's to become of merry old England, when its manor houses are all turned into manufactories, and its sturdy peasantry into pin-makers and stocking-weavers? I have looked in vain for merry Sherwood, and all the greenwood haunts of Robin Hood; the whole country is covered with manufacturing towns. I have stood on the ruins of Dudley Castle, and looked around, with an aching heart, on what were once its feudal domains of verdant and beautiful country. Sir, I beheld a mere campus phlegrae; a region of fire; reeking with coal-pits, and furnaces, and smelting-houses, vomiting forth flames and smoke. The pale and ghastly people, toiling among vile exhalations, looked more like demons than human beings; the clanking wheels and engines, seen through the murky atmosphere, looked like instruments of torture in this pandemonium. What is to become of the country with these evils rankling in its very core?' [8]

Here the imagery and topography anticipate Disraeli's portrayal of the Black Country in *Sybil*, which was to cause a literary sensation a quarter of a century later. Bracebridge's revival of the feudal custom of distributing alms at his gate anticipates the Conservative 'Young England' programme that Disraeli romanticized in *Coningsby* (1844). This is not without its problems, however, since in the *Sketch Book* the Squire admits that he now only invites the 'decent part' of the neighbouring peasantry into his home. He had once tried to keep open house, but found it overrun with beggars and vagrants. The ' "simple true-hearted peasantry" ', who would once have looked up to their simple true-hearted squire, are on the way out: ' "They have become too knowing, and begin to read newspapers, listen to ale house politicians, and talk of reform" ' (945–6).

For all his nostalgia for Merry England, the author of the *Sketch Book* remains an American tourist who has no intention of settling down amid the scenes he so much admires. He is proud of American democracy and even of his nation's Puritan heritage. Despite his affection for Squire Bracebridge, he knows that England's future lies with Mr Faddy and his like. (Christmas at Dingley Dell in deepest rural Kent is also a sentimental indulgence on Dickens's part, though no less enjoyable for that.) What is taken for granted in the *Sketch Book* is a nation divided between country and city, between agriculture and industry, between Cavalier and Roundhead, and between Tory and Whig. The Yankee outsider is free to indulge his emotional preferences without bearing any of the consequences of actually taking sides.

The form of the Geoffrey Crayon volumes—a miscellany of linked essays, travelogues, anecdotes, character sketches, and interpolated tales—represents a fictional innovation even if it has sometimes been mistaken for documentary writing. The looseness of structure in the *Sketch Book* and *Bracebridge Hall* was imitated by Mary Russell Mitford and, much later, by Elizabeth Gaskell in *Cranford* (1853). Mitford, initially a poet and playwright, set out to produce 'essays and characters

and stories, chiefly of country life, in the manner of the "Sketch Book",
but without sentimentality or pathos' in what became the five volumes of
Our Village (1824–32).[9] The village and its history were 'half real and half
imaginary', and it was not until the fifth volume that Mitford identified it
as her home village of Three Mile Cross in Berkshire, divulging what must
long have been an open secret.[10] Like Geoffrey Crayon, she is a con-
noisseur of English rural scenery. A landscape forms a 'pretty English
picture',[11] and the village itself 'sits for its picture'.[12] For public consumption Mitford praised Washington Irving's 'delightful but somewhat
fanciful writings' (144), although she privately dismissed them as
'maudlin trash'.[13] Jane Austen's portrayal of the English countryside was
much more to her taste. *Our Village* begins with an effusive tribute to
what can only be the portrayal of Highbury in *Emma* (it doesn't fit any of
the other Austen novels): 'nothing is so delightful as to sit down in a
country village in one of Miss Austen's delicious novels, quite sure before
we leave it to become intimate with every spot and every person it contains' (2). This is disconcertingly inaccurate (we cannot be said to make a
very wide acquaintance with the villagers of Highbury), but typically
Mitfordian in its invocation of a kind of literary picturesque. On a walk in
the meadows in 'The Cowslip-Ball', she feels 'out of this world' like
'Robinson Crusoe in his lonely island' (37). The landscape is experienced
as if it were already a text from English fiction.

   The countryside represented in Mitford's work is peaceful, unchanging, and uninterrupted even by the rumblings of reactionary squires. Its
variety is that of the 'dappled things' Gerard Manley Hopkins would later
celebrate in his sonnet 'Pied Beauty'. In 'shady and yet sunny' Berkshire,
'the scenery, without rising into grandeur or breaking into wildness, is so
peaceful, so cheerful, so varied, and so thoroughly English' (131). The
seasons roll round in their regular course and, for the most part, conflict
and rivalry are confined to the annual cricket match with the next village.
(Mitford is one of the earliest and best writers on village cricket.) The
busy life of Reading, only three miles away, was the subject of a separate,
long-forgotten book, *Belford Regis* (1835). There is no agricultural
machinery in 'Our Village', despite the popular agitation in Berkshire
which led to the so-called Captain Swing riots. In her 1832 volume,
Mitford briefly outlines the riots which had disturbed the even tenor of
'peaceful and happy England', bringing home 'to our very household
hearths' horrors normally connected with the 'sister island' of Ireland.
Three Mile Cross is 'in the centre of the insurgents', Mitford alarmingly
reports, though fortunately it has remained unaffected by political

meetings, marches, or machine-wrecking.[14] Her story 'The Incendiary: A Country Tale' is powerfully reassuring, since what it describes is not a politically motivated rick-burning but a traditional rural comedy of errors in which a hayrick is accidentally set alight by a farmer's daughter fumbling around in search of a love letter in the dark. The rights and wrongs of the wider conflict are quickly forgotten in the story of this clumsy, lovelorn country girl.

Like the *Sketch Book*, *Our Village* was widely read throughout the nineteenth century, influencing poets such as Tennyson and Clough and novelists such as Gaskell, Eliot, and Trollope.[15] While it is ostensibly neutral in political terms, Mitford's image of a picturesque and timeless England is heavily committed to maintaining the illusion of social harmony. 'Fears that cannot be resolved are replaced by stories for which she can imagine a happy ending,' as one critic has written.[16] Everything in *Our Village* is consistent with Edmund Burke's view of English society as an 'old establishment', possessed by the current generation as a 'body and stock of inheritance' and devoid of alien influence.[17] Revolutionary upheavals, like Hazlitt's 'materials for romance', belong to other countries or the distant past. Mitford's vision of rural England is thus clearly aligned with the Romantic Toryism of Burke and Walter Scott, even though her Toryism is beneath the surface. The author of *Our Village* was also a successful historical dramatist, the author of plays on classical and Italian Renaissance themes. If one side of Romantic Toryism was its aspiration towards a timeless present in which history could be turned back or stopped in its tracks, the other side was its harking back to the civil strife and national divisions of a more or less remote past.

Walter Scott and English Romance

Walter Scott did not invent the historical romance. Rather, he was the first great writer to seize on its potential as a dramatic narration of national history, a modern commercial equivalent of the old national epic. Scott's Waverley novels started out as the romance of Scotland, but of a Scotland that was now part of the United Kingdom, so that the hero was generally a young adventurer from south of the border. But Scott soon broke with this pattern, and with *Ivanhoe* (1819), the tenth in the series, he turned the adventure tale into a 'foundation epic of England'.[18]

Scott's principal predecessor in English historical romance was the Suffolk-born Clara Reeve, author of *The Old English Baron* (1777), which portrays the struggles of Edmund Twyford, a fifteenth-century dispossessed nobleman, to regain his family estates. The theme of overcoming usurpation and restoring a lost inheritance had already been adapted to the novel by Fielding and Smollett; it would become the standard plot device of the Waverley novels. First the young hero must find out who he is, then he must show the courage and endurance needed to defeat the enemies who have traitorously dispossessed him. *The Old English Baron* copies the plot of Shakespeare's *Hamlet* in so far as Edmund Twyford learns from a ghost of his father's murder. Later Edmund must fight a trial by combat, but ultimately he is dependent on the national sense of fair play as represented by the old Baron Fitz-Owen, who voluntarily resigns the property which he discovers is not legally his.

Clara Reeve was, like Jane Austen and Charlotte Brontë, an Anglican vicar's daughter, and *The Old English Baron* was first published under the title *The Champion of Virtue*. Conceived as an 'English Gothic' tale in reaction to the foreign setting of Horace Walpole's *The Castle of Otranto*, Reeve's rather wooden narrative ends in a strong affirmation of Christian benevolence. Fitz-Owen is 'English', above all, in his liberality, righteousness, and respect for the law. In a rhapsodic deathscene, Reeve observes of Fitz-Owen that 'happy are the descendants of such a father!...they will remember him, and be ashamed to degenerate from their ancestor.'[19] This stress on the moral obligations conferred by one's ancestry is not found in earlier eighteenth-century fiction, though it is a major element in Charlotte Smith's *Marchmont* (discussed in Chapter 4), as well as in Scott's fiction beginning with *Waverley*. Scott's heroes in his Covenanting and 'Jacobite' novels, notably *Waverley; or 'Tis Sixty Years Since* (1814), *Old Mortality* (1816), *Rob Roy* (1817), and *Redgauntlet* (1824), are profoundly influenced by what their ancestors did in the Civil Wars one, two, or three generations earlier. Family history imposes an inherited, even racial loyalty on the individual, who becomes embroiled in an age-old political conflict regardless of his own wishes.

At the beginning of *Waverley* we learn that Charles II took refuge at the family mansion of Waverley-Honour after the Battle of Worcester, and that one of the sons of the family was killed in his defence. Some three generations later young Edward Waverley is brought up as a loyal Hanoverian, but he falls for the romance of Jacobitism and deserts from the British Army to join forces with Bonnie Prince Charlie. Thanks to his Cavalier lineage, his allegiance is highly prized. His subsequent ordeal leading to rehabilitation and a royal pardon makes him a symbol of the burial of Jacobite divisions and the strengthening of the United Kingdom after 1745. From his sixty years' retrospect, Scott's narrator judges that, once the 'romance' of Waverley's youth has ended, his historical role is to represent the resolution of inherited conflicts in the building of a new, modern Scotland.[20]

Scott believed that his native country had changed beyond recognition during the previous sixty years, but he would not have said the same of England. In the Dedicatory Epistle to *Ivanhoe* he compared the eighteenth-century Highlands to the world of the Iroquois and Mohawks, a barbaric society in need of colonial suppression. Scotland had now 'caught up' with England, moving from primordial savagery to the status of a modern bourgeois society. But Scott, the great national writer of modern bourgeois society, had no interest in describing his own times. His mission, instead, was to turn historical memory into the material of modern popular entertainment. In *Old Mortality* he begins by visiting the neglected graves of the Covenanters who had died fighting for freedom of worship against the forces of Charles II. The old man tending the graves is based on one Robert Paterson, whom Scott claimed to have met in the 1790s. History here is a matter of intimate tradition and of respect for the dead, though Scott recasts it as romantic adventure. When he turned to English history the novelist was prepared to look much further back, 'amidst the dust of antiquity', as he put it;[21] later he would move forward from the medieval chivalry of *Ivanhoe* to Queen Elizabeth's court and eventually, in *The Fortunes of Nigel* (1822), *Peveril of the Peak* (1823), and *Woodstock* (1826), to seventeenth-century England. Like the young Waverley, Scott believed that romantic fiction was 'of all themes the most fascinating to a youthful imagination' (76), and he offered nineteenth-century versions of the romances of Tasso and Spenser which his hero is shown devouring in his youth. Scott's antiquarianism in his English novels is manifestly faked, although his novels of eighteenth-century Scotland lay some claim to linguistic plausibility and historical accuracy. In the latter he could draw on living traditions and surviving dialects; but the English novels are comparatively superficial entertainments evoking the nation's aristocratic and Royalist past. They were the first of Scott's romances to fall out of critical favour after his death.

For the Victorian critic Archibald Allison, the period portrayed in *Ivanhoe* was 'one in which great national questions were at stake, and the conversations and characters afforded the means of bringing them prominently before the mind of the reader'; and the result was a novel which, like *Old Mortality*, exhibited 'the perfection of historical romance, so far as subject goes'. Yet Allison had to admit that the later English novels from *Kenilworth* (1821) to *Woodstock* were often 'insupportably dull'. The dialogue in these books was 'a jargon mixed up of scraps and expressions from old plays or quaint tracts, such as no man on earth ever did speak, and which it is only surprising a man of his sagacity should have supposed they ever could'.[22] To Leslie Stephen, a slightly later critic, the English novels were 'stucco-work of a highly crumbling and unstable tendency', which had 'rightly descended from the library to the school-room'.[23] *Ivanhoe*'s reputation has never wholly recovered from strictures like these.

Ivanhoe expresses Scott's belief that the union of the native Saxons with the Norman invaders was the key to the formation of English identity, just as the reconciliation of Highlanders and Lowlanders was the key to modern Scotland. His portrayal of twelfth-century England as a recently colonized province with an insurmountable cultural, political, and linguistic barrier between the Norman overlords and their Saxon serfs was to have a vast influence on later historiography, whether or not it is good history.[24] In *Ivanhoe* Scott invites us to sympathize with the oppressed peasants under the 'Norman yoke' (225) much as he sympathizes with the defeated Highlanders. In each case, he portrays a crisis of instability and near-anarchy which can only be overcome by deliberate moves to build national unity. But the issue of Saxons and Normans is for the most part fully presented in the opening chapters of *Ivanhoe*. Scott's romantic plot then leads in a rather different direction.

Chapter seven of *Ivanhoe* begins with a passage of scene-setting worthy of a professional historian. It uses the sufferings of ordinary people to define the state of the nation or, in Thomas Carlyle's famous phrase which may have been inspired by Scott, the 'Condition of England'. In *Redgauntlet* the revolutionary leader Hugh Redgauntlet describes the 'state of this nation' as being analogous to the 'florid colour of a feverish patient'.[25] The same medical and diagnostic metaphor is present in *Ivanhoe*:

The condition of the English nation was at this time sufficiently miserable. King Richard was absent a prisoner, and in the power of the perfidious and cruel Duke of Austria. Even the very place of his captivity was uncertain, and his fate but very imperfectly known to the generality of his subjects, who were, in the meantime, a prey to every species of subaltern oppression. . . . To augment their misery, a contagious disorder of a dangerous nature spread through the land; and, rendered more virulent by the uncleanness, the indifferent food, and the wretched lodging of the lower classes, swept off many whose fate the survivors were tempted to envy, as exempting them from the evils which were to come. (65–6)

Carlyle would later describe the condition of England in 1839 as one of 'sad social pestilence'. Scott's 'contagious disorder' plays much the same role in medieval England as the outbreak of typhus fever in Edinburgh that Carlyle traced to a 'poor Irish widow' who had infected seventeen of the fellow citizens who refused her appeal for charity. Carlyle attributes this disaster to the 'government of the Poor by the Rich' under the banner of 'laissez-faire'.[26] In *Ivanhoe* the King whose absence is blamed for many of England's miseries reappears under the banner of *Le Noir Faineant*, literally the 'do-nothing' black knight—a medieval anticipation of the nineteenth-century doctrine of laissez-faire.

Barely one paragraph after this, Scott switches into what he called the 'Big Bow-wow strain' of epic romance—the strain that prompts him to draw some of his chapter epigraphs from the *Iliad*.[27] The narrator transports us to the 'singularly romantic' scene of the tournament held in Prince John's presence at Ashby-de-la-Zouch, which has 'attracted universal attention'—it is as if the whole people, young and old alike, have joined this 'immense confluence of persons of all ranks'—and soon miraculous feats are being performed by the champions of the downtrodden Saxons (66). The crippling social tensions are temporarily relieved by a symbolic jousting-match in which Ivanhoe, the young and unknown Saxon hero who calls himself the Disinherited Knight, overcomes his Norman foes. The ethic of chivalry is manifestly inadequate to deal with the social injustices Scott has outlined, but, after all, he is writing an adventure romance and not a historical tract for his times.

Edmund Burke in *Reflections on the Revolution in France* had based the conservative idea of liberty on the idea of inheritance: 'The very idea of the fabrication of a new government is enough to fill us with disgust and horror. We wished at the period of the [English] Revolution, and do now wish, to derive all we possess as *an inheritance from our forefathers*.'[28] Scott's historical fiction puts an extraordinary emphasis upon inheritance and lineage, but his conservatism is significantly different from Burke's. Burke had written when it seemed possible that the contagion of revolutionary France might spread to England, but Scott's generation lived in the knowledge that Britain had defeated its continental enemies and that its monarchy and aristocracy remained intact. Victory over Napoleon might even be compared to the Crusade against the arch-infidel Saladin. It is, therefore, no accident that Ivanhoe is a returning crusader whose eyes are gradually opened to the ills of his native country. It is true that he belongs to the remnant of the Saxon nobility, grimly hanging on to what is left of their feudal possessions, but Scott sees that their day is over. The imperial unity foreshadowed by the crusading armies represents England's future. Cedric, the Saxon chief, believes he is the representative of the old English nation, so that his kidnapping and imprisonment in Front-de-Boeuf's castle ought to give him the status of an important political prisoner. But all the Normans want is to extract a ransom and to rape Rowena, his ward. Cedric, in any case, has divided his followers by disowning Ivanhoe for going on the Crusades, thus separating him from his beloved Rowena. Athelstane, her intended bridegroom, is a renowned Saxon warrior but little else. Eventually he is exposed as the cock that will not fight against its Norman masters.

The Normans, brought to England a century earlier by William the Bastard, are still ruthless pillagers and conquerors. Prince John intends to usurp his brother's throne. His followers are cynically contemptuous of their own chivalric code, and only De Bracy, declining to take part in an assassination attempt on the King, stands by his oath of knighthood and draws the line at thuggery and 'highway practice' (299). There is virtual gang warfare across the countryside, involving a group of robbers who describe themselves as 'poor and disinherited' (105) as well as the Sherwood Forest outlaws and the Templar Brian de Bois-Guilbert with his gang of pretended outlaws. Scott draws on English eighteenth-century fiction both in his scenes of highway robbery and in the attempted rape of two young women, Rowena and Rebecca. When Bois-Guilbert tries to rape Rebecca, the novel's interest shifts away from the Saxon-Norman split to the 'disinherited and wandering' English Jews (97), of whom she is one, and to the Templars with their 'immense possessions in every kingdom of Europe' (202). The Templars, who acknowledge no ties of family or state, are the harbingers of a new order looking beyond the Middle Ages to Napoleon's attempted unification of Europe and (perhaps) to the modern world of rapacious global capitalists and international civil servants.

So, although the Saxon–Norman conflict is the official national-historical issue around which *Ivanhoe* revolves, Scott's interest in this conflict seems perfunctory at best. He had described his heroes as 'very amiable and very insipid sort of young men'; and, beginning with Hazlitt's essay on 'Why the Heroes of Romance are Insipid', their passivity has been a perennial item of critical discussion.[29] We may say that Scott's heroes are insipid because they are respectable nineteenth-century young gentlemen (with whom his readers could easily identify) dressed up as actors in history, but Ivanhoe seems like a burlesque even of the normal Scott hero. So marked is his passivity that he is first discovered lying prone, whether from exhaustion or depression, at the foot of a sunken cross near his father's house. He enters and leaves the house incognito and spends much of the remainder of the novel prostrate, carried from place to place in a litter as he is cured by Rebecca of the wound he receives at the tournament. It is true that we twice see him in his appointed role as a champion on horseback, as if he only comes to life when encased in steel from top to toe. The qualities which have brought him high in King Richard's counsels are never on display. In his second fight with Bois-Guilbert he is 'scarce able to support himself in the saddle' (390) and too weak to strike an effective blow. The day is saved, and Rebecca vindicated, by an act of God, since the Templar is seized by an apoplexy in the moment of combat.

Ivanhoe's subsequent marriage to the fair, blue-eyed Rowena, 'mild, timid, and gentle' (190) thanks to her Saxon blood, has also disappointed virtually every reader. The author felt obliged to defend himself in his 1830 Introduction for not pairing his hero off with Rebecca rather than Rowena. Ivanhoe's reconciliation with his father and his consequent marriage have the blessing of King Richard, just as the marriages in *Kenilworth*, *The Fortunes of Nigel*, *Peveril of the Peak*, and *Woodstock* all receive the blessing of an English king or queen. We are finally told that Ivanhoe distinguished himself in Richard's service and 'might have risen still higher, but for [the King's] premature death' (401)—so he is floored again, metaphorically speaking, just as in his first appearance at the sunken cross. His prosperity depends entirely on Richard's return from the Crusades, but this return is curiously muted, less as a matter of subtle policy than as a result of Richard's indolence. He saves Ivanhoe's life at the tournament by taking the field in disguise as the 'Black Sluggard' (114). Very late in the novel he unveils himself, refusing the label of Richard of Anjou that Cedric wants to pin on him and declaring himself Richard of England. But his statesmanlike attempts to reconcile Saxon and Norman are largely aborted by his own failures of leadership. The narrator offers a merciless analysis of the meteoric reign of the 'lionhearted king' who was distinguished by the 'brilliant, but useless character, of a knight of romance' (365); for all Scott's outspoken Royalism, his fictions constantly expose the shortcomings of weak rulers. Richard's enemies act on the assumption that chivalry is dead and that 'These are not the days of King Arthur, when a champion could encounter an army' (134). Richard represents a brief but futile reversion to the world of Arthur. Ivanhoe, too, has left his Saxon forefathers behind in order to devote himself to useless chivalry. His heroism discredits the Saxon barons' Realpolitik and saves Rebecca from otherwise certain death; but this is only possible thanks to the way in which his life has been preserved by Rebecca, by the Saxon churls Gurth and Wamba, and by the stout English yeoman Locksley. Locksley, or Robin Hood, is acknowledged 'King of Outlaws' by Richard (360), and his management of his band of outlaws offers the real King a lesson in good government. But he too is a curiously muted figure. The burden of true heroism—heroism of character—in *Ivanhoe* falls entirely on the saintly Rebecca.

Rebecca comes into the novel together with her father Isaac, the Jew of York whose moneylending keeps Prince John and his minions afloat. The vehement anti-Semitism aimed at Isaac comes from 'Norman, Saxon, Dane, and Briton' alike (61). Scott clearly deprecates the 'despotism of religious prejudice' (195), though Isaac is portrayed as a stereotypically grasping and avaricious Jew who has come to England to make his fortune. What John Ruskin was to say rather dubiously of Scott's Puritans— that they are 'formal and slavish', whereas his Cavaliers are 'free and masterful'—is most certainly true of the contest between Isaac and the treacherous Norman knights.[30] Isaac frequently falls back on Old Testament invocations, and when he is called before the Grand Master of the Templars he shows 'all the submission of oriental slavery': 'No naked slave, ushered into the presence of some mighty prince, could approach his judgment-seat with more profound reverence and terror than that with which the Jew drew near to the presence of the Grand Master' (308). Here Scott's polished and flattering periods mock at Isaac's obsequiousness. In this scene, as in the torture scenes at Front-de-Boeuf's castle and in the sadistic preparations for Rebecca's death, the novelist seems to relish the sight of Jewish prostration and terror.

But Rebecca shows a spirit of heroism which rises above both her family inheritance and the Jewish religious forms. Faced with threats of rape, abduction, and execution over a slow fire she shows 'that strong reliance on heaven natural to great and generous characters' (196), something which Scott differentiates sharply from from Isaac's gabbled prayers and invocations. She has the moral authority to denounce the 'fantastic chivalry' of the Christian knights (250) and to tell Bois-Guilbert that a woman's endurance of suffering surpasses all the male's 'vaunted courage' (344). At the same time, she devotes herself to healing men wounded in combat and has to call on the ethic of chivalry to save her own life. But she has no belief in the restoration of order promised by Richard's return, and her eventual decision to leave England passes a final judgement on the nation. Richard's clash with the Templars is referred to the Pope for arbitration, making the point that even a king who believes in reconciling Saxons with Normans does not yet have full dominion in his own land. Rebecca decides to emigrate because, as a 'land of war and blood', England remains an unsafe place for her: ' "The people of England are a fierce race, quarreling ever with their neighbours or among themselves, and ready to plunge the sword into the bowels of each other. Such is no safe abode for the children of my people," ' she tells Rowena (399). The Jews could only prosper under the protection of a strong central authority, but Richard remains the ineffectual monarch who, when ambushed by his enemies, had to rely on the clown Wamba to blow the horn and summon the men of Sherwood to his assistance. W. M. Thackeray wrote a sequel to *Ivanhoe*, *Rebecca and Rowena* (1850), in which a dissatisfied and no longer passive Ivanhoe leaves England in search of his dark-haired siren. Thackeray had perceived how far Scott's epic romance of English national identity turns away from its ostensible subject in another direction. The pattern is repeated, as we shall see, in his seventeenth-century romance *Peveril of the Peak*.

Royal Costume Dramas

The heroine of *Kenilworth* is Amy Robsart, who has secretly married the Earl of Leicester. The events of the novel supposedly take place at the time of the Queen's progress to Kenilworth Castle in 1575, but a series of wild anachronisms emphasize the difference between this 'merry England' romp and Scott's earlier novels.[31] Robsart's marriage to the future Earl had been publicly acknowledged in 1549, and she had died in 1560; Leicester's possible marriage to the Queen had been discussed by the Privy Council in 1566; and Shakespeare, not born until 1564, appears in *Kenilworth* as a fashionable young playwright who had already written *A Midsummer Night's Dream* and (what we now know to have been one of his last plays) *The Winter's Tale*. Even setting aside the confusion of dates, *Kenilworth* takes episodes from proverbial English history, like that of Raleigh's cloak, and translates them into a melodramatic tale teetering always on the brink of absurdity.

Scott knew very well that he could only approach the romance of English history belatedly and at second hand. Just as Locksley in *Ivanhoe* represented the legendary Robin Hood, the pageant put on for the Queen's visit to Kenilworth Castle includes the figures of Merlin and the Lady of the Lake. A company of 'true-hearted men of Coventry' (362) portray the Saxons' defeat of the Danes, and Elizabeth moralizes on the attributes her people have inherited from the ancient Britons, Romans, Saxons, and Normans. Merlin in a sycophantic address to the Virgin Queen describes multiracial England as 'in some measure the muster of the perfections of the other nations' (351–2). But, while Scott celebrates Elizabethan England's imperial power and national pride, he shows it as being ridden with villainy and corruption, while the Queen is a control-freak whose diplomacy and cunning are at the mercy of her capricious vanity. *The Fortunes of Nigel* portrays her weak-minded, irresolute successor James I. In *Woodstock* both the debauched Cavalier Prince Charles and his arch-enemy Cromwell are shown as weak and vacillating. The latter novel ends with the old Royalist knight Sir Henry Lee and his faithful dog dying of happiness at the moment of Charles II's triumphant return to London at the Restoration; one reason for their happiness, we might think, is that they will not have to live through the dreary excesses of the Restoration monarchy. *Peveril of the Peak* begins at the Restoration and ends with a long and tedious outline of manoeuvrings at Court during the Popish Plot of 1678–9. None of these novels can be said to flatter the reigning monarch. Yet in each of them the protagonist's quest for a personal interview with the monarch is the hinge on which the plot turns.

Peveril of the Peak ends, predictably enough, with the King conferring his blessing on a 'roundheaded alliance'—the marriage of Julian Peveril, the descendant of an old Cavalier family, to the daughter of the staunch Puritan Major Bridgenorth.[32] The warring Derbyshire estates of Martindale (Cavalier) and Moultrassie (Puritan) are joined together by this marriage, but, as so often, Scott presents this final token of national reconciliation with offhand unconcern. He cares, and we care, remarkably little about the happiness of his insipid hero and dutiful but beautiful heroine. One reason for this is that in *Peveril*, as in *Waverley* and *Ivanhoe*, there is a dark heroine as well as a light heroine vying for the protagonist's affections.

In *The Hero of the Waverley Novels* Alexander Welsh argues that Scott's fiction typically balances the official hero against a 'dark hero', who is not to be confused with the villain—an outlaw whose 'intentions are "good", though fierce and mistaken'.[33] Vich Ian Vohr in *Waverley*, Burley in *Old Mortality*, Rob Roy, Hugh Redgauntlet, Richard the Black Knight and Locksley in *Ivanhoe*, Leicester in *Kenilworth*, and Bridgenorth in *Peveril* could be said to belong to this type. Then there is the 'light heroine' whom the official hero, the blond hero, must marry; she is usually a kind of sister to him, an adopted member of his own family.

This is true of Rowena, of Alice Lee in *Woodstock*, of Alice Bridgenorth, and several others. Amy and Tressilian have a similar relationship in *Kenilworth*—Tressilian obtains her father's power of attorney in order to plead Amy's case before Queen Elizabeth—but they are not able to marry. Scott's novels therefore run counter to traditional romance and aristocratic values in that they seem to favour inbreeding and endogamy. Scott did not invent the kind of plot that skirts the notion of incest by introducing a hero and heroine who are virtually brother and sister, but he did a great deal to popularize it.

Scott's acknowledged indebtedness to Maria Edgeworth's fiction is relevant here. Edgeworth's *The Absentee* (1812) may be read as a response to an earlier 'national tale' by Sydney Owenson (Lady Morgan), *The Wild Irish Girl* (1806), in which the hero, an Anglo-Irish landowner brought up in England, falls in love with and marries a Gaelic princess. Edgeworth's young Anglo-Irishman Lord Colambre can also be said to fall in love with Ireland, but his chosen bride is the woman he has been brought up to think of as his orphaned first cousin, Grace Nugent. Colambre's mother holds the traditional aristocratic belief that 'first cousins should never marry, because they form no new connections to strengthen the family interest, or raise its consequence'.[34] Grace, therefore, is forbidden territory, all the more so when it turns out that she is supposedly illegitimate. Edgeworth's hero eventually marries her, just as he would have done in one of Scott's romances, but in Scott we are usually aware of romantic exogamy—the spiritual and sexual attraction of opposites—as a force pulling the hero away from marriage to a member of his own family. Yet in Scott the sovereign power of romantic exogamy is almost always denied.

Waverley falls deeply in love with Flora MacIvor, the Celtic beauty who helps to lure him onto the side of the rebels, though she acknowledges no sexual interest in him and eventually retires to a nunnery in France to lament over her brother's political martyrdom. Ivanhoe is resolutely unmoved by the passionate, raven-haired Rebecca. Julian Peveril is loved both by Alice, a fair Englishwoman, and by the mysterious Zarah or Fenella who is both Celtic and Oriental—a combination, as it were, of Flora and Rebecca. Zarah, a character confessedly based on Goethe's Mignon, is a double agent inserted into the household of the Roman Catholic Countess of Derby under the pretence of being deaf and dumb. She is the daughter of a Manx father and an Oriental mother. At home on the Isle of Man she is associated with Celtic legend and regarded as a child of the elves. In London she exploits her sexuality by dancing before the King and ensnaring the Duke of Buckingham, whereas Alice, the light heroine, fails to captivate either the King or Buckingham despite the attempts of her kidnappers to prostitute her at court. Only the dark heroine has sexual magnetism, and only the hero (for whom she sacrifices everything) is impervious to it. Moreover, the light heroine confirms national identity and the dark heroine challenges it. By marrying the light heroine who belongs to an estranged branch of his own family, the hero does his duty for England, reclaiming his inheritance and unifying a divided estate. But the Scott of the English novels is bored by this very proper fable, and yearns for his Celtic-Semitic heroine who represents both the spirit of romance and the defeated subjects of imperial power.

At times Scott, like some of the male novelists who succeeded him (notably Thackeray and Trollope), affects not to care for the narrative of courtship. His readers demand a suitably romantic climax, and he is willing to provide one, but with an air of masculine unconcern that almost destroys the mood. He equivocates about Ivanhoe's prospect of marital happiness with Rowena, and at the end of *Old Mortality* he invents a frivolous female reader, Miss Martha Buskbody, whose persistent questioning elicits the details of the hero's marriage from a disengaged and supercilious narrator. Does this mean that the story Scott really cares about is that of his male protagonist's reintegration into the nobility and recovery of his hereditary rights?[35] (Naturally in the process he must acquire a trophy wife.) This may be so, but there is something faked in the very idea of nobility in Scott. He could celebrate aristocratic values, just as he could celebrate Scottish national difference, precisely because they seemed to be disappearing and could be invested with fondness and nostalgia. In one of his earliest pieces of writing he set out his aim of contributing to the history of his native country, 'the peculiar features of whose manners and character are daily melting and dissolving into those of her sister and ally'.[36]

The son of an Edinburgh advocate, Scott was quintessentially a middle-class writer, and there is much evidence that his main concern was with achieving commercial prosperity through appealing to readers who were both predominantly middle class and predominantly English. Heinrich Heine argued that, where Cervantes had introduced a democratic element into romance, Scott, writing for the 'prosaic *bourgeoisie*', had restored to romance its aristocratic element.[37] Thus the Waverley novels turn feudal Scotland into an adventure playground where his readers can imagine living a more colourful, a more strenuous, and a more exciting life. Martin Green has commented that 'There is a fatal gentility to the

Waverley enterprise; one aspect to it is a game with chivalric trappings for readers who make their money in trade—a literary equivalent for the social pursuit of titles and coats of arms'.[38] In *Guy Mannering* (1815) the young Harry Bertram, brought up in Holland, now a captain in the Indian Army, approaches his ancestral estate on the Solway Firth, and Scott, exaggerating his hero's sufferings, shamelessly pulls out all the stops:

And thus,—unconscious as the most absolute stranger, and in circumstances which, if not destitute, were for the present highly embarrassing; without the countenance of a friend within the circle of several hundred miles; accused of a heavy crime; and, what was as bad as all the rest, being nearly penniless,—did the harassed wanderer for the first time, after the interval of so many years, approach the remains of the castle where his ancestors had exercised all but regal dominion.[39]

'All but regal dominion': the dream, ultimately, is not one of aristocratic obligations and responsibilities but of absolute power. The downtrodden member of the middle classes hopes to become king of all he surveys.

Scott was an ardent monarchist. He had begun life as a successful poet, and in 1813, shortly before the publication of *Waverley*, he turned down the laureateship. But this did not prevent him from becoming a favourite of the Prince Regent, to whom he was presented two years later. He was made a baronet in 1820, the first novelist to receive a knighthood. His contemporary William Maginn wrote *Whitehall; or, The Days of George IV* (1827), a burlesque poking fun at Scott's eagerness to kowtow to royalty. George IV, for his part, donned the kilt (made fashionable by *Waverley*) on his sole visit to Scotland in 1822. After a state banquet in Edinburgh, Scott took home the wineglass in which the King had just pledged the health of his people, but the novelist accidentally broke the glass, and was thrown into despair. (Leslie Stephen commented on this incident that 'that wretched bit of mock loyalty amounts almost to a national misfortune'.[40]) Scott also asked for, and received, permission to dedicate the collected Waverley novels to George IV. The dedication is considerably more fulsome than the dedication to *Emma* that the King, as Prince Regent, had extracted from a manifestly embarrassed Jane Austen. It is, however, as an entertainer, not as a patriot or historian, that Scott puts himself forward as a candidate for royal patronage. Far from expressing servility, he offers himself as the people's choice, backed, like a modern prime minister, by the votes of ordinary readers:

The Author of this Collection of Works of Fiction would not have presumed to solicit for them your Majesty's August Patronage, were it not that the perusal has been supposed in some instances, to have succeeded in amusing hours of relaxation, or relieving those of languor, pain, or anxiety; and therefore must have so far aided the warmest wish of your Majesty's heart, by contributing in however small a degree to the happiness of your people. (1829)[41]

This dedication marks one of the very few significant instances of royal patronage in English prose fiction, but in literary history it is a dead end. We have seen that in each of Scott's English novels the plot leads up to a personal interview with the sovereign, who (for the moment at least) reaffirms his subject's liberties. The absence of comparable portraits of any contemporary monarch, or even of an ideological role for the monarchy, in fiction before and after Scott's time is very noticeable. Kings and queens could be openly presented in the historical romance, but not in English domestic fiction, where the reader is barely even conscious of their absence. But Scott's example suggests that, even for the novelist who is a monarchist and a Tory romantic, the fictional portrayal of royalty has certain dangers. Scott's show of loyalty towards George IV does not disguise the fact that he claims absolute dominion over his own fictional creation, and is confident of being a much wiser ruler than most English kings. As a novelist he is nobody's subject.

Disraeli and Bulwer-Lytton

Early in 1826, Scott made a famous entry in his journal after reading Jane Austen's *Pride and Prejudice* for the third time:

That young lady had a talent for describing the involvements and feelings and characters of ordinary life which is to me the most wonderful I ever met with. The Big Bow-wow strain I can do myself like any now going, but the exquisite touch which renders ordinary commonplace things and characters interesting from the truth of the description and the sentiment is denied to me.[42]

It was the 'Big Bow-wow strain' that ushered in the Victorian novel. According to the critic R. H. Horne, Scott's achievement in historical romance bred 'hundreds of imitators' throughout the civilized world: 'Everybody thought he could write an historical novel.'[43] Horne's contemporary Archibald Allison noted that since the advent of historical romance the sentimental fiction of Fanny Burney, Ann Radcliffe, Charlotte Smith, and even Samuel Richardson had become 'wellnigh unreadable'. Writing in 1845, Allison saw the historical romance as a contemporary political force, since Scott's conservatism had counteracted the democratic tendencies of sentimental romance and had even 'gone far to neutralise the dangers of the Reform Bill'.[44] Not surprisingly, Scott's English followers contained more than one outspoken Tory.

Edward Bulwer-Lytton, originally elected to Parliament in 1831 on a Reform ticket, later became a minister alongside Benjamin Disraeli in Lord Derby's Conservative government. Bulwer-Lytton's enormous literary output includes a study of the national character, *England and the English* (1833), mainly notable for its anticipations of Disraeli's political philosophy. Like his much greater contemporary, Bulwer-Lytton was a monarchist who warned against the power of an overweening aristocracy or property-holding class. The 'aristocracy of shopkeepers' that would come to power under a republic would be just as bad, he argued, as an oligarchy of nobles.[45] It needed a royal prerogative to keep the aristocracy in check; as Bulwer-Lytton put it in his unvarnished way, 'Better one despot, than a reign of robbers' (373). Thus Bulwer-Lytton, soon to be followed by Disraeli, neatly reversed the traditional Whig argument for a constitutional monarchy in which aristocratic government served to protect the nation from the absolutist tyranny it had suffered under the Stuarts. Bulwer-Lytton and Disraeli responded to the French Revolution and the British experience of parliamentary reform by reverting to the 'King versus Parliament' debates of the seventeenth century, but taking the Royalist side and warning against the power of the Whig House of Lords rather than the House of Commons. Bulwer-Lytton called on his readers to 'rally round the Throne' (373), while Disraeli argued that, despite all appearances, the real tendency of nineteenth-century political movements was towards a strengthening of the monarchy.

The new party alignments were foreseen by Disraeli in one of the most striking of nineteenth-century political texts, his *Vindication of the English Constitution* (1835). Here the Tories are the 'national party' while the Whigs are denounced as a 'small knot of great families, who have no other object but their own aggrandisement, and who seek to gratify it by all possible means'.[46] The Whigs had secured the Hanoverian succession by a *coup d'état* in 1714 just as their republican forebears in the Long Parliament had carried out a *coup d'état*. Only the monarchy could stand above class interests to represent the nation as a whole; and the monarchy would find its voice in a rejuvenated Tory party. Following the *Vindication*, large tracts of Disraeli's political novels would be given over to his rewriting of English history in the interests of Tory democracy. Behind his invocation of the royal prerogative as a counterweight to the Whig doctrine of civil and religious liberty is his sense of a broad crisis of nationhood, summed up in the title of his best-known novel, *Sybil or The Two Nations* (1845).

Both Disraeli and Bulwer-Lytton invoke the idea of national character, which had become a major concept of European political and social debate. Their sense of national character grows out of the much older analogy between the nation (or state) and the family. Disraeli in the *Vindication* echoes Burke in proclaiming that England's greatest statesmen had 'looked upon the nation as a family, and upon the country as a landed inheritance' (24). What happens, then, if there is manifest unfairness in the way the inheritance is shared out? Disraeli blamed the growing national unrest on the effects of a century and a half of Whig dominance.

But Disraeli was not much concerned with the English class structure in the modern sense of the term. Instead, the *Vindication* looks at the function and destiny of what he calls the 'great national institutions' (181). (Disraeli was one of the first writers to popularize this sense of the term 'institution'.) First, there are the political institutions deriving from the medieval model of the three estates of the realm. For Disraeli the three estates are the clergy, the lords, and the commons, each of which he describes as a 'class of the nation invested with political rights'. (Bulwer-Lytton had also started from the three estates, but his were the monarchy, aristocracy, and commons, implying that the monarchy was a sectional interest within the nation rather than the only body standing above class and sectional interests.) The three estates provide the structure of Disraeli's trilogy of 'Young England' novels: *Coningsby or the New Generation* (1844) concerned with the aristocracy, *Sybil or The Two Nations* concerned with the people, and *Tancred or The New Crusade* (1847) concerned, in a much looser sense, with the clergy.

According to Disraeli, the eighteenth-century Whigs had converted England into a 'Venetian republic' where the king was only a nominal head of state and the aristocracy held all the political power. This analysis remains influential, since it was repeated without acknowledgement in J. H. Plumb's seminal study of *The Growth of Political Stability in England 1675–1725* (1967). There was a largely ineffectual opposition led by the Tory country gentlemen in the House of Commons, sometimes with the King's backing. For the most part, the rotten boroughs and pocket boroughs in the gift of the great landed families allowed the Whigs to command a majority in both Houses of Parliament. But, though the Whigs dominated two of the nation's three political institutions, their 'object of establishing an oligarchical republic' amounted to a declaration of war against the nation as a whole, in Disraeli's view: 'The Whig party has ever been odious to the English people, and...in the long run, the

English nation declares against them' (181). The 'nation' as Disraeli understood it was more than the apparatus of the state, but it was not to be arrived
at simply by counting heads among the population. Instead, it resided in the
'great national institutions' which it was the Tories' task to defend:

It is these institutions which make us a nation. Without our Crown, our Church,
our Universities, our great municipal and commercial corporations, our Magistracy, and its dependent scheme of provincial polity, the inhabitants of England,
instead of being a nation, would present only a mass of individuals governed by a
metropolis, whence an arbitrary senate would issue the stern decrees of its harsh
and heartless despotism. (181–2)

Here nationhood—that which gives England its 'national character'—is
something that intervenes between the Whigs' 'arbitrary senate', on the
one hand, and the people conceived as a 'mass of individuals' on the other.
Disraeli feared that senate and populace were headed for a disastrous
collision, akin to the French Revolution of 1789, unless the Tories, the
'really democratic party of England' (183), could come to the rescue.

   Nothing, then, could be more misleading than the simple theory of
the 'two nations' announced in Sybil by the popular radical Stephen
Morley—though, as often as not, it has been held to sum up Disraeli's
legacy as a novelist. In this famous and eloquent passage from the novel,
the young Charles Egremont has complacently remarked to two strangers
he encounters in the ruins of Marney Abbey that Queen Victoria reigns
over 'the greatest nation that ever existed':

'Which nation?' asked the younger stranger, 'for she reigns over two.... Two
nations; between whom there is no intercourse and no sympathy; who are as
ignorant of each other's habits, thoughts, and feelings, as if they were dwellers in
different zones, or inhabitants of different planets; who are formed by a different
breeding, are fed by a different food, are ordered by different manners, and are
not governed by the same laws.'
   'You speak of—' said Egremont, hesitatingly.
   'THE RICH AND THE POOR.'
   At this moment a sudden flush of rosy light, suffusing the grey ruins, indicated
that the sun had just fallen; and through a vacant arch that overlooked them,
alone in the resplendent sky, glittered the twilight star. The hour, the scene, the
solemn stillness and the softening beauty, repressed controversy, induced even
silence. The last words of the stranger lingered in the ear of Egremont; his
musing spirit was teeming with many thoughts, many emotions; when from the
Lady Chapel there rose the evening hymn to the Virgin. A single voice; but
tones of almost supernatural sweetness; tender and solemn, yet flexible and
thrilling.[47]

In Morley's outburst the two 'nations'—aristocracy and people or bourgeoisie and proletariat, it hardly matters—are segregated from one another as ominously as in the contemporary writings of Karl Marx. Morley's rhetoric draws upon Thomas Carlyle's social criticism in *Sartor Resartus*, *Chartism*, and *Past and Present*, rather than upon Disraeli's own writings. Egremont, at this point a political innocent, is learning about the depth of popular resentment from Morley, but Morley's vision is subtly undermined by a series of symbolic reminders of the three estates which, ultimately, make up one nation rather than two. The ruined abbey and the hymn to the Virgin link nineteenth-century class conflict to the splits in English Christianity going back to the Reformation: if the abbeys had not been ruined, Disraeli implies, there would be no such unbridgeable gap between rich and poor. The solemnity of the scene not only 'represses controversy' but points to a possible role both for the third estate, the clergy, and for the third volume of the trilogy Disraeli is writing. Meanwhile the figure of Queen Victoria reigning over a single but divided nation gives place to the 'single voice' of Sybil, the 'daughter of the people' who is (unknown to herself) a dispossessed aristocrat like one of Scott's protagonists. Metaphorically speaking, Disraeli's nun-like heroine hints at the potential reunification not only of the 'two nations' but of the three estates. Taken together, indeed, *Sybil* and *Tancred* seem to suggest that the bitter class divisions of the nineteenth century may prove a less intractable problem than the religious schisms embodied in England's identity as a Protestant nation.

We must wonder, then, why Disraeli's image of the 'two nations' became so resonant. In part this was due to the urgency of its historical context, in part to the repetition of a familiar fictional pattern. *Coningsby*, the first novel in the trilogy, had defined Carlyle's 'Condition of England Question' as the discrepancy between 'moral civilisation' and material wealth;[48] but *Sybil* portrays Chartism, the exploitation of the industrial workers, and the poverty caused by depression of trade in terms that would soon be echoed in the novels of Elizabeth Gaskell and Charles Kingsley. Disraeli's starving workers mount a plebeian insurrection that could be seen to presage a new Civil War. The rioters emerge from a kind of workers' republic ruled over by the despotic master-craftsman 'Bishop' Hatton, at Wodgate in the heart of the Black Country. Here there are no landlords, no churches, no large factories, no magistrates, no schools, and no political institutions, so that 'Labour reigns supreme' (203). It is the 'ugliest spot in England' (202). Even Stephen Morley is appalled by it. The plebeian insurrection soon collapses, however, and Wodgate is revealed as a plague-spot of anarchy and lawlessness rather than the capital of a separate 'nation'.

There are strong historical precedents for seeing England as having been divided into two 'nations' at earlier crises in its history, as Disraeli was well aware. There were the Puritan and Royalist Englands of the Civil War, which had given birth to the two-party system in which Disraeli was such a passionate partisan. Before the Civil War, there were the Catholic and Protestant Englands of the Reformation, and the Saxon and Norman Englands that Scott believed had persisted side by side after the Conquest. The novels of Disraeli's trilogy, especially *Sybil*, allude richly to each of these conflicts. The term 'Saxon', in particular, is used to evoke a cultural and racial stereotype that remains pertinent in the nineteenth century. In *Coningsby*, the manufacturer Oswald Millbank boasts of 'Saxon industry competing successfully with Norman manners' (165). His daughter Edith is the 'daughter of a Saxon', hence her Saxon name (162). In *Sybil* the preacher Aubrey St Lys possesses the 'beauty of the noble English blood', 'the Norman tempered by the Saxon' (140). Queen Victoria, on the other hand, is 'fair and serene, [with] the blood and beauty of the Saxon', and her historic task is to 'break the last link in the chain of Saxon thraldom' (67). Not only is Sybil herself shown reading Augustin Thierry's *History of the Conquest of England by the Normans* (1825), but her father, the Chartist Walter Gerard, insists upon its contemporary relevance: ' "It must interest all and all alike... for we are divided between the conquerors and the conquered" ' (213). Sybil has inherited her father's convictions that the gap between the classes is as impassable as the ancient gulf between Saxon and Norman, and that the people in the nineteenth century are as brutalized as Saxon peasants. Gerard glories in the notion that his forebears were 'peasants and the sons of peasants' (416), one of whom was a bowman at Agincourt. But Gerard is not in fact of peasant stock, and in Disraeli's fiction, we soon realize, no family pedigree is what it seems.

The supposedly ancient Norman families of the Egremonts and de Mowbrays in *Sybil* are impostors, the possessors of stolen lands and faked armorial bearings. The Egremonts owe their wealth to a 'confidential domestic' or upper servant under Henry VIII, who came in for a share of the great land-grab caused by the dissolution of the monasteries in the 1530s. They changed their name from Greymount to the pseudo-French Egremont and in the Civil War, 'pricked by their Norman blood' as Disraeli mockingly says, they fought as Royalists (35). (Fearing that the Stuarts might be planning to repossess the Church lands, they later sided with the Whigs.) Lord de Mowbray, who styles himself as a 'descendant of the first crusaders' (143), is an even more recent creation. The pseudo-Norman aristocracy is opposed by the Gerards, whose pseudo-Saxon pretensions Disraeli punctures a good deal more gently. Thanks to Walter Gerard's aristocratic appearance and manner, it is no real surprise that he eventually turns out to be both the descendant of a medieval abbot and the rightful Lord de Mowbray. Immediately before Sybil speaks of the English people and claims to be the 'daughter of their blood' (160) we are introduced to her dog Harold, 'a young bloodhound of the ancient breed, such as are now found but in a few old halls and granges in the north of England' (156). This pedigree pet with a royal Saxon name is the embodiment of true social instincts. He snarls at the pacifistic villain Stephen Morley and rushes to rescue Charles Egremont from Morley's clutches. (Gerard, by contrast, has no suspicions of Morley.) Morley, possibly the novel's only genuine Saxon, is guilty not only of political chicanery but of attempted rape and attempted murder.

If Harold instinctively knows the difference between the base Morley and the noble Egremont, Egremont too is something of a bloodhound, as is shown by the powerful attraction he feels towards both Gerard and his daughter. The plot of *Sybil* thus works to undermine both the 'two nations' theory and the notion that the modern rich and poor are the descendants of Normans and Saxons respectively. Both theories are, in effect, myths subscribed to by Disraeli's Chartists and radicals rather than expressions of his own political faith. Sybil herself is apparently a reader of *Ivanhoe* as well as of histories of the Norman Conquest. When Morley tries to blackmail her with promises to save her father in exchange for sexual favours, she retorts that ' "I have read of something of this sort … this bargaining of blood, and shall I call it love? But that was ever between the oppressor and the oppressed" ' (368). She is, then, the descendant of Rebecca in the hands of Bois-Guilbert.[49] Her name is that of a mysterious prophetess, and the fact that Disraeli never says who her mother was (she is simply the 'daughter of the people') might suggest a dark heroine in the Scott mode, but she is at best a light heroine in disguise—an 'embodiment of pure value', in one critic's words, and an aristocrat in love with Charles Egremont.[50] Inevitably she must lose her belief in the doctrine of class struggle. Disraeli's earliest readers were aware that the marriage plot of *Sybil* had not, in fact, unified the two nations; it was meant, instead, to undermine the 'two nations' theory.[51] Sybil rejects Morley for Charles Egremont because she no longer views the split between the rich and poor in the light of 'that sentiment of unmingled hate and scorn which she associated with Norman conquerors and feudal laws' (349–50). She believes that the English nation can be saved (even as its class divisions are perpetuated) by one-nation Toryism.

From *Vivian Grey* to *Tancred*: Aristocracy and Empire

Disraeli, like Bulwer-Lytton, started out as a member of the so-called 'silver fork' school of novelists of the English upper class and fashionable metropolitan life. But he also looked passionately beyond England. After travelling to the Middle East he produced a prose version of the Byronic Grand Tour in his novel *Contarini Fleming* (1832). *Alroy* (1833) is a romance, complete with historical notes modelled on Scott's, in which a twelfth-century Jewish prince briefly creates a Middle Eastern empire. With the hero's pilgrimage to Jerusalem in *Tancred*, the third volume of the 'Young England' trilogy, Disraeli went beyond Byronic travel fiction to write—and, indeed, to invent—the political romance of nineteenth-century British imperialism.

Aristocratic settings are commonplace in the Gothic romance and even in the Jacobin novelists of the 1790s. Fielding, Smollett, and Richardson before *Sir Charles Grandison* rarely moved higher than the gentry, but the novels of Burney, Edgeworth, Charlotte Smith, and their contemporaries had depicted lords and baronets in ever-increasing numbers. With the French Revolution, the ethos and plight of the aristocracy came to the fore as the traditional social structure was overturned. The abolition of hereditary titles in France causes alarm in the breast of Smith's Miss Fairfax, in *Desmond* (1792): ' "Only suppose the English mob were to get such a notion, and...begin the same sort of thing here!" '[52] But the English mob never did get such a notion. Instead, the 'silver fork' fiction that arose after the victory of Waterloo and the restoration of the Bourbon monarchy showed a parvenu fascination with the smallest details of manners and dress, encouraging a slavish worship of aristocratic opulence. Disraeli's first novel, *Vivian Grey* (1826), told its readers that in order to enter high society, 'a man must either have blood, a million, or a genius'.[53] This was followed by *The Young Duke* (1829), a piece of fiction memorably deflated by Disraeli's father Isaac, who is said to have asked, ' "What does Ben know of dukes?" '[54] Vivian Grey nurses a Dick Whittington-like ambition, and when asked what he aims to become, he replies airily, ' "Oh! Lord Mayor of London, I suppose" ' (74). He turns to the study of politics, and wins the confidence of the Marquis of Carabas whom he persuades to head a parliamentary coalition grandly called 'The New Union'. But Vivian is a political impostor, and the second half of the novel sends him, unmasked and disgraced, into European exile. The Duke of St James's in *The Young Duke*, by contrast, is shown spending, gambling, and womanizing at great length before belatedly developing a social conscience. His maiden speech in the House of Lords, portrayed as the testament of a born-again idealist, is in favour of Catholic Emancipation. Disraeli never comments on the timeliness of his conversion to this cause, which comes at the height of his pecuniary embarrassments caused partly by the arrears of rent on his Irish estates.

In *Vivian Grey* Disraeli had outlined the formula for the fashionable novel of the time: 'three volumes, one half of which contain the adventures of a young gentleman in the country, and the other volume and a half the adventures of the same young gentleman in the metropolis' (24). For 'the country' Disraeli tends to substitute a portrayal of his young gentlemen first of all at boarding school, and then as participants in country weekends or shooting-season holidays. Nevertheless, each of his novels briefly alludes to the motif of the rural idyll which plays a significant role in *Coningsby* and *Sybil*. Vivian early displays his unscrupulous adroitness by faking Washington Irving's autograph at a young lady's request; later he is shown visiting a country cottage, 'the very model of the abode of an English husbandman' (55), when it has just been stripped by the bailiffs. Ruined abbeys provide the setting for emotional scenes in *The Young Duke* and *Contarini Fleming* as well as in *Sybil*. In the 'Young England' trilogy Disraeli varies his fiction of young politicians on the make with pictures of agricultural distress and of model industrial settlements framed by a pastoral landscape.

Coningsby marks the perfection of the political plot that Disraeli had begun to devise in *Vivian Grey* and would reuse in *Sybil*. The emergence of the young hero's capacity for leadership, his admission into the counsels of the aristocracy, his meeting with a powerful stranger, and his break with his political mentor are all part of the formula. In *Coningsby* and *Sybil* this plot becomes the vehicle for Disraeli to expound his political ideas and to show the energies of heroic youth turning to the cause of national relief and regeneration. Formally the plot is concerned with the maturation of the young hero, ending in a symbolic marriage; in fact, prematurity is the essential feature of Disraeli's novels, and the spiritual direction of 'Young England' remains as uncertain as that of Vivian and the Duke of St James's. The reappearance of Harry Coningsby and

Charles Egremont as married young politicians in *Tancred* is both disconcerting and disillusioning, since there is little or nothing to show that they have become potential future statesmen rather than Westminster lobby-fodder like the backstairs fixers Rigby, Tadpole, and Taper. Rigby, the author of 'slashing articles' and the man employed 'to do the dirty work' in *Coningsby*, is a man 'destitute of all imagination and noble sentiment' (10, 410). Coningsby, Egremont, and Tancred have imagination and noble sentiment in abundance, but its practical application remains entirely a matter of faith.

Much of the drama of *Coningsby* lies in the protagonist's struggle with his grandfather Lord Monmouth, a Regency buck who prefers actresses and prostitutes to fashionable society, and lives for preference in southern Italy rather than in his grand English mansions. But Monmouth, a cold, distant tyrant who greets his schoolboy grandson with a bow such as 'Louis Quatorze might have bestowed on the ambassador of the United Provinces' (18), cannot bear to relinquish his political power at home. Though a Tory, he embodies all the arrogance of Disraeli's 'Venetian' Whigs. His eventual decision to disinherit Coningsby arises from a family feud of which Coningsby had his first inklings when he saw his mother's portrait hanging in the house of the Whig manufacturer Oswald Millbank. (Dickens uses the same device of the mother's portrait discovered in a strange house in *Oliver Twist* and *Bleak House*.) Coningsby breaks with his grandfather by refusing to stand against Millbank, who is the sitting MP for the Darlford constituency where the Tory nomination is in Monmouth's gift. After Monmouth's death, his now disinherited grandson is free both to marry Edith Millbank and to succeed her father as Darlford's MP. Benefiting from a combination of good luck and sacrificial benevolence as miraculous as anything in Scott, Coningsby then regains his inheritance thanks to the generosity of Lord Monmouth's natural daughter.

We see Coningsby visiting his contemporaries in their various country houses, all of which make a favourable contrast with the soulless luxury of Lord Monmouth's country seat. The excursion to Eustace Lyle's estate of St Geneviève seems to allude to the visit to Sotherton in *Mansfield Park*, though Disraeli shows none of Austen's mastery of dramatic effect. St Geneviève was a Royalist house besieged by the Parliamentary forces in 1643, but Lyle, a Roman Catholic, reverts to a much earlier age, attempting to reconstruct feudal social relationships by means of a ceremonial almsgiving two days a week. Later in the novel Coningsby spends a merry Christmas at St Geneviève, a brief episode heavily reminiscent of

Bracebridge Hall. But this backward-looking paradise is set against a very different rural idyll, the model industrial settlement of Oswald Millbank.

Travelling across a Sherwood-like ancient forest, Coningsby meets the mysterious horseman Sidonia, who pronounces that ' "The Age of Ruins is past. Have you seen Manchester?" ' (113). Our hero arrives in the northern metropolis only to be told by a mill-owner that ' "Manchester is a dead letter" ' (155), and that he should see Millbank instead. Millbank is not a city but an industrial village in a 'green and silent valley' which remains unpolluted since Oswald Millbank ('Millbank of Millbank') uses an unspecified process to 'consume his own smoke' (158, 161). But Millbank is not satisfied with his soundless and odourless hive of industry surrounded by 'broad plains', 'green lanes', and 'running streams' (169), since he has also bought a Tudor mansion at Hellingsley, next door to Coningsby Castle, which in its lush Englishness pointedly recalls the world of the *Sketch Book* and Jane Austen's Donwell Abbey. As Disraeli writes, 'The beautiful light of summer had never shone on a scene and surrounding landscape which recalled happier images of English nature, and better recollections of English manners, than that to which we would now introduce our readers' (354). Eton, Westminster, Coningsby Castle, St Geneviève, Manchester, Millbank, Hellingsley: the England of *Coningsby* unfolds like one of Washington Irving's tourist itineraries, although the itinerary extends from the playgrounds of the upper classes to the manufacturing districts of Lancashire and the West Midlands.

These districts are no less compelling for being, as Lady Marney observes in *Sybil*, 'very disagreeable' (105). Disraeli's technique in *Sybil* is one of pastoral inflation followed by deflation. From Lord Marney's country seat he takes us upstream past the Abbey farm and Abbey mill (reminiscent of Donwell in *Emma* with its Abbey-Mill Farm) to the deserted ruins where Egremont meets Sybil and her companions; but he also takes us downstream to the town of Marney. The Abbey farm is the scene of a recent rick-burning, which Lord Marney is determined to regard as being purely accidental. (Mary Mitford's tale of 'The Incendiary' gives precisely the explanation of a rick-burning incident that Lord Marney would have wanted to hear.) The rick-burning is evidently an act of sabotage and the perpetrators have most likely come from the town. Marney provokes Disraeli's most openly rhetorical assault on the 'rural idyll' convention:

The situation of the rural town of Marney was one of the most delightful easily to be imagined. In a spreading dale, contiguous to the margin of a clear and lively stream, surrounded by meadows and gardens, and backed by lofty hills, undulating and richly wooded, the traveller on the opposite heights of the dale would often stop to admire the merry prospect, that recalled to him the traditional epithet of his country.

Beautiful illusion! For behind that laughing landscape, penury and disease fed upon the vitals of a miserable population! (80)

Does Charles Egremont carry within him the solution to the people's misery? Despite his quarrels with Lord Marney, his elder brother, he becomes MP for the family borough (which is at Marbury, not Marney). Not once is this apostle of social welfare shown visiting his constituency or taking any interest in the people who regularly re-elect him to Parliament. Instead, he studies social conditions in Mowedale, where Walter Gerard is employed at a model factory which, in its rural setting, is another Millbank. When Egremont eventually makes a 'beautiful speech' in the Commons on the subject of the 1839 Chartist petition, Sybil congratulates him but adds that ' "They will listen to you, they will cheer you, but they will never follow you" ' (354). This is said before her conversion to Egremont's 'one-nation' outlook, but it is a convincing prophecy which only a generously inclined and biographically minded reader is likely to dismiss. However honourable and sympathetic a character, Charles Egremont is no Benjamin Disraeli.

In any case, Disraeli's aristocratic young Tories lack the most crucial element in his own identity—his Jewishness. The banker Sidonia (whose name itself suggests 'Disraeli'[55]) serves as a cosmopolitan Jewish mentor for the 'Young England' heroes. Sidonia stems from an old Spanish family that financed the Peninsular War and the Waterloo campaign, he is master of the learning of every nation, and he holds opinions that Disraeli may have found too radical for his Tory heroes. In *Coningsby* he is described as a specialist in the 'secret history of the world', a history in which, so he claims, 'the Jewish mind exercises a vast influence' (215, 246). Although he sends Harry Coningsby to Manchester, he is also close to the 'Venetian' Lord Monmouth, whose executor he becomes. His presence in *Coningsby* means that the novel cannot just be concerned with England's Saxon and Norman legacy, any more than *Ivanhoe* was. If the pampered Disraeli hero is a potential English statesman, Sidonia stands for the necessary link between national governance and imperial politics. But his presence in *Coningsby* is largely symbolic,[56] and he does not reappear until *Tancred*, where he supports the hero's Middle Eastern venture.

In his role as political talent-spotter Sidonia sees that Tancred, though 'as ignorant of the world as a young monk', possesses 'all the latent qualities which in future would qualify him to control society', and he introduces Tancred to Egremont.[57] It is through Sidonia's eyes that we are encouraged to see Coningsby (who briefly studies for the Bar) as a potential Lord Chancellor, Egremont as a future prime minister, and Tancred as a future archbishop. But Sidonia's function is also to point his young admirers in a particular direction, as when he tells Tancred (who is obsessed with the idea of a religious pilgrimage) that ' "All is race; there is no other truth" ' (149).

In *Sybil*, where Sidonia is absent, the 'meeting with the stranger' is the scene at the ruined abbey already discussed. It is tempting to imagine that Sybil, the 'Saxon Rebecca',[58] has, if not Semitic, at least Mediterranean connotations: she is, after all, a Catholic convert whose nun-like beauty is never described as 'Saxon'. But this only emphasizes the mystery of her parentage, since as we have seen she is motherless. Walter Gerard laments that the 'daughter of the people' ' "cannot look to marriage: no man that she could marry would be worthy of her" ' (347). As a worshipper of the Virgin whose name is inherited from her father's, not her mother's 'race' (215), she herself seems to be almost of virgin birth. Disraeli could have solved the mystery of Sybil's own 'worth' by providing her with a foreign mother, as George Eliot would later do for Daniel Deronda. Instead, it is given to Disraeli's third hero, Tancred, to fall in love with a Jewess who represents the 'perfection of oriental beauty' (187–8).

Sidonia makes no attempt to initiate the Little Englander Harry Coningsby into the 'secret history of the world' of which he is master. But he seeks to awaken imperial ambitions in Tancred, Lord Montacute, who turns down a seat in Parliament in order to retrace the steps of his ancestor who was a Crusader. (The Montacutes are, apparently, of genuine Norman blood.) The novel's subtitle, 'The New Crusade', suggests that his mission to the Holy Land might be an imperial adventure in the grand tradition of Napoleon's opening-up of Egypt—a suggestion implied, if also burlesqued, by the presence in the opening pages of a French ex-army chef with the 'grand air of the Imperial kitchen' (6). But Tancred's actual deeds in the East bear little relation to his noble ambitions. The structure of the 'Young England' trilogy is eventually undermined by its third hero, who travels in search of a new Jerusalem which he finds but does not conquer.

The explicit aim of his pilgrimage is to seek religious enlightenment and a cure for Victorian England's spiritual blindness. Such a cure must be sought, he believes, in the Bible lands, and its basis is the idea of Hebrao-Christian unity that had earlier been preached in *Sybil* by the

Anglo-Catholic Aubrey St Lys. Tancred eventually experiences a religious revelation, not at the Church of the Holy Sepulchre in Jerusalem (with its exclusively Christian associations) but on Mount Sinai. Here, feverish from a recent battle-wound, he is spoken to by an angel. He never returns to the Anglican communion, and his mission to reunite all the 'people of the Book', including Jews and Muslims, must have posed a formidable challenge even to the broadest of Broad Churches. But the fact that he is engaged on something more than a merely spiritual pilgrimage is evident to Sidonia and his Eastern associates, if not to Tancred himself. Sidonia views it as an attempt to penetrate the 'great Asian mystery' (124), and Tancred's friend the Emir Fakredeen calls it a 'religious-politico-military adventure' (439)—and, he might have added, an erotic adventure as well.

In Jerusalem everyone assumes that the young tourist is on a diplomatic mission, if not a British spy. Among the Bedouin, he becomes known as Queen Victoria's brother. He is captured and imprisoned in the hope that his ransom will pay for English rifles to fight against the Turks, and then he is taken to Lebanon to preside over an alliance between Muslims and Maronite Christians. For reasons never wholly clear, he persuades Fakredeen to accompany him to the mountain redoubt of the warlike Ansarey, the last surviving worshippers of the ancient Greek pantheon ruled over by the exotic Queen Astarte. Here the Queen falls in love with Tancred, who finds himself organizing her defences against the Turkish army sent to free Eva, her captive, with whom he himself is in love. Fakredeen presents himself as the ally of Tancred, Astarte, and Eva, and apparently betrays all three; but finally Fakredeen, Tancred, and Eva are reunited. No wonder the confused hero continues to ask himself 'Why was he there? Why was he, the child of a northern isle, in the heart of the Stony Arabia ... ?'(264).

In the novel's final scene, Eva's challenge to Tancred seems to contain Disraeli's summing-up of his hero's hectic odyssey:

'Your feelings cannot be what they were before all this happened; when you thought only of a divine cause, of stars, of angels, and of our peculiar and gifted land. No, no; now it is all mixed up with intrigue, with politics, and management, and baffled schemes, and cunning arts of men. You may be, you are, free from all this, but your faith is not the same. You no longer believe in Arabia.' (485)

Tancred responds by making passionate love to Eva and saying that he has 'no kindred, no country' (486), a disavowal that is openly mocked when, in the novel's last line—and in a remarkable contrast to the upbeat endings of *Coningsby* and *Sybil*—we hear that his parents have just

arrived in Jerusalem.[59] Will he return with them to England? Have they
come to Jerusalem as pilgrims, tourists, or (as at least one recent critic
assumes) as imperial pro-consuls?[60] Does Disraeli mean to imply a symbolic marriage between the Christian hero and the Jewess? Will love or
filial obedience triumph? The novelist will not say.[61] Eva, who has all
along been engaged to her cousin, remains ambiguous and noncommittal,
while Tancred is still immature, unfulfilled, and possibly in leading-
strings to his provincial English origins. His new crusade, in Michael
Ragussis's words, 'can look like either the discovery of an ancient
genealogy or the renunciation and betrayal of European and Christian
values'.[62] Disraeli's later novel *Lothair* (1870) sends its hero to Jerusalem
on an equally muddled and puzzling quest.

Nevertheless, Tancred is clearly the precursor of British imperial
expansion. In *Alroy* Disraeli's twelfth-century hero had voiced the ideal
of a universal empire, which 'must not be founded on sectarian prejudices
and exclusive rights'.[63] Tancred's ecumenical quest for Hebrao-Christian
unity fits in with the political requirements of empire. Eva, who believes
that 'Asia and the North' must always be at war, is shown as being
adamantly opposed to the extension of European colonialism to the
Middle East (217); but probably she is another yielding heroine like Sybil,
whose opposition to sexual union and political alliance with the
Disraelian hero is stated only to be overcome. When her Machiavellian
stepbrother Fakredeen shows Tancred the ruined city of Petra (the last
vestige of an ancient empire), he tries to tempt Disraeli's hero with the
vision of an Asian Empire ruled over by Queen Victoria. Here we have
something like Disraeli's own ambition as the future world statesman
who would have Victoria declared Empress of India:

'[T]he game is in our hands, if we have energy. There is a combination which
would entirely change the whole face of the world, and bring back Empire to the
East. . . . Let the Queen of the English collect a great fleet, let her stow away all her
treasure, bullion, gold plate, and precious arms; be accompanied by all her court
and chief people, and transfer the seat of her empire from London to Delhi. There
she will find an immense empire ready-made, a firstrate army, and a large rev-
enue. In the meantime I will arrange with Mehemet Ali. He shall have Bagdad and
Mesopotamia, and pour the Bedoueen cavalry into Persia. I will take care of Syria
and Asia Minor. The only way to manage the Affghans is by Persia and the Arabs.
We will acknowledge the Empress of India as our suzerain, and secure for her the
Levantine coast. If she like, she shall have Alexandria as she now has Malta: it
could be arranged. Your queen is young; she has an *avenir*. Aberdeen and Sir Peel
will never give her this advice; their habits are formed. They are too old, too
rusés.' (262–3)

Folie de grandeur is mixed here with a startling premonition of the 'Great Game' of Asian imperialism that would be played later in the century by Britain and Russia, and in our time by the United States. The passage seems less like the thoughts of Fakredeen or Tancred than a secret message from Disraeli to the Queen whom he doubtless thought of as one of his readers. He then sends Tancred and Fakredeen to the court of Astarte, who is a kind of displaced Queen Victoria. As a motif of imperial romance this would be repeated much later in the century, and at a more popular level, by H. Rider Haggard in *King Solomon's Mines* (1886) and *She* (1887). The ending of *Tancred* is cryptic and unsatisfactory because Disraeli can neither commit his hero to the 'great Asian mystery'—which, as we shall see later in *Daniel Deronda* and Kipling's *Kim*, would involve becoming a kind of double agent and losing his national identity—nor can he bring him back to the English world of Coningsby and Egremont.

Scott and Disraeli are both flawed novelists, but their Romantic Toryism had a lasting impact on the English novel's representation of national identity. The Romantic Tory begins by idealizing such 'true' or 'native' English qualities as a green and temperate English landscape, a feudal aristocracy and monarchy, or a sturdy Saxon peasantry. But these domestic idylls offer too little to the Romantic imagination, which must soon look for further fields to conquer. Hence the appeal of the overseas empire. The materials of romance, as Hazlitt observed, are once again sought outside England. The portrayal of the monarch—in Disraeli's case, the invisible Queen Victoria—is replaced by an exotic, erotic, and highly susceptible foreign queen. But imperial romance is a more complex process than the simple negation of Englishness that was found in the Gothic novelists. Will the Englishman abroad take part in the construction of a greater England, or will he (it is invariably he) become engulfed by the equivalent of Disraeli's Asiatic, Semitic mystery? The later classics of imperial fiction such as Kipling's *Kim* and Forster's *A Passage to India* explore this conflict of identity which was already anticipated in Disraeli's novels.

Tory Daughters and the Politics of Marriage: Jane Austen, Charlotte Brontë, and Elizabeth Gaskell

I N *Marriage* (1818) by the Scottish novelist Susan Ferrier, Lord Courtland demands that his daughter should make a traditional aristocratic marriage:

'She shall marry for the purpose for which matrimony was ordained amongst people of birth—that is, for the aggrandisement of her family, the extending of their political influence—for becoming, in short, the depository of their mutual interest. These are the only purposes for which persons of rank ever think of marriage.'[1]

Since this is a novel, we may be sure that Lord Courtland will be disappointed. The idea that young lovers are bound to defy social convention is one of the generic requirements of fictional romance, but the novels of Jane Austen and her contemporaries such as Maria Edgeworth and Susan Ferrier reflect specific anxieties about marriage in the early nineteenth century. The English aristocracy, having seen the flower of the French nobility sent to the guillotine in the Terror, was determined to defend its political power and to ensure its own survival. At the same time, the middle-class pattern of companionate marriage was becoming increasingly dominant, and novels did much to propagate this middle-class ideal.[2]

Although the novel and drama throughout history can be taken as advocating love matches and companionate marriage, such marriages in fiction invariably have an allegorical dimension. If literature asserts the right of two individuals to choose one another freely, it also tends to reveal the special appropriateness and poetic justice of the choices they make. Shakespeare's *Romeo and Juliet* is not merely an individual love tragedy; it tells us that family vendettas are evil, and would have done so even if the lovers had survived and ended happily. Aristocratic marriage is arranged, negotiated, and authorized, at least by the bride's parents;

fictional marriages involve either filial rebellion or, at the very least, the exercise of independent judgement by the hero and heroine. But the fact that novel heroines usually marry for love does not prevent these marriages from bearing a political as well as a moral significance. The normal pattern is one in which selfish and short-sighted family interests are set against the wider social interests that the lovers embody and the novelist implicitly or explicitly endorses.

Is there a 'national interest' in marriage? Before the Victorian period, the politics of marriage in English fiction mainly reflect internal divisions within the aristocracy and gentry. There were few successors to *Pamela*, in which the cavalier Mr B is redeemed by marrying his Puritanical serving-maid. Clarissa's rebellion is against a caste marriage dictated by the 'family fault', the Harlowes' greed to acquire more land. In *Tom Jones* Squire Western is a landed gentleman anxious to enlarge his estate and willing, therefore, to marry his daughter to Mr Allworthy's heir whoever that heir may be. Legal and economic changes in the eighteenth century gave increasing importance to the concentration and augmentation of landed estates.[3] The most successful practitioners of aristocratic marriage as recommended by Lord Courtland were perceived as being the ruling Whig dynasties, the 'small knot of great families' later to be lampooned by Disraeli.

For all their sympathies with the French Revolution, the English 'Jacobin' novelists of the 1790s such as Charlotte Smith, Thomas Holcroft, and Robert Bage produced parables of a reformed aristocracy rather than visions of an aristocracy overthrown by the people. In Smith's *The Old Manor House*, Orlando's marriage to Monimia and his inheritance of Rayland Hall represent the renewal of the estate which gives the book its title. Thomas Holcroft's *Anna St Ives* (1792) shows the heroine, a baronet's daughter, rejecting an arranged marriage with Coke Clifton, an unscrupulous libertine, who (as she complains) 'acts more from the love of his rank and family, that is of himself, than of me'.[4] Her preference is for the lower-class radical Frank Henley, a 'true liberty boy' for whom (in Clifton's colourful idiom) a 'Lord is a merry andrew', and 'a Duke a jack pudding' (94). But Anna refuses to disobey her father by eloping with Henley, and shoulders the burden of Clifton's moral rehabilitation, a task in which she finally succeeds. The hero of Robert Bage's *Hermsprong* (1796), by contrast, is a mysterious American republican, the owner of 60,000 acres on the Potomac, whose stay in England leads to suspicions that he is a Jacobin and a French spy. His chosen enemy is the tyrannical mine-owner Lord Grondale, who has him charged with sedition. All too predictably, Hermsprong turns out to be the rightful Lord Grondale. He marries his cousin and settles in England as a reformed, radical lord with a popular appeal that augurs well for the maintenance of the class system.

The Jacobin writers were without aristocratic connections, although their novels tend to suggest that an enlightened aristocracy could still form the backbone of the English nation. Charlotte Smith was born into the minor gentry and married a City merchant. Holcroft had worked as an actor, shoemaker, and stable boy, while Bage was a Quaker factory-owner. Jane Austen, who possessed a copy of *Hermsprong*,[5] came from a solidly genteel background and was strongly anti-Jacobin. Her characters are far more ill at ease in fashionable society than those of the Jacobin novelists whose radical politics she so disliked. The Jacobins remembered the anti-Royalist origins of the Whig party and dreamed of an alliance between radicals and reformed Whig aristocrats. For Austen, however, the eighteenth-century division between the Tory country gentry and the ruling Whig aristocracy was a deeply personal matter.

Austen has been described as the 'Tory daughter of a quiet Tory parson', and her novels as 'Tory pastorals'.[6] Although party names never appear in her fiction, the stinging portrayal of an aristocratic *grande dame* such as Lady Catherine de Bourgh implicitly involves party politics. Austen was a daughter of the clergy and a partisan of the devout, patriotic lower gentry, while Charlotte Brontë, who differs from her in so many respects, resembles her in being a Tory clergyman's daughter. Austen's Catherine Morland and Brontë's Caroline Helstone are the daughters of country parsons, as is Margaret Hale at the beginning of Elizabeth Gaskell's *North and South* (1855). Gaskell, Charlotte Brontë's friend and biographer, was the daughter of a Unitarian minister.

Austen's and Brontë's novels reflect their authors' rural and Anglican backgrounds in their concern with patriotism, paternalism, pastoralism, and the moral accountability of the individual. Patriotism is a stronger emotion in Austen and Brontë than in most English women novelists before or since. Austen lived through the Napoleonic Wars and had brothers in the navy; Charlotte Brontë, born in 1816, reflects some of the chauvinistic prejudices of a generation growing up in the aftermath of a successful war. There was an intense loyalist reaction to the French Revolution and the threat posed by Napoleon's armies, 'orchestrated by the rich', as one historian writes, but spreading to all classes.[7] Jacobin novelists like Charlotte Smith tried to warn their readers against the dangers of nationalism, balancing England against France and Royalism against republicanism. The heroine of Smith's *Marchmont* studies

English history and concludes that, for one who has gone beyond the abridged histories written for children, since the reign of Elizabeth I 'there is hardly an interval that can be read with pleasure'.[8] Jane Austen's outspokenly Royalist teenage *History of England*, admittedly a burlesque, reveals the 'strong political opinions' which later mellowed into her family's moderate Toryism.[9] Charlotte Brontë, the daughter of an Irish father and a Cornish mother, idolized the Anglo-Irish Duke of Wellington, the victor of Waterloo who later became Tory prime minister. Wellington and his sons are the central figures of the fantasy world of the Glass Town (later Angria) created by Charlotte and her brother Branwell in their youth. At the age of 13 Charlotte copied out Walter Scott's tribute to Wellington in his *Life of Napoleon Bonaparte*, adding the following exclamation: 'If he saved England in that hour of tremendous perils, shall he not save her again?'[10] The Victorian critic Leslie Stephen saw Charlotte Brontë as a typical example of the 'patriotism of the steeple'.[11]

As the phrase implies, the Church of England parson had a recognized duty to support the monarchy and the ruling class, and (at least in times of crisis) to preach patriotism and social obedience to his flock. Patriotism went with paternalism, the clergyman's duty to oversee the lives of his congregation and to act as its spiritual father. The priest's personal authority was also vested by proxy in his family—primarily his wife, but also his daughter. 'Clergyman's wife' is the role that the fashionable Mary Crawford in *Mansfield Park* will do almost anything to avoid, both in the play of *Lovers' Vows* and in reality. In *North and South*, Margaret Hale, returning from the metropolis to her father's parish of Helstone in the New Forest, anticipates the 'delight of filling the important post of only daughter in Helstone parsonage'.[12] The social standing and duties of a clerical family were taken very seriously by Victorian readers. The paternalism of the clergy was pastoral in two senses of the word: not merely caring and guiding, but, for these early nineteenth-century novelists, also essentially rural. Edmund Bertram ardently wishes for a country living, disregarding Mary Crawford's hints that it would be more suitable to become a celebrated preacher in a large town. Jane Austen was a child of Steventon Rectory, Charlotte Brontë of Haworth Parsonage, both of which have come to represent country idylls of a sort, though in very different kinds of rural landscape. Helstone in *North and South*, which Margaret makes sound 'like a village in a tale rather than in real life', is 'one of the most out-of-the-way places in England' (9, 17). Margaret also likens it to a 'village . . . in one of Tennyson's poems' (10), reminding us not only of the poetic tradition of the rural idyll but of Tennyson's experience as the son of a Lincolnshire rector. The word 'provincial' seems apt for the country villages of Austen, Brontë, and Gaskell (and also of Mary Russell Mitford), although provincialism as a geographical concept only gradually came to the fore in nineteenth-century fiction. The Dashwood family's move to Devonshire is the principal early event in *Sense and Sensibility* (1811), but the West Country setting has no impact on the novel's universalizing title or on its concern (like *Pride and Prejudice*) with 'truths universally acknowledged'. The case is very different with the Hales' move from deepest Hampshire to blackest 'Darkshire' (industrial Lancashire) in *North and South*, a novel written half a century later which has English provincial geography inscribed in its very title.

Traditionally the Church was a vocation open to the younger sons of the landed gentry. Members of the clergy were Oxford or Cambridge graduates, but increasingly the clergy formed a separate caste, recognizably genteel but often with very tenuous links to the owners of land. As eighteenth-century laxity gave way to nineteenth-century evangelical piety, there was a growing mental alienation between the parson and the lord of the manor. The clergyman's life came to be associated with genteel poverty and a lack of ruling-class privilege. A clergyman with marriageable daughters might find himself considerably embarrassed unless his daughters could themselves marry clergymen. Jane Austen remained single, Charlotte Brontë eventually married the Reverend Arthur Nicholls, and Elizabeth's Gaskell's husband was, like her father, a Unitarian minister.

The English courtship novel, with its strong appeal for female writers and readers, reflects the tension between the traditional definition of womanhood in terms of the marriage market, and women's demand for moral independence and self-respect. That marriage is a kind of market is rarely forgotten in these novels. A gentleman, it is assumed, must prefer a rich bride to a poor one, while for women a freely chosen marriage partner can bring about a dramatic fall in social status and family prospects. Jane Eyre's grandfather cuts her mother off without a shilling because of her impolitic marriage to Mr Eyre, a poor curate in a large manufacturing town; this is why, orphaned in early childhood, Jane is brought up as a despised outcast in the home of her well-to-do relations. Catherine Morland in *Northanger Abbey* is a clergyman's daughter who is mistaken for a rich heiress during her visit to Bath because she enjoys the Allens' patronage; when her real situation is discovered, she is immediately ostracized by her suitor's family. Margaret Hale in *North and South* is brought up by her Aunt Shaw in fashionable Harley Street, where she is expected to contract an advantageous marriage. Once she has found a wealthy suitor, however, the clergyman's daughter must remain on her guard. Jane Eyre is saved at the last minute from a bigamous marriage, and Catherine Morland must come to terms with her tyrannical father-in-law. The situation turns to tragedy in George Eliot's *Daniel Deronda* (1876), where Gwendolen Harleth, a poor clergyman's niece, is urged by her uncle to marry Henleigh Grandcourt, the heir of a family of Whig grandees. The name Grandcourt, an ironic echo of Richardson's Sir Charles Grandison, represents the collapse of the ideal of the perfect English gentleman: perfect in appearance, he is, as we quickly realize, rotten to the core, and he already has a clutch of illegitimate offspring. But in *Daniel Deronda*, as in the courtship novels of Austen, Brontë, and Gaskell, the focus is on the psychology of the heroine who emerges from a background of genteel poverty. For all their individual differences, these heroines resemble one another in being outside the charmed circle from which aristocratic brides are chosen. They have no obvious dynastic responsibilities, and the marital expectations that have been formed about them are of the vaguest. They are, therefore, relatively free, and conscious of their freedom; and, coming from staunch Protestant backgrounds, they possess a moral conscience and a desire to take personal responsibility for their own lives. The aim of the fictional plot in the courtship novel is not simply to portray the heroine's growth towards self-fulfilment and a settled happiness. The happy ending translates her moral assets into material ones, suggesting that—in fiction at least—virtue has its earthly reward.

In its simplest form, the happy ending of the courtship plot rewards the most morally deserving pair of lovers while thwarting all rival claimants. The politics of the happy ending depends upon its relationship to the conventional hierarchy of wealth and breeding. Most often, as we have already seen, the established social power is unexpectedly reaffirmed while the aristocracy is revitalized by an infusion of social responsibility and Christian virtue—the typical dowry, as it were, of a clergyman's daughter, even though the latter may be (like Jane Eyre) an heiress in disguise. Novelists like Austen and Charlotte Brontë lead us through romantic complications, intricate false alarms, and delicate misunder-standings to an endorsement of Tory England.

Jane Austen's Lessons in Englishness

Catherine Morland is a young girl bored with her parents—'plain matter-of-fact people'[13]—and disappointed with life in the rectory. She turns, instead, to the Gothic fiction of Ann Radcliffe and her successors, dreaming of sensational and romantic incidents in foreign settings. When she leaves her quiet country village for fashionable Bath, she laments that the journey is made in 'uneventful safety' with no highway robbers to enliven the route (6). From Bath she goes on, at Henry Tilney's invitation, to his family home of Northanger Abbey, described as 'one of the finest old places in England' (114); but she experiences Northanger as an exotic Gothic mansion of the kind she has read about in *The Myseries of Udolpho* and its imitators such as *Castle of Wolfenbach*, *Necromancer of the Black Forest*, and *Orphan of the Rhine*. When Henry Tilney learns of her suspicion that unspeakable atrocities are hidden at Northanger, he issues a magisterial rebuke, telling her, in effect, that she is lacking in patriotism as well as in good sense. She has forgotten her own identity:

'Dear Miss Morland, consider the dreadful nature of the suspicions you have entertained. What have you been judging from? Remember the country and the age in which we live. Remember that we are English, that we are Christians. Consult your own understanding, your own sense of the probable, your observation of what is passing around you—Does our education prepare us for such atrocities? Do our laws connive at them? Could they be perpetrated without being known, in a country like this, where social and literary intercourse is on such a footing; where every man is surrounded by a neighbourhood of voluntary spies and where roads and newspapers lay everything open?' (163)

Who, then, are the Tilneys? At Bath, Catherine is too inexperienced to be certain about them, but she, and we, learn a good deal from her selfish, scheming friend Isabella Thorpe and her brother. When Catherine believes herself to have been rebuffed by the Tilneys, Isabella leaps in to denounce them: 'It was all pride, pride, insufferable haughtiness and pride! She had long suspected the family to be very high, and this made it certain' (103). Similar feelings are expressed in almost all Austen's novels, suggesting the author's personal investment in this standard complaint against the wealthy and powerful. But the Thorpes also have a strong desire to be noticed by the Tilneys, thanks to Isabella's opinion that '"after all that romancers may say, there is no doing without money"' (116). John Thorpe, who calls General Tilney '"A very fine fellow; as rich as a Jew"' (76), cultivates his acquaintance over the billiard table. Since he aims to marry Catherine himself, he fills the General's ear with tales of her supposed wealth. General Tilney then invites her to Northanger, and encourages her interest in his son Henry.

The General boasts that he is the owner of 'as considerable a landed property as any private man in the county' (143). (Here the phrase 'private man' denotes that he is a commoner, not a member of the peerage, though it strongly hints that a peerage is what he deserves.) He stays up late at night poring over political pamphlets, being deeply concerned with national affairs. Henry, too, launches into a 'short disquisition on the state of the nation', presumably modelled on his father's views, but as his hearers are young women he finds it is a short step from politics to silence (90). There is a certain contradiction between the urgency of the General's pamphlets and Henry's complacency, in his rebuke to Catherine, about the liberty and benevolence enjoyed by the English people.

The question of Henry's credibility is of some moment in the novel, since—mistaken though Catherine was in concluding that General Tilney must have murdered his wife—Catherine later discovers that she has 'scarcely sinned against [the General's] character, or magnified his cruelty' (206). Both here and elsewhere the novelist is silent about the political parties her characters support, yet it is evident that General Tilney is a party man of one sort or another. In the light of Austen's later novels it will become evident that he represents the overbearing Whig oligarchy as against the Morlands' rural and clerical Toryism, and that the ruling Whigs stand in need of the moral reclamation that Catherine will bring by marrying Henry.

There is something very telling about the smoking-room camaraderie of the General and John Thorpe, who are in most respects natural enemies. Like parliamentary opponents in England's generally cosy two-party system, they prefer one another's company to the more complicated world outside in which life is something more than a game of billiards. At another level their man-to-man relationship is a recurring structural feature of Austen's plots. Thorpe, guilty of 'vanity and avarice' (204), is a rogue and an upstart whose careless irresponsibility causes Catherine a great deal of pain. General Tilney, for his part, exhibits several of the traditional Deadly Sins, including pride, wrath, and gluttony as well as avarice. If Thorpe is a bounder, the Tilneys are prigs—both the dom- ineering father, and the pedantic son who is constantly correcting his sister's, and Catherine's, language and tastes. In a sequence that recurs in *Sense and Sensibility*, *Pride and Prejudice*, *Mansfield Park*, and *Emma*, the heroine is first wooed by the bounder but eventually gives her heart to the prig. The bounder and the prig were first joined as a pair in Austen's unfinished early novel 'The Watsons', where the notorious ladies' man and card-player Tom Musgrave goes about in company with the haughty, reserved Lord Osborne. It is Osborne of whom Emma Watson observes that 'He would be handsome enough even though he were *not* a lord, and, perhaps, better bred'—one of the more outspoken expressions of Austen's resentment against aristocratic manners.[14]

Unlike the novels of Charlotte Smith and Walter Scott, *Northanger Abbey* is silent about the Tilney family's history. This deliberate omission is typical of Austen's fiction. Stately homes with names like Northanger Abbey and Donwell Abbey invoke the medieval, monastic past, but only at Sotherton in *Mansfield Park*—a former Royalist house with a chapel built in the reign of James II—is the house's history spelt out. The Elliots in *Persuasion* are the only Austen family whose elaborate (and Royalist) ancestry is recounted, though not with the romantic expansiveness of similar passages in *Marchmont* or *Waverley*. Sir Walter Elliot could 'read his own history with an interest which never failed', we are told, but all that Austen's reader is offered is a tight-lipped summary of his entry in the Baronetage.[15]

Sir Walter's pompous obsession with aristocratic lineage is evident in his comment that the naval captain Frederick Wentworth ' "was nobody ... quite unconnected; nothing to do with the Strafford family" ' (19). It would, however, be naive to think that Austen's choice of the name Wentworth for the hero of *Persuasion* had nothing to do with the Straffords. In her early *History of England* she ardently defended Thomas Wentworth, the first Earl of Strafford and the architect of Charles I's design for absolute government. The American scholar Donald Greene has shown that the Strafford connection in Austen's novels can be traced back to the thirteenth century, when one Robert Wentworth married an heiress called Emma Wodehous. Their grandest descendant was Charles Watson Wentworth of Wentworth Woodhouse, Marquess of Rockingham, Prime Minister, and political head of the Whig aristocracy, who died when Austen was seven.[16] Thus a single entry in the *Peerage of England* yields Wentworth, Woodhouse, and Watson as potential fictional names. Other Austen names with strong Whig associations are Bertram, Brandon, Churchill, Dashwood (though Sir Francis Dashwood of the Hell-Fire Club became a Tory), D'Arcy, Fitzwilliam, Russell, and Steele. Sir Walter Elliot's snobbish observation that Frederick Wentworth was not one of the Strafford family implies strongly that his friend Lady Russell must be one of the Whig Russells. And it is she who persuades Anne Elliot not to jeopardize her dynastic interest by marrying Wentworth, a decision that brings Austen's heroine years of unhappiness.

In Austen's novels, a critic has argued, 'the significance of marriage as a relationship between individuals ... is always subordinate to its significance as a relationship between families'.[17] Austen's characters, though strongly individualized, are not carried away by the anarchy of romantic love. The Whig names mentioned above occur in *The Watsons*, *Sense and Sensibility*, *Pride and Prejudice*, *Mansfield Park*, *Emma*, and *Persuasion*—in all the novels, in fact, except *Northanger Abbey* and the unfinished *Sanditon*. At the same time, there is an important variation in Austen's marriage plots, some of which are (broadly speaking) endo-gamous—as in Edmund Bertram's union with his cousin Fanny—and some exogamous. Endogamous marriage implies the purification and consolidation of a house, a dynasty, or a community. It is a defensive, protective measure. Exogamous marriage is a union of opposites—political, social, and temperamental—injecting new blood into one of the nation's old or ruling families. After *Northanger Abbey*, it is in *Pride and Prejudice* and *Persuasion* that we find the most striking examples of exogamous marriages calculated to humanize the aristocracy.

The culminating marriages in Austen's fictions are socially and eco-nomically far more advantageous to the heroine than the hero. Moreover, exogamous marriage is fraught with danger in her novels. To marry openly for economic advantage like Charlotte Lucas in *Pride and Pre-judice* is to invite the novelist's withering scorn; and the bridegroom's choice of a low-ranking bride can signify moral weakness as well as moral strength. This is implied in the opening sentence of *Mansfield Park*, where Miss Maria Ward of Huntingdon, 'with only seven thousand pounds', has had 'the good luck to captivate Sir Thomas Bertram'.[18] The fact that Mr Bennet in *Pride and Prejudice* has also married beneath him (in every sense) as a result of being 'captivated by youth and beauty' suggests that a man or woman foolish enough to be easily 'captivated' by the opposite sex is headed for disappointment.[19] Austen's heroines must resist easy captivation and must appear to disregard material considerations, so that their ability to contract a wealthy marriage is a tribute to their integrity alone. The heroine who rejects the handsome cavalier (or bounder) in favour of the unbending man of virtue (or prig) is set to fulfil her destiny.

'Her knowledge of Richardson's works was such as no one is likely again to acquire,' wrote Austen's nephew.[20] But what characterizes Austen's masculine cavaliers is not the single-minded pursuit and diabolical persistence of a Robert Lovelace but vacillation, self-contradiction, and inconsistency. Neither Willoughby, Wickham, Henry Crawford, nor Frank Churchill is truly a dominant male. Willoughby's name suggests his plia-bility as well as alluding to the would-be rapist Sir Clement Willoughby in Burney's *Evelina*. In *Sense and Sensibility* Willoughby and Sir John Middleton are the Dashwood family's country neighbours in Devon, and

Donald Greene points out that Thomas Willoughby, the first Lord Middleton, was a distant relative of Austen's on her mother's side.[21] Sir John Middleton is a personification of the ideal country squire. John Willoughby, however, is a man-about-town who foresakes a love match for traditional aristocratic marriage.

Willoughby comes upon the impoverished Marianne Dashwood for the first time when she has fallen and twisted her ankle, so that she is literally swept off her feet and carried home. He is heir to a nearby property, one of several locations where he pursues his expensive tastes in horses, carriages, and guns. Sir John Middleton twice describes him in Richardsonian style as the 'boldest rider in England'.[22] He offers Marianne a horse, and is also a notable dancer, causing her to exclaim that ' "that is what a young man ought to be" ' (77). Unlike almost all previous novelists Austen does not give him the opportunity to attack her heroine's chastity, which is just as well since Marianne would certainly have succumbed. She fails to recognize that his careless extravagance with horses and women will force him in the end to marry for money. He is a landed gentleman in straitened circumstances and his behaviour is caste-determined rather than chivalrous.[23] In a heavily contrived sequence, he reappears at what he thinks is Marianne's deathbed and confesses his real motivation to her sister Elinor; the result is to reveal him as spoilt, weak, and selfish, but not wholly evil or unprincipled. He marries the wealthy and appropriately colourless Miss Grey, and lives (we are told) 'to exert, and frequently to enjoy himself. His wife was not always out of humour, nor his home always uncomfortable; and in his breed of horses and dogs, and in sporting of every kind, he found no inconsiderable degree of domestic felicity' (367). Austen feels no great animus against this young man who eventually retreats into the customary pursuits of the Tory country squire.

All that we are told of Willoughby's politics is that he is 'in the opposition' to Mr Palmer, a fashionable and haughty young man who is standing for Parliament. Palmer is 'always going about the country canvassing against the election' (136); he is an ardent newspaper reader, and has no interest in rural pursuits. Nevertheless, he moves in the same circles as the country squire Sir John Middleton, being brother-in-law to Lady Middleton. Willoughby is apparently the Tory and Palmer the Whig, although the novel (originally written before *Northanger Abbey*) lacks a clear party-political meaning. What is crucial, however, is the rivalry and enmity between Willoughby and Sir John Middleton's close friend Colonel Brandon. In the past Willoughby has seduced and abandoned Brandon's female ward, leading them to fight a duel, and now they are rivals for Marianne's love. If Willoughby is a cavalier rogue, Brandon (who is named after Charles I's executioner) is manifestly a Roundhead and a prig. Readers have usually felt cheated when Marianne Dashwood finds herself able to forget Willoughby and to love Colonel Brandon. There are, perhaps, political as well as emotional reasons why this plot resolution is unsatisfactory. Austen's determination to end the novel with a version of the Cavalier–Roundhead alliance cannot alter the fact that Brandon, Middleton, and (in his final incarnation) Willoughby are all country squires representing broadly similar values and interests. The social tension between Marianne and Brandon is not great enough to become a focus of romantic interest.

In contrast to *Sense and Sensibility* there is no mistaking the meaning of Elizabeth Bennet's exogamous marriage in *Pride and Prejudice*, since Mr Darcy and his aunt belong to the wealthiest section of the landed gentry. The sheer grandeur of Darcy's country seat is revealed when Elizabeth makes her tour into Derbyshire and reflects, in a moment of telling excitement, that 'to be mistress of Pemberley might be something!' (211). Until this point, Lady Catherine (a peeress in her own right as well as a baronet's widow) has received, in one critic's words, 'all of the opprobrium we are never permitted to aim directly at Darcy or his parents, or at great gentry families in general'.[24] As well as being a symbolic monster, she is at the centre of a knot of Whig dynasties. Her brother is 'Lord——' (149) and her sister was Lady Anne Darcy. Lord——'s younger son is Colonel Fitzwilliam, and—since it is also Mr Darcy's first name—we may deduce that the name that is left blank is Fitzwilliam. Austen could not have put it in her novel because William, Earl Fitzwilliam, a Whig cabinet minister in 1806, was still alive. Robert D'Arcy, Earl of Holdernesse, another Whig cabinet minister, had died in 1778.[25]

Pride and Prejudice begins with a mother anxious to marry off her daughters. Of the three eligible gentlemen who come on the scene, the cold, tongue-tied Darcy appears the least attractive. His friend Bingley is handsome, lively, fond of dancing, and will marry the heroine's sister; he is Tom Musgrave to Darcy's Lord Osborne. The third man is Wickham, the dashing young army officer whom even the sharp-eyed Elizabeth finds instantly captivating. Elizabeth is powerless to see through his insinuations, lies, and malice against Darcy, and she would surely have been hurled into an unsuitable match (like her father) had not Wickham been so easily diverted towards the heiress Miss King, who in due course rejects him. By this time he is clearly revealed as a cavalier rogue and an inveterate gambler, debt-bilker, and seducer. Lydia Bennet, however, not only marries but tames him, turning him into a harmless country squire whose greatest feat will be to ' "kill more birds on the first of September, than any body else in the country" ' (274). Once again the Cavalier's sting has been drawn.

Wickham is the son of the estate manager at Pemberley, and godson to Darcy's father who has supported him through school and university. The Darcys' patronage has produced in him not gratitude but an intense, almost fratricidal hatred of Fitzwilliam Darcy, the unchallenged heir to Pemberley. In fact, Wickham's profligacy together with his jealousy and resentment suggest that, in his own eyes, he too had a claim to the estate. A more melodramatic novelist than Austen would have made him a bastard offspring of the great estate and Darcy's unacknowledged half-brother. It is he, unsurprisingly, who alerts Elizabeth to the endogamous marriage that Darcy is expected to make with his cousin Miss de Bourgh.

Had Wickham been Darcy's half-brother, his very existence, let alone his conduct, would have suggested the aristocratic degeneracy of the Darcy-Fitzwilliams, and Lydia's marriage to him would have provided a direct symbolic parallel to Elizabeth's marriage to Darcy. But Austen is more subtle than this. Darcy's condemnation of Wickham's behaviour is thoroughly vindicated, and the threat to the future of Pemberley is represented instead by Lady Catherine and her daughter Miss de Bourgh, who exemplify the paradox of high-born ill-breeding and bad manners of which Austen was always sharply aware. In terms of literal 'breeding'—blood, or dynastic succession—Miss de Bourgh is evidently degenerate. Mr Collins sycophantically describes her as having 'that in her features which marks the young woman of distinguished birth' (58), but she strikes the sharp-eyed Elizabeth as being 'pale and sickly', 'thin and small' and, worst of all, 'insignificant-looking' (142). As for Lady Catherine, her bad manners have apparently rubbed off on her nephew Darcy. Elizabeth not only rejects his first proposal, but rebukes him for not making it in a 'more gentleman-like manner' (168)—as Wickham would presumably have done. Austen then introduces Darcy's long letter of explanation and self-justification—a fictional contrivance as transparent as Willoughby's confession—to allow him to exculpate himself. The purpose of the letter is to show that his faults of behaviour stem from priggish rectitude and not from aristocratic ill-breeding, since Elizabeth can learn to love priggish rectitude. But Elizabeth is also determined to force Darcy and his family to treat her on terms of equality.

Austen's greatest confrontation between the gentry and the Whig aristocracy comes when she states her right to marry Darcy, telling Lady

Catherine that ' "He is a gentleman; I am a gentleman's daughter; so far we are equal." ' Lady Catherine's reply is meant to be crushing: ' "True. You *are* a gentleman's daughter. But who was your mother? Who are your uncles and aunts? Do not imagine me ignorant of their condition." ' (308). Mr Bennet has lost caste by marrying beneath him; the Fitzwilliams, by implication, never do. But if Elizabeth feels the resentment of a humble squire's daughter against the arrogance of the great Whigs, she is also displaying the toughness and pride that fit her to become mistress of Pemberley. Something is rotten at the great estate, for reasons in the past that remain hidden. Darcy has responded to his father's failure with Wickham by becoming priggish, defensive, and reserved, but he instinc- tively responds to Elizabeth's integrity and submits to being teased by her sportive irreverence. She alone, it seems, can counteract the Whig Ascendancy's inbreeding and bring life back to Pemberley. For all her claims to equality, the point of her marriage is that it is splendidly unequal, and it is this that, of all Austen's novels, brings *Pride and Prejudice* closest to fairy tale.

Traditionally the courtship novel traces the heroine's life from an initial displacement, as she leaves her childhood home, to the final redisposition caused by her marriage. Jane Austen, whose plots are never predictable, plays subtle variations on this pattern. In *Pride and Prejudice* the heroine is not displaced initially, but—where Austen's other heroines are content to range around southern England—her social ascent into the aristocracy is paralleled by her geographical adventure northwards from the Home Counties to Pemberley in Derbyshire. *Mansfield Park* begins with Fanny Price's move from Portsmouth to Mansfield, but once there she will not be dislodged. The male characters in *Mansfield Park* and *Emma* travel widely but on the periphery of the narrative action, while the heroines stay put and finally contract endogamous marriages. Fanny at last makes her home in the parsonage just across the park from the main house at Mansfield, while Emma Woodhouse contrives to stay under her father's roof even after her marriage. *Persuasion*, Austen's last completed novel, constitutes a return to the story of movement, travel, and exogamous marriage. For this reason I will discuss it before *Mansfield Park* and *Emma*.

Broadly speaking, *Persuasion* reverses the situation of *Pride and Pre- judice*. Anne Elliot is a baronet's daughter rather than the child of genteel poverty like Marianne Dashwood and Elizabeth Bennet, and it is the hero, not the heroine, who is socially ascendant. The Elliots' background is that of an old Royalist family of assiduous courtiers, 'serving the office of High Sheriff, representing a borough in three successive parliaments, exertions of loyalty, and dignity of baronet, in the first year of Charles II' (1–2). We may presume that they have subsequently become Whigs, since (as we have seen) the closest family friend, Lady Russell, bears the name of a great Whig dynasty. Sir Walter, however, is a degenerate knight and an ageing dandy who has squandered his family's once impressive political influence. In the middle of the Napoleonic Wars his haughty condescension towards Admiral Croft, the Trafalgar veteran who leases his bankrupt estate, suggests that his ancestors' dignity and 'exertions of loyalty' have given place to an overweening family pride.

We are told very little about Frederick Wentworth's family. His parents are dead, but since his elder brother was a curate it is very probable that, like Jane Austen's naval brothers and like Nelson, the hero of Trafalgar, he was a clergyman's son. In 1806 he proposed to Anne Elliot, who loved him but was persuaded to turn him down. At the time he may have seemed a penniless adventurer, but eight years later the opportunities of war and his own courage and skill have made him a wealthy commander. Wentworth is in some ways a stereotypical romantic idol—intelligent, generous, and considerate, but also handsome, ruthless, and masterful. His relationship with Anne is more sexually charged than any other in Jane Austen, and the revival of their love affair after eight years of bitter estrangement moves the novel towards a powerful emotional climax. Yet *Persuasion*'s final sentence balances the ideas of 'domestic virtue' and 'national importance' in reviewing Anne's future as a sailor's wife (219). Her marriage, it would seem, has national as well as domestic significance.

Yet this brings us up against the self-imposed limitations of Austen's fiction, since she can merely hint at the national importance of the fighting services. There is a strong awareness of social change, of a movement from 'the old English style' to 'the new' (33) in *Persuasion*; but while the naval officers symbolize this change, they cannot determine its direction. The fragment of *Sanditon*, which Austen did not live to finish, suggests that she may have been about to turn her attention to the commercial classes. In neither novel are the stately houses and their owners as formidable as they once were.[26] It would be fascinating to know whether *Sanditon*, like *Persuasion*, would have been a portrait of the hero as bounder rather than the hero as (like Edmund Bertram and Mr Knightley) gentlemanly prig. The last sentence of *Persuasion* observes that the drawback of being a sailor's wife is Anne Elliot's 'dread of a future war' (219), and the novelist could not have foreseen that the long peace after

Napoleon's defeat was likely to condemn Frederick Wentworth to a humdrum and largely inactive future. Perhaps, like those other would-be dominant males Willoughby and Wickham, he would have to settle for country sports.

Mansfield Park and *Emma*: Closing the Gates

It is in *Mansfield Park* and *Emma*, novels with a more didactic edge than *Pride and Prejudice* or *Persuasion*, that Austen most fully outlines the good principles and good manners that, in her view, should characterize the English gentry. The legend that *Mansfield Park* is 'about ordination' is apparently based on a misreading of one of Austen's letters, yet its persistence is revealing. The novel sets out the clergy's 'national importance' very deliberately, as may be seen from Edmund Bertram's observation that ' "it will . . . be every where found, that as the clergy are, or are not what they ought to be, so are the rest of the nation" '. Edmund contrasts the clergy, who are charged with embodying 'good principles', with the aristocracy who are the 'arbiters of good breeding' (121). For the most part, the aristocracy and gentry here and in *Emma* fail to live up to these ideals. There is a defensive aspect to these novels, the sense of a self-protective retreat behind park gates by the representatives of virtue, and this is largely due to Austen's decision to conclude each novel with an endogamous marriage. The good principles of Edmund and his bride Fanny Price have their effect within the family, but Edmund is not even shown exerting his influence over a congregation or a parish, let alone the nation at large.

In *Mansfield Park* the English ruling class is represented through the portrayal of three substantial landowning families and their failed mutual alliances. Maria Bertram marries Mr Rushworth for dynastic reasons but then elopes with Henry Crawford, bringing about a divorce between the Bertrams and the Rushworths and ruining the possibility of a double alliance between the Bertrams and the Crawfords. The Rushworths are the wealthiest of the three families, with an ancient and venerable Royalist history. Fanny Price is stirred by this history, but she finds to her disappointment that the built-in chapel of their house at Sotherton has no royal associations, being a last-ditch addition built just before the Glorious Revolution. In the seventeenth century the Rushworths would have been Jacobite Tories, but the change that has led to the desertion of the chapel and the abolition of family prayers has also apparently led to a change of party allegiance. Sir Thomas Bertram, a Member of Parliament, wants an alliance with Mr Rushworth because he is 'in the same interest' as well as residing in the same county; Rushworth, therefore, is the likely candidate for the pocket borough that Sir Thomas controls (73, 182).[27]

At the beginning of the novel the evidence suggests that the Bertrams, Rushworths, and Crawfords are all Whig families. The Bertrams inhabit a 'spacious modern-built house' (80), which we deduce must have been built out of the proceeds of the family's Antiguan sugar plantation. They are never described as an ancient family, so it is likely that the Mansfield estate, the baronetcy, and their seat in Parliament have all been bought by the same means. (It is because Mansfield Park is 'an estate without land' that Mary Crawford must resort to trying to hire a cart at harvest-time.)[28] Sir Thomas, or perhaps his father before him, is likely to have belonged to the 'West Indian' group of some sixty MPs inclined to the Whig interest.[29] Parliamentary duties take him regularly to London until the falling returns from Antigua force him to go out and take control of his plantation. Sir Thomas's heavy-handed sense of moral and commercial responsibility contrasts sharply with what we hear of Admiral Crawford, a libertine and 'man of vicious conduct' (174) who manifestly fits the stereotype of a freethinking, amoral Whig grandee. (His children regard the Church as a joke even though one of them, Mrs Grant, has married into it.)[30] Henry Crawford, described by his sister Mary as 'the most horrible flirt that can be imagined' (75), owns a large estate at Everingham in Norfolk, while it is Admiral Crawford's influence in high places that is needed to get William Price his naval promotion.

At the end of the novel Sir Thomas, 'sick of ambitious and mercenary connections' (455), has retired to Mansfield for good, thus concluding his long conversion from Whig parliamentarian, absentee landlord, and plantation owner to a gentle knight of the shires—though presumably he still draws the majority of his income from the West Indies. One recent critic has described Mansfield Park, with its gates metaphorically closed, as a little 'utopia of Tory reform'; the force of this description is that the Bertrams have thrown off the Crawfords and Rushworths and, with them, the corruptions of the Whig Ascendancy.[31]

It is true that the Bertrams' transformation in *Mansfield Park* is explicitly cast in moral and religious, rather than social and political, terms. Most of the novel's minor characters seem to have been constructed on the 'Seven Deadly Sins' principle.[32] Chapter one introduces Sir Thomas's 'pride' (42), Lady Bertram's sloth—she is 'remarkably easy and indolent' (42)—and Mrs Norris's avaricious 'love of money' (45); soon afterwards the gluttonous Dr Grant arrives at the parsonage. Julia's envy is manifest once Henry begins paying attention to her sister. Henry is the representative of lust. Wrath is possibly the exception among these medieval sins, since the Bible recognizes a righteous anger; not only are Christians meant to live in fear of the wrath of the Lord, but Fanny can justifiably display the 'dignity of angry virtue' (327). Fanny's ideal, much strengthened by her visit to her home at Portsmouth, is of Mansfield Park as a spacious, serene environment, yet it is often a quarrelsome, bad-tempered place, the setting for Maria's 'vexation and anger' (100), for Julia's 'vexed' and 'hasty' temper (128), and Mrs Norris's numerous appearances 'red with anger' (233), while the nearby parsonage resounds with Dr Grant's quarrels with his wife when the dinner is off. Fanny's self-repression also involves a good deal of anger management. We read of her as being 'almost vexed into displeasure and anger' against Edmund (414), and what (almost) arouses her righteous anger is the real or apparent failure of others to fulfil their moral obligations.

Moral imperatives, such as Edmund's pronouncement about the importance of the clergy being what they 'ought to be', echo even more resoundingly in *Mansfield Park* than in Austen's other novels. Fanny 'will be what [she] ought to be' to Mrs Norris (60); Mrs Grant's manners are 'just what they ought to be' (95); Fanny fears that 'Henry does not think as he ought, on serious subjects' (347); and Tom Bertram, the Regency buck and spendthrift heir, finally becomes 'what he ought to be, useful to his father' (447). The Prices' home in Portsmouth is an 'abode of noise, disorder, and impropriety' where 'nothing [is] done as it ought to be' (381). For those incapable of becoming what they ought to be, the novel's last chapter offers a small orgy of judgement and retribution. The evils finally brought to book have already been most amply revealed in *Mansfield Park*'s most celebrated episode, that of the amateur theatricals.

The link between upper-class immorality and the rage for private theatricals had been publicized by contemporary evangelicals, and it has been argued that Austen's fictional demonstration of this link shows her 'Tory preference for the soberer *mores* of the gentry against those of the Whig aristocracy'.[33] (Against this, however, we need to remember her comment that the 'itch for acting' is universal among young people (147), and the fact that there were theatricals in Austen's own family.) One of the main functions of the theatricals in *Mansfield Park* is to sharpen the opposition between thoughtless, gilded ruling-class youth and Fanny, the pious poor relation with stage fright, whose cramped, noisy home at

Portsmouth could never be converted into a theatre. Fanny during the theatricals at Mansfield appears like Richardson's Pamela, the lowly Puritanical member of the household who must always say no to her superiors however much pressure she is under. Her perception of profaneness and immorality is the traditional English Puritan objection to the stage. (She is also, like many Puritans, a consummate dissembler, so that nobody ever suspects her love for Edmund.) The theatricals are abruptly terminated by Sir Thomas's return so that, as the novelist puts it, 'Under his government, Mansfield Park was an altered place' (211); but it takes some time, and a series of melodramatic developments, for the reign of moral obligation over theatricality, of the pulpit over the stage, to finally assert itself. In the new climate Mansfield is thoroughly purged and Fanny achieves her aim of marriage to her cousin, but the wider destiny of the Bertram family must be taken on trust. They are dependent on their slave plantation in the West Indies, since the Bertrams have gained no new source of income either through business activity or marriage. Moreover, the yields from Caribbean plantations were in steep decline in the early nineteenth century.[34] Neither Sir Thomas nor his sons seem capable, at the end of the novel, of showing the enterprise and initiative needed to diversify the family fortunes. Unless unforeseen circumstances come to the rescue, this 'Tory utopia' can only stagnate.

Emma Woodhouse's pride, her delight in matchmaking, and her patronage of Harriet Smith help to disguise the fact that in *Emma* we are at a much greater distance from the ruling aristocracy than in *Mansfield Park*. The village of Highbury, less than half a day's ride from London, is perilously close to the world of 'trade'. Although Highbury contains the ancient manor of Donwell Abbey, its owner, George Knightley, lives off his own land without the conspicuous display that the Bertrams' colonial estate makes possible at Mansfield. It is one of Austen's sly jokes that the chivalrously named Mr Knightley keeps 'no horses' and rarely uses his carriage, 'having little spare money' (223). Aristocratic display is personified by Frank Churchill, the young, adopted heir who brings several horses with him on his visits to Highbury, and is always riding across country. Churchill represents worldliness, fine manners, and the rootlessness of a wealthy playboy, but his eventual choice of a bride shows his indifference to the idea of aristocratic marriage.

Mr Elton, the heroine's first suitor, angrily observes when his proposal is rejected that 'Every body has their level' (151). The comedy of *Emma* is that each of the young people eventually finds his or her level, which in Elton's case is that of trade and new-rich vulgarity. We should remember, however, that Emma's own fortune has presumably come from a similar source several generations back. Here is one critic's reconstruction of her family's probable origin:

we may assume that the progenitor of the Hartfield Woodhouses was a younger brother in a landed family, who entered trade, made his fortune, purchased the Hartfield estate (from the Knightleys, no doubt) and settled in Highbury...the Woodhouses in fact stand in almost the same position as the Westons, the Coles, and the Sucklings of Maple Grove.[35]

The Woodhouses' landed property is a 'sort of notch' in the Donwell estate, though it is large enough for stock-rearing (154–5). (Emma's bone-idle, valetudinarian father boasts of the quality of Hartfield pork, though it is impossible to imagine him as a pig farmer.) The handsome fortune that she stands to inherit comes from 'other sources' (155), but Mr Woodhouse in any case feels that there should be no marrying or giving in marriage; he wants to keep his remaining daughter for himself. Emma, in turn, rejects the prospect of marriage but uses matchmaking, or the fantasy of matchmaking, to exert control over her social inferiors. Meanwhile she attracts the attentions not just of the priggish Mr Elton, but of Frank Churchill, who flirts with her as cover for a secret alliance that he dares not reveal to his own family.

Frank is the product of a misalliance between Captain Weston, a young army officer, and Miss Churchill, 'of a great Yorkshire family', whose name suggests the Duke of Marlborough and his Whig dynasty. The Churchills, 'full of pride and importance', regard Captain Weston as an 'unsuitable connection'(46)—in effect, a bounder—but after his wife's death they spare no effort to adopt his son. Frank has been brought up by his grandmother, and has taken her name. Once Mr Elton is got out of the way, there is a sense in which *Emma* portrays the heroine's choice between the Knightleys and the Churchills, between the Toryism of Donwell Abbey and Whig cosmopolitanism, even though this choice of manners and values is not literally a choice between two suitors. The crisis comes during Emma's single venture outside Highbury—a very modest excursion to Box Hill—but it has been prepared for by Frank's offhand and infrequent visits to the village. He fritters away his life in parties of pleasure at what Knightley calls the 'idlest haunts in the kingdom', and in Knightley's eyes he is, like his mother's family, 'proud, luxurious, and selfish' (163). Emma, like the rest of Highbury, wishes to think well of such a dashing young man, but they only know him through his 'fine flourishing letter[s]' postponing his visits. Emma calls him amiable; Knightley disagrees: ' "No, Emma, your amiable young man can be amiable only in French, not in English. He may be very 'aimable', have very good manners, and be very agreeable, but he can have no English delicacy towards the feelings of other people; nothing really amiable about him" ' (166). 'English delicacy' here is the quality of the morally scrupulous, sympathetic, and socially aware English gentleman—a figure who is both a paragon in himself and an appropriate mentor for others. It is what Knightley has in common with Edmund Bertram. In fact, the phrase sounds so natural and so well-earned in George Knightley's mouth that we are apt to forget its novelty. Coming from a character who, in Emma's view, represents 'true gentility, untainted in blood and understanding' (353), it marks Jane Austen's standard of manners.

Some forty years before *Mansfield Park* and *Emma*, Lord Chesterfield's *Letters to His Son* (1774) had idealized the manners of the French aristocracy. For Chesterfield, to be 'both *respectable et aimable*' was 'the perfection of a human character'.[36] The Tory Samuel Johnson declared that the *Letters* taught 'the morals of a whore, and the manners of a dancing master'.[37] (Chesterfield, though he became a Tory, was brought up as a Whig grandee.) It might have been Austen's admiration for Johnson that led her to make Frank Churchill, who is determined to put on a ball at Highbury, appear in the novel as a kind of dancing master. Knightley refers to him with the slightest hint of a sneer as a 'gallant young man' (298) and, when Frank's secret understanding with Jane Fairfax begins to appear, it becomes a case of 'gallantry and trick' (344).

Knightley's praise of 'English delicacy' comes in a novel written at a period of intense English patriotism, in the year of the Battle of Waterloo. 'Delicacy' is not, perhaps, a word that is often associated with the English temperament, although delicacy of observation, humorous characterization, and moral discrimination are the hallmarks of Jane Austen's fiction. Her lightness of touch and the moral and social decorum surrounding her plots distinguishes her novels from most of the fiction of the later eighteenth century, heavily laden as it is with sexual melodrama and Gothic sensationalism. The 'gallantry' of Frank Churchill is a case in point, since he is evidently a sincere, generous-minded, and good-hearted young man even if his ardour and thoughtlessness tie him up in knots. He keeps his promise to marry Jane and, unlike the gallants who proliferate in eighteenth-century novels, he makes no attempt to seduce any of his female admirers. His 'French manners' are therefore harmless. He does, however, display a careless lack of respect for his elders that Austen perhaps associates with Jacobinism and French republicanism. When he patronizes the village shop he boasts that he is showing himself a 'true citizen of Highbury', a phrase with a suspiciously Gallic flourish even though Emma responds by praising his 'patriotism' (211). On the day that she admires Donwell Abbey with its embodiment of 'English verdure, English culture, English comfort', Frank quarrels with Jane Fairfax and announces that he is 'sick of England' (359).

Knightley, it goes without saying, is never sick of England; he is a country gentleman, not a cosmopolitan aristocrat, and nor does he ever appear (as Frank does) to be cross, heated, hasty of speech, or emotionally out of control. His 'English delicacy' is at one with the emotional reserve that would become a proverbial quality of the English gentleman, as we shall see in later chapters. His long-delayed proposal, delivered in what Austen calls his 'plain, unaffected, gentleman-like English' (432), begins with the words ' "I cannot make speeches, Emma" ' (417), an example of the national weakness for understatement that has so often upset foreign audiences. (The speech that follows includes his statement that 'I have blamed you, and lectured you, and you have borne it as no other woman in England would have borne it', an admission that he has in his time made many speeches.) What does Emma say in reply? 'Just what she ought, of course. A lady always does' (418). Her reply is a model of English propriety and 'amiability', but we are not told what she says. To divine it is left to the reader's own innate standard of delicacy.

In terms of a conventional upper-class alliance, that of George Knightley and Emma Woodhouse could hardly be bettered. The two leaders of Highbury society are joined together in a union that will restore the 'notch' that the Woodhouses have cut out of the Donwell estate. Yet the marriage is effectively endogamous, since the two families are already related by marriage and Knightley is an old and intimate friend of Emma's father. His brother is her brother-in-law, and he has been a kind of uncle to her. Their 'perfect happiness' (465) stands in tacit contrast to the destiny of Frank and Jane, passionate lovers whom nobody would expect to be perfectly happy. Even so, Mr Woodhouse will only agree to the marriage on condition that Knightley moves from Donwell to Hartfield, where his presence may help to deter the chicken-thieves who are plaguing the neighbourhood. The chicken-thieves may or may not be identified with the gypsies who earlier threatened Harriet Smith, giving Frank Churchill the chance to rescue her. Mr Woodhouse's timorousness represents the defensiveness of Highbury society, a society notable for its reluctance to admit even wealthy outsiders, though the latter eventually succeed in gaining entry. Emma's marriage thus confirms the image of

Highbury as a 'Tory utopia' and a citadel against change, even though its genteel society can only survive by constantly redrawing its boundaries.

Jane Eyre's Pilgrimage of Identity

Charlotte Brontë thought of herself as the antithesis of Jane Austen— passionate where Austen was restrained and decorous, plebeian where Austen was ladylike—and in some ways this is true. But the Brontë sisters were also the daughters of an Anglican vicar, and Charlotte, for all her sympathy with oppressed womanhood, was a political conservative and an ardent admirer of Walter Scott. It has been claimed that what happens in her novels is 'a marriage of identifiably bourgeois values with the values of the gentry or aristocracy'—a figurative political marriage, in fact.[38] Moreover, her writings are full of outspoken (though often ambivalent) patriotic feeling. Jane Eyre's chequered path leads towards emotional fulfilment in marriage with a reformed rake who has learned to prefer English domesticity and Christian penitence to foreign adventures and aristocratic libertinism. This most widely read of all English novels engages deeply with issues of English history and national identity.

Jane Eyre's whole life has been determined, as we gradually realize, by a series of rash and impolitic marriages in the preceding generation. Her mother, Jane Reed of Gateshead, married a poor curate. Jane as a displaced orphan came under the protection of her Uncle Reed, who in turn left her to his widow's tender mercies. Mrs Reed, who hated her husband's family, is ultimately punished by the fate of her three children, John Reed who falls into disgrace and commits suicide, Eliza who becomes a Catholic nun, and Georgiana who tries to elope with a young lord. If this were not enough, there is discord in Jane's father's family, since her Uncle John has failed in business and could not repay the capital invested by his brother-in-law Mr Rivers. Late in life, John Eyre becomes a successful Madeira merchant, but his quarrel with Rivers is never made up; hence he leaves all his money to Jane Eyre instead of dividing it equally between his nieces and his nephew St John Rivers. Jane's family history is blighted by family squabbles and disastrous alliances long before she becomes aware of the novel's most sensational example of a bad marriage, Edward Rochester's long-hidden union with the Jamaican Bertha Mason.

Edward Fairfax Rochester is named after a famous Restoration courtier and rake, and one of the leading Parliamentary generals. (At a different allegorical level, Rochester is the hard 'rock' for Jane to base her life on, not a breaking 'reed' or a 'river' for her to drown in.) His ancestor Damer de Rochester died on the Civil War battlefield of Marston Moor. The union of the Royalist Rochesters with the Fairfaxes has evidently come about more recently, since the housekeeper at Thornfield Hall, doubtless a poor relation, is Mrs Fairfax. The latter sees fit to remind Jane, Mr Rochester's newest employee, that 'Gentlemen in his station are not accustomed to marry their governesses'.[39] Jane soon jumps to the conclusion that he intends to marry Blanche Ingram (a peer's daughter with a fashionably French name) 'for family, perhaps political reasons; because her rank and connexions suited him' (215). Both partners are, she thinks, acting in conformity to ideas and principles instilled into them in childhood: 'All their class held these principles' (216). But the recklessness with which the Rochesters were prepared to apply the principle of aristocratic marriage is something of which Jane has no conception. Edward, a younger son, was sent out to Jamaica, where his father's old acquaintance Mr Mason was a sugar planter. Edward's marriage to Bertha Mason was encouraged by all parties, even though they knew that there was congenital insanity in Mason's family. (Bertha is a 'Creole', which means that she and her family would have been classed as white plantation owners, but her mixed-race background is blamed for her insanity.)[40] When Rochester first sees Bertha she is the belle of Jamaican society, and Brontë is notoriously vague about the process of mental degeneration after her marriage which leads to her virtual imprisonment at Thornfield. On separate occasions she tries to kill Jane, Rochester, and her brother Richard Mason, and eventually she succeeds in burning the house down. Before she learns of Bertha's existence, Jane remarks of the relationships among her master's guests at Thornfield that 'They generally run on the same theme—courtship; and promise to end in the same catastrophe—marriage' (227–8). Despite her light-hearted play on the innocent meaning of 'catastrophe' as the outcome of a dramatic plot, the moral is clear: marriage, it would seem, is invariably catastrophic.

No wonder, then, that Jane, the orphan child of the Eyres and the Reeds, enters the novel as a self-proclaimed outcast. When in *Northanger Abbey* Henry Tilney tells Catherine Morland to remember that she is English, he assumes her underlying conformity with the 'national character', a settled constitution temporarily obscured by her Gothic enthusiasms. According to Henry she need only consult her 'understanding' and 'observation' to see things in their right perspective again. But Catherine's Gothicism pales beside the tortured imagination of Jane Eyre, who hides herself away from her adopted family and questions her identity to its foundations. She feels herself to be a changeling, 'half fairy, half imp', she is the 'scapegoat of the nursery', and she is an 'uncongenial alien' both within the family circle and on her first arrival at Lowood school (46–8, 98). To the extent that *Jane Eyre* is a feminist novel, her sense of alienness recalls the argument, put forward half a century earlier in Mary Wollstonecraft's writings including her unfinished novel *The Wrongs of Woman* (1798), that since women have no political rights they have no country.[41] But Jane at the age of 10 is denied her rights within the family because she is a child, not a woman; and she is also a voracious, if unsophisticated, child reader whose knowledge of Oliver Goldsmith's *Roman History* enables her to cast her cousin John as Nero or Caligula, and herself as a rebel slave.[42] Behind the oppression and victimhood of the novel's opening pages we can just about glimpse the solidly middle-class upbringing, nourished by the classics on Mrs Reed's bookshelf and the servants' folk tales and fairy tales, that strengthens Jane's determination not to become poor or lose caste. (Had it not been for this determination, she would have been sent to join her Eyre relations in Madeira; Mrs Reed ignorantly assumes that they are beyond the pale of respectability.) Jane's childhood reading projects her into distant lands despite her refusal to go to Madeira. Hidden in the window-seat she sits 'cross-legged, like a Turk' (39) and absorbs the descriptions of Arctic seabirds in the second volume of Thomas Bewick's *History of British Birds*. The icy scenes of Norway and the Arctic Ocean in Bewick's engravings recur in her dreams and, later, in the desolate landscapes and seascapes of her watercolours.[43] Jane's watercolours could be described as self-portraits in a white, polar space, an imaginative geography so far removed from her native English countryside as to be barely capable of human settlement.

There is, however, another kind of geography in the novel that the young Jane does not yet understand. At every stage she is a chosen pilgrim following a predestined path, so that, while her imagination continues to construct fictional versions of herself, her true identity is gradually revealed. The sequence of place names in the narrative—Gateshead, Lowood, Thornfield, Whitcross and Ferndean—suggests a symbolic pilgrim's progress. At each stage she must undergo spiritual trials, beginning with her ordeal in the Red Room at Gateshead and culminating in the passionate temptation scenes of her courtships with Rochester and Rivers. Like the narrative of Bunyan's Pilgrim, Jane's story is set in an allegorical landscape which both is and is not England. Its dimensions of time and space are fictitious, since neither the novel's chronology nor its topography are consistent. The date of 1808, established by the fact that

St John Rivers presents Jane with a newly published first edition of Scott's *Marmion*, does not fit in with other parts of the action. When Jane is sent to Lowood she says that she 'brushed up [her] recollections of the map of England' (120), yet the novel's meticulous details of journey times and distances travelled by the stagecoach cannot be plotted on any map.[44]

Jane has her first lesson in English history soon after arriving at Lowood School. The girls are studying the reign of Charles I but Jane has, as yet, no opinion on the great question of the Civil Wars. Instead, she reports Helen Burns's measured but Royalist view:

'I was wondering how a man who wishes to do right could act so unjustly and unwisely as Charles the First sometimes did; and I thought what a pity it was that, with his integrity and conscientiousness, he could see no farther than the prerogatives of the Crown. If he had but been able to look to a distance, and see how what they call the spirit of the age was tending! Still, I like Charles—I respect him—I pity him, poor murdered king! . . . How dared they kill him!' (89)

Helen, who stands for stoical resignation and Christian forgiveness, takes a far more balanced view of the regicide than, say, Jane Austen in her *History of England*. The passage is a model of the capacity for judicious appraisal that Brontë's heroine needs to learn after her furious rebellion at Gateshead. But it seems like a digression until Jane comes under the spell of Rochester, whose full name (as we have seen) evokes both sides in the Civil Wars. The style of courtship that Rochester adopts with Blanche Ingram clearly belongs to a Cavalier hero: it is a style which 'if careless and choosing rather to be sought than to seek, was yet, in its very carelessness, captivating, and in its very pride, irresistible' (214). Blanche plays along in an equally cavalier style: 'She appeared to be on her high horse tonight; both her words and her air seemed intended to excite not only the admiration, but the excitement of her auditors: she was evidently bent on striking them as something very dashing and daring indeed' (208).

From a nineteenth-century point of view Blanche's manners, like her name, are those of the francophile Whig aristocracy. It is her wealth and breeding, not her conduct or morals, that distinguish her from Céline Varens, the actress who was Rochester's French mistress (he has had others in Germany and Italy) and mother of his ward Adèle. Jane finds in Adèle a 'superficiality of character, inherited probably from her mother, hardly congenial to the English mind' (176)—a distinction recalling Mr Knightley's 'English delicacy' but cast, as often in Charlotte Brontë, in invidiously racial terms. It could apply equally to Blanche Ingram, though Blanche appears at Thornfield not as a French orphan needing an English governess, but as one of a group of guests who between them comprise a peeress, a local magistrate, an army officer, and a Member of Parliament. Evidently they have shared political interests with their host, from which we are excluded: we hear only that 'Colonel Dent and Mr Eshton argue on politics; their wives listen' (205). Jane's mockery of Rochester's 'aristocratic tastes' and 'impetuous republican answers' make it evident that he and his friends represent the Whig aristocracy, a conclusion already implied by his West Indian connections (308).

The deepening love between Jane and Rochester is one of the English novel's crowning examples of an exogamous sexual romance based on the attraction of social and historical opposites. In a novel where the representation of otherness takes on a global and racial perspective—ranging from Rochester's first marriage in Jamaica to Jane's imaginary journeys to Turkey and the Arctic—the depth of apparent opposition between the lovers draws on Jane's sense of psychic displacement stemming from her childhood. The orphaned clergyman's daughter casts herself as Rochester's 'plebeian bride' (308). If he is a Cavalier, she is a Puritan with a 'plain, Quakerish' appearance and an 'earnest, religious energy' (287, 310). He likes dressing up, playing the parts of an Eastern emir and a condemned highwayman in charades with Blanche and then disguising himself as a fortune-teller, while her direct and unadorned gaze is 'the very sublime of faith, truth, and devotion' (310). He is an unscrupulous would-be bigamist who attempts to deceive her; she is a clairvoyant who sees through his disguises, although she cannot penetrate the secret of his marriage to Bertha. When, at last, she flees Thornfield she thinks of herself as going to the scaffold, as if—like Helen Burns's Charles I—not all her integrity and conscientiousness could open her eyes to what was coming.

Jane's departure from Thornfield, which is initiated by a supernatural voice and concluded by a miraculous reunion with her own family, is one of the most pilgrimage-like episodes in the novel. She escapes from Rochester only to find herself being endogamously courted by St John Rivers, the country vicar and Puritan saint who is also her cousin. Where Rochester would have lured her into a bigamous marriage, Rivers proposes a mere marriage of convenience, not a love match or a union likely to lead to offspring. Rochester's marriage to Bertha Mason was intended to carry colonial wealth back to England, while Rivers plans to export evangelical spirituality to India and tells Jane it is her duty to help him. Had Jane still felt herself 'a wanderer on the face of the earth' (256), she would surely have accepted.

What Jane detects in Rivers is the self-mortifying patriotism of the new breed of British imperialists. He hates the family Christmas that she prepares for her new-found cousins and, as she reflects, 'the Himalayan ridge, or Caffre bush, even the plague-cursed Guinea swamp, would suit him better' (419). He thinks of himself as an 'alien from his native country', but Jane's perception of his 'austere patriot's passion for his fatherland' (380, 426–7) is a sign of her own growing patriotism, which has its roots in Rochester's attempt to make her his English bride. The night of her (false) betrothal, when '[a] splendid Midsummer shone over England' (276) and she and Rochester embrace under an old chestnut tree to the sound of a nightingale, is a moment of emotional homecoming, even though the tree is split in two by lightning immediately afterwards. Rochester begins his proposal by threatening to send her away to become a governess with the O'Galls of Bitternutt Lodge, Ireland; Jane, not noticing that she is being teased, replies that the sea voyage would serve as a barrier '[f]rom England and from Thornfield', as well as from himself (279). The next day Rochester tells Adèle that Jane is from 'Elf-land' (296), but then asserts that he 'would not exchange this one little English girl for the Grand Turk's whole seraglio' (296–7).

It would seem that Rochester, having tired of European mistresses, is keen to replace his Creole wife with one of pure English race.[45] After coming back from Jamaica, he spent ten years travelling in Europe and making love among the continental aristocracy. He tells how Céline Varens charmed his 'English gold' out of his 'British breeches pocket' (170) and how he has brought her daughter back to grow up in the 'wholesome soil of an English country garden' (176), but he retains a villa in the south of France where he would like to keep Jane away from prying eyes. When she leaves Thornfield, she is convinced that he will return to his continental haunts; after all, travel and sexual licence are part of his way of life.[46] But he shuns the ruling-class company he has formerly kept, and (like Jane behind the window curtain at Mrs Reed's) shuts himself away in the isolated manor of Ferndean, a damp, low house in the middle of a gloomy forest. Jane finally joins her blind and maimed lover in a home where she cannot roam in the hills or even gaze out from the battlements over a wide landscape as she had done at Thornfield. The country whose geography had earlier been implausibly stretched is now contracted to a remote, self-enclosed hermitage where nobody (it seems) any longer cares about Mr Rochester and his bride.

Their life at Ferndean is, however, one of repatriation and restoration. Thanks to her Madeiran uncle who is closely linked to the Jamaican plantocracy, Jane brings Rochester a second Caribbean fortune. He has come to see his confinement at Ferndean as a form of divine punishment for his libertinism, and, before reaching a state of penitence, he has cursed and lamented like Job:

'Jane! you think me, I dare say, an irreligious dog...I did wrong: I would have sullied my innocent flower—breathed guilt on its purity: the Omnipotent snatched it from me. I, in my stiff-necked rebellion, almost cursed the dispensation: instead of bending to the decree, I defied it. Divine justice pursued its course; disasters came thick on me: I was forced to pass through the valley of the shadow of death. *His* chastisements are mighty; and one smote me which has humbled me for ever. You know I was proud of my strength: but what is it now, when I must give it over to foreign guidance, as a child does its weakness? Of late, Jane— only—only of late—I began to see and acknowledge the hand of God in my doom.' (471)

His blindness is the blindness of Samson, who also found himself under 'foreign guidance' (the guidance of strangers), but Jane's arrival at Ferndean puts him back into familiar English hands. As his nurse she restores him to happiness and the power of sight, and as his wife she bears his children, though the novel takes no interest in the children or their future. Yet, as is shown by the curiously dislocated tone of her confession, 'Reader, I married him' (474), Jane both enjoys her heart's desire— England and Mr Rochester—and remains somehow alienated in her enjoyment. She is mistress of Ferndean, but her world has manifestly diminished since the burning down of Thornfield, where she first dreamed of marrying her aristocratic lover. There is an ambivalence about the ending of *Jane Eyre* which looks forward to Brontë's last novel, *Villette* (to be discussed in Chapter 10), the confessional narrative of an Englishwoman who both remains single and chooses to live overseas.

The Cromwell of the North

Since Charlotte Brontë's first novel, *The Professor*, remained unpublished during her lifetime, we may say that Elizabeth Gaskell, six years older than Brontë, introduced the portrayal of the northern industrialist, as well as of the Manchester working class, into English fiction. Her first Manchester novel *Mary Barton* (1848) was followed by *North and South*, where the courtship plot suggests an allegorical healing of geographical and class divisions (though the title was invented by Charles Dickens when the novel was serialized in his journal *Household Words*).

The contrast between the rough world of northern industry and the genteel 'aristocratic' South is at the heart of Gaskell's liberal middle-class outlook.

Gaskell had earlier portrayed the genteel middle classes fallen on hard times in *Cranford*, her linked collection of stories reminiscent of Mitford's *Our Village*. Here there is no geographical opposition of North and South, but simply a group of respectable old ladies living on reduced incomes in a small town twenty miles from the city of Drumble, the centre of 'that "horrid cotton trade" ' and one of Gaskell's fictive incarnations of Manchester.[47] The Cranford ladies pride themselves on their high-born connections—'though some might be poor, we were all aristocratic' (3)— and their ideal of good manners is that of Lord Chesterfield's letters. The principal characters, Miss Jenkyns and Miss Matty, are the daughters of the deceased rector. When the bank in which Miss Matty has invested fails, she resorts to an upmarket form of trade, selling specialist teas, to make ends meet. But her long-lost brother comes back from India and saves her from this temporary descent into shopkeeping. He is by no means as 'rich as a nabob', but thanks to his mercantile activity in the East Miss Matty is once again able to 'live... "very genteelly" at Cranford' (217).

The quoted phrases illustrate how Gaskell turns the language of gentility into a defensive class idiom, fortified, as it were, with inverted commas. The utopia of the Cranford middle classes depends upon their refusal to acknowledge their lower-class neighbours, with the partial exception of shopkeepers and servants. In *North and South*, Margaret Hale has no such defences. At Helstone in Hampshire, where her father is rector, she relapses into solitude, failing (apart from her charitable visits to outlying cottages) to do anything to alleviate the village's wretched backwardness. She never acts on her resolution to become a teacher at the village school, despite her father's rebukes. When the family moves to Milton-Northern the bigoted matriarch Mrs Thornton regards her as an idle product of the 'aristocratic counties' who speaks like a 'duke's daughter' and is fit for nothing but to go 'angling after husbands' (89, 225).

Mrs Thornton, however, is the mother of Milton's most successful manufacturer, and the social distance between the Thorntons and the Hales—like similar class divisions in Charlotte Brontë's *Shirley* (1849)— is shown as being directly connected to the divisions of the Civil Wars and, before that, of the Saxons and Normans. In her *Life of Charlotte Brontë*, Elizabeth Gaskell noted that the West Riding of Yorkshire was full of descendants of those who 'served under Cromwell at Dunbar, liv[ing] on the same lands as their ancestors occupied then ... there is no part of England where the traditional and fond recollections of the Commonwealth have lingered so long'.[48] Roundhead affiliations underlie the radical republicanism of Hiram Yorke, the hereditary landowner in *Shirley*, and Yorke Hunsden, the mill-owner in *The Professor*. Yorke and Hunsden boast of their Saxon roots, just as John Thornton in *North and South* speaks of his 'Teutonic blood' (407). Thornton openly declares his admiration for Oliver Cromwell, telling Margaret that ' "Cromwell would have made a capital mill-owner ... I wish we had him to put down this strike for us" ' (146).[49] Thornton derives his political creed from his 'Teutonic' ancestry, supporting the regionalism of the Saxon Heptarchy against the remote London government introduced by the Normans.

When Thornton speaks of Cromwell as a capital mill-owner, Margaret coldly replies that ' "Cromwell is no hero of mine" ' (146). She is the granddaughter of Sir John Beresford, a knight of the shires identified as a Tory and a Royalist by his favourite toast of 'Church and King, and down with the Rump' (50). Margaret's Aunt Shaw has married an army general and lives a fashionable London life, while her mother has been condemned to rural shabby-gentility by her marriage to the Reverend Dr Hale. Having been brought up both in Helstone Parsonage and with her cousins in Harley Street, Margaret has experienced the two poles of genteel existence. Her cousin Edith marries a Scottish army captain, and Margaret receives a proposal from his brother, the ambitious barrister Henry Lennox. Her rejection of this potential second alliance registers her distaste for metropolitan values, but in defying class and family conventions she is retreading the path that her mother and brother have taken.

Mrs Hale has merely married a clergyman against her family's advice, but their son Frederick is an outlaw living in exile. A former naval officer convicted of mutiny, he is now serving with the Spanish army. Margaret's efforts to clear his name are unavailing, and in the end he renounces his English identity, marrying a Spanish Catholic and saying that he wishes to 'unnative himself' and would not take a pardon under any circumstances (413). Frederick's rebellion against the state is paralleled by Mr Hale's defection from the English Church, leaving the family's traditional Tory gentility in a state of utter collapse. A crisis of conscience leads him to resign his living and move to Milton, where he earns his living as tutor to John Thornton, who sees classical learning as a passport to the gentility from which he has been excluded.

The Thorntons and Hales, then, exemplify a process of class displacement and replacement. Margaret is deeply stirred by the sense of power that she finds in Thornton and his fellow factory-owners, while he and his mother pretend to believe that the gentry and aristocracy have outlived their usefulness. Mrs Thornton, in her middle-class pride, boasts that

'Go where you will—I don't say in England only, but in Europe—the name of John Thornton of Milton is known and respected amongst all men of business. Of course, it is unknown in fashionable circles,' she continued, scornfully. 'Idle gentlemen and ladies are not likely to know much of a Milton manufacturer, unless he gets into parliament, or marries a lord's daughter.' (134)

Despite his desire for classical learning, Thornton remains true to his creed that 'A man is to me a higher and a completer being than a gentleman' (195–6), yet neither he nor his mother would think it odd if he were to marry a lord's daughter.

When Margaret moves from the New Forest to Milton-Northern she feels a sense of physical affliction, a 'stupor of despair' that she breathes in with the polluted city air:

The heavy smoky air hung about her bedroom, which occupied the long narrow projection at the back of the house. The window, placed at the side of the oblong, looked to the blank wall of a similar projection, not above ten feet distant. It loomed through the fog like a great barrier to hope. (75)

The manufacturers, blinded by pride and their contempt for their factory hands, have ignored the human cost of their work and power. Margaret, however, becomes a kind of social worker, moving at ease (as she did not feel able to do in her Hampshire village) among the ordinary people. Her friendship with Jessy Higgins, the factory girl who is dying of an industrial lung disease, is based on a sense of equality and not of religious charity. People are dying all around her—during the eighteen months or so of narrative time there are, in true Victorian fictional style, no less than seven deaths—but Margaret grows in stature. When a crowd of striking workers storms the factory gates she alone shows heroism and presence of mind, although she also feels a 'deep sense of shame' at her public exposure to the 'unwinking glare of many eyes' (229). Her godfather, an Oxford don, jokes that Milton has turned her into a 'democrat', a 'red republican', and a 'socialist' (397). But what Milton-Northern actually finds in her is 'breeding', the traditional aristocratic fearlessness and integrity which inspires respect, not mockery. Dr Donaldson, the (presumably Scottish) doctor, describes her as a 'thoroughbred creature' (150), suggesting an inherited toughness which underlies her social position as a former clergyman's daughter. This discovery of identity provides the ground for her eventual marriage to Thornton.

North and South, unlike the novels of Austen and Brontë, is manifestly a tract for its times and a political parable. Necessarily it concludes with a political marriage calculated to resolve the national divisions that the novel has so fully expounded. By the time that Margaret is ready to accept Thornton's love, he has lost caste by being driven to the verge of bankruptcy while she has risen by inheriting a fortune, which includes slum property at Milton-Northern and the freehold of Thornton's mill. Margaret brings to the marriage 'breeding', a new injection of capital, and a concern for the welfare of all classes in society; Thornton brings the commercial initiative and ruthlessness that were driving Victorian England forward. The story, however, concludes before the marriage has actually taken place, and we are not told anything of the couple's future. One of Elizabeth Gaskell's friends 'remarked grimly to [her] that she doubted whether Margaret would ever be happy with Thornton, though she had no doubt as to his future bliss'.[50]

North and South has been called a 'Victorian *Pride and Prejudice*',[51] although Gaskell was far too intelligent to pretend that the social issues raised in her fiction could be easily laid to rest. Her novel *Sylvia's Lovers* (1863) is one of a number of later Victorian works which undermine any suggestion that the nation could be unified by marriage. After *Jane Eyre* and *North and South*, the great English courtship novels would end in frustration, bewilderment, and even tragedy. 'Reader, I married him' becomes an ominous refrain in the context of George Eliot's *Middlemarch* and *Daniel Deronda* and, still more, Thomas Hardy's novels.

'Turn Again, Dick Whittington!': Dickens and the Fiction of the City

I F any single writer has been said to embody the Englishness of the English novel it is Dickens. The novelist George Gissing wrote of his great predecessor that 'No man ever loved England more'.[1] G. K. Chesterton called him 'the most English of our great writers'.[2] Dickens's reputation rests above all on his characters, who are portrayed with marvellous vividness and symbolic power, and in a register that veers melodramatically between satire and sentiment. Their variety is that of a whole nation—of a nation centring on its metropolis—but the nation in Dickens's novels is sharply divided between public and private spheres, one of which inspires his mockery and the other his reverence. Many of his most famous satirical creations gleefully debunk the professional classes and holders of minor public office—beadles, midwives, lawyers, clerks, schoolteachers, and ministers of religion—and figures such as Bumble, Gradgrind, and Squeers have become proverbial monsters outliving the fictional contexts in which they first appeared. Their power over the lives of Dickens's ordinary heroes and heroines produces a sense of monstrous oppression and injustice. Dickens, then, is a radical novelist, but his reflection of national character has certain manifest limitations. Gissing wrote that 'his art, splendidly triumphant, made visible to all mankind the characteristic virtues, the typical shortcomings, of the homely English race'.[3] The key word here is 'homely'. He has no interest in the ceremonial aspects of English history or the national life, nor is his fiction international in outlook. What he wishes most for his protagonists is an untroubled, unambitious domestic happiness. He is the novelist as instinctive republican but also as Little Englander.

George Orwell contrasted Dickens's lack of 'vulgar nationalism' with the jingoism of his Victorian contemporaries:

never anywhere does he indulge in the typical English boasting, the 'island race', 'bulldog breed', 'right little, tight little island' style of talk....He is very much an Englishman, but he is hardly aware of it—certainly the thought of being an Englishman does not thrill him. He has no imperialist feeling, no discernible views on foreign politics, and is untouched by the military tradition.[4]

Orwell's generalization can only be applied to Dickens the novelist, since as a journalist he certainly expressed imperialist feelings. It has been said that his 'sympathy for the downtrodden poor at home is reversed abroad'.[5] He joined in the outcry against the perpetrators of the 1857 Indian Mutiny, and as a public figure he was prominent in recommending emigration to the white dominions such as Australia. Yet Dickens was also the author of A Child's History of England (1853), a work which became notorious for its exposure of the barbarities of past times and its mockery of the idiocies of English kings. Despite some dutiful praise of King Alfred and the sturdy Saxon race, the Child's History is English history written from a deliberately childlike point of view. Nothing could be less like an approved adult textbook for children.

The split between the public and the private spheres in Dickens's fiction can be related to a split in his own personality between the adult and the child. For all his greatness as a novelist, his fiction does not express his public persona as fully as Scott's or Fielding's does. Any biography of Charles Dickens will reveal his restlessness of spirit, his flair for publicity, his relentless ambition, and his capacity for overwork to the point of self-destruction. His novels, however, uphold the values of patience, humility, steadfastness, and, above all, of self-effacing retirement. David Copperfield, the one Dickens hero who becomes a successful novelist, is an amiable figure completely lacking his creator's driven and demonic temperament. Some of his other protagonists become prosperous businessmen, but none has any idea of serving the nation or taking public office. His novels set public vice against private virtue, so that typically they start in the mode of parody and end in the mode of romance.[6] Oliver Twist (1838) is the first example of the characteristic Dickens plot and, it has been argued, the 'one novel which he wrote over and over again' throughout his subsequent career.[7] Its opening chapters telling of Oliver's early childhood under the regime of the New Poor Law are one of the most savagely effective political satires ever written in the form of fiction. Yet Oliver at the end of the novel is still a child, and there is no reason to suspect that he will do anything spectacular or noteworthy in his adult life.

Citizens and 'Public Characters'

Many of Dickens's most famous characters are Londoners. For the staunch republican William Hazlitt, the citizens of a great city such as London were inherently more advanced and more progressive than their country cousins. Hazlitt rejected William Wordsworth's representation of men in cities as being anonymous and isolated from one another, like wild beasts; a Londoner was a sort of 'public creature', a member of a 'visible body-politic, a type and image of that huge Leviathan the State'. The Londoner in his view was a natural republican just as the country-dweller was a natural monarchist.[8] Hazlitt's essay 'On Londoners and Country People', from which these quotations are taken, was collected in *The Plain Speaker* (1826). It may be seen as anticipating the change from fiction largely dealing with the country gentry and their dependents (including those who, for one reason or another, move to the city) to the metropolitan novel of Dickens and his contemporaries with its wider and more demotic range of characters. The city is also the place where people can most easily change their status, leaving behind the stratum into which they were born.

Dickens did not envisage *The Pickwick Papers* (1836–7) as his first novel—though it certainly grew into that—but as letterpress to illustrate a series of comic prints. On a simplified view, his career as a novelist stretches from *Oliver Twist* and *Barnaby Rudge* (which was conceived, but not actually written, at the same time as *Pickwick*) to his last completed novel *Our Mutual Friend* some thirty years later. Young Oliver Twist begins as a mere 'item of mortality', an entry in the workhouse ledger in an unidentified country town, and makes what Dickens calls his 'first Entry into Public Life' when he is apprenticed to Mr Sowerberry the undertaker.[9] As a funeral attendant he becomes a familiar figure on the streets, standing on the lowest rung of the ladder leading to the giddy heights occupied by Mr Bumble the parish beadle, whose official 'stateliness and gravity' (as the narrator tersely informs us) far exceeds that of 'judges of the law, members of parliament, ministers of state, lord mayors, and other great public functionaries' (221). But Oliver's fortunes take a decisive turn when he runs away from Mr Sowerberry's and reaches a milestone which tells him he is seventy miles from London:

London—that great large place!—nobody—not even Mr Bumble—could ever find him there! He had often heard the old men in the workhouse, too, say that no lad of spirit need want in London; and that there were ways of living in that vast city, which those who had been bred up in country parts had no idea of. It was the very place for a homeless boy, who must die in the streets unless someone helped him. (97)

London, as the legendary Dick Whittington had found, is the place for the orphan, the 'lad of spirit', the restless adolescent who up to now has only been humiliated and downtrodden. Once in the city his public career can only flourish and broaden, yet the ideas of public life and citizenship have far more sinister connotations in Dickens than they do for a commentator such as Hazlitt.

When Noah Claypole follows Oliver Twist to London, adopts a false name, and joins Fagin's gang of thieves, Dickens sardonically describes him as having become a 'public Character in the Metropolis' (376). A 'public character' in his novels is as often as not someone with a police record, a notorious impostor, rogue, or confidence trickster. In *Our Mutual Friend* (1864–5) the Limehouse criminal Rogue Riderhood describes himself to Lawyer Lightwood as a 'Waterside character' (152), while the grave-robber in *A Tale of Two Cities* (1859) owns to being an 'Agricultooral character'.[10] Not surprisingly, Dickens's heroes and heroines do their best to shun publicity, so that the happy endings to most of his novels combine prosperity with complete obscurity. The phrase 'public character' in his fiction is tarnished by its association with crime even when it is applied to someone who is completely innocent. Thus Sir John Chester in *Barnaby Rudge* (1841) tells Gabriel Varden (whose name has been in the newspapers after giving evidence in court) that he has become 'quite a public character'.[11] When Mr Micawber, the Australian magistrate, is described by his wife as an 'important public character', we cannot but remember his past as an inveterate sponger and debt-bilker in London.[12] In *Our Mutual Friend* a book containing portraits of people of fashion is described as illustrating 'public characters' (410), hinting at the narrator's contempt for wealthy and fashionable society. The phrase occurs very naturally in a plot linking the pompous and respectable face of society to the criminal underworld. Dickens may be most renowned for his creation of characters, yet to be called, or to call oneself a 'character' in his novels is usually undesirable. Dickens's love of London must, therefore, be squared with his profound distrust of urban society and citizenship. What is most remarkable (as we shall see) is that in novel after novel he alludes to the legend of Dick Whittington, London's archetypal Lord Mayor who, above all, stands for Hazlitt's idea of the Londoner as a 'public creature'.

The English *Bildungsroman*

At least five of Dickens's novels, *Oliver Twist*, *Nicholas Nickleby*, *Martin Chuzzlewit*, *David Copperfield*, and *Great Expectations*, formally belong to the category of the male *Bildungsroman* or novel of education, typically the story of a young man from the provinces growing up and finding his way in society. The Dickensian *Bildungsroman* not only comes after Fielding and Smollett but after the great French novelists, Stendhal and Balzac, yet it is closer to folk tale and fairy tale than to the masterpieces of French realism. The typical Dickens hero (David Copperfield is the exception) is an orphan who inherits a fortune rather than using his character and abilities to secure a position in society, as the novelist himself had to do. Dickens's novels thus exhibit a 'recognition-inheritance pattern' like those of Fielding and Scott, a kind of plot that has been regarded as peculiarly English.[13] In English fiction the 'European' type of *Bildungsroman* is represented by the story of Thackeray's Arthur Pendennis (and of Charlotte Brontë's Lucy Snowe, to be discussed in the next chapter).

The hero of William Makepeace Thackeray's *Pendennis* (1850) is a gentleman's son, the heir to a country estate, and an Oxbridge graduate ('Oxbridge' seems to be a Thackerayan coinage) when he first moves to London. Like Lucien Chardon in Honoré de Balzac's *Illusions perdues* (1839), he is a provincial man of substance, not a friendless orphan. Like Lucien, too, he is a talented journalist but a morally tarnished human being, and he enters the metropolis in a state of intense excitement, as if he has reached the ultimate proving-ground both of his manhood and his ambitions. Driving into London on a stagecoach is a kind of initiation: 'from his place on the coach-roof the eager young fellow looked down upon the city, with the sort of longing desire which young soldiers feel on the eve of a campaign'.[14] Soon he has turned himself from an obscure provincial poet into a sketch writer and a fashionable novelist. Eventually he becomes a Member of Parliament. One might think that he has broken out of the rural gentry into a new world where class divisions are relatively fluid and reputations are made and broken overnight, but this is not the whole story.

It is Pendennis's friend George Warrington who takes him to a newspaper office and extols the revolutionary power of the press: ' "Look at that, Pen," Warrington said. "There she is—the great engine—she never sleeps. She has her ambassadors in every quarter of the world—her couriers upon every road. Her officers march along with armies, and her envoys walk into statesmen's cabinets"' (i. 313–14). The press with its 'ambassadors' and 'officers' is like an alternative state apparatus, a literary republic with global imperial ambitions. But Pendennis becomes a stylish belle-lettristic essayist, not a thunderous leader writer like Warrington. His job is to remind his paper's readers that it is 'written by gentlemen for gentlemen' (i. 330). Pendennis the fashionable essayist is seen from Thackeray's disillusioned perspective as a personification of opportunism and selfishness, not of stern ambition and a noble mission. He is a 'man and a brother' but not a 'hero' (ii. 394). His heavily auto-biographical first novel is the story of a prime minister's son whose rival is a young duke. (Doubtless Thackeray was cocking a snook at the more established Disraeli and his novel *The Young Duke*.) Pendennis's party allegiances change with the fluctuations of fashionable political opinion, and when Laura, his stepsister and future wife, innocently remarks that he must intend 'to do a great deal of good to the country' by going into Parliament, he covers his sense of shame with the remark that women should not meddle in politics (ii. 301).

Thackeray famously regretted the Victorian prurience that prevented him from portraying his hero's young manhood as explicitly as Fielding had done: 'Since the author of *Tom Jones* was buried, no writer of fiction among us has been permitted to depict to his utmost power a MAN. We must drape him, and give him a certain conventional simper' (i, p. xviii). So Pendennis is not actually allowed to make love to his lower-class inamorata Fanny Bolton, but this is not the only respect in which his military assault on London turns into something approaching a fiasco. He remains a country gentleman at heart, and, far from committing himself to the democracy of city life, he prefers to remain a prince in his family's eyes. Finally he marries the long-suffering Laura and returns to the values he once learned from his mother, a 'country bred woman' for whom the 'book of life' told 'a different story to that page which is read in cities' (i. 70). Pendennis's metropolitan adventures are only a detour. London for both Dickens and Thackeray was the 'modern Babylon',[15] but their protagonists often seem to languish there like the Israelites in captivity.

Pendennis's story may be viewed as either one of failure in the city or of exploiting the city, of taking its gifts of celebrity and riches while reserving oneself for a finer and more permanent life elsewhere. Subsequent English attempts at the form of the metropolitan *Bildungsroman* tend to explore one or the other of these alternatives, although H. G. Wells in *Tono-Bungay* (1909) and *The New Machiavelli* (1911) shares some of Thackeray's ambivalence. In *Tono-Bungay* (to be further discussed in

Chapter 12) the narrator, George Ponderevo, is jauntily shown London by his uncle Edward, the novel's principal spokesman for the 'Romance of Commerce':

'The richest town in the world, the biggest port, the greatest manufacturing town, the Imperial city—the centre of civilization, the heart of the world! See those sandwich men down there!...It's a wonderful place, George—a whirlpool, a maelstrom! whirls you up and whirls you down.'[16]

George works to build up his uncle's patent medicine business before devoting himself to technological invention and scientific research, a pursuit that enables him to survive the collapse of Edward's grossly inflated financial empire. George is neither a future Lord Mayor nor a prospective down-and-out wearing sandwich boards. His research takes him away from London and from England, but he has to acknowledge the truth that science and learning are, as his uncle tells him, luxuries ultimately paid for by 'Enterprising businessmen' (136). In Wells's œuvre *Tono-Bungay* had been preceded by *Love and Mr Lewisham* (1900), a story of metropolitan failure, and *Kipps* (1905), based on a Dickensian inheritance plot. It is, therefore, notable that George Ponderevo is an orphan who owes his chance in life to the accident of being an entrepreneur's nephew.

As we shall see in Chapter 11, the classical story in late Victorian English fiction is one of thwarted ambition in the English provinces. The provincial novelists include those, like George Eliot and Arnold Bennett, whose own lives present a tale of metropolitan success. Arnold Bennett's first novel, *A Man from the North* (1898), introduces its protagonist as the 'kind of youth of whom it may be said that he is born to be a Londoner'.[17] Richard Larch comes to the city in search of literary fame, but his projected book remains unwritten, as does his friend Aked's study of 'The Psychology of the Suburbs'. Bennett's best-known novels are set in the Potteries, but those with a London background such as *Riceyman Steps* (1923) are local and, as it were, suburban in character.

A different kind of transposition is seen in Thomas Hardy's *Jude the Obscure* (1895), where Christminster (Oxford), not London, is Jude Fawley's 'centre of civilization'. Hardy describes Jude with his dream of classical learning as 'a species of Dick Whittington whose spirit was touched to finer issues than a mere material gain'.[18] Jude's failure as a potential Dick Whittington is most abject, since his proletarian origins bar him even from entering the colleges of Christminster. But the idea that a material success like that of the legendary Lord Mayor would be unduly vulgar, and that the novelist should be concerned with 'finer issues', brings us back to Dickens's wrestling with the Whittington story.

Ragged Dick and the Master's Daughter

Dick Whittington is first of all a historical figure, one of innumerable country boys who have risen to become rich City merchants. Just why the third son of Sir William Whittington of Pauntley, Gloucestershire, should have achieved proverbial fame is not obvious, even though he was three times Lord Mayor at a time when the mayoralty was the only significant temporal office in the land not in the gift of the king. London since the beginning of the thirteenth century had been, in effect, a self-governing commune or miniature republic in which distinction was open to anyone on merit. Thomas Deloney's story of Simon Eyre, the penniless apprentice who tricked the master of a foreign ship into selling him his whole cargo on credit, has the authentic ring of mercantile capitalism, as we saw in Chapter 2. Eyre is a 'spiv' owing his success to quick thinking and confidence trickery, while Whittington's story radiates an essential innocence. A drooping boy (as Wordsworth described him in *The Prelude*)[19] rather than a self-made man, he turns his rags into riches thanks to good luck (the cat) and predestination (the message of the bells). By marrying his master's daughter he plays a part in the dynastic succession of an established mercantile family, the Fitzwarrens. Dickens rejects some aspects of the Whittington story while incorporating the legend into the recognition-inheritance pattern of his novels, a pattern in which it is the just distribution of existing wealth and not the creation of new wealth that matters.

There was a portrait of Whittington with cat in the Mercers' Hall as early as 1536, little more than a century after the death of the historical Sir Richard.[20] His story was embellished and retold in Elizabethan plays and ballads. Thomas Heywood's version of his *Famous and Remarkable History* (1636/7) speaks of his arrival in London: 'to beg he was ashamed, to steal he did abhor: two days he spent in gaping upon the shops and gazing upon the buildings feeding his eyes but starving his stomach.'[21] An eighteenth-century chapbook version of the same events turns him into the hero of a moral fable with obvious possibilities for fictional development:

He strolled about the country as ragged as a colt, till he met with a waggoner who was going to London, and who gave him leave to walk all the way by the side of his waggon without paying for his passage, which pleased little Whittington very much, as he wanted to see London sadly, for he had heard that the streets were paved with gold, and he was willing to get a bushel of it; but how great was his disappointment, poor boy! when he saw the streets covered with dirt instead of gold, and found himself in a strange place, without a friend, without food, and without money.[22]

From 'little Whittington's' ironic discoveries it is not a long step to Oliver Twist learning the realities of life in the metropolis.

If Whittington has no friends when he reaches the city, neither has he any real enemies. Although he is bullied by the kitchen maid, he is allowed to place his cat as a lucky investment in his master's argosy to the Barbary coast. It is Dick's impatience that moves him to run away. The message of Bow Bells that he heard on Highgate Hill was recalled by William Wordsworth in *The Prelude* (1805) and by Scott in *Rob Roy* (1817), as well as by Dickens on numerous occasions. At the beginning of *Rob Roy*, Francis Osbaldistone refuses to follow his father's profession as a City banker, deciding instead to try to reclaim his family's estate in Northumberland. As he climbs Highgate Hill he hears the 'admonitory "Turn again," erst heard by [the] future Lord Mayor', but takes no notice.[23] The destiny of the Scott hero lies in the Borders and Highlands, not in London, although it may involve shady metropolitan financial transactions. Osbaldistone's route up the Great North Road is travelled in reverse in a number of Scott's novels, including *The Heart of Mid-Lothian*, *The Fortunes of Nigel*, and *Peveril of the Peak*. But the protagonists go to London to plead for their established rights in Scotland or the North of England, not to seek new fortunes.

Dickens's heroes, like Scott's, despise the mercantile ambitions symbolized by the Whittington legend, although for very different reasons. Scott's heroes want to become romantic aristocrats, while the Dickensian protagonist wants to enjoy a simple private happiness. In Scott the inheritance to which the hero has been born takes the form of landownership, while Dickens's protagonists are rewarded with an income sufficient to make them persons of leisure. Members of the aristocracy and the criminal classes may be closely allied in plotting the protagonist's downfall. The reason why Dickens's allusions to the Whittington legend are so often facetious or satirical in tone is that its innocent aspirations have been irrevocably blocked by the modern reality of metropolitan corruption. For honest Joe Willet in *Barnaby Rudge*, for example, the message of the bells is not the simple negative that Scott's protagonist heard. In fact, there is no message:

He went out by Islington and so on to Highgate, and sat on many stones and gates, but there were no voices in the bells to bid him turn. Since the time of noble

Whittington, fair flower of merchants, bells have come to have less sympathy with humankind. They only ring for money and on state occasions. Wanderers have increased in number; ships leave the Thames for distant regions, carrying from stem to stern no other cargo; the bells are silent: they ring out no entreaties or regrets; they are used to it and have grown worldly. (237)

Most telling here is Dickens's sombre reference to the crowded emigrant ships, leaving London for more distant Eldorados. Dickens sends the Micawbers, the Peggottys, and Little Em'ly to Australia, and Martin Chuzzlewit and Mark Tapley in search of fool's gold to the United States. Little Nell and her grandfather in *The Old Curiosity Shop* (1841) also flee from London. Of these characters, only Joe Willet (who volunteers for the army and fights in the American War of Independence) and Martin Chuzzlewit are able to return to the city and come into an inheritance. It is the city slicker Montague Tigg, not anyone more creditable, who envisages Martin and his friend Tom Pinch as 'a pair of Whittingtons'.[24] Similarly, in *Oliver Twist* it is not Oliver but Bill Sikes, after the murder of Nancy, who finds himself powerless to escape from the environs of London once he has passed the 'stone in honour of Whittington' (424). In *The Old Curiosity Shop* Whittingtonian hopes are put in the mouth of the petty rogue Dick Swiveller, who thinks that if he goes to Highgate 'Perhaps the bells might strike up "Turn again, Swiveller, Lord Mayor of London"'.[25] Richard Carstone in *Bleak House* (1852–3) dreams idly of miraculous good fortune like that of his 'namesake Whittington'.[26] Oliver Twist's fate sums up what could be taken as Dickens's general advice to homeless orphans in his novels: whatever you do, steer clear of London. At Sowerberry's he has already been ill-treated in the kitchen by Noah and Charlotte. On the Great North Road at Barnet, some way before Highgate, he is accosted by the Artful Dodger, taken to the metropolis, and shown into the thieves' kitchen presided over by Fagin (where Nancy, however, does not ill-treat him). Oliver's career in crime reaches its logical ending when, wounded by a pistol shot after being forced to take part in an attempted burglary, he is left for dead in a ditch and disappears for six whole chapters. He is brought back to life thanks to the recognition-inheritance plot, and from this point on he is a country gentleman in the making.

Nicholas Nickleby, in Dickens's next novel, takes public employment as a Yorkshire schoolteacher and as secretary to a Member of Parliament, but gives up both positions in disgust. Eventually he finds complete satisfaction as a humble clerk to the Cheeryble brothers, who are ultra-benevolent London merchants. More to his surprise than ours, they entrust him with their fortune, but he moves to Somerset and runs their business from a great distance. It is not until Dickens's middle period that he seems able to dispense with the Cheeryble brothers' miraculous benevolence and to show characters relying on their own resources. His reckoning with the Whittington theme is summed up in his middle-period and later novels, beginning with *David Copperfield* and *Dombey and Son*.

David Copperfield (1849–50) is sufficiently autobiographical for it to have been rather awkward for its author to portray his hero as another Whittington. Nevertheless, David is constantly shown travelling the road to Highgate (the home of Steerforth, of Dr Strong and, for a time, of Betsy Trotwood) and looking down from its hill; moreover, his early sufferings as a 'ragged way-worn boy forsaken and neglected' (863) are never forgotten even though he finds a fairy godmother in his aunt. For most of the voluminous narrative David lives a life of gentility and growing prosperity. It is when he has become an established writer and an employer of servants that his domestic 'page', later to be transported for theft, is shown quarrelling with the cook like a 'perfect Whittington, without his cat, or the remotest chance of being made Lord Mayor' (691). Nevertheless, the young David is identified by Uriah Heep as a fellow 'upstart' (760), and David succeeds where Uriah fails in marrying their respective masters' daughters, Dora Spenlow and Agnes Wickfield. To add to his rival's sense of injury, David eventually takes Agnes for his second wife while Uriah languishes in prison. As a respected novelist, David also manages to achieve his ambition of becoming 'learned and distinguished' (155) while remaining wholly within the domestic sphere; Dickens does not show him as being in any respect a public figure. There are other possible Whittingtons in *David Copperfield*, since Tommy Traddles is finally about to become a judge, while Micawber's faith that 'something will turn up' has been duly rewarded in Australia. But when David comes back to England after three years abroad, he reflects that 'both England and the law appeared to me to be very difficult indeed to be taken by storm' (822).

Since Dickens increasingly saw the English state as a monstrously corrupt social organism, resistant to change—with its age-old corruption symbolized by institutions such as the Court of Chancery in *Bleak House*—it was the 'master's daughter' theme, rather than the hero's accession to public power and success, that continued to attract him to the Whittington story. The potential complexity of this theme is evident from the case of Estella in *Great Expectations* (1861): initially identified as the stepdaughter of Miss Havisham who is Pip's supposed patron, she is secretly a daughter to two of his 'masters', Magwitch (her actual father) and Jaggers (who lives with her mother). Pip's own story is a bleak negation of Whittington's, since the magical benefaction that makes him a London gentleman leads only to disillusionment and ruin, followed by many years of working overseas as a humble clerk. Finally Pip does, apparently, turn again, and Dickens notoriously revised his original ending to hint that his hero may at last succeed in marrying Estella.

The Dickens novel which returns most insistently to the Whittington theme is not, however, *Great Expectations* but *Dombey and Son* (1848), the story of a great City merchant told from the perspective of the master's daughter rather than of the outsider who aspires to marry her. It is here, almost uniquely, that Dickens tackles a City mercantile theme head-on. Once again, he is concerned with the problems of dynastic succession and not with making new money. Since (in the words of Whittington's Victorian biographers) the folk tale clearly implies that 'The children of successful men are rarely as energetic as their fathers',[27] Mr Dombey's misplaced determination to make his son his successor disregards the collective experience of the very entrepreneurial capitalism of which he is a figurehead. Had he been alive to the need for new blood in his family firm, he would have understood the value of his despised daughter Florence as the conduit for a potential son-in-law. Carker, who is Dombey's rival and would-be successor, is as blind as his master in that he targets his illicit desires at the latter's wife rather than his daughter. Carker for most of the novel seems a much more serious proposition than Walter Gay, the adopted son of the 'old-fashioned' (that is, near-bankrupt) shopkeeper Sol Gills. Walter's 'Whittingtonian hopes'[28] reflect the parental expectations of Gills and his friend Captain Cuttle rather than his own more modest ambitions. The fiction that he might be a future Lord Mayor is, as one critic says, 'shamelessly repeated' whenever his future is discussed or Florence's name is mentioned.[29] Moreover, the legend is twinned with a second, much more banal story, that of the coal-whipper who married the 'lovely Peg', daughter of the master of a Newcastle collier. As an office boy at Dombey and Son, Walter naturally falls in love with Florence although he is aware of the legend's apparent absurdity. But Dombey and Carker ship him off to the Caribbean in the ironically named *Son and Heir*, removing him from the action for a large part of the novel; and Dickens's original plan, in any case, was to disappoint all Walter's hopes in the manner of the Richard Carstone plot of *Bleak House*.[30] The novelist relented, at first allowing Walter to marry Florence without her father's knowledge once she has been cut out of the patriarchal succession, and then letting him succeed both in winning recognition as Dombey's son-in-law and in rebuilding the shattered family 'Edifice' (877). The problem here is that, like Nicholas Nickleby earlier, Walter has moved with his wife to the country while somehow controlling a new business in the heart of the city. He has more than his love for Florence in common with the unworldly Paul Dombey, who was his father's hoped-for successor. The ending of *Dombey and Son* reveals Dickens's extraordinary difficulties in reconciling his attachment to the Whittington legend with his rejection of the commercial enterprise culture. Nevertheless, he continued to produce ever more complex transmutations of the folk tale until his last completed novel, *Our Mutual Friend* (1864–5).

The Metropolitan Labyrinth

In modern times, Dickens had written in *Barnaby Rudge*, the bells only ring for money and on state occasions; but there are no state occasions in his novels, nor does he show much interest in the idea of the bells ringing for money. In Chapter 76 of *Barnaby Rudge* it is not Bow Bells but the bells of St Sepulchre Without Newgate that ring for Dickens's Londoners. St Sepulchre's bells, as a London historian writes, tolled 'with appalling frequency as the condemned from Newgate passed on their way to Tyburn'.[31] Their message to the condemned man is not 'Turn again!' but rather an incessant reminder that he is about to be, as Dennis the hangman would say, 'turn'd off'. That the bells tolling for ragged pilgrims to the metropolis might be those of St Sepulchre is clearly known to Harriet Carker in *Dombey and Son*, who watches helplessly as the 'stragglers' come wandering into London, passing her house at the city's edge on the Great North Road:

Day after day, such travellers crept past, but always, as she thought, in one direction—always towards the town. Swallowed up in one phase or other of its immensity, towards which they seemed impelled by a desperate fascination, they never returned. Food for the hospitals, the churchyards, the prisons, the river, fever, madness, vice, and death,—they passed on to the monster, roaring in the distance, and were lost. (480)

This passage seems almost out of place in *Dombey and Son*, evoking as it does the sombre worlds of *Oliver Twist*, *Barnaby Rudge*, and Dickens's last novels. The figuration of London as a cannibalistic 'monster', like the Minotaur at the heart of the labyrinth, suggests that those who enter the city do so only to become sacrificial victims. There is no escape, since the wanderers creep past in one direction only. The phrase (or cliché) 'a labyrinth of streets' proved irresistible to Dickens from *Oliver Twist* onwards.[32] The novels in which metropolitan labyrinths are evoked are themselves unprecedentedly labyrinthine, since any Dickens plot is full of complications, entanglements, obstructions, blind alleys, and doublings back. For Dickens, secrecy was of the essence of metropolitan living. A famous passage in *A Tale of Two Cities* (1859) describes the myriad of secrets enclosed in the 'darkly clustered houses' seen by a traveller entering a great city at night: 'Something of the awfulness, even of Death itself, is referable to this', the narrator adds (14–15). These are private secrets, the secrets of isolated individual hearts all hidden from one another, but as Dickens's characters gravitate towards 'the hospitals, the churchyards, the prisons', many private secrets are destined to be made public.

A city traditionally contains a walled citadel at its centre, but in Dickens's novels the centre of the metropolitan labyrinth is typically a prison or criminal underworld cut off from the ordinary urban life surrounding it. Mr Pickwick is sent to the Fleet Prison, and Fagin in *Oliver Twist* is last seen in the condemned cell, but the prison as the city's symbolic centre is first seen in *Barnaby Rudge*, where the main aim of the Gordon rioters is to liberate the inmates of Newgate and other jails. *Barnaby Rudge* grows out of the 'Newgate novels' of Dickens's contemporaries such as Bulwer-Lytton and Harrison Ainsworth, all of whom looked back to Scott, who had portrayed Edinburgh's Tolbooth prison as the 'Heart of Mid-Lothian' in the novel of that name. Scott in *The Fortunes of Nigel* portrays both imprisonment in the Tower, and the existence at the heart of Jacobean London of a criminal 'Alsatia' or no-go area such as we find in *Oliver Twist*. Dickens's later novels often surround a central prison with the labyrinthine apparatus of law and government, as in *Little Dorrit*, where the debtors in the Marshalsea Prison are subject to the do-nothing philosophy of the Circumlocution Office; *Great Expectations*, where entry and exit from Newgate and the hulks are controlled by the law business of Jaggers and Wemmick in Little Britain (the name of an actual London street); and *A Tale of Two Cities*, where the prison is the Bastille rather than Newgate. *Bleak House* may be added to this list, although the labyrinthine apparatus of the Court of Chancery belongs to the civil rather than the criminal law.

When George Gissing called Dickens the champion of the 'homely' English race, he will have had in mind that the novelist's most righteous characters are those who, like Harriet Carker and Esther Summerson, steer clear of the metropolis. The privacy of the family hearth is a sacred space for Dickens, although there are as many evil families as good ones in his fiction. And there are restless, unhappy individuals in Dickens's good families, like Richard Carstone in *Bleak House*, who head for the city and are sucked into its labyrinth. The bells hold no message for Richard, or, to put it another way, he lacks the Dickensian narrator's ability to see into the city's mysteries.

The narrator stands both inside and outside the labyrinth. Dickens himself was famously obsessed with pacing the London streets. Master Humphrey, the initial narrator of *The Old Curiosity Shop*, is a self-portrait whose 'constant pacing to and fro' and 'never-ending restlessness' (1) are at one with the city to which he belongs. It was said by Dickens's friend George Augustus Sala that he 'knew all about the back streets behind Holborn, the courts and alleys of the Borough, the shabby sidling streets of the remoter suburbs, the crooked little alleys of the City, the dank and oozy wharfs of the water-side'.[33] The novelist's walks brought him into contact with London's sordid, soulless, and criminal side but also with its endless repetitions, circularities, and, to use the Dickensian word, coincidences— for, as a character says in *Nicholas Nickleby*, there is not 'such a place in all the world for coincidence as London is' (530). The Dickens narrative is made of these coincidences, which both consolidate the city's labyrinthine structure and hint at a path of escape from it. The escape is triumphant in an early work such as *Nicholas Nickleby*, but in the later, darker novels it is increasingly subdued. Always it is an escape into an oasis of domestic privacy, offering no prospect of public recognition. Esther Summerson, the heroine of *Bleak House*, moves from her adopted family's home near St Albans—close enough to London for the city's glow to be visible at night—to a second 'Bleak House' which is smaller, more rural, more provincial, and more secure from intrusion. (Allan Woodcourt, the rising young metropolitan doctor who marries her, will surely find his gifts wasted in such an isolated spot.) Various critics of *Bleak House* have suggested that Esther represents the biblical Esther, who was also illegitimate and who married a king and saved her people.[34] But Esther cannot redeem the English nation any more than the novel's archetypal London waif, Jo the crossing-sweeper, is (as the rogue Harold Skimpole slimily predicts) 'reserved like Whittington to become Lord Mayor of London' (436).

The Phantom Merchant

Our Mutual Friend presents Dickens's most intricate transmutation of the Whittington theme at the same time that it portrays a city on the point of collapse. In this novel there are no massive institutions such as a prison, a government department, the Dombey 'Edifice', or a court of law. The lawyers, Lightwood and Wrayburn, have little or no work; fortunes are built out of dust; the upstart City merchant Veneering is a man of straw; and the novel's only 'prison' is the home of the dust-heaps—a dumping-point for the waste that the city continually produces but cannot expel—which is popularly known as 'Harmony Jail'. The novel's last chapter is called 'The Voice of Society', but society in effect has no voice.

With its array of small and large businesses, including a bone-shop, a doll's dressmaker, and a crooked moneylender, *Our Mutual Friend* constitutes a return to the mercantile city. But the novel's two large concerns, the 'drug-house' of Chicksey, Veneering, and Stobbles and old Harmon's dust-contracting business, are both eventually sold off. Veneering, once the traveller or commission-agent of the drug-house, has bought out his partners, set himself up in a 'bran-new house' and entered fashionable society. In due course he becomes a Member of Parliament, but his firm, his household, his circle of friends, and his pretensions as a public figure are all as insubstantial as his furniture: 'For, in the Veneering establishment...all things were in a state of high varnish and polish...the surface smelt a little too much of the workshop and was a trifle stickey' (17). By the end of the novel the Veneering establishment is ready for the rubbish heap.

Old Harmon has built what might seem a more durable fortune out of the city's waste. He dumps it at Battle Bridge just north of King's Cross, a 'tract of suburban Sahara, where tiles and bricks were burnt, bones were boiled, carpets were beat, rubbish was shot, dogs were fought, and dust was heaped by contractors' (42). The waste that Harmon collects is fig-ured variously as dust, ashes, rags, bones, and waste paper. Other waste products are suggested by the scavenger's cart, used for street cleaning, into which Silas Wegg is finally deposited with a 'prodigious splash' (770), and by the drowned bodies salvaged by scavengers as they float down the Thames. There is, of course, money in dirt, and the novel can be read as, like the Whittington legend, a quest for the city's hidden gold. The principal (Harmon) plot hinges on disguise, multiple identity, and the confused destination of the Harmon fortune. The 'master's daughter' theme undergoes new complications as the story develops.

The question of what exactly London's streets are paved with is the subject of a dialogue between Mr Podsnap, the chauvinistic middle-class Englishman, and his French dinner guest:

'And Do You Find, Sir,' pursued Mr Podsnap, with dignity, 'Many Evidences that Strike You, of our British Constitution in the Streets Of The World's Metropolis, London, Londres, London?'

The foreign gentleman begged to be pardoned, but did not altogether understand. . . .

'I Was Inquiring,' said Mr Podsnap . . . 'Whether You Have Observed in our Streets as We should say, Upon our Pavvy as You would say, any Tokens—'

The foreign gentleman with patient courtesy entreated pardon; 'But what was tokenz?'

'Marks,' said Mr Podsnap; 'Signs, you know, Appearances—Traces.'

'Ah! Of a Orse?' inquired the foreign gentleman. (136)

Podsnap thinks that the streets might be paved with evidences of the British Constitution, but all that the French visitor can find there is horse manure, yet another component of the waste that has made Harmon's fortune. The British Constitution, notoriously unwritten, is a kind of gold standard for Podsnap: it applies everywhere, even though the Frenchman (and, by implication, Dickens) can find it nowhere. The city's gold, however, has been turned into paper, another incipient waste-product. Old Harmon's fortune is tied up in legal documents of doubtful worth—neither the will that has been made public nor the one that Wegg and Venus find on the dust-heap is actually valid. Bella Wilfer reads (significantly, in her evening paper) of gold being 'taken to the Bank' (666–7), but the City's actual financial medium is now 'scrip' or share certificates and receipts. Dickens's narrator grandiloquently informs us that 'As is well known to the wise in their generation, traffic in Shares is the one thing to have to do with in this world' (118). Veneering's business success earns him a place among the 'Fathers of the Scrip-Church' (610), a company doubtless including present and future Lord Mayors. The original dictionary meaning of 'scrip' is scrap or waste, as in a scrap of paper, and the city's scrip is constantly turned into scrap, producing '[t]hat mysterious paper currency which circulates in London when the wind blows' (147).

Among the other products blown about by the wind are sawdust, and, very likely, bran. Dickens refers to the Veneerings and their wealth as 'bran-new' (17) rather than 'brand-new,' probably because of the dictionary sense of 'bran' as 'muck, excrement, filth.' Then, no doubt, there are rags, since, as Mortimer Lightwood puts it, 'everything wears to rags' (96). Since rags and sawdust are used in paper-making it is no coincidence that the novel contains a paper mill, close to Plashwater Weir Mill Lock on the Thames. The rural reaches of the Thames ought to be well outside the city's reach, but they are not, since, as we are told, the towpath prowled by the murderous schoolmaster Bradley Headstone is marked out by posts bearing the City of London shield. The towpath is but an extension of the streets, while the paper mill helps to recirculate London's waste. Within this 'beleaguered city' (147), is there any gold to be found? Dickens's plot prepares a fairy-tale answer to this question. Mr Boffin, known as the Golden Dustman, turns out to be true gold in every sense—he is the legal inheritor, not merely the guardian, of old Harmon's wealth, yet he gives it all back to Harmon's son—and John Harmon marries his master's adopted daughter, Bella Wilfer, who is a 'most precious and sweet commodity that was always looking up, and that never was worth less than all the gold in the world' (667). The position of the master's daughter as a bargaining counter in what is essentially the process of commercial succession could not be more clearly put, yet Dickens's ostensible meaning is that Bella is anything but a commodity.

John Harmon as a young man quarrelled with his father and went out to farm in South Africa. At the age of 28 he returns to London in disguise, believing that his father's estate has been willed to him on condition that he marries a young lady whom he has never met. But he and the sailor with whom he has exchanged identity, George Radfoot, are kidnapped, drugged, and left for dead in London's docklands. Harmon manages to escape drowning in the Thames, but remains under cover, giving false testimony at the inquest into the death of Radfoot, who has been identified as the heir to the Harmon fortune due to the papers found on his body. He takes a position as clerk to Mr Boffin, while at the same time Bella Wilfer, whom old Harmon had designated as his daughter-in-law, enters the Boffin household as an adopted daughter. Harmon makes love to Bella and eventually succeeds in marrying her under a false name. Nevertheless, he has married his 'master's' adopted daughter while Bella, also an upstart, has married the master's son. She would never have knowingly married the man to whom she had been left 'in a will, like a dozen of spoons' (45).

Harmon's real identity remains hidden from his wife for several years (and for some 300 pages) even though, as we eventually learn, he was recognized by the Boffins almost from the start. He spends years pretending to commute every day from suburban Blackheath to a 'China house' in the City. Where Dick Whittington's future identity was known even to Bow Bells, John Harmon the phantom City merchant is not even known to his family lawyer. He is not so much a figure of doubtful identity as a virtual non-presence or nonentity—the perpetual third party or spiritual absentee implied by the phrase 'our mutual friend' itself.

By the end of the novel, the dust-heaps have been cleared away in exchange for a paper fortune, while the gold that was supposedly at the city's centre has disappeared. Veneering, the potential Lord Mayor, is on the brink of bankruptcy and will be forced to flee to Calais and live off his wife's diamonds. In *Our Mutual Friend*, written at the culmination of Dickens's dazzling career and at the height of his powers, mercantile ambitions are dismissed as so much chaff and the novelist seems to revel in the integrity of idleness. John Harmon clearly has no intention of engaging in business, so that his future existence is that of a gentleman of leisure like the briefless barrister Eugene Wrayburn. After his 'downward slide' from the house where he was drugged and kidnapped into the Thames, Harmon recalls that 'a heavy horrid unintelligible something vanished, and it was I who was struggling alone there in the water' (363). It is the aim of all Dickens's protagonists to shrug off the heavy, unintelligible weight of a city where the bells have 'grown worldly' and the noble merchant of the Whittington legend has given place to a phantom. The homeliness and domesticity of Dickens's family idylls is the result of his disillusionment with the effects of wealth and power on the England that idolized him.

At Home and Abroad in Victorian and Edwardian Fiction: From *Vanity Fair* to *The Secret Agent*

WILLIAM MAKEPEACE THACKERAY, born in Calcutta in 1811, might have become the first great novelist of Anglo-India. His father, an East India Company official, died when he was 3, and in 1817 he was sent back to England. In his early twenties he lost the money he had inherited from his father, partly as a result of the collapse of Indian investments, and he never returned to the East. Since Thackeray is a satirist who manifestly loves and admires what he pokes fun at, it is significant that his juvenilia includes *The Tremendous Adventures of Major Gahagan* (1838), a hilarious send-up of the military memoir which in some ways anticipates the *Boy's Own Paper* style of imperial romance. (Who can forget the siege of Futtyghur, when the gallant British officer commanding the defence takes off the trunks of 134 enemy elephants with a single cannon shot?) In *Vanity Fair* (1848) Jos Sedley, the Indian nabob with the 'honourable and lucrative post' of Collector of Boggley Wallah,[1] is another figure of fun even though Thackeray's father had held the title of Collector. Major Dobbin is posted to Madras, and plans to devote the rest of his life after retiring from the army to writing a history of the Punjab. But, out of more than sixty chapters, only one is set in India, and that is mainly devoted to home thoughts from abroad.

The Empire of the Novel

Although the action of *Vanity Fair* mostly takes place in and around London, we can never forget that Thackeray's London is the centre of a global economy and the capital of a large empire. Dobbin and his friend George Osborne have served in Canada, the West Indies, and Central America before taking part in the Battle of Waterloo. Jos Sedley brings back a black servant from India, as well as the curry and green chillis that so upset Becky Sharp. Becky's husband Rawdon Crawley becomes governor of Coventry Island, a tropical outpost supplying guava jelly and cayenne pepper to metropolitan dinner tables. The spoils of empire are most evident in the lavish and gaudy furnishings, the costumes, jewellery, and headwear of *Vanity Fair*, since of all male novelists Thackeray is the most alive to women's fashions. When Becky Sharp daydreams about Jos before their first meeting, she imagines herself riding an elephant and clothed in 'an infinity of shawls, turbans and diamond necklaces' (22). Turbans are sported by several of Thackeray's females, including the colonel's wife, Mrs O'Dowd, who wears a turban with a bird-of-paradise feather. The most showily dressed of all Thackeray's characters is the 'Hottentot Venus', Miss Swartz, who appears 'in her favourite amber-coloured satin with turquoise bracelets, countless rings, flowers, feathers, and all sorts of tags and gimcracks, about as elegantly decorated as a she chimney-sweep on May-day' (200). Old Mr Osborne regards her as one of the spoils of empire, although his son George is more choosy. George has in the past made love to a judge's daughter at Demerara and a beautiful quadroon at St Vincent. For his wife, however, he demands a white English girl, just as Amelia Sedley's parents are greatly relieved that their son Jos has not brought them an Indian daughter-in-law. The gorgeous visual display of empire has to be set against the characters'—and their author's—unremitting racism. Nobody sees anything wrong in the fact that Miss Swartz has to pay double fees to attend Miss Pinkerton's school. And old Mr Osborne's multicultural bluster—' "I ain't particular about a shade or two of tawny" ' (222)—is simply a manifestation of his mercantile vulgarity and greed.

Vanity Fair balances gentility against wealth, racial purity against empire, but also England against Europe. The European theme enters the novel with the stock-market panic following Napoleon's return from Elba in 1814, when Mr Sedley's investments are wiped out and Amelia is no longer regarded as a suitable match for George. But Europe is already present in the person of Becky Sharp, the daughter of a drawing master and a French opera singer with republican and Bonapartist tendencies. When Becky gets rid of her prize copy of Johnson's Dictionary as she leaves Miss Pinkerton's academy, it is Englishness as well as scholarship that she throws out of the carriage window. She will end up in exile in France and Germany, where she poses as an English lady before going to live among the wealthy ex-colonials of Bath and Cheltenham. Before that, however, her career as a courtesan brings her to the heights of English society at what Thackeray portrays as one of its greatest periods of profligacy, the period of England after Waterloo.

Thackeray wishes to be thought the least Puritanical of novelists, for all his vagueness about Becky's, and Arthur Pendennis's, presumed sexual misconduct. His first full-length novel, the Defoe-like *Memoirs of Barry Lyndon, Esq.* (1844), traces the adventures of a professional gamester across Europe, and the same gambling streak reappears in George Osborne and Becky Sharp. Their immorality is patent, yet Thackeray feels considerable admiration for them so long as they keep ahead of the game. His refusal to 'cajole the public into a sermon' and his insistence that 'sick-bed homilies and pious reflections are...out of place in mere story-books' (179) put him somewhere between the English moral allegorist—'Vanity Fair', after all, is an allusion to John Bunyan—and the 'cynical Frenchman' in the following quotation:

The observant reader, who has marked our young Lieutenant's previous behaviour...has possibly come to certain conclusions regarding the character of
Mr Osborne. Some cynical Frenchman has said that there are two parties to a
love transaction: the one who loves, and the other who condescends to be so
treated.... But this is certain, that Amelia believed her lover to be one of the most
gallant and brilliant men in the empire: and it is possible Lieutenant Osborne
thought so too. (115)

Here the French nation's wisdom in matters of love is acknowledged but immediately patronized to—and by a narrator who sounds as knowing and disillusioned as any Frenchman. But the image of George Osborne as 'one of the most gallant and brilliant men in the empire' resounds with imperial pride even if the 'empire' is an empire of vanities. Thackeray's romantic irony and narrative sleight of hand, as exhibited in this passage, are an essential part of *Vanity Fair*'s brilliant and compelling entertainment.

In some respects, the novel portrays England and its empire as manifestly a sham. Becky's opportunity to rise in society comes from her employment as a governess at Queen's Crawley in Sussex, but the family home of the Crawleys is more like a run-down colonial estate than a gentleman's park in the Home Counties. Seen through Becky's eyes, its rustic squalor is as outlandish as the ruined Irish estates of Maria Edgeworth's novels. Yet Sir Pitt Crawley, who is a high sheriff and rides in a golden coach, comes from a long line of time-servers whose very names—John Churchill Crawley, Walpole Crawley, and Bute Crawley—show how the family has always toadied to the party in power. Sir Pitt, though 'a dignitary of the land, and a pillar of the state' (82), is a mean, illiterate curmudgeon. He would have been bankrupted long ago were it not for the £1,500 a year he receives from the slave owner Mr Quadroon in exchange for a pocket borough. It is through Sir Pitt that Becky gains access to Rawdon Crawley and then to Lord Steyne, leading to her ascent to a level of society so august that Thackeray hardly dares to name it.

Lord Steyne, who is descended from the druids and owns castles and palaces all over the British Isles, stands for the bloated and degenerate Whig aristocracy. He is the provider of Becky's diamond earrings and the 'superb brilliant ornament' which adorns what Thackeray calls her 'famous frontal development' (481, 184), as if her bosom, suitably clad, were itself a sign of Britain's imperial splendour. But Lord Steyne is also Lord of the Powder Closet, 'one of the great dignitaries and illustrious defences of the throne of England' (481). Thanks to him, Becky is presented at court, giving her the opportunity of entering the royal apartments with a swagger that 'would have befitted an empress' (478). When the King or, as Thackeray calls him, the 'Imperial Master' briefly appears in the audience chamber, the usually ebullient narrative voice is cowed and silenced: 'The dazzled eyes close before that Magnificent Idea. Loyal respect and decency tell even the imagination not to look too keenly and audaciously.... but to back away rapidly, silently, and respectfully, making profound bows out of the August Presence' (482). Is Thackeray laughing behind his sleeve here? We cannot tell. Certainly he is unsparing about Mr Osborne, of whom he says that 'Whenever he met a great man he grovelled before him, and my-lorded him as only a free-born Briton can do' (119). Thackeray himself seems to grovel before royalty, yet a nation stuffed with power and self-satisfaction is transfixed under his gaze until we perceive it as no more than a freak show, a box full of puppets strutting their way through a pompous charade that presages the vanity of human life and the impermanence of empires. The death of the gallant, flawed George Osborne on the field of Waterloo is to some extent the novelist's retribution for his heartless flirtation with Becky, yet it also portends the eventual passing away of the British Empire, which will fall just as Napoleon fell. But there is life after such a bereavement, as Thackeray shows through Amelia's gradual return to happiness.

The certainty of eventual political decline is an implicit element in Thackeray's allegory, even though Sir Pitt Crawley's prophecy of the 'speedy ruin of the Empire' (696) when he loses his two pocket boroughs as a result of the 1832 Reform Bill is manifestly absurd. We may consider, for example, the complex irony of the novelist's allusion to Lady Hester Stanhope: 'Lady Hester once lived in Baker Street, and lies asleep in the wilderness' (504). Baker Street (slightly to the west of the Anglo-Indian quarter of London popularly known as the 'Black Hole') had recently been rebuilt, much to Thackeray's disgust, while Lady Hester, a precursor of Becky Sharp at her most magisterial, had kept house for William Pitt when he was prime minister. Her subsequent adventures were familiar to Thackeray and his readers from Alexander Kinglake's bestselling *Eōthen* (1844), a romantic traveller's account of the ruined empires of the East. Kinglake had visited her at Palmyra (Tadmor), once the home of the legendary Queen Zenobia. All this lies behind Thackeray's observation that

Some day or other (but it will be after our time, thank goodness) Hyde Park Gardens will be no better than the celebrated horticultural outskirts of Babylon, and Belgrave Square will be as desolate as Baker Street, or Tadmor in the wilderness.... It is all vanity to be sure: but who will not own to liking a little of it? (503–4).

Baker Street, a construction site in Thackeray's time, will go full circle until it becomes once again a waste of builder's rubble; and the very novel that he is composing will be forgotten like waste paper. Thackeray's amusement at the spectacle of English society is always tinged with melancholy. The nation at the height of its power and prosperity after Waterloo is like a gambler on a winning streak, but *Vanity Fair* is full of reminders of the world beyond England. Jos's Indian servant goes back to Calcutta; the author of a pious tract called the 'Washerwoman of Finchley Common' becomes Lady Hornblower of Cape Town; Becky Sharp becomes so notorious that her doings are reported in the *New York Demagogue*; and Amelia and Dobbin are eventually reunited on the quayside at Ostend. Thackeray writes of Becky's life in exile that 'Those who know the English colonies abroad know that we carry with us our pride, pills, prejudices, Harvey-sauces, cayenne-peppers, and other Lares, making a little Britain wherever we settle down' (650). England in *Vanity Fair* is a bubble that will one day burst, while Thackeray, in spite of himself, seems to anticipate that the English novel may eventually become a novel of uprooted and cosmopolitan Englishness.

Charlotte Brontë and Nationalities in Conflict

In 1852 when he visited the southern United States, Thackeray wrote of the black slaves that 'They are not my men and brethren, these strange people with retreating foreheads, with great obtruding lips and jaws: with capacities for thought, pleasure, endurance, quite different to mine'.[2] Yet Thackeray, while an imperial racist, treats the question of national differences within Europe rather lightly. The same cannot be said of the major women novelists who were his contemporaries. Charlotte Brontë's strong feelings, not to say prejudices, about national character are evident throughout her writings. The narrator in 'Ashworth', an unfinished novel written in her mid-twenties, declares that 'Ferocity, treachery, and turbulence are strong characteristics' of the Irish and the French nations,[3] while in her last novel *Villette* (1853) both a place and a family are named Bretton (Britain). George Eliot contributed to the contemporary intellectual debate about national character in her late essay 'The Modern Hep! Hep! Hep!' (1879), which belongs with the statements of political thinkers and historians such as Mill, Bagehot, Ernest Renan, and J. R. Green. The essay reflects the commitment to the idea of Jewish nationality that inspired Eliot's *Daniel Deronda* (1876), while outlining her belief in the ultimate triumph of cosmopolitanism and the fusion of races and nationalities.[4] But the time is not yet ripe for cosmopolitanism, in Eliot's view. Instead, a 'too rapid effacement of those national traditions and customs which are the language of the national genius—the deep suckers of healthy sentiment' would lead to the moral degradation of society.[5] For this reason, Eliot warns against mass immigration, which would put the 'distinctive national characteristics' of a historic people such as the English 'in danger of obliteration by the predominating quality of foreign settlers' (283)—an early instance of the anti-immigration scaremongering that would become associated a century later with the Conservative politician Enoch Powell.

Even more strikingly, Eliot's idealistic rhetoric has the effect of elevating nationality into a kind of secular religion:

The eminence, the nobleness of a people, depends on its capability of being stirred by memories, and of striving for what we call spiritual ends—ends which consist not in immediate material possession, but in the satisfaction of a great feeling that animates the collective body as with one soul....It is this living force of sentiment in common which makes a national consciousness....A common humanity is not yet enough to feed the rich blood of various activity which makes a complete man. The time is not come for cosmopolitanism to be highly virtuous, any more than for communism to suffice for social energy. (264–5).

Here it may be that Eliot's anxiety to repudiate 'communism' as a source of social belief has led her to confuse nationalism with national consciousness—to confuse a conscious political ideology, that is, with an innate feeling of national solidarity or belonging. For if 'national consciousness' is to serve spiritual ends and to play its part in the making

of the 'complete man', then it must take on at least one characteristic of
a political ideology: it must be something that we are, in principle, free to
accept or not to accept. The supposed author of 'The Modern Hep! Hep!
Hep!' is Theophrastus Such, a metropolitan bachelor who speaks of his
Midland upbringing where he learnt the 'alphabet' of his native England.[6]
But he must be prepared to learn other languages beside his mother
tongue if he is to present himself as a disinterested observer of the 'varying
genius of nations' (286), rather than as a blinkered nationalist. This leaves
open the possibility that an individual like Eliot's protagonist Daniel
Deronda could be reared within one national consciousness but end up by
choosing another. Choice of nationality is one of the principal themes in
major novels by both Charlotte Brontë and George Eliot.

Charlotte Brontë's first novel to be published after *Jane Eyre* was
Shirley (1849), a historical novel of the West Riding set, like the early
chapters of *Vanity Fair*, in the period of the Napoleonic Wars. From one
point of view *Shirley* may be described as 'defiantly regional'.[7] The
Yorkshire manufacturers, infuriated by the disruption of trade caused by
the British naval blockade of European ports, support the anti-war party
and are bitterly hostile to the patriotic fervour sweeping across England in
response to Wellington's Peninsular campaign. The textile workers are so
ground down by economic hardship that 'For a morsel of meat they
would have sold their birthright', according to Brontë's narrator.[8]
Yorkshire independence is personified in the squire and mill-owner Hiram
Yorke, a radical republican whose family is the oldest in the district and
who denounces England as a 'king-ridden, priest-ridden, peer-ridden
land' (41). Yorke switches at will from standard English to 'Yorkshire
Doric' (289), while the workers who attack a mill belonging to his friend
Robert Moore announce their onslaught with a 'West Riding-clothing-
district-of-Yorkshire rioters' yell' (271–2).

Orthodox patriotism in *Shirley* is represented by the Anglican
clergyman Dr Helstone, who regards the Duke of Wellington as 'the soul
of England' (28). Helstone as the representative of the established Church
is naturally a Tory, while Moore and Yorke are 'bitter Whig[s]' (27),
and the weaver Mike Hartley, a leader of the rioting workers, is an
Antinomian, a Jacobin, and a would-be regicide. Thus the issue of
wartime patriotism sets London against Yorkshire, Anglican against
Dissenter, monarchist against republican, and Tory against Whig. But
Shirley is not simply a novel of domestic division, even though the
divisions will apparently be healed by the lifting of the blockade in 1812
and the subsequent Tory–Whig marriage of Caroline, Helstone's niece,

to Robert Moore. Brontë introduces a more international theme with the
baiting of Malone, the Irish curate, in the opening chapter. The final
resolution of the double courtship plot involves Robert and Louis Moore,
two brothers of half-Belgian descent who speak French at home and
who are shown hesitating between emigration to the United States and
settlement in Yorkshire.

Shirley is, paradoxically, more cosmopolitan in outlook than a novel
that was evidently influenced by it, Elizabeth Gaskell's *Sylvia's Lovers*
(1863). Set in the 1790s in the East Yorkshire town of Monkshaven
(Whitby), *Sylvia's Lovers* portrays the violent controversy aroused by the
use of the pressgang to man British warships during the Napoleonic
campaigns. Daniel Robson, the ringleader of an anti-pressgang riot, is an
ex-whaler who has chopped off his own finger and thumb to avoid service
in the American War twenty years earlier. Neither Robson nor his fellow
townsmen are Jacobins or 'bitter Whigs', however; they are 'John Bullish'
patriots, happy to support the war as long as they are not personally
forced to fight in it.[9] Robson's daughter Sylvia, believing that her lover
Charley Kinraid is dead at sea, agrees to marry Kinraid's rival Philip
Hepburn, who has never told anyone that he saw Kinraid being seized by
the pressgang. Kinraid reappears, exposing Hepburn's lying and cow-
ardice, but then, in a Scott-like romantic sequence, Philip changes his
name, joins the army, and saves Kinraid's life at the siege of Acre. Philip's
penitent return to England is compared to the story of Guy of Warwick,
who came back from the Crusades to live as a travelling hermit. Charley
Kinraid rises in the navy to become an officer and a gentleman, so that
both he and Philip may be said to have come to manhood as a result of
being forced to fight for the nation. The narrative focus, however, remains
on Sylvia, who stays at home in Monkshaven abandoned by both her
lovers. The daughter born to Sylvia and Philip emigrates to America, just
as Hiram Yorke's children end up scattered across the globe. Both
novels, for all their defiant regionalism, seem to suggest that regionalism
has little future.

When, in the opening scene of *Shirley*, the curates Donne and Sweeting
turn on the Irishman Malone, their dispute is summarized as follows: 'He
reviled them as Saxons and snobs at the very top pitch of his high Celtic
voice; they taunted him with being the native of a conquered land. He
menaced rebellion in the name of his "counthry," vented bitter hatred
against English rule; they spoke of rags, beggary, and pestilence' (5). Here
Malone's patriotic fury is reminiscent of Captain Macmorris's 'Who
talks of my nation?' in Shakespeare's *Henry V*. The use of dialect spelling

to represent Malone's speech suggests Brontë's concern to de-centre the 'English rule' that comes from the metropolis, since *Shirley* is also full of so-called 'Yorkshire Doric', and Yorkshire like Ireland is referred to as a country. As Robert Moore's foreman Joe Scott says, 'We allus speak our minds i' this country; and them young parsons and grand folks fro' London is shocked at wer "incivility"' (44). The 'young parsons' Donne and Sweeting are themselves notably uncivil, as we have seen, but as representatives of the Church they stand for the centralized state and the suppression of national and regional differences.

In the event, the future of Yorkshire separatism lies in the hands of Caroline Helstone, the Tory vicar's daughter, and the landowner Shirley Keeldar. Brontë's twin heroines, who are both Yorkshirewomen and, therefore, 'compatriots' (165), marry the immigrant brothers Robert and Louis Moore. The destiny of these two couples, however, is to become naturalized citizens of a new, industrialized England arising out of the ashes of the immemorial countryside. Caroline, Shirley, and Louis Moore take a mutual delight in the West Riding legends of Robin Hood; Louis's sense of affinity with the 'ghost of the Earl of Huntingdon' (408) almost leads him to seek his fortune in the virgin woods of America, but instead he settles down as a lord of the manor and local magistrate, more a Sheriff of Nottingham than a denizen of the greenwood. His brother Robert Moore, the mill-owner, apparently plans to cut down part of Nunnwood forest, one of Robin Hood's haunts. His plan to double the size of his mill involves the enclosure of Nunnely Common and the building of a housing estate in Fieldhead Hollow. The result of his new-found prosperity after the end of the blockade is that, as he boasts to Caroline, ' "The copse shall be firewood ere five years elapse: the beautiful wild ravine shall be a paved street" ' (509). The workers who inhabit his new estate will doubtless be imported from elsewhere.

There is certainly no sentimental attachment to local independence in Charlotte Brontë's juvenilia, such as the interminable 'Glass Town Saga' written in collaboration with her brother Branwell. These stories reveal an imagination obsessed with urbanization, colonization, and empire-building. They tell of the construction in the heart of Africa of the Glass Town, capital of the English colony of Angria; of the appearance there of the Duke of Wellington and his sons; and of the rivalry between Angria and its rebellious offshoot Northangerland. Angria, with its English-style parliament, monarchy, and aristocracy, is half imperial fantasy and half a parallel-world fiction of an allegorical toy England. If Northangerland is Yorkshire, the wars that threaten to tear the colony apart specifically allude to the seventeenth-century Civil Wars and the Wars of the Roses. The Angrian saga was written before Charlotte Brontë's crucial residence in Brussels as a student and English teacher, which brought the themes of cosmopolitanism and the conflict of nationalities into her writing. Brussels is the setting of her rejected first novel *The Professor* as well as providing the model for the city in *Villette*, her mature masterpiece.

In *The Professor* William Crimsworth, the younger brother of a York-shire mill-owner, goes to Brussels to teach English on the advice of his mentor Yorke Hunsden, an industrialist and republican radical. Hunsden appears by turns as saviour, demonic tempter, 'Saxon' Englishman, and cosmopolitan wanderer, while Crimsworth ultimately aspires for recognition as an English gentleman. Where Hunsden claims to be a 'universal patriot' and world citizen, Crimsworth sees his Belgian hosts through a veil of racial prejudice and religious bigotry. His pupils' 'true Flamand physiognomy' betrays their intellectual inferiority, or so he thinks; and the continental climate is to blame for their 'deformity of person and imbecility of intellect'.[10] Brontë herself had expressed similar views in letters home, describing the 'national character of the Belgians' as 'a character singularly cold, selfish, animal and inferior'.[11] But the accusation of coldness is mutual, since Crimsworth's Belgian colleague M. Pelet describes him as a 'cold, frigid islander' (89). The same stereotype is present in *Villette*, where the English heroine Lucy Snowe—herself cold, secretive, and emotionally repressed—describes the Anglo-Scottish Graham Bretton as a 'cool young Briton' who is as impassive as the 'pale cliffs of his own England'.[12]

The idea of emotional reserve and self-suppression as defining features of the English character was implicitly present in Jane Austen's Mr Knightley. Maria Edgeworth had commented in *The Absentee* that 'however reserved the English may be in manner, they are warm at heart',[13] while Thackeray in *Pendennis* remarks on the 'Curious modesty, strange stoical decorum of English friendship!' (ii. 325). In *The Professor*, when Crimsworth and Hunsden are shown parting from one another after a meeting in Brussels, 'With a simultaneous movement each turned his back on the other. Neither said "God bless you," yet on the morrow the sea was to roll between us' (234). Elizabeth Gaskell writes of John Thornton and his mother in *North and South* that 'a stranger might have gone away and thought that he had never seen such frigid indifference of demeanour between such near relations' (252). In *Shirley*, Caroline Helstone's mother remarks on the 'reserve of English manners and the decorum of English families' (298). When in *Villette* Lucy and her godmother Mrs Bretton are reunited after ten years, all that passes between them is summed up as 'few words and a single salute' (249). The phrase 'stiff upper lip' is mid-Victorian, though it is credited to the American poet Phoebe Cary rather than to an English writer.

While often seen as a sign of emotional inadequacy—of the kind that would lead Edwardian novelists such as E. M. Forster and D. H. Lawrence to send their characters to the Catholic Mediterranean countries to find a sensual awakening denied to them at home—the habit of English reserve is also a form of power, an expression of the governing mystique of an imperial elite or of the spiritual arrogance and superiority of successful middle-class Puritans like Hunsden and Thornton. To show English reserve means to refuse to betray emotional weakness or openness to persuasion by subordinates, so that it is clearly linked to a habit of class decorum and respectability ('Not in front of the servants'). In this vein Rudyard Kipling, for example, could write of an effusive greeting between an Indian father and son, both native officers who had served under the British, that 'they embraced as do father and son in the East' (52).[14] This passing remark, which embodies the very English reserve to which it silently alludes, is a reminder of Kipling's intense suffering as a child who was sent back from the warmth of India to the cold English schooling that was seen as a prerequisite for a future imperialist.

Self-suppression is scarcely characteristic of the male protagonists of eighteenth-century English fiction—of a Lovelace, a Tom Jones, or a Roderick Random. It may be seen, rather, as a female attribute, the public face of the suffering, endurance, and deprivation undergone by a heroine such as Clarissa. Novels, however, reveal their protagonists' suppressed feelings, and Charlotte Brontë above all develops the contrast between her characters' outward mask and their raging inner life. At the same time, she portrays self-suppression as a generalized code of conduct applicable to the more Puritanical members of both sexes. Female stoicism and male undemonstrativeness now look remarkably similar. As an indication of national character, English self-suppression receives what is perhaps its fullest statement in the early twentieth century, in the writings of Ford Madox Ford. Ford's essay *The Spirit of the People* (1907) illustrates the theme with two anecdotes, each concerning an inter-generational and filial or quasi-filial relationship like the meeting between Lucy and her estranged godmother in *Villette*. In the first anecdote, a young volunteer comes back from the Boer War maimed and crippled, and is met at the station by his father. The only words spoken are ' "Hullo, Bob!" ... "Hullo, Governor!" '. The second anecdote tells of an English gentleman's frigid and virtually silent parting from his ward, with whom he has fallen in love and who is being sent on a round-the-world voyage in order to cover up their passion. Their parting, once again, is at a railway station.[15] This anecdote famously became the germ of Ford's novel *The Good Soldier* (1915), where the silent parting takes place between Edward Ashburnham, who has served in India, and Nancy Rufford, who is on her way there. Ford's view of English reserve, like Kipling's, suggests that it is part of the cultural apparatus of military and imperial power.

In *The Professor*, however, Crimsworth's outward coldness and silence is principally a sign of his Puritanical seriousness and the intensity of his inner life. He undergoes solitary spiritual struggles, hears angelic and demonic voices, and eventually finds his path to redemption when he meets a Swiss Protestant, Frances Henri, whom he marries and brings back to England. They settle down in a picturesque Yorkshire cottage close to Hunsden, who has retired from trade to a region unspoilt by 'the smoke of mills' (246). Frances rapidly turns into a conservative rural English housewife, rebuking Hunsden's cosmopolitanism in terms very like those later to be used by George Eliot's Theophrastus Such. '"Sympathies so widely diffused must be very shallow"' (230), she remarks. But Hunsden remains the novel's most intricate and disturbing character, a Yorkshire industrialist who is also a cosmopolitan intellectual, a hereditary landowner doubling as Mephistophilian outcast.

Where Crimsworth falls in love with a Protestant and moves back to England, *Villette* is a novel of expatriation in which the English heroine agrees to marry a continental Jesuit whose anglophobia has earlier roused her to fury. Harriet Martineau, in a contemporary review, described Brontë's portrayal of life in a foreign *pension* in a 'third-rate capital' as something new in English literature, while at the same time detecting a vein of religious zealotry in Lucy Snowe's gloomy Protestantism and her passionate hatred of the Catholic Church.[16] The difficulty of controlling the balance and tone of a first-person narrative, already apparent in *The Professor* and *Jane Eyre*, is exacerbated in *Villette* by Lucy's manifest duplicity and secretiveness. Lucy's vehement anti-Catholicism is at once a measure of the attractions of the Catholic faith, and a cover for her rejection of English identity. Or we could say that Lucy manages to separate the core of her national identity—her Protestant faith—from any sentimental or material attachment to England as a cultural or political nation.

Lucy's life, like Crimsworth's and Jane Eyre's, is a pilgrimage, but the pilgrimage cannot end in marriage to a Protestant since her love for

Graham Bretton is unrequited. Having arrived unknown and almost penniless in Labassecour (Belgium), she is taken on at Madame Beck's *pension* and, after a number of trials, promoted to the position of class teacher. Here she is entirely at the mercy of an employer who is advised (if not controlled), as she gradually discovers, by the fiery anti-English chauvinist M. Paul and the other members of a Jesuit 'junta' headed by the priest Père Silas. Lucy passes all the tests set for her by Madame Beck and her confederates, matching her employer's remorseless system of espionage with her own vigilant counter-espionage. She is a spy in enemy territory working only for herself and, perhaps, for her Protestant God. But her intense loneliness leads to a double crisis of loyalties. First, in an intensely dramatic scene, she turns to the Catholic confessional in search of spiritual comfort, but resists the tempting welcome offered by Père Silas. Then, reunited with her English godmother, she refuses the opportunity offered by the Comte de Bassompierre (formerly known to her as Mr Home, a plain Scotsman) to become governess to his daughter Paulina, whom Lucy has known as a child.

To become Paulina's governess would be to become 'British' again, but Lucy is not prepared to do this if it means living as a subordinate in someone else's household. She prefers her hard-won professional status at Madame Beck's, even though she is dependent on her tyrannical employer's favour. The choice is, admittedly, complicated by the fact that Paulina will eventually marry Graham Bretton; but Graham's coldness towards Lucy embodies a wider truth, which is that the Labassecour Jesuits take her more seriously than her reserved English friends do. To the Jesuits she is, at least, a spiritual prize worth capturing; to the English, however superficially kind they may appear, she remains (as she feels) ultimately negligible and insignificant.

Lucy's melodramatic confession to the priest is not without its unconscious comedy. Père Silas tells her that ' "You were made for our faith . . . Protestantism is altogether too dry, cold, prosaic for you" ' (234), but Lucy recognizes his flattery as the voice of Satan. Later her fellow teacher M. Paul becomes fascinated by her inner fire, but it is his candour and outspokenness, the reverse of priestly flattery or English nonchalance, that win her heart. Trained by the Jesuits, he is a 'religious little man, in his way', attracted to the 'self-denying and self-sacrificing part of the Catholic religion' (279), and since—like Lucy and Madame Beck—he is also a dedicated voyeur, he subjects her to obsessive, unremitting scrutiny. In his more dictatorial moods Lucy sees him as a petty Napoleon; she, by analogy, must be the Wellington whom the young Charlotte Brontë had idolized. It is because, unlike Graham, he regards her as fully his equal that his hostility slowly changes into love and true friendship. But then Brontë unexpectedly sends off M. Paul, as Jane Austen had sent Sir Thomas Bertram, to attend to a Caribbean estate, so that he stays in Guadeloupe for three years and is, apparently, drowned on the way home. The novelist tantalizes us with the potential political allegory of a cosmopolitan, Catholic–Protestant marriage, only to withdraw it.

Villette may, of course, be read as a feminist manifesto, since M. Paul has freed Lucy from Madame Beck's and set her up as an independent schoolmistress prior to his departure. In the view of one recent critic, 'it may not be entirely a tragedy if M. Paul *is* killed by a storm and does not return from dominating West Indian blacks to marry the Lucy he calls "sauvage" '.[17] But we must also consider that marriage to a subject of the monarchy of Labassecour (even allowing for M. Paul's professed republican and cosmopolitan sympathies) would involve a degree of personal commitment in the conflict of nationalities that Brontë is happy for her heroine to avoid. As a humble foreigner in Labassecour she has been free to mock the country's King and Queen (whom she sees at a concert) and to take no interest in politics or public life. She is present only as an uninvited spectator at the patriotic festival in the park—attended by the Brettons and her other English friends—which forms one of the novel's great closing scenes. Lucy can remain independent, separate, and effectively stateless as a Protestant expatriate, though at the cost of staying childless and unaffiliated even to a specific Protestant sect. (One reason why the 'junta' thought her susceptible to conversion to Catholicism was that she was observed as worshipping indiscriminately at the Presbyterian, Lutheran, and Episcopalian chapels in the city, denying herself even the support of church membership.) She tells M. Paul that 'doubtless there were errors in every Church, but I now perceived by contrast how severely pure was my own' (516); but strictly speaking she has no church, only an entirely subjective system of beliefs. She is a spiritual exile who needs no homeland and no alliances, so long as her inner Protestantism is preserved intact. Her personal faith, attested to by the references to *The Pilgrim's Progress* that frame her narrative, may be the last sign of her Englishness, but it is a sufficient one. Her unsectarian but rigidly Protestant pilgrimage corresponds closely to the neo-Puritan fiction of some of Brontë's successors, notably the early George Eliot, whose heroines do not confront Catholic Europe but stay in the English provinces that Lucy has long left behind.

Xenophobia and Liberalism: Anthony Trollope and George Eliot

Two major novels of the 1870s, Anthony Trollope's *The Way We Live Now* (1875) and George Eliot's *Daniel Deronda* (1876), convey diametrically opposed attitudes to the question of English identity. *The Way We Live Now* is a notably xenophobic moral fable, portraying a degenerate nation at the mercy of foreign crooks and speculators, many of whom are, or are rumoured to be, Jewish. *Daniel Deronda*, by contrast, is famous for its depiction of Jewish culture and heritage through the perspective of a protagonist brought up under the assumed identity of an English gentleman. In the former novel, London society and the British economy are in danger of being taken over by unscrupulous international capitalists thanks to the English aristocracy's loss of moral fibre. In the latter, the same aristocracy is shown as being aggressively outward-looking, exporting its best and worst qualities to other lands.

The central figure of *The Way We Live Now*, the financier Augustus Melmotte, is a rogue with no fixed identity who has come to England after the collapse of an earlier venture, a 'great continental assurance company' based in Paris and Vienna.[18] On his arrival Melmotte has declared 'that he had been born in England, and that he was an Englishman' (30), but nobody seems to believe him. He is accompanied by his Jewish wife, whom he met and married in Frankfurt, and by his daughter Marie, the child of an earlier relationship. Some say that he is Jewish, others that he is the son of a New York Irishman named Melmody. He and his wife were known as Jews at Frankfurt and as Christians in Paris. When he makes an impromptu speech to the electors of Westminster, Melmotte boasts that he is 'an Englishman and a Londoner' (484). It is an identity from which he cannot escape except by committing suicide.

In his portrayal of London society, Trollope surrounds Melmotte with a number of other foreign immigrants—Germans, Jews, and Americans—only two of whom settle down to English respectability. Frederick Alf, the newspaper owner, was born a German Jew but 'knew England as only an Englishman can know it' (13); he speaks of himself and Melmotte as 'brother adventurers' (38), though eventually they become bitter rivals. Brehgert, the Jewish banker, fails in his attempt to marry the well-born Georgiana Longestaffe and loses money in Melmotte's enterprises, but remains a comfortable denizen of English middle-class suburbia. Two of Melmotte's other fellow adventurers disappear altogether: Cohenlupe, the Jewish financier, swindler, and Member of Parliament, and Herr Vossner, the German manager of the Beargarden club. Croll, Melmotte's commercial secretary, who speaks with a German-Jewish accent, eventually moves with Mrs Melmotte to New York. Then there are Trollope's two American characters, Fisker, the San Francisco railway promoter, and Winifred Hurtle, who claims to be either widowed or divorced (though in fact she is neither) and comes to London to beg the Englishman Paul Montague to marry her. She returns to the United States with Fisker and Marie, Melmotte's daughter, and Trollope seems to feel that England is well rid of all of them.

The plot of *The Way We Live Now* hinges on two kinds of speculation, speculation in heiresses and speculation in railway shares, and these are shadowed by a third, purely wasteful form of speculation, the games of chance played every night by Trollope's young English aristocrats at the Beargarden Club. For these young sprigs gambling is 'an institution, like primogeniture', since matters can always be put right by marrying a commercial heiress (435). The Beargarden is full of gossip about 'the great Marie-Melmotte plate' (76), a metaphorical horse race in which the hoped-for prize is Marie's father's fortune. Predictably, the idea that mutual love or even mutual liking should enter into the calculations of aristocratic marriage is widely dismissed as absurd; and equally absurd is the idea that City investors should know anything of the reality (or otherwise) of the businesses in which they own shares. Trollope's accounts of the directors' meetings leave us in doubt as to whether the shares in Melmotte's South Central Pacific and Mexican Railway scheme actually exist, let alone whether a railway is being built. But this does not prevent Melmotte from being elected to Parliament.

Trollope's representative of traditional English integrity in *The Way We Live Now* is the squire and backwoodsman Roger Carbury, the owner of Carbury Hall in Suffolk and country cousin of Lady Carbury and her wastrel son Sir Felix. Lady Carbury belongs to the modern world of publicity, corruption, and self-advertisement, while Roger lives a comfortably old-fashioned life on what is apparently a flourishing estate. Roger, who has all the xenophobia of the traditional Tory squire, sees Melmotte as a self-evident fraud; but he is also an unwanted bachelor grown old before his time, a remnant of Old England manifestly irrelevant to the 'way we live now'. Nevertheless, his hatred of modernity finally bears fruit. Paul Montague, a native Englishman who has moved to California, comes back to London, escapes from his entanglement with Winifred Hurtle, and sells his interest in the railway just in time. A career in the City is his for the asking, but he prefers to marry Henrietta and settle at Carbury Hall. Above all, he patiently listens to Roger's final homily about the necessity of living within his income. Trollope, blithely overlooking the long history of rural capitalism, profit fluctuations, enclosures, property sales, evicted tenants, and bankrupted estates, represents speculative finance as an alien intrusion into the English countryside. His novel was published at the beginning of the great agricultural depression of the late nineteenth century, which fundamentally altered the way of life of most rural landowners. For its earliest readers as well as for later ones, *The Way We Live Now* offered the consolations of a vanished age.

In the opening scene of *Daniel Deronda*, the heroine Gwendolen Harleth is shown gambling in the casino of a German spa. Soon afterwards she, like Paul Montague, has to listen to lectures on the need for domestic economy. Her family's wealth, which is ultimately derived from the West Indies, has suddenly been lost in mining speculations. Gwendolen has earlier been asked by her cousin Rex Gascoigne what she wishes to do in life: her answer, that she may 'go to the North Pole, or ride steeplechases, or go to be a queen in the East like Lady Hester Stanhope', perfectly catches the recklessness of her character.[19] She is the spoilt child of a cosmopolitan upbringing who finds herself reduced to shabby-genteel poverty in a country cottage. From this she might be saved by a wealthy marriage, and the novel's allegory rests on the contrast between two possible male contenders for her hand, Daniel Deronda and Henleigh Grandcourt.

Daniel is the ward of Sir Hugo Mallinger, a prominent Whig baronet with Norman and crusading ancestors. Like Disraeli's young aristocrats, he is determined to broaden his social experience in the hope of discovering a political mission, but he rejects Sir Hugo's ossified Whiggism in order to become a Zionist, not a Disraelian Tory. Unaware of his Jewish identity, he finds a mentor in the unworldly religious fanatic Mordecai Cohen, and a potential bride in Mordecai's sister Mirah. Eventually he learns his own, hitherto secret, family history.

Daniel's story is what one critic has called a 'chivalric quest', a 'romantic search for a father, an identity, and a mission'.[20] Such a quest is reminiscent of the Scott romance, and it is no surprise that, when Daniel saves Mirah from drowning, his friends immediately link her to Rebecca in *Ivanhoe*. But Eliot portrays Deronda's quest as part of the late nineteenth-century struggle between nationality and cosmopolitanism that she was to analyse in *Impressions of Theophrastus Such*. Georgiana Longestaffe in *The Way We Live Now* suggests that racially mixed marriages will soon become commonplace owing to the 'general heaving-up of society' (461), though she lacks the resolution to go through with one herself. *Daniel Deronda* contains a love affair leading to what is expected to be a successful mixed marriage between the heiress Catherine Arrowpoint and the musical maestro Klesmer, described as a 'felicitous combination of the German, the Sclave, and the Semite' (77). Klesmer's vision of the global future is one of a 'fusion of races' (284), though Eliot, doubtless, regarded the Klesmer–Arrowpoint marriage as courageous but premature. In any case, more than the logic of her own plot indicates that Daniel Deronda is likely to marry Mirah Cohen rather than Gwendolen Harleth. It was a bold enough step for an established Victorian novelist to create a hero who is brought up as an English gentleman but subsequently embraces his Jewish identity; but it would have been much bolder to allow the same hero to wed an English girl. Gwendolen may once have dreamed of being a 'queen in the East', but Daniel's choice of Mirah Cohen is as inevitable as Ivanhoe's rejection of the Jewish Rebecca for Saxon Rowena.

Daniel's Jewish odyssey takes him to Genoa to meet his dying mother (who is now a Russian princess) and then to Mainz for an encounter with Joseph Kalonymos, a friend of his grandfather. It is to Kalonymos that Daniel announces that he will take up his grandfather's mission of racial leadership, although in a secular, nationalist form. As he later tells Gwendolen, 'The idea that I am possessed with is that of restoring a political existence to my people, making them a nation again, giving them a national centre, such as the English have, though they too are scattered over the face of the globe' (875). Daniel has earlier urged Gwendolen to seek a refuge from her personal troubles in 'the higher, the religious life, which holds an enthusiasm for something more than our own appetites and vanities' (507–8). The implication is that, for him, Zionism offers the same resources of spiritual energy as the English Puritanism that Eliot had explored in her earlier novels (to be discussed in the next chapter). But his Zionism is a product of Eliot's political as well as her religious imagination, although it involves a projection of identity beyond any to which the novelist herself could lay claim.

It was only from the standpoint of a cosmopolitan liberal—a standpoint of whose shortcomings she was well aware—that George Eliot could call herself a Zionist; the cause of the Jews could never be that of her own people. (In this respect she is as close, perhaps closer, to Gwendolen Harleth than she is to Deronda.) Considered as an English novel, *Daniel Deronda* therefore belongs to the enterprise of what has been called 'positive orientalism', the romantic identification with the

East which had earlier inspired Kinglake's *Eōthen* and Disraeli's *Tancred*, and would later be pursued by Kipling and E. M. Forster.[21] Like other forms of 'positive orientalism', Daniel's proposed mission to the East is something of an imperial crusade as well as a journey of self-discovery. It is no accident that his adopted English family has crusading ancestors. Although the novel remains deliberately unspecific, Daniel's desire to restore a political existence to the Jewish people and to bring them back to nationhood can only be accomplished by liberating Jewish Palestine from Ottoman rule and from Muslim religious hegemony. Daniel learns to revere his grandfather who 'mingled all sorts of learning . . . like our Arabic writers in the golden time' (791), yet, like Lucy Snowe's expatriation, his renunciation of English identity is far from complete.

Daniel's Zionism, however, is set against the Englishness of Henleigh Grandcourt, an altogether stronger, crueller, and colder personality than Trollope's aristocratic playboys. Henry James described Grandcourt (who is a wealthy kinsman of Sir Hugo Mallinger) as a representation of 'the most detestable kind of Englishman', 'a consummate picture of English brutality refined and distilled';[22] these judgements, delivered at the time of the novel's first publication, suggest that he is both a symbol of national character and a figure whom James found unpleasantly realistic. Grandcourt is well travelled—he enjoys yachting in the Mediterranean and has gone tiger-hunting in India—and his dictatorial manner towards his subordinates suggests the corruptions of imperialist power rather than of a stagnant aristocracy. Gwendolen's uncle, an Anglican clergyman, considers that Grandcourt's rank exempts him from the 'ordinary standard of moral judgements': 'the almost certain baronet, the probable peer, was to be ranged with public personages, and was a match to be accepted on broad general grounds national and ecclesiastical' (176–7). This means that for Gwendolen to become Grandcourt's wife is a matter of patriotic duty rather than personal preference. Eliot's portrayal of 'English brutality' in *Daniel Deronda* lends weight to Daniel's renunciation of his English identity. Yet here, as in *The Way We Live Now*, the novelist's moral allegory considerably oversimplifies the issues involved in the choice of nationality.

James, Conrad, and Internal Exile

Although he lived in England for much of his adult life, it was only in his seventies, during the First World War, that Henry James took out British citizenship. The primary setting of his novels is usually outside England, and not all his works contain English characters. There is, at most, an 'English period' in James's career consisting of novels such as *The Princess Casamassima* (1886), *The Tragic Muse* (1890), *The Spoils of Poynton* (1897), and *The Turn of the Screw* (1898), together with numerous short stories. Perhaps more characteristically Jamesian is a novel such as *The Ambassadors* (1903), where England is merely a point of first contact for his naive American hero whose determination to 'prove the note of Europe' will inevitably take him to Paris.[23]

James, no doubt consciously remembering Dickens, wrote that 'The simplest account of the origin of *The Princess Casamassima* is ... that this fiction proceeded quite directly, during the first year of a long residence in London, from the habit and the interest of walking the streets'.[24] The 'international theme' which is James's hallmark is represented in this novel by a group of violent anarchists, apparently made up of foreigners who have barely assimilated into English life, and by the two protagonists, the Princess Casamassima and Hyacinth Robinson. The Princess, whom Hyacinth sees as 'the most beautiful woman in England' (316), is an Italian-American separated from her Roman husband; and Hyacinth, the 'little bookbinder', is, in effect, a Parisian transported to England. Both characters tend to interpret English society with the help of the novels they have read. Hyacinth, for example, recognizes the saintly slum visitor Lady Aurora as an example of 'that "best breeding" which he had seen alluded to in novels portraying the aristocracy' (266), while the Princess Casamassima finds the idea of Lady Aurora alone in her 'great dull house' 'quaint and touching, like something in some English novel' (432). (It is not clear what novels they have been reading; the Princess's view of Lady Aurora suggests Dickens's Florence Dombey, but Florence is not, of course, an aristocrat.) James himself seems to draw on his reading of *Daniel Deronda* in his portrayal of another character, Captain Godfrey Sholto, who is a paler, less commanding version of Grandcourt:

Sholto was a curious and not particularly edifying English type (as the Princess further described him); one of those strange beings produced by old societies that have run to seed, corrupt, exhausted civilisations. He was a cumberer of the earth, and purely selfish, in spite of his devoted, disinterested airs. He was nothing whatever in himself, and had no character or merit save by tradition, reflection, imitation, superstition.... He had travelled all over the globe several times, 'for the shooting', in that brutal way of the English. That was a pursuit which was compatible with the greatest stupidity. (352)

If Lady Aurora represents the idea of good breeding, Sholto, together with the working-class revolutionary Paul Muniment, stands for English brutality. Muniment's sister regards her brother as a future prime minister, while the Princess's judgement that he must be a 'first-rate man' because he is 'such a brute' (579) expresses admiration as well as irony. Another character, the Cockney beauty Millicent Henning, is presented as a symbol of the 'vulgarities and curiosities', the 'brutality' and 'knowingness' of plebeian London (93). English brutality has its uses, however. We do not doubt Millicent's assertion that, given the chance, she would defend Hyacinth Robinson like a tiger. And Lady Aurora is of the opinion that the English aristocracy would not give up their privileges as readily as their French counterparts—they would 'stay at home and resist' rather than rushing to emigrate (140). The 'brutal way of the English' is an expression of their power.

   That power is, of course, barely challenged by an underground anarchist movement which, here as in Joseph Conrad's *The Secret Agent*, is shown as consisting of a handful of cosmopolitan sentimentalists and malcontents. The leader is Diedrich Hoffendahl, a German who moves undercover from country to country and who may receive financial backing from the Princess. The movement's chief adherents in England, apart from Paul Muniment, are the French political exile Eustache Poupin and the German Schinkel. We are told of Poupin, to whom Hyacinth owes his entry into the London bookbinding trade, that his 'humanitary zeal was as unlimited as his English vocabulary was the reverse' (116). Madame Poupin speaks virtually no English, and has no friends among the 'cold insularies' (117). Poupin remains a French patriot—'If I suffer, I trust it may be for suffering humanity, but I trust it may also be for France', he declares (290)—and James wrily presents him as an example of the bittersweetness of exile. He would not welcome a political amnesty at home, since he would lose his character as a refugee and martyr. Poupin lives in a state of frozen identity, of identity that remains fixed and that forbids the openness to new experiences which James as a novelist values above all else. As the latter wrote in the preface to *The Princess Casamassima*, the agents in any drama 'are interesting only in proportion as they feel their respective situations', and it is those who possess 'the power to be finely aware and richly responsible' who feel most (35). Hyacinth possesses this fine awareness, but his capacity to act is almost paralysed by it. Paul Muniment, the political man of action, also has a good deal of awareness (which is why Hyacinth looks upon him as a friend), but is expert at suppressing it. Hyacinth's eventual tragedy stems from his inability to repress his sympathies as Muniment or Poupin would have done.

The dilemma posed by Hyacinth's dual national identity is a central though largely submerged theme in *The Princess Casamassima*. As the narrator says, 'He knew he looked like a Frenchman, he had often been told so before, and a large part of the time he felt like one—like one of those he had read about in Michelet and Carlyle' (102). Michelet and Carlyle were the two great popular historians of the French Revolution, in which Hyacinth's maternal grandfather, a watchmaker, was killed on the barricades. Hyacinth's paternity, however, remains mysterious. His English adoptive mother, 'Pinnie' the dressmaker, has supplied him with 'a hundred different theories of his identity' (166). What we know is that his mother came to England, took a lover from among the English aristocracy, and was later condemned to life imprisonment for murdering him. If Hyacinth is the child of this relationship, his English relatives have clearly repudiated him. Hyacinth, then, is a protagonist who 'didn't really know whether he were French or English, or which of the two he should prefer to be' (127).

What bulks more largely in the novel, however, is his uncertainty about whether or not he wishes to be taken for an aristocrat. Paul Muniment sees him as a 'duke in disguise' (445), and it is because he would not look out of place at a fashionable reception that the anarchists give him the task of publicly assassinating an English duke. Nevertheless, he is increasingly torn by the conflict between his democratic loyalties, which have led him to pledge his life to the anarchist underground, and his growing revulsion against the doctrine of material equality and the cult of plebeian revenge. James makes much of the ideological torment of the young man who is drawn to both sides in a violent class struggle, and all Hyacinth's friends are aware of his tergiversations. The tension between the 'English' and 'French' sides of his identity, however, is something that he keeps to himself. His grandfather's death as a political martyr and his mother's 'suffering in an alien land' and her 'unspeakable, irremediable misery' (127) give him a personal motive for carrying out the terrorist act for which he has been chosen. If he was caught and had to pay the extreme penalty, he could draw on the pride of his forebears and the exaltation of the suicide bomber. But he dreads 'the idea of a *repetition*' (582), of being seen to perform an act that could simply be blamed on a hereditary taint drawn from his French mother. It is because she, in her French way, has murdered an English aristocrat in a *crime passionnel* that he feels unable to murder an English duke in cold blood.

James's masterly unravelling of this drama makes much of the fact that Hyacinth's loyalty to the secret oath he has taken long outlives his belief in revolutionary politics. An unyielding sense of honour prevents him from accepting the pragmatic opt-outs offered by some of his English friends. The compromise that he arrives at is at once delicate and brutal. Delicate, because by committing suicide he ironically fulfils his mission of killing at least a spiritual adherent of the reactionary upper classes. We cannot say, therefore, that by refusing to take the life of an English duke he has chosen his English paternal inheritance as against the Frenchness that has earlier defined him. But the novel's denouement also has a shocking brutality, since what the Princess sees when she discovers his body is 'a horrible thing, a mess of blood, on the bed, in his side, in his heart' (590). The scene has echoes both of Henry Wallis's popular painting of *The Death of Chatterton* (1856) and of Jacques-Louis David's *The Assassination of Marat* (1793), but it is more disgusting and less heroic than either pictorial representation. Hyacinth's tragedy is that he is caught between opposing ideologies, incompatible ideas of honour, and contending national identities.

As the story of an international anarchist group planning a terrorist attempt in London, *The Princess Casamassima* invites comparison with the English masterpiece of another immigrant novelist, Joseph Conrad. *The Secret Agent* (1907) has a remarkably cosmopolitan cast of characters, including members of an international Red Committee, the personnel of a foreign embassy, and an Anglo-French pornography merchant, Adolf Verloc. Many of the novel's locations suggest the world of the new immigrant, rather than a settled community of political refugees: the embassy building, a police station, a bed-sitting room, an underground beer hall, an Italian restaurant, as well as a clandestine political meeting at Mr Verloc's shop. Conrad's revolutionaries are kept under surveillance by the police, an organization which as Verloc remarks is common to every country, as well as by the European governments lobbying for international action for the 'suppression of political crime'.[25] Nevertheless, the novel's pivotal event is the bomb explosion in Greenwich Park which the Assistant Commissioner in charge of the investigation memorably describes as a 'domestic drama' (181).

'Heredity' is as important in *The Secret Agent* as it was in *The Princess Casamassima*, but it is no longer the inheritance of supposed national characteristics such as the French penchant for revolutionary violence that is at stake. Instead, we are exposed to the universal pseudo-scientific discourse about human pathology favoured by the exiled anarchist Alexander Ossipon, who loftily classifies Verloc's English wife Winnie and her retarded brother Stevie as mental and moral 'degenerates'. Conrad, however, ironizes this universal language of science—which is the target of the otherwise meaningless attack on the Greenwich Observatory—while suggesting that the familiar English characteristics of reticence and self-suppression play an important part in the action. The Assistant Commissioner's idea of a 'domestic drama', as the context makes clear, is of a drama confined within the nation as well as within the family. Faced with an outrage that will be blamed by the press on mysterious 'foreign anarchists', his words are chosen to reassure the British government that what has taken place is entirely within the competence of the Metropolitan Police.

In the dramatis personae of *The Secret Agent*, the manifestly non-English characters such as Ossipon, Michaelis, Yundt, and Vladimir are counterbalanced by Winnie, Winnie's mother, her brother Stevie, and Inspector Heat. The other main characters cannot be so easily classified as 'foreign' or 'domestic'. The arch-terrorist bomb-maker known as the Professor is given no surname, and his parentage is described as 'obscure' (68). His diminutive stature, spectacles, and high domed forehead may suggest a stereotypical foreign intellectual, but there are reasons for doubting this, as we shall see. The Assistant Commissioner is technically British, but has made his name as a colonial official in the tropics. He has a 'foreign-looking' appearance (175) and, when he appears in her shop, Winnie Verloc instantly assumes that he is a newly arrived political refugee. Adolf Verloc has done military service in the French Army and is the 'obscure familiar of at least two Embassies' (46). In marrying Winnie he has taken one of the quickest routes to social integration available to an immigrant, that of the lodging-house tenant who weds his landlady's daughter. When confronted by Mr Vladimir, the shady foreign diplomat, he states forthrightly that he is 'English' and a 'natural-born British subject' (27).

Verloc's use of the term 'British subject' marks the transition from the nineteenth-century idea that nationality is a matter of 'national character' to the twentieth-century world in which identity may be conferred by a passport or other official document. Since he has the 'air of moral nihilism' common to those who live off the 'vices, the follies, or the baser fears of mankind' (21), it is by no means clear that Verloc's proclaimed legal status corresponds to his real identity. Nevertheless, his life as a secret agent fits in perfectly with what Conrad identifies as the 'prudence', 'respectability', and 'reticence' of the English middle classes. The novel's fullest statement about his and Winnie's married life takes the form of an ironic obituary tribute:

Except for the fact that Mrs Verloc breathed [she and her husband] would have been perfectly in accord: that accord of prudent reserve without superfluous words, and sparing of signs, which had been the foundation of their respectable home life. For it had been respectable, covering by a decent reticence the problems that may arise in the practice of a secret profession and the commerce of shady wares. To the last its decorum had remained undisturbed by unseemly shrieks and other misplaced sincerities of conduct. (213)

The decorum of the English family goes together with the English people's 'idealistic conception of legality' and their 'scrupulous prejudices', which both the terrorist Professor and the agent provocateur Mr Vladimir see as political obstacles (67). Verloc scorns these idealistic prejudices yet secretly shares them, so that he remains sublimely unaware that his wife could be capable of murdering him to avenge her brother's death. But the murder and Winnie's subsequent suicide are the acts of a woman who is, like her husband, a kind of secret agent. She does not go to the police or denounce her husband with 'unseemly shrieks', but keeps her revenge to herself. All that the world ever learns of the affair comes from the newspaper report of the 'Suicide of Lady Passenger from a cross-Channel Boat', which concludes that her 'act of madness or despair' is destined to remain mysterious (246).

Conrad himself was (as has often been remarked) a kind of secret agent. His English marriage to Jessie George and the start of his literary career both took place in 1895, after twenty years at sea. Born of Polish parents in the Ukraine, he had been a British subject since 1886. Conrad settled in England for the last three decades of his life, but England (as opposed to Englishmen) appears in his fiction only rarely, and usually as an alienated and sinister environment. *Heart of Darkness* (1902), the story of a journey to central Africa, begins on the Thames estuary with the reminder that 'this also . . . has been one of the dark places on the earth'.[26] The London of *The Secret Agent* is still a dark place, a city where the façade of respectability can easily break down and nobody feels truly at home. In a powerful image of the dissolution of traditional family structures, Winnie's mother is ejected from Mr Verloc's residence and is put into an almshouse. Soon Winnie finds herself 'alone' in a city which 'rested at the bottom of a black abyss from which no unaided woman could hope to scramble out' (218). The novel's final image of metropolitan alienation is the meeting of two of the surviving revolutionaries, Ossipon and the

Professor, who share this condition of internal exile. Ossipon now seems destined for the 'black abyss' of unemployment, while the Professor moves unseen and unsuspected among the city crowd, a suicide bomber who might blow himself up at any moment.

Ossipon is a washed-up immigrant, and the Professor speaks of England and its social institutions with a cold detachment that suggests he is essentially stateless. Nevertheless, his roots are in provincial Puritanism of a recognizably English type:

His father, a delicate dark enthusiast with a sloping forehead, had been an itinerant and rousing preacher of some obscure but rigid Christian sect—a man supremely confident in the privileges of his righteousness. In the son, individualist by temperament, once the science of colleges had replaced thoroughly the faith of conventicles, this moral attitude translated itself into a frenzied puritanism of ambition. He nursed it as something secularly holy. (73)

In this passage the Professor appears as the perverse offspring of the spotless provincial idealists of Victorian fiction such as Eliot's Felix Holt and Hardy's Clym Yeobright, whom we shall consider in the next chapter. His secret, ruthless ambition recalls that of Godwin Peak in George Gissing's *Born in Exile* (1892). It is as if he has strayed into the cosmopolitan, nomadic world of the modern metropolis from a very different kind of novel, where the search for 'something secularly holy' would arise out of a much more traditional framework of English domestic life.

Puritan and Provincial Englands: From Emily Brontë to D. H. Lawrence

THOMAS CARLYLE, echoing the tones of a revivalist preacher, declared in 1845 that 'The Age of the Puritans is not extinct only and gone away from us, but it is as if fallen beyond the capabilities of memory herself... Its earnest Purport awakens now no resonance in our frivolous hearts.'[1] The 'Age of the Puritans' may be said to have ended with the birth of the modern English nation in 1688, the year of John Bunyan's death as well as of the Whig triumph which Thomas Babington Macaulay and others celebrated as the 'English Revolution'.[2] In Victorian England Macaulay's progressive or 'Whig' interpretation of history found at least as many adherents as Carlyle's harking-back to an epic past, yet Macaulay found it curiously difficult to shake off the memory of seventeenth-century Puritanism. His uncompleted *History of England* (1848–61) begins with a lengthy discussion of the 'State of England in 1685', and terminates less than twenty years later with William III's death in 1702. Looking for the beginnings of the two-party system, Macaulay suggests that the division of English politics between progressives and conservatives began with the meeting of the Long Parliament in October 1641.[3]

Carlyle as a young man had planned to write an essay on the Civil War and the Commonwealth as a reflection of 'some features of the national character'; what he eventually produced was his edition of *The Letters and Speeches of Oliver Cromwell* (1845), a work of biography rather than history.[4] The idea that history could be explained by 'character'—whether the character of individuals, a nation, or an age—was one of the great commonplaces of nineteenth-century thought. It joins political history to literary narrative, emphasizing history's relationship to the novel rather than to drama. Walter Bagehot, for example, found Macaulay's *History of England* too theatrical: brilliant in its portrayal of politics as spectacle, it was deficient in character analysis. For Bagehot the 'form and life' of the Civil War was that of the 'two great characters—the Puritan and the

Cavalier' to which no English historian had yet done justice. The Cavalier was eager, impulsive, 'open to every enjoyment', 'brave without discipline', 'noble without principle'; the essence of Puritanism lay in its 'passionate, deep, rich, religious organization'.[5] Later in the century John Richard Green's *Short History of the English People* (1874) included a highly influential analysis of 'Puritan England', while another English historian, W. E. H. Lecky, declared that 'We are Cavaliers or Roundheads before we are Conservatives or Liberals'.[6]

According to J. R. Green, the 'Puritan gentleman' was characterized by independence, moral fervour, social or at least spiritual egalitarianism, domestic tenderness, and sobriety of speech and costume.[7] This is an ideal type that consciously or unconsciously mirrors the Puritan protagonists of George Eliot's fiction, culminating with Dorothea Brooke in *Middlemarch* (1871–2). Dorothea, who is descended from a 'Puritan gentleman who served under Cromwell', displays a 'hereditary strain of Puritan energy'.[8] She is regarded with a mixture of awe and exasperation by her more conventional sister Celia, and—the unmistakable badge of the Puritan heroine—she has 'that kind of beauty which seems to be thrown into relief by poor dress' (1). (Less ceremoniously, one of the characters of Eliot's *The Mill on the Floss* (1860) observes of Maggie Tulliver that she looks best in 'shabby clothes'.[9]) In the scene where Dorothea and Celia try on their mother's jewels, Celia finds 'a strong assumption of superiority in [Dorothea's] Puritanic toleration, hardly less trying to the blond flesh of an unenthusiastic sister than a Puritanic persecution' (8). Eliot has no sooner identified Dorothea as a Puritan character than she stresses the contradictory and self-divided nature of Puritan beliefs.

A Puritan is always strung between extremes. This chapter began with Carlyle's contrast between Puritanism's 'earnest Purport' and 'our frivolous hearts', a passage exhibiting the necessary hypocrisy of revivalism or what is now called religious fundamentalism. The Puritan preacher is duty-bound to exaggerate, since the challenge he has accepted is to testify to the 'true faith' at a time of permanent crisis. He must convince his hearers that he shares their real or imagined mental struggles. The godly are engaged in battle with the ungodly, but they must also be perpetually on guard against ungodliness in themselves. The preacher's claim to speak the truth rests on his double assertion that, while he too is a sinner, anything that conflicts with his words must inevitably be false.

The true faith, for Protestants, has its source in the Bible; but the Bible had always needed to be supplemented both by the words of the preacher and, as literacy spread in England, by propagandist pamphlets and the growing genre of devotional fiction, especially fiction written for children. In a well-known scene in *Wuthering Heights*, the young Catherine and Heathcliff are shown hitting one another with the two devotional texts, *The Helmet of Salvation* and *The Broad Way to Destruction*, that they have been given to lighten their Sunday afternoon. It is possible that some of the greatest English nineteenth-century novels originated in their authors' rejection of the religious propaganda fed to children.

The Victorian novelists of Puritan England portray institutional Puritanism as an obsolete, dying culture, confronted by new and usually more frivolous influences but lingering on among the older generation throughout the English provinces. At the same time, the Puritan character or 'temper' remains alive and vital, as long as it can be separated from the religious dogma with which it was historically associated. What links the newer Puritanism to the old is often the tenacious genealogy of close-knit Puritan families. Many of the 'Puritan' novels show an antiquarianism verging on historical romance: for example, Dinah Morris, the young Methodist preacher in George Eliot's *Adam Bede* (1859), can only have flourished before 1803 when the Methodist Conference banned female preachers.

After 1688 Puritanism would always remain a minority element and oppositional force in English life, as the labels 'Dissent' and 'Nonconformity' indicate. Split into contending sects, with its leadership unsanctioned by the crown and its adherents debarred from the universities, Nonconformity could never succeed in disestablishing the Anglican Church. Nor, unlike English Catholicism, could it claim the support of an established (if defeated and marginalized) section of the aristocracy. At most, Dissenting congregations could build an alliance with Whig radicalism in order to exercise an influence far beyond their actual numbers. The latter were greatly increased by the Methodist secession from the Church of England in 1791, as Methodism spread rapidly among the urban poor. Soon Nonconformists were wrestling with the new breed of Anglican Evangelicals to save the souls of the new industrial classes. In Victorian England they had also to compete with a growing band of secular missionaries, such as teachers, doctors, social workers, trade unionists, and also novelists.

Poverty, or at least the appearance of poverty, has a general moral value in Christian teaching, since the poor man is closer to the kingdom of heaven. Nineteenth-century fiction portrays poverty as a spiritual ideal— as in Dickens's 'good poor men' like Mr Plornish and Stephen Blackpool— much more often than it shows the reality of poverty. In *Felix Holt, the Radical* (1866), for example, George Eliot portrays the generational gulf between an old-fashioned radical Nonconformist preacher, Rufus Lyon, and Felix Holt, his future son-in-law. Felix wants to improve the state of the workers through education, and he is willing to sacrifice his own moderate prosperity in order to go and live among them. Earlier English fictional heroines such as Pamela, Elizabeth Bennet, and Jane Eyre had had to prove their fitness for wealth and social position, but Esther Lyon, Rufus's stepdaughter, realizes that in order to marry Felix she must show that she is 'fit for poverty'.[10]

The choice of poverty is also a choice of provincialism. Even in *Middlemarch*, where Dorothea is born into the country gentry and eventually marries a young politician, the world of the novel is completely cut off from the metropolitan circles that Eliot herself inhabited. The novel is a self-conscious 'Study of Provincial Life', celebrating characters who live 'hidden lives' and perform 'unhistoric acts' (896). In the early George Eliot, as well as in Emily Brontë, Thomas Hardy, Arnold Bennett, and D. H. Lawrence, provinciality is indicated through the characters' varying use of regional dialects and also of biblical language. These novels are enlivened both by the directness of demotic speech and by the scriptural idioms familiar from clerical discourse. Novelists like Brontë and Hardy bring folk culture and biblical language into direct collision, giving rise to charges of barbarity and obscenity.

Wuthering Heights and *The Mill on the Floss*

Wuthering Heights (1847) has always been understood as a provincial novel, portraying violent and brutal extremes of behaviour and set in a wildly romantic landscape. Charlotte Brontë's preface to the second edition of her sister's work describes it as the 'rude and strange production' of a 'home-bred country girl': its language and manners must appear 'in a great measure unintelligible, and—where intelligible—repulsive', to those unacquainted with the West Riding.[11] The primitiveness of the Yorkshire moors is registered through the eyes of the southern-bred Lockwood, a gentleman who is free to come and go as he pleases. Brontë's characters, however, are lost to sight the moment that they stray beyond the moorland setting. The novel's confined topography is in sharp contrast to the cosmopolitan settings and incessant journeyings of the Gothic and Jacobin fiction to which it is indebted.

Wuthering Heights is, first and last, a ghost story. Lockwood, snowed in as a result of his uninvited social call at Wuthering Heights, fights (or dreams that he fights) with Catherine Earnshaw's ghost at the window pane. The novel's final paragraph depicts the graves of Catherine, Heathcliff, and Edgar Linton, with the narrator wondering how we could ever have imagined 'unquiet slumbers' for those buried there (300). It is his encounter with Catherine's ghost that makes Lockwood curious to hear her story from Brontë's principal narrator Nelly Dean; once the story is over, these tortured spirits can be laid to rest. The central figure of *Wuthering Heights* is Heathcliff, a man who—like the hero of such a Gothic novel as Matthew Lewis's *The Monk*—has allegedly sold his soul to the devil and become a fiend in human shape. But *The Monk* was set in seventeenth-century Germany and Spain and its plot involved a corrupt prioress, the tortures of the Inquisition, and the hero's discovery in his last agonies that he had raped his sister and murdered his mother. These things were not likely to happen (or so Catherine Morland was assured in *Northanger Abbey*) in the Midland counties of a respectable Protestant England. But could ghosts and fiends be roaming the moors of wildest Yorkshire?

The sensational Gothic material in *Wuthering Heights* is balanced by its status as a tale of courtship and domestic passion. The striking two-part structure, with bitter conflict in the first generation and gradual reconciliation in the second, had been anticipated in at least one earlier courtship novel, *A Simple Story* (1791) by Elizabeth Inchbald, the author of the English version of Kotzebue's *Lovers' Vows* which was performed at Mansfield Park. *A Simple Story* is set among the Catholic aristocracy, with a plot that moves between fashionable London, a large country house, and a lonely retreat in Northumberland. In the first part, the heroine falls in love with Dorriforth, a Catholic priest, and marries him when he succeeds to a peerage; but the marriage breaks down irretrievably. In the second part, the couple's daughter succeeds in gaining recognition from her father, who has disowned her. Much of the novel's drama hinges upon Dorriforth's Jesuitical self-righteousness and his emotional dependence on his confessor. In *Wuthering Heights*, provincial Puritanism to some extent takes the place of *A Simple Story*'s high-bred Catholic spirituality.

'Wuthering', glossed as a 'significant provincial adjective' (2), is the first of the numerous dialect words to be singled out by Brontë's narrator. Wuthering Heights is owned by gentleman farmers, as is shown by the standard English spoken by Heathcliff, the master of the house; the name Hareton Earnshaw and the date 1500 are carved over the front door. On his first visit Lockwood speaks to Heathcliff and then to Joseph, the misanthropic old servant whose 'pious ejaculation' (2) introduces the role he will play throughout the novel—that of a Puritan fundamentalist voicing his grumbling disapproval of everything that takes place. In the third chapter Joseph reappears as a lay preacher, caught in a pen-and-ink cartoon in Catherine Earnshaw's diary. The children have been forced to listen for three hours to Joseph's Sunday sermon.

On fine Sundays the family goes to Gimmerton chapel, where the preacher is the Reverend Jabes Branderham; on wet days they must make do with Joseph. Catherine's diary is written in the margins of one of Branderham's published sermons. When Lockwood falls asleep over the diary, he dreams that he is accompanying Joseph (who carries a pilgrim's staff) to hear Branderham preach. Seized by a 'sudden inspiration' in the church, Lockwood denounces Branderham as the 'sinner of the sin that no Christian need pardon' (19), while the minister responds by excommunicating his attacker. The sermon ends in fighting and uproar, until Lockwood is awoken by the rattling of a branch against his window, but the branch, in his next dream, becomes Catherine's ghost.

Joseph's sermon and Jabes Branderham's address to the chapel at Gimmerton thus set a Puritanical devotional context for the love story of *Wuthering Heights*. Catherine's diary records how she and Heathcliff, a castaway of Asian or American descent brought back from Liverpool by the late Mr Earnshaw, decided to rebel against the tyranny of her brother Hindley Earnshaw. Later, Catherine tells the housekeeper Nelly Dean of her love for Heathcliff—though her declaration is shadowed by her decision to abandon him for Edgar Linton:

'My love for Linton is like the foliage in the woods. Time will change it, I'm well aware, as winter changes the trees—my love for Heathcliff resembles the eternal rocks beneath: a source of little visible delight, but necessary. Nelly, I *am* Heathcliff—he's always, always in my mind—not as a pleasure, any more than I am always a pleasure to myself, but as my own being—' (73)

Catherine's words take *Wuthering Heights* beyond Puritanism to a kind of neo-paganism or romantic nature worship, but they are poetic metaphors rather than inspired truths, and at some level they are deeply false. Heathcliff, for his part, loves Catherine but never identifies his being with her.[12] Catherine is as cruel and, in the end, as self-destructive as her brother Hindley. She recklessly betrays both Heathcliff and Linton. Heathcliff, by contrast, reckons up everything, stores up his revenge, and in the end exacts every penny he is owed. Catherine learns to fear him as a 'fierce, pitiless, wolfish man' (90) as he takes control of Wuthering

Heights and becomes a 'cruel hard landlord' (174). He is the sinner against the Holy Ghost whom Joseph and Jabes Branderham wished to see excommunicated. This means that the romantic passion of Catherine and Heathcliff is not a bond between eternal soul-mates, as Catherine once thought, but a union of opposites, a Puritan–Cavalier love tragedy in which the vengeful Puritan outcast tries to drag his former lover down the 'broad way to destruction'.

This opposition between Heathcliff and Catherine is to some extent masked by the more obvious opposition between Wuthering Heights and Thrushcross Grange, between the savage, brutal, Earnshaws (including Heathcliff, who is an Earnshaw by adoption) and the polite, respectable, namby-pamby Lintons. The more that Catherine seems to identify with the family into which she has married, the more Heathcliff accepts his demonic role of eternal excommunication. When Nelly piously tells Heathcliff that it is for God to punish the wicked, he retorts that ' "God won't have the satisfaction that I shall" ' (53). After Catherine's death we are told that he has become a kind of Satanist, shutting himself up and 'praying like a methodist: only the deity he implore[s] is senseless dust and ashes; and God, when addressed, [i]s curiously confounded with his own black father!' (153). Nelly and Joseph think that conscience has 'turned his heart to an earthly hell' (289). He teaches Hindley's son to call him 'Devil daddy', but is himself haunted by Catherine's ghost.

But Heathcliff's elaborate plan of revenge cannot prevent a growing alliance between the Earnshaws, who are 'remnants of the old yeoman class of independent farmers', and the Lintons, who are genteel land-owners.[13] The Lintons inhabit a house and park rather than a farm kitchen, but Hindley Earnshaw's banishment of his servants to the 'back-kitchen' has already started his family on the path of gentrification. He is entirely in favour of his sister marrying Edgar Linton. Edgar seems to live in genteel idleness and doubtless employs a farm manager; he is delicate enough to catch pneumonia as a result of staying out late to see the end of the harvest. The Earnshaws' life is not wholly dissimilar, since neither Hindley nor Heathcliff, when master of Wuthering Heights, appears to engage in manual labour.

Heathcliff's death sums up the novel's themes of dynastic succession, sin and punishment, excommunication, and devil-worship. He has made arrangements for an un-Christian burial, with his body 'carried to the churchyard in the evening' (297) and no minister present. Lockwood's elegiac visit to the graveyard to view the three headstones is preceded by another, far more discordant oration spoken by Joseph over Heathcliff's dead body. Joseph has invariably called on God to 'spare the righteous, though he smote the ungodly' (75), and now he believes his prayers have been answered. His words, in broad dialect, are reported by Nelly, the peasant woman who has taught herself middle-class manners and speech:

'Th' divil's harried off his soul,' he cried, 'and he muh hev his carcass intuh t' bargin, for owt Aw care! Ech! what a wicked un he looks girnning at death!' and the old sinner grinned in mockery.

I thought he intended to cut a caper round the bed; but suddenly composing himself, he fell on his knees, and raised his hands, and returned thanks that the lawful master and the ancient stock were restored to their rights. (298)

Here Nelly effortlessly puts 'the old sinner' in his place, turning his moment of triumph into a grotesquely blasphemous outburst. Whether or not he really intended to 'cut a caper', the lay preacher and self-elected saint stands as a blatant example of Puritan hypocrisy. Emily Brontë, as we have seen, was an Anglican vicar's daughter who would have had little sympathy with Joseph's Nonconformity; Lockwood is tellingly vague about whether Joseph attends a Methodist or Baptist chapel at Gimmerton. Charlotte Brontë's warnings about the 'unintelligibility' and 'repulsiveness' of *Wuthering Heights* may be taken to apply to Hindley's brutality and Heathcliff's devilry, but they apply equally to the uncouth, curmudgeonly, and perpetually dissenting Joseph. He represents the novel's most extreme example of Yorkshire provincialism and hell-fire Puritanism.

Like *Wuthering Heights*, George Eliot's *The Mill on the Floss* is a tragic novel of overmastering passion set in a markedly provincial landscape. While the moors in *Wuthering Heights* form a passive, if bleak and forbidding, environment, the alluvial plain of the Floss finally takes command at the end of the novel when there is a devastating flood. St Ogg's and the river mouth, however, are based not on Eliot's native landscape of Warwickshire (the Loamshire of *Adam Bede*, *Felix Holt*, and *Middlemarch*) but on Gainsborough and the Humber estuary, with which she was much less familiar. Critics have noted the unreality of the flood episode.[14] The provincial world of *The Mill on the Floss* is, ultimately, a more artificial and less compelling literary creation than Emily Brontë's West Riding or Thomas Hardy's Wessex.

Eliot does not use a dramatized external narrator like Lockwood. Instead, there is a pervasive contrast between the provincial insider's viewpoint, represented by the nervous sensitivity and rural isolation of Maggie Tulliver's childhood, and the broader, more judicious perspective of the third-person narrative voice. The unsophisticated language and manners of the Tullivers and Dodsons are presented with wonderful comic intimacy, as if through Maggie's clear-eyed youthful perceptions; but at other times the narrator assumes a quasi-scientific, generalizing authority, alternately praising and disparaging, and always somewhat condescending. Maggie's story thus belongs to 'the history of unfashionable families' (272), and the scene of her childhood is one of 'oppressive narrowness' (254–5). It is as if Charlotte Brontë's preface to her sister's novel had got into the text. The tone of dispassionate social and ethnographic observation soon modulates into the personal impressions of Eliot the moralist:

Observing these people narrowly . . . one sees little trace of religion, still less of a distinctively Christian creed. Their belief in the Unseen, so far as it manifests itself at all, seems to be rather of a pagan kind; their moral notions, though held with strong tenacity, seem to have no standard beyond hereditary custom. You could not live among such people . . . you are irritated with these dull men and women, as a kind of population out of keeping with the earth on which they live—with this rich plain where the great river flows for ever onward, and links the small pulse of the old English town with the beating of the world's mighty heart. A vigorous superstition, that lashes its gods or lashes its own back, seems to be more congruous with the mystery of the human lot, than the mental condition of these emmet-like Dodsons and Tullivers. (254)

'You could not live among such people': after what has gone before, this has a startling vehemence. It leads to the classification of the Dodsons and Tullivers as 'emmet-like', a simile with scientific associations (since antlike creatures can only be closely observed through a microscope or magnifying-glass), but still strongly expressive of Eliot's impatience with provincial narrowness.

   The author of this passage was an agnostic intellectual who (as she wrote in a letter) sought to find the 'lasting meaning that lies in all religious doctrine'.[15] Her characterization of the Dodsons and Tullivers contrasts Christianity with paganism, and vigorous superstition with sluggish inertness. (Somewhere behind it lurks the distinction between a 'great river' flowing with its customary tranquillity, and a river in flood.) What is odd about this train of reflection is that, though it condemns the Tullivers for having 'no standard beyond hereditary custom', it functions as a commentary on one of the novel's decisive acts, which does indeed seem to be prompted by a 'vigorous superstition': Mr Tulliver's curse on his rival John Wakem, which he causes to be written down in the family Bible. The curse marks an obsession with vengeance which, as in *Wuthering Heights*, works itself out over two generations. Tom Tulliver's emotional life is entirely consumed by his determination to get back Dorlcote Mill and avenge his father, regardless of the suffering this brings to himself and his family.

In constructing her plot around a vendetta and a 'family curse', Eliot underlines her belief that the fiction of provincial realism ought to echo the great tragic themes of classical drama and myth—a belief shared by Thomas Hardy, and later by Arnold Bennett. The 'history of unfashionable families' possesses a tragic sublimity even if it is the 'unwept, hidden sort' of tragedy (183). The novel's tragic form also means that the continuity of its provincial world will be shattered, and the narrowness of the Dodsons and Tullivers changed beyond recognition. The first sign of this lies in the individual spiritual development undergone by both Maggie and Tom, for all their differences from one another.

Eliot has defined the Dodsons' and Tullivers' torpid religion as a hitherto uncharted variety of Protestantism.[16] Maggie's intense spirituality is entirely self-taught, emerging from her reading of an illustrated Bible in her infancy and, later, from her discovery of Thomas à Kempis's *Imitation of Christ* in a parcel of old books. Maggie dreams of a life of abject renunciation, self-denial, and self-humiliation, an ideal all too obviously reflecting her passionate attachment to her cruel and unfeeling brother. But her openness to sexual passion leads to her involvements with Philip Wakem, the son of the hated John Wakem, and with the unscrupulous Stephen Guest. Fittingly, she admires the 'dark unhappy' heroines of Scott such as Rebecca and Flora MacIvor (312), and Philip with some truth accuses her of self-torture and self-repression.

George Eliot, the daughter of an evangelical land agent, became a rationalist and agnostic in adult life, but her sense of supernatural sanctions never deserted her. Walking with the poet and critic F. W. H. Myers in a Cambridge college garden, she is said to have spoken 'with terrible earnestness' of the concepts of God, Immortality, and Duty—'how inconceivable was the *first*, how unbelievable the *second*, and yet how peremptory and absolute the *third*'.[17] If the element of self-punishment here suggests Maggie Tulliver, the need to cling to an idea of unquestioning rectitude suggests Tom. It is this that enables him to wipe out the memory of his father's bankruptcy and to return to Dorlcote Mill, rejecting what might have been a far more prosperous career in his uncle's expanding business. At the same time, he becomes an unloved and unlovable recluse who restores the family's good name while cutting himself off from the family itself. Maggie's weakness is that in the very moment of rebelling against Tom's rigid morality she has an irresistible need to humiliate herself before him, as if he were 'a reflection of her own conscience' (456). It is 'as if he were a prophetic voice predicting her future fallings' (370). Tom is a far more decisive figure in her life than either Philip or Stephen, not to mention the Anglican clergyman Dr Kenn who might have become her third lover. His self-righteousness and her urge towards submission and self-humiliation represent two warring but, in the end, inseparable aspects of English Puritanism.

Tom Tulliver is an embodiment of what E. M. Forster, in his 'Notes on the English Character' (1926), would call the 'undeveloped heart'. Forster said of the 'undeveloped heart' that 'it is not that the Englishman can't feel—it is that he is afraid to feel'.[18] Tom is like Heathcliff in becoming a ruthless, hard-headed businessman in order to achieve his private ends, yet he is a son and brother rather than a demonic, mysterious man from nowhere. His 'narrowness of imagination and intellect' (430) is a product of exactly the same upbringing as Maggie's. Maggie, who like her author believes in the 'Blessed influence of one true living soul on another',[19] repeatedly comes to Tom for an understanding and forgiveness which he cannot or will not provide. At one point she denounces him as a pitiless 'Pharisee' (326), but usually these scenes end with her in floods of tears. Maggie's tearfulness is, perhaps, easily aroused—she cries, as we have seen, over Washington Irving's *Sketch Book*—but it is a sign of her tenderness of conscience, the 'divine presentiment' that she has of the 'sacredness of life' (432). She becomes an outcast in St Ogg's as a result of her refusal to marry Stephen, and her final decision to renounce him on the night of the flood is sealed by her involuntary recollection of some words of Thomas à Kempis. She returns to Dorlcote and tries to rescue Tom, while he at last abandons the grinding Mill (the mechanical instrument of retribution) and submits himself to the flood of dammed-up feeling. Eliot's self-divided Puritanical soul-mates are, therefore, drowned together.

Two Victorian Job Stories

Loamshire and Barsetshire are the two 'bastard counties' added by the mid-Victorian novelists Eliot and Trollope to the map of England. Anthony Trollope's Barsetshire novels begin with *The Warden* (1855) and *Barchester Towers* (1857). Of one of the later novels in the series, *Framley Parsonage* (1861), he recalled that

as I wrote it I became more closely acquainted than ever with the new shire which I had added to the English counties. I had it all in my mind—its roads and railroads, its towns and parishes, its members of Parliament, and the different hunts which rode over it. I knew all the great lords and their castles, the squires and their parks, the rectors and their churches.[20]

As an Ordnance Survey map of the conventional English middle-class novel this could hardly be bettered. It also shows why, for all his attachment to locality, Trollope is not a genuinely provincial novelist. His subject is the ruling class, portrayed over a greater or more detailed sociological range than in Fielding or Jane Austen, and more soberly and realistically than in Disraeli's novels. Trollope follows Disraeli and Thackeray in reintroducing his cast of aristocrats and prominent public figures in novel after novel, creating a continuous social world in which the protagonist of one novel reappears as a background character in the next. Moreover, his 'new shire' could be almost anywhere in England's agricultural heartland even though Barchester, its cathedral city, has often been equated with Salisbury. His rural world is structured by familiar national oppositions—between the Broad Church and the Evangelicals, between the squires and the great lords, between Tories and Whigs—and Trollope is a master of the established conventions of English novel-land. In *Doctor Thorne* (1858) Frank Gresham, the young Tory heir, is 'every inch a Gresham', a member of a family that 'had from time immemorial been handsome': 'it is he who is to be our favourite young man, to do the love scenes, to have his trials and his difficulties, and to win through them or not, as the case may be', the narrator adds.[21] The novel is largely concerned with dynastic marriage, and, needless to say, Frank falls in love with, and finally marries, the one woman who can save his family's bankrupt estate.

George Eliot's fiction has its share of conventional English ladies and gentlemen, and of plots based on hidden identity and the mysteries of inheritance. But Eliot at the start of her career set out to widen the novel's social range, going beyond the 'boundaries of an ancestral park' to the 'midland villages and markets' where the narrator of her last book, *Impressions of Theophrastus Such* (1879), locates his 'native England'.[22] From *Scenes of Clerical Life* (1858) onwards, she frequently draws attention to the ordinariness of her characters and their low social standing. There is 'a pathos in their very insignificance'.[23] This discovery of complexity in simplicity is part of the democratization of the English novel, a movement to which Eliot signally contributed. But it is also characteristic of the traditional literary pastoral. Eliot is closest to pastoral in *Adam Bede* and in *Silas Marner* (1861), a brief tale which, like Trollope's *The Warden*, is manifestly based on the Job story.[24]

In Trollope's novel, the Reverend Septimus Harding, a humble and inoffensive widower, is denounced in the national press for holding the comfortable position of warden of Hiram's Hospital, a charitable institution intended to benefit the poor. He resigns his post although his ecclesiastical supporters, like false comforters, want him to put up a fight. Archdeacon Grantly, his worldly son-in-law, finds his meekness ' "enough to provoke Job" ' (161), as if Grantly, not Harding, were the Job figure. Harding is eventually restored to modest prosperity thanks to a second sinecure at St Cuthbert's, a tiny city parish consisting only of a few houses next to the cathedral. The roof-beams at St Cuthbert's have two gargoyles at each end, with 'two devils and an angel on one side, two angels and a devil on the other' (183), suggesting both the symmetry of Trollope's plot and the tug-of-war between God and Satan that initiated the story of Job.

Harding at the end of *The Warden* is a lesser man in material terms but greater in spirit. Similarly, the arrival of the foundling child Eppie serves to compensate Silas Marner, George Eliot's lonely cottager and handloom weaver, for the theft of a hoard of gold sovereigns. In each novel, the innocent love of a young girl softens the outlines of the Job story and leads to the hero's reconciliation with his enemies. Harding's daughter shares his sufferings, but eventually marries the Puritanical reformer who had inspired the press campaign against his wardenship. Eppie stays with Silas until her marriage despite an attempt by Godfrey Cass, a local gentleman farmer, to reclaim her as his daughter.

Where the Barchester of *The Warden* was manifestly a contemporary cathedral city, *Silas Marner* is set fifty years in the past in the 'rich, central plain of what we are pleased to call Merry England'.[25] The 'odour of Christmas cooking' is in the wind (119), and Eppie finds shelter with Silas on New Year's Eve; the fact that Eliot's tale is an example of the Victorian Christmas story adds to its pastoralism. Reversing the flow of history and the general movement of population in the Industrial Revolution,[26] Silas is a fugitive from a great city with 'currents of industrial energy and Puritan earnestness' (33). Unjustly expelled from the Dissenting congregation of Lantern yard in the 'city of destruction' (207), he comes to the village of Raveloe to pursue his livelihood as a handloom weaver, a profession that had effectively disappeared in the half-century separating the time of the story from its composition. Soon he becomes a miser and a recluse, cut off from his neighbours both by his occupation and by his Puritanical dedication to independence and self-sufficiency.

The God of Lantern Yard was a hard, 'unpropitious deity' (22), while Raveloe is a benighted village knowing little more than the primordial 'fetishism' of the 'gods of the hearth' (221). That it is a place of spiritual darkness is emphasized by the novel's brilliantly imagined night scenes, such as the New Year's Eve dance, the evening in the village pub, and the glimpse of Silas worshipping his gold by the light of his cottage hearth. Nevertheless, Raveloe enjoys the prosperity of 'Merry England', and the 'careless abundance' of its rich, fertile lands leads to good neighbourliness and a surplus available for charitable giving (22). When the Puritanical Silas enjoys a surplus, he hoards it up for himself until the hoard is stolen. It could be objected that his is not a true Job story since he loses his Lantern Yard faith and worships his own pagan 'gods of the hearth', first the gold and then Eppie. At last, thanks to Eppie, he becomes a full member of the village community, recovers his lost gold, and learns Christian charity. Only the sufferings of Godfrey Cass's abandoned wife and his unwanted child speak of the actual experiences of the poor in this patently idealized countryside.

Loamshire and the Puritan Temper

Like *Romola* (1863), her historical novel set in fifteenth-century Florence, *Silas Marner* was an eddy in the main current of George Eliot's fiction leading from *Scenes of Clerical Life* to *Middlemarch*. Her major novels all follow the programme of missionary realism that she had set out in her review-essay 'The Natural History of German Life' (1856). Here she attacks Dickens's novels for their romantic and melodramatic caricatures of the urban poor, and accuses socialist thinkers of stereotyping the proletariat whose interests they champion. The duty of the novelist is to portray 'the people as they are', not an ideal or sentimental travesty, so that the reader's 'sympathies' are extended to the actual plight of the poor.[27] Eliot's implied reader, then, is a potentially liberal-minded and socially conscious member of the middle class. Left to themselves, however, such readers would be liable to languish in an original condition of (individual or class) selfishness or 'egoism'; the novelist ought to further their moral development towards a state of altruism, or caring for others. To understand other people in the way that we understand the characters in a novel is (Eliot believes) necessarily to sympathize with them and care about their fate.

Sympathy-extension, however, is not merely an external duty imposed upon the novelist, since it is built into Eliot's narrative method. Her omniscient narrators move about from one character or social group to the next, recording their private gossip, and overhearing what they have to say about one another. Individual moral development is measured on a scale ranging from egoism to altruism, so that the moments of greatest psychological drama in her novels are moments in which her characters' sympathies are unexpectedly extended. Typically this happens through silent communication, mediated by eye-contact between two individuals.[28] These mutual gazes in her novels vary greatly in openness and intensity, ranging from the shifty, furtive, and superficial to the profoundly emotional and direct. At the higher end of the range is the exchange of looks between a spiritual mentor and a character assuming the humble position of discipleship. Usually mentor and disciple are of opposite sexes, so that the scene is a sublimation of fiction's more conventional motifs of sexual romance. What happens is a kind of seduction of the spirit.

The figure of the clergyman or religious mentor plays a major part in Eliot's fiction, although most of her clergy fall far short of her altruistic ideal. Perhaps the earliest of her characters to possess the gift of communicating sympathy is the evangelical Mr Tryan in 'Janet's Repentance', the most substantial of the three tales that constitute *Scenes of Clerical Life*. Tryan is regarded by Eliot's provincial Anglican community as a zealot and a prig, but he is able to help Janet Dempster to achieve a reconciliation with her brutal, dying husband. The evangelical clergyman has made the transition from Puritanical preacher to mentor and healer, a man whose sympathetic nature can inspire sympathies in others. His role is a mirror image of the role that Eliot claims for the novelist. Tryan's successors in her fiction include Dinah Morris, the Methodist preacher in *Adam Bede*; the Independent minister Rufus Lyon and his radical protégé Felix Holt; and Dorothea in *Middlemarch*, who is married to a clergyman of the most unsympathetic sort.

The farmhouse, not the country house, is at the centre of *Adam Bede*, Eliot's first full-length novel, and this alone was a momentous departure in English fiction. The Poysers are much lower on the social scale than the Earnshaws of *Wuthering Heights*, and their farm kitchen brings together Dinah Morris, a former mill-worker turned preacher, and the illiterate, empty-headed Hetty Sorrel. The fact that Hetty has 'never read a novel' means that she cannot understand the real meaning of the attentions that Arthur Donnithorne, a young army captain, is paying to her;[29] moreover, Eliot unsparingly describes her as a 'little trivial soul' who lacks the maternal instinct and is indifferent to the 'joys and sorrows of foregone generations' (340, 284). The Poysers of Hayslope are tenant-farmers who regard their landlords, the Donnithornes, with a 'whispering awe' as they ride by on horseback like gods in human shape (80). Dinah, however, speaks of the rich and poor as equals, since, as she asserts in her sermon on the village green, ' "God's love turns poverty into riches" ' (31). Her egalitarianism comes from her experience as a mill-worker, while she has turned to Methodism because it is the religion of the poor. She is at odds with the ingrained deference and subordination of the farming community, since, as Martin Poyser remarks, ' "It's on'y tradesfolks as turn methodists; you niver knew a farmer bitten wi' them maggots" ' (190).

But Dinah, as we have seen, is also a historical curiosity in a novel published nearly sixty years after the Methodist Church banned women preachers. She dresses with archaic plainness, and to Eliot's Victorian readers she must have seemed almost as old-fashioned as a seventeenth-century witch. Arthur Donnithorne, the Cavalier villain, is also something of a stock figure. As heir to the estate he is universally liked for his generosity, his jokes, and his 'free manners' (86). As an officer and sportsman he feels 'very heroic' as he strides towards the stables (124), and at first he is revered by his social inferiors such as the carpenter Adam Bede. But ultimately Arthur is a hero only to himself. He would like to be the 'model of an English gentleman', but his tragic flaw is his 'reliance on his own virtues' and his 'confidence that his faults were all of a generous kind' (124–5). Just as he enjoys an unearned income, he believes that he will always have a credit balance in the moral bank. Arthur is not a cold-hearted ladies' man, but he cannot resist temptation when it is offered to him.

Adam Bede, then, contains manifest representatives of the Cavalier and the Puritan tempers, but it is not a Cavalier-and-Puritan love story. Far from putting up a show of resistance, Hetty Sorrel is an eager and cooperating victim in her own seduction. Not only is she one of Eliot's rural pagans but she is represented as a hard, selfish young woman, more a sexual animal than a civilized human being. It is only after she has abandoned her baby and left it to die that she begins to learn a measure of sympathy for others.

The Bede family household provides an alternative focus to the Poysers' farm kitchen. Adam's father, like Hetty's, was a drunken good-for-nothing, but Adam is devoted to self-improvement and the gospel of work. Doctrinally, he is no Puritan but a Broad Church Anglican. But his development through the novel exemplifies the characteristics of J. R. Green's 'Puritan temper', and it is this that (once his infatuation with Hetty has run its painful course) makes him a suitable mate for Dinah. When he becomes Arthur Donnithorne's estate manager, he demonstrates his independence and sense of equality by standing up to his employer both physically and morally. Hetty, he tells Arthur, is ' "more nor everything else to me, all but my conscience and good name" ' (307); there is a Puritanical scrupulousness about these two exceptions. He has a 'devout mind' even if he is 'impatient of devout words', and, as Eliot puts it, 'his tenderness [lies] very close to his reverence' (392). His domesticity finds expression in his close attachment to a domineering mother, a relationship anticipating that of Paul and Mrs Morel in D. H. Lawrence's *Sons and Lovers* (1913).

Adam Bede ends, like *Silas Marner*, with the gradual healing of a broken rural community. The two most disruptive influences, Arthur and Hetty, are banished to the remotest reaches of the British Empire, Arthur as a regular army officer on an overseas posting and Hetty as a reprieved child-murderer sentenced to transportation. (Only Arthur, now a fever-shattered colonel, ever returns home.) Dinah stays in Hayslope but as a wife and mother, since she can no longer follow her vocation as a preacher. Mrs Bede has recommended her son to Dinah as a ' "husband . . . as isna just the cut o' thysen" ' (494), and for most of the novel they are apparently opposites, with Dinah devoted to her ministry and Adam content to be a good workman. But once their courtship is concluded they are one and the same, just as rural England's divisions have been mended. The novel is, as the title indicates, Adam's story—the narrator claims to have heard it from him in old age—and Adam reinstates the traditional rural order by eventually forgiving his former rival for Hetty's love. Arthur Donnithorne may have squandered his moral capital but he still owns the countryside.

Where *Adam Bede* differs from Eliot's later novels is that, for all its endorsement of the the Puritan temper, it ends with a withdrawal into private life. Arthur has had to give up his ambition of becoming a Member of Parliament, while Dinah's ministry is at an end. These characters' lives will henceforth only concern their immediate neighbours. But in *Felix Holt* Eliot wrote that 'there is no private life which has not been determined by a wider public life' (43), and her later protagonists, especially Felix Holt and Daniel Deronda, normally attempt to influence public life in their turn. Dorothea in *Middlemarch* marries Casaubon because she thinks she can help him in a piece of outstanding intellectual work. It is these characters' sense of duty, 'peremptory and absolute', that forces them to act in ways that confound expectations and help to destabilize traditional provincial society.

Returned to its context, Eliot's pronouncement about public and private life in *Felix Holt* refers not so much to broad social and historical relationships as to specific dirty deeds in the past. *Felix Holt* and *Middlemarch* have complicated and artificial plots involving an element of mysterious identity and petty crime; and they also offer a somewhat satirical view of political developments in the 1830s, the local manifestations of national history. In *Felix Holt*, Harold Transome's decision to stand for Parliament as a Radical candidate complicates the normal straight fight between Whigs and Tories. During the election campaign the Dissenting minister Rufus Lyon challenges his Anglican counterpart to a public debate on the 'Constitution of the true Church'. The result is to some extent a novel of ideas in the Disraeli tradition, an attempt to initiate a public debate beyond the confines of fiction. Eliot went on to write an 'Address to Working Men, by Felix Holt', published in *Blackwood's Magazine* the year after Disraeli's Second Reform Act.

Harold Transome, newly returned from the Middle East, is a political opportunist, a domestic tyrant, and a subtler representative of the careless immorality that Eliot had portrayed in Arthur Donnithorne. He is, however, a successful businessman rather than a dashing young heir, since he has the 'energetic will and muscle, the self-confidence, the quick perception, and the narrow imagination which make what is admiringly called the practical mind' (93). In politics, however, his tactical manoeuvring stands in sharp contrast to the principled radicalism of Rufus Lyon and Felix Holt, the respective embodiments of the old and the new versions of the Puritan temper. Lyon, an 'old-fashioned Puritan' (49), is a pedantic but lovable fundamentalist preacher. His stepdaughter Esther ignores her father's doctrines, refuses to become a member of his chapel, and is a devoted reader of Byron. But she is also a typical George Eliot heroine in being, in the critic Leslie Stephen's words, a 'woman in need of a confessor'.[30]

Felix Holt, though a political rather than a religious leader, lives a life of self-denial and Puritanical rectitude. He works as a watch-mender to support his widowed mother, since he refuses to profit from his father's pill-vending business, which he regards as dishonest. Felix, burdened with a spiritual independence that has led him to despise the 'new prosperity of Dissent' (45), is one of what George Gissing would later call the 'unclassed'. Eliot at one point shows him addressing a political meeting together with a working-class trade unionist, a stereotypical proletarian with an appearance of 'mere acuteness and rather hard-lipped antagonism'. Felix, by contrast, manifests the 'look of habitual meditative abstraction from objects of mere personal vanity or desire, which is the peculiar stamp of culture' (247). He is one of those 'men of culture' to whom Matthew Arnold would soon be appealing in *Culture and Anarchy* (1869). Whether, before *Culture and Anarchy*, Eliot's phrase 'the peculiar stamp of culture' had quite the snobbish ring it would later acquire is difficult to say; what is notable, however, is that in earlier times Felix's 'look of habitual meditative abstraction' would have been the sign of a religious vocation, so that the value put on 'culture' is part of the secularization of religion in Eliot's writing. Felix has told Esther that he aims to become a 'demagogue of a new sort; an honest one, if possible, who will tell the people they are blind and foolish, and neither flatter them nor fatten on them' (223). Here the message of the 'honest demagogue' resembles that of the fundamentalist preacher in everything except its appeal to reason rather than biblical authority. The preacher tells the people that they are miserable sinners; Felix's rather less acceptable message is that they are uneducated boors who do not deserve the vote. Rufus Lyon, an inveterate proponent of universal suffrage, is a more genuine democrat than his future son-in-law.

Felix's addresses to working men seem unlikely to have much practical effect, although he does prompt an 'inward revolution' (388) in Esther Lyon. He is sent to prison after a misguided attempt to take control of a Radical mob on election day. In the end he, Esther, and Rufus leave Loamshire for an unnamed industrial town, after Esther has turned down the Transome fortune to which it is revealed she is the legal heir. This ending, as one critic has written, combines the 'narrative pleasure of apparent change with the satisfying reassurance of the essential stability of things', since Loamshire is left to the Tories after the protagonists' departure.[31] Before they begin their new life, Felix marries Esther in the local Anglican church, in a remarkably implausible manifestation of ruling-class magnanimity and national solidarity. The narrator observes that 'Every one in those days was married at the parish church' (397), although Felix and Esther need only have waited two or three years for the passage of the 1837 Civil Marriages Act, after which, as the son and daughter of Dissenters, they would have been expected to marry at Rufus Lyon's chapel. But since it is an Anglican wedding 'Even very great people, like Sir Maximus [Debarry] and his family, went to the church to look at this bride, who had renounced wealth, and chosen to be the wife of a man who said he would always be poor' (397). Perhaps the Debarrys (the local Tories) might have been less complacent if the former watch-mender had said he intended to get rich.

Neither *Middlemarch* nor *Daniel Deronda* has a fairy-tale ending like *Felix Holt*. *Middlemarch* is a great Victorian classic, and it is also, as its subtitle tells us, a 'Study of Provincial Life', but it portrays provincial life at a higher social level, and in a vein that is closer to the novels of Trollope than to Eliot's earlier fiction. Both Hayslope and the Treby Magna of *Felix Holt* are more topographically distinctive than the town of Middlemarch and its surrounding countryside. *Middlemarch* centres on the local gentry, the clergy, and the urban middle classes, with doctors, an industrialist, a banker, and a land agent among its characters. Puritan tenderness is represented by Dorothea Brooke, with her thwarted determination to make a success of her marriage to Casaubon, the unfeeling clergyman and desiccated scholar; her second husband will be Will Ladislaw, Casaubon's scapegrace and somewhat Cavalier relative. The banker Nicholas Bulstrode, by contrast, has followed what Eliot regarded as the typical itinerary of the rising Nonconformist businessman. Formerly a Dissenter and Calvinist, he cements his position in Middlemarch by joining the Church of England and supporting its militantly evangelical wing.[32] In the novel we see him trying to stage-manage the appointment of an evangelical candidate to the post of hospital chaplain, and ultimately he is unmasked as a fraud and a hypocrite and forced to leave Middlemarch. But, if provincial life no longer has a place for this pretended embodiment of Puritan rectitude, the other remaining principal characters—Lydgate the doctor, Dorothea, and Ladislaw—are like him in seeking their fortunes elsewhere. Casaubon, Lydgate, and Ladislaw have intellectual ambitions which, in any case, look beyond Loamshire, while Fred Vincy, the manufacturer's son who does fit easily into the provincial horizon, is roundly condescended to by the narrator. As in *The Mill on the Floss*, the 'provincial life' of *Middlemarch* never quite escapes the stigma of provincial narrowness.

Pilgrims and Preachers: Thomas Hardy

Of all major English novelists, Hardy is the most determinedly provincial. He is, unapologetically, a novelist not of England but of 'Wessex'—less the ancient Saxon kingdom than a fictional place which, as he wrote of Christminster in *Jude the Obscure* (1896), 'in its entirety existed nowhere else in the world but between the covers of [my novels]'.[33] Wessex is rural, old-fashioned, a last redoubt of folk customs, and full of enclaves like Egdon Heath and the forests around Hintock which at first sight seem hardly touched by the nineteenth century. Hardy often suggests that the people of Wessex represent elemental human nature, so that 'dramas of a grandeur and unity truly Sophoclean' are played out among them.[34] But they are also geographically isolated, with only the vaguest sense of what lies beyond Wessex. While the realm of nature in Hardy transcends the local and particular—it is 'conterminous with the universe in space, and with history in time'[35]—his more ambitious characters do not look to the nation or the national metropolis as the arena in which their desires might be satisfied. Tess Durbeyfield and Angel Clare accompany the milk churns to their local railway station, since London is the market to which the Vale of the Great Dairies sends its produce, but it never occurs to the lovers themselves to go there. Jude Fawley is a 'sort of Dick Whittington', but Christminster (or Oxford), not London, is his city of light. In *The Return of the Native* (1878) the great city where Clym Yeobright has lived, and where Eustacia Vye longs to go, is not London but Paris.

Nevertheless, Tess and Angel's trip to the station and Eustacia's dreams of Paris indicate Hardy's pervasive concern with the mobility and rootlessness of modern life. His most widely read novels do not verge on historical fiction, as George Eliot's do. Tess has passed the sixth standard in the National School (which should not be confused, however, with a post-1870 Board School) and has thought of becoming a teacher; Jude lives to see the birth of the university extension movement and the beginnings of mass higher education. Even Hardy's traditional rural crafts are not always what they seem. Diggory Venn the reddleman is, we are told, 'one of a class rapidly becoming extinct in Wessex, filling...the place which, during the last century, the dodo occupied in the world of animals'.[36] But Venn is a prosperous farmer who takes up the reddle trade for a time because he fancies a wandering life, not a traditional reddleman. He is a bit like the weekend hobbyists of the late twentieth century who set out to reopen disused railway lines and to revive the age of steam.

If Venn is (once we penetrate his disguise) as modern as any of Hardy's characters, he is also presented as a countryman and, therefore, a natural antiquarian. Modern Wessex deliberately and self-consciously lags behind the modern city. This is why Clym Yeobright's return from Paris to Egdon creates such expectations—the local labourers talk about it 'as if it were of national importance' (128)—and why his relapse into the traditional and lowly occupation of furze-cutting is felt to be so disturbing. As Hardy says of Clym, 'Mentally he was in a provincial future, that is, he was in many points abreast with the central town thinkers of his date' (196), but until the end of the novel he fails to act like someone influenced by town thought. As for Hardy himself, he is manifestly not a metropolitan intellectual like George Eliot, but nor is he as countrified as Clym. His novels record the struggle between archaism and modernity in the countryside, and it is in this context that Puritanism, at first a rather marginal presence in Hardy's fiction, comes to the fore in his last novels *Tess* and *Jude*.

Hardy began with an unpublished novel, *The Poor Man and the Lady*, which he later described as a 'sweeping dramatic satire of the squirearchy and nobility, London society, the vulgarity of the middle class, and political and domestic morals in general'. His views at that time were 'obviously those of a young man with a passion for reforming the world'.[37] *Tess* and *Jude* show that he never lost his passionate hatred of social injustice, yet, compared to his predecessors in nineteenth-century fiction, Hardy the novelist is curiously unpolitical. His literary success began not with a social-problem novel but with a sentimental rural idyll, *Under the Greenwood Tree* (1872). This was followed by a metafictional romance, *A Pair of Blue Eyes* (1873)—metafictional in the sense that the heroine, Elfride Swancourt, is herself a romantic novelist—in which class politics are represented by the 'Saxon versus Norman' convention inherited from Disraeli and Scott. 'Elfride' is a Saxon-sounding name, while 'Swancourt' combines Anglo-Saxon and Norman roots. Elfride's two principal suitors are Henry Knight, a London barrister and journalist, and Stephen Smith, an architect's assistant whose father was a humble stonemason. (Hardy eventually revised the text to remove many of the dialect forms from the Smith family's speech.) The novel is set in Endelstow, 'a parish on the sea-swept outskirts of Lower Wessex'.[38] The local landowner is Lord Luxellian, a Cornish name, but the working people of Endelstow are represented as being of Saxon, not Celtic, origin, and the central confrontation between a Smith and a Knight reproduces the Saxon-Norman opposition almost too literally. Hardy's best-known invocation of Norman ancestry is in *Tess*, which begins with Parson Tringham, mounted on horseback, encountering John Durbeyfield the carter, who at this moment is symbolically on foot. Tringham, an antiquarian, addresses Durbeyfield as 'Sir John' and tells him he is the lineal descendant of Sir Pagan d'Urberville, a Norman knight. The family 'declined a little in Oliver Cromwell's time, but to no serious extent', and was rewarded for its Royalism by Charles II (14). Durbeyfield has no sooner listened to this genealogy than, spurred by an ancestral memory, he sends for a horse and cart and is driven round the village. Much more will be heard in the novel of the bloody legend of the 'd'Urberville coach', but Hardy, in one of his most sardonic asides, also indicates the pointlessness of Parson Tringham's revelation: 'So much for Norman blood unaided by Victorian lucre' (25).

As the name 'Sir Pagan' and the d'Urberville family history suggest, there is a theme of rural paganism (much more heavily emphasized here than in George Eliot) and also a contrast of Cavalier and Puritan types running through Hardy's novels. The Durbeyfields' marauding Norman ancestor may have been a pagan in the sense of following the unscrupulous, lawless conduct of one living in a Hobbesian state of nature, and there is a hint that the Victorian d'Urbervilles, who have bought the family name, are similarly disposed. But 'paganism' in Hardy usually means the pre-Christian superstitions of the Wessex countryside. His characters are closer to the land than those of any earlier English novelist, largely because they are shown working on the land. Tess, for example, mixes up the scriptures she has learnt at school with the '[p]agan fantasy of their remote forefathers' which Hardy says is natural to field labourers (124). Giles Winterbourne in *The Woodlanders* (1887) appears at harvest time as an emanation of nature, a 'fruit-god' or 'wood-god' who 'looked and smelt like Autumn's very brother' (305, 235). Hardy sometimes refers to pre-Christian religious practices and rites, as with the 'Druidical mistletoe' which persists in the primeval forest of the Chase where Tess is raped (47). On other occasions he portrays secular folk rituals such as the skimmington ride in *The Mayor of Casterbridge* (1886).

The contrasted sets of Cavalier and Puritan male characters in Hardy include Damon Wildeve and Clym in *The Return of the Native*, Henchard and Farfrae in *The Mayor of Casterbridge*, Fitzpiers and Winterbourne in *The Woodlanders*, and Alec d'Urberville and Angel Clare in *Tess*. 'Puritan' in this context does not necessarily mean a religious affiliation; in *Tess* it is Alec, not Angel, who briefly becomes a Puritan preacher. Angel Clare and Giles Winterbourne are identifiable as Puritans largely because of their sexual fastidiousness, as when Giles, ill with fever, refuses to share a cottage, let alone a bed, with his lover Grace Melbury when she flees to him for shelter in the depths of winter. One of Hardy's most distinctive character types, however, is the post-Puritan preacher in the style of Felix Holt. Clym Yeobright is the grandson of a curate and the son of a narrowly possessive, Puritanical mother; he comes back from Paris, fired with the brotherhood of man, to the remote community of Egdon, a heathen 'world's end' (417) where there is little or no churchgoing because the church is too far away. Eventually Clym announces his intention to 'keep a night-school' (413), and he becomes an 'itinerant open-air preacher and lecturer on morally unimpeachable subjects' throughout Wessex: 'He left alone creeds and systems of philosophy, finding enough and more than enough to occupy his tongue in the opinions and actions common to all good men' (423). Hardy has, perhaps, a Socratic ideal in mind, but Clym's avoidance of religious or political controversy suggests that the action of preaching is more important to him than any message he might have for his hearers.

Clym's successor as a secular preacher and lecturer is Jude Fawley; and one thing that both men have in common is their inability to dispense with religious language and, above all, the language of the Book of Job. They see themselves as reliving the story of Job.[39] Clym quotes the Book of Job at least once—' "I have made a covenant with mine eyes; why then should I think upon a maid?" ' (412)—and Jude does so repeatedly. Clym's life and preaching might suggest the possibility of a direct progression from the paganism of Egdon Heath to a provincial future of rational agnosticism, as if doctrinal Christianity had been superseded or sidelined. But *Jude the Obscure* (1896) permits no such conclusion.

Biblical texts play a crucial role in both *Tess* and *Jude*, most notably in the Pauline epigraph to *Jude*, 'The letter killeth', and in the work of the sign-painter in *Tess*, who puts the words 'THY, DAMNATION, SLUMBERETH, NOT' on a stile (97). When he turns to a nearby wall, he begins to write out the seventh commandment but hesitates over the word 'adultery'. Hardy's defence of Tess's moral innocence is evident from the novel's subtitle—'A Pure Woman'—although the concept of purity is naturally ambiguous. A 'pure woman' means, in one of its senses, the quintessence of womanhood, but the supposed purity of Nature is frequently called into question. Very early in *Tess* we encounter the name of one of the two public houses of Marlott, the Pure Drop, suggesting both the natural purity of water and the artificial purity of fermented and distilled liquors, but in any case carrying a warning against adulteration.

In *Tess of the d'Urbervilles* a standard of rigid Puritanism is represented by Angel Clare's father, the Reverend Mr Clare of Emminster, whose name we first hear from the sign-painter. He is an 'uncompromising Evangelical' and a strict Calvinist, a 'man of fixed ideas' (137), who punishes Angel for his loss of faith by refusing to allow him to follow his brothers to university. Alec d'Urberville, like the sign-painter, comes under his spell and becomes an unlicensed preacher. Hardy tells us that in Alec's conversion 'animalism had become fanaticism', and 'Paganism Paulinism', but it is all 'the mere freak of a careless man in search of a new sensation' (344, 364). Mr Clare, unlike his priggish elder sons and their friend Mercy Chant, is shown as being capable of human sympathy. It is unlikely, however, that—like the Broad Church vicar of Marlott—he would have accepted Tess's christening of her ailing infant Sorrow as possessing religious validity. Tess's do-it-yourself baptism is evidence of her struggle to reconcile pagan and Christian feelings, but she, like Alec and Angel, tends to vacillate unpredictably between paganism and Puritanism.

Tess's history in some respects recalls Hetty Sorrel's story in *Adam Bede*, although Tess is a devoted mother and her child dies from natural causes. Like Hetty, Tess is able to claim that she would have known how to defend herself against seduction had she been a lady, because ladies 'read novels that tell them of these tricks' (100). Tess's 'purity', that is, could have been defended had she known about trickery, but such knowledge would also have compromised her innocence. The tragedy of her marriage to Angel is that she stoops to the trickery of concealing her past. When she tells him on their wedding night of her rape by Alec, he rejects her in horror, yet when he sees her the next morning, 'She looked absolutely pure. Nature, in her fantastic trickery, had set such a seal of maidenhood upon Tess's countenance that he gazed at her with a stupefied air' (269). Hardy will, of course, have remembered the biblical text that 'To the pure all things are pure', yet his reference to Nature's 'fantastic trickery' is not simply ironic. The previous day, before Tess makes her confession, Angel notices Tess's resemblance to the seventeenth-century d'Urberville ladies whose portraits hang on the wall. In particular, he looks at the picture of a Cavalier dame with a low-cut bodice whose 'long pointed features, narrow eye, and smirk' are 'suggestive of merciless treachery' (247). Could she be implicated in the 'dreadful crime' (committed by one of the male d'Urbervilles) that lies behind the legend of the coach (244)? Hardy never wholly dismisses the superstition that Tess's fate is ultimately determined by her heredity, and that her purity is compromised by the guilt of her aristocratic forebears. In the end she murders Alec, as one of her Caroline ancestors might have done.

Angel Clare has rejected the doctrines of the established Church, yet he has all the scruples of the Puritan conscience. He is the prisoner of a rigid Pauline morality in his admiration of 'spotlessness' and hatred of 'impurity' (256). His infatuation with Tess is based on his misreading of her as a pagan Artemis or Demeter rather than a penitent 'Magdalen' (153). Once he learns her true history, his callous abandonment of her comes to seem repellent even to his father. Alec eventually gives up his preaching and comes to take Angel's place, blaming Tess for this spiritual somersault:

'Tess, ever since you told me of that child of ours, it is just as if my feelings, which have been flowing in a strong puritanical stream, had suddenly found a way open in the direction of you, and had all at once gushed through. The religious channel is left dry forthwith; and it is you who have done it!' (369–70)

Alec's hypocrisy has at least this element of truth, that in *Tess of the d'Urbervilles* Christianity is tried and found wanting. It is for this reason that Tess and Angel finally fetch up at Stonehenge, the legendary altar of pagan sacrifice, and that when his heroine is executed for murder Hardy concludes that ' "Justice" was done, and the President of the Immortals, in Aeschylean phrase, had ended his sport with Tess' (446). If *Tess* caused some disquiet among its early readers, it was because Hardy was so clearly saying that there was no just God.

Although *Jude the Obscure* provoked a still more savage outcry, it is ostensibly neo-paganism, or the attempt to go beyond Christianity, that is put on trial in Hardy's last novel. The representative of neo-paganism is Sue Bridehead, the intellectual who persuades Jude to drop his deep-rooted Christian piety and to give up his intention of training for the ministry. An older, more instinctive rural paganism is personified by Jude's wife Arabella, who cheerfully commits bigamy but then, after her second husband's death, becomes for a time a devout evangelical. Arabella, who originally seduced Jude and later reseduces him, is like a comic version of Alec d'Urberville. No sooner has she seen Jude again than she abandons her devout widowhood, announcing her apostasy by throwing her bundle of religious tracts into a hedge. In a novel even more full of spiritual vacillations than *Tess of the d'Urbervilles*, her apostasy is the cue for Sue Bridehead to return to a hysterical, self-denying form of religious faith.

It is, however, Jude who (as Sue remarks) knows his Bible intimately and is always quoting it. In his youth, Jude's capacity for religious devotion is manifested through his adulation of Christminster, which he sees as the 'heavenly Jerusalem'.[40] But there are two sides to Christminster, the Christian and the pagan, since it is at once an 'ecclesiastical romance in stone' and a centre for the study of pagan literature (43). Hence the ghosts that Jude summons up on his first arrival in the city include not only the great divines but the mockers of Christianity such as the historian Edward Gibbon. Christminster is the source of Sue's pagan statues of Greek gods and of the Voltairean rationalism that she has picked up during her relationship with a former undergraduate. When Jude arranges to meet her for the first time, their rendezvous is at the Martyrs' Cross, but Sue insists on moving further down the street; later, when Jude invites her to go and sit in Melchester cathedral, she prefers the railway station since the cathedral has 'had its day' (154). She thinks of

Jude as 'a man puzzling his way along a labyrinth from which one had one's self escaped' (157). But neither of them has in fact escaped. As Jude later laments, ' "Perhaps the world is not illuminated enough for such experiments as ours! Who were we, to think we could act as pioneers!" ' (372). As so often in Hardy, the failure of Sue's and Jude's neo-pagan experiment in free love is partly put down to their ill-omened family heredity. It is also due to the 'labyrinth' of Christminster, which they are unable to forget as they move disconsolately from one Wessex town to another in search of employment. When the couple try to make some money at Kennetbridge fair, they do it by selling 'Christminster cakes'. The colleges offer Jude his most skilled work as a stonemason even though they will not admit him as a student. His self-identification with the biblical Job is graphically announced when, having been summarily rejected by the Master of Biblioll College, he responds by chalking the following text on the college wall: ' "*I have understanding as well as you; I am not inferior to you: yea, who knoweth not such things as these?*"— Job, xii 3' (138). The moment of his arrival back in the city, on the day of the academic procession, is that in which he discovers his vocation as a public speaker on behalf of the working classes, like Felix Holt and Clym. Previously he was known as the 'Tutor of St Slums' (344); now Tinker Taylor, one of his old drinking companions, responds to his confession of spiritual despair with the words ' "Well preached!" ' (346). Finally Jude dies repeating a text from Job that has appeared once before in the novel: ' "*Let the day perish wherein I was born . . . Wherefore is light given to him that is in misery, and life unto the bitter in soul?*" ' (423–4). These last words are not the sign of a return to the faith, but rather, as one critic has remarked, a 'blasphemous parody of Job's legend'.[41] Neither Puritanism nor paganism can comfort the modern Job, who dies without any hope of a redeemer.

Although Hardy's renunciation of prose fiction after *Jude* has been taken as a retreat in the face of the storm of protest that the novel aroused, it is hard to see how he could have continued with the plan of the Wessex novels. In *Jude*, provincialism like Puritanism had become an empty shell. The hero's ambitions, like Whittington's, were focused on a city, and at one point Hardy thought of naming him 'Jack England'. The characters no longer speak a pure Wessex dialect, like the Dorsetshire of *Tess*,[42] and their increased mobility is emphasized by their endless railway journeys. Their confinement to the region of Wessex is increasingly artificial, and Hardy has some difficulty in preventing Jude and Sue from going to seek anonymity in London. Of Jude as a boy we were told that 'his dreams were once as gigantic as his surroundings were small' (41). Logically such a protagonist ought to leave his province behind even if he was destined eventually to return to it.

Puritanism as an Anachronism

Puritanism in Thomas Hardy is represented by itinerant preachers and by Anglican evangelicals such as Mr Clare, but not by the Dissenting churches. The latter became a substantial political force in the late nineteenth century owing to the extension of the franchise. They were a mainstay of Gladstonian Liberalism and, later, of the Labour movement, and their influence remained strong in English provincial fiction down to Winifred Holtby's *South Riding* (1936), where one of the main characters is a local councillor and Methodist lay preacher. Yet the Puritan faith was held to be increasingly anachronistic. Its internal decay is memorably registered in the novels and autobiographical writings of William Hale White, the Bedford shopkeeper's son who wrote under the pseudonym 'Mark Rutherford'. As a young man White was expelled from theological college for questioning the authority of the scriptures, and in *The Autobiography of Mark Rutherford* (1881) he wrote that it took Wordsworth's *Lyrical Ballads* to show him what true religion might mean: 'Wordsworth unconsciously did for me what every religious reformer has done,—he re-created my Supreme Divinity; substituting a new and living spirit for the old deity, once alive, but gradually hardened into an idol.'[43] Mark Rutherford's novels include *The Revolution in Tanner's Lane* (1887), which begins in 1814 and has a second part set in the early 1840s, and *Clara Hopgood* (1896), also set in the 1840s. Zachariah Coleman, the protagonist of the earlier part of *The Revolution in Tanner's Lane*, is a descendant of the seventeenth-century Puritans who becomes involved in radical politics and eventually suffers imprisonment. His political beliefs grow naturally out of his membership of an Independent chapel, since the Independents were by tradition Cromwellian republicans. His minister, the Reverend Thomas Bradshaw, is related to Bradshaw the regicide. Zachariah is a democrat because he believes in the spirit of the people, not in deferring to the will of the majority; as Rutherford comments, 'He believed in the people, it is true, but it was a people of Cromwellian independents.'[44] The second part of the novel portrays the disillusionment of the next generation, when parliamentary reform has been achieved and a new kind of Dissenting minister begins to meddle in electoral politics.

Here the setting is the provincial town of Cowfold, where the Independent congregation of Tanner's Lane is headed by the Reverend Thomas Broad, whose name is clearly a satire on the Anglican 'Broad Church'. Broad doubts the wisdom of 'sermons against covetousness, or worldliness, or hypocrisy' (284), since they might upset the businessmen whose pew rents pay his salary. He refuses to support the radical candidate in a bitterly fought local election, leading to a riot in which (in an echo of *Felix Holt*) Rutherford's new protagonist, George Allen, becomes unwillingly caught up. George rejects the 'gospel according to Tanner's Lane' (296) and finally emigrates to America, while the protagonist of *Clara Hopgood* also leaves England to give her life in the struggle for Italian independence.

For most of the nineteenth century, the moral values affirmed by English novelists were largely synonymous with Christian values, however broadly interpreted. But authors born after 1850 brought a distinct air of secularism into their fiction. George Gissing, according to his friend Morley Roberts, 'had no religion', and regarded religious faith as 'a curious form of delusion almost ineradicable from the human mind'.[45] In Gissing's *The Unclassed* (1884) the protagonist, Osmond Waymark, is 'a student of ancient and modern literature, a free-thinker in religion, a lover of art in all its forms, a hater of conventionalism'.[46] Waymark's scepticism also extends to politics, since he is a disillusioned ex-socialist. Aestheticism is his new creed, so he writes a novel about the London poor which is intended to tell the 'absolute truth' no matter how hideous and repellent it may be (201). Unsurprisingly, it falls dead from the press, but, like the secular homilies of a Felix Holt or a Clym Yeobright, its most striking resemblance is to a Puritan sermon. One of Waymark's friends tells him that ' "It was horrible in many parts, but I was the better for reading it" ' (282), while another predicts that ' "Such a book will do more good than half a dozen religious societies" ' (201). Waymark has an unhappy relationship with the devout Maud Enderby, whose 'overpowering consciousness of sin' he regards as 'an anachronism in our time' (213); eventually he marries the reformed prostitute Ida Starr. Nevertheless, his own urge to bear witness to the full degradation of the working classes seems to reflect a transferred religious impulse.

Gissing's most influential exploration of the fate and function of the contemporary novel came in *New Grub Street* (1891). His major novel on religious themes, however, is *Born in Exile* (1892), where Godwin Peak, a declared secularist and freethinker, poses as a Christian apologist and prepares to train for the ministry as a result of his infatuation with Sidwell Warricombe, a provincial middle-class Anglican girl. Peak first sets eyes on Sidwell at a prize-giving ceremony at Whitelaw College, Kingsmill (based on Owens College, later Manchester University, which Gissing attended). He is the orphaned son of a radical father—hence his name Godwin—and arrives at Whitelaw on a scholarship. Although his social circle throughout the novel consists of his former fellow students from the college and their friends, he can never rid himself of his double sense of intellectual superiority and social inferiority: he is 'born in exile' from his true place in society, while they are not.[47] He leaves Whitelaw on a somewhat perverse matter of principle and goes to work as an industrial chemist, a vocation he evidently despises. When he meets Sidwell again he abandons his job and settles in her home town of Exeter, hoping that his metropolitan reputation as a freethinking intellectual will not have reached the distant cathedral city. Once again, his decision strikes the reader as perverse, and a contemporary reviewer pointed out that Peak 'was far more likely to attain the social position he coveted by persevering in his own work than by masquerading as a clergyman'.[48]

But Peak is not short of self-justifications for the path he has chosen. There is, he persuades himself, no other way in which he could have been allowed to share the 'benevolence' and 'gentle sympathies' of the wealthy and cultured middle classes (185). At the same time, he sees through the shallow self-deceptions resorted to by Christian believers unable to face up to the challenge of nineteenth-century biological discoveries. Peak helps Sidwell's father, Martin Warricombe, to retain his faith in creationism even though he himself believes in none of his own arguments. Since hypocrisy is normal in this society, he thinks, his own much more blatant hypocrisy is validated by the intellectual effort it takes to sustain it and the penalties attached to being found out. This gives an extra edge to the contempt he feels for the glib posturing of the fashionable Broad Churchman, the Reverend Bruno Chilvers, who maintains that ' "The results of science are the divine message of our age ... Less of St Paul, and more of Darwin! Less of Luther and more of Herbert Spencer!" ' (377). As Peak tells Sidwell after his disgrace, ' "I criticise myself ceaselessly; expose without mercy all those characteristics which another man would keep out of sight" ' (437). It may be said that he has inherited the spiritual pride which was the besetting sin of the old Puritans, although his motto is not 'holier than thou' but 'cleverer than thou'. The novel's poignancy lies in the reader's gradual realization that Peak is a sentimentalist and something of a moral coward, not the exceptional person he believes himself to be. Forced to leave Exeter, he becomes an analyst in a chemical factory at St Helen's in Lancashire, soon to become one of the centres of modern industrial technology in Britain. But Peak has no place in this emerging world. No sooner has he inherited a small legacy than he gives up his job, leaves the country, and spends the remainder of his life in continental boarding houses, thus deserting the new professional and productive middle classes to follow the old ideal of gentlemanly idleness. If Christianity is an anachronism in *Born in Exile*, so ultimately is Godwin Peak.

Gissing's protagonists, it sometimes seems, will go to almost any lengths to protest against and defy their manifest social destiny. Their perversity contrasts sharply with the acts of submission and renunciation portrayed in the novels of Arnold Bennett, whose characters typically accept the limitations of circumstance and the lessons of duty and humility enjoined by provincial Nonconformity. The Bennett of *Anna of the Five Towns* (1902), *The Old Wives' Tale* (1909), and *Clayhanger* (1910) remains unsurpassed as a realistic novelist of industrial and commercial England. Heroism in his novels is largely the heroism of self-restraint. *The Old Wives' Tale* traces the lives of two sisters, Sophia and Constance Baines, the rebel and the stay-at-home. Sophia elopes to Paris while Constance spends all her life in the Staffordshire Potteries, but both, in the end, exemplify what Bennett in *Anna of the Five Towns* calls 'the profound truth that a woman's life is always a renunciation, greater or less'. This 'truth' is something that Anna Tellwright, in the earlier novel, has 'sucked in with her mother's milk'.[49] However offensive it may have seemed to the feminists of Bennett's time, it is fundamental to the provincial Methodist culture that the novelist portrays in great depth. Anna, born into the Methodist 'Old Guard', has a father whose 'holy valour for the pure doctrine' (31) is equalled only by his financial stinginess. The miser and the swindler are, in Bennett's view, typical products of a decaying Puritanism.

The Nonconformist minister, a crucial character in *Felix Holt* and *The Revolution in Tanner's Lane*, plays almost no role here. Religious feeling in *Anna of the Five Towns* is stirred up by a visiting revivalist—an evident mountebank—while the resident minister's address is summed up as 'vapid, perfunctory, and fatigued' (77). The only aspect of religious fervour that Bursley's Methodists seem to carry over into their working lives is an unflinching, unforgiving self-righteousness. Anna Tellwright falls from favour when she shows compassion for Willie Price, a manufacturer's son who admits to helping to forge the signature on a commercial bond. She finds Henry Mynors, Price's commercial and sexual rival, guilty of Phariseeism, yet she eventually marries Mynors. But Anna never becomes a chapel member, since the Methodists have no place for one who has 'fraternized with sinners, like Christ' (199). Their religion is idolatry.

D. H. Lawrence's provincial background was very similar to Bennett's, as he acknowledged in 1912 when he read *Anna of the Five Towns* during the first of his numerous periods of residence outside England. Bennett's attack on the Nonconformist tradition did not go far enough, according to Lawrence in one of his letters:

I am so used to the people going by outside, talking or singing some foreign language, always Italian now: but to-day, to be in Hanley, and to read almost my own dialect, makes me feel quite ill. I hate England and its hopelessness. I hate Bennett's resignation. Tragedy ought really to be a great kick at misery. But *Anna of the Five Towns* seems like an acceptance—sò does all the modern stuff since Flaubert. I hate it. I want to wash again quickly, wash off England, the oldness and grubbiness and despair.[50]

Lawrence's fiction from *Sons and Lovers* (1913) to *Lady Chatterley's Lover* (1928) claims to reject the whole inheritance of English Puritanism, yet he was a prophetic novelist who saw the novel itself as a kind of Bible. The Puritan inheritance is what Paul Morel is born to in *Sons and Lovers*, since his mother Gertrude 'came of a good old burgher family, famous independents who had fought with Colonel Hutchinson, and who remained stout Congregationalists'.[51] Lawrence outlines the emotional gulf separating Gertrude from her coal-miner husband Walter Morel in a series of stereotypical Puritan–Cavalier contrasts. Gertrude's father George Coppard 'ignored all sensuous pleasure', while she is 'a puritan, like her father, high-minded, and really stern' (18). Walter Morel is a ladies' man of partly French ancestry who runs a dancing-class, notorious for its 'carryin's-on', in the mining village (22). In his youth he was 'a choir-boy with a beautiful voice, and had taken solos in Southwell Cathedral' (28); his background is Anglican where she is descended from Cromwellian Independents. Gertrude briefly, and disastrously, sees Walter as a chivalrous knight-errant who 'risked his life daily, and with gaiety' in the coal mine (19). But once they are married they quarrel bitterly over money, since Walter is a spendthrift with no scruples about borrowing and then telling lies about what he has done. Gertrude is a believer in scrimping and saving for deferred gratifications, but, as she says to herself, ' "I wait...I wait, and what I wait for can never come" ' (13).

In the first chapter of *Sons and Lovers* the history of the Morels' married life is framed within the story of a single weekend, that of the August fair known as the wakes, originally a religious festival. Walter spends all day at the fair serving at the bar to add to his wages, while Gertrude is reluctantly dragged there late in the afternoon by her children. The next day Walter goes off on a jaunt to Nottingham with a crony, comes back heavily drunk, and locks his pregnant wife out in the moonlight:

The moon was high and magnificent in the August night. Mrs Morel, seared with passion, shivered to find herself out there in a great white light, that fell cold on her, and gave a shock to her inflamed soul. . . . She became aware of something about her. With an effort she roused herself to see what it was that penetrated her consciousness. The tall white lilies were reeling in the moonlight, and the air was charged with their perfume, as with a presence. Mrs Morel gasped slightly in fear. She touched the big, pallid flowers on their petals, then shivered. . . . Except for a slight feeling of sickness, and her consciousness in the child, herself melted out like scent into the shiny, pale air. After a time the child, too, melted with her in the mixing-pot of moonlight, and she rested with the hills and lilies and houses, all swum together in a kind of swoon. (34–5)

This is Gertrude's own 'wake' in the religious sense of a watch or vigil at night. Paul, Lawrence's protagonist, is the unborn child in her womb, and the symbolism of the pollen, of which 'she drank a deep draught', almost suggests an immaculate conception. It is clear from this scene that Paul is to be his mother's, not his father's child. Gertrude is the bearer of the Puritan inheritance, but her sensations in the moonlight reveal that she is open to the neo-pagan nature mysticism which, for Lawrence, is destined to transcend and supersede orthodox Christianity. Paul Morel, the first of Lawrence's post-Christian heroes, grows up in the mining village, and it is from the Nottinghamshire landscape that he imbibes all his knowledge of nature. He hopes to make his name as a landscape painter and fabric designer, proving that he has wider horizons than the earlier generations who worked on or underneath the land. The novel's final scene shows him leaving for the city, his childhood at last over. Like the novelist himself, Paul both rejects the Puritan tradition and turns his back on the English provinces. There are signs in Lawrence's last works of a possible reconciliation with England and with his Puritan inheritance, but such a reconciliation could never come.

From Forster to Orwell: The Novel of England's Destiny

A T the end of the nineteenth century, Krishan Kumar has claimed, 'English intellectuals and artists—historians, political theorists, literary and cultural critics, composers, poets and novelists—for the first time began an inquiry into the character of the English people as a nation—as a collectivity, that is, with a distinct sense of its history, its traditions and its destiny'.[1] Such an inquiry was hardly unprecedented, as this book has shown. In early twentieth-century fiction it was pursued with greater self-consciousness than ever before, but also in an increasingly sceptical and critical spirit. If any novelist of the time was dedicated to investigating the English character it was E. M. Forster, but Forster wrote in 'What I Believe' (1939) that 'I hate the idea of causes, and if I had to choose between betraying my country and betraying my friend, I hope I should have the guts to betray my country'.[2]

Early in Forster's *The Longest Journey* (1907) the protagonist, Rickie Elliot, is being shown around Sawston School, a Jacobean foundation that is now a boarding school for the upper-middle classes. Rickie, who will become a teacher at Sawston, is deeply ambivalent about the public-school ethos. But as he looks reverentially at a fragment of Jacobean brickwork he and his guide, the schoolmaster Herbert Pembroke, are joined in a moment of sympathy:

The two men, who had so little in common, were thrilled with patriotism. They rejoiced that their country was great, noble, and old.

'Thank God I'm English,' said Rickie suddenly.

'Thank Him indeed,' said Mr Pembroke, laying a hand on his back.

'We've been nearly as great as the Greeks, I do believe. Greater, I'm sure, than the Italians, though they did get closer to beauty. Greater than the French, though we do take all their ideas. I can't help thinking that England is immense. English literature certainly.'[3]

This scene could not have appeared in a mid-Victorian novel, since characters in Victorian fiction do not feel the need to launch into patriotic rhapsodies. They might, like Lucy Snowe, defend their country in the heat of a passionate argument with foreigners, but they do not appraise and describe their Englishness as Rickie does. Herbert Pembroke, who is a conventional Victorian, quickly removes his hand from Rickie's back, since he 'found such a patriotism somewhat craven'. 'Genuine patriotism', he reflects, 'comes only from the heart' (51). What offends Herbert is Rickie's air of judicious, comparative judgement, as if the English were no more than temporary victors in a kind of European champions' league. The shadow of liberal internationalism lurks behind Rickie's words. In the very moment of affirming his national identity he is implicitly setting himself above the provinciality of petty nationalism.

It is true that Rickie's outburst of patriotism originates in a spontaneous, almost visceral feeling and that Herbert initially shares it. Herbert seems to view patriotism as being like religious faith in coming from the heart, while Rickie is experimenting with patriotism as a substitute for religion. He is an orthodox, undemonstrative Anglican who regards his faith as 'personal, and the secret of it useless to others' (51–2). His patriotism, on the other hand, is something he feels an urge to confess. Unlike the Puritan heroes and heroines of earlier novels, an early twentieth-century protagonist like Rickie feels driven to explore his patriotism rather than his religious beliefs.

In England before the First World War the power and wealth of the Empire were at their height, yet there was a new awareness of competition between the European powers. There was red all over the globe, but the German domination of Central Europe led the British government, for the first time, to enter into defensive alliances with France and Russia. What we find in the Edwardian novelists' view of England is often a sense of shrinkage. It is not just that (Kipling apart) they tend to be exclusively concerned with the national homeland, feeling little interest in or loyalty towards the outer reaches of empire. The homeland too seems small and fragile, something that can be protectively encircled by the imagination. The threat to England comes, in part, from cosmopolitanism and globalization, as George Eliot had foreseen; but it also comes from the emergence of rival great powers with its message of England's impending relative decline. Rickie, for example, is shown contemplating England's 'immensity', but all he feels certain about is the canon of English literature. The love of England that openly speaks its name in this manner is an anxious, protective love.

The fiction of the last decades of the nineteenth century includes a remarkable series of apocalyptic fantasies portraying England's future collapse. Some of these were scare stories warning of a possible German invasion, such as Sir George Chesney's *The Battle of Dorking* (1871). Others were more far-sighted. William Morris's *News from Nowhere* (1890) evokes a future Communist England in which industrialism, urbanization, and centralized government have miraculously been abolished. Morris's post-industrial pastoral utopia was a rejoinder to Richard Jefferies' *After London, or Wild England* (1885), a tale of semi-barbarous adventures in a future England shattered by natural disasters. Jefferies' well-born hero emerges from a series of feudal entanglements strongly reminiscent of Scott's *Ivanhoe* to embark on a solo voyage towards the ruins of London, a poisonous quagmire from which he escapes at the risk of his life. The idea of a future England as a hostile, strange, and terrifying environment is a reversal of the imperial adventure story in which intrepid explorers go out from the homeland to bring civilization to the uttermost ends of the earth. H. G. Wells's *The War of the Worlds* (1898) depicts a series of Martian landings in England as an act of imperial conquest, in which the 'natives' are overcome by the awesome firepower of extra-terrestrial invaders. Wells's most uncanny vision of a future England, however, came in his first scientific romance, *The Time Machine* (1895).

In his early drafts of *The Time Machine* Wells had thought of sending his explorers backwards as well as forwards in time. In one version his Time Traveller is attacked by a Puritan preacher and by one of Cromwell's Ironsides in the year 1645, while in another rejected draft the protagonist theorizes about the historical split in English society between the 'sombre, mechanically industrious, arithmetical, inartistic' Puritan type, and the 'pleasure-loving, witty and graceful type that gives us our clever artists ... some of our gentry, and many an elegant rogue'.[4] The split between the Cavalier and the Puritan, as well as that between the leisured and the working classes, undoubtedly lies behind the two distinct post-human species, the Eloi and the Morlocks, in the published version of *The Time Machine*. The most striking feature of Wells's portrayal of an English landscape three-quarters of a million years in the future, however, is the biological degeneration of the inhabitants and the death of historical memory. The Eloi and Morlocks live among the ruins of a future civilization which had, apparently, reverted to a pastoralism not unlike that of Morris's utopia. The same myth of a somewhat sinister 'greening' of England in the coming centuries is found in W. H. Hudson's *A Crystal Age* (1887), set thousands of years in the future in a small, isolated community living in a dilapidated country house. Once again, historical memory has vanished. The plot hinges on the apparent sterility of the people of the future, for whom the means of reproduction has become a terrifying mystery. The need to counteract fears of species death and infertility may also underlie a cluster of well-known English social novels of the turn of the twentieth century, novels that conclude not with a marriage but with the achievement of parenthood. The child's arrival suggests the renewal of the evolutionary 'struggle for existence' in which the novel's protagonist has manifestly failed. These novels include Arnold Bennett's *A Man from the North*, H. G. Wells's *Love and Mr Lewisham* (1900), Forster's *The Longest Journey* and *Howards End* (1910), and, in the succeeding generation, George Orwell's *Keep the Aspidistra Flying* (1936). *Howards End*, the closest of these works to Hudson's *A Crystal Age*, uses the figures of a revitalized country house and a child born out of wedlock to symbolize the nation's future. *Howards End* is one of a series of Edwardian novels attempting to 'discern England's destiny'—its potential, that is, for further evolution.[5] Typically, these novels combine a moral critique of the nation's current prosperity with a sense of foreboding about its future.

The plot of *Howards End*, it has been observed, 'is about the rights of property, about a destroyed will-and-testament and rightful and wrongful heirs',[6] and in this it resembles innumerable English novels going back to the eighteenth century. In *Howards End*, however, Forster employs a kind of nature-mysticism that makes the house seem greater and more meaningful than the families who own and occupy it. During his last year as a pupil at Tonbridge School he had written a prize essay on 'The influence of climate and physical conditions upon national character',[7] and the narrator of *Howards End* speaks warmly of a Shropshire mansion, 'unintellectual but kindly', which is a product of the times when 'architecture was still an expression of the national character'.[8] Howards End, the house in Hertfordshire, also expresses an aspect of national character, one that Forster's heroine, Margaret Schlegel, hopes will become 'the future as well as the past' (316). It is an image of a true England constructed, as a critic has put it, 'on the basis of its aversion to the real one'.[9] Like other Edwardian novelists of England's destiny, Forster aims to strike a prophetic note without abandoning the conventions of fictional realism for those of utopian romance or futuristic fantasy.

The Progressive Theory of History

The Edwardian novelists' concern with England's destiny reflects the widespread consensus at the beginning of the twentieth century about the progressive nature of human history. Civilization, it was held, was perpetually moving forward, and England, thanks to the long period of peace, prosperity, and imperial expansion under Queen Victoria, was for the time being in civilization's vanguard. The keynote of English history was the peaceful reconciliation of tradition and progress.[10] In contrast to the tyrannous, bloodthirsty, and insurrectionary politics of mainland Europe, Ford Madox Ford wrote in *The Spirit of the People* (1907), 'the Englishman sees his history as a matter of a good-humoured broadening down of precedent to precedent, a broad and tranquil stream of popular advance to power in which a few negligible individuals have lost upon the block their forgotten heads'.[11] This was the 'evolutionary' view of English history, summed up for Ford's generation by J. R. Green's *Short History of the English People* and for a later generation by G. M. Trevelyan's *History of England* (1926). It was what the Tory historian Herbert Butterfield, in an influential critique, called the 'whig interpretation of history'.[12] Ford, a brilliant commentator on this view of English history, contrasted its complacency with the opinion of an unnamed German professor that 'One becomes almost ill in reading your history, with its records of murders and beheadings'.[13]

G. M. Trevelyan's English history, as we shall see later in this chapter, was read or reread by Virginia Woolf while she was writing her last novel, *Between the Acts* (1941). If any historian was able to give comfort to English hearts during the dark days of the Battle of Britain in 1940, it was surely Trevelyan. His theory of English history was of the gradual consolidation of the British nation and the gradual transition from hereditary despotism to a healthy and prosperous democracy. Not only was Britain the 'mother of Parliaments', but the result of imperialism and sea-power was that the Englishman's outlook was 'universal' as well as insular.[14] That it was hard to disagree with such apparently self-evident propositions was acknowledged by Butterfield, who wrote in 1944 that the 'whig interpretation' was effectively the 'English' interpretation of English history, since there was nothing 'worth considering on the other side'— there was no distinctively Tory version of England's history.[15] There was, of course, no shortage of attempts to write a Tory history, including two by well-known novelists: C. R. L. Fletcher and Rudyard Kipling's *A School History of England* (1911), and G. K. Chesterton's *A Short History of England* (1917). Butterfield's view was that the 'real tory alternative' was to write English history, as Sir John Seeley had done in *The Expansion of England* (1883), as the story of imperial conquest and settlement. Kipling and his collaborator had certainly done this, but the story of empire written from a British patriotic point of view was, according to

Butterfield, simply another version of the familiar celebration of freedom and constitutional democracy. (The chief beneficiaries of British rule in India, for example, were held to be the three hundred million people of the subcontinent.)[16] As Butterfield wrote without discernible irony, 'Perhaps only in the shock of 1940 did we realize to what a degree the British Empire had become an organization for the purpose of liberty.'[17] Butterfield's influence, however, was to spur later historians to mount precisely the kind of critique of the 'whig interpretation' that he had suggested was impossible.

At the beginning of the century the progressive theory of English history was, if not refuted, certainly brought into question by several Edwardian novelists. The first of these, chronologically speaking, was Ford Madox Ford, whose view of English history appears in his historical and topographical survey of *The Cinque Ports* (1900) as well as in his non-fiction trilogy *England and the English*, consisting of *The Soul of London* (1905), *The Heart of the Country* (1906), and *The Spirit of the People*. Ford, the son of a German immigrant, was known to Edwardian readers by his real name of Ford Madox Hueffer. He is hard to pin down, since he could put on a brilliant impersonation of an English country gentleman while claiming in *The Spirit of the People* to write of England as an outsider, 'a man of no race and few ties' (171). Later he would emigrate to France and to the United States, and it is his view of immigration and emigration that most strikingly contrasts with conventional patriotic history.

The progressive theory of national development was often also a racial theory, since Victorian historians liked to trace the English love of freedom back beyond Magna Carta to the institutions of the Teutonic tribes who became known as Anglo-Saxons. J. R. Green, for example, notoriously claimed that English history began after the departure of the Romans with the landing of the first band of Teutonic invaders at the 'sacred' spot of Ebbsfleet in Kent.[18] Trevelyan, a more conventional historian, begins with the 'Mingling of the Races', a process that, he claims, lasted from the dawn of history until the Norman Conquest. Both writers are mainly concerned with the story of a settled and (in ethnic terms) largely homogeneous nation; Green, for example, rejects Walter Scott's theory of the long separation between Saxons and Normans. Ford, by contrast, regards the English people as dynamic rather than stable, as a community forever in flux rather than rooted and settled. His conclusion in *The Heart of the Country* is that ' "change, change, change," is the note of all country-sides',[19] while in *The Soul of London* he argues that Londoners are not natives but temporary visitors. As for the Cinque Ports at the narrowest point of the English Channel, they were 'the door through which the course of empire had fared westward'; England itself was 'perhaps, but the door for a larger movement'.²⁰ In *The Spirit of the People* he describes the English as 'a people descended from Romans, from Britons, from Anglo-Saxons, from Danes, from Normans, from Poitevins, from Scotch, from Huguenots, from Irish, from Gaels, from modern Germans, and from Jews' (44), indicating that significant immigration had continued up to the time when he was writing. But his vision is of peoples finding in England 'no home, but a hotel' (54)—of a movement of continuous passage whose ultimate destination is apparently North America and the other lands open to white settlers. England is an island upon which 'the hordes of European mankind have rested during their secular flights westward in search of the Islands of the Blest' (46). The immigrants who have come to England are precisely the restless and adventurous types whose descendants are most likely to move on further. Ford's history is at once poetic and imperialist—he describes the Englishman as the 'eternal frontiersman of the world' (51)—but he celebrates England for the role it has played in the broad process of European expansion rather than for its peculiar national destiny.

If 'whig history' was inherently the history of a settled, largely Anglo-Saxon, people, it was also inherently Protestant. The Whigs owed their power to the constitutional monarchy established after 1688, while the Tories remained compromised by associations with Jacobitism and with the Stuart kings, the last of whom, James II, was a practising Catholic. In his trilogy of historical novels *The Fifth Queen* (1906–8), Ford became the first twentieth-century novelist to look at English history from an imagined Catholic perspective. The novels are set not in the time of the Stuarts but a century earlier, when the first of many failed attempts to reverse the English Reformation was supposedly inspired by Henry VIII's fifth wife Katharine Howard. Ford regarded Henry's chief minister Thomas Cromwell, rather than his descendant Oliver Cromwell, as England's greatest Protestant nation-builder. Katharine's antagonist, therefore, was the 'great man . . . who welded England into one formidable whole'.²¹

Unlike his later masterpieces *The Good Soldier* (1915) and *Parade's End* (1924–8), Ford's attempt to dramatize sixteenth-century power politics is, at best, of minor interest. Nevertheless, there is a memorable moment in *The Fifth Queen* when Katharine and Henry VIII share a vision of the 'blessed Utopia of the lost islands', a world that is not only lost to the papal realm but to the English people as well. The idea of a Utopia alludes to Henry's former chancellor Sir Thomas More, but this Utopia, Katharine tells the King, is not to be found in a distant ocean but 'hidden in this realm of England'.[22] Ford's image of the Fortunate Isles or 'Islands of the Blest' is, therefore, a symbol of what England has lost in its triumphant assertion of Protestantism and progress. It is, like Forster's Howards End, a glimpse of a true England constructed in opposition to the real England.

Forster and the 'Undeveloped Heart'

In general, the progressive theory of English history looks with favour on the physical transformation of the landscape in the process of urban and industrial development. To Forster, however, this was a negation of the true England. 'Into which country will it lead, England or suburbia?' the narrator of Howards End asks of a Hertfordshire railway station (16). His characters leave English suburbia for Italy in Where Angels Fear to Tread (1905) and A Room with a View (1908), while Rickie Elliot in The Longest Journey identifies rural Wiltshire as the 'heart' of England (132). The belief that England, ideally, consists of unspoilt countryside was expressed much more stridently in the two pageant plays that Forster later wrote, 'The Abinger Pageant' (1934) and 'England's Pleasant Land' (1940); the latter includes Jerry the Builder's derisive song 'Ripe for development'.[23] 'Development', in Forster's view, should be a spiritual and moral, not primarily a physical and mechanical, process, and it should begin with the individual. In his brief essay 'Notes on the National Character' (1926) he observed that middle-class Englishmen graduate from school and university with 'well-developed bodies, fairly developed minds, and undeveloped hearts'.[24] 'Development' here is not something imposed from the outside, nor does it consist in violent change from one state to another. It is a bringing-out of innate capacities.

Forster's tendency to blame the shortcomings of the English character on the practice of sexually segregating adolescents in boarding schools reflects twentieth-century notions of child psychology and sexual freedom. Manifestly it corroborates Ford's account of the English habit of emotional self-suppression, which was discussed in Chapter 10. Both writers seem to imply that 'Englishness' is largely a masculine condition. Thus the victory of the Schlegel sisters in Howards End has been seen as Forster's declaration that 'England must and shall return to the keeping of women, out of the custody of men'.[25]

The first two sections of The Longest Journey, 'Cambridge' and 'Sawston', represent the university and the public school respectively.

Sawston School, modelled on Tonbridge School which Forster himself attended, is represented as a breeding-ground for missionary imperialism rather than for genuine patriotism. In *Where Angels Fear to Tread* the protagonist, Philip Herriton, also lives in Sawston, suggesting that the names have a symbolic value (if Herriton indicates 'inheritance', then Sawston indicates 'source') and also pointing towards a more traditional explanation of English emotional inhibition. The novel concerns the Herritons' disastrous attempts to 'rescue' their widowed daughter-in-law Lilia, who falls in love with a penniless Italian, and her baby son. Philip's mother and sister are ironclad Protestants, while their friend Caroline Abbott, travelling to Italy to save a 'little soul' from a working-class Catholic upbringing, sees it as her duty to 'champion morality and purity, and the holy life of an English home'.[26] Philip, the supercilious aesthete, contrasts the two nations: 'There [in England] we plan and get on high moral horses. Here we find what asses we are, for things go off quite easily, all by themselves' (112). In fact, however, it is much worse than this, for Forster's melodramatic plot associates the Italians with warmth, directness, and vitality, and the Puritanical English with coldness, hypocrisy, and death. Sawston thus stands for the provincial Puritan mentality.

All Forster's early fiction involves violent deaths, which are arbitrary and undermotivated but carry a heavy thematic significance. *The Longest Journey* contrasts the deaths of Rickie and his crippled daughter with the survival of his illegitimate half-brother Stephen Wonham, a drunken but fertile Wiltshire yokel. Rickie's death in a railway accident in which he saves Stephen's life is modelled on a similar episode in a novel whose author Forster much admired, George Meredith's *Beauchamp's Career* (1875). Here Nevil Beauchamp, a naval officer, turns against his own class to become a quixotic champion of the proletariat and is eventually drowned while rescuing a working-class boy whom the narrator calls an 'insignificant bit of mudbank life'.[27] Stephen Wonham, however, is loaded with authorial significance. He is a product of Wiltshire, the novel's English heartland; he is untouched by Puritanism or by public-school discipline; he leaves the home of his genteel foster parents, the Failings, to work on the land; and he is a winner (as his name indicates) where Rickie is a loser in the evolutionary struggle for existence that the novel tacitly portrays. Although Stephen is uneducated and inarticulate he is credited with what in effect is the novel's final soliloquy:

He was alive, and had created life. By whose authority? Though he could not phrase it, he believed that he guided the future of our race, and that, century after century, his thoughts and passions would triumph in England. The dead who had evoked him, the unborn whom he would evoke—he governed the paths between them. By whose authority? (288)

The 'authority' is manifestly the novelist's, since Stephen, loved by Rickie and unspoilt by middle-class morality, is the chosen representative of England's destiny.

This passage from the end of *The Longest Journey* exemplifies Forster's technique of presenting his novels' intellectual and ideological message in a questioning, indirect manner. His narrative voice is much less obtrusive than George Eliot's air of moral and social omniscience or Meredith's bantering whimsy, though both survive as influences. Meredith's aim, as he wrote in *Beauchamp's Career*, was to appeal to the 'conscience residing in thoughtfulness' (443); Forster's unemphatic narrative presence does this much more successfully. H. G. Wells, a leading apologist for the novel of ideas, wrote that, in an age of shifting and unstable values, it was inevitable that the 'splintering frame' of the novel should 'get into the picture'.[28] Forster, unlike Wells or D. H. Lawrence, was remarkably skilful at presenting the frame as if it were the picture. He learned to disguise a didactic and thesis-ridden narrative as a simple record of his characters' thoughts and feelings.

In *Howards End* the masculine Wilcoxes, representatives of the 'undeveloped heart', are opposed to the Anglo-German Schlegel sisters, whose father was a Prussian military officer turned university lecturer. The Schlegels are financially independent thanks to the fortune left by their English mother. They stand for metropolitan culture and a certain degree of cosmopolitanism, while Henry Wilcox is a director of the Imperial and West African Rubber Company, a firm which also employs his two sons. Forster's epigraph 'Only connect . . .' and Margaret Schlegel's marriage to Henry Wilcox represent the symbolic conjunction of culture and business. Between the Schlegels and the Wilcoxes is the divisive presence of Leonard Bast, an insecure, oversensitive clerk who aims to better himself. *Howards End* is thus a novel with a programme, just as Disraeli's fiction had been. One question that it asks in remarkably rhapsodic terms is, 'To whom does England belong?':

England was alive, throbbing through all her estuaries, crying for joy through the mouths of all her gulls, and the north wind, with contrary motion, blew stronger against her rising seas. What did it mean? For what end are her fair complexities, her changes of soil, her sinuous coast? Does she belong to those who have moulded her and made her feared by other lands, or to those who have added nothing to her power, but have somehow seen her, seen the whole island at once, lying as a jewel in a silver sea, sailing as a ship of souls, with all the brave world's fleet accompanying her towards eternity? (165)

England here is a feminized national body whose ownership is disputed between two highly romanticized factions or castes, the nation-builders and those capable of imagining the nation—the soldiers, that is, and (as the Shakespearian cadences intimate) the poets. But this division not only simplifies but, in some respects, actually falsifies the national conflict that the novel presents.

The opposition between 'art' and 'commerce' is at the centre of a novel published shortly before *Howards End*, John Galsworthy's *The Man of Property* (1906), later incorporated into *The Forsyte Saga* (1922). Galsworthy's concern with national allegory was evident from the title of his first novel, *The Island Pharisees* (1904). Jolyon Forsyte, the patriarchal figure in *The Man of Property*, embodies 'all that unconscious soundness, balance and vitality of fibre that made of him and so many others of his class the core of the nation'.[29] The Forsytes are prosperous City men, solicitors, company directors, and estate agents. According to young Jolyon (here, as often, the author's mouthpiece), 'It's their wealth and security which makes everything possible; makes your art possible, science, even religion, possible' (202). Much the same function is assigned to the Wilcoxes in *Howards End*. In both novels, too, there is a crisis of inheritance coinciding with the passage from the Victorian era to the twentieth century. The younger generation lacks its predecessors' 'unconscious soundness' and 'balance', threatening to wreck the nation's harmony. Soames Forsyte, who abuses his wife and quarrels with the architect of his luxurious country mansion, plays a somewhat similar role to Forster's volatile Charles Wilcox, the elder son who is disgraced and imprisoned for manslaughter.

The Wilcoxes draw on the Kiplingesque, military values of empire although they have no military or civil service connections. Paul, the younger son, is sent out to Nigeria in accordance with his father's belief that ' "England will never keep her trade overseas unless she is prepared to make sacrifices" ' (123–4), but it is the family's investments in rubber plantations that are primarily at stake. Similarly, Henry Wilcox has been unfaithful to his wife 'in a garrison town in Cyprus' (230), but he must have been there on business since he is no soldier. (He has shares in a Greek currant farm.) He has married into an old gentry family which, rather curiously, has both Quaker and military connections. Ruth, his wife, had a brother who was killed overseas, and was herself expected to marry a soldier. Margaret Schlegel, the intellectual whose liberal guilt leads her to declare that 'More and more do I refuse to draw my income and sneer at those who guarantee it' (164), argues that the commercial Wilcoxes and the military caste are one and the same: ' "If Wilcoxes hadn't worked and died in England for thousands of years, you and I couldn't sit here without having our throats cut. There would be no trains, no ships to carry us literary people about in, no fields even. Just savagery" ' (164). The novel, however, implies that Margaret, the former Prussian officer's daughter, is attributing to the Wilcoxes qualities of honour and military discipline they do not possess. In Forster's melodramatic denouement, Charles Wilcox impetuously unsheathes the Schlegels' ancestral German sword to administer a horsewhipping to Leonard Bast, who promptly dies of heart failure. Charles's swordplay is apparently seen as cowardly and un-soldierlike by the jury who convict him of manslaughter.

If the Wilcoxes and Schlegels in *Howards End* sum up the division of the English middle class, the condition of the ordinary people is symbolized by Leonard Bast, 'one of the thousands who have lost the life of the body and failed to reach the life of the spirit' (109). He belongs to the third generation of a family who had to leave the land for the cities. Despite his admiration for George Meredith's *The Ordeal of Richard Feverel* (1859) in which, as he says, the hero finally 'gets back to the earth' (111), Leonard's weak heart reveals the extent to which he has 'lost the life of the body'. Forster's hopes for the future centre on the representative of the next generation of Basts, the child whom Leonard has fathered on Helen Schlegel and who is last seen growing up at Howards End. Howards End with its wych-elm tree set with pigs' teeth was the family home of Ruth Wilcox, whose reverence for the past, Forster writes, constitutes 'that wisdom to which we give the clumsy name of aristocracy' (22). But Howards End is no more than a modest farmhouse, and Ruth is the bearer of the spiritual essence, not the reality of aristocratic culture.[30] The house has passed through the hands of the Wilcoxes, who are described as 'destroyers' of the earth (301), but in the end it will be left to the Schlegels and Basts. Forster writes of the 'Imperial' type, a type that 'breeds as quickly as the yeoman, and as soundly', that 'the earth that he inherits will be grey' (301). *Howards End* concludes with a fragile and rather mawkish attempt to turn back imperial development thanks to the recovery of an England capable of restoring the life of the body and holding the suburbs at bay. There is, in the words of the Woodman in 'The Abinger Pageant', '*another England, green and eternal*'; a corner of Hertfordshire that is, so to speak, still Heartfordshire.[31]

Wells and Lawrence

The themes of destructive imperialism and a possible return to the land can be traced in two of Forster's contemporaries, H. G. Wells and D. H. Lawrence. Wells's *Tono-Bungay* (1909) ends with the hero, a scientist and engineer, leaving England behind on the first voyage of an experimental naval destroyer. His comic romance *The History of Mr Polly* (1910), however, shows the protagonist, a downtrodden small shopkeeper, escaping into a romance world of cakes and ale in an English country inn. The transition from satirical comedy to dream romance in *Mr Polly* influenced later English novelists, notably George Orwell in *Coming Up for Air* (1939), but there is no such escape on offer in *Tono-Bungay*.

In Wells's major novel of England's destiny, Edward and George Ponderevo, the patent-medicine tycoon and his nephew, are fugitives from the countryside who come to London to seek their fortunes. George, Wells's narrator, is a social observer who casts his observations in the scientific language he has learned as a biology student. His concern is with shapes and structures, with social anatomy and taxonomy. Pre-industrial England had a clearly articulated structure, which he calls the 'Bladesover system' after the great country house where his mother was housekeeper. The nation's commercial and industrial development has covered the land with hypertrophied and potentially cancerous urban sprawl, while many of the country estates have been bought up by a new, 'pseudomorphous' gentry, often of Jewish descent.[32] Edward Ponderevo, whose name implies foreign origins, also becomes the 'pseudomorphous' owner of a large country house.[33] When Edward's business collapses he flees to France to escape his creditors, while George at the end seems ready to emigrate to the United States, since (thanks to the Admiralty's lack of interest) his experimental warship 'isn't intended for the empire, or indeed for the hands of any European power' (389). *Tono-Bungay* began life as a serial in Ford Madox Ford's *English Review*, and it seems that George, like the European immigrants whom Ford described in *The Spirit of the People*, is following the course of empire westwards.

There is, then, a fluid indeterminacy about George's concern with England's future. Early in the novel he uses the analogy of an early form of slide projector:

The new order may have gone far towards shaping itself, but just as in that sort of lantern show that used to be known ... as the 'Dissolving Views', the scene that is going remains upon the mind, traceable and evident, and the newer picture is yet enigmatical long after the lines that are to replace those former ones have grown bright and strong, so that the new England of our children's children is still a riddle to me.... In the meantime the old shapes, the old attitudes remain, subtly changed and changing still, sheltering strange tenants. (15–16)

Wells's choice of the 'Bladesover system', the land tenure of the ruling classes (and specifically of the Whig aristocracy) as the foundation for this social model suggests that he views the commercial development and financial corruption of modern England in a similar way to Trollope in *The Way We Live Now*. George Ponderevo, however, lacks the basic soundness of Trollope's erring Paul Montague, let alone his straitlaced Roger Carbury. George's narrative begins with his offhand confession that, in the course of an illegal prospecting mission, he once murdered an African native. Later in a moment of introspection he comments that 'It may be I see decay all about me because I am, in a sense, decay' (382). As one critic has observed, 'it is difficult to guess where Wells's ostensible purpose in writing the book—exposure of the condition of England— leaves off, and a more uncanny, undiluted fascination with evil takes over'.[34] George is at once a Fellow of the Royal Society and a desperate adventurer, a devotee of impersonal scientific truth and a designer of warships. Both his marriage and his love affair with the aristocratic Beatrice Normandy are childless and sterile. He has little, if any, personal stake in the 'new England of our children's children' about which he speculates so freely.

The source of the Ponderevos' intoxicating rise to power and wealth is not a constructive scientific invention but a trashy patent medicine. The novel portrays a spectacle of unbridled capitalism which is, apparently, leading the nation to ruin. The name Bladesover suggests 'the poised sickle of Father Time', as one critic remarks, and also the flaming sword guarding a paradise to which modern humanity can never return.[35] The title of the penultimate chapter is 'Love among the Wreckage', and this is succeeded by the voyage of the destroyer down the Thames, a voyage which seems to George 'to be passing all England in review.... To run down the Thames so is to run one's hand over the pages in the book of England from end to end' (382–4). England here has become a history book or a museum, while the panorama seen from the river is a 'London symphony' (a phrase that inspired the London Symphony of the composer Ralph Vaughan Williams). The first movement of Wells's 'symphony' invokes the royal and religious associations of Kew and Hampton Court, while the second movement includes Parliament, New Scotland Yard, the Inns of Court, and the City. But the third part 'is beyond all law, order and precedence, it is the seaport and the sea'; it is the chaotic hub of modern global capitalism, and, beyond it, 'windy freedom and trackless ways' (386–7). So *Tono-Bungay* with its 'Dissolving Views' ends with an allegory suggesting England's dissolution.

D. H. Lawrence knew the novels of Forster and Wells, and his work alternates between Forsterian optimism and the pessimism of *Tono-Bungay*. The central symbol of *The Rainbow* (1915) consciously or unconsciously alludes to Forster's image in *Howards End* of the 'rainbow bridge' which connects the 'prose in us with the passion': 'Without it we are meaningless fragments, half monks, half beasts, unconnected arches that have never been joined into a man' (174). Lawrence uses the rainbow symbol primarily to signify the achievement of sexual connection between man and woman, but it also stands for the succession of generations and for an apocalyptic reconstruction of English society. So, at the novel's conclusion, his heroine Ursula Brangwen sees 'in the rainbow the earth's new architecture, the old, brittle corruption of houses and factories swept away, the world built up in a living fabric of Truth, fitting to the over-arching heaven'.[36] Lawrence embraces transcendental religion where Wells embraces social science, but both are prophetic novelists, as this passage suggests.

Lawrence wrote in an autobiographical essay that the countryside surrounding the Nottinghamshire mining district where he grew up was 'still the old England of the forest and agricultural past'. It was 'the old agricultural England of Shakespeare and Milton and Fielding and George Eliot'.[37] But in *The Rainbow* the immemorial rural past has been brought to an end by the building of a canal around 1840, to carry barges to and from the rapidly expanding collieries. In the next generation, Tom Brangwen of the Marsh Farm marries a Polish immigrant. Tom's marital happiness is largely inarticulate and instinctive, but in each succeeding generation there are greater obstacles to sexual and emotional fulfilment. Thus Will Brangwen is 'aware of some limit of himself, of something unformed in his very being, of some buds which were not ripe in him, some folded centres of darkness which would never develop and unfold whilst he was alive in the body' (210). When Will's daughter Ursula, at the age of 15, first meets the Anglo-Polish Anton Skrebensky, she feels that he is one of the 'Sons of God' (292), but they soon prove to be sexually, intellectually, and emotionally incompatible. Ursula is moved by her generation's feminism and by her experiences outside the home as a teacher and a university student; Anton, an orphan, becomes an army officer and transfers his affections from his family to his regiment. Ursula is in search of self-fulfilment, while Anton finds his fulfilment in devotion to the state. As he prepares to go out to India, Ursula foresees his role as a Kiplingesque servant of empire:

He would become again an aristocrat, invested with authority and responsibility, having a great helpless populace beneath him. One of the ruling class, his whole being would be given over to the fulfilling and the executing of the better idea of the state. And in India, there would be real work to do. The country did need the civilization which he himself represented: it did need his roads and bridges, and the enlightenment of which he was part. . . . But that was not her road. (443–4)

Ursula rejects Anton just as Jane Eyre rejects the missionary St John Rivers, and her final vision of the rainbow confirms that she has been right to do so. In Lawrence's sequel *Women in Love* (1920), Ursula finds personal fulfilment with Rupert Birkin, but the couple (a schoolteacher and a school inspector) give up their jobs, leave the country, and resign any responsibility for England's future. They 'want to be disinherited', Birkin says.[38]

Anton Skrebensky's spiritual successor in *Women in Love* is Gerald Crich, the ex-army officer who takes over his father's business and ruthlessly stamps his will and authority on the coal mines. Faced by a 'world of creeping democracy', he imposes a ruthlessly efficient, autocratic regime:

There was a new world, a new order, strict, terrible, inhuman, but satisfying in its very destructiveness. The men were satisfied to belong to the great and wonderful machine, even whilst it destroyed them. It was what they wanted. . . . Otherwise Gerald could never have done what he did. (244, 260)

It has been objected that this passage bears no relation to actual social history, since there was intense industrial militancy among the mineworkers in the early twentieth century.[39] But Lawrence was writing during the First World War, so that this aspect of the novel may be read as a displaced response to the mass self-sacrifice entailed in trench warfare. Gerald is a military officer transferring the lessons of military discipline to the coalfields (where they probably would not have worked), but the destructive social machinery that he creates has numerous twentieth-century parallels. And Gerald himself is a symbol of death, failing as a lover and eventually committing suicide.

The First World War kept Lawrence in England like a prisoner, and after 1918 his spiritual odyssey took him to Italy, Australia, and the United States. *The Lost Girl* (1920) and some of his stories depict English heroines who, like Forster's Lilia Herriton, take a one-way trip to Italy.

But in *Lady Chatterley's Lover* (1928) the novelist returned to England with a redemptive sexual romance of love in a modern Sherwood Forest. For Lawrence as a child, as he later recalled, 'the mines were, in a sense, an accident in the landscape, and Robin Hood and his merry men were not very far away'.[40] Mellors, the gamekeeper who makes love to Connie Chatterley in his woodland hut, is a kind of Robin Hood, with the maimed coal-owner Sir Clifford Chatterley as the Sheriff of Nottingham.

Lady Chatterley's Lover is, self-consciously, a novel written in the aftermath of the Great War. The sharp, brittle surface of Lawrence's later narrative style masks a crisis of language, since 'All the great words, it seemed to Connie, were cancelled for her generation: love, joy, happiness, home, mother, father, husband, all these great, dynamic words were half dead now, and dying from day to day'.[41] But the word 'England' carries a much greater emotional charge in *Lady Chatterley's Lover* than in *The Rainbow* or *Women in Love*: 'England my England! But which is *my* England?' the narrator asks (162). The Chatterleys of Wragby try to straddle agricultural and industrial England, preserving the old oak forest on their estate which Clifford sees as 'the old England, the heart of it' (44); but Clifford's father, who 'stood for England and Lloyd George as his forebears had stood for England and St George' (12), has been forced to fell much of the timber for trench-props. The novel shows Connie's return to the forest, where she becomes pregnant with Mellors's child; and it also endorses Mellors's prophecy of the coming death of the industrial system.

Connie Chatterley, daughter of a Fabian mother and a titled Royal Academician, has lived in Germany as a young woman. Like the Schlegel sisters she has what Lawrence calls 'the cosmopolitan provincialism of art that goes with pure social ideals' (6). Clifford Chatterley too is an intellectual, a younger son who has become the heir of Wragby after his brother's death; he is ill-suited to his role as a landowner even before he is crippled in the trenches. Lawrence's greatest difficulty, as he worked through the several successive drafts of *Lady Chatterley's Lover*, was with the character of Mellors. Like Robin Hood he is a gentleman in disguise, a former army officer who is content with his job as a servant on the Chatterley estate.[42] His reversion to Nottinghamshire dialect is a deliberate choice, since he has learnt to speak Standard English. In some respects he is a humanized, more potent version of Anton Skrebensky, since for all his sexual vitality and independence he subscribes, or part of him subscribes, to an ethic of service. He leaves the Wragby estate for a job that he has been given by an old army contact, working as a farm labourer in preparation for a future in which he and Connie will become smallholders.

In the family where Mellors is last seen lodging, there is a 'long gawky lass training for a school-teacher' (313) whom he helps with preparing her lessons, but Lawrence, himself a former teacher, cannot really imagine a constructive role for the schoolteacher in building the new England. The utopia of which Mellors dreams will find its salvation in the body rather than the mind, in aesthetics rather than education or politics; it will not be an educated England. Like the future imagined in William Morris's utopian romance, it will be a land of rich architecture, dignified manual labour, and beautifully dressed people—but not too many of them. Connie's right to experience sexual fulfilment and give birth to a child is part of the basic justification that Lawrence offers for her triumphant adultery, but sex in the future will be 'unnatural' in the sense of being separated from procreation. As Mellors says to Connie when they are naked together in the forest, ' "An' clean the country up again. An' not have many children, because the world is overcrowded" ' (229).

Virginia Woolf: The Splintering Frame

The social novels of Forster, Wells, and Lawrence pursue their questioning of England's destiny within the broad framework established by their predecessors in fiction. *Tono-Bungay* and *The Longest Journey* are examples of the *Bildungsroman*; *Howards End*, *The Rainbow*, and *Women in Love* are in large measure novels of courtship; and *Lady Chatterley's Lover* is Lawrence's attempt to defy the traditionally tragic outcome of the European novel of adultery. At the same time, the three authors were manifestly ill at ease with these inherited structures. Wells's case is the most blatant, since he quarrelled with Henry James over the art of fiction, and later wrote that *Tono-Bungay* was the nearest he had come to 'a deliberate attempt upon The Novel'.[43] Forster as a novelist relapsed into silence after *A Passage to India* (1924), while Lawrence's fiction like Wells's became increasingly propagandistic. Some of Lawrence's finest later work was in the form of fables and short stories. Meanwhile, the outspoken sexual vocabulary of *Lady Chatterley's Lover* cut it off from the English reading public for more than thirty years.

Forster, Wells, and Lawrence were anxious to avoid the leisurely historical retrospect of so many Victorian novels, which both begin and end in a world that the writers acknowledge has already disappeared. Virginia

Woolf shared her predecessors' explicit concern with 'the way we live now', but believed that only new and experimental fictional structures could render it adequately. Nevertheless, her early novels *The Voyage Out* (1915) and *Night and Day* (1919) are manifestly continuous with Edwardian fiction. Throughout her career she remained a literary intellectual appealing to Meredith's 'conscience residing in thoughtfulness', and she was as deeply concerned with national history and destiny as any of her contemporaries.

This concern, it is true, is one that both she and her characters sometimes seem inclined to repudiate. In her political essay *Three Guineas* (1938) Woolf affirmed that 'as a woman, I have no country.... As a woman my country is the whole world'.[44] English history and the English literary canon, she argued, were oppressively dominated by men. This may be why her characters find so little inspiration in the compulsory study of history. Rachel Vinrace in *The Voyage Out* is unenthusiastic about Gibbon's *Decline and Fall*, while in *Night and Day* (1919) a reluctant Cassandra Otway is told to read Macaulay's *History of England*. Miss Kilman is employed to teach history to Clarissa Dalloway's daughter in *Mrs Dalloway* (1925). Kitty Malone in *The Years* (1937) has a tutor whose *Constitutional History of England* is prescribed reading. Woolf evidently sympathizes with these bored and put-upon young minds. At Cambridge the protagonist of *Jacob's Room* (1922) is set an essay on whether history is the same thing as the biographies of great men, a question that doubtless meant more to him than to Woolf's young ladies. Woolf herself sometimes mocked the conventions of male biography, of which her father, Leslie Stephen, the editor of the *Dictionary of National Biography*, was an acknowledged master. And yet she makes her peace with historical writing in her last novel, *Between the Acts* (1941), where Lucy Swithin is an ardent student of history, and the plot is based on the performance of a pageant representing English history from its earliest times. Moreover, this pageant has a female author.

The Voyage Out satirizes conventional English patriotism in the person of Richard Dalloway, a Tory politician later to reappear in *Mrs Dalloway*. The Dalloways, shipboard companions of Rachel and her father, fondly contemplate 'the line of conservative policy, which went steadily [backwards] from Lord Salisbury to [King] Alfred'.[45] Richard is an ardent imperialist who can conceive 'no more exalted aim' than to be a citizen of the Empire. But his female listeners are unimpressed and, for his part, he complains that ' "I have never met a woman who even saw what is meant by statesmanship" ' (69). Richard and his ideology then smartly leave the ship, which is carrying a group of British settlers and holidaymakers to Brazil. The narrative 'voyage out' is one-way, and some of the passengers will never return.

But this is almost the only significant instance where one of Woolf's narratives ventures outside Great Britain. London and, specifically, Westminster, are 'the very centre of it all' in *Night and Day* and again in *Mrs Dalloway*.[46] *Orlando* (1928) begins in a great country house whose grounds contain a hill crowned by an oak tree from which 'thirty or perhaps forty' English counties and the peaks of Scotland and Snowdonia can be seen (a botanical and geographical impossibility).[47] In less whimsical vein, Kitty Malone climbs to a hilltop on her husband's estate in the spring of 1914 and lies there listening to 'the land itself, singing to itself, a chorus, alone'.[48] These scenes seem to confess what one critic has called Woolf's 'deep and perhaps helpless love of England'.[49] They prepare us for the social and historical panorama presented in microcosm in *Between the Acts*, which is Woolf's most direct exploration of national destiny.

Between the Acts is the story of a village pageant and a country house-party at Pointz Hall in the 'very heart of England'.[50] It sounds like a recipe for complacent nostalgia, and one contemporary critic, the American Malcolm Cowley, described it as a portrait of 'England under glass'.[51] But the date, June 1939, should give us pause, and Woolf's opening sentence ironizes her whole conception: 'It was a summer's night and they were talking, in the big room with the windows open to the garden, about the cesspool' (3). A new municipal cesspool or sewage works is being built to serve the expanding local population now that a car factory and an aerodrome have been sited nearby. (Luckily none of these things can be seen from the windows of Pointz Hall, but then the house is built in a hollow.) Mr Oliver, a retired Indian civil servant, observes that the site for the cesspool is 'on the Roman road': 'From an aeroplane, he said, you could still see, plainly marked, the scars made by the Britons; by the Romans; by the Elizabethan manor house; and by the plough, when they ploughed the hill to grow wheat in the Napoleonic wars' (3–4). This is the novel's first historical panorama, taking us from the ancient Britons to the Napoleonic Wars which enabled the newly rich Olivers to buy their country estate. It suggests a neatly stratified sequence of development, a series of 'scars' clearly marked out in time and space. The landscape seen from the aeroplane, the annual pageant (acted by villagers but watched by the local gentry), and the building of the cesspool all point to one thing: the progressive theory of English history.

Progressive history is implied by the biographies of Palmerston and Garibaldi in the library at Pointz Hall, although the twentieth-century Olivers are portrayed as hidebound reactionaries. It is present in the 'Outline of History' that Lucy Swithin is reading (10), and which enters the narrative through her interior monologue. This 'Outline' has been taken to suggest H. G. Wells's bestselling account of world history published in 1920. The passages that Lucy remarks, however, have a specifically English focus that can be traced to the early chapters of Trevelyan's *History of England*. Woolf's diaries and notebooks show that she was reading Trevelyan's history during the last months of 1940.

George Macaulay Trevelyan, to give him his full name, was six years older than Virginia Woolf. Both were born into almost exactly the same segment of the English upper-middle classes, the so-called 'intellectual aristocracy' grouped around London and Cambridge. Trevelyan was the great-nephew of Lord Macaulay and the son of Sir George Otto Trevelyan, a Liberal cabinet minister and Lord Macaulay's biographer. The 'whig interpretation of history' ran in Trevelyan's blood, but it did not endear him to English novelists. Wells in *The New Machiavelli* (1911) had called him 'one of those unimaginative men of letters who are the glory of latter-day England'.[52] Trevelyan and Woolf were slightly acquainted, and cordially disliked one another. When Trevelyan became Master of Trinity College, Cambridge, in 1940, Woolf wrote in her diary that he was the 'complete Insider', 'the perfect product of the Universities'. Her father had also been an 'Insider':

Insiders write a colourless English. They are turned out by the University machine. I respect them. Father was one variety. I dont love them. I dont savour them. Insiders are the glory of the 19th century. They do a great service like Roman roads. But they avoid the forests and the will o' the wisps.[53]

Three weeks later, when Coventry Cathedral had just been destroyed by German bombers and she was about to finish a draft of *Between the Acts*, she wrote more appreciatively of the *History of England*: 'And pin my faith still to Trevy's history. And now return to that' (339). Trevelyan, she thought, occupied a 'low rung' on the ladder of art, but nevertheless she copied passages from his history into her notebooks.

Woolf's comparison of the 'Insider' to a Roman road reminds us of the Roman road which is the site for the cesspool in *Between the Acts*. Woolf associates Roman roads with conventional male history and biography, as when Bernard in her novel *The Waves* (1931) speaks of the 'biographic style . . . laid like Roman roads across the tumult of our lives'.[54] Roman roads were laid across the primeval forest, or what Trevelyan calls the 'virgin woodland wilderness of all England',[55] which appeals to Lucy Swithin as she reads her 'Outline of History': ' "England," she was reading, "was then a swamp. Thick forests covered the land. On top of their matted branches birds sang . . ." ' (196). The pageant in *Between the Acts* is held on an open-air terrace framed with trees, and it begins with an empty stage and the producer, Miss La Trobe, hiding behind a tree. A small girl representing England emerges from behind the bushes. In *Between the Acts* the primordial essence of England is represented as a feminized virgin forest.

Village pageants had earlier appeared in John Cowper Powys's novel *A Glastonbury Romance* (1932) and Anthony Powell's *From a View to a Death* (1933), and, as we have seen, E. M. Forster had written two historical pageants. One of Woolf's working titles was simply 'The Pageant'. Her innovation was to imagine a pageant with a female author, Miss La Trobe, who presents a highly ambitious and implicitly feminist version of English history. Its principal episodes parody upper-class fiction and drama from the periods of the three great female reigns, those of Queen Elizabeth, Queen Anne, and Queen Victoria. The pageant's most dramatic and experimental moment comes at the end, with the scene described in the programme as 'Present time. Ourselves' (158). Some of the audience want a grand ensemble with the Union Jack and the army and navy, as in the popular Empire Day celebrations of the period.[56] But Miss La Trobe offers nothing of the kind. At first the stage is empty and the audience are left to their own devices, but then the actors suddenly reappear, holding up mirrors which are pointed at the audience. These offer a splintered, discordant, almost Cubist version of social reality, a vision of modern people as '*orts, scraps and fragments*' (169). There follows a well-meaning speech by the local vicar, rudely interrupted by a flight of warplanes roaring overheard. We are back amid the ominous uncertainties of June 1939.

Woolf's eventual title for her novel refers to the deceptive interlude between two world wars, as well as to what seems a brief intermission in the marital conflict of the young couple at Pointz Hall, Isa and Giles Oliver. The novel mirrors the play—the actors holding up mirrors to the audience suggest the troubled mutual gaze between the writer and her readers—while Miss La Trobe, the play's author and producer who is last seen beginning to devise her next drama, is also an important fictional character and symbol. Her name suggests a troubador or wandering minstrel, but like Lucy Swithin she retains a female connection to the primeval forest. (The words 'arboreal' and 'arboretum' are near-anagrams of La Trobe.) She first appears in the novel 'pacing to and fro between the leaning birch trees' (57), and by the end of the performance her fidgety anxiety and rootedness to one spot have worn a hole in the grass, rather as if she were a tree herself. Another female figure, Lady Haslip, is also connected to the forest. We are never told her maiden name, but she is described as 'indigenous' and 'prehistoric' (183) and compared to an 'uncouth, nocturnal animal, now nearly extinct'. Her marriage with the local peer has 'obliterated in his trashy title a name that had been a name when there were brambles and briars where the Church now stood' (84). Miss La Trobe and Lady Haslip are two of Woolf's 'Outsiders', women who—unlike the male builders of cesspools and Roman roads—have barely emerged from the forest.

Between the Acts, then, may be seen (as one recent critic has put it) as an attempt to re-establish a vision of national identity based on 'pastoral memory' in opposition to the nationalism of Britain's imperial mission.[57] To this extent it returns to the programme of *The Longest Journey* and *Howards End* and, to a certain extent, of *Lady Chatterley's Lover*. But *Between the Acts* is far from echoing the complacency of those twentieth-century historical pageants which 'managed to represent hundreds of years of English history by suggesting that all the important things had stayed the same'.[58] Far from being reassuring, the novel's natural symbolism is deeply unsettling, resisting any cosy or idealized version of the primeval forest. On the one hand, the warplanes fly overhead 'in perfect formation like a flight of wild duck' (174); on the other, 'nature' is represented by a chorus of birds 'attacking the dawn like so many choir boys attacking an iced cake' (7), by a snake which has been suffocated in the act of swallowing a toad, and by a flock of starlings whose 'quivering cacophony' (188–9) as they settle on a tree is as raucous and violent as a dive-bomber attack. The symbolism serves as a background to Isa Oliver's emotional turmoil as she considers her unfaithful husband, with whom she expects to end that day in an act of love from which 'another life might be born' (197).

What is implicit at the end of the novel is that any child about to be born to the Olivers will grow up in a very different world, since the genteel life of Pointz Hall has no immediate future. From late 1939 onwards some 2,000 English country houses were requisitioned by the War Ministry, mostly for the use of the Air Force, and Pointz Hall, being close to an aerodrome, is highly likely to be one of these.[59] The novel offers no intimations of this, but it shows Pointz Hall as being caught between the male brutality of impending war (including the report of the gang-rape of a girl in a London barracks and news of Nazi atrocities) and the primordial brutality of nature. The artificially prolonged serenity of the country-house weekend will soon be shattered. Meanwhile Miss La Trobe is planning her next play—not a historical pageant this time, but an elemental drama set in prehistoric times in a 'land merely, no land in particular' (189). *Between the Acts* thus ends by suggesting that the pageant of national history as seen by an 'Insider' such as Trevelyan is now effectively over. The nation has a future, but Woolf (who committed suicide immediately after finishing the novel) implies that the future will be nasty, brutish, and very likely short.

From England as a Family to England as Nightmare: George Orwell

George Orwell's early novels set in England are a mixture of nightmare and dream romance, of gloomy realism and quixotic rebellion. Gordon Comstock in *Keep the Aspidistra Flying* (1936) is at the mercy of the 'money-god' of bourgeois respectability symbolized by the aspidistra, the indestructible rubber plant that he calls the 'flower of England': 'It ought to be on our coat of arms instead of the lion and the unicorn. There will be no revolution in England while there are aspidistras in the windows.'[60] George Bowling in *Coming Up for Air* (1939) is possessed by the power of prophecy which turns him into a modern Cassandra, 'the only person awake in a city of sleep-walkers'. 'It seemed to me that I could see the whole of England', he writes, 'and all the people in it, and all the things that'll happen to all of them;' and what he foresees is war, Fascism, and destruction.[61] These pre-war novels prepared the ground for *Nineteen Eighty-Four* (1949), yet Orwell's most devastating vision of England and its destiny was also influenced by his experiences as a combatant in the Spanish Civil War and as a civilian in wartime England.

Homage to Catalonia (1938), his account of the Spanish War, ends with Orwell returning to his homeland disillusioned and physically shattered, the victim of political betrayal as well as a Fascist bullet. Landing at Dover, he travels through the Kent countryside, 'probably the sleekest landscape in the world', to

the huge peaceful wilderness of outer London, the barges on the miry river, the familiar streets, the posters telling of cricket matches and Royal weddings, the men in bowler hats, the pigeons in Trafalgar Square, the red buses, the blue policemen—all sleeping the deep, deep sleep of England, from which I sometimes fear that we shall never wake till we are jerked out of it by the roar of bombs.[62]

The language of sleep, dreaming, and waking is always significant in Orwell, so it is notable that, after two years of vehement opposition to the coming 'imperialist war', he himself awoke one morning in the summer of 1939 after a dream which revealed to him that he was really a loyal British patriot at heart. A year later he wrote the first of his two extended essays on Englishness and the national character, *The Lion and the Unicorn: Socialism and the English Genius* (1941). Early in this essay he relives the moment of re-entry into England that he had described in *Homage to Catalonia*: 'When you come back to England from any foreign country, you have immediately the sensation of breathing a different air.'[63] The air is soporific, but also gentle. The 'gentle manners' of the English are, Orwell says, common to all classes (57). He calls England 'the most class-ridden country under the sun' (67), but does not remark on the fact that, in earlier times, the phrase 'gentle manners' would have suggested a purely sociological observation of upper-class behaviour. Instead, England's gentleness leads him to say that 'the nation is bound together by an invisible chain' (67), and, in one of his most famous pronouncements, to reduce national tensions to a family quarrel (74).[64]

Anthony D. Smith has remarked that the metaphor of the family is indispensable to nationalism,[65] and the fact that the family–state analogy was already a commonplace will have recommended it to Orwell as a political pamphleteer. But his development of the metaphor in *The Lion and the Unicorn* reveals the eye of the novelist, not the political theorist or propagandist. (Doubtless it is a sign of Orwell's republicanism that his national family has no father or mother, but orphans are commonplace in classic English novels.) The passage runs as follows:

England is not the jewelled isle of Shakespeare's much-quoted passage, nor is it the inferno depicted by Dr Goebbels. More than either it resembles a family, a rather stuffy Victorian family ... with all its cupboards bursting with skeletons. It has rich relations who have to be kow-towed to and poor relations who are horribly set upon, and there is a deep conspiracy of silence about the source of the family income. It is a family in which the young are generally thwarted and most of the power is in the hands of irresponsible uncles and bedridden aunts. Still, it is a family. It has its private language and its common memories, and at the approach of an enemy it closes its ranks. (68)

Searchlight Books, the series for which Orwell wrote his essay on the English character, was devised in response to the Battle of Britain, but earlier in 1940 he had used the same title, 'The Lion and the Unicorn' for a very different project. It is hard to read his picturesque account of the national family without recalling his unfulfilled plan, announced in letters to his friends in 1939 and 1940, to write a huge novel which he called a 'family saga'.[66]

Orwell scholars have been quite dismissive about this unwritten work, for which only a few notes survive. His biographer Bernard Crick calls it a 'socialist Forsyte Saga', while the editor of his *Complete Works* speculates that he must have planned it 'when time lay heavy on his hands' at Wallington, the remote Hertfordshire village where he lived in 1939–40.[67] Orwell's notes for the long novel that he abandoned describe a stuffy, shabby-genteel family in which his unnamed hero (referred to as 'H') is brought up by his elderly, conservative aunts. The stifling atmosphere of his childhood was to have been conveyed through a series of catchphrases, proverbs, and commonplaces, which Orwell carefully jotted down. The notes deal with H's sexual frustration and confinement within the family, but they also show him as being destined, like Orwell himself, to become a volunteer in the Spanish Civil War. There is a scene at Charing Cross Station in 1918 where H, presumably still a schoolboy (certainly he is too young to fight), catches sight of an older cousin in officer's uniform being brought back from France on a stretcher. He contrasts the soldier's lot with his own comfort, and the notes state that 'His death in Spain in 1937 is a direct result of this vision'.[68] There is very little more, though it is hard to believe that his death would have ended the story.

Orwell's unwritten novel has a bearing on a crucial contradiction in *The Lion and the Unicorn* and its successor *The English People* (1947)— the fact that these essays purport to describe a settled and permanent national character at a time not merely of domestic political change, but of invasions, foreign wars, and the mass displacement and emigration of peoples across Europe. Orwell is much less alive to the possible implications of mass immigration than Ford Madox Ford had been in *The Spirit of the People*, although Ford was writing in what came to be seen as the golden years of stability before the First World War. Admittedly, in *The English People* Orwell acknowledges that the 'chances of war' have 'brought to England, either as soldiers or as refugees, hundreds of thousands of foreigners who would not normally have come here, and forced them into intimate contact with ordinary people'.[69] But he plainly envisages these 'foreigners' as being like the US forces stationed in Britain—temporary visitors, that is, like himself and his fellow international volunteers in Spain, who would eventually depart having made no impact on the national character. The idea of national identity as involving voluntary identification and partial or temporary affiliation to a national community does not seem to occur to him. Instead, the 'English character' that he describes is organic and permanent. England, he writes in *The Lion and the Unicorn*, 'like all living things', has 'the power to change out of recognition and yet remain the same' (78).

But in *Nineteen Eighty-Four* England has not remained the same. Orwell's most influential novel is a dystopian satire in which the nation has been replaced by Airstrip One, the third most populous province of Oceania (a superpower formed by the absorption of the British Empire into the United States).[70] In theory Oceania should differ sharply from a traditional political empire, since the new state has no capital and none of its 300 million inhabitants feel that they are a 'colonial population' ruled from a distance (167). Thus Airstrip One has a manifestly British rather than American urban landscape, even though its currency is the dollar. But for all its size Oceania, with its leader called Big Brother, is a vast parody of the nuclear family. When Winston Smith, Orwell's hero, attempts to rebel against it he is caught, imprisoned, tortured, and re-educated by a single individual, who plays the role of a stern but understanding father. Oceania so far as Winston is concerned is a family with O'Brien in control.

Since it is designed to supplant both family and nation, Oceania systematically destroys conventional family and national structures. Children are taught to spy on and betray their parents, sex between married couples is overseen by the state, and the very name of England has been successfully expunged. Winston, aged 39, reflects that in his childhood 'Even the names of countries, and their shapes on the map, had been different. Airstrip One, for instance, had not been so called in those days: it had been called England or Britain, though London, he felt fairly certain, had always been called London' (29). His uncertainty is telling. The lingua franca of Oceania is still called English, but is rapidly being replaced by Newspeak, and the original texts of English literature will be destroyed once they have been translated into the new language. The concept of a national origin is perpetuated only in the name of the state ideology, Ingsoc, which means English socialism. (One must wonder what the state ideology is called in Oceania's other provinces.)

Orwell in *The Lion and the Unicorn* had written blithely of an English socialist revolution in which 'the Stock Exchange will be pulled down, the horse plough will give way to the tractor, the country houses will be turned into children's holiday camps, the Eton and Harrow match will be forgotten, but England will still be England' (78). In *Nineteen Eighty-Four*, however, 'England' is like Winston's glass paperweight enclosing a fragment of coral, a 'tiny crinkle of pink' resembling a rosebud or a heart (177). At times Winston dreams that his whole life is inside the paperweight, but at the moment of his arrest the Thought Police smash it to pieces. 'England' survives as a place only in Winston's memory, but, as we soon discover, his innermost feelings and memories can be altered and tampered with by O'Brien. The destruction of the nation's military and ecclesiastical history is made evident when Winston visits Victory Square (formerly Trafalgar Square). The church of St Martin-in-the-Fields has become a propaganda museum, while the figure of Big Brother has been placed on what was formerly Nelson's column. Nearby is an equestrian statue which Winston is able to identify as that of Oliver Cromwell. Orwell's appendix on 'The Principles of Newspeak' states that 'Considerations of prestige made it desirable to preserve the memory of certain historical figures, while at the same time bringing their achievements into line with the philosophy of Ingsoc' (251). Cromwell's imposition of a Puritan tyranny in place of the British monarchy makes him an appropriate forerunner of Big Brother.

At least the names, if not the works, of the great English writers are expected to survive. Orwell's appendix mentions Shakespeare, Milton, Swift, Byron, and Dickens. The poet Ampleforth is imprisoned for failing to find a substitute for the word 'God' in his corrected version of one of Kipling's poems (it has to rhyme with 'rod'). After Winston dreams of the 'Golden Country'—a Home Counties rural landscape—he wakes up 'with the word "Shakespeare" on his lips' (28). The narrator offers no comment, but it is evident that Shakespeare here stands for Englishness.[71] Later, Orwell's protagonist enters one of 'the drinking-shops which the proles frequented ("pubs", they called them)' (71) and questions an old man about his memories of the past. To him, the old man's stream of personal recollections is 'nothing but a rubbish-heap of details' (77), although the reader is likely to judge otherwise. Winston at his most optimistic believes that the people must one day awaken and that 'If there was hope, it lay in the proles' (175). They are at least fecund, while his love for Julia is barren. O'Brien tells Winston that he is the 'last man', and that 'Your kind is extinct; we are the inheritors' (217). In fact, the national inheritance is left to be contested between the Machiavellian tyrants of the Inner Party and the despised, uneducated proles. If anything of the English nation remains undestroyed, it will have to be recovered from the 'rubbish-heap of details' (such as the old man's memories) that members of the Party have overlooked as insignificant. Among the fragments that have survived unnoticed both in the intellectual and the popular memory are snatches of an old nursery rhyme, 'Oranges and lemons', with its litany of London church bells. But the rhyme ends with 'Here comes a chopper to chop off your head' (82), which in itself symbolizes Orwell's gloomy prophecy of England's destiny.

Throughout his life he took a strong interest in what he called 'Utopia books', including the late nineteenth-century apocalyptic fantasies mentioned at the beginning of this chapter. Wells's *When the Sleeper Wakes* (1899), a vision of a twenty-first-century totalitarian state brutally suppressing an underclass of industrial workers, made a particularly strong impression. *Nineteen Eighty-Four* belongs in this tradition and, like some of its predecessors, it is awkwardly poised between imaginative fiction and a book of essays, between satire and political prediction or warning. At the same time, *Nineteen Eighty-Four* is a novel of England's destiny in a sense that is not true of its great dystopian rival, Aldous Huxley's *Brave New World* (1932). The latter, though mainly set in London, portrays a world state in which national loyalties have lost all meaning and global travel and interchange are frequent. In *Nineteen Eighty-Four*, however, the setting is claustrophobically confined to Airstrip One, to London, and then to a single cell in the heart of a vast Ministry building ('Room 101'). National loyalties still exist, but they have been perverted. The people of Oceania never mix with foreigners and are forbidden to learn foreign languages. England has undergone a traumatic revolutionary process—an atomic bomb has fallen on Colchester, and there has been street-fighting in London—and the common people are constantly whipped up into ecstasies of nationalist hysteria. Their assumed loyalty is to Oceania not to England, but the fact that this loyalty is purely synthetic may offer hope for the future. Winston reflects that 'They were not loyal to a party or a country or an idea, they were loyal to one another' (135). If this is true of the ordinary people, then what remains of England is still a family, with the Party and Inner Party as its jailers.

Orwell's gifts as a novelist have frequently been underestimated, but his promise was nevertheless unfulfilled. The example of *Nineteen Eighty-Four* suggests that the fiction of England's destiny could no longer be contained within the frame of the orthodox English novel, as Forster, the Wells of *Tono-Bungay*, Lawrence, and Woolf in *Between the Acts* had tried to do. There have been few, if any, fictional successors in this tradition. Visions of a future England have, instead, proliferated in the subgenres of science fiction and apocalyptic fantasy, including the novels of John Wyndham, J. G. Ballard, and many others. The moral seriousness of Orwellian satire gives place to a much lighter vein of futuristic farce in a more recent novel such as Julian Barnes's *England, England* (1998). The virtual demise of 'England's destiny' fiction is, however, a reflection of Britain's decline as a world power as well as of purely formal limitations. The idea that England's destiny must ultimately be decided elsewhere is, of course, hinted at in several of the novels discussed in this chapter, as well as in the fiction of empire to which Forster and Orwell also contributed. It was left, however, to one of Orwell's contemporaries, the critic and novelist V. S. Pritchett, to argue that the 'England's destiny' novel had ceased to be an adequate representation of 'the way we live now'. 'The great English subject, and at any rate the great subject which includes a picture of society,' Pritchett wrote in an essay collected in 1965, 'lies outside England, simply because English life itself has for long been parasitic on life abroad and does not wish to recognise the fact.'[72]

From Kipling to Independence:
Losing the Empire

I T was not until the British Empire was nearing its end that it became both a major presence in English fiction and a controversial topic in the discussion of English identity. Before Rudyard Kipling's birth in 1865 the English, in Sir John Seeley's words, had 'conquered and peopled half the world in a fit of absence of mind'.[1] There had been representations of British seafaring, trading, plantation-owning, and colonial administration in English novels since the seventeenth century, yet these activities were mostly taken for granted and nearly always kept in the background. The heroes of the early journey novels and rogue novels were likely to visit Britain's overseas settlements, but not to stay there except as fugitives from British justice. In the novel of courtship, the need to manage a colonial estate provided a convenient explanation for a lover's or father's absence. Early Victorian novels such as *David Copperfield*, *Mary Barton*, and Charles Kingsley's *Alton Locke* (1850) end with the emigration of characters who cannot find a suitable place in English society. By the end of the nineteenth century, the emphasis was no longer on the wealth to be garnered from colonial exploitation but on imperialism as an extension, or even a quintessence, of the national identity.

In 1869 John Seeley, formerly a professor of Latin at University College, London, was appointed Professor of Modern History at Cambridge. Seeley made little impact as a historian until 1883, when his lectures on *The Expansion of England* offered a fundamental challenge to the conception of the modern British nation put forward by Macaulay and his successors. The proper subject for English historians, in Seeley's view, was not the domestic politics of the British Isles but the 'Greater Britain' or 'vast English nation' spread all over the globe. England, Seeley argued, was now and in the future 'wherever English people are found' (88–9, 141). Seeley's confidence in the strength of imperial institutions makes him an intellectual forerunner of the twentieth-century Commonwealth; he was strongly opposed to the conventional liberal view that the white-settler colonies were likely to follow the United States in seeking a complete separation from the mother country. Jacques Turgot, the late eighteenth-century French statesman, had observed that colonies were 'fruits which cling to the tree only till they ripen'.[2] Seeley responded with his famous distinction between the first British empire, which culminated in the loss of the American colonies, and the second empire which had accrued since Britain's defeat of Napoleon. The second empire, including Australia, Canada, New Zealand, and South Africa, formed a single political unit that could be held together by modern communications, British naval supremacy, and the granting of dominion status and limited self-government. But Seeley saw a profound difference between the white-settler dominions and the most populous and, potentially, the wealthiest British possession—the Indian subcontinent. India, he concluded, was not and could not become part of 'Greater Britain'; it was a conquered territory that must always remain outside the limits of English nationality. Seeley was aware that British rule in India could not be sustained indefinitely, although he thought British influence there might be as long-lasting as Latin civilization in Europe.

The Expansion of England appeared just before the late nineteenth-century European 'scramble for Africa', which added further large 'non-English' territories to the British Empire. Within little more than a dozen years, the fictional representation of Central Africa passed from the epic romance of H. Rider Haggard's *King Solomon's Mines* (1886)—the prototype of the modern imperial adventure story based on a confrontation between barbaric and mysteriously glamorous natives and intrepid white explorers—to the withering disillusionment of Joseph Conrad's *Heart of Darkness* (1902). The Polish-born Conrad became deeply familiar with the Malay Archipelago during his years at sea, but made a single inland voyage into Central Africa. Haggard, born in Norfolk, spent six years in South Africa before returning home to establish himself as a popular novelist. His life story could be seen as a mirror image of that of the bestselling South African novelist Olive Schreiner, whose *The Story of an African Farm* (1883) was published during her eight-year residence in England. The contrast between the homeland and foreign territory is straightforward in Haggard, perhaps less so in Schreiner. Rudyard Kipling, who was born in Bombay, educated in England, and employed as a journalist in India until the age of 24, was a fervent British imperialist in the Seeley mode, as his *School History of England* (1911) shows. His emotional and imaginative loyalties, however, were more tangled than perhaps he was aware.

Anglo-Indian fiction begins with a thrilling adventure romance in the tradition of the earlier English rogue novel, Philip Meadows Taylor's *Confessions of a Thug* (1839). Kipling's first novel, *The Light That Failed* (1890), explicitly rejects the genre of the adventure romance even though its hero, Dick Heldar, is twice shown in the thick of imperial battles in the Sudan. Perhaps the strongest impression left by *The Light That Failed* is that of Heldar and his fellow war correspondents living bored, frustrated, drink-sodden lives in London, where they are subject to the wiles of cruel and deceitful women as they wait for their next imperial mission. Domesticity is for women, the novel implies, while masculine self-respect demands a life of overseas action. The deliberately outlandish names and nicknames of Kipling's male characters—Heldar, Torpenhow, Keneu, the Nilghai—imply their alienation from the English (or any other) motherland. *Kim* (1901), too, is a very male book, and much closer to adventure romance than *The Light That Failed*. The novel of courtship was not a significant presence in Anglo-Indian fiction until Forster's *A Passage to India* (1924). Forster and his successors explore, but almost invariably reject, the possibility of a composite 'Indian English' identity which must be traced back to *Kim*; and the author of *Kim* is the only significant English writer from the period of empire who may also be classed as an Indian writer. Although he settled in Sussex from 1902 onwards, Kipling does not fit easily into the insular English literature of his time, and he remains a kind of test case for the complexity of national identities in colonial and postcolonial literature. His greatest contribution to English fiction takes the form of an 'Indian English' novel that is entirely set in India, and in which the hero, said to be an Englishman, is an orphan born and raised in India of Irish parentage.

Kim and 'Indian Englishness'

Almost the first thing we learn about Kipling's protagonist is that 'the English held the Punjab and Kim was English'.[3] Yet as a boy he lives in a purely Asian environment where he speaks Urdu and Hindustani as well as English, and is known as 'Little Friend of all the World'. Later, his career and prospects depend on his ability to pass as an Indian native. Kim knows nothing of England itself except what he hears from a drummer boy who has grown up in the suburbs of Liverpool, and this is so far outside his experience that he refuses to believe it. As an orphan brought up by an Indian woman, his only proofs of his Englishness are his birth certificate, his white skin, and two other mementoes left behind by his father. His nationality is confirmed when he shows these documents to the Catholic chaplain of his father's old regiment, but no sooner is his identity validated than he begins to question it, a questioning from which he will never escape.

In *Kim*, unlike traditional English fiction, race and nationality are therefore problematic from the start. Differences of identity are constantly highlighted and explained, and the narrative logic is one of inescapable hybridity and divided allegiances. The novel is full of ideological statements about Europeans and Orientals masquerading as truisms and commonplaces. Some of these reflect a callow European ignorance which the narrator uses to satirical effect—as when the Reverend Bennett pompously opines that 'one can never fathom the Oriental mind' (77)—but most carry Kipling's manifest endorsement. Kim's restlessness and impatience, his horror of snakes, and his dislike of a vegetarian diet are all, supposedly, inherited traits of the 'white man'. At the same time, his future lies among the elite of Anglo-Indian civil servants who combine strong ethnographic interests with a genius for secret intelligence work. Since their vocation is to fathom the 'Oriental mind' to its depths, they alone can fully appreciate the value of Kim's local knowledge and his Indian upbringing. The 'white man' as both secret agent and imperial master must not only recognize the alienness of the 'Indian' character: he must be able to assume that character, with none of the defects of imperfect imitation that Kipling exploits for comic effect when an Indian poses as a European.

The more Kim is trained to act like an imperial ruler, the more paradoxical his Englishness seems. But it was paradoxical at the outset, since the 'Little Friend of all the World' is the son of an Irish father, and Kipling makes several derogatory references to Kim's Irish blood. Nevertheless, the novelist was manifestly aware of the part played by the Irish in building the empire. In Thackeray's *Vanity Fair* the regimental commanding officer Major O'Dowd and his wife are Irish, and in 1830 Irish troops constituted over 40 per cent of the British Army.[4] The elite Anglo-Indian academy that Kim attends, St Xavier's at Lucknow, is a mission school run, we must assume, by Irish Catholics. Kim is recommended to go there by Father Victor, the Catholic priest of the Mavericks, whose regimental banner consists of a 'great Red Bull on a background of Irish green' (70). Kim has known the symbol of the Red Bull on a green field since his earliest childhood, and it may be taken to signify British imperial dominance over Ireland, though a bull was also the symbol of the Irish High Kings.[5] The ambiguity of Kim's parentage suggests a mirror image of this regimental device, with the colours reversed to represent his father Kimball O'Hara as an Irishman in British India. We do not know for certain whether Kim's mother, who is named as Annie Shott, was Irish, English, or (as Kim's stepmother somewhat unreliably claims) a half-caste Indian. But Kim, as a child with a British Army provenance and a white skin, is English by imperial definition.

The novel begins with a visit to the 'Wonder House' or ethnographic museum in Lahore, whose curator had been Kipling's own father. A passion for ethnography links the scholarly curator to such key figures in the British secret service as the spymaster Colonel Creighton, Kim's immediate mentor Hurree Babu, and his teacher Lurgan Sahib, whose house in Simla is another museum of native treasures. Kipling himself regarded his task as a journalist and author in India from 1882 to 1889 as a kind of ethnography. In a letter home written at the age of 20 he evokes the exoticism of Indian life:

Underneath our excellent administrative system; under the piles of reports and statistics; the thousands of troops; the doctors; and the civilian runs wholly untouched and unaffected the life of the peoples of the land—a life as full of impossibilities and wonders as the Arabian nights. . . . immediately outside of our own English life, is the dark and crooked and fantastic, and wicked, and awe inspiring life of the 'native'. Our rule, so long as no one steals too flagrantly or murders too openly, affects it in no way whatever—only fences it around and prevents it from being disturbed.[6]

From this there arises almost inevitably the fantasy of the imperial ruler as Haroun al-Raschid, the Caliph of the *Arabian Nights* who wanders in disguise among his subjects in order to find out what they will say and do when he is not watching them. Kipling's own experiences may have been 'only a queer jumble of opium-dens, night houses, night strolls with natives' and so forth, but they are a preparation for Kim, the small boy whose apparent insignificance is a new version of the Englishman in Oriental disguise, a role pioneered by the mid-Victorian Arabist Sir Richard Burton.[7] Like the curator of the museum, Kim seeks a knowledge of 'all India', the India he sees symbolically 'spread out to right and left' (56) as he travels on the Grand Trunk Road. In a novel that is (as Kipling himself confessed) 'nakedly picaresque and plotless', his survey of India takes shape as a pilgrimage.[8] It involves inevitable self-questioning and should lead to self-knowledge, but this knowledge eludes him, so that the English identity confidently announced at the beginning is finally left in limbo.

Kim's initial decision to leave Lahore in the service of the Tibetan Lama who is searching for the 'River of the Arrow' lays him open to the full variety and multitudinousness of Indian life, which is symbolized by the Grand Trunk Road, 'such a river of life as nowhere else exists in the world' (51). Soon he begins his self-questioning—' "This is the great world, and I am only Kim. Who is Kim?" ' (101)—and Kipling suggests that such freewheeling 'speculation as to what is called personal identity' (156) is an Asian, not a European characteristic, presumably because it fits the experience of hybrid and subject peoples. Elsewhere Kipling wrote that in India 'everyone is the son of some father—and writes his father's name down when he writes his own',[9] and Kim's journey becomes a search for surrogate parents on both sides. Four of his substitute fathers— the horse dealer Mahdud Ali, Creighton, Lurgan, and Hurree Babu—ease his way into the secret service, while the Lama pays for his European education at St Xavier's College out of monastic funds. The narrative skips very quickly over Kim's years at St Xavier's, concentrating on the school holidays and the six-month furlough he is allowed after leaving school, so that the influence of his European mentors and the character-forming effects of the mission school are largely hidden from the reader. At 17 Kim is much the same young trickster and scapegrace that he was at 13, although he has done well at school and has learnt that 'One must never forget that one is a Sahib, and that one day, when examinations are passed, one will command natives' (107). Already his exploits as an apprentice spy have earned him the 'Departmental praise' of which Kipling says that 'Earth has nothing on the same plane to compare with it', though it can also be a 'deadly pitfall' (184). So little are the effects of his schooling and of this 'ensnaring praise' allowed to interfere with our view of Kipling's protagonist that to the end of the novel it remains a shock to hear him addressed by his fellow Europeans as 'O'Hara', not 'Kim'.

Kim apparently spurns maternal ties. His mother died of cholera when he was 3, while his half-caste stepmother has been broken down by opium addiction; so little does he regard her that he never bids her goodbye or tries to contact her after leaving Lahore. The aged Rani from Kulu nurses him through his illness at the end of the novel and looks upon him as a son, although Mahdud Ali comments sardonically that 'Half Hind seems that way disposed' (235). It has been said that, allegorically at least, Kim is 'free to suckle, as it were, on Indian breasts',[10] yet it is possible that he harbours a deeply repressed desire for his lost birth mother. (The same may be said of Dick Heldar in *The Light That Failed*.) When in order to disguise his movements he acts the part of a sleepwalker, he gives out the 'terrible, bubbling, meaningless yell of the Asiatic roused by nightmare', shouting out the word '*churel*'. The narrator, having described the yell as meaningless, proceeds to explain what it means: 'A *churel* is the peculiarly malignant ghost of a woman who has died in child-bed' (117–18). Was Kim's mother pregnant when she died of cholera, and why was the 3-year-old boy left as an only child? Clearly the novel offers no answers to these questions, but Kim seems deeply irritated by women who offer him maternal attentions. 'How can a man follow the Way or the Great Game when he is so-always pestered by women?' he expostulates: 'When I was a child it was well enough, but now I am a man and they will not regard me as a man' (214). When he leaves the plains for the Himalayas the narrator reminds us of the proverb 'Who goes to the hills goes to his mother' (192), but in the hills he meets the Woman of Shamlegh, who makes him address her as 'Sister' rather than 'Mother'. The Woman of Shamlegh sees through his disguises and subjects him, for almost the first time, to female influence, but he ignores her sexual advances. (It is Hurree Babu rather than Kim who may have enjoyed her favours.) Kim has been described as learning the lesson of sexual self-denial necessary to an imperial ruler in this episode, but it is likely that he is not ready for sexual initiation, since his battle is still with the image of the mother.[11]

After nursing him back to health on his return to the plains, the Rani says, 'Let him go. I have done my share. Mother Earth must do the rest'. Still weak, he throws himself upon the breast of 'Mother Earth':

There stood an empty bullock-cart on a little knoll half a mile away . . . and his eyelids, bathed in soft air, grew heavy as he neared it. The ground was good clean dust—no new herbage that, living, is half-way to death already, but the hopeful dust that holds the seeds of all life. He felt it between his toes, patted it with his palms, and joint by joint, sighing luxuriously, laid him down full length along in the shadow of the wooden-pinned cart. And Mother Earth was as faithful as the Sahiba. . . . His head lay powerless upon her breast, and his opened hands surrendered to her strength. The many-rooted tree above him, and even the dead man-handled wood beside, knew what he sought, as he himself did not know. Hour upon hour he lay deeper than sleep. (235)

Kim is not yet weaned from the Indian motherland, from Indian earth. He is on the verge of adulthood, but no more. The symbolism of the empty bullock-cart reminds us of his father's regimental banner, but the brown Indian dust has replaced the banner's field of Irish green. The Lama, meanwhile, has found his 'River of the Arrow' and plunged into it, only to be saved from drowning and brought back to watch over Kim in his illness. In the novel's final sentence the Lama smiles 'as a man may who has won salvation for himself and his beloved' (240). The ending recalls *The Pilgrim's Progress*, where the pilgrims arrive on the river bank and have to wait to be ferried across to the Celestial City of their salvation. Whether or not the Lama believes that he and Kim will enter the river, Kim seems likely to be about to give him the slip (or, perhaps, to mourn his death) before distinguishing himself in the secret service. But Kipling cannot envisage Kim's life after the point where he must choose between the secret service and the Lama's service, so that the novel fails to turn into an adult *Bildungsroman* and remains a kind of children's literature.

As an 'Englishman' whose motherland is India Kim is like Strickland, the British agent who features in a number of Kipling's stories and who is proud of having had an Indian wet-nurse. Zohreh T. Sullivan detects a 'characteristic indecisiveness and glide' in Kipling's narrative voice, as it shifts from objective to subjective and from omniscience to lyrical impressionism, revealing 'a kind of evasiveness that raises issues and problems it does not intend to resolve',[12] and Kim's national identity is one of these problems. His 'Indian Englishness' is sharply but not always convincingly distinguished from that of the educated, Westernized Indian Hurree Babu, a graduate of Calcutta University whose (not necessarily unrealistic) ambition is to become a Fellow of 'the Royal Society, London, England' (219). Hurree comes from the Bengali middle class which was to lead the fight for national independence, but he is a loyal British agent and a reliable and resourceful player of the imperial 'Great Game'—in fact, he is a better and more experienced agent than Kim. But Kipling cannot resist laughing at him, since in Edward W. Said's words he is, in part, 'the ontologically funny man, hopelessly trying to be like "us"'.[13]

Does Kim's Irish or half-Irish birth make him more authentically English than the 'brown Englishman'[14] Hurree? If Kim becomes a Sahib who can pass as a native, Hurree is a skilled impersonator who completely deceives Kim with his disguise as a 'Dacca drug-vendor' (182). Unlike Kim, he does not have to dye his skin in order to pass as a 'native', but nor can he bring off the 'British' act to perfection, as the mission-educated Kim O'Hara presumably can. When Kim leaves school Hurree tells him that 'If you were Asiatic of birth you might be employed right off; but this half-year of leave is to make you de-Englishized, you see?' (155). It is also true that Kim is still only playing at the Great Game as a hero of schoolboy fiction might, while Hurree and his colleagues live in constant danger for little reward. When Kim asks agent E23 if the government offers no protection to its foot soldiers in the Great Game, the reply is conclusive: ' "We of the Game are beyond protection. If we die, we die. Our names are blotted from the book. That is all" ' (168). It has been said that Kipling's novel itself is a kind of Great Game, but this can only be true so long as the reader shares Kim's determinedly innocent perspective rather than that of his fellows.[15]

The general aim of East India Company officials was, reportedly, to 'make [their] lakhs of rupees and come home'. Later, the career officers of the Indian Civil Service went out 'not to settle but to serve their time'.[16] Southern England was full of retired colonials, and it was here that Kipling himself settled immediately after the publication of *Kim*. But the concept of 'Indian Englishness' implies that, in fiction at least, Kim and his Anglo-Indian mentors Lurgan and Creighton could never go back to Hampshire or Sussex. If the 'Indian English' ought to stay in India, the 'English Indian' Hurree Babu is inherently capable of emigrating to England and, by doing so, becoming English. Two generations later, he might well have done so, since there are many comparable figures in more recent English novels. *Kim* is thus a prototype, not merely of Anglo-Indian fiction, but of the multicultural English novel of the later twentieth century. At the same time, Kipling's inability to allow his protagonist to grow up (and also his own inability to develop as an adult novelist after *The Light That Failed* and *Kim*) arises from the parting of the ways represented by his decision to leave India, where Kim (whether or not he is true to the Lama) is bound to stay. *Kim* has been seen as a novel that 'announces, even as it laments, Kipling's choice of England over India', but as a novelist he never really came back to the English homeland.[17]

Forster, Personal Relationships, and Indian Nationalism

Only twenty-three years separate the publication of *Kim* and *A Passage to India*, but Forster's Anglo-India is sclerotic and verging on senility, a setting not for glad confident youth but the cynical middle-aged. Ronny Heaslop, the youngest of the Europeans in Forster's Chandrapore, is recognized by his elders as 'one of us', which is not surprising since he constantly defers to their seniority and parrots their words.[18] Ronny's assertion that 'No one can even begin to think of knowing this country until he has been in it twenty years' (29) pays lip-service to a wealth of experience like Kim's, while revealing that the imperial mind has no use for fresh approaches or new ideas. Ronny's code of behaviour is the opposite of the 'show of manly independence' (33) that, as he notes with considerable alarm, is becoming commonplace among educated Indians. Even Forster's liberal hero Cyril Fielding has come late to India, and is no longer a young man. There is a clear implication that India, the oppressed nation, represents youth, while its British rulers are hidebound, embittered, and old before their time. But Forster's principal symbol of the mystery of India is not the thronged and vibrant Grand Trunk Road but the Marabar Caves, dark, claustrophobic, indistinguishable from one another, and unquestionably very ancient.

There had always been anti-imperialist feeling among a liberal and radical minority in England. To hold down an empire by military force was felt to be demeaning; the overriding motive was material greed; and the freedoms taken for granted by British citizens were bought at the price of colonial oppression. The economist J. A. Hobson wrote in *Imperialism: A Study* (1902) that 'Not five per cent of the population of our Empire are possessed of any appreciable portion of the political and civil liberties which are the basis of British civilization'. English society at home was corrupted both by the spoils of empire and by the political influence of retired colonial officials, so that 'the spirit of Imperialism poisons the springs of democracy in the mind and character of the people'.[19] Hobson's Liberal 'Little Englandism'[20] was widely shared in the last years of the British Empire, and a number of English novelists after Kipling presented the imperial frame of mind as a distortion, even a debasement, of the national character. The growth of national independence movements all over the world suggested that the struggle to maintain the empire was both thankless and doomed.

The question whether liberal concessions or brutal repression will do more to avert an ultimate bloodbath is much on the minds of the characters of *A Passage to India* and George Orwell's *Burmese Days* (1934). *A Passage to India* begins ominously with a group of Indian Muslims arguing about whether it is possible to be friends with an Englishman. Ronny Heaslop tells Adela Quested, the young woman newly arrived from England, that 'We're not pleasant in India, and we don't intend to be pleasant' (50). The Indian Hamidullah observes that people like Ronny 'come out intending to be gentlemen, and are told it will not do' (13). In public, at least, the rules of English decency and gentlemanly conduct no longer apply, and *A Passage to India* asks whether they can still be maintained in the private sphere.

What have come to be known as 'Bloomsbury' ethics—the valuing of individual feeling and passionate commitment over group discipline and impersonal duty—grew out of the traditional idealism of literary culture and, especially, the novel. Forster's liberal beliefs do not substantially differ from the implicit values of earlier novels—even a novel such as *Kim*—which privilege unorthodoxy over orthodoxy, passion over self-interest, and loyalty to one's innermost convictions over loyalty imposed from outside. In fiction the unorthodox individual is almost invariably vindicated, proving to be more far-sighted—and ultimately, therefore, more public-spirited—than hidebound officialdom. The tragedy of Ronny and Adela is that at home they were liberal idealists who were initially drawn together by their mutual belief in the 'sanctity of personal relationships' (82). In India, however, where they are constantly on display and there is no space for private life, they are socially ill at ease, emotionally repressed, and frequently irritated with one another. The disintegration of their love affair (like that of Ursula Brangwen and Anton Skrebensky in Lawrence's *The Rainbow*) illustrates Hobson's thesis that imperialism was a 'depraved choice of national life'.[21] As for Fielding, 'He was not unpatriotic, he always got on with Englishmen in England, all his best friends were English' (61), but his disgust with the lack of privacy among the British colonial officials leads him to seek friendship among the Indians of Chandrapore. It may be said that Ronny, Adela, and Fielding are all products of the English middle class, and that what they lack is the training and conviction to act as members of a masterful, self-possessed ruling elite. Ronny Heaslop is a government officer who has set out, in his dogged and unappealing way, to acquire aristocratic mastery; Fielding, a schoolmaster, would like to remain a middle-class liberal. Neither is particularly successful, and Forster's novel tells of the failed courtship between Ronny and Adela and of the temporary intimacy between Fielding and a young Muslim, Dr Aziz.

The name Adela Quested denotes a heroine who is not only mar-riageable but should be destined for a politically and morally meaningful alliance; and Forster takes care to have Mrs Turton, Chandrapore's senior memsahib, remark on the peculiarity of her name (28). But 'Miss Quested' is a plain young woman, unattractive both to the Indian characters and to Fielding, who tries to befriend her when the English turn against her. It is her misfortune to suffer a hysterical delusion that Aziz has assaulted her in the Marabar Caves, while her refusal to sustain her accusation in court shows that she continues to put truth to her private feelings over the imperial ruling-class code which dictates that an Indian, having been accused of the attempted rape of a white woman, must be savagely punished. The possibility of sexual relations between the novel's

English and Indian characters is thus reduced to an isolated rape fantasy, although there is at least a pale reflection of Forster's own homosexuality in Fielding's Indian friendships. Adela, once abandoned by Ronny, is, apparently, no longer marriageable in Anglo-Indian terms. Her offence is to have imagined an interracial sex relationship that did not in fact take place. The supposed degradation involved in such a mixing of identities (whether actual or potential) became a standard topic of colonial fiction. Forster traces its impact on the entirely innocent Aziz, who is wrongly accused and imprisoned for assault. At a personal level he may feel able to forgive the English people he formerly considered his friends; politically, however, he abandons his position of benevolent neutrality and becomes an outspoken nationalist.

A *Passage to India* thus portrays Aziz's progress from 'English Indian' to Indian identity—'I am Indian at last' (288), he tells himself in the novel's final section—and, through him, foretells the failure and imminent collapse of the British Raj. But the novel also deflates the pieties of Indian nationhood, both through the world-weary ironies of the narrative voice and through Fielding's explicit mockery. Forster's message seems to be that India, like the Marabar Caves, can never be firmly grasped but must always lead to uncertainty, metaphysical confusion, and anticlimax. The Indian reality, though dazzling on the surface, is ultimately depressing. 'The fissures in the Indian soil are infinite' (288) the narrator observes, and, though Forster is not more critical of India than of England, his tone in writing about it is less affectionate. While much of the narrative is apparently told from Aziz's point of view, there is always an underlying sympathy for Fielding's deflating scepticism. Moreover, the two men's perspectives are more deeply irreconcilable than appears at first sight. Forster introduces their final confrontation by saying that 'Each had hardened since Chandrapore, and a good knock-about proved enjoyable', and the tone of their argument is friendly enough; but, unless we accuse Fielding of supercilious insincerity, their disagreement hardly leaves room for compromise:

India a nation! What an apotheosis! Last comer to the drab nineteenth-century sisterhood! Waddling in at this hour of the world to take her seat! She, whose only peer was the Holy Roman Empire, she shall rank with Guatemala and Belgium perhaps! Fielding mocked again. And Aziz in an awful rage danced this way and that, not knowing what to do, and cried: 'Down with the English anyhow. That's certain. Clear out, you fellows, double quick, I say. We may hate one another, but we hate you most. If I don't make you go, Ahmed and Karim will, if it's fifty five-hundred years we shall get rid of you, and then'—he rode against him furiously—'And then,' he concluded, half kissing him, 'you and I shall be friends.' (316–17)

For Forster, writing after the First World War as an admirer of H. G. Wells's *The Outline of History* (1920), nationhood may have seemed a jaded and tarnished political aspiration, a source of hatred, hypocrisy, and bloodshed rather than enlightened personal relationships. But Fielding after leaving Chandrapore has, we are told, 'thrown in his lot with Anglo-India' (314)—the Anglo-India in which 'God save the King' is the 'Anthem of the Army of Occupation', and Christianity is valued by someone like Ronny only 'as long as it endorsed the National Anthem' (26–7, 51). Through Fielding, Forster would certainly like to hint at the existence of a world beyond nationality, an overarching cosmic reality to which, he suggests, Hindu spirituality could give access, for all the quaintness of Hindu beliefs in both Western and Muslim eyes. Fielding and Aziz evidently share the narrator's half-mocking, half-admiring affection for Professor Godbole's other-worldly innocence, just as Kipling is careful to indulge Kim's reverence for the Lama. Mrs Moore, the dying English lady, becomes the vehicle of a European counterpart of Godbole's detachment from the life of politics and personal relationships, a detachment that is both sublime and manifestly frustrating.

'Would he to-day defy all his own people for the sake of a stray Indian?' (314), Fielding asks himself during his last meeting with Aziz. By now he is married to Mrs Moore's daughter and has perhaps acquired some of the mother's detachment. When he mocks Aziz's nationalism he chooses to ignore the gulf between the English, for whom nationhood is an established right, and Indians for whom it is a necessary aspiration. Both here and in *Burmese Days* the aspiration to nationhood is echoed in miniature by the middle-class Indians' desire to be admitted to the whites-only English Club. Since Fielding's belief in Aziz's innocence has led him to resign from the Club at Chandrapore, he is at liberty to despise the privilege of membership. Forster, too, seems to alternate between a search for significance beyond and above the political realm, and an occasional (if surely unthinking) reversion to national stereotypes. In the role of narrator he invokes the 'Oriental mind' to explain the behaviour of Aziz and his friends, sometimes explicitly but sometimes more insidiously. Thus he writes at the beginning of chapter 31 that 'Aziz had no sense of evidence. The sequence of his emotions decided his beliefs, and led to the tragic coolness between himself and his English friend' (265). Aziz may be jumping to a wrong conclusion (he thinks that Fielding's bride is Adela

Quested), but his supposed lack of a sense of evidence implies that his
'Asiatic' temperament negates his Western medical and scientific training.

A few pages later Forster takes on the role of cultural diagnostician,
explaining Aziz's mistake with a resoundingly clinical metaphor: 'Suspicion
in the Oriental is a sort of malignant tumour, a mental malady, that makes
him self-conscious and unfriendly suddenly; he trusts and mistrusts at the
same time in a way the Westerner cannot comprehend. It is his demon, as
the Westerner's is hypocrisy' (272). One would guess that some experience
of personal hurt might have led Forster to write this passage, but its even-
handedness is only apparent and it has the effect of reducing Aziz and
Fielding to well-meaning but blinkered representatives of their respective
nations and races. Like George Eliot, Forster believes that the world is not
yet ready for cosmopolitanism, and may never be so. After the final confrontation between Fielding and Aziz over the question of nationhood it is
their horses, the earth, and even the Indian sky that force them apart,
insisting that this is neither the time nor the place for cross-cultural
friendship to ripen. In a novel whose plot hinges on Adela's disastrous
passage to India and her ignominious return home, Forster leaves it to his
readers to judge whether or not the English should go back to England.

Last Rites in the East

For Orwell in *Burmese Days*, the Indian Empire is a 'despotism with theft
as its final object'.[22] His theme, unlike Forster's, is the corruption and
despair brought about by colonial exile. Not only are his principal characters timber merchants rather than imperial civil servants, but they hate
Burma a good deal more virulently than the Burmese hate the British. Flory,
Orwell's protagonist, has been fifteen years in Burma and tells his friend
Dr Veraswami that the imperialists' motto is ' "In India, do as the English
do" ' (140); Veraswami comments with amused sympathy that ' "You
English have the sense of smell almost too highly developed. What torments
you must all suffer in our filthy East!" ' (138). In psychological terms,
Orwell presents the experience of the colonist in terms of a sadomasochistic
addiction; politically, he portrays a mutual stand-off leading to an explosion of violence and self-destruction. His own five years' service with the
Indian Imperial Police offers some kind of guarantee that the bigotry,
foul language, and race hatred of the English colonists in Kyauktada are
historically authentic. The extent of Forster's decorousness and circum-
spection in *A Passage to India* becomes painfully evident.

Flory is a secret intellectual and a rebel, but his life is outwardly almost indistinguishable from that of his fellow countrymen. In between visits to his timber camp he spends his days drinking at the English Club and his nights with a native mistress whom he despises. He is anxious to impress Elizabeth Lackersteen, the young Englishwoman who comes to Burma in search of a husband, but mistakenly assumes that, like Adela Quested, she wants to be shown the 'real' East. Elizabeth, however, is for the most part frightened and disgusted by what she sees. She is mystified by Flory's enthusiasm for the Burmese people and their culture, though she does seem to detect that it is not entirely genuine. Despite the use of Burmese vocabulary to create a local atmosphere in the novel, neither Flory nor Orwell himself betrays any strong desire to experience or understand the country in depth. Compared with Aziz and his friends, the three main Burmese characters, Veraswami, U Po Kyin, and Ma Hla May, are all stereotypes. Flory's identification with Burma is a product of his self-hatred and hatred of his fellow countrymen rather than of any genuine love for the exotic. Coming back from England to Burma he realizes that 'This country which he hated was now his native country, his home' (68), but this is represented as the negative identification of a lonely exile rather than a statement of hybrid Englishness like Kim's.

The principal aim of Orwell's three Burmese characters is, more or less, the same: to get into the English Club. Flory unsuccessfully proposes Veraswami for membership in response to the new government policy intended to break down racial apartheid; Ma Hla May breaks into the club garden and later interrupts an English church service to press her claims to be recognized as Flory's wife; and U Po Kyin, by far the worst and most crooked of the three, finally secures election. Before this, the Club has been besieged by native rioters. Sacrosanct in *A Passage to India*, the imperial enclosure is threatened by a penetration that at least one of the English residents, Elizabeth's aunt Mrs Lackersteen, sees in explicitly sexual terms. Earlier we have been told that 'To her mind the words "sedition", "Nationalism", "rebellion", "Home Rule", conveyed one thing and one thing only, and that was a picture of herself being raped by a procession of jet-black coolies with rolling white eyeballs' (131); during the siege she gives way to uncontrolled hysteria. The fantasy of interracial rape is no longer a personal aberration, as it was for Adela Quested; with Mrs Lackersteen it becomes the acknowledged essence of the colonial relationship. In Orwell's novel there is no question of innocently discussing whether the Burmese and the English can be friends.

The relationship between Flory and Dr Veraswami is clearly modelled to some extent on that of Fielding and Aziz, but it is not a relationship between equals because Veraswami's passionate admiration for the English has, we are told, survived 'a thousand snubs from Englishmen' (38). His love for the colonial masters is essentially abject. Orwell offers a neat allegory of this when Elizabeth and Flory, out hunting together, succeed in slaughtering a pair of green pigeons even though, as Flory says, ' "It's murder to shoot them" ': ' "The Burmese say that when you kill one of these birds they vomit, meaning to say, 'Look, here is all I possess, and I've taken nothing of yours. Why do you kill me?' " ' (156–7). Veraswami, typically, promises that he would not actually come to the English Club if he were to be elected; simply to be allowed to pay the subscription would be privilege enough. The English, however, have more respect for the Macchiavellian U Po Kyin than for Veraswami who shows genuine goodwill towards them. It is taken for granted among Orwell's colonists that 'India is going to the dogs' and that the 'British Raj is finished' (28), and suicides in the Anglo-Indian community are, we are told, quite common. The novel ends on an appropriately self-destructive note with the murder of one of the English settlers followed by Flory's suicide.

The 'English character' is manifestly out of place in Orwell's Burma, where supposedly upright English gentlemen become brutal, cynical, foul-mouthed, and deceitful. Flory, however, continues to believe in an unspoilt and innocent form of Englishness to which he could have access by marrying Elizabeth, who is newly arrived from the homeland: 'She had brought back to him the air of England—dear England, where thought is free and one is not condemned forever to dance the *danse du pukka sahib* for the edification of the lower races. . . . Just by existing she had made it possible for him, she had even made it natural to him, to act decently' (144). Flory's self-deception here is blatant, since Elizabeth's ability to fit in as a 'burra memsahib' is never in doubt. She becomes the wife of the Deputy Commissioner and, Orwell writes, 'a certain hardness of manner that always belonged to her' becomes accentuated (272). Like the 'hardening' of Fielding and Aziz at the end of *A Passage to India*, this implies a loss of youthful sensitivity and openness, but it is also a hardening into the stereotypical national identities imposed by the conflict between the colonial rulers and their subjects. It is a hardening from which the young Kim remains protected throughout Kipling's novel. But in the very act of portraying the hardening of character Forster and Orwell keep alive the notion that national character could remain softer and more malleable, or at least more benign. The writing of *Burmese Days* can therefore be seen to have freed Orwell to leave his Burmese experience behind in writings such as *The Lion and the Unicorn* where he would invoke the ideas of English decency and the fresh English air as if they were eternal values, untarnished by Britain's imperial history. It needs some effort to remember that these ideas had first appeared in his fiction in the consciousness of a self-deceived, self-hating, and ultimately suicidal colonial exile.

Orwell and his contemporaries in the 1930s can have had no intimations of the impending conquest of South-East Asia by the Japanese, to be followed by the partition of the subcontinent and the founding of independent India and Pakistan in August 1947. But Forster's and Orwell's novels bear witness that the Indian Empire was manifestly failing and that the Englishness of the imperial ruling class was doomed to travesty and self-betrayal. Above all, the fear and disgust provoked by interracial sex in these novels reveals that there can be, politically speaking, no 'marriage' between English and Indian or other colonial identities during the period of British rule. The theme of interracial rape is replayed in post-war fiction such as Doris Lessing's *The Grass is Singing* (1950), set in southern Africa, and Paul Scott's melodramatic 'Raj Quartet' (1966–75) set in India. Western sexual indulgence is a prominent motif in Anthony Burgess's *Malayan Trilogy* (1956–9), with its final volume suggestively named *Beds in the East*. Lessing's portrayal of white farmers shows a society in which the attachment to England is purely sentimental. Her heroine thinks of herself as British although neither she nor her parents have ever been to England, and their true identity is 'white South African'.[23] Both the Burgess trilogy and Scott's finest novel, *Staying On* (1977), are deliberate elegies for the empire. Burgess's hero Victor Crabbe and Scott's Tusker Smalley exemplify a condition that was, perhaps, already implicit in the earlier colonial novels: their very 'Englishness' prevents them from taking the more sensible course and returning home. Obstinacy, eccentricity, self-indulgence, and a curious idealism all play a part in this. In Fielding, Flory, and now Crabbe and Smalley, permanent colonial and postcolonial exile becomes the last resort of a form of character seen by the novelist as typically or essentially English.

Many of the themes of Burgess's *Malayan Trilogy* are brought together in a long dialogue in the third volume between Victor Crabbe and the Chinese expatriate Lim Cheng Po, a dialogue in which Crabbe's sense of imperial responsibility is confronted by his adversary's world-weary cynicism. When Crabbe describes himself as a 'typical Englishman of my class—a crank idealist' and wonders what he is doing in Malaya, Cheng Po replies for him: ' "Deriving an exquisite pleasure out of being misunderstood. Doing as much as you can for the natives" (he minced the word like a stage memsahib) "so that you can rub your hands over a mounting hoard of no appreciation." [24] There is an element of play-acting here—the two men relaxing in wicker chairs feel themselves 'begin to enter a novel about the East' (418)—and Burgess, who spent six years in the colonial service, evidently sees Crabbe as a successor to Forster's Fielding. A schoolteacher who later becomes a provincial education officer, it is his love for Malaya that leads him to reject the prospect of a headmastership back in England although his wife Fenella longs to go home. Like Flory he has a native mistress, a Burmese dance hostess who makes him feel that he is 'somehow piercing to the heart of the country, of the East itself' (38). But he has come too late to the East. The Malayan jungle is in the grip of Communist insurgents, the British are preparing to leave (his task as Chief Education Officer is to hand over to his Malay deputy), and racial tension is growing as the Malays try to take back power from the Chinese, Sikh, and Tamil communities that have flour-ished under the empire. Crabbe's former college friend Hardman tells him that independence should be granted right away: ' "It's probably going to be a hell of a mess, but that's not the point. Whether the fruit's going to be good or rotten, the time is ripe" ' (288). In Crabbe's reflections the perception of imperial twilight becomes an occasion for self-pity: 'If you loved, your love was rarely returned. Malaya didn't want him' (325). But whether or not Malaya wants him, he is obstinately determined to stay in Malaya.

The reason he gives himself for staying is the classic justification for liberal imperialism: to help the development of a new nation. He holds an interracial 'bridge party' (another echo of Forster's Chandrapore) and tells his guests that nation-building requires the emergence of a secular state, intermarriage, and the creation of an indigenous culture capable of voicing the sense of nationhood. He discovers a young musical prodigy, Robert Loo, whose compositions, he believes, give expression to a 'national image' (417); but nobody else perceives this, and Loo goes on to write second-rate pastiches of Hollywood film music. Crabbe's other personal and political initiatives end in similar indignity and farce. His fate has been predicted very early in the trilogy by his Indian colleague Mr Raj: ' "The country will absorb you and you will cease to be Victor Crabbe. You will less and less find it possible to do the work for which you were sent here. You will lose function and identity. You will be swallowed up and become another kind of eccentric" ' (175). Burgess's achievement in the *Malayan Trilogy* is to have absorbed much of the linguistic and cultural profusion of the East into what remains very recognizably an English novel, but his hero in the end is almost literally swallowed up by Malaya. His undignified, accidental death stands as a symbol of the British imperium which was always doomed to dissolve, leaving barely a wrack behind. His character is memorable in proportion to its futility, and what Burgess calls the 'romantic dream' (334) of liberal imperialism dies with it.

In Paul Scott's *Staying On* the grand themes of Burgess's imperial lament are virtually forgotten. Compared to Victor Crabbe, Scott's hero Tusker Smalley, a retired colonel in the Indian Army, is a small-minded bigot. His death at Pankot in April 1972 from a massive coronary expresses the collective sclerosis of diehard Anglo-India, since Tusker's only real difference from his military contemporaries lies in his refusal to go home after independence. His growing perverseness and misanthropy are seen from several viewpoints, including those of his landlord and friend Mr Bhoolabhoy ('Billy-boy'), his wife Lucy, and their servant Ibrahim. The novel's pathos centres on the fate of Lucy, the daughter of an English clergyman who will be left to spend her widowhood isolated and poverty-stricken in a country for which she feels little affection despite having lived there for most of her adult life. She and Tusker are, as she says, 'people in shadow'.[25] Tusker, Lucy belatedly realizes, had never intended to go home: 'It was as though he bore a grudge against his own country and countrymen' (96). He was not an impressive man in his prime, but retirement a long way from England gives him the opportunity to act out a fantasy of cantankerous English eccentricity and to play the charade, as it were, of being the last Tory squire—for, however reduced his circumstances in India, he remains 'Tusker Sahib' and still has the glamour of being an ex-ruler.

With *Staying On* the colonial adventure that began as epic romance and foundered in disillusionment and despair had ended in a mixture of dark comedy and sentimental farce. Not only are Tusker and Lucy childless, but they do their best to ignore Pankot's small Eurasian community, who represent the hybrid identity produced by imperialism. For, Lucy reflects, the history of interracial sex that they represent was 'a physical connection between the races that had continually to be discouraged' (204–5). Her belief in racial purity is part of the fantasy of an 'English character' that could not easily be sustained in England itself, where (for example) Ibrahim's brother-in-law has settled as a slum landlord in Finsbury Park. *Staying On* is, perhaps, a novel of its time in implying that, in large part, Britain had simply washed its hands of the empire, with little consciousness of unfinished business left behind. Lucy, in the tradition of Sir John Seeley, would like to claim that the British have permanently altered India for the better—'There really wasn't a single aspect of the nice civilized things in India that didn't reflect something of British influence' (97), she consoles herself—but the novel seems to imply that 'Britishness' itself, and not just the remnants of Anglo-India, is rapidly dying out. When in the final sentence Lucy laments that Tusker has gone 'home' and left her stranded (255), the word signifies neither England nor India but simply the grave.

~ 14 ~

Round Tables: Chivalry and the Twentieth-Century English Novel-Sequence

I N twentieth-century English fiction there are novelists of expansion
and novelists of contraction. D. H. Lawrence's œuvre after the First
World War is an outstanding example of expansion through time
and space. It reflects Lawrence's restlessness as he journeyed to Australia,
New Mexico, and southern Italy; it explores his fascination with primitive
cultures and ideas of prehistory, and hints at transcendental realities
beyond the material world. Novels and stories like *The Plumed Serpent*
(1926) and *The Woman Who Rode Away* (1928) are fantastic fables
foretelling the defeat of Western civilization and European imperialism.
No novelist has done more to distance himself from his beginnings in
Victorian provincial realism, yet Lawrence in *Lady Chatterley's Lover*
executes a final if rather hesitant return to England.

In the work of Lawrence and other 'expansionist' novelists—Aldous
Huxley, Wyndham Lewis, H. G. Wells, and later in the century Doris
Lessing—the novel form itself comes under intense strain. Their fiction is
unstably poised between topical satire and dream romance, between the
'discussion novel' of ideas and visionary science fiction. But the majority
of twentieth-century English novelists did not follow their lead. Far from
representing an ever-widening circle of life and intelligence, their novels
portray a distinctly diminished social circle. Theirs is the fiction of what
one critic has called the 'shrinking island'.[1]

If the novelist's social range was shrinking, so was the novel itself as a
physical object. In the 1890s the Victorian circulating libraries lost their
virtual monopoly of the book market and the conventional three-volume
novel was replaced by single volumes which were far more attractive
to purchasers. Ambitious novelists continued to write long novels, and
many bestsellers were extremely bulky, but the average novel became
much shorter. By the middle of the twentieth century there was a striking

uniformity in the design of new novels, which rarely exceeded 250 pages. The younger English novelists of the 1930s and after rarely seem to have questioned this format. Graham Greene, for example, was even more cosmopolitan than Lawrence in his choice of settings, but his fiction regularly falls back on the disciplined plotting and melodramatic conventions of the thriller and the detective story. Evelyn Waugh's early novels *Decline and Fall* (1928) and *Vile Bodies* (1930) are tightly knit social comedies set among the English gentry and aristocracy; the same is true of Anthony Powell's *Afternoon Men* (1931) and *From a View to a Death* (1933). Like many of their contemporaries, Waugh and Powell present English society on a deliberately limited scale, as a small upper-class clique living a virtually self-contained life in defiance of a wider, rapidly changing world.[2] The aristocracy, once feared and respected, is now a dying breed treasured for its very absurdity. Its manners have been reduced to mannerisms, its habits of command to helpless and impotent gestures. Far from seeking revenge on their ancient enemy, the middle-class reading public were content to see the former ruling class turned into figures of fun, as was supremely the case in the master-and-servant comedies of P. G. Wodehouse.

But more serious ideas of national identity were at stake. The American narrator of Ford Madox Ford's *The Good Soldier* (1915) states in his opening paragraph that 'Six months ago I had never been to England, and, certainly, I had never sounded the depths of an English heart. I had known the shallows.'[3] Ford's embodiment of the 'English heart' is Edward Ashburnham, a member of the landed gentry and a captain in the Indian Army who eventually commits suicide. Ashburnham's successor in Ford's work is the much more likeable Christopher Tietjens, the protagonist of the *Parade's End* sequence, who observes in *No More Parades* (1925) that 'Our station in society naturally forms rather a close ring'.[4] The small circle or microcosm corresponds to the formal desire for a tight fictional plot at the same time that it appeals to a generation of novelists less curious about, and less confident in handling, the diversity of English society than their predecessors had been. The novel-sequences of Ford, Waugh, and Powell enable an extension of the timespan rather than a widening of the social range of single-volume fiction. Their novels suggest that England is run by an old-boy network based on 'private education, wealth, and pedigree'.[5] The novel-sequences tend to 'turn sequence into a cycle' through techniques of thematic repetition and temporal looping back.[6]

Nevertheless, the English upper classes as represented by Ford, Waugh, and Powell are not simply inward-looking. Protagonists like Tietjens and

Waugh's Guy Crouchback feel a kind of mission, if not to impose order, at least to bear witness to their inherited values. They are aware of living public lives in the sense that what they do is watched or noticed by the wider society, and they try to behave in their better moments like chivalrous English gentlemen. Mark Girouard has defined 'upper-class chivalry' in its early twentieth-century manifestations in the following terms: the chivalrous gentleman was brave, straightforward, true to his word, loyal to his friends and his country, and unfailingly protective of women, children, and animals.[7] Ford's Christopher Tietjens shows all these characteristics but is little appreciated for it, so that his loss of reputation is a measure of the corruption of the gentlemanly caste to which he belongs.

The Arthurian romances were the traditional source of ideas of chivalry for English writers. Throughout the nineteenth century poets and painters had popularized Arthurian themes, and Tennyson, the leading Victorian poet, devoted his major work to a reinterpretation of the Arthurian cycle. Malory's *Le Morte d'Arthur* (1485) and Tennyson's *The Idylls of the King* (1859–91) tell of the establishment of the Round Table with its fellowship, its ethic of chivalry, and its assertion of monarchical authority. The Round Table reaches its greatest glory in the Christian mission of the Grail, but at the same time the fellowship is being undermined by factionalism, infidelity, and betrayal. Once the Grail has been achieved, the story turns to tragedy as internal dissension leads to civil war, a disastrous last battle, and the death of Arthur. The Victorians, prompted by Tennyson, came to read the Arthurian cycle as a warning of Britain's possible destiny and, above all, of the dangers of imperial decay.

The Arthurian legends had been associated with Royalism ever since Henry VII, the first of the Tudor dynasty, had claimed to be descended from Arthur. Nevertheless, the principal source text, Malory's *Le Morte d'Arthur*, had long been out of favour. During the late seventeenth and eighteenth centuries—the period of the English Civil Wars, the Glorious Revolution, and the Jacobite rebellions—it languished unreprinted for more than a hundred years. Although Walter Scott in his youth made notes on Malory, *Le Morte d'Arthur* was not widely available to the reading public until the appearance of new editions during the period of Tennyson's boyhood.[8]

In fact, Tennyson was not the first laureate poet to consider rewriting the legends. Milton contemplated the story of Arthur as the subject for a proposed national epic.[9] Dryden wrote an Arthurian play, while the physician and courtier Sir Richard Blackmore produced two verse epics,

Prince Arthur (1695) and *King Arthur* (1697). Wordsworth once thought of writing 'on some British theme, some old | Romantic tale, by Milton left unsung'.[10] Scott's verse romances of sixteenth-century Scotland include the Arthurian-inspired *The Lady of the Lake* (1810). But prose fiction since Cervantes had prided itself on displacing the romances of chivalry, and before the twentieth century the Arthurian revival had very little impact on the novel. Smollett, who had translated the *History and Adventures of Don Quixote* (1755), went on to mock Arthurian feats of arms in *Sir Launcelot Greaves* seven years later. Tennyson's *Idylls of the King* was ridiculed in Mark Twain's *A Connecticut Yankee in King Arthur's Court* (1889), while chivalric romance was among Lewis Carroll's targets when, for example, he created the White Knight in *Alice's Adventures in Wonderland* (1865) and Tweedledum and Tweedledee in *Through the Looking-Glass* (1872). Bulwer-Lytton's *King Arthur* (1849) was not a novel but a much-ridiculed verse epic.[11] The one hero of Victorian prose fiction who seems indebted to Arthur is Charlotte M. Yonge's Sir Guy Morville in *The Heir of Redclyffe* (1853), who writes an Arthurian epic as a boy and later models for a picture of Sir Galahad; but his chivalry is confined to the domestic sphere. Yonge's novel was a favourite of William Morris and Edward Burne-Jones, two of the most influential figures in the tradition of Arthurian poetry and painting.[12] It was not until the twentieth century, long after the Arthurian legends had exhausted their poetic and pictorial appeal, that a significant body of Arthurian fiction began to appear. This ranges all the way from the modern rewriting of the legends as prose romance, most notably in T. H. White's tetralogy *The Once and Future King* (1938–58), to the diffused reflection of Arthurian themes in novels of contemporary life such as Virginia Woolf's *The Waves* (1931) and Iris Murdoch's *The Green Knight* (1993).

The long-delayed 'return of Arthur' in twentieth-century English fiction was by no means a purely literary phenomenon. Modern warfare and, above all, the introduction of conscription in 1916 brought the experience of soldiering home to everyone. Far from being absurdly antiquated, Arthurian romance became a symbol of all that was missing from the vast and deadly machinery of warfare which no longer discriminated between soldiers and civilians, or between brave fighters and expendable cannon fodder. At the same time, modern anthropological studies beginning with Sir James Frazer's *The Golden Bough* (1890–1915) revived interest in the Grail and other mystery elements of the Arthurian legends. The link between Arthurian romance and warfare is seen not just in novelists such

as Ford and Waugh but in the flawed, ambiguous writer and adventurer
T. E. Lawrence, who first visited the Middle East in connection with his
undergraduate thesis on Crusader castles. Later he became a member of
Lord Milner's imperialist pressure group known as the Round Table.
Lawrence's whole life, it has been said, was inspired by his 'mystical and
poetic conception of the Order of Knighthood' and by the personal ideal
of the medieval knight as 'clean, strong, just and completely chaste'.[13] In
Seven Pillars of Wisdom (1926) Lawrence recalls that, as he took part in
the Arab Revolt of 1917, he kept a copy of the *Morte d'Arthur* in his
saddlebags: 'It relieved my disgust.'[14] Lawrence distinguished between
two kinds of Englishmen: one, 'the John Bull of the books', a 'complete
Englishman' in his 'armoured certainty', is a kind of King Arthur. The
other, 'subtle and insinuating', whose 'own nature lay hid' as he directed
them secretly, is a Merlin-like magician and an evident self-portrait
(354–5). It led to what he called the 'rankling fraudulence' of his 'daily
posturing in alien dress, preaching in alien speech' (514). A British agent
posing as a Bedouin Arab just as Kim was able to pass for an Indian,
Lawrence represents the elements of imperialism, asceticism, and primi-
tivism that had come to cluster around the Arthurian legend.

Lawrence, for all his self-dramatization and self-pity, deplored the
betrayal of the Arabs by Britain and France; his ideal of chivalry was
not simply confined to national identity and the 'matter of Britain'. By
contrast, the need to identify the Arthurian legends with an approved
version of national origins led to the consolidation of the 'English' Arthur,
a figure who (as we saw in Chapter 2) was already present in Malory. By
an extraordinary historical reversal, T. H. White, for example, portrays
Arthur as a champion of the victorious Saxons instead of the defeated
Celts.[15] The historical conflict between Celt and Saxon is a principal
theme in the major twentieth-century novel to take the Arthurian legend
as its explicit subject, John Cowper Powys's *A Glastonbury Romance*
(1932). Powys (1872–1963) has recently been claimed as a Welsh writer,
although he was born in Derbyshire in 1872 and brought up in the West
Country. *A Glastonbury Romance* sets out to repossess not just the
Arthurian legend but England itself as a land for Celts rather than Saxons.

This huge narrative saga, a kind of grotesque parody of the sexual
obsessions, eccentric characterizations, and melodramatic confrontations
of Hardy's Wessex novels, portrays Glastonbury in Somerset as the
ancient refuge of the defeated Celts which has become, in modern times, a
tourist attraction and pilgrimage centre. The novel begins in Norfolk, in the
traditional heart of Saxon England, where the Crows are descended from

generations of yeomen. In moving to Glastonbury, Powys's protagonist John Crow has been preceded by his cousin Philip, an industrialist and modernizer who declares war on heritage culture and the conservation of outdated values. Philip Crow would like to cover the West Country with industrial plants such as the dye-works and tin mine that he owns, but he finds to his disgust that the most successful local enterprise is a souvenir factory turning out cheap figures of Arthur and Merlin. The factory is the brainchild of 'Bloody Johnny' Geard, the mayor of Glastonbury and a religious maniac, who builds new shrines connected to the Grail legend and institutes an annual fair and Arthurian pageant. John Crow deserts his Saxon imperialist cousin and joins forces with Geard.

The characters of A Glastonbury Romance are not so much reincarnations of the Arthurian world as its modern exploiters and devotees. They range from the Welsh antiquarian Owen Evans, a reader of Malory first encountered by John Crow at Stonehenge, to Geard with his vision of an English Celtic Revival that will restore Glastonbury to a central place in the spiritual history of Europe. Geard, whose name is a possible corruption of Galahad, is less interested in King Arthur and his court than in the story of the Grail which Joseph of Arimathea brought from the Holy Land to Glastonbury. In Geard's hands the Grail myth, which Powys believes to be of pagan Celtic ancestry, becomes the basis of a modern Christian heresy. Another element in the story is a Communist conspiracy bent on exploiting Geard's revelation for its own ends, so that at one point Glastonbury is declared an independent republic or commune with the religious heretic as its nominal president. In repossessing the Arthurian legends for Celtic Britain, Powys also seems intent on destroying their Royalist associations. Finally Bloody Johnny and his followers are overwhelmed by a great flood, suggesting the pagan forces of nature and the nature goddess that must eventually destroy modern society with its welter of rival ideological, scientific, and mystical cults. Having comprehensively exposed the false prophets of industrialism, socialism, and Christian occultism, Powys's final paean to Cybele, the goddess of fertility, expresses his wish to emerge in D. H. Lawrence fashion as a follower of the old pagan deities.[16] The Glastonbury legend with its national allegory of Saxon England versus Celtic Britain is eventually overshadowed by this vaguer and more primitivist ambition. But Powys's vast and portentous fictional canvas is also notable for its prolixity, idiosyncrasy, and lack of narrative tension.

John Cowper Powys was almost alone in exploring the modern, democratic ramifications of a legend usually noted for its aristocratic, conservative, and archaic elements. Where his idea of a modern 'round table' consists of a popular religious cult or a subversive political conspiracy, other novelists stress the Arthurian concern with closed circles and privileged elites. In this respect the relatively small number of novels explicitly concerned with rewriting the legend, such as Anthony Powell's *The Fisher King* (1986) and Iris Murdoch's *The Green Knight*, typify a much broader tendency in the fictional representation of modern English society. *The Green Knight* alludes to the legends of the Grail, Excalibur, and Balin and Balan as well as to that named in its title. But it is also, in part, a summation of the novelist's whole œuvre, in which Arthurian allusions are sparse or non-existent. Seen from the perspective of this very late novel, most of her fiction pursues recognizably Arthurian themes of sexual competition, brotherly strife, magical or charismatic authority, and quest romance within a small circle of upper-middle-class characters joined together by occult links of one kind or another. This is a stylization of tendencies present in some of the most influential earlier twentieth-century English novelists, from Virginia Woolf to the novel-sequences of Ford, Waugh, and Powell. For these writers, the working-out of individual destinies within a charmed circle is not merely a necessity imposed by the conventions of fictional plotting. It reflects their understanding of upper and cultivated middle-class English society as a confined and small-scale community.

In E. M. Forster's *A Room with a View*, Lucy Honeychurch envisions the middle class (or what Forster calls suburbia) as 'a circle of rich, pleasant people, with identical interests and identical foes. In this circle one thought, married, and died.'[17] Forster is a novelist of inclusion and expansion, taking Lucy to Italy, prefacing *Howards End* with his motto 'Only connect', and finally portraying English imperialism defeated by the multitudinousness of India. But Lucy's formulation suggests that, even in the more contracted novels of middle or upper-class life, there is a built-in source of dramatic tension, since she suggests that people of 'identical interests' must also have 'identical foes'. The round table is, by definition, both surrounded and likely to be infiltrated by its enemies. However securely established its characters appear, the upper-class novel continually returns to the idea of a potential Last Battle.

Symbolic Knighthood in Virginia Woolf

In a telling moment in Virginia Woolf's *Night and Day*, Ralph Denham, a lower-middle-class parvenu from suburban Highgate, stands in the darkness outside Katherine Hilbery's house in Chelsea and looks up at its lighted windows. The Hilberys' drawing-room, Ralph thinks, is a 'little sanctuary' of people whose 'identity was dissolved in a general glory of something that might, perhaps, be called civilization'. He himself is 'one of those lost birds fascinated by the lighthouse and held to the glass by the splendour of the blaze'.[18] There are, broadly, two notions of the civilized elite in Woolf's fiction—the traditional idea of a social hierarchy presided over by wealth, political power, and masculine virtue, and an alternative centring on art, female sensitivity, and personal relationships. It is often hard to separate these notions, since so many of Woolf's female characters are drawn to the traditional hierarchy symbolized in her novels by the political centres of Westminster and Whitehall. Whitehall in her novels is more than simply a bastion of patriarchal authority.[19] Katherine Hilbery lives in earshot of Big Ben, forming part of 'that centre which was constantly in the minds of people in remote Canadian forests and on the plains of India, when their thoughts turned to England' (44). As the granddaughter of a famous Victorian poet she occupies a house which has become a cultural shrine and belongs, so to speak, to English literature. All this is doubtless in Ralph's mind as he gazes up at her windows.

Night and Day is Woolf's only conventional novel of courtship, but the accepted customs of aristocratic and upper-middle-class England prove remarkably resilient throughout her fiction. Her characters, by and large, are waited on by servants, they dress for dinner and leave the gentlemen alone to drink their port afterwards. New generations are shown experimenting and breaking the rules, but the rules remain in the background. Parents and grandparents play an ever-expanding role in Woolf's later, more retrospective novels. The young protagonists are rebels searching for a more liberal way of life, but for the most part they continue to observe established conventions. What the narrator of *Night and Day* calls the 'great make-believe game of English social life' (193) is still being played. Woolf's fiction thus presents a mythologized ruling class as the defining location of national identity.[20] This is nowhere more explicit than in the most avant-garde and experimental of her novels, *The Waves* (1931).

The image of the circle is ever-present in Woolf's fiction. She imagines the work of art as being spherical in shape, 'one of those globed compacted things over which thought lingers, and love plays'.[21] In *Night and Day* Ralph Denham's friend Mary Datchet works for a political campaign whose office is dominated by a huge wall-map 'dotted with little pins' (238). Ralph, however, is neither an expansionist and conqueror nor a maker of maps. His own sense of symbolic space is expressed by the doodle he does for Katherine at the end of the book, consisting of a 'little dot with . . . flames round it' (457). The little round dot stands for their love, as Katherine implicitly understands: ' "Yes, the world looks something like that to me too," ' she tells him (458). Having at first felt excluded from the centre of civilization that he identified with the Hilberys' drawing room, Ralph has at last penetrated the ring of fire and reached the centre. In doing so, however, he may have lost the reformist zeal he once shared with Mary Datchet, a fellow outsider. Ralph and Mary belong to 'the class which is conscious of having lost its birthright' in the ruling structures of society: 'They were alike . . . in believing that it behoved them to take in hand the repair and reconstruction of the fabric of England' (203). But we suspect that Ralph, like many ambitious outsiders, will be satisfied by his personal accession to the ruling class.

In *The Waves* there are no true outsiders, although Louis, one of the group of six childhood friends whose interwoven voices constitute Woolf's narrative, is marked out from the others by his Australian identity. For all their individual differences (and despite the fact that only two of them are described as the 'sons of gentlemen') from a purely sociological standpoint the six characters are virtually identical.[22] Their lifelong friendship grows out of their shared devotion to a seventh figure, Percival, who dies young and whose voice is never heard. The image that Woolf repeatedly uses for her group of six (Bernard, Jinny, Louis, Neville, Rhoda, and Susan) is that of the circle. As children they sit together in a ring, and Louis believes that by describing their union in words he can forge it into a 'ring of steel' (33). Twice in the novel they gather around a restaurant table, where they are like a 'seven-sided flower' (108), but also inside a 'globe whose walls are made of Percival, of youth and beauty' (124). These moments of union and temporary coalescence are set against their increasingly anguished experiences of separation, fragmentation, and fear of mental breakdown. The sense of order created by their self-identification as a group contrasts sharply with the solitude and unrest that they must undergo individually. Woolf's subject, inspired by her own episodes of mental illness, is the creation of a community of friends that can overcome individual isolation and terror.

At the centre of this most introverted and psychologically complex of Woolf's novels is the figure of Percival, who represents, quite explicitly, the hero of Arthurian legend. He is a modern version of Malory's Sir Percivale de Galis and of Wagner's Parsifal, just as Joyce's Leopold Bloom is a modern Ulysses. Percival is also a twentieth-century Crusader, a servant of the British Empire who goes out to India and dies, as he has lived (that is, as he has lived in his friends' imaginations) on horseback. Very early in the novel the group of six identify him as a man of action and a natural leader. For Louis, 'his magnificence is that of some medieval commander. . . . he will certainly attempt some forlorn enterprise and die in battle' (31). He is a 'hero' (105), a protagonist of romance who 'inspires poetry' (33). The weakness of the novel is that Percival manifestly has nothing in common with the six characters who are devoted to him, so that we cannot believe he would have chosen them as friends. But Woolf certainly intends to ironize the friends' hero-worship, since Percival is killed in a horse-racing accident and not in battle.

While Bernard compares Percival's fate to the inglorious death of King William III (who was thrown from his horse when it stumbled on a molehill), Neville paints it as a poignant scene of imperial self-sacrifice: 'They carried him to some pavilion, men in riding-boots, men in sun helmets; among unknown men he died' (129). These fellow sahibs and racing companions are unknown to Neville and his friends but not, one imagines, to Percival. The pathos of Percival's death as seen by the group of six back in England underwrites his transformation from a reckless and unfortunate subaltern to a knight permanently encased in shining armour. Hence Bernard's dying words at the end of the book: 'It is death against whom I ride with my spear couched and my hair flying back like a young man's, like Percival's, when he galloped in India' (256). Bernard's self-dramatization is in keeping with the rapt, poetic style of *The Waves*, but there is a thin line between the noble pathos that Woolf intends and the traditional English novel's mockery of chivalric romance. Bernard as a long-haired old buffer riding for a fall is a bit like Carroll's White Knight.

The Novel-Sequences

Ford Madox Ford's *Parade's End*, Evelyn Waugh's *Sword of Honour* (1952–61), and Anthony Powell's *A Dance to the Music of Time* (1951–75)—sequences of four, three, and twelve volumes respectively—are among the major achievements of twentieth-century English fiction. Central to each of them is the experience of participating in a world war, so that the narrow social circle of the principal characters is necessarily, even pitilessly exposed to modern global realities. The novel-sequence (reminiscent, in some ways, of Thackeray and Trollope) avoids the artificiality of modern single-volume fiction in which the social milieu is rigidly circumscribed, usually by a plot device such as a sea voyage—as in

Woolf's *The Voyage Out* and Powell's *The Fisher King*—or a country-house weekend. It is what distinguishes Waugh and Powell from authors sometimes compared to them such as Ivy Compton-Burnett, Henry Green, and Muriel Spark, in whose novels characters brought together by family relationship, similarity of situation, or pure accident are held rigidly in place within an institution such as a village, a school, a literary circle, or a residential building for young ladies. The characters may come and go from this campus or precinct, but the narrative itself rarely if ever steps outside it. Such novels make up in intensity of focus what they lack in rounded characterization, and they may, indeed, be written in the belief that a coherent and integrated personal identity is an anachronism in the modern novel. However well we think we know other people, these novels imply, they can only be known as they appear in particular contexts and particular roles. C. P. Snow in *Strangers and Brothers* (1940–70) showed how an eleven-volume sequence might be constructed out of a series of such deliberately circumscribed vignettes. Perhaps the most successful of Snow's individual volumes is *The Masters* (1951), a political thriller with a timespan of a few weeks during which the action never strays beyond the gates of a single Cambridge college.

What Snow offers, apart from simple entertainment, is social history (as underlined in an 'Appendix' to *The Masters*)[23] and a shrewd but limited form of worldly wisdom. But the title *Strangers and Brothers* at least hints at the romance roots of the modern English novel-sequence. The sequences by Ford, Waugh, and Powell have numerous preoccupations in common, all of them manifestly paralleling the themes of Arthurian legend. There is a band of two or more brothers-in-arms who are destined to grow apart and possibly fight with one another; a close link with a leader who is at once friend, father-substitute, protector, and enemy; a relationship with a harpy or powerfully evil woman involving emotional torment and sexual betrayal; devotion to a higher cause sanctioned by supernatural forces whether Christian or pagan; and a last battle in which the hero's legacy, and with it the 'matter of Britain', are determined. It is true that the 'last battle' is not portrayed in the apocalyptic terms found in Malory and Tennyson, or indeed in Bernard's final vision of death in *The Waves*. It is more likely to be presented as a conventional struggle over inheritance, succession, and the stewardship of property. Seen as a whole, this complex of themes takes shape as an elegy for a dying aristocracy.

The sequences of Ford, Waugh, and Powell are conservative and even diehard in their ideology. The novelists' social vision is nostalgic and somewhat alarmist, since they apparently failed to anticipate that distinctions of class and wealth would survive such twentieth-century developments as the break-up of country estates and the disappearance of live-in servants. They themselves belonged to the upper-middle class rather than the aristocracy, although Powell married into the aristocracy and Waugh had numerous aristocratic friends. Ford and Waugh shared a literary and artistic background. Ford, born in 1873, was the son of the music critic of *The Times* and grandson of the painter Ford Madox Brown; Waugh, born thirty years later, was the son of a publisher and was educated at a minor public school and Oxford. Powell, born into a military family and educated at Eton and Oxford, worked as a young man in the film industry. Most of all, their army service in early middle age links these three novelists together and strikingly differentiates them from most of their contemporaries and predecessors in English fiction. Ford enlisted in 1915, at the age of 42, when he could easily have found secure occupation on the home front; he was gassed and invalided out of the army two years later. Waugh and Powell were in their mid-thirties at the start of the Second World War. Waugh saw active service with the Royal Marines in Crete, Yugoslavia, and elsewhere, while Powell worked for the Intelligence Corps in London. In all three writers the broad social realities of modern England are set against the closed world of the army regiment with its rigid hierarchy, its proud traditions, its brutality and pettiness, and its all-male comradeship. The modern conscript army embodies a clash between aristocracy and democracy in which democracy might still be contained and held at bay.

It may have been his experience of army service that kept Evelyn Waugh—who was hardly one of nature's moderates—from joining the lunatic fringe of modern conservative thought that finds literary expression in non-realistic genres such as the mythological romance and the 'paranoid' thriller, where sinister and occult conspiracies are threatening to take over the nation. Nevertheless, the opposition between Christianity and Communism in Waugh's trilogy could be compared to such 'evil empire' fantasy fiction as J. R. R. Tolkien's immensely popular *The Lord of the Rings* (1954–5). Perhaps the most blatant example of paranoid conservative fantasy by a respected writer is to be found in *That Hideous Strength* (1945), the third novel in the 'space' trilogy by Tolkien's friend and associate C. S. Lewis. Where the earlier volumes in Lewis's trilogy had taken his hero to Malacandra and Perelandra (Mars and Venus), *That Hideous Strength* stages the battle to save England from a Satanic conspiracy entirely in the city of Oxford, where both Lewis and Tolkien taught English literature. In a novel based explicitly on the occult elements of Arthurian romance, the forces of scientific research, social planning, bio-engineering, and corporate enterprise—the agenda, more or less, of C. P. Snow and of post-war Labour governments—are opposed by the secret realm of Logres with its 'unbroken succession of Pendragons'.[24] Beginning with the discovery of Merlin's tomb, *That Hideous Strength* rewrites the whole of English history as a struggle between the preservers and destroyers of the Arthurian legacy. Ford, Waugh, and Powell also offer a view of England that is conservative, mystical, romantic, elegiac, and patriarchal to the point of misogyny. But in their worlds, unlike those of the thriller and the mythological romance, heroism is so compromised as to be virtually impossible. The reality of modern warfare replaces the delusion that salvation might be won by galloping into battle.

Ford Madox Ford and the Last of England

'Chivalry' is a word that plays little part in Ford Madox Ford's vocabulary, although critics instinctively reach for it to describe the character of his protagonist Christopher Tietjens. Malcolm Bradbury, for example, spoke of Tietjens's 'chivalric and ancient notions of male honour and nobility', of the ' "chivalric" act' he performs in marrying his wife Sylvia when she is pregnant by another man, and of his 'irritating chivalry' in refusing to divorce her once she has deserted him.[25] Tietjens, as we have seen, embodies the gentlemanly ideal defined by the historian Mark Girouard, but this does not make him a respected companion or a member of an order of contemporary knights dedicated to a common purpose. Instead, he becomes widely distrusted. His wife, the principal object of his chivalry, hates and despises him. In the army he proves to be a 'good soldier' but receives a series of humiliating postings and is frequently threatened with official disgrace. Hardly anyone except his lover Valentine Wannop believes in him or takes him at face value. To be a chivalrous gentleman in Ford's modern England is not to have a seat at the round table but to be, in Tietjens's words, 'a sort of lonely buffalo: outside the herd' (137).

But if Tietjens is a spiritual outsider, he is invariably represented as belonging to a tight social circle. In the opening sentence of *Parade's End* he is one of 'two young men . . . of the English public official class' (3)—the other is his colleague Macmaster—setting off by train for a country weekend. Macmaster, a Scot, is of humble origins and owes his social position to a loan from Tietjens's mother; he is destined to become one of Tietjens's many betrayers. Tietjens is the youngest son of a Yorkshire country gentleman, but his wish is to be remembered as a kind of Anglican saint, one who was 'able to touch pitch and not be defiled': this, he high-mindedly assumes, has been the 'desire of every English gentleman from Colonel Hutchinson onwards' (200–1). (Colonel Hutchinson, the Parliamentary commander and regicide, was known from his wife's *Memoirs* first published in 1806.) Tietjens thus associates the idea of the gentleman with Puritanical moral integrity rather than inherited social rank. His eccentricity and unworldliness are the marks of a dying breed, since for a long time neither he nor his brothers seem to be capable of producing children. He likes to fancy himself 'the last surviving Tory', a member of an extinct species like the megatherium (527, 646).

Tietjens's Toryism is basic to his character. It is one of the first things we learn about him, and it fits his position as a scion of the Yorkshire squirearchy. Others define him as a Tory: Macmaster, for example, who is 'a Whig by conviction, by nation, by temperament' (61), and Valentine, the suffragette who tells him that ' "I've never met a Cambridge Tory man before. I thought they were all in museums and you work them up again out of bones" ' (145). It is typical of Ford to provide such confirmatory touches, but his pervasive use of interior monologue as a narrative device means that, for the most part, we must take Tietjens's Toryism at his own valuation. No one ever challenges the idea that Toryism like Tietjens's is virtually extinct and that he himself may be its last embodiment. His elder brother, Mark, is as dyed in the wool as he is. Ford's intense focus on his protagonist's private obsessions, together with the use of narrative flashbacks, foreshortening, and interior monologues, gives to Tietjens's isolation and his capacity to be generally misunderstood a pathos it does not always deserve. The myth of his being politically, socially, and morally a last survivor is essential to the spell he exerts over the reader.

Thanks to a series of radical time-compressions, each volume in the tetralogy comes to a relentlessly melodramatic climax of a kind more familiar on the stage than in the novel. The whole dramatic situation between the characters has substantially been outlined by the end of the first volume, *Some Do Not* ... (1924), but events and assumptions are continually re-evaluated as Ford belatedly supplies the reader with crucial narrative information, which is gradually and somewhat artificially drip-fed into Tietjens's interor monologues, producing a jigsaw-puzzle effect. *Some Do Not* ... brings the main characters together on a country-house weekend in Sussex at midsummer 1912, when Tietjens first meets

Valentine and Macmaster encounters his future wife, Mrs Duchemin. Tietjens and Valentine, driving a horse and cart in the early morning mist, are run into by a car driven by his godfather General Campion, an accident that reverberates throughout the succeeding volumes since Campion immediately concludes that Tietjens is conducting an adulterous affair. Meanwhile, Tietjens's estranged wife, Sylvia, is considering returning to her hated husband, since her Catholic principles forbid divorce.

The second part of *Some Do Not...* takes place on the last day of Tietjens's army leave in 1917 before being sent back to France. He has to sort out his personal affairs with Sylvia, to meet the banker whose refusal to honour one of his cheques threatens to ruin his social reputation, and to attend for an interview at the War Office. He asks Valentine to become his mistress on his last night before returning to the front but, as we learn much later, their desires are thwarted. *No More Parades* (1925) shows him at the base camp in France. Sylvia, on a highly irregular visit, tries to engineer a reunion with him but apparently becomes Campion's lover instead. Campion, Tietjens's commanding officer, orders him back to the front line, where his desperate experiences are recalled in *A Man Could Stand Up* (1926). The latter novel shows Tietjens's long-delayed reunion with Valentine on Armistice Day 1918, but it is not until *The Last Post* (1928) that we learn that on the same night Christopher was summoned to his brother Mark's bedside. *The Last Post* (which some editors have excluded from the sequence as not being part of Ford's original conception) brings the main characters together at a remote Sussex farmhouse on the day of Mark's death shortly after the war.

Even the briefest plot summary brings home the extent to which *Parade's End* is constructed, not around a 'band of brothers' or fellow officers, but in terms of relationships within a single extended family. There are wider social groupings on display, such as the Golf Club at Rye in *Some Do Not...* and the men under Tietjens's command at the base camp in *No More Parades*, but as often as not they simply lead back into the family. Moreover, the characters who do not belong to his circle never take on the individuality of Tietjens's own extended family members. Ford's organizing principle is thus one of filiation rather than the affiliation which is central to Waugh's *Sword of Honour* and Powell's *The Music of Time* as well as to the legendary Arthurian Round Table.[26] The apparent closeness of the Tietjens family circle is reinforced by Sylvia's malicious suggestion that Christopher's relationship with Valentine is incestuous. Both Christopher's brother Mark (a high-ranking civil servant) and his godfather Campion use their influence to get his army postings changed. After sending him to the front line, Campion—ostensibly to avoid any suspicion of favouritism—refuses Christopher the citation he has rightfully earned for bravery under fire. Ford's plot thus puts Tietjens at the mercy of a general who is at the same time his godfather, his commanding officer, and his wife's latest admirer.

For most of *Parade's End*, the family structure does little or nothing to mitigate Christopher Tietjens's isolation. Christopher, Mark, and their father barely communicate with one another, while Christopher's remaining two brothers and his sister are killed in the First World War. Both his father and his surviving brother are willing to credit the most damaging rumours about Christopher's behaviour. Christopher rarely sees his wife and never sees his son, while Sylvia's time is divided between adulterous liaisons and spiritual retreats organized by the Catholic Church. His attitude of old-fashioned chivalry cuts him off even more sharply from his fellows. In *Some Do Not...* he helps two militant suffragettes to escape from the outraged members of Rye Golf Club and from the police, thus earning himself a reputation as a philanderer and a secret radical. Instead of seeking to escape from his unhappy marriage, he tries to behave scrupulously towards both Sylvia and his new lover Valentine. One of the most convincing aspects of the novel is Sylvia's rage at finding herself the object of his elaborate knight-errantry. Perhaps he deserves, in his turn, to suffer her vindictive malice. If Christopher's battle against female enchantment recalls one of the major themes of Arthurian romance, it also seems at times a thinly disguised idealization of Ford's own sexual conduct; the scandalous rumours surrounding his protagonist were directly paralleled in Ford's own life. Yet, for all its suspicion of special pleading, *Parade's End* portrays its hero as a quixotic knight-errant embodying the noblest aspects of upper-class English identity.

In a moment of intense patriotism at the outbreak of war in 1914, Christopher foresees certain humiliation for the nation he loves: 'We were fitted neither for defeat nor for victory; we could be true to neither friend nor foe. Not even to ourselves' (200). Here his personal isolation is a reflection of England's plight. Nevertheless, the tetralogy works its way towards a certain kind of brotherhood and family reconciliation, since Christopher and Mark come closer together after the deaths of their father and brothers. But the cost of this reconciliation is the sense of national betrayal they both share. At the outbreak of war the two men are loyal and dedicated civil servants, but at its end they have resigned in disgust. In *The Last Post* we learn that Mark was paralysed by a stroke (or, alternatively, that he retreated into an oath of silence) in response to the supposed betrayal of France by Britain and America at the end of the war. Christopher resigns after discovering that his work as a government statistician has been used to double-cross the French. Mark's awareness of national disgrace finds expression in the phrase 'The last of England', and the Last Post, blown by a drunken bugler on Armistice Night, again makes him think of 'The Last of England' (234, 787).

'The Last of England' necessarily alludes to the famous painting by Ford Madox Brown, the novelist's grandfather, of emigrants leaving the English homeland. *Parade's End*, however, concludes with a withdrawal into the English countryside rather than an escape from it. Christopher's ideal is summed up in the seventeenth-century Anglican poet George Herbert and his retreat to a country parsonage, and he blames Disraeli, the 'jerry-building Jew', for inspiring England's imperial ambitions: '"Damn the Empire!"' he reflects. '"It was England! It was Bemerton Parsonage that mattered!"' (639). Mark also retreats to a cottage in Sussex. He takes no interest in the family estate to which he is the heir, although the fate of Groby and its Great Tree is much on Christopher's mind. Since one of the puzzles of *Parade's End* is the extent to which it appears to be at odds with Ford's earlier assertions, in *The Spirit of the People* and elsewhere, of the intrinsically changing and transient nature of English identity, it is important to note that neither the tree nor the Tietjenses themselves are native to England. The Great Tree is a cedar imported from Sardinia, not a Forsterian wych-elm or an English oak. The Tietjenses (as their name reveals) are Dutch opportunists who came to England with William III at the time of the Glorious Revolution. As Protestants who were able to dispossess the Stuart-supporting Catholic owners of Groby they became subject to an ancestral curse, laid down by the seventeenth-century author of 'Speldon on Sacrilege' who denounced the seizure of Catholic lands. Christopher's knight-errantry is rooted in guilt and superstition, since he believes that each of his ancestors who lived at Groby has 'died of a broken neck or a broken heart' (189). Moreover, the persecution of British and Irish Catholics continues in the twentieth century and is, Ford implies, part of the dark underside of British imperialism. Sylvia's mentor Father Consett is hanged during the Great War for refusing to divulge the confessions of Irish Republican prisoners. This atrocity plays its part in Sylvia's devastating rants against the Tietjenses and their values. It reflects the extraordinary ambivalence of Ford Madox Ford, a novelist who in *The Critical Attitude* (1911) had contrasted the 'insularly English novel' with the works of Joseph Conrad and Henry James which were, he said, in the 'mainstream of the current of

European literature'.[27] Ford's artistic affiliations were with Conrad and James, but *Parade's End*, for all its narrative experimentation and psychological complexity, is full of insularly Anglo-Saxon attitudes. It is hard to say whether or to what extent these are ironized. Ford's Irish contemporary Mary Colum suggestively remarked that *No More Parades* did not seem to be a 'thoroughgoing English book', but rather 'the work of one of those aliens in the British Empire, Celt or Semite, who in their souls resent what England stands for'.[28] Ford himself, when he wrote the novel, had already left England.

Had the sequence ended with *A Man Could Stand Up* as he originally intended, Ford's ambivalence would have remained entirely unresolved. *The Last Post* offers a kind of solution, since the object of Christopher's quixotic quest can now be seen as the return of Groby to Catholic hands and the lifting of the curse. Mark reflects on what would be needed to redeem England from 'ruin at home and foreign discredit':

The old governing class to which he and his belonged might never return to power but, whatever revolutions took place—and he did not care!—the country must return to exacting of whoever might be its governing class some semblance of personal probity and public honouring of pledges.... A state of war obviously favour[ed] the coming to the top of all kinds of devious storm petrels; that was inevitable and could not be helped. But in normal times a country—every country—was true to itself. (807–8)

England's finest hour, according to Mark in this remarkably optimistic passage, would be found in peace, not war. And the country, once true to itself, would no longer be seen as an oppressor. The condition of this romantic ideal is that the split between Catholic and Protestant, which has reigned since the Reformation, should at last have been healed. Mark tries to achieve this by marrying his Catholic mistress and by making Groby over to Christopher, who in turn allows Sylvia and his son to live there. But Sylvia rents out Groby to the rich Americans who promptly cut down the Great Tree. We are allowed to suppose that Mark's death may give Christopher the opportunity to repossess the estate and preserve it for his son or stepson (his paternity is never wholly clear). But Christopher's son, brought up as a Catholic, has become a Communist at university, while Sylvia may still be capable of springing some nasty surprises.

W. H. Auden, in a (not always reliable) summary of the plot of *Parade's End*, saw the ending of *The Last Post* in remarkably positive terms:

Yet, at the end of the tetralogy, one feels the curse has been lifted. Sylvia can do no more harm, Christopher knows that he is the father of her child, a nice boy who will make a good heir to Groby, and that his father did not, as it had been believed, commit suicide, and Valentine is about to have a child. His honor remains unimpaired, but his sufferings have made him humble; the one real defect in his character as a young man, his arrogance, is gone.[29]

One reason for distrusting this account is that *The Last Post* is structured around Mark's dying monologue and Christopher is absent until the end. It is significant that he has redeemed himself in his elder brother's eyes, but the final verdict on the beleaguered Tory gentleman and soldier striving to make his peace with England's Catholic past remains as uncertain as ever. In *No More Parades* Christopher was shown trying to look after the 2,000 men in his care at the base camp in France as if they were an extended family, but after the Armistice he rejects any kind of public-service role and becomes a private entrepreneur exporting antique furniture. We cannot exactly describe the England of *Parade's End* as a family with the wrong members in control, since the dour, introspective Tietjenses seem largely unfitted to exercise any kind of control. Their record in the civil service is less impressive than the stubborn eccentricity of their withdrawal from society in order to preserve their integrity and honour.

Mark reflects in *The Last Post* that 'All the Tietjenses were born with some sort of kink. It came from the solitude maybe, on the moors, that hard climate, the rough neighbours—possibly even from the fact that Groby Great Tree overshadowed the house' (797). It would seem, however, that the Tietjens 'kink' owes little or nothing to these ostensible causes. Mark and Christopher were very easily recruited into the upper echelons of the civil service, and their idiosyncrasies do not seem to spring from the Yorkshire locality which, throughout the tetralogy, Ford only represents by hearsay. Their 'solitude', perhaps, is that of the Dutch Protestant family who uprooted themselves with·William III and took over land which did not belong to them. Mark and Christopher have spent their working lives in Whitehall and appear to be at home there, but somehow—as we see from the obsessive recirculation and recall of private memories and feelings in their interior monologues—they have gone on speaking in their own private language regardless of their neighbours. It is this instinctive inbreeding that constitutes Ford's critique of the English ruling class. Meanwhile the threat to Groby and what it represents is brought home by the ludicrous proposal of Sylvia's American (and presumably Catholic) tenants, the de Bray Papes, to turn the Yorkshire estate into a Regency theme park with powdered footmen and the tenants' children kneeling in reverence as the lady of the manor passes by in her coach and six. Despite the vague hopes of redemption placed on Christopher and his son, this Marie Antoinette-style fantasy is the novel's only detailed suggestion of a possible future for the landed gentry.

Evelyn Waugh: Dishonouring the Sword

The theme of the Catholic aristocracy winning back one of the great English estates provides the underlying plot of Evelyn Waugh's *Brides-head Revisited* (1945). Although Brideshead at the beginning and end of the book has been requisitioned by the army during the Second World War, the flame in the house's private chapel is kept burning just as—to paraphrase the novel's final descriptive paragraph—it burned for the medieval knights who went on the Crusades. There is none of Ford's tentativeness and uncertainty in this novel, which Waugh in his 1959 preface memorably described as a 'panegyric preached over an empty coffin'. He had anticipated that after the war 'the ancestral seats which were our chief national artistic achievement were doomed to decay and spoliation like the monasteries in the sixteenth century', and so had written a novel deliberately defying this trend. In later life Waugh half disowned *Brideshead Revisited* with its blatant contribution to the late twentieth-century cult of the English country house.[30]

The palatial mansion of Brideshead is not, like Groby, a gloomy product of civil war and Catholic dispossession. Instead, it is the seventeenth-century home of the Flyte family, Marquises of Marchmain, who were Anglicans until the current Lord Marchmain's marriage into the Catholic aristocracy.[31] It is Lady Marchmain's family who are connected to the old world of chivalry and whose flame burns in the Brideshead chapel. The house is a curious mixture of real and fake traditions. The novel's prologue shows it being revisited by Captain Charles Ryder, Waugh's protagonist, and his sidekick Lieutenant Hooper who is a symbol of the new lower-middle-class world. Ryder and Hooper are, at one level, obvious representatives of a nation divided between Cavaliers and Roundheads, as their names indicate. Yet Hooper is no New Model zealot but a lazy, unprofessional soldier, while Ryder is a 'romantic', a parvenu would-be aristocrat, and (now that the war has come) a self-appointed representative of ancient military tradition. In a kind of threnody for a vanished order he contrasts his boyhood dreams with what he takes to have been Hooper's: 'The history they taught [Hooper] had had few battles in it but, instead, a profusion of detail about humane legislation and recent industrial change. Gallipoli, Balaclava, Quebec, Lepanto, Bannockburn, Roncevales, and Marathon—these, and the Battle in the West where Arthur fell . . . sounded in vain to Hooper' (15). Ryder's list of battles starts with names that might feature on a regimental banner but ends with the death of Arthur, invoked in Tennysonian cadences.

Waugh and his characters look back to the world of chivalric romance and legend through nineteenth-century spectacles. Just as Ford Madox Ford wrote a life of Ford Madox Brown, one of Waugh's early books was his biography of Brown's fellow Pre-Raphaelite D. G. Rossetti. Rossetti's paintings of Arthurian scenes, including his series of murals for the Oxford Union in 1856, are burlesqued in Waugh's *A Handful of Dust* (1934), where Tony Last's ruinous divorce leads to his expulsion from Hetton Abbey, a neo-Gothic mansion built in 1864 with gaudily decorated bedrooms named 'Morgan le Fay', 'Guinevere', and the like. Tony has been told that 'Big houses are a thing of the past in England'. Belatedly he is forced to realize that his battle with his estranged wife leaves no room for chivalry. As Waugh writes in a characteristic passage of medievalist fantasy, 'A whole Gothic world had come to grief . . . there was now no armour glittering through the forest glades, no embroidered feet on the green sward; the cream and dappled unicorns had fled'.[32] Finally Tony retreats to the Amazon jungle, where he has a vision of a lost medieval city and is taken prisoner by a mad Englishman who makes him read aloud the complete works of Dickens from end to end. Waugh's hero goes full circle back, not to the Middle Ages, but to 1864.

In *Brideshead Revisited* Charles Ryder meets Sebastian Flyte at Oxford and falls in love, as he thinks, with Brideshead and everything it represents. He finds his *métier* as an architectural painter and undergoes an aesthetic conversion from the functionalist 'puritanism' of those arbiters of modern English taste, John Ruskin and Roger Fry, to the Baroque extravagance of the Flytes' family mansion (79). The opposition between Puritanism and the Cavalier ethic in the novel is, however, far more entangled than it appears from the initial contrast of Hooper and Ryder. When Ryder begins an adulterous affair with Julia, Sebastian's sister, he is shocked and incredulous at the sudden reawakening of her Catholic piety. Later on he objects to the parish priest's attempts to secure Lord Marchmain's deathbed repentance. His rationalistic fervour has more than a hint of the Protestant denunciation of Popery. Julia deserts him, but when he revisits Brideshead as an army captain he says a prayer in the chapel, 'an ancient, newly-learned form of words' (370), implying that he has undergone a belated Catholic conversion. Waugh frequently suggests that there is an inner spirituality to the Catholic faith to which his protagonist, for all his love of Brideshead, has been impervious. This final twist in which the 'Cavalier' Ryder rejects both modern rationalism—seen as belonging to the Philistine, destructive world of Hooper—and his inherited Protestantism illustrates the romantic unreality of *Brideshead Revisited*, a novel which (for all its fascination) is much inferior to the later *Sword of Honour* trilogy as a chronicle of aristocratic England's decline and fall.

Sword of Honour, too, has had its detractors. Waugh's friend Lady Diana Cooper wrote to him after the first volume that ' "I thought that you were going to give us a modern *War and Peace*, but it's much more like *Mrs Dale's Diary*" '.[33] This is unfair (*Mrs Dale's Diary* was a popular radio serial) but not irrelevant. Waugh's own explanation of the novel was that it was 'a description of the Second World War as it was seen and experienced by a single, uncharacteristic Englishman'.[34] The epic sweep and historical vision of Leo Tolstoy's masterpiece (a historical novel written from a fifty-year retrospect and describing events that took place before the author was born) were not, perhaps, available to Waugh, who drew directly on his own service with the Royal Marines. But *Sword of Honour* is more than a fictionalized memoir thanks to its complex, unfolding moral theme. An essential part of Waugh's plan is the background of literary romance involving the idea of medieval chivalry in general and the Arthurian legends in particular. Waugh's 'uncharacteristic Englishman' is Guy Crouchback, a self-effacing Catholic who has spent the pre-war years living in exile, and apparently at a loose end, in Italy. His soul, as we learn at the beginning of *Men at Arms* (1952), has been a 'wasteland' for years, but, aged 35, he responds instantly to the announcement of the Nazi-Soviet pact in 1939: 'The enemy at last was plain in view, huge and hateful, all disguise cast off. It was the Modern Age in arms.'[35] Before leaving for England he visits the tomb of the English Crusader Sir Roger de Waybroke and runs his finger along the knight's sword. This is the trilogy's 'sword of honour' (a phrase which normally signifies the award made to the best cadet in the annual passing-out parade at the military academy of Sandhurst). Guy's house in Italy is known as the Castello Crouchback, while his family home, abandoned during his childhood, is a medieval fortified mansion built around two quadrangles with a collection of swords and other weapons hanging in the great hall. He is, then, a modern knight whose personal Holy Grail is his religious and ideological war against Communism and (to a considerably lesser extent) Nazism.

There are many parallels between Guy Crouchback and Christopher Tietjens—their naivety and occasional childishness, their cuckoldry and failed marriages, their Christian piety, their dedication to obsolete ideals—but Guy is much more clearly identified as a modern Knight of the Round Table than Ford's protagonist. The 1965 'final version' of the trilogy goes so far as to retitle book three of *Unconditional Surrender* (1961) 'The Last Battle'.[36] In *Men at Arms* Guy's first social circle is Bellamy's, the London club to which his family have always belonged and which he periodically revisits throughout the trilogy; but Bellamy's is linked to his pre-war state, and his closest associate there is Ian Kilbannock, the journalist and Scottish peer whose aim is to become 'one of the soft-faced men who did well out of the war' (*M* 26). Guy's military initiation comes with his first regiment, the Halberdiers, whose officers' mess is Waugh's closest equivalent to the Arthurian Round Table. At the same time, there is a farcical discrepancy between Guy's dream of belonging to a high company of warriors and the reality. As a volunteer in his mid-thirties he soon becomes known as 'Uncle', an old crock and a potential invalid. During the horseplay which is part of his first guest night in the officers' mess he sustains a knee injury which puts him out of action for weeks. Apthorpe, the other middle-aged subaltern in his company, represents an even more surreal version of Guy's military fantasy. But Apthorpe's comic battle with his brigadier which enlivens the tedium of military training is succeeded by the pointlessness of his death in a West African hospital, where he is killed, apparently, by the effects of a bottle of whisky thoughtlessly smuggled in by Guy. The mission that has taken them to West Africa—the 1940 commando assault on Dakar—is a military fiasco. Guy, who has approached it in the manner of a *Boy's Own*-style adventure, displays bravery under fire and saves his brigadier's life, but the night raid for which he has volunteered is an unofficial sideshow, and it leads to his expulsion from the Halberdiers.

There is a narrative of belated growing-up throughout *Men at Arms*. The Halberdiers are shown training at a requisitioned preparatory school under the command of Brigadier Ben Ritchie-Hook, recognizably a mad headmaster. At Dakar Ritchie-Hook joins the men on Guy's landing-craft and uses the occasion to collect a scalp or 'coconut', the head of an unfortunate Negro soldier. (This immoral and illegal expedition recalls the dark side of the medieval Crusades, commemorated across the centuries in English pub signs like the Turk's Head and the Saracen's Head.) Guy cannot be blamed for Ritchie-Hook's atrocity, and when he smuggles the whisky in to Apthorpe he does so with the encouragement of a superior officer; both incidents, however, reflect the gathering sense of dishonour surrounding his personal mission. A narrative model tacitly underlying the trilogy is the Arthurian story of Sir Gawain and the Green Knight, with the three tests that Gawain has to pass to escape execution. (He passes, but somewhat equivocally, so that one of the Green Knight's three sword strokes cuts open the skin of his neck.) Guy's first test, in effect a double test, takes place at the end of *Men at Arms*. His second test comes during the withdrawal from Crete at the end of *Officers and Gentlemen* (1955). The third and most serious test comes towards the climax of the final volume, *Unconditional Surrender*. Early in this volume Waugh writes that 'In the recesses of Guy's conscience there lay the belief that somewhere, somehow, something would be required of him; that he must be attentive to the summons when it came. . . . All that mattered was to recognize the chance when it offered.'[37] Once again there is a double test, as we shall see. Guy's conduct falls short of the standards of perfect heroism, but he is not dishonoured.

In general, Waugh's moral commentary is remarkably sparing. In a narrative that uses none of the experimental technical devices of Ford Madox Ford, the work of discrimination is nevertheless left to the reader. After Apthorpe's death, for example, Guy is harangued by a senior officer, but feels no sense of shame:

He felt shaken, as though he had seen a road accident in which he was not concerned. His fingers shook but it was nerves not conscience which troubled him; he was familiar with shame; this trembling, hopeless sense of disaster was something of quite another order; something that would pass and leave no mark. (*M* 242).

A Victorian novelist could not have described an incident such as this in third-person narrative without passing judgement on it, but how far we may trust Guy's intuitions at such moments is never made clear. Doubtless he has encouraged Apthorpe's dipsomania, but is he or is he not his brother's keeper? Where Ford Madox Ford seems tacitly to endorse his misunderstood hero, Waugh's laconic style suggests a world of moral uncertainty in which traditional notions of authority—whether that of a military commander or an omniscient fictional narrator—no longer apply. Such uncertainty has a precedent in the medieval romances in which the hero is plunged into a world of evil enchantments where nothing is what it seems.

There is another kind of evil enchantment in war fiction, when writers attempt to convey the physical experience of coming under fire. Ford's evocation of the impact of shelling in *No More Parades* is a tour de force of impressionist style. Waugh is at his most virtuoso in the extraordinary cluster of images used to describe a bombing raid on central London in the Blitz:

The sky over London was glorious, ochre and madder, as though a dozen tropic suns were simultaneously setting round the horizon; everywhere the searchlights clustered and hovered, then swept apart; here and there pitchy clouds drifted and billowed; now and then a huge flash momentarily froze the serene fireside glow. Everywhere the shells sparkled like Christmas baubles. . . .

Guy was momentarily reminded of Holy Saturday at Downside; early gusty March mornings of boyhood; the doors wide open in the unfinished butt of the Abbey; half the school coughing; fluttering linen; the glowing brazier and the priest with his hyssop, paradoxically blessing fire with water. . . .

A crescent scream immediately, it seemed, over their heads; a thud which raised the paving-stones under their feet; a tremendous incandescence just north of Piccadilly; a pentecostal wind; the remaining panes of glass above them scattered in lethal splinters about the street.[38]

These passages are interspersed with nonchalant, tight-lipped dialogue, as Guy and Ian Kilbannock do their best to dissemble the experience of awe and terror in the middle of the bombing. They are officers and gentlemen displaying what Ford had called the 'peculiarly English habit of self-suppression in matters of emotion' to the point of caricature. The dialogue expresses schoolboy one-upmanship and a literary class code, uniting Guy and Ian against inferior breeds such as 'progressive novelists in firemen's uniform' and air raid wardens: when the two men disagree over which Romantic painter would have caught the scene best, Guy 'would not accept correction on matters of art from this former sporting-journalist' (*O* 9). The series of descriptive images in the passage clearly begins with the pictorial—'ochre and madder' are artists' colours—but it proceeds through memories of Guy's Catholic public school (about which we otherwise hear very little) and an evocation of the Christian year from Christmas to Pentecost, the day of the descent of the Holy Ghost. The half-submerged images of the congregation, the open doors, and the passing of the holy fire through the church suggest not just the Catholic ritual but Malory's description of the coming of the Grail to Camelot:

Then anon they heard cracking and crying of thunder, that then thought the place should all to drive. In the midst of this blast entered a sunbeam more clearer by seven times than ever they saw day, and all they were alighted at the grace of the Holy Ghost. . . . Then there entered into the hall the Holy Greal covered with white samite, but there was none might see it, nor who bore it. . . . And when the

Holy Greal had been born through the hall, then the Holy Vessel departed suddenly, that they wist not where it became: then had they all breath to speak.[39]

Waugh was, no doubt, aware that T. S. Eliot in his poem 'Little Gidding' (1944) had used mystical Christian symbolism to evoke the bombing of London. Beneath the superficial jokiness of this opening scene of *Officers and Gentlemen* is the sense of Guy's rededication to his spiritual quest. (From his later perspective, as we shall see, he is still living in a 'Holy Land of illusion' (O 240) or enchantment.)

As if reflecting both the terror of war and its banality, *Sword of Honour* blends its moments of almost visionary solemnity with long episodes of broad farce. The first section of *Officers and Gentlemen*, featuring Ritchie-Hook as the leader of the commando unit Hookforce, is titled 'Happy Warriors'. While Guy is training in the Hebrides and waiting for action in Egypt the narrative turns aside to pursue the adventures of Trimmer, a war hero invented entirely by the media (represented here by the 'former sporting-journalist' Kilbannock). British propaganda requires a dashing, lower-class commando leader, and Trimmer, on the strength of one botched and shameful episode, becomes a national celebrity. Even Guy's saintly father is taken in by the newspaper stories about the former hairdresser. As Mr Crouchback naively reflects, 'When the country needs them, the right men come to the fore. . . . He downs his scissors and without any fuss carries out one of the most daring exploits in military history' (O 152). In *Officers and Gentlemen* not only is the 'hero' not a real hero, but constant transformations of identity mean that nobody is what he seems to be. Apthorpe's old African comrade 'Chatty' Corner becomes King Kong, while Guy, as he approaches Corner's Hebridean lair, becomes Browning's medieval knight Childe Roland. But at the end of the novel the make-believe world of Hookforce is exposed to an unsparing test of reality, in the doomed Cretan adventure which ends in headlong retreat.

Waugh's Cretan narrative has been criticized for its inexplicitness,[40] but the moral judgements passed on the characters, though cryptic, can hardly be missed. Major Hound tells Colonel Tickeridge that ' "They say it's *sauve qui peut* now" ', to which Tickeridge, every inch a Halberdier, replies ' "Don't know the expression" ' (O 179). Hound is manifestly a 'lost soul' (177), whether or not he is one of two people murdered by the ruthless *sauve qui peut* expert Ludovic. Then there is Ivor Claire, the dashing commando whom Guy hero-worships in the earlier part of *Officers and Gentlemen*: 'Ivor Claire, Guy thought, was the fine flower of them all. He was quintessential England, the man Hitler had not taken into account, Guy thought' (O 114). In his 1965 revision Waugh cut out the final 'Guy thought' which he doubtless found overemphatic, but it underlines the extent to which his protagonist has been taken in by an officer whose civilian avocation, appropriately enough, was showjumping. Claire leaves his men to their fate in Crete in order to avoid being taken prisoner himself, abandoning the 'path of honour' (O 221) while Guy, who also escapes back to Egypt, manages to preserve his honour. During the battle of Crete Guy comes upon the body of a dead Catholic soldier, who reminds him of Sir Roger de Waybroke and whose identity tag he secures, intending to return it to headquarters. But in Cairo he entrusts it to the socialite Julia Stitch, who destroys it under the impression that it is a deposition concerning Ivor Claire.

Guy is unaware of Julia's treachery—his disenchantment proceeds at a different pace from the reader's—but his recuperation in Cairo coincides with a momentous world event, Hitler's invasion of Russia, which all but destroys his personal crusade. During the two years (1939–41) of the Nazi-Soviet Pact, Guy has sought to defend Christendom against the 'Modern Age in arms', but once Britain is allied with the Soviet Union his sense of being part of a national crusade disappears: 'he was back after less than two years' pilgrimage in a Holy Land of illusion in the old ambiguous world, where priests were spies and gallant friends proved traitors and his country was led blundering into dishonour' (O 240). The happy warrior is now disenchanted. His growing detestation of the wartime alliance is suggested in book one of *Unconditional Surrender*, 'State Sword', where the central symbol is an actual sword manufactured at the King's command in 1943 for presentation to Stalin as a gift to the people of Stalingrad.[41] This 'sword of honour', put on display in Westminster Abbey, is supposed to have been suggested to the King by Trimmer. But, whatever the moral fate of the nation, in *Unconditional Surrender* Guy's personal honour is once again (almost) vindicated.

Guy was most closely identified with the nation's war aims when Britain was fighting alone against the Axis powers. He reflects (in a passage that Waugh deleted in 1965) that 'There was in romance great virtue in unequal odds' (M 174). Once Russia and America have joined in on Britain's side victory is certain, but Guy's Catholic chivalry makes him increasingly isolated. He is no longer a Halberdier and cannot rejoin his old battalion even when he comes across them fighting a rearguard action in Crete. Like most of the British land forces he is condemned to long years of tedium and inactivity. Soldiers, he reflects, 'should be laid away in their boxes in the nursery cupboard' between engagements; they should 'repose among the briar like the knights of the Sleeping Beauty' (*O* 84). In *Unconditional Surrender* his romantic reveries are contrasted with the dark romanticism of Ludovic, the increasingly paranoid officer who becomes a bestselling novelist. Ludovic's childhood has 'furnished few models of chivalry' (*U* 37), but he makes his name with *The Death Wish*, a melodramatic tale of the pre-war cosmopolitan aristocracy. (According to Waugh's friend and biographer Christopher Sykes, the novel and its success are a send-up of *Brideshead Revisited*.)[42] Another crucial character in *Unconditional Surrender* is Guy's estranged wife, Virginia, who finds herself pregnant with Trimmer's child and, having failed to procure an abortion, decides to go through with the birth. Guy, as a Catholic, will not divorce his wife and, to his friends' dismay, he agrees to a reconciliation. After he has been posted to Yugoslavia Virginia converts to the Catholic faith, gives birth, and is promptly killed by a flying bomb. Guy's legal son and heir escapes uninjured. As Guy's brother-in-law resentfully concludes somewhat later, ' "things have turned out very conveniently" ' for Waugh's protagonist (239).

At the time of his reconciliation with Virginia, he is forced to defend his actions by a friend who finds his behaviour foolish and deluded. To her charge that ' "men aren't chivalrous any more" ', he replies that

'Knights errant . . . used to go out looking for noble deeds. I don't think I've ever in my life done a single, positively unselfish action. I certainly haven't gone out of my way to find opportunities. Here was something most unwelcome, put into my hands; something which I believe the Americans describe as "beyond the call of duty"; not the normal behaviour of an officer and a gentleman; something they'll laugh about in Bellamy's.' (*U* 151)

If chivalry sets Guy apart from his fellow clubmen and brother officers, it also compensates for the virtual impotence of which Virginia accuses him. In an outburst reminiscent of Sylvia Tietjens she denounces his whole 'over-bred and under-sexed' race: ' "You're dying out as a family," she continued. . . . "Why do you Crouchbacks do so little——ing?" ' (*U* 146). At the end of *Unconditional Surrender* Guy has fathered two more sons after the war, although in the 1965 revision of the text Waugh significantly removed this detail. Guy has found a successor without actually begetting one.

Guy's chivalry is put to a different kind of test in Yugoslavia. As in his previous military exploits his success is equivocal and he is shown to be well intentioned but blundering and naive. He flies from the Italian city of Bari (a port that he associates with the Crusades) to take up his post as liaison officer with the Communist partisans, who constitute a new kind of secret society or round table from which he is firmly excluded. His old regimental colleague Frank de Souza arrives on a short visit and achieves a level of access to the partisan leaders that Guy can only envy: 'They trusted him and treated his advice with a respect they would not have accorded to Guy or even Brigadier Cape; or for that matter to General Alexander or Mr Winston Churchill' (U 207). De Souza, of course, is a Communist Party member, and other British officers—like the major at Bari who is shown 'dispatching royalist officers—though he did not know it—to certain execution' (U 234) do the Communists' bidding. Guy, however, tries to save the lives of a group of Jewish refugees whom the partisans allege to be guilty of collaboration and class treachery. He saves all but two of them since, led astray by personal kindness, he foolishly compromises their spokeswoman Madame Kanyi and her husband.

Guy's thoughtlessness in this case, like his chivalry in taking on Virginia's child, should be judged according to the spiritual principle expressed by his devout Catholic father in his last letter to his son. 'Quantitative judgements don't apply,' Mr Crouchback wrote. 'If only one soul was saved that is full compensation for any amount of loss of "face"' (U 17). If this principle applies positively in Guy's reconciliation with Virginia it also applies negatively, so that the rescue of the vast majority of the Jewish refugees is no compensation for his failure to protect the Kanyis. Doubtless Guy is a victim of his times and of the death of chivalry in the modern world, a conclusion that is reinforced by the novel's ironic final scene of a commando reunion at the time of the Festival of Britain. Waugh's comment on the state of the nation at the beginning of this scene—'In 1951, to celebrate the opening of a happier decade, the government decreed a Festival' (U 237)—is commendably restrained. But the mid-century celebrations of an ageing group of happy warriors are overshadowed by our memory of Madame Kanyi's last words to Guy, a speech that once again illustrates Waugh's deft modulation from melodrama and farce to romantic moral seriousness.

Shortly before Guy's last meeting with the Jewish refugee, Ritchie-Hook has been killed leading a suicidal attack on an enemy strongpoint in an operation which, as he well knows, is only a publicity stunt put on by the partisans to impress visiting dignitaries. Now Guy's moment of self-understanding is prompted by the words of a woman who knows him only slightly:

'It seems to me there was a will to war, a death wish, everywhere. Even good men thought their private honour would be satisfied by war. They could assert their manhood by killing and being killed. They would accept hardships in recompense for having been selfish and lazy. Danger justified privilege. I knew Italians—not very many perhaps—who felt this. Were there none in England?'

'God forgive me,' said Guy. 'I was one of them.' (*U* 232)

It does not matter that Guy has not actually killed anyone. In Mr Crouchback's dogmatic moral terms, what must really count is that, although Guy's attempts to rescue two damsels in distress (Virginia and Madame Kanyi) both failed, one of the women died in the Catholic faith. Catholic and non-Catholic readers may differ sharply as to whether this affects the value of his actions, but, as we have seen, Guy's knight-errantry is surrounded by ambiguities from beginning to end. Waugh allows the actions and events of the trilogy to speak for themselves, and his only attempt to enforce a final verdict comes through the words of Madame Kanyi. Her judgement applies to the whole history of aristocratic chivalry and the romance of the knight in shining armour, not simply to one uncharacteristic Englishman's battle against the 'Modern Age'.

Anthony Powell: A Guest at the Arthurian Table

The twelve volumes of *A Dance to the Music of Time* follow the changing fortunes of a largely aristocratic circle of young men growing up in the 1920s, and of their older counterparts who have fought in the First World War. The sequence traces their lives through to the beginnings of old age, bringing them into contact with the hippy generation of the 1960s. The narrator Nicholas Jenkins remains fascinated by his Etonian contemporaries Peter Templer, Charles Stringham, and Kenneth Widmerpool, the first two of whom perish in the Second World War. Further links are made through Jenkins's father (an army officer), at Oxford, at the dances and balls of 1920s London, and in the bohemian and artistic world where Jenkins finds employment. Out of these overlapping circles come the sequence's epic talkers—the alcoholic Stringham, the composer Hugh Moreland, and the failed novelist X. Trapnel—together with the women who haunt them, above all Pamela Flitton who marries Widmerpool and destroys the manuscript of Trapnel's last novel. Widmerpool himself, the 'Frog Footman' whose unstoppable rise to power and fame is unaffected by farcical episodes of humiliation and self-abasement, is the great comic figure of the series. From volume to volume his metamorphoses provide an endless supply of gossip reported to us by the self-effacing but wonderfully observant narrator.

Powell creates a conspectus of English upper-class eccentricity while at the same time portraying a feature of the national culture rather little emphasized by earlier novelists: its endemic revivalism. The atmosphere of the novels is deeply literary, with allusions to classical and neoclassical sources, to Robert Burton's seventeenth-century *Anatomy of Melancholy* (from which the later volumes in the sequence occasionally take long quotations), and to medieval romances of various kinds. Nicholas Jenkins has a mythical ancestor, the Celtic warlord Llywarch the Old who is described as 'a discontented guest at the Arthurian table'.[43] Llywarch's discontent suggests that of his fellow Welshman Perceval, the archetypal hero at the centre of Powell's later novel *The Fisher King*, which is a deliberate rewriting of Arthurian myth. In *The Fisher King* Valentine Beals, a popular novelist whose latest work is *Lancelot's Love Feast*, explains that Perceval was turned down for the Round Table because he was 'too young, too uncouth, too lacking in the sort of chic required of an Arthurian knight'.[44] It may be pressing too hard to insist on a parallel with the self-effacing and generally underestimated narrator of *The Music of Time*. More striking is Powell's very detailed allusion in the final volume of the sequence, *Hearing Secret Harmonies* (1975), to another of the classic romances of chivalry, Ariosto's epic poem *Orlando Furioso* (1532).

In *Hearing Secret Harmonies* it is Widmerpool, in his last incarnation as the follower of a magic cult, whose madness is likened to that of Orlando, one of Charlemagne's knights. Orlando 'drops out', as Powell puts it, and roams naked through the countryside after he has been abandoned by his beloved Angelica. Widmerpool, similarly, is found 'waging war against a society he had renounced' after his wife's suicide.[45] Orlando is eventually rescued thanks to the persistence of Astolpho, an English duke, who travels to the moon and retrieves his comrade's wits from what Powell calls the Valley of Lost Things. There are various possible candidates for the role of Astolpho in *Hearing Secret Harmonies* (and in any case Widmerpool's wits are irretrievably lost), but the English peer rummaging through the Valley of Lost Things—a kind of planetary junk-shop—suggests the patient, almost scholarly restorative acts of Powell the novelist and his narrator. What the dance of time has taken away from us can be recovered through the medium of fiction. The image suggests eternal recurrence and a cyclical view of history, but it also suggests the retrieval, almost the resurrection, of a lost aristocratic England. *The Music of Time* is itself cyclical, with its final images of a winter bonfire and workmen standing round a brazier returning us to the

opening pages of *A Question of Upbringing* (1951) written a quarter of
a century earlier. Within the fifty-year timespan of his story Powell also
portrays the cycle of artistic taste and cultural consumption, as the
forgotten novelists and painters of Jenkins's youth come back into fashion,
a process described by the narrator as 'not so much a Resurrection as a
Second Coming' (*HSH* 227).

Powell's characters give the impression of forming a well-defined social
circle although on closer inspection it may seem that this circle exists only
in the mind of Jenkins, the narrator. The idea of a community held
together by the mysterious and fantastic conjunctions thrown up by the
'music of time', and not just by sociological proximity, is both a structural
necessity of the sequence and a recurring Jenkinsian hobby horse. The
image of a tournament or chivalric competition involving Jenkins and his
contemporaries is first used by Sillery, the Oxford tutor, who speaks of
the 'glittering prizes' open to 'those with stout hearts and sharp swords'
(*AW* 120). Sillery takes it for granted that the young knights in this
competition will also be his protégés; and in Powell's world a stout heart
and sharp sword count for little unless one is born with, or can acquire,
the credentials necessary to enter the contest in the first place. Except in
childhood, adolescence, and old age, the world of *The Music of Time* is
largely metropolitan. Within it, the narrator observes how people in
certain professions, notably politicians, writers, and musicians, tend to
form small cliques or 'charmed circles'.[46] Jenkins is adept at penetrating
into or at least overhearing the talk in such circles, which are bound
together by the mysterious quality of 'influence' first identified by the
dottily eccentric Uncle Giles: 'It was an article of faith with [my uncle]
that all material advancement in the world was a result of influence, a
mysterious attribute with which he invested, to a greater or lesser degree,
every human being on earth except himself.'[47] Giles's philosophy is
endorsed by the single-minded careerist Widmerpool, who patronizingly
declares that ' "Brains and hard work are of very little avail, Jenkins,
unless you know the right people" ' (*QU* 133).

In Powell's narrative the 'right people' keep on encountering and
re-encountering one another, sometimes at large social gatherings such as
country-house weekends, fashionable parties, and public dinners, but also
as a result of chance proximity during an air raid or in the street. Evelyn
Waugh believed that the often fortuitous narrative connections in *The
Music of Time* were a kind of 'genuine social realism', as well as satisfying
the artificial necessities of the novelist's art: the degree of personal
interplay between the characters would not have been possible, he

thought, either in the 'looser society' of the United States or the 'tighter society' of Western Europe.[48] The connections are, of course, all made by Jenkins the narrator, and their prominence results from his usually very rigorous selection and foreshortening of the details of his experience. The more unlikely his encounters, the greater their occult resonance. In *Hearing Secret Harmonies* the Reverend Paul Fenneau tells Jenkins of his 'deeply held conviction...as to the repetitive contacts of certain individual souls in the earthly lives of other individual souls' (*HSH* 120). Fenneau is a figure specially invented for Powell's final volume—though he claims to have been a contemporary of Jenkins's at university, we have never heard of him previously—and we might therefore view him with suspicion as a medium for authorial self-justification. But he is also the last in a series of recurring characters—notably Myra Erdleigh, Dr Trelawney, and Scorpio Murtlock—who appear in the sequence as Merlin-like wizards and mages, aware of the workings of destiny that determine the recurrence of individual characters and events. Thus, on the one hand, we have the sociological shrewdness of Kucherman, the Belgian liaison officer in *The Military Philosophers* (1968), who instantly understands the extent to which the British ruling class is a closed circle: ' "Your fathers were in the War Office too," ' he tells Jenkins, who seems almost dumbfounded by this observation.[49] On the other hand there is Myra Erdleigh casting Pamela Flitton's horoscope, identifying her as being 'under Scorpio' and as possessing 'many of the scorpion's cruellest traits'. ' "I fear she loves disaster and death," ' Mrs Erdleigh adds (*MP* 136), thus setting out the plot line for the next two novels and preparing the ground for Pamela's eventual successor, Scorpio Murtlock.

Although *The Music of Time* cannot be reduced to Arthurian allegory—its characters and situations are much too various for that—in the early novels Powell's Camelot is Stourwater, the country mansion of the tycoon Sir Magnus Donners where Jenkins is an infrequent and marginal guest. Stringham and Widmerpool are quick to join Donners's circle. The house itself is a neo-Gothic folly which strikes Jenkins as a 'Hollywood film set' rather than a home: 'Here was the Middle Age, from the pages of Tennyson or Scott, at its most elegant.'[50] Donners likes to take his friends on a tour of the 'dungeons' and to tie up some unsuspecting young lady guest; Widmerpool, on Jenkins's first visit, confesses that he has just rescued a damsel in distress (he has paid for Gipsy Jones's abortion) and then backs his car, an unruly charger, into a Gothic flowerpot. At Stourwater Jenkins meets Jean Templer, his first love, who is 'like a great lady in a medieval triptych or carving' (*AW* 141), while her admirers—her victims, as he comes to think—are 'gothic too, beings carved on the niches and corbels of a medieval cathedral to arouse at once laughter and horror'.[51] During Jenkins's second visit to Stourwater in *The Kindly Ones* (1962), his wife Isobel is reminded of the *Morte d'Arthur*'s Castle of Joyous Gard with its associations of Arthur and Guinevere. On this occasion in the summer of 1939 Sir Magnus's guests dress up in a game of charades based on the medieval Seven Deadly Sins, a game that is finally broken up by the sudden arrival of Widmerpool in battledress, 'a sinister, threatening figure, calling the world to arms' (*KO* 136). With the onset of war, both Donners and, in due course, Widmerpool move to Whitehall, which now takes over the position of Camelot. Soon Widmerpool rather than Donners appears as the sequence's representative of worldly power, in effect its King Arthur.

Widmerpool is initially a social outsider, despised at Eton for his physical awkwardness but also because he is the son of a liquid manure merchant. His almost manic determination to succeed, first manifested at school in his indomitable cross-country running in all weathers, is finally encapsulated in the reported circumstances of his death: he is struck down by a heart attack while out jogging with the other members of Murtlock's commune, his last words being ' "I'm leading, I'm leading now" ' (*HSH* 249). If Widmerpool must always fight his way to the front of the pack, he is also, in Jenkins's words, 'an archetypal figure, one of those fabulous monsters that haunt the recesses of the individual imagination' (*MP* 202). He of all Powell's characters is, in the terms set out in the eleventh volume, a 'temporary king' or carnivalesque figure whose absurd coronation is a sign of the world having been turned upside down.[52]

Powell's achievement has been seen as to some extent an imitation of Proust's *A la recherche du temps perdu*, to which Jenkins pays generous tribute in *The Military Philosophers*. But the comparison is at best superficial.[53] Powell's subject is not the recovery of Proustian lost time, but the tragicomedy of repetition and recurrence as seen in the English governing class across half a century. He is self-consciously in the English tradition, despite his disparaging remarks about such predecessors as Trollope, Woolf, and D. H. Lawrence. From the moment when Jenkins, as a would-be novelist, begins to 'brood on the complexity of writing a novel about English life', we are aware that the society he is describing has a national idiosyncrasy quite as marked as that of Proust's French aristocracy. Jenkins continues with the reflection that 'Intricacies of social life make English habits unyielding to simplification, while understatement and irony—in which all classes of this island converse—upset the normal emphasis of reported speech' (*AW* 38). The opacity of English life meets its match in Powell's scrupulously elaborate, often ponderous style, with its air of self-mockery which exerts an irresistible hold over the novelist's devotees.

Consider the opening of *The Soldier's Art* (1966)—to do Powell justice he must be quoted at length:

When, at the start of the whole business, I bought an army greatcoat, it was at one of those places in the neighbourhood of Shaftesbury Avenue, where, as well as officers' kit and outfits for sport, they hire or sell theatrical costume. [. . .] The deal was negotiated in an upper room, dark and mysterious, draped with skiing gear and riding breeches, in the background of which, behind the glass windows of a high display case, two headless trunks stood rigidly at attention. One of these effigies wore Harlequin's diagonally spangled tights; the other, scarlet full-dress uniform of some infantry regiment, allegorical figures, so it seemed, symbolising dualisms of the antithetical stock-in trade surrounding them ... Civil and Military ... Work and Play ... Detachment and Involvement ... Tragedy and Comedy ... War and Peace ... Life and Death ...

An assistant, bent, elderly, bearded, with the congruous demeanour of a Levantine trader, bore the greatcoat out of a secret recess in the shadows and reverently invested me with its double-breasted, brass-buttoned, stiffly pleated khaki folds. [. . .] In a three-sided full-length looking-glass nearby I [. . .] critically examined the back view of the coat's shot-at-dawn cut, aware at the same time that soon, like Alice, I was to pass, as it were by virtue of these habiliments, through its panes into a world no less enigmatic.

'How's that, sir?'

'All right, I think.'

'Might be made for you.'

'Not a bad fit.'

Loosening now quite slowly the buttons, one by one, he paused as if considering some matter, and gazed intently.

'I believe I know your face,' he said.

'You do?'

'Was it *The Middle Watch*?'

'Was what the middle watch?'

'The show I saw you in.'

I have absolutely no histrionic talent, none at all, a constitutional handicap in almost all the undertakings of life; but then, after all, plenty of actors possess little enough. There was no reason why he should not suppose the Stage to be my profession as well as any other. [. . .] Accepting the classification, however sobering, I did no more than deny having played in that particular knockabout. He helped me out of the sleeves, gravely shaking straight their creases.

'What's this one for?' he asked.

'Which one?'
'The overcoat—if I might make bold to enquire?'
'Just the war.'
'Ah,' he said attentively, '*The War*...'[54]

We notice in this lovingly drawn-out scene the blatancy of the symbolism of the tailor's dummies, the element of literary fantasy introduced by the allusion to Lewis Carroll, and the orotund narrative phrasing set off against drably monosyllabic dialogue. The latter's effect of comic understatement depends entirely on the presence and absence of italics (*The Middle Watch*, *The War*) to suggest inflections of the spoken voice. This passage bears on one of Powell's great themes, the extent to which the life of the English ruling class has become a charade or costume drama whose real significance remains hidden. Jenkins claims to be disdainful of Sir Magnus's playacting at Stourwater, but he spends much of the 1930s writing filmscripts and is an unfailing guide to the roles played by his contemporaries and the disguises in which they appear.

With Powell's war trilogy (*The Valley of Bones*, *The Soldier's Art*, and *The Military Philosophers*) the costume drama becomes more ominous. Going through his deceased uncle's effects in 1939, Jenkins discovers Uncle Giles's officer's commission from Queen Victoria, and wonders what sort of figure he himself will cut as a soldier. In the event he undergoes regimental training but spends most of his time as a staff officer in intelligence and Allied liaison in London. He witnesses the rapid rise of Widmerpool, whose position as a colonel attached to the prime minister's office leads directly to his post-war career as a Member of Parliament, knight, and life peer. Widmerpool uses his position in the army to determine the fates of Jenkins's other schoolfriends Templer and Stringham, each of whom becomes, in his way, a hero.

We hear little about Templer's fate, killed on a secret mission in Eastern Europe after a change of political alliance at headquarters. He was apparently sacrificed, with Widmerpool's knowledge, in accordance with what Powell calls the 'military philosophy' of victory at all costs— the cynical reverse of Guy Crouchback's moral code. Needless to say, Widmerpool's unscrupulousness serves his own interests as well as the nation's. His betrayal of the chivalric ideal contrasts with the humility and saintliness of Stringham, the last scion of an old aristocratic family and by now a reformed alcoholic. Stringham joins up in the ranks, and Widmerpool has him posted to the Far East where he will no longer be an embarrassment to his old schoolfellows. Jenkins tries to persuade him not to go, but Stringham, who identifies with Browning's doomed knight-errant Childe Roland, is adamant in accepting his destiny. He is captured at Singapore and dies in a Japanese prison camp; all that we learn from Powell's deliberately restrained presentation is that he 'behaved very well there' (*TK* 215). Stringham is the Christian hero of *The Music of Time*, whose forgiveness of his fellows extends even to Widmerpool. This makes it all the more ironic that Pamela Flitton, the evil woman of the later parts of the trilogy, is his niece.

In the novels of Ford, Waugh, and Powell the male companionship of the army is set against the machinations of a *femme fatale* from whom the protagonist finds it difficult if not impossible to extricate himself. Sylvia tortures and rails against Tietjens; Guy Crouchback is heartlessly betrayed by Virginia; and Nicholas Jenkins suffers deeply from the duplicity of Jean Templer. It is true that Tietjens and Jenkins eventually find happiness with somewhat more pallid 'good women'—Valentine and Isobel—reminding us of the contrast of Scott's dark and light heroines. Jenkins then employs all his powers of literary mythologization to describe the impact of Pamela, the sequence's second dark heroine, on Widmerpool (whom she eventually marries) and her other victims. Pamela is compared to Circe, Judith, Delilah, Salome, and Le Belle Dame sans Merci,[55] but above all she is portrayed as Morgan le Fay, the sister and inveterate enemy of King Arthur and the Round Table.

The last three novels of *The Music of Time* are dominated by Pamela and another new character, the novelist X. Trapnel who appears in person only in *Books Do Furnish a Room* (1971). Trapnel is never seen without a theatrical prop, his swordstick with its knob carved in the shape of a skull. His seduction of Pamela makes him Launcelot to Widmerpool's King Arthur, and to this extent Pamela is his Guinevere. The swordstick is a magical sceptre like Excalibur—while Trapnel holds it, he is an up-and-coming novelist, but without it he is lost—and Pamela increasingly appears not just as a vengeful mistress but as the evil sister of Arthurian legend. She appears at a funeral early in the novel as an 'appropriate attendant on death', and her wartime sex life is described as 'gladiatorial'.[56] Unforgettably, Trapnel tells Jenkins what Pamela is like in bed: ' "She wants it all the time, yet doesn't want it. She goes rigid like a corpse" ' (*BFR* 239). At the culmination of *Books Do Furnish a Room* she throws the manuscript of Trapnel's new novel into the Regent's Canal, claiming that it is not worthy of him, and Trapnel throws in his swordstick after it: 'A mystic arm should certainly have risen from the dark waters of the mere to receive it. That did not happen' (*BFR* 237). Trapnel, it seems, is essentially a second-rate novelist, a poseur who was at his best holding court in the Hero of Acre pub in Fitzrovia, the district that had taken over from Bloomsbury as the post-war headquarters of literary London. He is one of the 'great egoists' (*BFR* 167) of *The Music of Time*, an actor or role-player rather than an artist. After his death he becomes a literary legend and the subject of the biography that the American Gothic scholar Russell Gwinnett eventually publishes as *Death's-Head Swordsman*. He is present in spirit at Pamela's death in Gwinnett's arms in *Temporary Kings* and, perhaps, at the death of Widmerpool in *Hearing Secret Harmonies*.

Pamela as sadist and necrophiliac initiates both Trapnel and Widmerpool into what one critic calls 'The Abyss of Carnality', a darker costume drama hidden beneath the social surface.[57] This corrupt sexual masquerade (which parallels Proust's portrayal of the French aristocracy) is a sign of what Jenkins calls 'the general disintegration of society in its traditional form' (*AW* 128). In one of his numerous Gothic similes, he compares both society between the wars and (by extension) his own narrative to a ride on a ghost train rushing headlong past frightening obstacles towards a 'shape that lay across the line' (*CCR* 221). The image suggests the decadent, gaudy unreality of fashionable upper-class society while leaving it ambiguous whether the corpse on the line portends a final apocalyptic collision, or simply one more macabre element in the charade. Nevertheless, from the point of view of Jenkins's sanity, moral scruple, and good humour, the energies unleashed by Pamela and Widmerpool are self-destructive and do not in the end prevail. Jenkins is fully aware of the absurdity of his old schoolfellow's final incarnation as the populist Lord 'Ken' Widmerpool, a 'man in a life-and-death grapple with the decadent society round him' (*TK* 20). Jenkins, too, sees revival and resurrection as features of late twentieth-century English life, alongside its undeniable decay.

In *Hearing Secret Harmonies* Scorpio Murtlock and his followers form a 'sacred circle' (*HSH* 156) so that they can indulge in group sex at an ancient monument known as the Devil's Fingers. Nearby is another prehistoric site, the Whispering Knights, where a group of treacherous knights were turned to stone by a witch. The two images sum up the more sinister side of *The Music of Time*. But against them should be put the elements of rebirth in Powell's final volume, such as the revival of Trelawneyism, the rediscovery of Edgar Deacon's pictures, and the publication of Gwinnett's biography of Trapnel. New characters from the young generation, like Murtlock and the Quiggin twins, take up roles left vacant by those who have gone before. If death and, above all, the death of Widmerpool is the inevitable outcome, the novels also harbour eccentric mystics such as Trelawney and Murtlock who deny the reality of death. Jenkins's own narrative quest is inconclusive, since the full truth beneath the costume drama can, it is hinted, never be known. With his insatiable appetite for gossip he has apparently penetrated the scandalous sexual secrets of most of his fellows, proving himself to be, in his way, as much of a voyeur as Widmerpool at his most debauched. At the same time, his observation that, while 'few subjects are more fascinating than other people's sexual habits from the outside', most people's sex life remains mysterious—especially that of those who 'seem to make most parade of it'—remains valid (MP 113–14). Jenkins is obsessed with recording these past events which, on his own account, can never be fully understood, while he seems completely uninterested in the future and in his own family—traits which suggest, as one critic has sharply observed, that 'all is not quite right with his world'.[58]

Nevertheless, Powell's achievement is more subtle in one crucial respect than those of Ford and Waugh, since Jenkins, his 'uncharacteristic Englishman', is not himself the centre of the fictional circle. That place must be ceded to Widmerpool, the self-absorbed 'man of the will' who is the most protean of Powell's characters since he seems to sum up the whole costume drama in his own person. Finally he becomes a deluded and cheated holy man, a King Arthur who has voluntarily thrown away his sword by putting himself in the power of Pamela's successor Scorpio Murtlock. Unlovable, gauche, self-destructive, and unstoppable, Widmerpool is not merely Powell's crazed knight and carnival king but, perhaps, the English novel's most telling embodiment of post-imperial, post-aristocratic national delusions. In the moment of his death he is still out in front, so he thinks, and holding the torch for a new generation to whom he is little more than a laughing stock.

Inward Migrations: Multiculturalism, Anglicization, and Internal Exile

K ARIM AMIR, the narrator of Hanif Kureishi's *The Buddha of Suburbia* (1990), introduces himself as 'an Englishman born and bred, almost. I am often considered to be a funny kind of Englishman, a new breed as it were, having emerged from two old histories. But I don't care—Englishman I am (though not proud of it), from the South London suburbs and going somewhere.'[1] As critics have noted, the much-quoted opening passage of Kureishi's novel has the quality of a mission statement for a new world in which cultures and traditions are intermingled and hybrid fusion is the norm.[2] Nevertheless Karim, born in London of an Indian father and an English mother, is an Englishman by any standards except those of the racial extremist. His Englishness, as he acknowledges, is a given identity, not a matter of choice. Writing for an American readership in 1964, the novelist John Fowles set out to distinguish English from British identity, describing the latter as 'an organizational convenience, a political advisability, a passport word'. His definition of Englishness, though conservative and racially exclusive in its orientation, clearly includes Karim: 'It is having at least two grandparents out of four English; having lived at least half one's life in England; having been educated at an English school; and of course having English as a mother tongue.'[3] Fowles's stipulation of two grandparents out of four introduces a racial element while allowing for the possibility of mixed parenthood which must be part of any healthy and dynamic community. What are we to make, however, of first-generation immigrants for whom England must necessarily be a country of adoption? According to Fowles, only their children or grandchildren may become English. Is the 'organizational convenience' of Britishness the most to which they can aspire, or do people become English by self-identification? The novel of immigration—now recognized as the most vital form of English fiction at the beginning of the twenty-first century—considers these questions.

The 'Buddha of suburbia' in Kureishi's novel is not Karim but his father Haroon, who meets none of Fowles's conditions but is more proud of his Englishness than his son is. Haroon and his brother Anwar have chosen Britain over India, living, so far as they could, 'like Englishmen' (64) in the South London suburbs for some twenty years. Haroon, with an English wife and an English mistress, brings up his children to consider themselves English despite the hostility of their racist neighbours. At the same time, he trades on his Indian origins by setting up as a guru expounding Eastern religion and philosophy to the inhabitants of sub-urbia. His desire to be English is inseparable from his ambivalence about being English. We may say, perhaps, that for Haroon and other members of post-imperial immigrant groups national and racial origins are a source of local identification, since he willingly accepts that Indians and English are destined to live side by side in the wider society to which he now belongs. His residual anti-English feeling is not unlike the forms of class, caste, and regional hostility that English society has long learned to accommodate.

Throughout his childhood in India Haroon was convinced of his superiority to the British rulers, a feeling that was confirmed when he came to their home country and saw, for the first time, English people doing menial jobs and living in poverty. He wants both to be Indian and to make a better job of being English than most of the English do. His son has inherited his belief that the British were 'exhausted now; their Empire was gone; their day was done and it was our turn' (250). Haroon, an office worker, could move to England easily because there was a demand for his labour there; and he inhabits modern London which, in the words of one recent literary historian, is 'no longer the centre of an empire', but 'an international city of racial and cultural mixtures'.[4]

Hanif Kureishi emerged as a critic of traditional ideas of English national identity in *The Rainbow Sign* (1986), an essay published at the height of Margaret Thatcher's Conservative revival and just a few years after rioting devastated the poorest areas of Britain's inner cities. According to Kureishi, the racism and xenophobia of ordinary people gave the lie to George Orwell's praise of English gentleness and tolerance. Black British people wanted the social justice they were denied, not a show of tolerance and condescension. Most of British society, in Kureishi's view, had yet to learn that 'being British isn't what it was. Now it is a more complex thing, involving new elements'.[5] In terms of public debate, the acceptance of multiculturalism soon became part of the liberal orthodoxy of British society, although the 'mainstream' English novel was slow to register much change. In 1996 the critic James Wood noted a turn towards 'novels of Englishness—rather than English novels', but judged that 'what most of these books proved was that English writing in the last thirty years has largely failed to tell convincing national stories'. Wood blamed this failure on 'the weight of tradition'.[6] It could be argued that he was looking in the wrong place and that the fiction of immigrant communities in England deserved far more attention than it was then receiving. By the time that Wood was writing there was already a century-old tradition of novels about immigration into Britain.

Earlier generations had had a rather different idea of the 'new England' of the twentieth century that was waiting to be discovered and recorded in literature. A significant example is J. B. Priestley's *English Journey* (1934), published six years before Orwell's celebration of Englishness in *The Lion and the Unicorn*. Like Orwell, Priestley was both a successful novelist and a lover of 'little England'—that is, of non-expansionist, non-imperial England.[7] But much of what he noted in his tour of the country was neither the legacy of traditional England nor of the empire. Its 'real birthplace', instead, was America:

This is the England of arterial and by-pass roads, of filling stations and factories that look like exhibition buildings, of giant cinemas and dance-halls and cafés, bungalows with tiny garages, cocktail bars, Woolworths, motor-coaches, wireless, hiking, factory-girls looking like actresses, greyhound racing and dirt tracks, swimming pools, and everything given away for cigarette coupons. (401)

Predictably Priestley complains that the new England of global capitalism, the internal combustion engine, and Art Deco is 'lacking in character' (405). The people in this mechanized landscape are dwarfed by the buildings, and, whether dolled up 'like actresses' or hidden away in their cars, they do not inspire patriotic feeling. Set beside the poverty and industrial depression that Priestley described in Lancashire and the North-East, the prosperous London suburbs, 'built-up areas', and dormitory towns are featureless and bland, a cheap, tasteless mixture of imported styles spreading like a blight across the countryside.

Priestley begins *English Journey* with a trip to Southampton, but while he notes the romance of the great ocean liners he could have no intimation that, fifteen years later, this would be the port of disembarkation for thousands of first-time immigrants into Britain. Instead, he refers disparagingly to cheap stores selling 'the brittle spoils of Czecho-Slovakia and Japan', and to gramophones playing 'tunes concocted by Polish Jews fifteen stories above Broadway' (16–17). It is not until he reaches his home town of Bradford in Yorkshire that Priestley reminds us that cheapness of manufacture is essential to the success of any industrial and trading nation. Moreover, imitation and immigration go together. Bradford in the nineteenth century underwent a 'friendly invasion' of 'intelligent aliens', German and German-Jewish merchants, so that 'in those days a Londoner was a stranger sight than a German' (158, 160).[8] But in the twentieth century, Priestley reports, the city has become more provincial and less cosmopolitan. Priestley never reconciles his admiration for the 'leavening process' of immigration with his professed Little Englandism. Nor does his concern with the decay and demoralization of the old industrial centres lead him to analyse the relationship of the regions to the metropolis. His journey begins and ends in London, but he cannot wait to get out of the city. Priestley, unlike Ford Madox Ford in *England and the English*, does full justice to provincial England, especially England north of the Trent; and he implies very strongly that the heart of the country is to be found not in the metropolis, nor in suburbia, but in the provinces.

Both Priestley and Ford are writers whose ideas of national identity are intimately tied up with geography and symbolic space. Priestley's journey round England is, very roughly, a circle described clockwise; it is a way of defining the territorial limits or beating the bounds of a country surrounded on three sides by water. Ford's interests are not so much territorial as atmospheric. He is in search of a series of auras, of evanescent presences: the 'soul of London', the 'heart of the country', the 'spirit of the people'. Both approaches take for granted a feeling of ownership. There is, apparently, nothing provisional or precarious about the writers' claim to be English, although Ford, as the son of a German father, could easily have aligned himself with Priestley's 'intelligent aliens'. As for Priestley, he described himself in 1973 as 'an Englishman writing about the English',[9] and few men have better embodied the popular image of the born-and-bred Yorkshireman. Nevertheless, he was brought up by a stepmother and one of the few things we know about his real mother is that she grew up among Irish immigrants.[10] The most influential twentieth-century writers on Englishness display a security of possession that it is possible they do not entirely feel. They have more in common than at first appears with Kureishi's Karim Amir, that 'Englishman born and bred, almost'.

In the fiction of immigration there is a logical distinction between the novel of the first generation, focusing on new immigrants, and the work of second-generation novelists like Kureishi whose experience is at first sight more thoroughly multicultural. But although there are clear examples of 'first generation' and 'second generation' novels, in most cases the distinction collapses. The children of immigrants reimagine the lives of their parents; many novels share an equal focus on parents and children, or on the established immigrant community and new arrivals; and only the Caribbean community has produced an extensive literature of direct testimony about the first-generation immigrant experience. What most novels of immigration have in common, however, is their sense of spatial confinement. Sometimes the passage to England is described, but there is little or no sense of geographical exploration within England. The characters are held within a highly specific local space, or what the language of imperialism would call a settlement or outpost. One of the most striking features of the fiction of immigration into Britain is the overwhelming presence of working-class London as a setting, including the recurrence, over more than a century, of particular areas such as Whitechapel and Spitalfields in the East End. This is the setting of parts of Israel Zangwill's *Children of the Ghetto: A Study of a Peculiar People* (1892) and Salman Rushdie's *The Satanic Verses* (1988), as well as of more local fiction such as Farrukh Dondy's *Come to Mecca* (1978) and Monica Ali's *Brick Lane* (2003). The long history of Spitalfields as an immigrant space is evident when Rushdie describes the Jamme Masjid mosque in the 'borough of Brickhall', a building 'which used to be the Machzikel HaDath synagogue which had in its turn replaced the Huguenots' Calvinist church'.[11]

The history of the streets around Petticoat Lane and Brick Lane is not that of a ghetto in the strict sense of the word—an area to which Jews or other ethnic groups are forcibly restricted—but rather what Zangwill termed an 'Alsatia', a terra incognita or no-go area confounding the expectations of conventional English society.[12] At the same time, the area is necessarily a forcing-house for the process that Zangwill calls Anglicization. It is where the imported norms of immigrant culture begin to break down since, as one character asserts in Monica Ali's novel about 1980s Bengali immigrants, ' "This is England . . . You can do whatever you like" '.[13] But 'Anglicization' is a controversial and contested idea which has different meanings for different immigrant groups. In the vocabulary of imperialism it was normally applied to the attempts of the colonizers to stamp out indigenous culture, and for this reason 'de-Anglicization' became a rallying cry for nationalists in Ireland and elsewhere. Colonial immigrants to Britain were mostly impervious to the rhetoric of 'de-Anglicization', otherwise they would not have come. For them, Anglicization often meant a painful adjustment of their high expectations, as overseas British subjects, to the sordid domestic reality.

There are, however, well-documented contrasts between the experience of Caribbean and other immigrant communities whose whole existence was a result of the British Empire, and those like the Whitechapel Jews whose traditional way of life owed little or nothing to British influence. Nevertheless, all these immigrant groups faced a common enemy in the white racism which tried to prevent their assimilation into British life.

Israel Zangwill: The Trauma of Anglicization and the Conflict of Loyalties

To Israel Zangwill's contemporaries at the end of the nineteenth century, the idea of Whitechapel as an Alsatia or terra incognita would have suggested a new variety of the 'slum novel' of the London proletariat. *Children of the Ghetto* came after the East End novels of Walter Besant and George Gissing, which focus on relations between the urban poor and the conscience-ridden middle classes. In Besant and Gissing, as later in Rushdie, there is a degree of spatial overlapping, with the middle-class characters entering the East End as welfare workers, slum landlords, or novelists in search of copy, while the East Enders make occasional riotous and destructive forays into the more fashionable parts of the city. *Children of the Ghetto* was succeeded by the novels of the so-called 'Cockney school', in which the denizens of particular parts of East London (although ethnically indistinguishable from the rest of the English working class) are treated as virtual ghetto-dwellers because of their poverty and cultural isolation. Arthur Morrison's *A Child of the Jago* (1896) identifies a small area in Shoreditch as the centre of criminal London, a site of moral darkness such as Dickens had portrayed in *Oliver Twist*. The heroine of Somerset Maugham's melodramatic first novel *Liza of Lambeth* (1897) is an archetypal daughter of the slums. Dialect is a crucial element of the working-class 'reality' presented in these novels, which did much to pioneer the modern transcription of Cockney speech.[14] Morrison used Cockney phonetic distortion in the title of one of his earliest stories, 'Lizerunt' (Eliza Hunt) in *Tales of Mean Streets* (1894). He presented himself as a social explorer revealing the shocking truths of an area of society completely unknown to middle-class readers. Such readers needed to be reminded that 'For the existence of this [the Jago], and for the evils it engendered, the community was, and is, responsible; so that every member of the community was, and is, responsible in his degree'.[15] The ideas of community and responsibility are much less straightforward in *Children of the Ghetto*, where, despite the novel's emphasis on new generations growing up in London, the majority of the characters are not and do not claim to be English.

In *Children of the Ghetto* Zangwill's appeal is not to the national conscience but, first and foremost, to that of the established Jewish community in Britain. His narrative is divided into two parts, 'The Children of the Ghetto' and 'The Grandchildren of the Ghetto', with the grandchildren's history being defined as 'mainly a history of the middle-classes' (323). Among immigrant groups, this split between an affluent middle class and a new population languishing in desperate poverty is highly unusual. The long history of Jewish settlement in Britain, with its well-established presence in industries such as banking and tailoring, was disrupted in the late nineteenth century by the flood of new immigrants from Central and Eastern Europe. Many of the new arrivals, unlike Gissing's and Morrison's Cockney East Enders, were skilled workers who could expect a relatively swift transition to steady employment and respectability. Those who remained unsettled frequently moved on to the United States. This means that, like the Caribbean immigrants of Samuel Selvon's *The Lonely Londoners* (1956), Zangwill's Whitechapel Jews are economic migrants drawn by their belief in the 'auriferous character of London pavements'.[16] There are distant echoes of the Whittington story in *Children of the Ghetto*, which ends with its heroine, Esther Ansell, forced to decide whether to rejoin her family (who have moved from the Whitechapel slums to Chicago) or to marry her wealthy, Oxford-educated, middle-class Jewish suitor in London.

Zangwill's fiction has a strongly ethnographic dimension, but it also confronts the immigrants' mixture of love and hate, pride and shame, in their ethnicity. Above all, Zangwill is concerned with conflicts within the immigrant community and the way that these are stirred up by the community's representation in realistic fiction. The very people who would welcome an outsider paying tribute to their cultural 'peculiarity' (as George Eliot had done for the East End Jews in *Daniel Deronda*) are ready to persecute one of their own number who does the same thing. Zangwill's earliest fictional work was the anonymous, privately pub-lished *Motso Kleis, or the Green Chinee* (c.1882) which, he later said, was 'widely denounced by Jews, and widely bought by them'; in particular it was denounced for its use of 'jargon' (Yiddish), which was thought to expose the immigrants' barbarity and illiteracy.[17] Language and the authority of narration are again central issues in *Children of the Ghetto*. Esther Ansell, brought up in Whitechapel but later 'rescued' by a Jewish philanthropist, publishes an anonymous novel, *Mordecai Josephs*, which scandalizes 'West-End Judaism' (325). ' "It's plain treachery and disloy- alty, this putting of weapons into the hands of our enemies" ' (329), is a typical response to Esther's faithful reproduction of the multilingual Whitechapel idiom. In creating Esther, Zangwill was drawing both on the fate of his earlier novel and on the tragic life of the novelist and poet Amy Levy (a product not of the ghetto but of Newnham College, Cambridge), who committed suicide after her novel *Reuben Sachs* (1888) was attacked by Jewish critics, including Zangwill himself. *Children of the Ghetto* was written immediately after these disturbing events, and it became part of the process by which they could be conveniently forgotten. It rapidly became a bestseller, making Zangwill's reputation with a wider public while encountering only mild criticism in the Jewish press.[18]

Children of the Ghetto was commissioned by the Jewish Publication Society of America, which wanted a Jewish counterpart to Mrs Humphry Ward's popular study of East End philanthropy and religious doubt in *Robert Elsmere* (1888). Much to Zangwill's annoyance, the Jewish Publication Society added a glossary to the first American edition of the novel; but he was soon reluctantly forced to create his own glossary for subsequent editions, and he also revised the text, cutting down on the use of Yiddish vocabulary.[19] Zangwill's approach to fiction reflects his journalistic background and his intention of documenting typical phases of Jewish London life. The plot is based on a series of family melodramas like a modern soap opera, and chapter-titles such as 'The Purim Ball', 'Sugarman's Bar-mitzvah Party', and 'The Hebrew's Friday Night' sug- gest the author's investment in the more picturesque aspects of Jewish culture. Book two with its portrait of middle-class Jewry opens con- troversially with a Christmas dinner party rather than a Jewish festival. Esther's position as a clandestine novelist living quietly and demurely with the wealthy Goldsmith family reflects the 'double life' she has led and the 'two tongues' she has spoken ever since she first went to school in Whitechapel. As a girl she not only reads her brother's *Boys of England* comic, but secretly obtains a New Testament. Her Jewish identity is 'always at the back of her consciousness', yet she becomes a patriotic English girl happy in her knowledge that 'the English language was the noblest in the world' and that her ancestors have 'always beaten the French' (151–2). Her crime as an adult is to use the form of the English novel to portray a generation of new immigrants who have yet to become as Anglicized as she is.

Apart from Esther's story, two of the other plot lines in *Children of the Ghetto* are concerned with religious fundamentalism, which would become one of the most sensitive issues in the novels of Rushdie and Kureishi a century later. Esther's suitor Raphael Leon edits a paper, *The Flag of Judah*, partly financed by Henry Goldsmith (the host at the Christmas dinner party) with a paradoxical mission to defend Jewish orthodoxy. In the earlier part of the novel Hannah Shemuel, a rabbi's daughter, finds her happiness in love thwarted by an obscure but draconian provision of Jewish religious law. Her lover wants her to elope to America so that they can get married under a more liberal dispensation, but at the last minute she remains true to her father's faith. This sentimental tragedy of non-assimilation became central to the dramatized version of the novel.

In itself, *Children of the Ghetto* cannot be described as a neglected literary classic, but it is a pioneering work of extraordinary interest and continuing relevance. The controversies within the Jewish community that it reflects were paralleled more than a century later when Monica Ali's bestselling *Brick Lane*, set in the same part of Whitechapel, was condemned by Muslim community representatives for its 'insulting and shameful' depiction of Bengali immigrants.[20] The author, it was claimed, knew little of the community represented in her 400-page novel; equally relevant, perhaps, was the fact that the novel's strongly feminist and integrationist values clearly challenged fundamentalist orthodoxy. Probably the *Brick Lane* controversy would have attracted little notice had it not been for the precedent of *The Satanic Verses*, which was denounced all over the world and burnt by Muslim protesters in Britain once its author had received a religious death sentence in 1989. (The opening sequence of *The Satanic Verses* shows its two protagonists, Gibreel Farishta and Saladin Chamcha, suffering a kind of fall from the heavens and fetching up in contemporary London, but Rushdie is not an immigrant novelist, influential as his London scenes have been. The controversy over the novel relates to its dream sequences set in the Arabian peninsula.) The motives of the British anti-Rushdie protesters in London were portrayed with a certain sympathy in Hanif Kureishi's immigrant novel *The Black Album* (1995). It seems likely that immigrant fiction will always retain the capacity to disturb some of its readers, since it explores issues of national and cultural identity which give rise to profound and passionate disagreement. The example of *Children of the Ghetto* is a reminder that fiction dealing with the trauma of migration and resettlement has a long history.

Metropolitan Alienation

When Esther belatedly confesses to Raphael that she is the author of *Mordecai Josephs*, she declares that

'I wrote it and I glory in it. Though all Jewry cry out "The picture is false," I say it is true. So now you know the truth. Proclaim it to all Hyde Park and Maida Vale, tell it to all your narrow-minded friends and acquaintances, and let them turn and rend me. I can live without them or their praise. Too long they have cramped my soul. Now at last I am going to cut myself free.' (428)

The city here is the place of judgement, but also the place of freedom. Even if 'all Hyde Park and Maida Vale' point the finger of censure at her, Esther can survive their condemnation. The figure of the writer in the metropolis has long been a central trope in immigrant fiction: the writer as truthful witness and potential betrayer of her community's secrets, but also as a solitary outcast cherishing her loneliness amid the city's anonymity. The freedom the city offers is, as often as not, the freedom to fantasize, and the fantasies it breeds are often outrageous, from visions of drugged hallucination, unlimited sexual possibility, and mental break-down to those of terrorist violence and civil war. While Esther's defiance of her own community in the above quotation suggests the extent to which she has become Anglicized, we may suspect that it is Anglicization as a negative identification, the product of disillusionment and disgust rather than a genuine reaching out towards a non-Jewish mode of life. Her confession is made privately to Raphael—a dissident intellectual who takes a strong interest in her—and her moment of defiance leads to a renewed discovery of love and comradeship within the Jewish community, which proves to be less narrow-minded than she had feared. This senti-mental ending suggests that Esther's rebellion is, in the end, little more than a family quarrel. She does not suffer permanent intellectual isolation of the kind depicted in the novels of Zangwill's contemporary George Gissing.

Gissing in his time was a much less popular writer than Zangwill, but his presentation of metropolitan alienation and the separation of the intellectual from the community anticipates the artistic introversion and solipsism of some of the most famous twentieth-century fiction: the novel as, first and foremost, a 'portrait of the artist'. Any artist who is, in Gissing's sense, 'unclassed'—who has turned against the section of society from which he or she came—is by definition a kind of migrant, whose work is likely to be either a record or, at least, a product of the experience of displacement. Such displacement is an individual act, in sharp contrast to the fates of 'displaced persons', refugees, economic migrants, and the like. At times, however—as with the movement of Caribbean writers to Britain after the Second World War—it takes on the appearance of a group phenomenon. In such cases, the fiction of individual isolation influences, and is influenced by, the fiction of immigration. It becomes hard to distinguish between the portrayal of London, for example, as a city of the uprooted, the bewildered, and the lost, and novels of immigrant communities where (as one critic has said of first-generation Caribbean immigrant fiction) there is a 'notable absence of women, successful love relationships, or any organic family life'.[21]

In the twentieth century, both the novel as 'portrait of the artist' and the fiction of immigration tended to emphasize the cultural, economic, and political centrality of the metropolis. The collapse of the British and other European empires barely affected the global dominance of cities such as London, Paris, and New York. V. S. Naipaul, who came as a student from Trinidad, wrote retrospectively that

in 1950 in London I was at the beginning of that great movement of peoples that was to take place in the second half of the twentieth century—a movement and a cultural mixing greater than the peopling of the United States, which was essentially a movement of Europeans to the New World. . . . Cities like London were to change. They were to cease being more or less national cities; they were to become cities of the world, modern-day Romes, establishing the pattern of what great cities should be, in the eyes of islanders like myself and people even more remote in language and culture.[22]

For Naipaul the immigrant's sense of failure as he shivers in a cold, damp, and unwelcoming London bedsit leads to self-examination rather than to disillusionment with the city. He and his fellow immigrants are Dick Whittingtons drawn to the metropolis, and it is here that he discovers his identity as a writer, an identity that has nothing to do with Bow Bells. He remains an outsider in the city, he does not settle in it, but he returns again and again in his work to the moment of arrival and his bewilderment there.

One of the most remarkable novelists of metropolitan alienation in a London setting is Jean Rhys, who first came to England from Dominica as a teenager in 1907. Rhys's lonely heroines endlessly lament that they have no money. Rebelling against a background of family poverty and narrow horizons, they have succeeded only in bringing failure and degradation upon themselves. Julia Martin in *After Leaving Mr Mackenzie* (1930) rejects her family, survives a broken marriage in Germany and a series of failed liaisons in Paris, and returns to England to see her dying mother. The memory of her childhood in tropical South America takes on the quality of a lost paradise in contrast with her disconnected, dysfunctional, and emotionally paralysed life in London. Julia is defeated and goes back to Paris, but Anna Morgan, the first-person narrator of *Voyage in the Dark* (1934), retreats into drunkenness, illness, sleep, and inertia. Once again, she is obsessed by memories of the tropics. As a child growing up in colonial luxury, she rebelled against her family's Puritanical code of order and self-discipline and 'wanted to be black'. But now she is lonely, miserable, and unemployed in London, a city of greasy pavements, tasteless food, sordid lodging houses, and (two years before George Orwell's *Keep the Aspidistra Flying*) aspidistras in the hallway. 'Being black is warm and gay, being white is cold and sad,' she reflects during her downward slide towards prostitution and an illegal abortion.[23]

In the fiction of some of Rhys's successors, not only the displaced and tormented first-person narrator but the city itself is disintegrating and falling apart. The heroine of Anna Kavan's story 'Our City' (1945) is an immigrant 'from the other side of the world' (though Kavan herself was a British novelist born in France). The city, evidently wartime London, is 'full of the troops of a foreign army', while the protagonist, a mental patient in remission, is 'the city's outcast and prisoner'. She is, like Lazarus, risen from the dead—but still mentally half-dead—and ultimately she foresees an apocalypse of 'fire and brimstone from above' which will bring the city to an end.[24] Doris Lessing's *The Memoirs of a Survivor* (1974), a vision of a violent, anarchic future London, is similarly apocalyptic. Lessing, who described her arrival in London from southern Africa in *In Pursuit of the English* (1960) and elsewhere, shows a heroine who at the end is miraculously transported to another place, which may represent a world beyond the grave or a new stage in her spiritual migration.

Lessing and Kavan are writers whose concern with unusual psychic experience has led them from time to time into the realms of science fiction. For a more orthodox realist like the West Indian-born Caryl Phillips, there is no escape from the predicament of metropolitan alienation in 1950s London. Phillips has identified himself as a firm believer in the 'melting pot' idea of English cultural diversity,[25] but his first novel, *The Final Passage* (1985), portrays the suffering and delirium of an immigrant who cannot come to terms with her new environment. The small Caribbean island where Leila and her feckless husband grew up offered an intimate communal life shadowed by economic stagnation and endemic unemployment; the metropolis, by contrast, is a pitiless waste-land condemning its weaker inhabitants to self-destructive isolation. Leila, a born victim like Rhys's heroines, turns away the offers of help she receives and is last seen alone and destitute on Christmas Eve, locking the door of her bleak London flat against the world outside and burning her baby's clothes in the grate in a last attempt to keep warm. *The Final Passage* has been described as a novel about Phillips's parents, so his decision to end the story at this point may be seen as a deliberate turning of the narrative towards tragedy and away from the self-absorption of the 'portrait of the artist'. It leaves us with a numbing sense of the heroine's 'voicelessness' and her failure to discover or refashion her identity.[26]

V. S. Naipaul's career began with comic novels set in his native Trinidad and notable for their characters' rich fantasy lives. In 1967, however, he published *The Mimic Men*, which soon became notorious for its denunciation of the culture and politics of newly independent Caribbean states. The political memoirs of Naipaul's first-person narrator Ralph Singh are bracketed by lengthy descriptions of his life in London, first as a student and later as a deposed national leader in exile. He has come back to 'the final emptiness: London and the home counties' to take up the vocation of writing, but what he writes is a self-obsessed memoir rather than the broad history of the impact of European imperialism that he had originally planned.[27] Singh, who is, he says, 'too much a victim of that restlessness which was to have been my subject' (38), is rather evidently a thinly veiled projection of Naipaul himself at a particularly bleak stage of his literary odyssey. He is shown living alone in a suburban hotel amid the featureless twentieth-century landscape described by J. B. Priestley. He has no sense of belonging or membership of a community, nor any goal beyond that of completing his memoirs. But he does record with some pride that he is toasted as 'our overseas guest' by the landlady at the hotel's Christmas dinner (297).

Descended from Indian immigrant labourers (his name has been anglicized from Ranjit Kripalsingh), Ralph Singh in his final incarna-tion has fulfilled the 'fourfold division of life' prescribed by his Aryan ancestors, having been 'student, householder and man of affairs, recluse' (300). As a student he at first followed 'the god of the city' (22), walking London's streets and remembering its famous names much as Jude Fawley did at Christminster. But as the 'gold of the imagination' turned to the 'lead of reality' (13) he sought solace in sexual promiscuity. Next comes the narrative of his marriage to an English girl and his eventual divorce, together with his rapid rise as a populist leader on his home island of Isabella. Finally, overcome with self-disgust and world-weariness, he throws in his hand as a politician and retires to London. He turns into a secular, Westernized version of the Hindu 'Holy Man', but his message is that the migration of peoples is unnatural and fundamentally wrong. Like Rhys's heroines, Naipaul's introspective, self-pitying protagonist remains defined by his restlessness. An immigrant who is content to stay on as an 'overseas guest', he has found only a disconnected artistic identity in Britain.

Metropolitan Fantasies

In *The Pleasures of Exile* (1960) the novelist George Lamming spoke of the tension between the West Indian writer's need to 'win the approval of Headquarters' (England) and his responsibility to his own people.[28] Naipaul's Olympian prose in *The Mimic Men* and later books has secured his ready acceptance as a master of English fiction, but it is the novels of his compatriot Samuel Selvon that give expression to what Lamming called 'the people's speech'—a compound of Trinidadian and other dialects that constitutes the earliest literary form of black British English.[29] Naipaul's early novels of Trinidad life, *The Mystic Masseur* (1957) and *A House for Mr Biswas* (1961), are based on a 'trickster' hero, an ingenious and resourceful self-made man whose imagination is nourished by the distant influence of the metropolis. Selvon in *The Lonely Londoners* (1956) introduced a rather similar figure, Moses Aloetta, a Caribbean immigrant undergoing the transition from metropolitan alienation to belonging. The hero of Selvon's humorous, anecdotal third-person narrative bounces back after innumerable defeats, valiantly maintaining his vision of London as the immigrant's promised land. In the end, like Ralph Singh, he settles on the goal of writing his memoirs. Selvon's two sequels, *Moses Ascending* (1975) and *Moses Migrating* (1983), are instalments of these memoirs, portraying the hero's progress from homesick outsider to absurdly ultra-loyal black Englishman.

The folk-tale roots, both English and Caribbean, of Selvon's storytelling are never far from the surface. At the start of *The Lonely Londoners* Moses is hanging out at Waterloo Station—'Perhaps he was thinking is time to go back to the tropics, that's why he feeling sort of lonely and miserable'[30] — when he meets the newly arrived Henry Oliver, who immediately acquires the name of the quest-hero Sir Galahad. Moses warns Galahad that

Londoners will view him as a greedy, upstart Dick Whittington who has come to the city in search of wealth and women: 'So don't expect they will treat you like anybody special—to them you will be just another one of them black Jamaicans who coming to London thinking that the streets paved with gold' (25). Moses and Galahad soon become members of a mixed West Indian group known as 'the boys', and Selvon (who was himself of Asian descent) is studiously vague about his characters' racial identities.[31]

According to Moses, 'if it was that we didn't get together now and then to talk about things back home, we would suffer like hell.... Nobody in London does really accept you. They tolerate you, yes, but you can't go in their house and eat or sit down and talk. It ain't have no sort of family life for us here' (114). But while Moses acknowledges the poverty and exploitation of immigrant 'Brit'n', the fantasy life of 'the boys' as they come together to drink, joke, and exchange stories is at the heart of *The Lonely Londoners*. Moses becomes the 'master of ceremonies' (98) at their regular get-togethers, and his ten years in London are seen as a small epic of survival and adaptation.

Moses Ascending and *Moses Migrating* lack some of the casual, improvised grace of *The Lonely Londoners*. Moses becomes a property-owning British patriot and slum landlord, but is virtually imprisoned in his own basement after being outwitted by Bob, the white immigrant to London from Leicestershire whom he first employed as his Man Friday. By the end of the trilogy Moses is on the run from the police in both England and Trinidad. Selvon thus puts an abrupt end to the career of a hero who was able to boast in *Moses Ascending* that 'I have weathered many a storm in Brit'n, and men will tell you that in my own way I am as much part of the London landscape as little Eros with his bow and arrow in Piccadilly, or one-eye Nelson with his column in Trafalgar Square, not counting colour'.[32]

'Colour' is, of course, made to count throughout Selvon's trilogy, which aims to dissolve the cruelty and prejudice of British institutional racism into laughter. In *Moses Ascending* Galahad and some of the other 'boys' join the Black Panthers, challenging Moses, now a self-conscious memoirist, to show whether he is cut out to be a campaigning writer like the American James Baldwin or, as always seems more likely, a British Uncle Tom. When Moses puts up the bail money to get the Black Panther leaders out of prison, he declares with splendid absurdity that 'No Englishman with black blood in his veins can stand aside and see innocent victims hang' (96). His 'black Englishman' persona reaches its apotheosis at the Trinidad carnival in *Moses Migrating*, where he appears in state as a black Britannia with Bob and his wife Jeannie as his white slaves.

Selvon's comedy is set against the background of Britain's changing relationship with its ex-colonies, as highlighted in the 1960s by the country's economic crises and by the racist speeches of the Conservative politician Enoch Powell. Moses as a loyal black Englishman is torn between responding to Powell's call for the immigrants to return home, and a reluctance to desert 'Brit'n' in its hour of need: 'How would the country survive with all these blacks returning to the islands? When the streets were paved with gold they came a-running: now that the humble potato was princely they were rushing out to the Third World to eat rice instead, having made their kill in the British Isles'.[33] So Moses returns to Trinidad as a self-appointed ambassador for his adopted country, proclaiming that 'Johnny Walker was still going strong, that the British bulldog still had teeth, that Britannia still ruled the waves' (30). He wins a silver cup with his carnival float, but the reality is that, far from Bob and Jeannie being his slaves, he has become theirs. His fantasy of Britishness is just that—a fantasy—and, since he deserts his Trinidadian fiancée, a sterile one; it is not Moses who will be producing the next generation of black Englishmen. His glory, however, has been his ability to persuade himself, not just that he belongs in London, but that London belongs to him.

Fantasies of metropolitan assimilation and political resistance are presented in much more extreme terms in Hanif Kureishi's *The Black Album*, a novel of London in the late 1980s. On the one hand there are orgies of sex, rock music, and drug-taking, which Kureishi suggests might be the common experience of London teenagers; on the other hand, militant Islamic sects embody a much more fiercely Puritanical opposition to the metropolitan blurring of identities than Selvon's Black Panthers had done. Kureishi's protagonist Shahid Hasan is torn between his sexual infatuation with Deedee Osgood, his white teacher and girlfriend, and his involvement with a fundamentalist group. Shahid is also a writer whose intensity of observation fills Kureishi's third-person narrative with a poetry of imaginatively transformed urban spaces. Here he is waiting on an Underground platform:

Beneath the banality and repetition of this ordinary day there ran, like the warm inhabited tube tunnels under the city, flirtation, passion and the deepest curiosities.... Skirts, shoes, haircuts, looks, gestures: enticement and fascination were everywhere, while the world went to work. And such allure wasn't a preliminary to real sex, it was sex itself. Out there it was not innocent. People yearned for romance, desire, feeling. They wanted to be kissed, stroked, sucked, held and penetrated more than they could say. The platform of Baker Street Station was Arcadia itself.[34]

But the sexual pastoral is indulged only to be repudiated: 'What torrents of drug-inspired debris he had allowed to stream through his head! What banal fantasies he believed were visions! And on Baker Street Station too!' (130). Soon afterwards Shahid goes to a mosque, which is so full of different types and nationalities of men (we note that they are all men) that it could be anywhere. The mosque and its adherents stand apart from their profane locality, while Shahid's vision of a sexual Arcadia is tied to a particular place in the metropolis. His co-religionists may accuse him of sexual enslavement to Deedee, but it is because he is a would-be novelist with a passion for the details and fullness of experience that his commitment to the metropolis must win out, in the end, over his attempts at religious devotion. He comes to take pride in the 'seedy variety' of his part of the city, which in Cockney style he calls his 'manor': 'In London, if you found the right place, you could consider yourself a citizen the moment you went to the same local shop twice' (193). London offers the glamour of sex, drugs, and consumerism, of art and self-display, but it is also a place of belonging. It offers anonymity and local knowledge at the same time.

But also fear. Ralph Singh in *The Mimic Men* had sensed that London was a 'conglomeration of private cells', but Shahid is aware of a new degree of social breakdown, of which the street gangs and poverty-stricken housing estates are only symptoms. The world is 'breaking up into political and religious tribes', he thinks, so that even previously stable societies may be threatened with civil war (133–4). Shahid, split between two identities, himself embodies the conflict that he detects around him. Civil violence, hitherto mainly confined to futuristic fiction such as Lessing's *The Memoirs of a Survivor*, is always a possible dimension of metropolitan fantasy.

Immigrants in the 'Heart of England'

Until recently there was a remarkable shortage of novels of immigration set outside London. The attraction of the Whittington theme for writers and intellectuals remained as powerful as it was in the time of Thackeray and Dickens. In traditional English fiction the lure of the city was balanced by the representation of the English countryside as the place from which the novel's male protagonists came and to which most of them would eventually return. The countryside was associated with childhood, the city with the excitement and disillusionment of young adulthood, but the hero's reward repeatedly took the form of a country mansion, a wife and children, and a landed estate. Since the countryside in fiction is so often a place of absence, it is significant that the immigrant's remembered countryside is far away from England: hence the tropical landscapes of reverie in Jean Rhys's novels, and the cryptic, embittered childhood memories of Ralph Singh.

There is also the residual but strongly persistent idea, sanctioned by literature since the time of the Romantic poets, that the English countryside is the heartland of national identity. In the twentieth century it was most strongly expressed by the Georgian poets—an early example is Edward Thomas's *The Heart of England* (1906)—and their successors.[35] The 'unspoilt' countryside is opposed to the new England of suburban development and industrial sprawl—as in Forster and J. B. Priestley—but it is also seen as standing apart from the mixing of cultures in the cities. The more rural England is mythologized, the more it is likely to be feared or avoided by the immigrant writer. Thus the urbane, sophisticated V. S. Naipaul speaks in *The Enigma of Arrival* (1987) of Wiltshire, the 'ancient heart of England', as an 'unlikely setting' for what he calls his 'new life' (96). The 'ancient heart' is more than a historical and geographical metaphor. It implies the seat of patriotic emotions, and also the supposed stability and homogeneity of the rural population. *The Enigma of Arrival* deliberately sets out to dispel this view of the countryside. By contrast, Caryl Phillips's novel *A Distant Shore* (2003) is set in a former mining village where an illegal African immigrant is brutally murdered. The novel is at once an indictment of the racism and violence to be found outside the big cities, and an evocation of a changing England where the old division between town and country no longer applies. Novels of immigration set in the countryside can, indeed, be linked to an older kind of English writing summed up in the title of George Sturt ('George Bourne')'s classic memoir *Change in the Village* (1912). As Phillips's white narrator remarks, 'These days it's difficult to tell who's from around here and who's not. Who belongs and who's a stranger.'[36]

But if the countryside is the traditional English heartland, it is also a place where, to use Forster's term, the Englishman's 'undeveloped heart' may be cruelly exposed. Novelists in the English pastoral tradition tend to adopt the perspective of the misunderstood country people; thus Hardy in *Tess* and *The Woodlanders* contrasts the tragic nobility of his rural labourers with the careless insensitivity of the incoming middle classes. At the other extreme, recent immigrant novelists such as Phillips and Meera Syal portray the inbred racism of the English provinces. One of the first major novels touching on overseas immigration into the English countryside is D. H. Lawrence's *The Rainbow*, where the first chapter is entitled 'How Tom Brangwen married a Polish Lady'. The Brangwens, we are told in the novel's opening sentence, 'had lived for generations on the Marsh Farm', but it is Tom Brangwen, the youngest son, who takes over the farm.[37] His three elder brothers preferred to seek opportunities elsewhere. As a bachelor farmer, Tom is the last of his line until he meets Lydia Lensky, the Polish immigrant with whom he forms an almost wordless relationship. Their marriage is the start of a new dynasty whose fortunes are traced in *The Rainbow* and *Women in Love*, although the search for emotional and intellectual fulfilment that Lawrence traces in each generation inevitably takes Tom Brangwen's progeny away from the land, never to return.

Lydia Lensky's role in *The Rainbow* is symbolic but somehow incidental. Her Polish background apparently means nothing to her granddaughter Ursula, who is Lawrence's primary heroine and the spiritual heir of the Brangwens. The narrative of Ursula's unhappy love affair with Anton Skrebensky does not include any analysis of their shared immigrant heritage. Anton's dedication to his acquired British identity as an army officer and imperial servant is seen as an indictment of his undeveloped heart; Lawrence has little sympathy for his situation as an orphan child of Anglo-Polish parents. Ursula's own capacity for development towards emotional richness is, in effect, the sign of her passionate if inarticulate Brangwen ancestry.

What Lawrence did not and perhaps could not write is the story of the Brangwens as seen from the standpoint of the Lenskys and Skrebenskys. Not many English-born novelists have elected to portray the English from an 'alien' point of view, as Ford does in *The Good Soldier* and Forster to a lesser extent in *Howards End*. A distinguished mid-century example of immigrant fiction by an English-born writer is Philip Larkin's second novel *A Girl in Winter* (1947). In *Jill* (1946), a pioneering example of post-war campus fiction, Larkin had satirized the life of Oxford under-graduates as seen by a northern working-class freshman. Katherine Lind, the protagonist of *A Girl in Winter*, is a wartime (presumably Jewish) refugee working as a library assistant in a provincial city. This memorable novel suggests the potential loss to English fiction resulting from Larkin's decision to become a professional librarian and poet.

Larkin is vague and perhaps deliberately reticent about Katherine's origins. Her name sounds Nordic or Germanic, but her hosts during a

schoolgirl visit to England before the war thought that she might be
Catholic, implying German or Austrian nationality, and there is a hint
that she comes from the Rhineland. A German refugee at liberty in
wartime England must certainly be Jewish, but Larkin carefully avoids
giving her this label. The novel's formal structure traces her life on a
single winter day, with her pre-war visit to the family of her English 'pen
pal', Robin Fennel, being recalled in a long retrospect. Larkin hints
without actually stating that the upper-middle-class Fennels, who are not
a religious family, were dismayed by their belated realization that they
were entertaining a Jewish guest. Robin's future brother-in-law, an Aryan
type with 'cold blue eyes', does his best to ignore her, while her unguarded
response to being told that she is 'almost one of the family' evokes the
latent anti-Semitism in Robin:

'It would be amusing if I were,' said Katherine absently. 'Don't you think families
with a foreign side are more interesting? They become much stronger. And the
one branch can help the other.'
  'That's what the Jews think, isn't it,' he said rather distantly.[38]

This is the novel's sole reference to 'the Jews'.

Robin Fennel, supposedly destined for the Diplomatic Service, is the
cool young Briton, mocked by his sister Jane for his meticulously planned
career leading to marriage at the age of 30 and a decoration from the King.
Katherine thinks that 'he had puzzled her at first, because he was so very
English—how English she never realized till she met more English people—
but once she had got used to him he had been rather dull' (180). But Robin
is not what he seems. When he visits Katherine five years later he is a
common soldier absent without leave from his unit; he is on the verge of
an overseas posting and has turned into a boorish alcoholic. He is like
Powell's Charles Stringham (in *The Music of Time*), only much less
sympathetically presented. He has no appreciation of Katherine's difficulties, or of her own social displacement, which is much greater than his.
When Katherine first visited the Fennels she believed she was moving into
a 'world that might have been a country dance' (216), but Robin's English
gentlemanliness was cruelly deceptive. Katherine's summer of girlish
illusion has given place to the bleakest of realities, and Larkin's novel is
starkly at variance with the official mood of relief and self-congratulation
after the Second World War.

While Robin Fennel is not openly identified as anti-Semitic, Anita
Rutter, the heroine's best friend in Meera Syal's *Anita and Me* (1996), is
an English working-class teenager who becomes a 'Paki-bashing' racist.

At the same time, the novel depicts class hostility and resentment as the underlying forces fuelling racial antagonism. Meena Kumar's parents decided to settle in a terraced house in Tollington, a former Black Country mining village, because it was all they could afford when they first came to England in search of what Meena calls 'the promised gold beneath the dog shit on the streets'.[39] But the Kumars are plainly destined for the middle class: Meena's father works in an office, her mother is an infant teacher, and she eventually passes the eleven-plus to go to the local grammar school. The novel is an autobiographical account of Meena's pre-teenage years when she attends the village school (subsequently bulldozed by a property developer) and lives in what seems to her in retrospect to have been an idyllic, self-enclosed working-class community. Tollington, 'a forgotten village in no-man's land between a ten-shop town and an amorphous industrial sprawl' (135), is in a state of transition. The men are mostly out of work, while the local engineering factory takes on women only. At first Tollington is still just rural enough to remind Meena's mother of her Indian homeland, but by the end of the novel it has become part of the new England that Priestley foresaw, with new housing estates, bored teenagers, a supermarket, and a motorway.

Meena, caught between her upwardly mobile parents and their working-class neighbours, is 'a freak of some kind, too mouthy, clumsy and scabby to be a real Indian, too Indian to be a real Tollington wench' (149–50). She is not allowed to speak the Tollington dialect at home: ' "Just because the English can't speak English themselves, does not mean you have to talk like an urchin. You take the best from their culture, not the worst" ' (53), her mother tells her. As a 'Junglee' or wild, naughty child she is deeply attracted to Anita, the glamorous older girl who eventually falls for Sam Lowbridge, the leader of a gang of skinheads. But Anita and Sam are abused and deprived youths, while Meena's loving, supportive parents makes her realize that 'there was a corner of me that would be forever not England' (112). When Sam repeats the notorious racist political slogan of the 1960s—' "If You Want A Nigger For A Neighbour, Vote Labour!" ' (273)—and beats up a visiting Asian businessman, he earns Meena's hatred and contempt; but her relationship to Tollington can never be one of simple antagonism, since Tollington, she discovers, is as much part of England's imperial history as her own family is. A white neighbour suddenly addresses Meena's grandmother in Punjabi, while the last owner of the local coal mine, now a notorious recluse, turns out to be a Sikh like her own family. Meena eventually comes to a deliberately staged, somewhat unlikely understanding with

Sam, who gives her her first kiss and excuses his hostility to her as a matter of class, not race: ' "You've always been the best wench in Tollington. . . . But yow wos never gonna look at me, yow won't be stayin will ya? You can move on. How come? How come I can't?" ' (314). Sam and Anita can develop no further and must remain in Tollington, while Meena and her family prepare for the 'next reincarnation in our English life-cycle' (327)—a suburban house close to the grammar school, with plenty of Hindu neighbours. We could say that, like Israel Zangwill's novel, *Anita and Me* is a sentimental romance about the problems of Anglicization and leaving the ghetto. But Meena's ghetto, the 'tiny, teeming and intimate world' (250) that she recalls so vividly, is that of the beleaguered white rural working class.

V. S. Naipaul's Indian Summer

George Ponderevo, Wells's narrator in *Tono-Bungay*, compares the state of the English countryside to 'an early day in a fine October': 'The hand of change rests on it all, unfelt, unseen; resting for awhile, as it were half reluctantly, before it grips and ends the thing for ever.' Later in the novel he shows a village clergyman suddenly gripped by the realization that 'all his world lay open and defenceless, conquered and surrendered, doomed so far as he could see, root and branch, scale and form alike, to change'.[40] Yet Wells's countryside is also curiously slow to recognize change, and the same sense of artificially prolonged stagnation can be found in writing throughout the century. V. S. Naipaul's *The Enigma of Arrival* is set on a decaying Wiltshire estate which, as the narrator very clearly understands, has no future. The splendid manor house, underwritten by the wealth of empire, is an Arts and Crafts Movement creation dating from the time that Edwardian novelists such as Wells and Galsworthy depicted as the final Indian summer of the old rural order.

The narrator of *The Mimic Men* tells us that he once dreamed of retiring to an abandoned colonial plantation to write his planned history of modern imperialism. In this setting, Ralph Singh suggests, the reality of slavery and exploitation would have receded and the word 'agriculture' would have 'acquired its classical associations and lost its harsher island significance' (41). But this pastoral vision is a self-delusion—identified as such in *The Mimic Men* and, still more harshly, in Naipaul's later Caribbean novel *Guerrillas* (1975)—since the island's colonial history continues to fester. Nevertheless, it would seem that the Naipaul of

The Enigma of Arrival has succeeded in living out a pastoral fantasy very like Singh's.[41] The name of the Wiltshire village in which the narrator resides, Waldenshaw (a reminiscence of Thoreau's Walden), is an obvious pastoral touch. One of the difficulties in referring to *The Enigma of Arrival* as a pastoral, however, is its strongly autobiographical content. The novel's form recalls an earlier example of the fictional literary memoir, George Gissing's *The Private Papers of Henry Ryecroft* (1903)— originally to have been titled 'An Author at Grass'—but Naipaul, unlike Gissing, actually lived in the setting he describes. For much of the time it seems an excessive delicacy not to refer to the narrator as Naipaul, although the book is labelled a novel on its title-page.

When Naipaul first moves into his cottage on a Wiltshire estate he tends to read the landscape through literary spectacles, describing an old labourer as a 'Wordsworthian figure' and the seasonal rhythms of agriculture as being like a 'Book of Hours' (20). But these are naive perceptions, and the self-conscious literariness of his vision recedes as his intellectual and emotional intimacy with Waldenshaw grows. At a deeper level, the indebtedness to literary modes of vision remains. The Conradian idea of the 'secret sharer' underlies the affinities that the solitary, reclusive narrator feels for the neighbours he observes with such fascinated concentration: the garden-loving Jack, Pitton the groundsman, Les and Brenda the unhappily married couple, and, above all, the lord of the manor, a last decayed representative of the class of imperial rulers.

The landlord and the colonial immigrant are opposites, but each is to some extent the other's creation, and, moreover, both Naipaul and his landlord are writers of sorts. The landlord once had a reputation as a promising poet. In middle age Naipaul represents artistic success and his landlord artistic failure, so that the one travels the world on literary and journalistic assignments while the other shuns all mental activity and human contact, rarely stepping outside his mansion. One of the literary precedents shadowing Naipaul's characterization of his landlord is Yeats's poem 'Ancestral Houses', about the last days of the British ascendancy in Ireland. Yeats (who is never quoted in *The Enigma of Arrival*) contrasts the 'Bitter and violent men' who built the great estates with their puny, contemptible successors:

> O what if levelled lawns and gravelled ways
> Where slippered Contemplation finds his ease
> And Childhood a delight for every sense,
> But take our greatness with our violence?[42]

The neglected and shrunken Waldenshaw estate also becomes the source of the narrator's childlike sensual delight, a setting for imaginative rebirth as well as a symbol of post-imperial decrepitude.[43]

As he ponders the mystery of the manor and its landlord's inactivity, Naipaul turns to that central (if covert) obsession of traditional pastoral, the presence of death in Arcadia. His landlord has perhaps 'stalled in what might be considered a state of perfection' (254), and this may be equated with what, taking the longest possible view of English history, Naipaul calls the 'plateau of historical light' (50) stretching from the Saxons to the present. The idea of a new impending English dark age is written into the novel's rural landscape, since Waldenshaw is close to Amesbury, and 'It was to a nunnery in Amesbury that Guinevere, Arthur's queen, the lover of Lancelot, had retired when the Round Table had vanished from Camelot' (50). But for the work of change—including Naipaul's own immigrant presence there—Waldenshaw might be a place of refuge from impending barbarism as secluded and peaceful as Guinevere's nunnery.

For Naipaul, however, the immigrant rather than the slippered recluse is a universal figure, an Everyman, as we see in his reflections on the Giorgio de Chirico painting which gives the novel its title. Sometime in the classical period a traveller arrives by ship at an unknown Mediterranean port. He disembarks and plunges into the streets:

The mission he had come on—family business, study, religious initiation—would give him encounters and adventures. He would enter interiors, of houses and temples. Gradually there would come to him a feeling that he was getting nowhere; he would lose his sense of mission; he would begin to know only that he was lost. His feeling of adventure would give way to panic.

Finally the traveller returns to the 'quayside of arrival', but the ship has gone: 'The traveller has lived out his life' (92).

As it happens, this allegory of the 'enigma of arrival' strongly recalls the plot of George Lamming's *The Emigrants* (1954), an early novel of immigration to Britain by a Trinidadian novelist whom Naipaul considered an inferior rival.[44] *The Emigrants* begins with a ship arriving at a strange port in the French Caribbean. The transit passengers disembark, go into the town, and later rejoin their ship, which takes them to England. Lamming's account of their adventures in London conveys a strong sense of the city's strange and rather sinister interiors—those of an immigrant hostel, a workshop, an unlicensed hairdressing saloon, an Englishman's suburban house, and so on. In the end, the characters' sense of bewilderment is acute.

The symbol of this bewilderment is the narrator's fellow passenger Dickson, who becomes a down-and-out:

I had no great liking for Dickson, but I suddenly felt that Dickson's fate might in a way have been awaiting me, or any man who chose one country rather than another in the illusion that it was only a larger extension of the home which he had left. For it would be a lie to deny that on the ship and even in the hostel, there was a feeling, more conscious in some than others, that England was not only a place, but a heritage. Some of us might have expressed a certain hostility to that heritage, but it remained, nevertheless, a hostility to something that was already part of us.

But all that was now coming to an end. England was simply a world which we had moved about at random, and on occasions encountered by chance. It was just there like nature, drifting vaguely beyond our reach.[45]

Settlement at Waldenshaw is what saves Naipaul from this nightmare of displacement, so that England for him becomes 'a heritage' rather than a world in which he moves about at random. Near the end of *The Enigma of Arrival* there is a moving scene in which he receives the gift of an old neighbour's walking-stick. 'I will keep it as long as I live' (303), he declares, leaving us to wonder to whom he might, in his turn, pass it on. *The Enigma of Arrival* is itself a kind of legacy, a part of England left by an immigrant writer to his readers.

So far from being a deliberate move, V. S. Naipaul's arrival in Wiltshire was apparently an accident, caused by the failure of his plans to leave England altogether.[46] In 1969 he sold his London house, but a year later he came back. The narrator of *The Enigma of Arrival* begins to feel at home in Waldenshaw when he realizes that many of the other figures in his landscape are also incomers, who have no difficulty in accepting him as one of themselves. To the estate servants, he thinks, the manor house is a strange survival from more opulent times, 'like a barbarian coming upon an ancient Roman villa': 'on the manor Pitton, like the Phillipses, like me, was a camper in the ruins, living with what he found, delighted by the evidence of the life of the past' (212). The sense of camping among ruins, like so much else here, can be traced to earlier twentieth-century fiction: Lawrence, for example, begins *Lady Chatterley's Lover* with the sentiment that 'The cataclysm has happened, we are among the ruins, we start to build up new little habitats, to have new little hopes'.[47] Foremost among Lawrence's new hopes (as we saw in Chapter 12) was a renewal of sexual tenderness, whereas Salman Rushdie has alleged that the word 'love' does not appear in *The Enigma of Arrival*.[48] What Naipaul finds, instead, is a defiance of death and the sense of a new mission—no longer the wasted life of his allegorical traveller.

When Jack, the garden-lover (the term seems appropriate), knows that he is dying, he drives to his favourite pub on Christmas Eve for a last, determined public appearance. The narrator also describes the funeral observances for his sister in Trinidad, so that the novel's final section, 'The Ceremony of Farewell', balances the 'enigma of arrival'. The book's dedication—'In loving memory of my brother Shiva Naipaul' (here at least is the word 'love')—records a still more deeply felt loss: Shiva Naipaul, a novelist and journalist living like his older brother in England, died at the age of 40. Within this sombre perspective we can more fully appreciate the narrator's own joy at what he calls 'this gift of the second life in Wiltshire, the second, happier childhood as it were' (83), a rebirth all the sweeter for being necessarily transient. Waldenshaw for him is the happy valley, one of the traditional locations, together with the garden and the island, of utopia or paradise. The 'second chance' he has found there is a 'miracle' (96). It is in this countryside that Naipaul claims (in one critic's words) 'to have come, eventually taken root, and in his own way conquered'.[49]

Naipaul's way is more than a highly individual writer's eccentric odyssey, although as a first-generation immigrant he cannot speak directly for younger British-born writers. *The Enigma of Arrival* is his version of the dialectic of assimilation, self-assertion, and hybrid inheritance suggested by the following passage from Zadie Smith's *White Teeth* (2000), in which a British Asian teenager records her fascination with a middle-class white London family, the Chalfens:

She just wanted to, well, kind of, *merge* with them. She wanted their Englishness. Their Chalfishness. The *purity* of it. It didn't occur to her that the Chalfens were, after a fashion, immigrants too (third generation, by way of Germany and Poland, née Chalfenovsky) or that they might be as needy of her as she was of them. To Irie, the Chalfens were more English than the English.[50]

Englishness, as in so many novels about immigration, is at once a façade or sham and a deeply desirable, ever elusive goal for the incomer. And yet it could very easily be said of the narrator of *The Enigma of Arrival*, beating the bounds of his Wiltshire valley with an ancestral walking-stick, that he is 'more English than the English'. The creation of new identities and the surprising prolongation, or perhaps even usurpation, of older ones is at the heart of immigrant fiction. In the work of these writers the implicit subject matter of the whole tradition of the English novel—the creation, maintenance, decay, and cross-fertilization of the national identity—is at last made explicit.

Conclusion: On Englishness and the Twenty-First-Century Novel

IN 2001 Ian McEwan's novel *Atonement* was shortlisted for the annual Booker Prize. Starting with an epigraph from Jane Austen ('Remember that we are English...') and a long episode portraying a 1930s country-house party, it was the story of the childhood and youth of an English novelist—a novelist, moreover, of the generation before McEwan's own. *Atonement* proceeds to evoke the retreat to Dunkirk in 1940 and the arrival of the casualties from Dunkirk at St Thomas's Hospital in London. Apart from a brief concluding section dated 'London, 1999', all the narrated events take place well before McEwan's own birth in 1948.[1] Critics found nothing unusual in this degree of retrospective vision. Historical reconstruction had become such a regular feature of late twentieth-century English fiction that *Atonement* was not generally classed as a historical novel.

With the exception of some little-understood foreigners encountered by the British soldiers near Dunkirk, all McEwan's characters are English. *Atonement* was published at a time when self-consciously Anglocentric fiction (including a number of novels with 'England' or 'English' in their titles) was back in fashion. McEwan was concerned with class conflict within his country-house society, and with the contrast between the private world of upper-class manners and regimented mass institutions such as the army and the hospital. Dunkirk and its aftermath were presented as a time of national crisis successfully surmounted by most of his characters. One of *Atonement*'s few direct acknowledgements of the vast social changes that took place subsequently was the bare information that, in 1999, the country house of the opening section had been turned into a hotel. Presumably it would have been staffed by members of Britain's recent immigrant population, but that was not one of the novelist's concerns.

Lamenting the death of the American novelist Saul Bellow in 2005, McEwan wrote that 'In Britain we no longer seem able to write across the crass and subtle distortions of class—or rather, we can't do it gracefully, without seeming to strain or without caricature'.[2] It is equally true that in the half-century before the publication of *Atonement* much of the most celebrated English fiction had become inward-looking. It was concerned with revisiting the earlier tradition of the novel as well as the national past. What came to be known as 'historiographic metafiction' surrounded historical romance with reflexive commentaries on the nature of fiction and history, usually parodic in spirit. The historical pageant at the centre of Virginia Woolf's *Between the Acts* is an early forerunner of this trend, which became the basis of bestselling fiction in, for example, John Fowles's Victorian melodrama *The French Lieutenant's Woman* (1969) and Graham Swift's family saga *Waterland* (1983). But a novel need not be set in the past to be retrospective in temper. Many narratives of contemporary life reproduce familiar settings of 'English novel-land' such as the country house, or repeat the plot structures of classic English novels, or openly allude to the earlier tradition.

Novelists like Fowles, McEwan, and Swift write what has come to be known as 'literary fiction' as opposed to popular generic novels and romances. Paperback sales, film, television, and radio adaptations, and extended copyrights make the worldwide marketing of successful literary fiction as profitable today as it has ever been. The authors of modern literary fiction have themselves often had a literary education, and a significant number of them either start out as, or later become, teachers of literature or creative writing. An ever-increasing proportion of their potential readers have studied literature or other humanities subjects. Not surprisingly, there have long been allegations that the climate of literariness and the 'burden of the past' were stifling new fictional creation. The novelist A. S. Byatt, an acute commentator on the contemporary scene, discussed modern English novelists' uneasy relationship to tradition in her essay 'People in Paper Houses' (1979). She concluded with the admonition that 'to be [a good writer], whatever form you use, takes more primitive gifts of curiosity and greed, about things other than literature'.[3] But literariness is not so easily avoided. A case in point is the career of Kingsley Amis, whose first popular success was *Lucky Jim* (1954), a campus comedy in which the hero is a rebellious lecturer in medieval history.

Amis's public stance was relentlessly anti-academic and hostile to what he called literary self-consciousness. A champion of science fiction and other popular forms, he wrote in his introduction to *The Golden Age of Science Fiction* (1981) that literary self-consciousness means that your purpose ceases to be, say, just telling your story as effectively as you can; it comes to include doing what other people have decided you should be doing. A close and intricate relationship between novelists and academics means that the novelists are writing for the academics, not for anything as vulgar as fans.... the link with the readership is impaired.[4]

Before he became a successful novelist Amis taught for many years at University College, Swansea, and then at Cambridge. Philip Larkin, the poet and former novelist who was Librarian of Hull University, was one of his closest friends. Amis rejects a close and intricate relationship with academics, whom he regards, more or less, as parasites upon the creative artist; but his novels are deeply versed in earlier literature and his characters are sometimes enthusiastic readers. *Take a Girl Like You* (1960), the most ambitious of his early works, is a self-conscious rewriting of the Richardsonian novel of seduction. The heroine, Jenny Bunn, is a schoolteacher; the rakish Patrick Standish is a college lecturer. Jenny defends herself against Patrick's first attempt at seduction with the remark that ' "I've read about you in books" '. Her education puts her in a different category from an illiterate Victorian heroine such as Eliot's Hetty Sorrel, but she loses her virginity all the same. The novel's comic conclusion shows the couple, still unmarried, happily agreeing that 'those old Bible-class ideas have certainly taken a knocking'.[5] Jenny and Patrick embody a series of stereotypical Puritan–Cavalier oppositions— monogamy versus promiscuity, northern provincial versus southern metropolitan, honest sobriety versus drunken playacting, and so on—so naturally they find one another irresistible. The passionate and romantic conflicts of earlier English fiction have given way to an amusing and frivolous pastiche.

It is not only English novelists writing about English characters who feel the urge to rewrite the English tradition. V. S. Naipaul's *Guerrillas* (1975), for example, portrays a modern Heathcliff who—having taken a writing course and studied *Wuthering Heights*—sets up a Caribbean agricultural commune which he names Thrushcross Grange. Asya, the heroine of *In the Eye of the Sun* (1992) by the Egyptian-born novelist Ahdaf Soueif, is the daughter of a female English professor in Cairo. When she comes to England to write her doctorate at a northern provincial university, she sees herself as a successor to George Eliot's and Charlotte Brontë's heroines. She becomes involved with a sinister Englishman, Gerald Stone, whose name indicates the state of his heart as surely as it would in a Victorian melodrama. Asya, who is already married, realizes that she has stepped outside the English tradition to join Tolstoy's and Flaubert's heroines once she starts making love to Gerald—but she cannot entirely shake off the legacy of Maggie Tulliver and Dorothea Brooke. As an adulteress, she tells herself, 'you've joined Anna and Emma and parted company for ever with Dorothea and Maggie—although Dorothea would have understood—would she?' *In the Eye of the Sun* is not a novel of immigration, since after her doctorate Asya returns to Egypt to teach literature to a new generation of students, including Islamic fundamentalists whose declared motive is to learn the 'language of [the] enemy'.[6] Soueif's narrative spans the period of decolonization in the Middle East including the Nasser regime, the Suez invasion, the oil boom, and the Arab-Israeli wars. Asya's mother was originally inspired to study English literature by the sight of British women volunteers driving lorries for the Eighth Army in Cairo during the Second World War. That was a passing historical phase; so, we might conclude, is the 'postcolonial' world which has brought about her daughter's deep love for the English novel and her self-identification with its heroines.

The literariness of recent English fiction may also be a strictly temporary phenomenon. For many writers and critics it is associated with Postmodernism, an international style affecting all the arts which came to dominate cultural theory and critique from about 1970 onwards. But, although Postmodernism builds on the self-referentiality which is a perennial aspect of artistic forms, the English novel has been affected by specific local circumstances as national politics and the national economy have undergone profound and continuing changes. The agricultural and manufacturing base declined, the heritage and tourist industries grew in importance, and fiction often seemed to reinforce an essentially backward-looking national image. A novel like *Atonement* which revisits the English country house and the events of May 1940 is to a certain extent complicit in Patrick Wright's description of 'National Heritage' as 'the extraction of history—of the idea of historical significance and potential—from a denigrated everyday life and its restaging or display in certain sanctioned sites, events, images and conceptions'.[7] Novelists, however, are equally capable of satirizing the heritage industry, as Julian Barnes does in *England, England* (1998) where an entrepreneur buys up the Isle of Wight and converts it into 'England', a hugely successful tourist theme park, while the rest of the country, now known as Albion, is left to rot. Barnes's satire does not make economic sense (as was shown, for example, by the financial disaster of London's vaunted Millennium Dome in the year 2000) and so perhaps invites dismissal as a mere fantasy. But there is a danger for the English novel—as Barnes, for one, was evidently aware—in a self-conscious pursuit of Englishness that leads to the spiritual evacuation of ordinary, everyday England.

In more recent essays A. S. Byatt has defined a second major strand in modern English fiction, a strand that is metaphysical in its ambitions and that draws on the whole of human history and geography in tales which often specialize in 'tricks of consciousness, dreams, illusions'. The authors are 'fabulists' and their works, rather than dwelling on the English class system or the decline of the British Empire, are 'European fables'.[8] The novels that Byatt cites are often historical, with settings that include medieval Italy, fifteenth-century Cairo, eighteenth-century Germany, and elsewhere. They are 'European' in that they reflect the influence of European writers such as Italo Calvino, Albert Camus, Isak Dinesen, Günter Grass, Milan Kundera, and others. But Byatt might equally have mentioned the impact in Britain of Latin American 'magic realism' and of Postmodernist fiction from the United States.

In the British context, what Byatt and others call fable or 'fabulation' might also be seen as a revival of the romance. The romance tradition with its preference for the marvellous over the mundane is strongly present in such post-Second World War English novelists as William Golding, Iris Murdoch, Muriel Spark, and the later Doris Lessing. Broadly interpreted, most successful modern romances are fables about identity, some of which address issues of national identity. William Golding's early novels, for example, include two tales of castaways— *Lord of the Flies* (1954) and *Pincher Martin* (1958)—and a prehistoric romance, *The Inheritors* (1955). All three have been widely understood and analysed as moral parables about universal human nature, with the Englishness of Pincher Martin and the boys in *Lord of the Flies* being seen as a major contributing factor. 'Englishness' here, though not always in Golding's later work, is an end-of-Empire phenomenon reflecting the author's own Royal Navy experience; it is, therefore, in sharp contrast with the work of Byatt's 'European fabulists' (including Angela Carter, Penelope Fitzgerald, and Jeanette Winterson as well as Murdoch and Spark) who may be seen as reflecting a new sense of post-imperial national identity. The more recent novelists are writing in the context of Britain's membership of the European Union, a context which, if it does not mean the erasure of national identity, certainly entails its possible reduction to something like regional identity.

The revival of romance, and especially the recent popularity of historical romance, might be dismissed as simple escapism. The critic

Jason Cowley wrote in a review of Byatt's essays that the 'retreat into history' is evidence of a 'powerful loss of confidence in the fictional possibilities of England, particularly beyond the metropolis. One struggles to think of a handful of novelists who bring urgent news of our contemporary condition, in the way that Dickens must have done.' (But—for all his wealth of journalistic experience—Dickens in his own time was more often seen as a fabulist than as a faithful reporter on contemporary conditions.) Cowley concedes that one way of writing about the modern world is to 'write about the present through the aspect of the past, so that the novel becomes a kind of palimpsest'.[9] Among modern novelists, Angela Carter had a lifelong concern with rewriting the corpus of traditional folk tales and fairy tales; this is seen at its purest in *The Bloody Chamber* (1979). Her fiction continually returns to the contemporary, though in ways that are wholly different from the world of newspaper reporting.

Where Cowley was undoubtedly right was in urging that novelists should not lose sight of the 'fictional possibilities of England' and the changing nature of English identity. The work of a number of recent novelists, as well as historians and literary critics, points towards a much more open and hospitable definition of national identity than was found, for example, two or three generations ago in the writings of George Orwell and J. B. Priestley. The novelist and critic Peter Ackroyd—who is often seen as a conservative figure—acknowledges Ford Madox Ford as a precursor in his sketch of *Albion: The Origins of the English Imagination* (2002). Ackroyd defines Englishness as 'the principle of appropriation. It relies upon constant immigration, of people or ideas or styles, in order to survive.'[10] A new style of historiography is exemplified by Norman Davies in *The Isles: A History* (1999), a work whose very title bypasses the genre of histories of 'England' and 'Britain' to which it nevertheless belongs. Crudely summarized, Davies's theme is both the construction of a United Kingdom comprising the major part of what are sometimes called 'these islands', and the losses (and, to a lesser extent, gains) resulting from that kingdom's severance from Europe. For Davies, Britain's severance from Europe was not an inevitable consequence of geography or the national temperament, but—more or less—the chance outcome of the Hundred Years War and the Reformation. Henry VIII's adoption of Protestantism as the English state religion, in Davies's words, 'cut England off from the cultural and intellectual community to which she had belonged for nearly a thousand years; and it forced her to develop along isolated, eccentric lines. The English have had little chance but to take pride in their isolation and eccentricity.'[11] Davies seems to believe that the severance from Europe is almost over, with popular hostility to the European Union constituting a last rearguard action on behalf of an outdated national pride.

Davies is in full-scale reaction against the triumphalism of former British imperialism, but in some respects *The Isles* perhaps falls short of its best insights. Not only is 'England' in the above quotation still resolutely female, but national development is implicitly presented as a species of individual development leading to the emergence of a pronounced national character: insular, eccentric, and full of pride. We need to remember that Davies has suggested that this was largely accidental—less a matter of inbuilt 'character' than the emergence and, in the end, the conscious adoption of a particular identity. *The Isles*, unlike most previous national histories, is at bottom a story of changing identities rather than of the consolidation of the English character. In this book I have argued that the movement from 'character' to 'identity' as a framework for analysis reflects certain tendencies that had long been present in the tradition of English fiction, including the work of novelists who are well known for their commitment to the ideas of fictional character and characterization.

Virginia Woolf, for example, vowed in her essay 'Mr Bennett and Mrs Brown' (1924) 'never, never to desert Mrs Brown', whom she imagined as an ordinary old lady in a railway carriage and, therefore, as 'the spirit we live by, life itself'.[12] It is only by sticking to Mrs Brown that writers, apparently, can overcome the social stratification and compartmentalization that Woolf in her later essay 'The Niece of an Earl' (1932) saw as typifying English society. For Woolf, the idea that 'We are enclosed, and separate, and cut off' is a structural and sociological fact, which creates the multi-textured social reality that novelists delight in:

We are enclosed, and separate, and cut off. Directly we see ourselves in the looking-glass of fiction we know that this is so. The novelist, and the English novelist in particular, knows and delights, it seems, to know that Society is a nest of glass boxes one separate from another, each housing a group with special habits and qualities of its own.[13]

Woolf's example of such a little group, or groups, is contained in her rather whimsical phrase 'the nieces of Earls and the cousins of Generals' (216). This means that her notion of 'Society' as a 'nest of glass boxes' is double-edged, since at one level it removes any obligation for the novelist to write across the cruder boundaries of class and caste in search of a 'vision of plurality' such as Ian McEwan has attributed to recent

American fiction.[14] Woolf seems to have half hoped and half feared that the advance of democracy would trample down all minor social distinctions, rendering the 'English novelist' obsolete: 'Novels may be written as seldom and as unsuccessfully by our descendants as the poetic drama by ourselves' (219).

Woolf's doubts about the immediate future of the English novel were manifestly misplaced. At the same time, her reference to the 'looking-glass of fiction' is a reminder that what we recognize when we look in a mirror is identity, not character. The identities that she chose to highlight in her 1932 essay were already vanishing, yet it can be argued that her intuition about English society as represented in the novel is still largely correct. It is the contents of the 'glass boxes' that have changed, so that instead of the subtle class divisions of Woolf's world we now have 'identity boxes'. That is, they house the cultural, ethnic, regional, and gender identities of the mixed and changing English population that is charted, most notably, in the novel of immigration. The England of many recent novels is less a network of different kinds of character (despite the continuing importance of characterization in fiction) than a chequerwork of increasingly deliberate and self-conscious identities. While many of the novels referred to in Chapter 15 were essentially realistic reports bringing news of contemporary experience, the modes of romance and fable are equally able to represent an England in which conflicts of identity and intricate problems of self-recognition have become part of the social and cultural fabric.

Two recent novels by Marina Warner, *Indigo, or Mapping the Waters* (1992) and *The Leto Bundle* (2001), offer an imaginatively reworked and slightly askew version of English society as the backdrop for fables of identity, colonial and postcolonial in the case of *Indigo* and international and stateless (in the sense that modern refugees and asylum seekers are perceived as stateless) in *The Leto Bundle*. In the former novel, the imperial summer game is not cricket but 'Flinders', while in the latter England has become, once again, 'Albion', and one of the protagonists sits on a government committee in the newly created Department of Cultural Identities. ' "Some of us are mongrels, yes. Some of us aren't. Some of those don't wish to entertain the mongrelisation of the nation," ' Kim McQuy tells his fellow committee members.[15] Kim is the son of Leto, an adopted child from a war-torn part of the world who is also the age-old goddess of migrants and an outcast member of the classical mythological pantheon. Her arrival on the shores of Albion joins universal history to the strictly contemporary. Warner is a student of mythology and an intellectual commentator whose use of the term 'mongrelisation' explicitly alludes to postcolonial debates about multi-culturalism and hybrid identities. Her novel has a political edge in its protest against right-wing propaganda and popular hostility towards immigrants and asylum seekers.

In the development of the English novel, the concept of national character has given way to national identity and the questioning of identity has become increasingly explicit. That national identity is (at least) problematic is part of the burden of many of the great English nineteenth-century novels, from *Northanger Abbey* and *Jane Eyre* to *Kim*. The term itself, however, did not become current until more recently, and it is possible that its first appearances were in immigrant fiction. In Andrew Salkey's *Escape to an Autumn Pavement* (1960), the Jamaican narrator laments to his English girlfriend that ' "Can't you see that I don't belong anywhere? . . . Where does anybody actually come face to face with his national identity?" '[16] The idea that national identity is problematic is now very widespread, if not universal. We may be confident that twenty-first-century novelists will continue to participate in the making and remaking of English identity.

Notes

Introduction

1. E. P. Thompson, 'The Peculiarities of the English', in *The Poverty of Theory and Other Essays* (London: Merlin, 1978), 35–91.
2. Peter Brooks, *Reading for the Plot: Design and Intention in Narrative* (Cambridge, Mass., and London: Harvard University Press, 1992), 130.
3. Florence Noiville, 'Jonathan Coe, l'homme-orchestre', *Le Monde* (23 July 2004), p. viii: 'Que les "anglo-addicts" se rassurent. Le roman "made in England"—une appelation originale aussi authentique que le Pim's ou le Stilton—ne s'est jamais, lui, aussi bien porté' [' "Anglo-addicts" should take heart. The novel "made in England"—a label of origin as unmistakable as Pimm's or Stilton—is stronger than ever'].
4. Henry James, *Letters*, vol. iii: 1883–1895, ed. Leon Edel (London: Macmillan, 1981), 244; Milan Kundera, 'Wisdom of Being', *Guardian*, 27 January 1994, ii. 8.
5. Quoted in Ulick O'Connor, ed., *The Joyce We Knew* (Cork: Mercier, 1967), 97.
6. Cf. Jed Esty, *A Shrinking Island: Modernism and National Culture in England* (Princeton and Oxford: Princeton University Press, 2004), 1.
7. Bertrand Russell, *Autobiography* (London and New York: Routledge, 1998), 394.
8. Margaret Drabble, *The Ice Age* (New York: Popular Library, 1977), 15.
9. See Esty, *A Shrinking Island*, *passim*.
10. See e.g. Paul Langford, *Englishness Identified: Manners and Character 1650–1850* (Oxford: Oxford University Press, 2000).
11. Brooks, *Reading for the Plot*, 10.
12. Ibid. 26.
13. Krishan Kumar, *The Making of English National Identity* (Cambridge: Cambridge University Press, 2003).
14. Antony Easthope, *Englishness and National Culture* (London and New York: Routledge, 1999), 28.
15. See Linda Colley, *Britons: Forging the Nation 1707–1837* (New Haven and London: Yale University Press, 1992); and Gerald Newman, *The Rise of English Nationalism: A Cultural History 1740–1830* (London: Weidenfeld, 1987).

Chapter 1. The Novel and the Nation

1. The case is argued at length by Margaret Anne Doody, *The True Story of the Novel* (London: HarperCollins, 1997).
2. William Congreve, *Incognita*, in Paul Salzman, ed., *An Anthology of Seventeenth-Century Fiction* (Oxford and New York: Oxford University Press, 1991), 474.

3. Walter Scott, 'Essay on Romance' (1822), quoted in Alexander Welsh, *The Hero of the Waverley Novels* (New Haven and London: Yale University Press, 1963), 13.

4. Simon During, 'Literature—Nationalism's Other? The Case for Revision', in Homi K. Bhabha, ed., *Nation and Narration* (London and New York: Routledge, 1990), 144.

5. Ian Watt, *The Rise of the Novel: Studies in Defoe, Richardson and Fielding* (Harmondsworth: Penguin, 1963), 14.

6. *The Diary of Samuel Pepys*, ed. Robert Latham and William Matthews (London: Bell, 1976), ix. 313.

7. Walter Bagehot, *The English Constitution* (London: Watts, 1964), 248.

8. Virginia Woolf, 'The Niece of an Earl', in *The Common Reader*, vol. ii, ed. Andrew McNeillie (London: Vintage, 2003), 218.

9. Bagehot, *The English Constitution*, 266 n.

10. Virginia Woolf, 'The Reader', in ' "Anon" and "The Reader": Virginia Woolf's Last Essays', ed. Brenda R. Silver, *Twentieth Century Literature* 25: 3/4 (Fall/Winter 1979), 429.

11. J. B. Priestley, *Margin Released: A Writer's Reminiscences and Reflections* (London: Heinemann, 1962), 138.

12. Robert Louis Stevenson, 'A Gossip on Romance', in *Memories and Portraits* (London: Chatto, 1920), 151–67.

13. William Hazlitt, 'Standard Novels and Romances', in *Complete Works*, ed. P. P. Howe (London and Toronto: Dent, 1933), xvi. 9. Subsequent page references in the text are to this (earlier) version of Hazlitt's essay.

14. William Hazlitt, *Lectures on the English Comic Writers* (London: Oxford University Press, 1920), 138. These words do not appear in the earlier version.

15. George Eliot, 'The Natural History of German Life: Riehl', in *Works*, Warwick edn. (Edinburgh and London: Blackwood, 1891), xii. 490–1.

16. See especially Benedict Anderson, *Imagined Communities: Reflections on the Origin and Spread of Nationalism* (London and New York: Verso, 1983).

17. Franco Moretti, *Atlas of the European Novel 1800–1900* (London and New York: Verso, 1998), 20.

18. Paul Gilbert, 'The Idea of a National Literature', in John Horton and Andrea T. Baumeister, eds., *Literature and the Political Imagination* (London and New York: Routledge, 1996), 206, 211.

19. Krishan Kumar, *The Making of English National Identity* (Cambridge: Cambridge University Press, 2003), 22–3.

20. Ibid. 34.

21. Jonathan Swift, *Gulliver's Travels* (1726; London: Folio Society, 1965), 174.

22. Caryl Phillips, ed., *Extravagant Strangers: A Literature of Belonging* (London: Faber, 1998), p. xiv.

23. William Hazlitt, 'Wilson's Life and Times of Daniel Defoe' (*Edinburgh Review*, January 1830), in *Complete Works*, ed. P. P. Howe, xvi. 381.

24. Edmund Burke, *Reflections on the Revolution in France and on the Proceedings in Certain Societies in London Relative to that Event*, ed. Conor Cruise O'Brien (Harmondsworth: Penguin, 1968), 117, 285, 376.

25. Sir Walter Scott, *The Lives of the Novelists* (London: Dent, and New York: Dutton, 1910), 385.

26. Edward W. Said, *The World, the Text, and the Critic* (London: Faber, 1984), 16–22, esp. 20.

27. David Hume, 'Of National Characters' in *Political Essays*, ed. Knud Haakansson (Cambridge: Cambridge University Press, 1994), 78.

28. Perry Anderson, 'Nation-States and National Identity', *London Review of Books* 13: 9 (9 May 1991), 7.

29. See e.g. Paul Langford, *Englishness Identified: Manners and Character 1650–1850* (Oxford: Oxford University Press, 2000), 10.

30. Anderson, 'Nation-States', 7.

31. George Eliot, *Middlemarch: A Study of Provincial Life*, World's Classics edn. (London: Oxford University Press, 1947), 157.

32. Daniel Defoe, *The True-Born Englishman and Other Writings*, ed. P. N. Furbank and W. R. Owens (London: Penguin, 1997), 36.

33. Hume, 'Of National Characters', 85–6.

34. Langford, *Englishness Identified*, 300–1.

35. Anderson, 'Nation-States', 7.

36. Anthony D. Smith, *National Identity* (London: Penguin, 1991), 4, 71.

37. Anderson, 'Nation-States', 8.

38. John Stuart Mill, 'Representative Government' (1861), in *Utilitarianism, On Liberty, Considerations on Representative Government, Remarks on Bentham's Philosophy*, ed. Geraint Williams (London: Dent, and North Clarendon, Vt.: Tuttle, 1993), 391, 395.

39. Walter Bagehot, *Physics and Politics: or Thoughts on the Application of the Principles of 'Natural Selection' and 'Inheritance' to Political Society*, 6th edn. (London: Kegan Paul, 1881), esp. 37, 100, 147.

40. Ibid. 21.

41. Ibid. 40, 150.

42. Henry Fielding, *Joseph Andrews and Shamela*, ed. Arthur Humphreys, rev. edn. (London: Dent, and North Clarendon, Vt.: Tuttle, 1993), 47, 218.

43. The phrase was used by a contemporary German critic of Fanny Burney's fiction; Langford, *Englishness Identified*, 10.

44. Scott, *The Lives of the Novelists*, 46.

45. See Katie Trumpener, *Bardic Nationalism: The Romantic Novel and the British Empire* (Princeton: Princeton University Press, 1997), *passim*. The term 'national allegory' is specifically associated with the cultural theory of Fredric Jameson. See e.g. his *Fables of Aggression: Wyndham Lewis, the Modernist as Fascist* (Berkeley: University of California Press, 1979), 87–104.

46. Gerry Smyth, *The Novel and the Nation: Studies in the New Irish Fiction* (London and Chicago: Pluto, 1997), 20. Smyth is explicating Jameson's notion of national allegory.

47. H. G. Wells, *Tono-Bungay* (London: Macmillan, 1909), 3. Subsequent page references in text.

48. Woolf, 'The Niece of an Earl', 214–15, 216.

49. D. H. Lawrence, *Women in Love*, ed. Charles L. Ross (Harmondsworth: Penguin, 1986), 108–9.

50. Hazlitt, 'Standard Novels and Romances', 8.

51. The vexed question of Jonathan Swift's relationship to the novel form turns, in part, on the extent to which in book four of *Gulliver's Travels* he seems to be debunking the rational horses and the ideal of (so to speak) horsemanship.

52. Matheo Aleman, *The Rogue, or The Life of Guzman de Alfarache*, trans. James Mabbe (1623) (London: Constable, and New York: Knopf, 1924), i. 92, 242.

53. Claudio Guillén, *Literature as System: Essays toward the Theory of Literary History* (Princeton: Princeton University Press, 1971), 79–81.

54. See A. L. Blackburn, 'The Picaresque Novel' (unpublished Ph.D. thesis: University of Cambridge, 1963), 162.

55. These questions are further pursued in e.g. Nancy Armstrong, *Desire and Domestic Fiction: A Political History of the Novel* (New York and Oxford: Oxford University Press, 1987), and Ruth Bernard Yeazell, *Fictions of Modesty: Women and Courtship in the English Novel* (Chicago and London: University of Chicago Press, 1991). On English vs. continental fiction see ibid. 78–9.

56. Bagehot, *The English Constitution*, 248.

57. Jane Austen, *Mansfield Park*, ed. Tony Tanner (Harmondsworth: Penguin, 1966), 434.

58. Brian W. Downs, *Richardson* (London: Routledge, and New York: Dutton, 1928), 109.

59. For this term see Trumpener, *Bardic Nationalism*, 137.

60. Orwell, *The Lion and the Unicorn: Socialism and the English Genius*, in *Collected Essays, Journalism and Letters*, ii. 68, 84.

61. Woolf, 'The Niece of an Earl', 216–17.

62. Bagehot, *The English Constitution*, 94.

63. E. T. (Jessie Chambers), *D. H. Lawrence: A Personal Record*, ed. J. D. Chambers (London: Cass, 1965), 103.

64. Martin Green, *Dreams of Adventure, Deeds of Empire* (London and Henley: Routledge, 1980), 61.

Chapter 2. Cavaliers, Puritans, and Rogues

1. See William Baldwin, *Beware the Cat: The First English Novel*, ed. William A. Ringler, Jr., and Michael Flachmann (San Marino, Calif: Huntington Library, 1988), 75, 84.

2. Ibid. 77.

3. Geoffrey of Monmouth, *The History of the Kings of Britain*, trans. Lewis Thorpe (London: Folio Society, 1969), 189.

4. Eugène Vinaver, ed., *The Works of Sir Thomas Malory*, 3 vols. (Oxford: Clarendon Press, 1947), i, p. v.

5. Sir Thomas Malory, *Le Morte d'Arthur*, Everyman edn., 2 vols. (London: Dent, and New York: Dutton, 1906), i. 3. Subsequent page references in text.

6. Jane Austen, *Northanger Abbey*, Everyman edn. (London: Dent, and New York: Dutton, 1970), 22.

7. On Sidney's sources see Sir Philip Sidney, *The Countess of Pembroke's Arcadia (The Old Arcadia)*, ed. Katherine Duncan-Jones, World's Classics edn. (Oxford: Oxford University Press, 1994), pp. xi–xiii. Subsequent page references in text.

8. See David Margolies, *Novel and Society in Elizabethan England* (London and Sydney: Croom Helm, 1985), 46–63, for an extended analysis of Lyly's position.

9. Cf. ibid. 55.

10. John Lyly, *Euphues: The Anatomy of Wit and Euphues and His England*, ed. Edward Arber (London: Constable, 1904), 431, 451. Subsequent page references in text.

11. Thomas Nashe, *The Unfortunate Traveller*, in *Shorter Novels: Elizabethan*, Everyman edn. (London: Dent, and New York: Dutton, 1929), 265, 267. Subsequent page references in text.

12. Thomas Hobbes, *Leviathan*, ed. C. B. Macpherson (Harmondsworth: Penguin, 1968), 186, 188. Subsequent page references in text.

13. *The Unfortunate Traveller* remained unreprinted until 1883. On Deloney and Puritanism see Thomas Deloney, *Works*, ed. Francis Oscar Mann (Oxford: Clarendon Press, 1912), pp. ix–xi.

14. Cf. Robert Mayer, *History and the Early English Novel: Matters of Fact from Bacon to Defoe* (Cambridge: Cambridge University Press, 1987), 148–9.

15. On the merchant caste cf. Martin Green, *Dreams of Adventure, Deeds of Empire* (London and Henley: Routledge, 1980), esp. 20, 62.

16. The tale also appears in Boccaccio. See Baldwin, *Beware the Cat*, 89.

17. Thomas Deloney, *Jack of Newbury*, in Paul Salzman, ed. *An Anthology of Elizabethan Prose Fiction* (Oxford and New York: Oxford University Press, 1987), 356. Cf. Margolies, *Novel and Society*, 131.

18. Thomas Deloney, *Thomas of Reading*, in *Shorter Novels: Elizabethan*, 83. Subsequent page references in text.

19. Ernest A. Baker suggests that the industry's golden age was in the reign of Henry VIII a mere sixty years before Deloney was writing, but the novelist backdated it by some three centuries in order to make the clothiers' dependence on royal protection seem part of the ancient English constitution. Baker, *The History of the English Novel*, vol. ii: *The Elizabethan Age and After* (London: Witherby, 1929), 187.

20. Paul Salzman, *English Prose Fiction 1558–1700: A Critical History* (Oxford: Clarendon Press, 1985), 114.

21. *The Princess Cloria: or, The Royal Romance. . . . Written by a Person of Honour* (London: Wood, 1661), 'To the Reader'.

22. Quoted in James Sutherland, ed., *The Oxford Book of English Talk* (Oxford: Clarendon Press, 1953), 108–9.

23. John Locke, *Two Treatises of Government*, ed. Peter Laslett (New York: New American Library, 1965), 467.

24. Quoted in Salzman, *English Prose Fiction 1558–1700*, 209.

25. Matheo Aleman, *The Rogue, or The Life of Guzman de Alfarache*, trans. James Mabbe (London: Constable, and New York: Knopf, 1924), 93.

26. Thomas Dangerfield, *Don Tomazo, Or the Juvenile Rambles of Thomas Dangerfield*, in Paul Salzman, ed., *An Anthology of Seventeenth-Century Fiction*, (Oxford and New York: Oxford University Press, 1991), 364. Subsequent page references in text.

27. Spiro Peterson, ed., *The Counterfeit Lady Unveiled and Other Criminal Fiction of Seventeenth-Century England* (Garden City, NY: Doubleday, 1961), 184.

28. See Ernest Bernbaum, *The Mary Carleton Narratives, 1663–1673: A Missing Chapter in the History of the Novel* (Cambridge: Cambridge University Press, 1914); and, for a recent account, Josephine Donovan, *Women and the Rise of the Novel, 1405–1726* (New York: St Martin's, 2000), 72–3.

29. Salzman, *English Prose Fiction 1558–1700*, 238.

30. Richard Head and Francis Kirkman, *The English Rogue, Described in the Life of Meriton Latroon* (New York: Dodd, Mead, 1928), 21–2, 142. Subsequent page references in text.

31. Salzman, *English Prose Fiction 1558–1700*, 239.

32. Ibid. 228–9.

33. Aphra Behn, *The Plays, Histories, and Novels*, 6 vols. (London: Pearson, 1871), i. 346–7.

34. John Bunyan, *The Holy War*, ed. Roger Sharrock and James F. Forrest (Oxford: Clarendon Press, 1980), 121. Subsequent page references in text.

35. Aphra Behn, *Oroonoko, The Rover and Other Works*, ed. Janet Todd (London: Penguin, 1992), 108.

36. See Maureen Duffy's introduction to Aphra Behn, *Love-Letters Between a Nobleman and His Sister* (London: Virago, 1987), p. vii. Subsequent page references in the text to *Love-Letters* are to this edition.

37. See Miranda J. Burgess, *British Fiction and the Production of Social Order, 1740–1830* (Cambridge: Cambridge University Press, 2000), 47. According to Josephine Donovan, however, *Love-Letters* 'remains largely in the vein of the *chronique scandaleuse*'. Donovan, *Women and the Rise of the Novel*, 91.

38. Richardson's *Clarissa* would later begin with what is invariably described as the 'rencounter' between Lovelace and the hot-tempered James Harlowe, in which the latter draws his sword without provocation.

39. Virginia Woolf, *Women and Writing*, ed. Michèle Barrett (London: Women's Press, 1979), 91.

40. See e.g. A. A. Parker, *Literature and the Delinquent: The Picaresque Novel in Spain and Europe 1599–1753* (Edinburgh: Edinburgh University Press, 1977), 100–1.

41. John Bunyan, *The Life and Death of Mr Badman*, ed. James F. Forrest and Roger Sharrock (Oxford: Clarendon Press, 1988), 87. Subsequent page references in text.

42. Mercy's courtship by Mr Brisk in part two of *The Pilgrim's Progress* is (unusually for Bunyan) rather more fully dramatized, but Mercy rejects her hypocritical suitor.

43. For example, in *The Holy War* Wet-eyes is the son of Mr Repentance; his mother gave him his name in his cradle when she saw what he was like (101).

44. Wilton House was the home of Mary Herbert, Countess of Pembroke, sister of Sir Philip Sidney and niece to the Earl of Leicester. By naming his scabrous page Wilton, Nashe seems to express his hostility to Herbert and her literary circle. Robinson Crusoe is, as Defoe's character explains, Anglo-German, and Crusoe almost rhymes with Defoe. Moreover, Defoe plays on the association between Crusoe and crusade, as will be seen in Ch. 3.

45. See Franco Moretti, *The Way of the World: The Bildungsroman in European Culture* (London: Verso, 1987), esp. 185–6, 213–14.

46. John Bunyan, *The Pilgrim's Progress*, ed. Roger Sharrock (Harmondsworth: Penguin, 1965), 362. Subsequent page references in text.

47. According to Leopold Damrosch, Jr., his name represents human free will, 'fickle' but 'active and powerful', and he changes sides during the conflict. See Damrosch, *God's Plot and Man's Stories: Studies in the Fictional Imagination from Milton to Fielding* (Chicago and London: University of Chicago Press, 1985), 142, 146.

48. Bunyan, *The Holy War*, 256 n.

49. Damrosch, *God's Plot and Man's Stories*, 143, 149.

50. John Bunyan, *Grace Abounding to the Chief of Sinners*, ed. Roger Sharrock (Oxford: Clarendon Press, 1962), 93. Subsequent page references in text.

51. There is a Valley of the Shadow of Death in both books. The 'land of Darkness' in *The Holy War* (227) might be identified with Darkland in *The Pilgrim's Progress* (350).

52. See Christopher Hill, *Liberty Against the Law: Some Seventeenth-Century Controversies* (London: Penguin, 1997), 39–40.

53. William III's census found that in England in the 1690s there were only 108,000 male Nonconformists as against nearly 2.5 million Anglicans. Ernest Barker, *National Character and the Factors in Its Formation* (London: Methuen, 1927), 202.

Chapter 3. Cross-Grained Crusoe: Defoe and the Contradictions of Englishness

1. Linda Colley, *Britons: Forging the Nation 1701–1837* (New Haven and London: Yale University Press, 1992), 1.

2. Joseph Addison, Sir Richard Steele, and Eustace Budgell, *Sir Roger de Coverly*, ed. John Hampden (London: Folio Society, 1967), 35. Subsequent page references in text.

3. John Arbuthnot, *The History of John Bull*, ed. Alan W. Bower and Robert A. Erickson (Oxford: Clarendon Press, 1976), p. cii.

4. Ibid. 9.

5. See Jeannine Surel, 'John Bull', in Raphael Samuel, ed., *Patriotism: The Making and Unmaking of British National Identity*, vol. iii: *National Fictions* (London and New York: Routledge, 1989), esp. 6–7, 9.

6. James Joyce, *Ulysses: the Corrected Text*, ed. Hans Walter Gabler with Wolfhard Steppe and Claus Melchior (New York: Vintage, 1986), 346.

7. Claudio Guillén, *Literature as System: Essays toward the Theory of Literary History* (Princeton: Princeton University Press, 1971), 79–81. See Ch. 1 above.

8. Daniel Defoe, *The Farther Adventures of Robinson Crusoe, Being the Second and Last Part of his Life*, ed. George A. Aitken (London: Dent, 1895), 319. Subsequent page references in text.

9. Daniel Defoe, *The Life of Captain Singleton* (London: Dent, 1906), 6. Subsequent page references in text.

10. Daniel Defoe, *Memoirs of a Cavalier*, ed. James T. Boulton (London: Oxford University Press, 1972), 125. Subsequent page references in text.

11. See e.g. *Defoe's Review*, ed. Arthur Wellesley Secord (New York: Columbia University Press, 1938), 14, 167. Quoted in David Trotter, *Circulation: Defoe, Dickens, and the Economies of the Novel* (Basingstoke: Macmillan, 1988), 4.

12. Daniel Defoe, *The Complete English Tradesman* (Gloucester: Sutton, 1987), 212. Subsequent page references in text.

13. Daniel Defoe, *The Consolidator*, in Henry Morley, ed., *The Earlier Life and Chief Earlier Works of Daniel Defoe* (London: Routledge, 1889), 298.

14. Daniel Defoe, *The True-Born Englishman and Other Writings*, ed. P. N. Furbank and W. R. Owens (London: Penguin, 1997), 30, 36. Subsequent page references in text.

15. Daniel Defoe, 'Explanatory Preface' to *The True-Born Englishman* in *The Shortest Way With the Dissenters and Other Pamphlets* (Oxford: Blackwell, 1927), 23.

16. Ibid. 24.

17. Britannia's Song properly consists of lines 893–956 of the current Penguin text edited by Furbank and Owens, which however omits to begin a new paragraph when Satire resumes at line 957.

18. Daniel Defoe, *The Original Power of the Collective Body of the people of England*, in *The True-Born Englishman and Other Writings*, 92. Subsequent page references in text.

19. Daniel Defoe, *Serious Reflections during the Life and Surprising Adventures of Robinson Crusoe, With his Vision of the Angelic World*, ed. George A. Aitken (London: Dent, 1895), p. ix. Subsequent page references in text. This is the third volume in the Robinson Crusoe 'trilogy', following the *Life and Surprising Adventures*—the *Robinson Crusoe* that everyone knows—and the *Farther Adventures*.

20. Daniel Defoe, *Moll Flanders* (London: Dent, and New York: Dutton, 1930), 236.

21. Daniel Defoe, *Roxana: The Fortunate Mistress*, ed. Jane Jack (Oxford and New York: Oxford University Press, 1981), 260.

22. Daniel Defoe, *The History and Remarkable Life of the Truly Honourable Colonel Jack* (London: Folio Society, 1967), 317.

23. See e.g. Alan Downie, '*Robinson Crusoe*'s Eighteenth-Century Contexts', in Lieve Spaas and Brian Stimpson, eds., *Robinson Crusoe: Myths and Metamorphoses* (Basingstoke and London: Macmillan, 1996), 20.

24. Daniel Defoe, *Robinson Crusoe: An Authoritative Text, Contexts, Criticism*, ed. Michael Shinagel, 2nd edn. (New York and London: Norton, 1994), 31. Subsequent page references in text.

25. See David Fausett, *The Strange Surprizing Sources of Robinson Crusoe* (Amsterdam and Atlanta, Ga.: Rodopi, 1994), 167.

26. Cf. ibid.

27. Daniel Defoe, *A Journal of the Plague Year*, ed. Anthony Burgess and Christopher Bristow (Harmondsworth: Penguin, 1966), 119, 249. Subsequent page references in text.

28. Martin Green notes that 'Defoe or his characters *disguise* themselves as Quakers, in costume or dialect; but they also clearly regard Quakerism as the purest of moral positions'. Green, *Dreams of Adventure, Deeds of Empire* (London and Henley: Routledge, 1980), 87.

29. A. L. Morton, *The English Utopia* (London: Lawrence & Wishart, 1969), 131; Ian Watt, '*Robinson Crusoe* as a Myth', in *Robinson Crusoe*, ed. Shinagel, 299.

30. For a relevant discussion see Michael Seidel, 'Crusoe's Island Exile', in Richard Kroll, ed., *The English Novel*, vol. i: *1700 to Fielding* (London and New York: Longman, 1998), esp. 197. Seidel implies that, through his absence from England, Crusoe is able to sustain the capitalist and expansionist ideals of the Commonwealth.

31. Paul J. Korshin, *Typologies in England 1650–1820* (Princeton: Princeton University Press, 1982), 220. For a comparable argument see Tom Paulin, 'Fugitive Crusoe', *London Review of Books* 23: 14 (19 July 2001), 15–20.

32. Walter Raleigh, *The English Novel: A Short Sketch . . .*, 5th edn. (London: Murray, 1911), 133. Cf. James Joyce, 'Daniel Defoe', in *Robinson Crusoe*, ed. Shinagel, 323.

33. Leslie Stephen, 'Defoe's Novels' (1868), in Pat Rogers, ed., *Daniel Defoe: The Critical Heritage* (London and New York: Routledge, 1972), 176.

34. Ibid. 177.

35. Defoe, *The True-Born Englishman*, 36.

36. Coleridge's marginalia quoted in *Daniel Defoe: The Critical Heritage*, 85.

37. Cited in Harvey Swados, '*Robinson Crusoe*: The Man Alone', in Daniel Defoe, *Robinson Crusoe*, Signet edn. (New York: New American Library, 1961), 307–8.

38. Louis James, 'Unwrapping Crusoe: Retrospective and Prospective Views', in Spaas and Stimpson, eds., *Robinson Crusoe*, 6–7.

39. Samar Attar, 'Serving God or Mammon?', ibid. 91–2.

40. Quoted in Swados, '*Robinson Crusoe*: The Man Alone', 312.

41. Ibid. 307.

42. Manuel Schonhorn, *Defoe's Politics: Parliament, Power, Kingship, and 'Robinson Crusoe'* (Cambridge: Cambridge University Press, 1991), 154, 162.

43. Trotter, *Circulation*, 37.

44. This point is made by Sara Sancini, 'The Island as Social Experiment', in Marialuisa Bignami, ed., *Wrestling with Defoe: Approaches from a Workshop on Defoe's Prose* (Milan: Cisalpino, 1997), 40.

45. Cf. Ian Watt, '*Robinson Crusoe* as a Myth', 296: 'For Crusoe hard work seems to be a condition of life itself, and we notice that the arrival of Friday is a signal, not for increased leisure, but for expanded production.'

Chapter 4. Histories of Rebellion: From 1688 to 1793

1. Henry Fielding, *Joseph Andrews and Shamela*, ed. Arthur Humphreys, revised edn. (London: Dent, and North Clarendon, Vt.: Tuttle, 1993), 216.

2. Henry Fielding, *The Journal of a Voyage to Lisbon*, ed. Tom Keymer (London: Penguin, 1996), 7.

3. Henry Fielding, *The History of Tom Jones*, ed. R. P. C. Mutter (Harmondsworth: Penguin, 1966), 7. Subsequent page references in text.

4. Jane Austen, *The History of England* (London: Penguin, 1995).

5. For the fullest survey of these works see Laird Okie, *Augustan Historical Writing: Histories of England in the English Enlightenment* (Lanham, Md.: University Press of America, 1991).

6. Oliver Goldsmith, 'Preface to *The History of England*', in *Collected Works*, ed. Arthur Friedman (Oxford: Clarendon Press, 1966), v. 338, 339.

7. Thomas Babington Macaulay, like his near-namesake Mr Crawley, condemned Hume as a cunning advocate of Stuart absolutism and an opponent of liberty. See Duncan Forbes, 'Introduction', in David Hume, *The History of Great Britain: The Reigns of James I and Charles I* (Harmondsworth: Penguin, 1970), 49. On Hume's claim to impartiality see ibid. 44.

8. Quoted in J. W. Burrow, *A Liberal Descent: Victorian Historians and the English Past* (Cambridge: Cambridge University Press, 1981), 14.

9. Austen, *The History of England*, 15–16.

10. Okie, *Augustan Historical Writing*, 21, 32.

11. Ibid. 32, 20, 137.

12. William Godwin, 'Of History and Romance', in *Things As They Are or the Adventures of Caleb Williams*, ed. Maurice Hindle (London: Penguin, 1988), 367.

13. Burrow, *A Liberal Descent*, 18.

14. See ibid.

15. Hume, *The History of Great Britain*, 183–4. Subsequent page references in text.

16. On 'revolution' in Hobbes and Locke see R. C. Richardson, *The Debate on the English Revolution* (London: Methuen, 1977), 146.

17. 'Of National Concord', reprinted from the *British Magazine* (December 1760) in Oliver Goldsmith, *Works*, ed. Peter Cunningham (London: Murray, 1854), i. 288. This essay was attributed to Goldsmith posthumously, but the attribution is no longer accepted. Smollett has been suggested as its possible author.

18. Oliver Goldsmith, *The History of England, from the Earliest Times to the Death of George the Second*, 11th edn., 4 vols. (London, 1812), ii. 446–7.

19. Godwin, 'Of History and Romance', 367.

20. The search for the hand of God in political events was one of the principal means of consolation for the defeated Puritans after 1660. See Christopher Hill, *God's Englishman: Oliver Cromwell and the English Revolution* (Harmondsworth: Penguin, 1972), 228, 239–40.

21. Godwin, 'Of History and Romance', 372.

22. *The Princess Cloria: or, The Royal Romance ... Written by a Person of Honour* (London: Wood, 1661), 'To the Reader'.

23. 'The Double Marriage: or, the Fatal Release. A True Secret History', in Eliza Haywood, *Three Novellas*, ed. Earla A. Wilputte (East Lansing, Mich.: Colleagues, 1995), 105–41.

24. Aphra Behn, *Oroonoko, The Rover and Other Works*, ed. Janet Todd (London: Penguin, 1992), 140. Subsequent page references in text.

25. See S. J. Wiseman, *Aphra Behn* (Plymouth: Northcote, 1996), 85; and Janet Todd, 'Introduction' to Behn, *Oroonoko, The Rover and Other Works*, 19.

26. S. J. Wiseman argues that the plays 'increasingly invite the audience to take pleasure in the staged defeat of republicanism', a defeat expressed largely in terms of sexual humiliation and which indicates the 'powerful frisson' that the fascinating but repellent Puritan cause held for Behn and her contemporaries. Wiseman, *Aphra Behn*, 45.

27. See Ch. 1, n. 2 above.

28. Colonel Newport, born in 1623, was too young to have won his spurs in the Swedish Army, as Defoe's narrator does before returning to England in 1635. See Daniel Defoe, *Memoirs of a Cavalier*, ed. James T. Boulton (London: Oxford University Press, 1972), pp. vii–viii. Subsequent page references in text.

29. M. M. Bakhtin, 'Epic and Novel', in *The Dialogic Imagination: Four Essays*, ed. Michael Holquist, (Austin, Tex: University of Texas Press, 1981), 13.

30. Paul Hunter, quoted in Homer Obed Brown, '*Tom Jones*: The "Bastard" of History', *Boundary* 2 7: 2 (1979), 210.

31. Thomas Hobbes, *Leviathan*, ed. C. B. Macpherson (Harmondsworth: Penguin, 1968), 257.

32. Quoted in Gordon J. Schochet, *Patriarchalism in Political Thought: The Authoritarian Family and Political Speculation and Attitudes Especially in Seventeenth-Century England* (Oxford: Blackwell, 1975), 24.

33. Perez Zagorin, *A History of Political Thought in the English Revolution* (London: Routledge, 1954), 199.

34. John Locke, *Two Treatises of Government*, ed. Peter Laslett, revised edn. (New York: New American Library, 1965), 362. Subsequent page references in text.

35. See Schochet, *Patriarchalism in Political Thought*, 148–9, 198–9, 274.

36. Mary Astell's work is discussed in relation to Richardson in Jocelyn Harris, *Samuel Richardson* (Cambridge: Cambridge University Press, 1987), 18.

37. On dramatic metaphors see ibid.

38. Congreve's *The Way of the World* (1700), for example, has been described as a displaced representation of the Whig interpretation of the fall of the Stuarts; see Richard Braverman, *Plots and Counterplots: Sexual Politics and the Body Politic in English Literature, 1660–1830* (Cambridge: Cambridge University Press, 1993), 213.

39. Aphra Behn, *Love-Letters Between a Nobleman and His Sister* (London: Virago, 1987), 3.

40. William Congreve, *The Way of the World*, in *Restoration Plays*, Everyman's Library edn. (London: Dent, and New York: Dutton, 1968), 180.

41. Samuel Richardson, *Selected Letters*, ed. John Carroll (Oxford: Clarendon Press, 1964), 85–6.
42. Samuel Richardson, title-page to *Pamela; or, Virtue Rewarded*, ed. Thomas Keymer and Alice Wakely (Oxford: Oxford University Press, 2001), 1; and Richardson, *Familiar Letters on Important Occasions* (London: Routledge, 1928), p. 187.
43. Samuel Richardson, *Pamela*, vol. ii, Everyman's Library edn. (London: Dent, and New York: Dutton, 1914), 458. Subsequent page references in text as 'P2'.
44. Brian W. Downs, *Richardson* (London: Routledge, and New York: Dutton, 1928), 159. *Clorana* contains characters called Clarissa and Clementina, so that it may be a source for the names of two of Richardson's four heroines.
45. Samuel Richardson, *Clarissa*, 4 vols., Everyman's Library edn. (London: Dent, and New York: Dutton, 1932), i. 23. Subsequent page references in text.
46. Samuel Richardson, *The History of Sir Charles Grandison*, ed. Jocelyn Harris, 3 vols. (London: Oxford University Press, 1972), ii. 199. Subsequent page references in text.
47. Samuel Richardson, *Pamela, or Virtue Rewarded*, ed. Peter Sabor (Harmondsworth: Penguin, 1980), 82. Subsequent page references in text.
48. For an interpretation of *Sir Charles Grandison* as national allegory reflecting Richardson's Anglican and anti-Catholic bias see Ewha Chung, *Samuel Richardson's New Nation: Paragons of the Domestic Sphere and 'Native' Virtue* (New York: Lang, 1998), *passim*.
49. Margaret A. Doody, 'Introduction', in *Pamela, or Virtue Rewarded*, ed. Sabor, 9.
50. On this point see Michael Austin, 'Lincolnshire Babylon: Competing Typologies in Pamela's 137th Psalm', *Eighteenth-Century Fiction* 12: 4 (2000), 501–14.
51. Thomas Keymer, 'Introduction' to *Pamela*, ed. Keymer and Wakely, pp. x–xi, xix–xx.
52. Henry Fielding, *The True Patriot and Related Writings*, ed. W. B. Coley (Oxford: Clarendon, 1987), 13, 23, 31.
53. In *Natural Masques: Gender and Identity in Fielding's Plays and Novels* (Stanford: Stanford University Press, 1995), 162, Jill Campbell argues that Fielding's portrayal of the King's army as 'unruly, inchoate, and divided' implies that there is little to choose between the two sides. But there is no suggestion in *Tom Jones* that the King's cause is not just.
54. Thomas Cleary draws attention to the allusions to the War of Austrian Succession early and late in the novel, and concludes that its reference to the '45 must result from a hasty, last-minute revision of the book's central chapters. But the War of Austrian Succession had ended in 1748, the year before *Tom Jones* was published, and it seems equally possible that it was the early and late parts of the novel that were updated. We do not know whether the sub-theme of the '45 was belatedly added or whether material on the rebellion was actually removed from the story. See Thomas Cleary, 'Jacobitism in *Tom Jones*: The Basis for an Hypothesis', *Philological Quarterly* 52: 2 (1973), 239–51, esp. 239, 241.

55. See Martin C. Battestin, 'Tom Jones and "His Egyptian Majesty": Fielding's Parable of Government', *PMLA* 82: 1 (1967), 68–77.
56. Peter J. Carlton, however, argues that Tom's and Sophia's marriage represents the 'reconciliation of England's Stuart past with her Whig-Hanoverian present'. See '*Tom Jones* and the '45 Once Again', *Studies in the Novel* 20: 4 (1988), 371.
57. See John Barrell, *English Literature in History 1730–80: An Equal, Wide Survey* (London: Hutchinson, 1983), 199–200.
58. Laurence Sterne, *The Life and Opinions of Tristram Shandy, Gentleman*, ed. Graham Petrie (Harmondsworth: Penguin, 1967), 447. Subsequent page references in text.
59. Graham Petrie notes that Slop is a caricature of Dr John Burton, who was imprisoned during the 1745 rebellion at the instigation of Sterne's rigorously anti-Catholic uncle. See *Tristram Shandy*, 626 n.
60. Samuel Johnson, 'The Bravery of the English Common Soldiers', in *Johnson: Prose and Poetry*, ed. Mona Wilson (London: Hart-Davis, 1963), 627. An early text praising the bravery of English soldiers is Richard Hawkins's *A Discourse on the National Excellencies of England* (1658). See Peter Furtado, 'National Pride in Seventeenth-Century England', in Raphael Samuel, ed., *Patriotism: The Making and Unmaking of British National Identity*, vol i: *History and Politics* (London and New York: Routledge, 1989), 48.
61. T. Smollett, *The History of England from the Restoration to the Death of George the Second*, iv. 475.
62. Henry Mackenzie, *The Man of Feeling*, ed. Brian Vickers (London: Oxford University Press, 1970), 109.
63. Charlotte Smith, *The Old Manor House*, ed. Anne Henry Ehrenpreis (London: Oxford University Press, 1969), 523. Subsequent page references in text.
64. Cf. Loraine Fletcher, 'Four Jacobin Women Novelists', in John Lucas, ed., *Writing and Radicalism* (London and New York: Longman, 1996), 123.
65. See Jacqueline M. Labbe, 'Metaphoricity and the Romance of Property in *The Old Manor House*', *Novel* 34: 2 (2001), 216–31.

Chapter 5. The Novel of Suffering: Richardson, Fielding, and Goldsmith

1. T. Smollett, M.D., *The History of England from the Revolution to the Death of George the Second (Designed as a Continuation of Mr Hume's History)*, 5 vols. (London, 1796), iii. 357. Subsequent page references in text.
2. Oliver Goldsmith, *The Citizen of the World: or Letters from a Chinese Philosopher residing in London to his friends in the East* (London: Folio Society, 1969), 271–2.
3. See Laura Brown, *English Dramatic Form, 1660–1760: An Essay in Generic History* (New Haven and London: Yale University Press, 1981), 195–6.
4. Margaret Anne Doody, quoted in Miranda J. Burgess, *British Fiction and the Production of Social Order, 1740–1830* (Cambridge: Cambridge University Press, 2000), 77.

5. See Jonathan Lamb, *The Rhetoric of Suffering: Reading the Book of Job in the Eighteenth Century* (Oxford: Clarendon Press, 1995), esp. 4.

6. Smollett, *The History of England*, v. 381–2.

7. Ann Radcliffe, *The Mysteries of Udolpho*, Everyman edn., 2 vols. (London: Dent, and New York: Dutton, 1931), ii. 51.

8. Christopher Hill, 'Clarissa Harlowe and Her Times', in *Puritanism and Revolution* (London: Panther, 1968), esp. 351–5.

9. Samuel Richardson, *Clarissa*, 4 vols., Everyman edn. (London: Dent, and New York: Dutton, 1932), i. 33. Subsequent page references in text.

10. Among the critics who have commentated on Richardson's naming are Margaret Anne Doody, 'Richardson's Politics', *Eighteenth-Century Fiction* 2: 2 (1990), 121–4. Carol Kay considers that James Harlowe's name implies an association with Stuart tyranny: Kay, *Political Constructions: Defoe, Richardson, and Sterne in Relation to Hobbes, Hume and Burke* (Ithaca, NY, and London: Cornell University Press, 1988), 167. Paul J. Korshin, by contrast, sees Clarissa and Lovelace as theological 'type names'—Clarissa is 'the superlative of perfection', while Lovelace means 'bereft of the love of God': Korshin, *Typologies in England 1650–1820* (Princeton: Princeton University Press, 1982), 246.

11. Tom Keymer, *Richardson's 'Clarissa' and the Eighteenth-Century Reader* (Cambridge: Cambridge University Press, 1992), 157.

12. Samuel Richardson, *The History of Sir Charles Grandison*, ed. Jocelyn Harris, 3 vols. (London: Oxford University Press, 1972), i. 84. Subsequent page references in text.

13. Kay, *Political Constructions*, 170.

14. Quoted in Keymer, *Richardson's 'Clarissa'*, 119.

15. Recent criticism of *Clarissa* has largely avoided discussing this episode. According to Terry Eagleton, for example, Lovelace is a 'reactionary throwback, an old-style libertine or Restoration relic', and the 'mechanism of his downfall' shows the 'triumph of bourgeois patriarchy'. In that case Richardson should not have found it necessary to fall back on the reactionary aristocratic code to ensure Lovelace's punishment. Eagleton, *The Rape of Clarissa: Writing, Sexuality and Class Struggle in Samuel Richardson* (Oxford: Blackwell, 1982), 76.

16. Korshin, *Typologies in England*, 245.

17. Samuel Richardson, *Pamela, or Virtue Rewarded*, ed. Peter Sabor (Harmondsworth: Penguin, 1980), 43.

18. Martin C. Battestin, *The Providence of Wit: Aspects of Form in Augustan Literature and the Arts* (Oxford: Clarendon Press, 1974), 201.

19. I. A. Richards, *Beyond* (New York and London: Harcourt Brace, 1974), 48.

20. Battestin, *The Providence of Wit*, 199, 208.

21. Nevertheless the divine justice which Clarissa may expect is expressed by Lovelace's friend Belford in terms of an earthly metaphor. Warning that 'thou wilt certainly meet thy punishment . . . as she will her reward, HEREAFTER', he adds, '*It must* be so, if there really be such a thing as *future remuneration*' (iii. 456).

22. See Hill, 'Clarissa Harlowe and Her Times', 364.

23. See Korshin, *Typologies in England*, 250 n. A number of critics have analysed the role of the Job story in the plot of *Clarissa*. Lovelace, as Lois E. Bueler observes, explicitly identifies with Satan and pretends that his testing of the heroine's virtue is actually in her own interest; Bueler, *Clarissa's' Plots* (Newark, Del.: University of Delaware Press, and London: Associated University Presses, 1994), 55–6. Both the Harlowes and Anna Howe (who urges Clarissa to enter into a marriage of expediency with Lovelace after the rape) can be regarded as false comforters; see ibid. 67, and Tom Keymer, 'Richardson's *Meditations*: Clarissa's *Clarissa*', in Margaret Anne Doody and Peter Sabor, eds., *Samuel Richardson: Tercentenary Essays* (Cambridge: Cambridge University Press, 1989), 98–9.

24. Lamb, *The Rhetoric of Suffering*, 230; Robert A. Erickson, ' "Written in the Heart": *Clarissa* and Scripture', *Eighteenth-Century Fiction* 2: 1 (1989), 41.

25. Keymer, *Richardson's 'Clarissa'*, 212; Lamb, *The Rhetoric of Suffering*, 112.

26. Korshin, *Typologies in England*, 249.

27. Christopher Hill, *The English Bible and the Seventeenth-Century Revolution* (London: Allen Lane, 1993), 262.

28. Lamb, *The Rhetoric of Suffering*, 230.

29. Daniel Defoe, *Moll Flanders* (London: Dent, and New York: Dutton, 1930), 236.

30. Cited in Battestin, *The Providence of Wit*, 209.

31. Henry Fielding, *Amelia*, 2 vols. (London: Bell, 1914), i. 3. Subsequent page references in text.

32. Sarah Fielding, *The Adventures of David Simple*, ed. Malcolm Kelsall (Oxford: Oxford University Press, 1994), 334, 415.

33. Frances Sheridan, *Memoirs of Miss Sidney Bidulph, Extracted from her own Journal, and now first published* (London and New York: Pandora, 1987), 429. Subsequent page references in text.

34. Henry Fielding, *Amelia*, Everyman edn., 2 vols. (London and Toronto: Dent, and New York: Dutton, 1930), i, p. xv.

35. On the implausibility of the novel's denouement see Patricia Meyer Spacks, *Imagining a Self: Autobiography and Novel in Eighteenth-Century England* (Cambridge, Mass., and London: Harvard University Press, 1976), esp. 281, 285–6.

36. Brian McCrea comments on the improbability of this scene, though doubtless in Fielding's experience the necessity of kowtowing before the great was all too familiar. McCrea also remarks of Amelia that 'her virtue is lame because Fielding will not permit it to combat the vice it encounters'. See McCrea, *Henry Fielding and the Politics of Mid-Eighteenth-Century England* (Athens, Ga.: University of Georgia Press, 1981), 186–7.

37. Ibid. 187.

38. Mary Wollstonecraft, *Mary, A Fiction and The Wrongs of Woman*, ed. Gary Kelly (London: Oxford University Press, 1976), p. xxxi. Subsequent page references in text.

39. Lucius Apuleius, *The Transformations of Lucius, otherwise known as the Golden Ass*, trans. Robert Graves (Harmondsworth: Penguin, 1950), 214.

40. Oliver Goldsmith, *The Vicar of Wakefield*, Everyman edn. (London: Dent, and New York: Dutton, 1962), 56. Subsequent page references in text.

41. The fact that the Vicar's father was killed with Lord Falkland at the Battle of Newbury in 1643 means that Goldsmith's novel is set very early in the eighteenth century, at least fifty or sixty years before its publication date. Primrose is a contemporary of the controversialist William Whiston (1667–1752), some of whose opinions he shares.

42. For other accounts of Goldsmith's use of Job in *The Vicar of Wakefield* see Battestin, *The Providence of Wit*, esp. 198–9, 214; Korshin, *Typologies in England*, esp. 256; and Ronald J. Paulson, *Satire and the Novel in Eighteenth-Century England* (New Haven and London: Yale University Press, 1967), 270–4.

43. See Frank Morley, *Literary Britain: A Reader's Guide to Writers and Landmarks* (London: Hutchinson, 1980), 390–1.

Chapter 6. The Benevolent Robber: from Fielding to the 1790s

1. Henry Fielding, *The History of Tom Jones*, ed. R. P. C. Mutter (Harmondsworth: Penguin, 1966), 59. Subsequent page references in text.

2. Anthony, Earl of Shaftesbury, *Characteristics of Men, Manners, Opinions, Times*, ed. John M. Robertson (Indianapolis and New York: Bobbs-Merrill, 1964), 268, 317. Subsequent page references in text.

3. Thomas Hobbes, *Leviathan*, ed. C. B. Macpherson (Harmondsworth: Penguin, 1968), 161. Subsequent page references in text.

4. Cf. Douglas Hay, 'Property, Authority and the Criminal Law', in Hay et al., *Albion's Fatal Tree: Crime and Society in Eighteenth-Century England* (London: Allen Lane, 1975), 38. Hay argues that the property qualification existed to exclude ordinary people, who would inevitably have been of Hobbes's opinion, from jury service.

5. Bernard Mandeville, *The Fable of the Bees, or Private Vices, Public Benefits*, ed. Douglas Garman (London: Wishart, 1934), 88, 77.

6. Daniel Defoe, *Memoirs of a Cavalier*, ed. James T. Boulton (London: Oxford University Press, 1972), 12–13.

7. Oliver Goldsmith, *The Citizen of the World: or Letters from a Chinese Philosopher residing in London to his friends in the East* (London: Folio Society, 1969), 273.

8. Cf. Laura Brown, *English Dramatic Form, 1660–1760: An Essay in Generic History* (New Haven and London: Yale University Press, 1981), 198.

9. Patricia Meyer Spacks, *Imagining a Self: Autobiography and Novel in Eighteenth-Century England* (Cambridge, Mass., and London: Harvard University Press, 1976), 12.

10. Not only were the criminal biographies full of tall tales and inventions, but they incorporated such things as the life of Colonel Jack 'as written by himself'—a summary of Defoe's novel. See Capt. Charles Johnson, *A General History of the Lives and Adventures of the Most Famous Highwaymen, Murderers, Street-Robbers, & C.* (London, 1734), 117.

11. Johnson, *General History*, 1. The *Newgate Calendar* first published in five volumes in 1773 was a collation of Smith, Johnson, and some later publications. See J. L. Rayner and G. T. Crook, eds., *The Complete Newgate Calendar*, 5 vols. (London: Navarre Society, 1926).

12. John Gay, *The Beggar's Opera*, in John Hampden, ed., *The Beggar's Opera and Other Eighteenth-Century Plays* (London: Dent, and New York: Dutton, 1964), 127, 158.

13. Henry Fielding, *An Enquiry into the Causes of the Late Increase of Robbers and Related Writings*, ed. Malvin R. Zirker (Oxford: Clarendon Press, 1988), 73, p. lv (where the editor cites the *Whitehall Evening-Post*, 3–6 February 1750). For an exploration of Fielding's complex attitudes to crime see also Ian A. Bell, *Literature and Crime in Augustan England* (London and New York: Routledge, 1991), esp. 183–9.

14. Defoe in *An Essay upon Projects* advocates provincial banking and the improvement of the road system. His pamphlet *Street-Robberies Consider'd* (1728) advises people not to carry too much money around with them; see Peter Linebaugh, *The London Hanged: Crime and Civil Society in the Eighteenth Century* (London: Allen Lane, 1991), 211–12. Fielding wrote that the 'Wandering' of the poor was one cause of the 'Increase of Robbers'. Another reason for his somewhat alarmist view of the problem in 1751 was that, three years earlier, 54,000 men had been discharged from the army and navy after the Peace of Aix-la-Chapelle. Fielding, *Enquiry*, 75 n., 138.

15. Lincoln B. Faller, *Turned to Account: The Forms and Functions of Criminal Biography in Late Seventeenth- and Early Eighteenth-Century England* (Cambridge: Cambridge University Press, 1987), 178.

16. The highwayman's traditional show of gallantry towards his wealthy victims may be related to the fact that only the rich were likely to initiate the private prosecution needed to bring a thief to trial. See Hay, 'Property, Authority and the Criminal Law', 41–2.

17. Henry Fielding, *The History of the Adventures of Joseph Andrews and His Friend Mr Abraham Adams*, Signet edn. (New York: New American Library, 1960), 326. Subsequent page references in text.

18. Henry Fielding, *The History of the Life of the Late Mr Jonathan Wild the Great*, World's Classics edn. (London: Oxford University Press, 1932), 133. Subsequent page references in text.

19. For the real-life Tom Jones see Captain Alexander Smith, *A Complete History of the Lives and Robberies of the Most Notorious Highwaymen, Footpads, Shoplifts, and Cheats of Both Sexes*, ed. Arthur L. Hayward (London: Routledge, 1926), 177–80.

20. *The Life and Death of Gamaliel Ratsey*, Shakespeare Association Facsimiles 10 (London: Oxford University Press, 1935) (unnumbered pages). Ratsey also makes use of the classic phrase 'Stand and deliver'.

21. Smith, *Complete History*, 44.

22. See Joan Parkes, *Travel in England in the Seventeenth Century* (London: Oxford University Press, 1925), 154.

23. Edward Hyde, Earl of Clarendon, *The History of the Great Rebellion*, ed. Roger Lockyer (London: Oxford University Press, 1967), 456.

24. For Howard, see Johnson, *General History*, 160; for Cottington see Smith, *Complete History*, 325. Other Royalist highwaymen whose reputations survived into the eighteenth century include Nevison, Hind, Stafford, Frith, and Gilder-Roy. On the targeting of Cromwell Captain Johnson comments that 'the Writers of that Time...have probably made this Usurper and his Friends to be serv'd in this Manner much oftener than they really were' (311).

25. See for example Aphra Behn, *Love-Letters Between a Nobleman and His Sister* (London: Virago, 1987), 438: ' "you have attacked me on the King's high-way, and have robbed me of a heart." '

26. Samuel Richardson, *Clarissa*, ed. Angus Ross (Harmondsworth: Penguin, 1985), 165, 337.

27. Samuel Richardson, *The History of Sir Charles Grandison*, ed. Jocelyn Harris, 3 vols. (London: Oxford University Press, 1972), i. 197.

28. See Ruth Bernard Yeazell, *Fictions of Modesty: Women and Courtship in the English Novel* (Chicago and London: University of Chicago Press, 1991), 104–5.

29. According to Terry Castle in her study of this topic, the masquerade offers the 'image of an ecstatic anti-society' pervaded by a 'World-Upside-Down ambience' and threatening to undermine the dominant narrative ideology. Castle, *Masquerade and Civilization: The Carnivalesque in Eighteenth-Century English Culture and Fiction* (London: Methuen, 1986), esp. 92–3, 106, 120–1.

30. Ibid. 31, citing the *Gentleman's Magazine* of 1753. The culprits appeared before Justice Fielding.

31. Rt. Hon. Lord Lytton, *Paul Clifford*, Stevenage edn. (London: Routledge, n.d.), 217.

32. See Linebaugh, *The London Hanged*, esp. 184–9, for evidence that the highwaymen of the late 1730s were mostly unemployed tradesmen. By contrast, a number of the earlier figures celebrated in the criminal biographies were university graduates and/or younger sons of the gentry.

33. Lennard J. Davis, *Factual Fictions: The Origins of the English Novel* (New York: Columbia University Press, 1983), 123–5. See also Frederick R. Karl, *A Reader's Guide to the Development of the English Novel in the Eighteenth Century* (London: Thames & Hudson, 1974), 48–9.

34. Douglas Hay, 'Property, Authority and the Criminal Law', 18, 53.

35. Martin J. Wiener, *English Culture and the Decline of the Industrial Spirit 1850–1980* (Cambridge: Cambridge University Press, 1981), 8.

36. Daniel Defoe, *The Fortunes and Misfortunes of the Famous Moll Flanders*, ed. G. A. Starr, World's Classics edn. (Oxford: Oxford University Press, 1981), 280, 301.

37. Henry Fielding, *Amelia*, ed. Martin C. Battestin (Oxford: Clarendon Press, 1983), 97.

38. Tobias Smollett, *The Expedition of Humphry Clinker*, ed. Louis M. Knapp and Paul Gabriel Boucé (Oxford and New York: Oxford University Press, 1984), 150. Subsequent page references in text.

39. Fielding, *Enquiry*, 136.

40. Gay, *Beggar's Opera*, 127.

41. Smith, *Complete History*, 412.

42. Quoted in Linebaugh, *The London Hanged*, 203–4.

43. Smith, *Complete History*, 360.

44. See e.g. Faller, *Turned to Account*, 188; Linebaugh, *The London Hanged*, 217. Another writer who argues that the robber stands for 'true justice' is Graham Seal, *The Outlaw Legend: A Cultural Tradition in Britain, America and Australia* (Cambridge: Cambridge University Press, 1996), 200–1.

45. Smith, *Complete History*, 408.

46. [Thomas Percy, ed.], *Percy's Reliques of Ancient English Poetry*, Everyman edn., 2 vols. (London and Toronto: Dent, and New York: Dutton, 1906), esp. i. 115–16. On Robin Hood societies, see H. T. Dickinson, *The Politics of the People in Eighteenth-Century Britain* (Basingstoke and London: Macmillan, 1995), 98. Fielding satirized the semi-literate 'Robinhoodians' in the *Covent-Garden Journal*, in 1752; *The Works of Henry Fielding, Esq.*, ed. Leslie Stephen, vol. vi (London: Smith, Elder, 1882), esp. 31–6.

47. 'Prince of all robbers' is Ritson's phrase. [Joseph Ritson, ed.], *Robin Hood: A Collection of all the Ancient Poems, Songs and Ballads, Now Extant . . .* [1823] (Wakefield, Yorks: EP, 1972), p. x.

48. For 'Grandeur and Hospitality' see Johnson, *General History*, 19. It has been argued that the eighteenth-century versions of the legend show Robin's liberality as deriving less from a notion of social redistribution than from the 'aristocratic virtues of largesse and display'. In other words, his generosity towards the poor and deserving reflected a plebeian fantasy of how the rich and successful ought to behave. See R. D. Dobson and J. Taylor, *Rymes of Robin Hood: An Introduction to the English Outlaw* (London: Book Club Associates, 1976), 55.

49. Daniel Defoe, *The History and Remarkable Life of the Truly Honourable Colonel Jack* (London: Folio Society, 1967), 78, 98–9.

50. According to Colonel Jack, Pindar of Wakefield is on the road from Gray's Inn Lane to Kentish Town (ibid. 74). There is a Wakefield Street close to the modern Gray's Inn Road.

51. Gary Kelly, *The English Jacobin Novel 1780–1805* (Oxford: Clarendon Press, 1976), 38–40.

52. Ritson, understandably, strongly disliked *Caleb Williams*. On his relationship with Godwin see Bertrand H. Bronson, *Joseph Ritson: Scholar-at-Arms*, 2 vols. (Berkeley: University of California Press, 1938), i. 146. Godwin speaks of his research for *Caleb Williams* in his 1832 preface to *Fleetwood*. See William Godwin, *Things as They Are or the Adventures of Caleb Williams*, ed. Maurice Hindle (London: Penguin, 1988), 351–2.

53. Ibid. 224. Subsequent page references in text.

54. Pamela Clemit, *The Godwinian Novel: The Rational Fictions of Godwin, Brockden Brown, Mary Shelley* (Oxford: Clarendon Press, 1993), 53.

55. Sir Walter Scott, *Rob Roy*, ed. John Sutherland, Everyman edn. (London: Dent, and North Clarendon, Vt.: Tuttle, 1995), 24, 384.

56. Sir Walter Scott, *The Heart of Mid-Lothian*, ed. Tony Inglis (London: Penguin, 1994), 288.

57. W. Harrison Ainsworth, *Rookwood: A Romance* (London and New York: Routledge, n.d.), 163–4.
58. Ibid., p. xxxiii.
59. Charles Dickens, *Oliver Twist*, ed. Peter Fairclough (London: Penguin, 1985), 34–5. The preface first appeared in the third edition of the novel.
60. On *Oliver Twist* as Dickensian prototype see Anny Sadrin, *Parentage and Inheritance in the Novels of Charles Dickens* (Cambridge: Cambridge University Press, 1994), 146.

Chapter 7. Romantic Toryism: Scott, Disraeli, and Others

1. William Hazlitt, *Lectures on the English Poets and The Spirit of the Age* (London: Dent, and New York: Dutton, 1910), 228. Subsequent page references in text.
2. Jane Austen, *Northanger Abbey*, Everyman edn. (London: Dent, and New York: Dutton, 1970), 165. Subsequent page references in text.
3. Jane Austen, *Emma*, ed. Ronald Blythe (Harmondsworth: Penguin, 1966), 355. Subsequent page references in text.
4. Walter Scott, review of *Tales of My Landlord* in Scott, *On Novelists and Fiction*, ed. Ioan Williams (London: Routledge, 1968), 259.
5. See Malcolm Bradbury, *Dangerous Pilgrimages: Trans-Atlantic Mythologies and the Novel* (London: Secker, 1995), 69–73.
6. Washington Irving, *The Sketch Book of Geoffrey Crayon, Gent.* in *Washington Irving: History, Tales and Sketches* (New York: Library of America, 1983), 744. Subsequent page references in text.
7. See J. A. R. Pimlott, *The Englishman's Christmas: A Social History* (Sussex: Harvester, 1978), 79, 194.
8. Geoffrey Crayon, Gent., *Bracebridge Hall; or The Humorists*, 2 vols. (London: Murray, 1822), ii. 25, 28. Subsequent page references in text.
9. Mary Russell Mitford, letter of 16 January 1824 quoted in P. D. Edwards, *Idyllic Realism from Mary Russell Mitford to Hardy* (Basingstoke: Macmillan, 1988), 157.
10. Mary Russell Mitford, 'Introduction', in *Our Village: Sketches of Rural Character and Scenery*, 5th ser. (London: Whittaker, 1832), 3–4.
11. Mary Russell Mitford, *Our Village*, ed. Ernest Rhys (London and Felling-on-Tyne: Walter Scott, [1891]), 58. Subsequent page references in text are to this selection.
12. Mitford, *Our Village: Sketches of Rural Character and Scenery* (London: Whittaker, 1824), 273. P. D. Edwards notes the frequency with which Mitford evokes painters and paintings, especially of the Dutch school (*Idyllic Realism*, 8).
13. Quoted in Edwards, *Idyllic Realism*, 157.
14. Mitford, *Our Village*, 5th ser., 6–7.
15. See Edwards, *Idyllic Realism*, 2
16. Elizabeth K. Helsinger, *Rural Scenes and National Representation: Britain, 1815–1850* (Princeton: Princeton University Press, 1997), 129, 131.

17. Edmund Burke, *Reflections on the Revolution in France and on the Proceedings in Certain Societies in London Relative to that Event*, ed. Conor Cruise O'Brien (Harmondsworth: Penguin, 1968), 117, 285.

18. Martin Green, *Dreams of Adventure, Deeds of Empire* (London and Henley: Routledge, 1980), 128.

19. Clara Reeve, *The Old English Baron: A Gothic Story*, ed. James Trainer (London: Oxford University Press, 1967), 152.

20. Sir Walter Scott, *Waverley*, Everyman's Library edn. (London: Dent, and New York: Dutton, 1969), 406. Subsequent page references in text.

21. Sir Walter Scott, *Ivanhoe*, ed. Graham Tulloch (Edinburgh: Edinburgh University Press, 1998), 7. Subsequent page references in text.

22. [Archibald Allison], 'The Historical Romance', in *Blackwood's Edinburgh Magazine* 58: 359 (September 1845), 349, 352, 355.

23. Leslie Stephen, 'Some Words about Sir Walter Scott', in John O. Hayden, ed., *Scott: The Critical Heritage* (London: Routledge, 1970), 453, 457.

24. For a recent discussion see Norman Davies, *The Isles: A History* (London: Macmillan, 2000), 335–7.

25. Sir Walter Scott, *Redgauntlet: A Tale of the Eighteenth Century* (London: Black, 1932), 365.

26. Quotations from *Chartism* and *Past and Present* in Thomas Carlyle, *Selected Writings*, ed. Alan Shelston (Harmondsworth: Penguin, 1971), 156, 280. Carlyle alludes to Gurth the swineherd in *Ivanhoe* in order to illustrate the exploitation of the poorest workers. *Past and Present* (London: Chapman & Hall, 1889), 19.

27. *The Journal of Sir Walter Scott 1825–26* (Edinburgh and London: Oliver & Boyd, 1939), 135.

28. Burke, *Reflections on the Revolution in France*, 117.

29. Scott, review of *Tales of My Landlord* in *On Novelists and Fiction*, 240; Alexander Welsh, *The Hero of the Waverley Novels* (New Haven and London: Yale University Press, 1963), 53 and *passim*.

30. John Ruskin, *Modern Painters*, 5 vols. (London: Allen, 1906), iii. 288.

31. Walter Scott, *Kenilworth: A Romance*, ed. J. H. Alexander (London: Penguin, 1999), 1. Subsequent page references in text.

32. Sir Walter Scott, *Peveril of the Peak*, ed. Andrew Lang (London: Macmillan, 1910), 820.

33. Welsh, *The Hero of the Waverley Novels*, 59.

34. Maria Edgeworth, *Castle Rackrent and The Absentee*, Everyman's Library edn. (London: Dent, and New York: Dutton, 1910), 124.

35. Cf. Daniel Cottam, *The Civilized Imagination: A Study of Ann Radcliffe, Jane Austen, and Sir Walter Scott* (Cambridge: Cambridge University Press, 1985), 168. Cottam's general discussion of the clash of aristocratic and middle-class values in Scott and his contemporaries is richly suggestive.

36. Walter Scott, Introduction to *Minstrelsy of the Scottish Border*, quoted in David Daiches, 'Scott's Achievement as a Novelist', in D. D. Devlin, ed., *Walter Scott: Modern Judgements* (Nashville and London: Aurora, 1970), 39.

37. Heinrich Heine, Introduction to *Don Quixote* (1837), in Hayden, ed., *Scott: The Critical Heritage*, 304–5.

38. Green, *Dreams of Adventure, Deeds of Empire*, 104.

39. Sir Walter Scott, *Guy Mannering, or The Astrologer*, ed. Andrew Lang (London: Nimmo, 1898), 404.

40. Stephen, 'Some Words about Sir Walter Scott', in Hayden, ed., *Scott: The Critical Heritage*, 452. For Stendhal's account of the wineglass incident see ibid. 320–1.

41. Scott, *Waverley*, 1.

42. *The Journal of Sir Walter Scott 1825–26*, 135.

43. Richard Hengist Horne, ed., *A New Spirit of the Age* (1844) (London: Oxford University Press, 1907), 156.

44. [Allison], 'The Historical Romance', 345, 347.

45. Edward Lytton Bulwer, *England and the English*, ed. Standish Meacham (Chicago and London: University of Chicago Press, 1970), 372. Subsequent page references in text.

46. Disraeli the Younger, *Vindication of the English Constitution in a Letter to a Noble and Learned Lord* (1835) (Farnborough, Hants: Gregg International, 1969), 172–3. Subsequent page references in text.

47. Benjamin Disraeli, *Sybil or The Two Nations*, ed. Thom Braun (Harmondsworth: Penguin, 1980), 96. Subsequent page references in text.

48. Benjamin Disraeli, *Coningsby*, World's Classics edn. (London: Oxford University Press, 1931), 68. Subsequent page references in text.

49. Catherine Gallagher notes that Sybil has Jewish overtones, though by virtue of her association with the Blessed Virgin rather than with Rebecca; Gallagher, *The Industrial Reformation of English Fiction: Social Discourse and Narrative Form 1832–1867* (Chicago and London: University of Chicago Press, 1985), 213. See also n. 58 below.

50. Ibid. 214.

51. See e.g. Rosemarie Bodenheimer, *The Politics of Story in Victorian Social Fiction* (Ithaca, NY, and London: Cornell University Press, 1988), esp. 173–5.

52. Charlotte Smith, *Desmond*, ed. Antje Blank and Janet Todd (Peterborough, Ont.: Broadview, 2001), 73.

53. Rt. Hon. B. Disraeli, *Vivian Grey*, new edn. (London: Longmans, n.d.), 16. Subsequent page references in text.

54. Robert Blake, *Disraeli* (London: Eyre & Spottiswoode, 1966), 57.

55. Daniel R. Schwarz, 'Disraeli's Romanticism: Self-fashioning in the Novels', in Charles Richmond and Paul Smith, eds., *The Self-Fashioning of Disraeli 1818–1851* (Cambridge: Cambridge University Press, 1998), 62.

56. Michael Ragussis, *Figures of Conversion: 'The Jewish Question' and English National Identity* (Durham, NC, and London: Duke University Press, 1995), 188.

57. Rt. Hon. B. Disraeli, *Tancred or the New Crusade*, new edn. (London: Longmans, n.d.), 124. Subsequent page references in text.

58. Ragussis, *Figures of Conversion*, 190.

59. Cf. Blake, *Disraeli*, 205.

60. Daniel Bivona, *Desire and Contradiction: Imperial Visions and Domestic Debates in Victorian Literature* (Manchester and New York: Manchester University Press, 1990), 18, 24.

61. Cf. Bernard Semmel, *George Eliot and the Politics of National Inheritance* (New York and Oxford: Oxford University Press, 1994), 119.
62. Ragussis, *Figures of Conversion*, 199.
63. Rt. Hon. B. Disraeli, *Alroy. Ixion in Heaven. The Infernal Marriage. Popanilla*, new edn. (London: Longmans, n.d.), 141.

Chapter 8. Tory Daughters and the Politics of Marriage

1. Susan Ferrier, *Marriage, A Novel*, ed. Herbert Feltinek (London: Oxford University Press, 1971), 2.
2. See Robert Miles, *Jane Austen* (Tavistock: Northcote House, 2003), 23, 121. On companionate marriage see Lawrence Stone, *The Family, Sex and Marriage in England 1500–1800* (London: Penguin, 1990), 217–53.
3. Christopher Hill, *Puritanism and Revolution* (London: Panther, 1968), 352, citing H. J. Habakkuk.
4. Thomas Holcroft, *Anna St. Ives*, ed. Peter Faulkner (London: Oxford University Press, 1970), 158. Subsequent page references in text.
5. See Marilyn Butler, *Jane Austen and the War of Ideas* (Oxford: Clarendon, 1975), 85.
6. See Donald J. Greene, 'Jane Austen and the Peerage', in Ian Watt, ed., *Jane Austen: A Collection of Critical Essays* (Englewood Cliffs, NJ: Prentice-Hall, 1963), 161–3; Miles, *Jane Austen*, 148.
7. Gerald Newman, *The Rise of English Nationalism: A Cultural History 1740–1830* (London: Weidenfeld, 1987), 231.
8. Charlotte Smith, *Marchmont*, 3 vols. (Delmar, NY: Scholars' Facsimiles, 1989), ii. 45.
9. This is on the testimony of her nephew: J. E. Austen-Leigh, *A Memoir of Jane Austen* (London: Macmillan, 1906), 83–4.
10. Christine Alexander, ed. *An Edition of the Early Writings of Charlotte Brontë*, vol. i: *The Glass Town Saga, 1826–1832* (Oxford: Blackwell, 1987), 90, 124.
11. Leslie Stephen, 'Charlotte Brontë', in Barbara Timm Gates, ed., *Critical Essays on Charlotte Brontë*, (Boston: Hall, 1990), 26.
12. Elizabeth C. Gaskell, *North and South*, World's Classics edn. (London: Oxford University Press, 1923), 2. Subsequent page references in text.
13. Jane Austen, *Northanger Abbey*, Everyman edn. (London: Dent, and New York: Dutton, 1970), 48. Subsequent page references in text.
14. Jane Austen, 'The Watsons', in Austen-Leigh, *A Memoir*, 333.
15. Jane Austen, *Persuasion*, Everyman edn. (London: Dent, and New York: Dutton, 1970), 219. Subsequent page references in text.
16. Greene, 'Jane Austen and the Peerage', 155.
17. Daniel Cottam, *The Civilized Imagination: A Study of Ann Radcliffe, Jane Austen, and Sir Walter Scott* (Cambridge: Cambridge University Press, 1985), 99.
18. Jane Austen, *Mansfield Park*, ed. Tony Tanner (Harmondsworth: Penguin, 1966), 41. Subsequent page references in text.

19. Jane Austen, *Pride and Prejudice*, Everyman edn. (London: Dent, and New York: Dutton, 1960), 205. Subsequent page references in text.

20. Austen-Leigh, *A Memoir*, 54.

21. Greene, 'Jane Austen and the Peerage', 156. This Lord Middleton was unrelated to John Middleton, the seventeenth-century cavalry commander who joined the Royalists and was ennobled by Charles II.

22. Jane Austen, *Sense and Sensibility*, ed. Tony Tanner (Harmondsworth: Penguin, 1969), 76, 223. Subsequent page references in text.

23. See Claudia L. Johnson, *Jane Austen: Women, Politics, and the Novel* (Chicago and London: University of Chicago Press, 1988), 56.

24. Ibid. 89.

25. Greene, 'Jane Austen and the Peerage',155.

26. Cf. Johnson, *Jane Austen*, 165.

27. The phrase 'the same interest' has been strangely misunderstood by some of *Mansfield Park*'s editors, including Tony Tanner (458); its normal application is to party politics. See Igor Webb's discussion of *Mansfield Park* in *From Custom to Capital: The English Novel and the Industrial Revolution* (Ithaca, NY, and London: Cornell University Press, 1981), esp. 102–4.

28. See Miles, *Jane Austen*, 98.

29. See Webb, *From Custom to Capital*, 104.

30. Loraine Fletcher points out that Henry and Mary Crawford 'are never allowed to argue a sceptical point of view in religion or politics, though to speak and act as they do, they would have to have one'. Fanny blames Mary's frivolous impiety on her upbringing. Loraine Fletcher, *Charlotte Smith: A Critical Biography* (Basingstoke and London: Macmillan, 1998), 313.

31. See Ann Banfield, 'The Influence of Place: Jane Austen and the Novel of Social Consciousness', in David Monaghan, ed., *Jane Austen in a Social Context* (Basingstoke: Macmillan, 1981), 44; and Claudia Johnson, *Jane Austen*, 119.

32. For a general discussion of Austen's fictional use of the Deadly Sins see Donald Greene, 'Jane Austen's Monsters', in John Halperin, ed., *Jane Austen: Bicentenary Essays* (Cambridge: Cambridge University Press, 1975), 262–78.

33. Butler, *Jane Austen and the War of Ideas*, 231, 231 n.

34. Sugar prices plummeted in 1807, for example, at the time when the slave trade was outlawed. See Katie Trumpener, *Bardic Nationalism: The Romantic Novel and the British Empire* (Princeton: Princeton University Press, 1997), 177.

35. Shinobu Minma, 'Self-Deception and Superiority Complex: Derangement of Hierarchy in Jane Austen's *Emma*', *Eighteenth-Century Fiction* 14: 1 (October 2001), 62.

36. See Frank W. Bradbrook, *Jane Austen and Her Predecessors* (Cambridge: Cambridge University Press, 1966), 32.

37. *Boswell's Life of Johnson* (London: Oxford University Press, 1953), 188.

38. Terry Eagleton, 'Class, Power and Charlotte Brontë', in Gates, ed., *Critical Essays on Charlotte Brontë*, 54.

39. Charlotte Brontë, *Jane Eyre*, ed. Q. D. Leavis (Harmondsworth: Penguin, 1966) 294. Subsequent page references in text.

40. For discussion of these issues see Jenny Sharpe, *Allegories of Empire: The Figure of Woman in the Colonial Text* (Minneapolis and London: University of Minnesota Press, 1993), esp. 45–7.

41. Mary Wollstonecraft, *Mary, A Fiction and The Wrongs of Women*, ed. Gary Kelly (London: Oxford University Press, 1976), 159.

42. On the complexity of Jane's childhood self-identifications see Cora Kaplan, '"A Heterogeneous Thing": Female Childhood and the Rise of Racial Thinking in Victorian Britain', in Diana Fuss, ed., *Human, All Too Human* (New York and London: Routledge, 1996), esp. 181–8.

43. Chapter 1 of *Jane Eyre* incorporates verbatim quotations from Bewick. See Thomas Bewick, *History of British Birds*, vol. ii: *Water Birds* (Newcastle, 1804), p. xii.

44. Kathleen Tillotson writes that 'though everyone thinks of *Jane Eyre* as a Yorkshire novel, no district is specified and the name Yorkshire never appears.' Tillotson, *Novels of the Eighteen-Forties* (London: Oxford University Press, 1961), 90. We do know that the Gytrash is a 'north-of-England spirit' (143) and that Jane hears about it from Bessie, a native of Gateshead, which is presumably in the north. Lowood and Whitcross are cold, hilly, Pennine regions; Leeds and Sheffield seem to lurk behind the large towns of 'L——' between Lowood and Gateshead, and 'S——' close to Whitcross; but the distances between these places and Thornfield mean that England north of the Trent is simply not large enough to contain them all.

45. Cf. Sharpe, *Allegories of Empire*, 46.

46. Cf. Enid L. Duthie, *The Foreign Vision of Charlotte Brontë* (London and Basingstoke: Macmillan, 1975), 128–30. We are told that after their marriage Jane does travel, presumably with Rochester, to France and Germany.

47. Elizabeth Gaskell, *Cranford* (London: Hamish Hamilton, and New York: Pantheon, 1951), 87. Subsequent page references in text.

48. Elizabeth Gaskell, *The Life of Charlotte Brontë* (London: Smith, Elder, 1889), 23.

49. Blair Worden suggests that Thornton's 'iron' and 'rough' figure, bent on '"justice" and a "wise despotism"', is modelled on Thomas Carlyle's heroic view of the Protector in *Oliver Cromwell's Letters and Speeches* (1845). Worden, *Roundhead Reputations: The English Civil Wars and the Passions of Posterity* (London: Penguin, 2001), 286.

50. Cited by Coral Lansbury, *Elizabeth Gaskell: The Novel of Social Crisis* (London: Elek, 1975), 114.

51. Gaskell's biographer A. B. Hopkins, quoted by Rosemarie Bodenheimer, *The Politics of Story in Victorian Social Fiction* (Ithaca, NY, and London: Cornell University Press, 1988), 53 n.

Chapter 9. 'Turn Again, Dick Whittington!': Dickens and the Fiction of the City

1. George Gissing, *Charles Dickens: A Critical Study* (London: Blackie, 1898), 180.

2. G. K. Chesterton, *Charles Dickens*, 12th edn. (London: Methuen, 1919), 185.

3. Gissing, *Charles Dickens*, 84.

4. George Orwell, 'Charles Dickens', in *Collected Essays, Journalism and Letters*, 4 vols., ed. Sonia Orwell and Ian Angus (Harmondsworth: Penguin, 1970), i. 473–5.

5. Patrick Brantlinger, *Rule of Darkness: British Literature and Imperialism, 1830–1914* (Ithaca, NY, and London: Cornell University Press, 1988), 207.

6. On parody and romance see John Kucich, *Excess and Restraint in the Novels of Charles Dickens* (Athens, Ga.: University of Georgia Press, 1981), 245.

7. Anny Sadrin, *Parentage and Inheritance in the Novels of Charles Dickens* (Cambridge: Cambridge University Press, 1994), 146.

8. William Hazlitt, 'On Londoners and Country People', in *Complete Works*, ed. P. P. Howe (London and Toronto: Dent, 1933), xii. 77.

9. The quoted phrase is part of the title of chapter 4. Charles Dickens, *Oliver Twist*, ed. Peter Fairclough (London: Penguin, 1985), 68. Subsequent page references in text.

10. Charles Dickens, *Our Mutual Friend*, ed. Adrian Poole (London: Penguin, 1997), 152; Charles Dickens, *A Tale of Two Cities*, ed. Richard Maxwell (London: Penguin, 2000), 318. Subsequent page references to both novels in text.

11. Charles Dickens, *Barnaby Rudge: A Tale of the Riots of 'Eighty* (London: Oxford University Press, 1954), 577. Subsequent page references in text.

12. Charles Dickens, *The Personal History of David Copperfield* (London: Oxford University Press, 1948), 808–9. Subsequent page references in text.

13. See Franco Moretti, *The Way of the World: The 'Bildungsroman' in European Culture* (London: Verso, 1987), 205 and *passim*.

14. William Makepeace Thackeray, *Pendennis*, 2 vols., Everyman edn. (London and Toronto: Dent, and New York: Dutton, 1910), i. 283. Subsequent page references in text.

15. Dickens, *David Copperfield*, 530. Chapter 28 of *Pendennis* is entitled 'Babylon'.

16. H. G. Wells, *Tono-Bungay*, ed. Patrick Parrinder (London: Penguin, 2005), 90–1. Subsequent page references in text.

17. Arnold Bennett, *A Man from the North* (London: Methuen, 1912), 1.

18. Thomas Hardy, *Jude the Obscure*, ed. P. N. Furbank (London: Macmillan, 1974), 97.

19. William Wordsworth, *The Prelude or Growth of a Poet's Mind (Text of 1805)*, ed. Ernest de Selincourt (London: Oxford University Press, 1960), book vii, line 116.

20. Walter Besant and James Rice, *Sir Richard Whittington: Lord Mayor of London* (London: Wood, 1881), 134.

21. Henry B. Wheatley, ed., *The History of Sir Richard Whittington, by T. H.* (London: Villon Society, 1885), 6.

22. Ibid., p. xxxiii.

23. Sir Walter Scott, *Rob Roy*, ed. John Sutherland, Everyman edn. (London: Dent, and North Clarendon, Vt.: Tuttle, 1995), 23. Subsequent page references in text.

24. Charles Dickens, *The Life and Adventures of Martin Chuzzlewit*, ed. P. N. Furbank (London: Penguin, 1986), 157.

25. Charles Dickens, *The Old Curiosity Shop* (London: Panther, 1964), 333. Subsequent page references in text.

26. Charles Dickens, *Bleak House* (London: Oxford University Press, 1948), 60. Subsequent page references in text.

27. Besant and Rice, *Sir Richard Whittington*, 87.

28. Charles Dickens, *Dealings with the Firm of Dombey and Son: Wholesale, Retail and for Exportation* (London: Oxford University Press, 1950), 135. Subsequent page references in text.

29. Sadrin, *Parentage and Inheritance*, 51.

30. Based on a letter of Dickens to John Forster (July 1846). See Gissing, *Charles Dickens*, 78.

31. David Piper, *The Companion Guide to London* (London: Fontana, 1970), 386.

32. Numerous critics have written on Dickens's uses of the labyrinth topos. See e.g. J. Hillis Miller, *Charles Dickens: The World of his Novels* (Cambridge, Mass.: Harvard University Press, 1958); and Richard Maxwell, *The Mysteries of Paris and London* (Charlottesville, Va., and London: University Press of Virginia, 1992), both *passim*.

33. George Augustus Sala, *Charles Dickens* (London: Routledge, [1870]), 27.

34. See e.g. John Lucas, *Charles Dickens: The Major Novels* (London: Penguin, 1972), 99; and James Buzard, ' "Anywhere's Nowhere": *Bleak House* as Autoethnography', *Yale Journal of Criticism* 12: 1 (1999), 30–4.

Chapter 10. At Home and Abroad in Victorian and Edwardian Fiction

1. W. M. Thackeray, *Vanity Fair*, Everyman edn. (London: Dent, and New York: Dutton, 1963), 23. Subsequent page references in text.

2. Quoted in John Carey, *Thackeray: Prodigal Genius* (London: Faber, 1977), 24.

3. Charlotte Brontë, *Unfinished Novels* (Stroud: Sutton, 1993), 32–3.

4. On George Eliot and the idea of historical progress see Neil McCaw, *George Eliot and Victorian Historiography: Imagining the National Past* (Basingstoke: Macmillan, 2000), esp. 52.

5. George Eliot, 'The Modern Hep! Hep! Hep!' in *Impressions of Theophrastus Such*, *Works*, Warwick edn. (Edinburgh and London: Blackwood, 1901), xii. 285. Subsequent page references in text.

6. Eliot, *Impressions of Theophrastus Such*, 36.

7. Kathleen Tillotson, *Novels of the Eighteen-Forties* (London: Oxford University Press, 1961), 90.

8. Charlotte Brontë, *Shirley*, Everyman edn. (London: Dent, and New York: Dutton, 1969), 21. Subsequent page references in text.

9. Elizabeth Gaskell, *Sylvia's Lovers*, ed. Andrew Sanders, World's Classics edn. (Oxford: Oxford University Press, 1982), 95.

10. Charlotte Brontë, *The Professor* (London: Classics Book Club, 1951), 64, 95. Subsequent page references in text.

11. Charlotte Brontë, letter of July 1842, quoted in Enid L. Duthie, *The Foreign Vision of Charlotte Brontë* (London and Basingstoke: Macmillan, 1975), 30.

12. Charlotte Brontë, *Villette*, ed. Mark Lilly (Harmondsworth: Penguin, 1979), 73, 341. Subsequent page references in text.

13. Edgeworth, *Castle Rackrent and The Absentee*, Everyman edn. (London: Dent, and New York: Dutton, 1910), 88.

14. Rudyard Kipling, *Kim*, ed. Zohreh T. Sullivan, Norton Critical edn. (New York and London: Norton, 2002), 52.

15. Ford Madox Hueffer, *The Spirit of the People: An Analysis of the English Mind* (London: Alston Rivers, 1907), 148–50.

16. Harriet Martineau, review of *Villette* (1853) in Barbara Timm Gates, ed., *Critical Essays on Charlotte Brontë* (Boston: Hall, 1990), 254.

17. Susan Meyer, 'Colonialism and the Figurative Strategy of *Jane Eyre*', in Jonathan Arac and Harriet Ritvo, eds., *Macropolitics of Nineteenth-Century Literature: Nationalism, Exoticism, Imperialism* (Durham, NC, and London: Duke University Press, 1995), 160.

18. Anthony Trollope, *The Way We Live Now*, ed. Sir Frank Kermode (London: Penguin, 1994), 414. Subsequent page references in text.

19. George Eliot, *Daniel Deronda*, ed. Barbara Hardy (Harmondsworth: Penguin, 1967), 101. Subsequent page references in text.

20. Bernard Semmel, *George Eliot and the Politics of National Inheritance* (New York and Oxford: Oxford University Press, 1994), 18.

21. See Patrick Brantlinger, *Rule of Darkness: British Literature and Imperialism, 1830–1914* (Ithaca, NY, and London: Cornell University Press, 1988), esp. 178, 182.

22. '*Daniel Deronda*: A Conversation' [1876], in Henry James, *Selected Literary Criticism*, ed. Morris Shapira (London: Heinemann, 1963), 36–7, 46.

23. Henry James, *The Ambassadors* (Harmondsworth: Penguin, 1973), 5.

24. Henry James, 'Preface' (1909) to *The Princess Casamassima*, ed. Derek Brewer (London: Penguin, 1987), 33. Subsequent page references in the text are to this edition.

25. Joseph Conrad, *The Secret Agent* (Harmondsworth: Penguin, 1963), 23, 33. Subsequent page references in text.

26. Joseph Conrad, 'Heart of Darkness' in *Three Short Novels* (New York: Bantam, 1960), 4.

Chapter 11. Puritan and Provincial Englands: From Emily Brontë to D. H. Lawrence

1. Thomas Carlyle, *The Letters and Speeches of Oliver Cromwell*, ed. S. C. Lomas, 3 vols. (London: Methuen, 1904), i. 8.

2. Thomas Babington Macaulay, *The History of England from the Accession of James II*, 3 vols. (London and Toronto: Dent, and New York: Dutton, 1906), ii. 208.

3. Ibid. i. 82.

4. Carlyle, *Letters and Speeches of Oliver Cromwell*, p. xxi.

5. Walter Bagehot, 'Thomas Babington Macaulay' (1856), in *Selected Essays* (London: Nelson, n.d.), 309–17.

6. W. E. H. Lecky, *The Political Value of History* (1892), quoted in J. W. Burrow, *A Liberal Descent: Victorian Historians and the English Past* (Cambridge: Cambridge University Press, 1981), 14.

7. John Richard Green, *History of the English People* (London: Macmillan, 1879), iii. 13–19. This is a slightly extended version of the discussion which had appeared in the *Short History* five years earlier.

8. George Eliot, *Middlemarch: A Study of Provincial Life*, World's Classics edn. (London: Oxford University Press, 1947), 1, 3. Subsequent page references in text.

9. George Eliot, *The Mill on the Floss*, Everyman edn. (London: Dent, and New York: Dutton, 1908), 350. Subsequent page references in text.

10. George Eliot, *Felix Holt, the Radical*, ed. Fred C. Thomson (Oxford: Oxford University Press, 1988), 303. Subsequent page references in text.

11. Emily Brontë, *Wuthering Heights*, ed. Ian Jack (Oxford: Oxford University Press, 1955), 324–5. Subsequent page references in text.

12. Elizabeth K. Helsinger, *Rural Scenes and National Representation: Britain, 1815–1850* (Princeton: Princeton University Press, 1997), 175.

13. Ibid. 210–11.

14. On the problems of the flood episode, see George Eliot, *The Mill on the Floss*, ed. Gordon S. Haight (Oxford: Clarendon Press, 1980), 466–7.

15. Quoted in Basil Willey, 'George Eliot', in Gordon S. Haight, ed., *A Century of George Eliot Criticism* (London: Methuen, 1966), 263.

16. Book iv, chapter 1 of *The Mill on the Floss* is titled 'A Variation of Protestantism Unknown to Bossuet'.

17. Quoted in Willey, 'George Eliot', 259.

18. E. M. Forster, 'Notes on the English Character' in *Abinger Harvest and England's Pleasant Land*, ed. Elizabeth Heine (London: Deutsch, 1996), 5.

19. George Eliot, *Scenes of Clerical Life*, ed. Thomas A. Noble (Oxford: Oxford University Press, 1988), 263. Subsequent page references in text.

20. Anthony Trollope, *An Autobiography*, ed. Michael Sadleir and Frederick Page, World's Classics edn. (Oxford: Oxford University Press, 1992), 154.

21. Anthony Trollope, *Doctor Thorne*, ed. David Skilton, World's Classics edn. (Oxford: Oxford University Press, 1980), 7–8.

22. George Eliot, *Impressions of Theophrastus Such*, in *Works*, Warwick edn., 12 vols. (Edinburgh and London: Blackwood, 1901), xii. 36.

23. George Eliot, 'Amos Barton' in *Scenes of Clerical Life*, 37.

24. The contemporary *Times* reviewer E. S. Dallas was the first to identify Silas Marner as a Job figure: 'He is surrounded with comforters, most of whom are even less sympathizing than the comforters of Job, and he sinks into a deeper despair than that of the most patient of men, for, as we have said, he cursed and denied God in his affliction.' [Eneas Sweetland Dallas], review of *Silas Marner* [1861] in Haight, ed., *A Century of George Eliot Criticism*, 20.

25. George Eliot, *Silas Marner* (London: Nelson, n.d.), 119. Subsequent page references in text.

26. See Sally Shuttleworth, *George Eliot and Nineteenth-Century Science: The Make-Believe of a Beginning* (Cambridge: Cambridge University Press, 1986), 79.

27. George Eliot, 'The Natural History of German Life: Riehl', in *Works*, xii. 490–1. Subsequent page references in text.

28. See Patrick Parrinder, 'The Look of Sympathy: Communication and Moral Purpose in the Realistic Novel', *Novel* 5 (1972), 135–47.

29. George Eliot, *Adam Bede*, ed. Valentine Cunningham, World's Classics edn. (Oxford: Oxford University Press, 1996), 136. Subsequent page references in text.

30. Stephen, 'George Eliot', 142.

31. Ruth Bernard Yeazell, 'Why Political Novels Have Heroines: *Sybil*, *Mary Barton*, and *Felix Holt*', *Novel*, 18: 2 (1985), 140.

32. Cf. Martin J. Svaglic, 'Religion in the Novels of George Eliot', in Haight, ed., *A Century of George Eliot Criticism*, 291–2.

33. Florence Emily Hardy, *The Life of Thomas Hardy 1840–1928* (London: Macmillan, 1962), 278.

34. Thomas Hardy, *The Woodlanders*, ed. David Lodge (London: Macmillan, 1974), 38. Subsequent page references in text.

35. Thomas Hardy, *Tess of the d'Urbervilles* (London: Macmillan, 1968), 41. Subsequent page references in text.

36. Thomas Hardy, *The Return of the Native*, ed. Derwent May (London: Macmillan, 1974), 37–8. Subsequent page references in text.

37. Florence Emily Hardy, *Life*, 61.

38. Thomas Hardy, *A Pair of Blue Eyes*, ed. Alan Monford, World's Classics edn. (Oxford: Oxford University Press, 1985), 8.

39. Book v, chapter 1 of *The Return of the Native*, describing Clym's despair after his mother's death, is titled ' "Wherefore is Light given to him that is in Misery?" ' (Job 3: 20).

40. Thomas Hardy, *Jude the Obscure*, ed. P. N. Furbank (London: Macmillan, 1974), 97. Subsequent page references in text.

41. Joss Marsh, *Word Crimes: Blasphemy, Culture, and Literature in Nineteenth-Century England* (Chicago and London: University of Chicago Press, 1998), 318.

42. See ibid. 295, 321.

43. *The Autobiography of Mark Rutherford, Edited by his friend Reuben Shapcott* (London: Hodder & Stoughton, n.d.), 19.

44. Mark Rutherford, *The Revolution in Tanner's Lane* (London: Cape, 1927), 37. Subsequent page references in text.

45. Morley Roberts, ed., *The Private Life of Henry Maitland*, 2nd edn. (London: Eveleigh Nash, 1923), 112–13.

46. George Gissing, *The Unclassed* (London: Benn, 1930), 41. Subsequent page references in text.

47. George Gissing, *Born in Exile* (London: Nelson, n.d.), 266. Subsequent page references in text.

48. Unsigned review of *Born in Exile* in *The Times*, 1 July 1892, in Pierre Coustillas and Colin Partridge, eds., *Gissing: The Critical Heritage* (London and Boston: Routledge & Kegan Paul, 1972), 204.

49. Arnold Bennett, *Anna of the Five Towns* (Harmondsworth: Penguin, 1967), 235. Subsequent page references in text.

50. D. H. Lawrence, letter to A. W. McLeod, 6 October 1912, in Aldous Huxley, ed., *The Letters of D. H. Lawrence* (London: Heinemann, 1934), 64–5.
51. D. H. Lawrence, *Sons and Lovers* (Harmondsworth: Penguin, 1948), 14. Subsequent page references in text.

Chapter 12. From Forster to Orwell: The Novel of England's Destiny

1. Krishan Kumar, *The Making of English National Identity* (Cambridge: Cambridge University Press, 2003), 224.
2. E. M. Forster, *What I Believe* (London: Hogarth, 1939), 8.
3. E. M. Forster, *The Longest Journey* (Harmondsworth: Penguin, 1960), 50–1. Subsequent page references in text.
4. H. G. Wells, 'The *National Observer Time Machine*', in Harry M. Geduld, ed., *The Definitive Time Machine* (Bloomington and Indianapolis: Indiana University Press, 1987), 171.
5. The quotation is from Noel Annan, 'Kipling's Place in the History of Ideas', in Andrew Rutherford, ed., *Kipling's Mind and Art* (Edinburgh and London: Oliver & Boyd, 1964), 115. See also Richard Gill, *Happy Rural Seat: The English Country House and the Literary Imagination* (New Haven and London: Yale University Press, 1972), esp. 95–131; and Patrick Parrinder, 'Historical Imagination and Political Reality: A Study in Edwardian Attitudes', *Clio* 4: 1 (1974), 5–25.
6. Lionel Trilling, *E. M. Forster: A Study*, 2nd edn. (London: Hogarth, 1967), 102.
7. P. N. Furbank, *E. M. Forster: A Life*, vol. i: *The Growth of the Novelist (1879–1914)* (London: Secker & Warburg, 1977), 47.
8. E. M. Forster, *Howards End* (Harmondsworth: Penguin, 1941), 198. Subsequent page references in text.
9. David Gervais, *Literary Englands: Versions of 'Englishness' in Modern Writing* (Cambridge: Cambridge University Press, 1993), 76.
10. Cf. J. W. Burrow, *A Liberal Descent: Victorian Historians and the English Past* (Cambridge: Cambridge University Press, 1981), 297.
11. Ford Madox Hueffer, *The Spirit of the People: An Analysis of the English Mind* (London: Alston Rivers, 1907), 8. Subsequent page references in text.
12. H. Butterfield, *The Englishman and his History* (Cambridge: Cambridge University Press, 1944), 1–2.
13. Hueffer, *The Spirit of the People*, 3.
14. G. M. Trevelyan, *History of England* (London: Longmans, 1927), pp. xvii, xx.
15. Butterfield, *The Englishman and his History*, 2.
16. C. R. L. Fletcher and Rudyard Kipling, *A School History of England* (Oxford: Clarendon Press, 1911), 241.
17. Butterfield, *The Englishman and his History*, 81–2.
18. John Richard Green, *A Short History of the English People*, 2 vols. (London and Toronto: Dent, and New York: Dutton, 1915), i. 7.
19. Ford Madox Hueffer, *The Heart of the Country: A Survey of a Modern Land* (London: Alston Rivers, 1906), 211.

20. Ford Madox Hueffer, *The Cinque Ports: A Historical and Descriptive Record* (Edinburgh and London: Blackwood, 1900), 20.
21. Hueffer, *The Spirit of the People*, 71.
22. Ford Madox Ford, *The Fifth Queen* (Oxford: Oxford University Press, 1984), 163–4, 191.
23. E. M. Forster, *Abinger Harvest and England's Pleasant Land*, ed. Elizabeth Heine (London: Deutsch, 1996), 399.
24. E. M. Forster, 'Notes on the English Character', in *Abinger Harvest and England's Pleasant Land*, 4–5.
25. Martin Green, *The English Novel in the Twentieth Century [The Doom of Empire]* (London: Routledge & Kegan Paul, 1984), 56. Forster himself, however, happily spent the last two decades of his life in what was then the all-male institution of King's College, Cambridge.
26. E. M. Forster, *Where Angels Fear to Tread*, ed. Oliver Stallybrass (London: Penguin, 2001), 113. Subsequent page references in text.
27. George Meredith, *Beauchamp's Career* (London: Chapman & Hall, 1894), 506. Subsequent page references in text.
28. H. G. Wells, *Experiment in Autobiography: Discoveries and Conclusions of a Very Ordinary Brain (since 1866)*, 2 vols. (London: Gollancz and Cresset Press, 1966), ii. 495.
29. John Galsworthy, *The Man of Property* (Harmondsworth: Penguin, 1967), 85. Subsequent page references in text.
30. See Len Platt, *Aristocracies of Fiction*, 53.
31. Forster, *Abinger Harvest and England's Pleasant Land*, 349.
32. H. G. Wells, *Tono-Bungay*, ed. Patrick Parrinder (London: Penguin, 2005), 16. Subsequent page references in text.
33. See Bryan Cheyette, 'Introduction' to *Tono-Bungay*, ed. Cheyette (New York: Oxford University Press, 1997), pp. xxxi–xxxiv. Cheyette also discusses Wells's 'use of the language of socialist anti-Semitism' and observes that George's uncle is 'named after the reigning monarch, Edward the Seventh, who was...said to be in the hands of plutocrats which embodied the "Semitic" corruption of old England' (p. xxxiv). George is named after the Prince of Wales, who became King in 1911.
34. Daniel Born, *The Birth of Liberal Guilt in the English Novel: Charles Dickens to H. G. Wells* (Chapel Hill, NC, and London: University of North Carolina Press, 1995), 163.
35. Michael Draper, *H. G. Wells* (Basingstoke: Macmillan, 1987), 89.
36. D. H. Lawrence, *The Rainbow* (Harmondsworth: Penguin, 1949), 496. Subsequent page references in text.
37. D. H. Lawrence, 'Nottingham and the Mining Countryside', in *A Selection from Phoenix*, ed. A. A. H. Inglis (Harmondsworth; Penguin, 1971), 103, 106.
38. D. H. Lawrence, *Women in Love* (Harmondsworth: Penguin, 1960), 408. Subsequent page references in text.
39. See David Craig, *The Real Foundations: Literature and Social Change* (London: Chatto, 1973), 144–54.
40. Lawrence, 'Nottingham and the Mining Countryside', 103.

41. D. H. Lawrence, *Lady Chatterley's Lover* (Harmondsworth: Penguin, 1960), 64. Subsequent page references in text.

42. Cf. Scott Sanders, *D. H. Lawrence: The World of the Major Novels* (London: Vision, 1973), 181.

43. Wells, *Experiment in Autobiography*, ii. 503.

44. Virginia Woolf, *Three Guineas* (Harmondsworth: Penguin, 1977), 125.

45. Virginia Woolf, *The Voyage Out*, ed. Lorna Sage (Oxford: Oxford University Press, 1992), 51. Subsequent page references in text.

46. Virginia Woolf, *Night and Day* (Harmondsworth: Penguin, 1969), 44. Subsequent page references in text. The chimes of Big Ben are heard in both *Night and Day* and *Mrs Dalloway*.

47. Virginia Woolf, *Orlando: A Biography* (Harmondsworth: Penguin, 1967), 12–13, 230.

48. Virginia Woolf, *The Years*, ed. Hermione Lee (Oxford: Oxford University Press, 1992), 265.

49. Patricia Klindienst Joplin, 'The Authority of Illusion: Feminism and Fascism in Virginia Woolf's *Between the Acts*', in Margaret Homans, ed., *Virginia Woolf: A Collection of Critical Essays* (Englewood Cliffs, NJ: Prentice-Hall, 1993), 213.

50. Virginia Woolf, *Between the Acts*, ed. Frank Kermode (Oxford: Oxford University Press, 1992), 15. Subsequent page references in text.

51. Malcolm Cowley, review of *Between the Acts* reprinted in Robin Majumdar and Allen McLaurin, eds., *Virginia Woolf: The Critical Heritage* (London and Boston: Routledge, 1975), 448.

52. H. G. Wells, *The New Machiavelli* (London: John Lane, 1911), 254.

53. Anne Olivier Bell and Andrew McNeillie, eds., *The Diary of Virginia Woolf*, vol. v: 1936–1941 (London: Hogarth, 1984), 333, 337. Subsequent page references in text.

54. Virginia Woolf, *The Waves* (Harmondsworth: Penguin, 1964), 222–3. Subsequent page references in text.

55. Trevelyan, *History of England*, 87.

56. See Gillian Beer, 'Introduction' to Woolf, *Between the Acts*, ed. Beer and Stella McNichol (London: Penguin, 1992), p. xxxii.

57. Jed Esty, *A Shrinking Island: Modernism and National Culture in England* (Princeton and Oxford: Princeton University Press, 2004), 90.

58. Ibid. 59.

59. Christopher Woodward, *In Ruins* (London: Vintage, 2002), 235.

60. George Orwell, *Keep the Aspidistra Flying* (Harmondsworth: Penguin, 1962), 49.

61. George Orwell, *Coming Up for Air* (Harmondsworth: Penguin, 1962), 28–9, 224.

62. George Orwell, *Homage to Catalonia* (Harmondsworth: Penguin, 1962), 46.

63. George Orwell, *The Lion and the Unicorn: Socialism and the English Genius* in *Collected Essays, Journalism and Letters*, ed. Sonia Orwell and Ian Angus, 4 vols. (London: Secker, 1968), ii. 57. Subsequent page references in text.

64. In an earlier article Orwell had described parliamentary democracy and the two-party system as a family quarrel. See George Orwell, 'Caesarean Section

in Spain' [March 1939], in *Complete Works*, ed. Peter Davison, 20 vols. (London: Secker, 1998), xi. 332.

65. Anthony D. Smith, *National Identity* (London: Penguin, 1991), 79.

66. Orwell, *Collected Essays, Journalism and Letters*, i. 410.

67. Bernard Crick, *George Orwell: A Life* (Harmondsworth: Penguin, 1982), 389; Orwell, *Complete Works*. xv. 360.

68. Orwell, *Complete Works*. xv. 366.

69. George Orwell, *The English People*, in *Collected Essays, Journalism and Letters*, iii. 1.

70. George Orwell, *Nineteen Eighty-Four: A Novel* (Harmondsworth: Penguin, 1954), 150. Subsequent page references in text.

71. In *The English People* Orwell links Shakespeare to the nation's 'profound, almost unconscious patriotism'. *Collected Essays, Journalism and Letters*, iii. 7.

72. V. S. Pritchett, 'Conrad', in *The Working Novelist* (London: Chatto, 1965), 195.

Chapter 13. From Kipling to Independence: Losing the Empire

1. Sir J. R. Seeley, *The Expansion of England: Two Courses of Lectures*, 2nd edn. (London: Macmillan, 1897), 10. Subsequent page references in text.

2. Quoted ibid. 17.

3. Rudyard Kipling, *Kim*, ed. Zohreh T. Sullivan, Norton Critical edn. (New York and London: Norton, 2002), 3. Subsequent page references in text.

4. Peter Vansittart, *In Memory of England: A Novelist's View of History* (London: Murray, 1998), 142.

5. See Zohreh T. Sullivan, *Narratives of Empire: The Fictions of Rudyard Kipling* (Cambridge: Cambridge University Press, 1993), 149.

6. Letter of 1885–6, in *Kim*, ed. Sullivan, 267–8.

7. Ibid. 268. On Burton and *Kim* see e.g. Parama Roy, *Indian Traffic: Identities in Question in Colonial and Postcolonial India* (Berkeley: University of California Press, 1998), esp. 25.

8. Rudyard Kipling, *Something of Myself*, in *Kim*, ed. Sullivan, 277.

9. Letter of 1885–6, in *Kim*, ed. Sullivan, 269.

10. Suvir Kaul, '*Kim*, or How to Be Young, Male and British in Kipling's India', in *Kim*, ed. Sullivan, 429.

11. Sullivan, *Narratives of Empire*, 176.

12. Ibid. 173.

13. Edward W. Said, '[*Kim* as Imperialist Novel]', in *Kim*, ed. Sullivan, 340.

14. Blair B. Kling, '*Kim* in Historical Context', in *Kim*, ed. Sullivan, 300.

15. Edward W. Said, *Culture and Imperialism* (London: Vintage, 1994), 187–8.

16. Angus Wilson, quoted in Roy, *Indian Traffic*, 86.

17. Sullivan, *Narratives of Empire*, 148.

18. E. M. Forster, *A Passage to India* (Harmondsworth: Penguin, 1961), 26. Subsequent page references in text.

19. J. A. Hobson, *Imperialism: A Study* (London: Allen & Unwin, 1968), 116, 150.

20. See Jed Esty, *A Shrinking Island: Modernism and National Culture in England* (Princeton and Oxford: Princeton University Press, 2004), 25.

21. Hobson, *Imperialism*, 368.

22. George Orwell, *Burmese Days* (Harmondsworth: Penguin, 1967), 65. Subsequent page references in text. E. M. Forster had written of foreign residents in Egypt that 'in all cases they are aliens in Egypt and have come to exploit it'. Forster, *Government of Egypt* (Labour Research Department, 1919), quoted in Mohammad Shaheen, *E. M. Forster and the Politics of Imperialism* (London: Palgrave Macmillan, 2004), 62.

23. Doris Lessing, *The Grass is Singing* (London: Heinemann, 1973), 140.

24. Anthony Burgess, *The Long Day Wanes: A Malayan Trilogy* (London: Heinemann, 1984), 417. Subsequent page references in text.

25. Paul Scott, *Staying On* (St Albans: Granada, 1978), 40. Subsequent page references in text.

Chapter 14. Round Tables: Chivalry and the Twentieth-Century English Novel Sequence

1. Jed Esty, *A Shrinking Island: Modernism and National Culture in England* (Princeton and Oxford: Princeton University Press, 2004), *passim*.

2. Cf. Randall Stevenson, *The Last of England? The Oxford English Literary History*, vol. xii: *1960–2000* (Oxford: Oxford University Press, 2004), 398.

3. Ford Madox Ford, *The Good Soldier: A Tale of Passion* (Harmondsworth: Penguin, 1972), 11.

4. Ford Madox Ford, *Parade's End* (London: Everyman's Library, 1992), 373. Subsequent page references in text.

5. Stevenson, *The Last of England?*, 398.

6. Steven Connor, *The English Novel in History 1950–1885* (London and New York: Routledge, 1996), 139.

7. Mark Girouard, *The Return to Camelot: Chivalry and the English Gentleman* (New Haven and London: Yale University Press, 1981), 260.

8. There were new editions in 1816 and 1817. See ibid. 18, 42, 178.

9. See Stephanie L. Barczewski, *Myth and National Identity in Nineteenth-Century Britain: The Legends of King Arthur and Robin Hood* (Oxford: Oxford University Press, 2000), 17–18.

10. William Wordsworth, *The Prelude or Growth of a Poet's Mind (Text of 1805)*, ed. Ernest de Selincourt (London: Oxford University Press, 1960), book i, lines 179–80.

11. Barczewski, *Myth and National Identity*, 213.

12. Girouard, *The Return to Camelot*, 148.

13. Philip Knightley and Colin Simpson, *The Secret Lives of Lawrence of Arabia* (London: Nelson, 1969), 28.

14. T. E. Lawrence, *Seven Pillars of Wisdom: A Triumph* (Harmondsworth: Penguin, 1962), 495. Subsequent page references in text.

15. Barczewski, *Myth and National Identity*, 234.

16. John Cowper Powys, *A Glastonbury Romance* (Woodstock, NY: Overlook, 1996), 1118–20.

17. E. M. Forster, *A Room with a View* (Harmondsworth: Penguin, 1955), 117–18.

18. Virginia Woolf, *Night and Day* (Harmondsworth: Penguin, 1969), 366. Subsequent page references in text.

19. Contrast Rachel Bowlby, *Virginia Woolf: Feminist Destinations* (Oxford: Blackwell, 1988), 112.

20. Cf. Len Platt, *Aristocracies of Fiction: The Idea of Aristocracy in Late Nineteenth-Century and Early-Twentieth-Century Literary Culture* (Westport, Conn., and London: Greenwood, 2001), 116, 121.

21. Virginia Woolf, *To the Lighthouse* (Harmondsworth: Penguin, 1964), 218.

22. Virginia Woolf, *The Waves* (Harmondsworth: Penguin, 1964), 16. Subsequent page references in text. Compare Powell's *The Acceptance World*, where Nicholas Jenkins says of himself and Mark Members that 'Viewed from some distance off, Members and I might reasonably be considered almost identical units of the same organism, scarcely to be differentiated even by the sociological expert'. Anthony Powell, *The Acceptance World* (London: Fontana, 1974), 39. Subsequent page references in text are prefixed 'AW'.

23. C. P. Snow, *The Masters* (Harmondsworth: Penguin, 1956), 300–12.

24. C. S. Lewis, *That Hideous Strength* (London: Pan, 1955), 241.

25. Malcolm Bradbury, 'Introduction' to Ford Madox Ford, *Parade's End* (London: Everyman's Library, 1992), p. xxi.

26. During the ten years covered by *Parade's End*, Tietjens's father possibly commits suicide after listening to malicious gossip which leads him to believe that his son Christopher has disgraced himself. Christopher's saintly mother also dies, but he finds a substitute mother in the widow of his father's oldest friend, who is also Valentine's mother. Valentine herself is alleged by Sylvia to be Christopher's illegitimate half-sister, though it is also suggested that Christopher is actually Campion's son.

27. Ford Madox Hueffer, *The Critical Attitude* (London: Duckworth, 1911), 88–9.

28. Quoted in Max Saunders, *Ford Madox Ford: A Dual Life*, 2 vols. (Oxford: Oxford University Press, 1996), ii. 288.

29. W. H. Auden, 'Il faut payer', *Mid-Century* 22 (1961), 9.

30. Evelyn Waugh, *Brideshead Revisited: The Sacred and Profane Memories of Captain Charles Ryder* (Harmondsworth: Penguin, 1962), 8. Subsequent page references in text.

31. Christopher Sykes, *Evelyn Waugh: A Biography* (Harmondsworth: Penguin, 1977), 336.

32. Evelyn Waugh, *A Handful of Dust* (Harmondsworth: Penguin, 1951), 149, 151.

33. Sykes, *Evelyn Waugh*, 474.

34. Evelyn Waugh, Preface to *Sword of Honour: A Final Version of the Novels* (London: Chapman & Hall, 1965), 9.

35. Evelyn Waugh, *Men at Arms* (Harmondsworth: Penguin, 1964), 12. Subsequent page references in text are prefixed 'M'.

36. The status of the 1965 version is controversial, since Waugh made some savage and (many have thought) unnecessary cuts. For this reason I have generally preferred to make reference to the three novels as originally published; see notes 35, 37, and 38.

37. Evelyn Waugh, *Unconditional Surrender* (Harmondsworth: Penguin, 1964), 66. Subsequent page references in text are prefixed 'U'.

38. Evelyn Waugh, *Officers and Gentlemen* (Harmondsworth: Penguin, 1964), 9–10. Subsequent page references in text are prefixed 'O'.

39. Sir Thomas Malory, *Le Morte d'Arthur*, Everyman edn., 2 vols. (London: Dent, and New York: Dutton, 1906), ii. 171.

40. See Sykes, *Evelyn Waugh*, 560–1.

41. See ibid. 554.

42. Ibid. 567.

43. Anthony Powell, *The Valley of Bones* (London: Fontana, 1973), 7.

44. Anthony Powell, *The Fisher King* (London: Sceptre, 1987), 21.

45. Anthony Powell, *Hearing Secret Harmonies: A Novel* (London: Fontana, 1977), 32. Subsequent page references in text are prefixed 'HSH'.

46. Anthony Powell, *Casanova's Chinese Restaurant* (London: Fontana, 1974), 19. Subsequent page references in text are prefixed 'CCR'.

47. Anthony Powell, *A Question of Upbringing* (London: Fontana, 1974), 67. Subsequent page references in text are prefixed 'QU'.

48. Quoted in Isabelle Joyau, *Investigating Powell's 'A Dance to the Music of Time'* (Basingstoke: Macmillan, 1994), 78.

49. Anthony Powell, *The Military Philosophers* (London: Fontana, 1971), 151. Subsequent page references in text are prefixed 'MP'.

50. Anthony Powell, *A Buyer's Market* (London: Fontana, 1974), 194–5.

51. Anthony Powell, *The Kindly Ones* (London: Fontana, 1971), 183. Subsequent page references in text are prefixed 'KO'.

52. Anthony Powell, *Temporary Kings: A Novel* (London: Fontana, 1974), 11. Subsequent page references in text are prefixed 'TK'.

53. See Joyau, *Investigating Powell's 'A Dance to the Music of Time'*, 30.

54. Anthony Powell, *The Soldier's Art* (London: Fontana, 1968), 5–6.

55. See Joyau, *Investigating Powell's 'A Dance to the Music of Time'*, 130–1.

56. Anthony Powell, *Books Do Furnish a Room* (London: Fontana, 1972), 53, 69. Subsequent page references in text are prefixed 'BFR'.

57. Joyau, *Investigating Powell's 'A Dance to the Music of Time'*, 124.

58. Christopher Harvie, *The Centre of Things: Political Fiction in Britain from Disraeli to the Present* (London: Unwin, 1991), 211.

Chapter 15. Inward Migrations: Multiculturalism, Anglicization, and Internal Exile

1. Hanif Kureishi, *The Buddha of Suburbia* (London: Faber, 1990), 3. Subsequent page references in text.

2. See Susheila Nasta, *Home Truths: Fictions of the South Asian Diaspora in Britain* (Basingstoke: Palgrave, 2002), 199.

3. John Fowles, 'On Being English but Not British', *Texas Quarterly* 7: 3 (Autumn 1964), 154.

4. Bruce King, *The Internationalization of English Literature: The Oxford English Literary History*, vol. 13: *1948–2000* (Oxford: Oxford University Press, 2004), 2.

5. Hanif Kureishi, 'The Rainbow Sign', in *My Beautiful Laundrette and The Rainbow Sign* (London: Faber, 1986), 38.
6. James Wood, 'England', in John Sturrock, ed., *The Oxford Guide to Contemporary Writing* (Oxford: Oxford University Press, 1996), 140.
7. J. B. Priestley, *English Journey* (London: Heinemann, 1937), 416. Subsequent page references in text.
8. Cf. James Procter, *Dwelling Places: Postwar Black British Writing* (Manchester and New York: Manchester University Press, 2003), 175.
9. J. B. Priestley, *The English* (London: Heinemann, and Haarlem: Gottmer, 1973), 11.
10. J. B. Priestley, *Margin Released: A Writer's Reminiscences and Reflections* (London: Heinemann, 1962), 91.
11. Salman Rushdie, *The Satanic Verses* (London: Viking, 1988), 285, 461.
12. Israel Zangwill, *Children of the Ghetto: A Study of a Peculiar People*, ed. Mari-Jane Rochelson (Detroit: Wayne State University Press, 1998), 66. Subsequent page references in text.
13. Monica Ali, *Brick Lane* (London: Doubleday, 2003), 413.
14. See P. J. Keating, *The Working Classes in Victorian Fiction* (London: Routledge, 1971).
15. Arthur Morrison, 'Preface to the Third Edition' [1897], in *A Child of the Jago*, ed. P. J. Keating (London: MacGibbon & Kee, 1969), 39.
16. Zangwill, *Children of the Ghetto*, 85.
17. Mari-Jane Rochelson, 'Introduction' to *Children of the Ghetto*, 23–4.
18. See ibid. 26–7.
19. Ibid. 24.
20. See e.g. Ian Jack, 'It's only a novel...', *Guardian*, 20 December 2003, Review, 7. The condemnation was issued in the name of the Greater Sylhet Welfare and Development Council.
21. Nasta, *Home Truths*, 63.
22. V. S. Naipaul, *The Enigma of Arrival: A Novel in Five Sections* (Harmondsworth: Viking, 1987), 130. Subsequent page references in text.
23. Jean Rhys, *Voyage in the Dark* (London: Deutsch, 1967), 31.
24. Anna Kavan, *I am Lazarus: Short Stories* (London: Cape, 1945), 123, 134, 136.
25. See Caryl Phillips, ed., *Extravagant Strangers: A Literature of Belonging* (London: Faber, 1998), p. xiv.
26. C. L. Innes, 'Wintering: Making a Home in Britain', in A. Robert Lee, ed., *Other Britain, Other British: Contemporary Multicultural Fiction* (London and East Haven, Conn.: Pluto, 1995), 25.
27. V. S. Naipaul, *The Mimic Men* (London: Readers Union, 1968), 11. Subsequent page references in text.
28. George Lamming, *The Pleasures of Exile* (London: Joseph, 1960), 24.
29. Ibid. 45; King, *The Internationalization of English Literature*, 42.
30. Samuel Selvon, *The Lonely Londoners* (London: Longman Drumbeat, 1979), 10. Subsequent page references in text.
31. Nasta, *Home Truths*, 72.

32. Sam Selvon, *Moses Ascending* (London: Heinemann, 1984), 44. Subsequent page references in text.

33. Sam Selvon, *Moses Migrating* (London: Longman, 1983), 25. Subsequent page references in text.

34. Hanif Kureishi, *The Black Album* (London: Faber, 2000), 124. Subsequent page references in text.

35. See e.g. Judy Giles and Tim Middleton, eds., *Writing Englishness 1900–1950: An Introductory Sourcebook on National Identity* (London and New York: Routledge, 1995).

36. Caryl Phillips, *A Distant Shore* (London: Vintage, 2004), 3.

37. D. H. Lawrence, *The Rainbow* (Harmondsworth: Penguin, 1949), 7.

38. Philip Larkin, *A Girl in Winter* (London and Boston: Faber, 1975), 158, 160. Subsequent page references in text.

39. Meera Syal, *Anita and Me* (London: Flamingo, 1997), 31. Subsequent page references in text.

40. H. G. Wells, *Tono-Bungay*, ed. Patrick Parrinder (London: Penguin, 2005), 15, 274.

41. See e.g. Nasta, *Home Truths*, 120; Timothy F. Weiss, *On the Margins: The Art of Exile in V. S. Naipaul* (Amherst, Mass.: University of Massachusetts Press, 1992), 213. Selwyn R. Cudjoe in *V. S. Naipaul: A Materialist Reading* (Amherst, Mass.: University of Massachusetts Press, 1988), 213, calls *The Enigma of Arrival* 'the most intense of all [Naipaul's] fantasies'.

42. W. B. Yeats, *Collected Poems* (London: Macmillan, 1950), 225–6.

43. Contrast Salman Rushdie's assessment of the 'tiny world' in which *The Enigma of Arrival* is set as a mirror for its author's 'exhaustion and turning-towards-death'. Salman Rushdie, *Imaginary Homelands: Essays and Criticism 1981–1991* (London: Granta, 1991), 150.

44. Bruce King is one critic who has endorsed this judgement. King, *The Internationalization of English Literature*, 47.

45. George Lamming, *The Emigrants* (London and New York: Allison & Busby, 1980), 228–9.

46. Landeg White, *V. S. Naipaul: A Critical Introduction* (London and Basingstoke: Macmillan, 1975), 189.

47. D. H. Lawrence, *Lady Chatterley's Lover* (Harmondsworth: Penguin, 1960), 5.

48. Rushdie, *Imaginary Homelands*, 151.

49. Bruce King, *V. S. Naipaul* (Basingstoke and London: Macmillan, 1993), 148.

50. Zadie Smith, *White Teeth* (London: Penguin, 2001), 328.

Conclusion: On Englishness and the Twenty-First-Century Novel

1. Ian McEwan, *Atonement* (London: Cape, 2001), 351–72.

2. Ian McEwan, 'The Master', *Guardian*, 7 April 2005, G2, 2.

3. A. S. Byatt, 'People in Paper Houses: Attitudes to "Realism" and "Experiment" in English Postwar Fiction', in Malcolm Bradbury and David Palmer, eds., *The Contemporary English Novel* (London: Arnold, 1979), 41.

4. Kingsley Amis, 'Introduction' to *The Golden Age of Science Fiction*, ed. Amis (London: Hutchinson, 1981), 20.

5. Kingsley Amis, *Take a Girl Like You* (Harmondsworth: Penguin, 1962), 59, 317.

6. Ahdaf Soueif, *In the Eye of the Sun* (London: Bloomsbury, 1999), 723, 754.

7. Patrick Wright, *On Living in an Old Country: The National Past in Contemporary Britain* (London: Verso, 1985), 69.

8. A. S. Byatt, 'Parmenides and the Contemporary British Novel', *Literature Matters* 21 (December 1996), 6–8. See also Byatt's *On Histories and Stories: Selected Essays* (London: Chatto, 2000), *passim*.

9. Jason Cowley, 'How the Dead Live', review of *On Histories and Stories* by A. S. Byatt, *New Statesman* (4 December 2000), 51–2.

10. Peter Ackroyd, *Albion: The Origins of the English Imagination* (London: Chatto, 2002), 237. On Ackroyd's conservatism see Mette Bollerup Doyle, ' "The Mystical City Universal": Peter Ackroyd's London', *European English Messenger* 11: 1 (Spring 2002), 29–32.

11. Norman Davies, *The Isles: A History* (London: Macmillan, 2000), 434. Subsequent page references in text.

12. Virginia Woolf, 'Mr Bennett and Mrs Brown', in Woolf, *The Captain's Death-Bed and Other Essays* (London: Hogarth, 1950), 111.

13. Virginia Woolf, 'The Niece of an Earl', in Woolf, *The Common Reader*, vol. ii, ed. Andrew McNeillie (London: Vintage, 2003), 215. Subsequent page references in text.

14. See n. 2 above.

15. Marina Warner, *The Leto Bundle* (London: Chatto, 2001), 93.

16. Andrew Salkey, *Escape to an Autumn Pavement* (London: Four Square, 1966), 41.

Author Biographies

ACKROYD, PETER (1949–), biographer and historical novelist, born in London. He is the author of *Hawksmoor* (1985), *Chatterton* (1987), and many other novels, and his non-fiction includes *London* (2000) and *Albion* (2002).

ADDISON, JOSEPH (1672–1719), essayist. As Member of Parliament for Malmesbury from 1710 he held office under the Whigs. His papers on Sir Roger de Coverly and his friends were contributed to the *Spectator* (1711–12, 1714) while the Tories were in power.

AINSWORTH, WILLIAM HARRISON (1805–82), novelist, born in Manchester. His 'Newgate novel' *Rookwood* (1834) was followed by many other historical romances. A friend of Thackeray and Dickens, his popularity declined in later years.

ALI, MONICA (1967–), novelist, born in Bangladesh, resident in England since the age of 3, author of *Brick Lane* (2003).

AMIS, KINGSLEY (1922–95), novelist, born in London. His first novel *Lucky Jim* (1954) was written while he was a university lecturer at Swansea. Later works include *Take a Girl Like You* (1960), *The Anti-Death League* (1966), *The Alteration* (1976), *Russian Hide-and-Seek* (1980), and *The Old Devils* (1986), which won the Booker Prize. His son Martin Amis (b. 1949) is also a celebrated novelist.

ARBUTHNOT, JOHN (1667–1735), Scottish satirist and personal physician to Queen Anne. An associate of Pope and Swift in the Scriblerus Club, his series of pamphlets on 'the History of John Bull' was isued in 1712.

ARNOLD, MATTHEW (1822–88), poet, critic, and educationist, whose works include *Culture and Anarchy* (1869).

ASTELL, MARY (1666–1731), philosopher and feminist. Her most influential work was *A Serious Proposal to the Ladies* (1694), an argument for women's education.

AUSTEN, JANE (1775–1817), novelist, born in Hampshire, the daughter of an Anglican clergyman. Her principal novels are *Sense and Sensibility* (1811), *Pride and Prejudice* (1813), *Mansfield Park* (1814), *Emma* (1816), *Northanger Abbey* (1818), and *Persuasion* (1818). She began the unfinished *Sanditon* in 1817. Her juvenilia includes *A History of England*.

BAGE, ROBERT (1728–1801), novelist and paper manufacturer, born near Derby, best known for his 'Jacobin novels' *Man As He Is* (1792) and *Hermsprong; or, Man As He Is Not* (1796).

BAGEHOT, WALTER (1826–77), banker, political writer, and journalist who became editor of the *Economist* in 1860. He was author of *The English Constitution*

(1867) and *Physics and Politics* (1872). His essays on Dickens, Macaulay, Scott, and others were collected in *Literary Studies* (1879).

BALLARD, JAMES GRAHAM (1930–), novelist, born in Shanghai, China, resident in England from 1946. His novels include *The Drowned World* (1962), *Crash* (1973), *Concrete Island* (1974), and *Empire of the Sun* (1984).

BARNES, JULIAN (1946–), novelist, born in Leicester, author of *Metroland* (1980), *Flaubert's Parrot* (1984), *Staring at the Sun* (1986), *England, England* (1998), and other works.

BEHN, APHRA (1640–89), novelist, playwright, and outspoken Royalist. Her early life is obscure, but it is thought that she was born in Kent and visited Surinam. In 1666 she was sent to Antwerp as a government agent. From 1670 she was a leading writer for the London stage. Her principal novels are *Love-Letters Between a Nobleman and his Sister* (1684–7) and *Oroonoko* (1688).

BENNETT, ARNOLD (1867–1931), novelist, born in Staffordshire. He was author of *A Man from the North* (1898), *Anna of the Five Towns* (1902), *The Old Wives' Tale* (1908), *Clayhanger* (1910), *Riceyman Steps* (1923), and many other works. His criticism includes *Literary Taste* (1909).

BESANT, WALTER (1836–1901), novelist and historian of London, born in Portsmouth. Much of his fiction, beginning with *Ready Money Mortiboy* (1872), was produced in collaboration with James Rice (1844–82), with whom he also wrote a biography of *Sir Richard Whittington* (1881). His best-known solo novel is *All Sorts and Conditions of Men* (1882). He helped found the Society of Authors in 1883, and was knighted in 1895.

BLACKMORE, SIR RICHARD (1654–1729), physician and poet, author of *Prince Arthur* (1695) and *King Arthur* (1697), epics which have been seen as allegorical representations of the Glorious Revolution and the expulsion of the Stuarts.

BRADBURY, MALCOLM (1930–2000), novelist and critic, born in Sheffield, author of *Eating People is Wrong* (1959), *The History Man* (1975), and other novels. His non-fiction includes *The Modern British Novel* (1993) and *Dangerous Pilgrimages* (1994).

BRONTË, ANNE (1820–49), novelist, sister of Charlotte and Emily, author of *Agnes Grey* (1847) and *The Tenant of Wildfell Hall* (1848), both published under the pseudonym 'Acton Bell'.

BRONTË, CHARLOTTE (1816–55), novelist, sister of Emily and Anne, born near Bradford, Yorkshire, the daughter of an evangelical clergyman. In 1820 the family moved to Haworth parsonage. Charlotte was a pupil and, later, a teacher at Roe Head, and then studied French and taught English in Brussels (1842–3). She spent her remaining years at Haworth. During her lifetime she published *Jane Eyre* (1847), *Shirley* (1849), and *Villette* (1853) under the pseudonym 'Currer Bell'. Her first novel *The Professor* was published posthumously in 1857.

BRONTË, EMILY (1818–48), novelist and poet, sister of Charlotte and Anne, author of *Wuthering Heights* (1847) published under the pseudonym 'Ellis Bell'. She accompanied Charlotte to Brussels in 1842, but soon returned home and spent the rest of her life at Haworth.

BUNYAN, JOHN (1628–88), author and Nonconformist preacher, born near Bedford. He served in the New Model Army (1644–6), and was imprisoned in 1661 for denouncing the Church of England. He was not released until 1672. He wrote several books in Bedford Jail, including his spiritual autobiography *Grace Abounding* (1666) and *The Pilgrim's Progress* (1678). His later works include *The Life and Death of Mr Badman* (1680) and *The Holy War* (1682).

BURGESS, ANTHONY (John Burgess Wilson) (1917–93), novelist and critic, born in Manchester. His 'Malayan trilogy' *The Long Day Wanes*, consisting of *Time for a Tiger* (1958), *The Enemy in the Blanket* (1958), and *Beds in the East* (1959), was written while he was an education officer in Malaya and Brunei. His many later novels include *A Clockwork Orange* (1962) and *Earthly Powers* (1981).

BURKE, EDMUND (1729/30–97), Anglo-Irish politician and author, born in Dublin. A Member of Parliament from 1766, he expounded his political philosophy in *Reflections on the Revolution in France* (1790) and other works.

BURNEY, FRANCES (FANNY) (1752–1840), novelist, born in Norfolk. She was the author of *Evelina* (1778), *Cecilia* (1782), *Camilla* (1796), and *The Wanderer* (1814). She served as a keeper of the robes to Queen Charlotte (1786–91).

BUTTERFIELD, HERBERT (1900–79), historian, author of *The Whig Interpretation of History* (1931) and *The Englishman and his History* (1944). He was knighted in 1968.

BYATT, ANTONIA SUSAN (1936–), novelist and critic, born in Sheffield, sister of Margaret Drabble, author of *The Virgin in the Garden* (1978), *Still Life* (1986), and *Possession* (1990), which won the Booker Prize.

CARLYLE, THOMAS (1795–1881), Scottish biographer, historian, and social critic, author of *Chartism* (1839), *On Heroes, Hero-Worship and the Heroic in History* (1841), and *Past and Present* (1843), and editor of *Oliver Cromwell's Letters and Speeches* (1845).

CARROLL, LEWIS (Charles Lutwidge Dodgson) (1832–98), lecturer in mathematics at Oxford and author of *Alice's Adventures in Wonderland* (1865) and *Through the Looking-Glass* (1872).

CARTER, ANGELA (1940–92), novelist, born in Sussex, author of *The Magic Toyshop* (1967), *Heroes and Villains* (1969), *The Passion of New Eve* (1977), *The Bloody Chamber* (1979), *Nights at the Circus* (1984), and other works.

CAXTON, WILLIAM (c.1421–91), editor, translator, and printer, who established the first English printing press at Westminster in 1476. His edition of Malory's *Le Morte d'Arthur* was published in 1485.

CHESNEY, GEORGE TOMKYNS (1833–95), soldier and novelist, author of *The Battle of Dorking* (1871). He was knighted in 1890.

CHESTERFIELD, PHILIP DORMER STANFIELD, 4TH EARL OF (1694–1773), politician, author, and sometime patron of Samuel Johnson, whose *Letters* to his son were published posthumously in 1774.

CHESTERTON, GILBERT KEITH (1874–1936), political journalist, novelist, and poet, born in London. His books include *The Napoleon of Notting Hill* (1904), *Charles Dickens* (1906), and *A Short History of England* (1917).

CLARENDON, EDWARD HYDE, 1ST EARL OF (1609–74), Royalist politician, lord chancellor to Charles II from 1658 until his impeachment in 1667. His *History of the Rebellion and Civil Wars in England*, begun in the 1640s, was completed in exile in 1672 and published posthumously in 1702–4.

COLLINS, WILKIE (1824–89), novelist, born in London, author of *The Woman in White* (1860), *Armadale* (1866), *The Moonstone* (1868), and other 'sensation novels'.

COMPTON-BURNETT, IVY (1884–1969), novelist, born in Middlesex, author of *A House and Its Head* (1935), *Parents and Children* (1941), and many other works.

CONGREVE, WILLIAM (1670–1729), dramatist, born in Yorkshire and educated in Ireland. His novel *Incognita* (1692) was written before his success as a playwright, which began with *The Old Bachelor* (1693).

CONRAD, JOSEPH (Józef Teodor Konrad Nalecz Korzeniowski) (1857–1924), novelist, born in the Polish Ukraine. He joined the Merchant Navy in 1878, became a naturalized British subject in 1886, and settled in England from 1894. His novels include *Almayer's Folly* (1896), *Lord Jim* (1900), *Heart of Darkness* (1902), *Nostromo* (1904), *The Secret Agent* (1907), and *Under Western Eyes* (1911). He also wrote two novels in collaboration with Ford Madox Ford (q.v.).

DANGERFIELD, THOMAS (1654–85), informer and thief, born in Essex, probable author of *Don Tomazo, or The Juvenile Rambles of Thomas Dangerfield* (1680).

DEFOE, DANIEL (c.1660–1731), novelist, journalist, and satirist, born in London and educated for the Nonconformist ministry. He was the author of *The True-Born Englishman* (1701), *Robinson Crusoe* (1719), *Captain Singleton* (1720), *Moll Flanders* (1722), *Colonel Jack* (1722), *A Journal of the Plague Year* (1722), *Roxana* (1724), *Memoirs of a Cavalier* (1724), and numerous other works. The exact extent of his authorship is still debated among scholars.

DELONEY, THOMAS (c.1543–c.1600), novelist and balladeer, probably born in Norwich. He was the author of *Jack of Newbury* (1597), *The Gentle Craft* (1597–8), and *Thomas of Reading* (c.1598).

DHONDY, FARRUKH (1944–), novelist and short-story writer, born in India, resident in England since 1964. His collections of stories include *East End at Your Feet* (1976), *Siege of Babylon* (1977), and *Come to Mecca* (1978).

DICKENS, CHARLES (1812–70), novelist and journalist, born in Portsmouth. His works include *Sketches by Boz* (1836–7), *The Pickwick Papers* (1837), *Oliver Twist* (1837–8), *Nicholas Nickleby* (1838–9), *The Old Curiosity Shop* (1840–1), *Barnaby Rudge* (1841), *Martin Chuzzlewit* (1843–4), *Dombey and Son* (1848), *David Copperfield* (1849–50), *Bleak House* (1852–3), *A Child's History of England* (1851–3), *Little Dorrit* (1855–7), *A Tale of Two Cities* (1859), *Great Expectations* (1860–1), and *Our Mutual Friend* (1864–5). Most of his novels were serialized in monthly parts, although he also edited the weekly journals *Household Words* (1850–9) and *All the Year Round* (1859–70).

DISRAELI, BENJAMIN (1804–81), novelist and Conservative prime minister, born in London, author of *Vivian Grey* (1826–7), *The Young Duke* (1831), *Contarini Fleming* (1832), *Alroy* (1833), *Coningsby* (1844), *Sybil* (1845), *Tancred* (1847), *Lothair* (1870), and other works. He set out his political philosophy in *A Vindication of the English Constitution* (1835). Queen Victoria made him Earl of Beaconsfield in 1876.

DOYLE, ARTHUR CONAN (1859–1930), Scottish novelist and physician, resident in England from 1882. The detective Sherlock Holmes and his accomplice Dr Watson appeared in *A Study in Scarlet* (1887) and many later stories. He was knighted in 1902.

DRABBLE, MARGARET (1939–), novelist, born in Sheffield, sister of Antonia Byatt, and author of *The Garrick Year* (1965), *The Needle's Eye* (1972), *The Ice Age* (1977), *The Radiant Way* (1987), and other novels. She is editor of the 5th edition of *The Oxford Companion to English Literature* (1985).

EDGEWORTH, MARIA (1767–1849), Anglo-Irish novelist, born in Oxfordshire and educated in England, author of *Castle Rackrent* (1800), *Belinda* (1802), *Ennui* (1809), *The Absentee* (1812), and *Ormond* (1817). She spent much of her life in the family home at Edgeworthstown, County Longford.

ELIOT, GEORGE (Mary Ann Evans) (1819–80), novelist, born near Nuneaton, Warwickshire, author of *Scenes of Clerical Life* (1858), *Adam Bede* (1859), *The Mill on the Floss* (1860), *Silas Marner* (1861), *Romola* (1863), *Felix Holt the Radical* (1866), *Middlemarch* (1871–2), *Daniel Deronda* (1874–6), and *Impressions of Theophrastus Such* (1879). She lived together with the critic George Henry Lewes (1817–78).

FERRIER, SUSAN (1782–1854), Scottish novelist, author of *Marriage* (1818) and other works.

FIELDING, HENRY (1707–54), novelist, playwright, and London magistrate, brother of Sarah, born in Somerset. His career as a successful dramatist was terminated by the introduction of theatrical censorship in 1737. *Shamela* (1741), his burlesque of Samuel Richardson's *Pamela*, was followed by *Joseph Andrews* (1742), *Miscellanies* (1743) (including *Jonathan Wild the Great*), *Tom Jones* (1749), *Amelia* (1751), and the posthumous *Journal of a Voyage to Lisbon* (1755). His social and political tracts included *An Enquiry into the Causes of the Late Increase of Robbers* (1751).

FIELDING, SARAH (1710–68), novelist, sister of Henry, author of *The Adventures of David Simple* (1744–53) and other works.

FILMER, SIR ROBERT (*c*.1588–1653), political writer, whose *Patriarcha* was published posthumously in 1680.

FITZGERALD, PENELOPE (1916–2000), novelist, born in Lincoln. Her first novel was *The Golden Child* (1977). *Offshore* (1979) won the Booker Prize.

FORD, FORD MADOX (Ford Madox Hueffer) (1873–1939), novelist and essayist, born in Surrey. He collaborated with Joseph Conrad on *The Inheritors* (1901) and *Romance* (1903). His many novels include *The Fifth Queen* trilogy (1906–8), *The Good Soldier* (1915), and the *Parade's End* tetralogy (1924–8), in which he drew on his wartime service as an army officer. Among his non-fiction are the *England and the English* trilogy (1905–7) and *The Critical Attitude* (1911). He founded and edited the *English Review* (1908–9).

FORSTER, EDWARD MORGAN (1879–1970), novelist and essayist, born in London, author of *Where Angels Fear to Tread* (1905), *The Longest Journey* (1907), *A Room with a View* (1908), *Howards End* (1910), *A Passage to India* (1924), and the posthumously published *Maurice* (1971). His other works include two collections of essays, *Abinger Harvest* (1936) (including 'The Abinger Pageant') and *Two Cheers for Democracy* (1951). The second of his pageant plays was published as *England's Pleasant Land* (1940).

FOWLES, JOHN (1926–2005), novelist, born in Essex, author of *The Magus* (1966), *The French Lieutenant's Woman* (1969), and other works.

GALSWORTHY, JOHN (1867–1933), novelist and playwright, born in Surrey. His novels include *The Island Pharisees* (1904), *Fraternity* (1909), and *The Man of Property* (1906), the first of his Forsyte novels. He wrote the remaining eight volumes of the 'Forsyte Saga' after the First World War.

GASCOIGNE, GEORGE (*c*.1535–77), author and courtier, who wrote *The Adventures of Master F. J.* (1573) as well as poems, plays, and tracts.

GASKELL, ELIZABETH (1810–65), novelist, born in London but raised by her aunt in Cheshire. The daughter of a Unitarian minister, from 1832 she was a minister's wife in Manchester. Her works include *Mary Barton* (1848), *Cranford* (1851–3), *Ruth* (1853), *North and South* (1855), *Sylvia's Lovers* (1863–4), and *Wives and Daughters* (1864–6). She also wrote *The Life of Charlotte Brontë* (1857), and numerous short stories.

GAY, JOHN (1685–1732), poet and dramatist, author of *The Beggar's Opera* (1728).

GIBBON, EDWARD (1737–94), historian, author of *The History of the Decline and Fall of the Roman Empire* (1776–88).

GISSING, GEORGE (1857–1903), novelist, born in Wakefield, author of *The Unclassed* (1884), *Demos* (1886), *The Nether World* (1889), *New Grub Street* (1891), *Born in Exile* (1892), *The Whirlpool* (1897), *The Private Papers of Henry Ryecroft* (1903), and other works. His non-fiction includes a study of *Charles Dickens* (1898).

GODWIN, WILLIAM (1756–1836), novelist and political philosopher, husband of Mary Wollstonecraft and father of Mary Shelley, born in Cambridgeshire. He was the author of *An Enquiry Concerning Political Justice* (1793), *Things As They Are, or The Adventures of Caleb Williams* (1794), *St Leon* (1799), and *Fleetwood* (1805). His later works include a *History of the Commonwealth of England* (1824–8).

GOLDING, WILLIAM (1911–93), novelist, born in Cornwall. His novels include *Lord of the Flies* (1954), *The Inheritors* (1955), *Pincher Martin* (1956), *The Spire* (1964), and *Darkness Visible* (1979). He was awarded the Nobel Prize for Literature in 1983 and was knighted in 1988.

GOLDSMITH, OLIVER (*c*.1728–1774), Irish novelist, poet, and playwright, resident in London from 1756, author of *The Citizen of the World* (1762), *The Vicar of Wakefield* (1766), and of two histories of England (1764, 1771).

GREEN, HENRY (Henry Yorke) (1905–73), novelist, born in Gloucestershire, author of *Living* (1929), *Party Going* (1939), *Loving* (1945), and other works.

GREEN, JOHN RICHARD (1837–83), historian, author of *A Short History of the English People* (1874; expanded in later editions).

GREENE, GRAHAM (1904–91), novelist, born in Hertfordshire, author of *England Made Me* (1935), *Brighton Rock* (1938), *The Heart of the Matter* (1948), and many other works. He travelled extensively, and during his later years lived mainly in France.

HAGGARD, HENRY RIDER (1856–1925), novelist, born in Norfolk. He spent the years 1875–81 in South Africa, and later published *King Solomon's Mines* (1885) and *She* (1887). He was knighted in 1912.

HARDY, THOMAS (1840–1928), novelist and poet, born in Dorset. His novels include *Under the Greenwood Tree* (1872), *A Pair of Blue Eyes* (1873), *Far from the Madding Crowd* (1874), *The Return of the Native* (1878), *The Mayor of Casterbridge* (1886), *The Woodlanders* (1887), *Tess of the d'Urbervilles* (1891), and *Jude the Obscure* (1896).

HAYS, MARY (1759–1843), novelist, born in Southwark, author of *Memoirs of Emma Courtney* (1796) and *The Victim of Prejudice* (1799).

HAYWOOD, ELIZA (1693?–1756), novelist and playwright, probably born in Shropshire, author of *Love in Excess* (1719), *Anti-Pamela* (1741), *The History of Miss Betsy Thoughtless* (1751), and numerous other works.

HAZLITT, WILLIAM (1778–1830), critic and essayist, author of *Lectures on the English Poets* (1818), *Lectures on the English Comic Writers* (1819), *The Spirit of the Age* (1824), and many other works.

HEAD, RICHARD (*c*.1637–86?), writer and bookseller, born in Ireland, author of *The English Rogue* (1665) and *Jackson's Recantation* (1674). Later parts of *The English Rogue* were written by or in collaboration with Francis Kirkman (q.v.).

HERBERT, PERCY, 2nd BARON POWIS (1598–1667), politician and author of *Cloria and Narcissus* (1653–61). A Royalist Member of Parliament from 1620, his estates were confiscated in 1652–3.

HEYWOOD, THOMAS (*c*.1573–1641), playwright and poet, born in Lincolnshire, whose prose works include *The Famous and Remarkable History of Sir Richard Whittington* (1636/7). He also wrote several lord mayors' pageants in the 1630s.

HOBBES, THOMAS (1588–1679), philosopher, author of *Leviathan* (1651).

HOBSON, JOHN ATKINSON (1858–1940), economist and social theorist, author of *Imperialism* (1902).

HOLCROFT, THOMAS (1745–1809), novelist, playwright, and political radical, author of *Anna St Ives* (1792).

HOLTBY, WINIFRED (1898–1935), novelist and feminist, born in Yorkshire. Her novel *South Riding* was published posthumously in 1936.

HORNE, RICHARD HENGIST (1802–84), poet, playwright, and critic, author of *A New Spirit of the Age* (1844).

HUDSON, WILLIAM HENRY (1841–1922), author and naturalist, born in Argentina, resident in England from 1874 and naturalized as a British subject in 1900. His fiction includes *The Purple Land* (1885), *A Crystal Age* (1887), and *Green Mansions* (1904).

HUME, DAVID (1711–76), Scottish philosopher and historian, author of *A Treatise of Human Nature* (1739–40), *Essays, Moral and Political* (1741–8), and *The History of Great Britain* (1754–61).

HUXLEY, ALDOUS (1894–1963), novelist and essayist, born in Surrey. His novels include *Point Counter Point* (1928), *Brave New World* (1932), and *Eyeless in Gaza* (1936). He emigrated to California in 1937.

INCHBALD, ELIZABETH (1753–1821), novelist and playwright, born in Suffolk, author of *A Simple Story* (1791), *Nature and Art* (1796), and of the drama *Lovers' Vows* (1798), an adaptation from Kotzebue.

IRVING, WASHINGTON (1783–1859), American essayist and short-story writer, author of *The Sketch Book of Geoffrey Crayon* (1820), *Bracebridge Hall* (1822), and other works.

JAMES, HENRY (1843–1916), American novelist, resident in England from 1876 and naturalized as a British subject in 1915. His novels with English settings include *The Princess Casamassima* (1886), *The Tragic Muse* (1890), *The Spoils of Poynton* (1897), and *The Turn of the Screw* (1898).

JEFFERIES, RICHARD (1848–87), rural writer and novelist, born in Wiltshire, author of *Bevis* (1882), *The Story of My Heart* (1883), and *After London* (1885).

JOHNSON, CHARLES (fl.1724–34), criminal biographer, author of *A General History of the Robberies and Murders of the Most Notorious Pirates* (1724), and of a 1734 reprint of the highwayman biographies published by Alexander Smith (q.v.).

JOHNSON, SAMUEL (1709–84), poet, critic, lexicographer, and biographer, whose *History of Rasselas, Prince of Abyssinia* (1759) is his principal contribution to prose fiction.

KAVAN, ANNA (Helen Ferguson) (1901–68), novelist, born in France, author of *Let Me Alone* (1930), *A Stranger Still* (1935), *Ice* (1967), and other works. She lived continuously in London from about 1942.

KINGLAKE, ALEXANDER WILLIAM (1809–91), author of *Eōthen* (1844), a narrative of his travels in the Near East.

KINGSLEY, CHARLES (1819–75), novelist and Christian socialist, born in Devon. His novels include *Alton Locke* (1850), *The Water Babies* (1863), and *Hereward the Wake* (1865).

KIPLING, RUDYARD (1865–1936), novelist and poet, born in India, whose works include *Plain Tales from the Hills* (1888), *The Light That Failed* (1890), *Kim* (1901), *Puck of Pook's Hill* (1906), and (with C. R. L. Fletcher) *A School History of England* (1911). He lived in England continuously from 1899 and was awarded the Nobel Prize for Literature in 1907.

KIRKMAN, FRANCIS (1632–c.1680), bookseller and writer, author of *The Counterfeit Lady Unveiled* (1673) and author or co-author of the later parts of Richard Head's *The English Rogue*.

KUREISHI, HANIF (1954–), novelist and screenwriter, born in London, author of *The Buddha of Suburbia* (1990), *The Black Album* (1995), and the screenplays *My Beautiful Laundrette* (1986) and *Sammy and Rosie Get Laid* (1988).

LAMMING, GEORGE (1927–), Barbadian novelist and essayist, author of *In the Castle of My Skin* (1953), *The Emigrants* (1954), and *The Pleasures of Exile* (1960).

LARKIN, PHILIP (1922–85), poet, novelist, and librarian, born in Coventry. His novels *Jill* (1946) and *A Girl in Winter* (1947) preceded his recognition as a poet.

LAWRENCE, DAVID HERBERT (1885–1930), novelist, essayist, and poet, born in Nottinghamshire. His novels include *The White Peacock* (1911), *Sons and Lovers* (1913), *The Rainbow* (1915), *Women in Love* (1920), *The Lost Girl* (1920), *Aaron's Rod* (1922), and *Lady Chatterley's Lover* (1929). After 1919 he lived mainly in Italy, Australia, and New Mexico.

LAWRENCE, THOMAS EDWARD (1888–1935), soldier and author, who took part in the Arab Revolt in 1916–18 and described his adventures in *Seven Pillars of Wisdom* (1926).

LECKY, WILLIAM EDWARD HARTPOLE (1838–1903), Irish historian, author of *The History of England in the Eighteenth Century* (1878–90).

LENNOX, CHARLOTTE (c.1730–1804), novelist, born in Gibraltar, author of *The Female Quixote* (1752).

LESSING, DORIS (1919–), novelist, born in Iran and brought up in Southern Rhodesia. Her novels include *The Grass is Singing* (1950), the *Children of Violence* quintet (1952–69), *The Golden Notebook* (1962), *The Memoirs of a Survivor* (1975), and *The Good Terrorist* (1985). She also wrote *In Pursuit of the English* (1960).

LEVY, AMY (1861–89), poet and novelist, born in London, author of *Romance of a Shop* (1888) and *Reuben Sachs* (1888).

LEWIS, CLIVE STAPLES (1898–1963), writer, scholar, and Christian propagandist, born in Belfast. His fiction includes *Out of the Silent Planet* (1938), *Perelandra* (1943), *That Hideous Strength* (1945), and *The Chronicles of Narnia* (1950–6).

LEWIS, MATTHEW GREGORY (1775–1818), novelist, born in London, author of *The Monk* (1795).

LEWIS, PERCY WYNDHAM (1882–1957), artist and writer, born in Canada and raised in England, whose novels include *Tarr* (1918), *The Childermass* (1928), and *The Apes of God* (1930).

LOCKE, JOHN (1632–1704), philosopher, author of *Two Treatises on Government* (1689) and *An Essay Concerning Human Understanding* (1690). A political exile under the Stuarts, he returned to England in 1689.

LYLY, JOHN (1554–1606), author and playwright, whose prose fiction includes *Euphues, the Anatomy of Wit* (1578), which originated the style known as 'Euphuism', and *Euphues and His England* (1580).

LYTTON, EDWARD GEORGE EARLE LYTTON BULWER-, 1st BARON (1803–73), novelist and politician, born in London. His many novels include *Pelham* (1828), *Paul Clifford* (1830), and *Eugene Aram* (1832). He also published *England and the English* (1833), and served as a Member of Parliament (1831–41, 1852–66). He was raised to the peerage in 1866.

MABBE, JAMES (1571/2–1642?), translator, whose version of Aléman's *Guzman de Alfarache* appeared as *The Rogue* (1622).

MACAULAY, THOMAS BABINGTON, 1ST BARON (1800–59), historian, essayist, and
politician. After serving as a Whig cabinet minister he wrote *The History of
England* (1848–55). He was raised to the peerage in 1857.

MCEWAN, IAN (1948–), novelist, born in Hampshire. His fiction includes *The
Cement Garden* (1978), *The Child in Time* (1987), *Amsterdam* (1998), and
Atonement (2001). *Amsterdam* won the Booker Prize.

MACKENZIE, HENRY (1745–1831), Scottish novelist, author of *The Man of Feeling*
(1771).

MAGINN, WILLIAM (1794–1842), Irish journalist and poet, author of *Whitehall, or
The Days of George IV* (1827).

MALORY, SIR THOMAS (*c.*1415–71), author and Member of Parliament from 1445,
who was several times imprisoned. *Le Morte d'Arthur*, possibly written in the
Tower of London (1468–70), was printed by William Caxton in 1485.

MANDEVILLE, BERNARD (1670–1733), philosopher, author of *The Fable of the
Bees* (1714).

MANLEY, DELARIVIER (1670–1724), romancer and playwright, born in Jersey,
author of the *Secret History of Queen Zarah and the Zarazians* (1705), *Secret
Memoirs* (1709), and many other works.

MAUGHAM, WILLIAM SOMERSET (1874–1965), novelist and playwright, born in
Paris, author of *Liza of Lambeth* (1897) and *Of Human Bondage* (1915). He
qualified as a doctor in London but spent much of his life in France.

MEREDITH, GEORGE (1828–1909), novelist, born in Portsmouth, author of *The
Ordeal of Richard Feverel* (1859), *Beauchamp's Career* (1876), *The Egoist*
(1879), and many other works.

MILL, JOHN STUART (1806–73), philosopher and political theorist, author of
On Liberty (1859) and *Representative Government* (1861).

MITFORD, MARY RUSSELL (1787–1855), writer and playwright, born in Hampshire,
author of *Our Village* (1824–32) and *Belford Regis* (1835).

MORE, SIR THOMAS (1478–1535), author and statesman, executed for high treason
under Henry VIII. His *Utopia*, begun while he was an envoy in Flanders, was
published in Latin in 1516.

MORGAN, LADY (Sydney Owenson) (1776–1859), Irish novelist, author of *The
Wild Irish Girl* (1806) and *O'Donnel: A National Tale* (1814).

MORRIS, WILLIAM (1834–96), author and designer, born in Essex, whose prose
works include a number of historical romances and the utopian romance *News
from Nowhere* (1891).

MORRISON, ARTHUR (1863–1945), novelist, born in London. His fiction set in the
East End includes *Tales of Mean Streets* (1894), *A Child of the Jago* (1896), and
The Hole in the Wall (1902).

MURDOCH, IRIS (1919–99), novelist and philosopher, born in Dublin, author of *Under the Net* (1954), *The Flight from the Enchanter* (1955), *The Bell* (1958), *The Red and the Green* (1965), *The Green Knight* (1993), and many other works. She became a DBE in 1987.

NAIPAUL, SHIVA (1945–85), novelist and journalist, born in Trinidad, brother of V. S. Naipaul, author of *Fireflies* (1970), *The Chip-Chip Gatherers* (1973), and other works.

NAIPAUL, VIDIADHAR SURAJPRASAD (1932–), novelist and essayist, born in Trinidad, since 1950 mainly resident in England. His novels include *The Mystic Masseur* (1957), *A House for Mr Biswas* (1961), *Mr Stone and the Knights Companion* (1963), *The Mimic Men* (1967), *Guerrillas* (1975), *A Bend in the River* (1979), *The Enigma of Arrival* (1987), and *Half a Life* (2001). He was knighted in 1990 and awarded the Nobel Prize for Literature in 2001.

NASHE, THOMAS (1567–1601), novelist, satirist, and playwright, born in Suffolk, author of *The Unfortunate Traveller* (1594).

ORWELL, GEORGE (Eric Blair) (1903–50), novelist and political writer, born in Bengal, resident in England from 1904, author of *Burmese Days* (1934), *A Clergyman's Daughter* (1935), *Keep the Aspidistra Flying* (1936), *Coming Up for Air* (1939), *Animal Farm* (1945), and *Nineteen Eighty-Four* (1949). His non-fiction includes *The Road to Wigan Pier* (1937), *Homage to Catalonia* (1937), and *The Lion and the Unicorn* (1941).

PEACOCK, THOMAS LOVE (1785–1866), novelist and satirist, born in Dorset, author of *Headlong Hall* (1815), *Melincourt* (1817), *Nightmare Abbey* (1818), *Maid Marian* (1822), and other works.

PEPYS, SAMUEL (1633–1703), diarist and civil servant, whose *Diary* written in 1659–69 was first published in 1825.

PERCY, THOMAS (1729–1811), author of *Reliques of Ancient English Poetry* (1765). He was ordained in 1751 and became a Church of Ireland bishop in 1782.

PHILLIPS, CARYL (1958–), novelist and playwright, born in St Kitts and brought up in England. His novels include *The Final Passage* (1985), *Cambridge* (1991), and *A Distant Shore* (2003), and he has edited the anthology *Extravagant Strangers* (1997).

POWELL, ANTHONY (1905–2000), novelist, born in London, author of *Afternoon Men* (1931), *Venusberg* (1932), *From a View to a Death* (1933), *Agents and Patients* (1936), and the twelve-volume sequence *A Dance to the Music of Time* (1951–75). His last novel was *The Fisher King* (1986).

POWYS, JOHN COWPER (1872–1963), novelist, born in Derbyshire, author of *Wolf Solent* (1929), *A Glastonbury Romance* (1932), *Weymouth Sands* (1934), and many other works.

PRIESTLEY, JOHN BOYNTON (1894–1984), novelist and playwright, born in Bradford, author of *The Good Companions* (1929), *Angel Pavement* (1930), *The Image Makers* (1968), and other novels. His non-fiction includes *The English Novel* (1927), *English Journey* (1933), *The English* (1973), and an autobiography, *Margin Released* (1962).

RADCLIFFE, ANN (1764–1823), novelist, born in London, author of *The Romance of the Forest* (1791), *The Mysteries of Udolpho* (1794), *The Italian* (1797), and other Gothic romances.

REEVE, CLARA (1729–1807), novelist, born in Suffolk, author of *The Champion of Virtue* (1777), which was republished in the following year as *The Old English Baron: A Gothic Story*.

RHYS, JEAN (Ella Gwendoline Rees Williams) (1890–1979), novelist, born in Dominica, educated in England, where she resided from 1928 onwards. She was the author of *Quartet* (1928), *After Leaving Mr Mackenzie* (1930), *Voyage in the Dark* (1934), *Good Morning, Midnight* (1939), and *Wide Sargasso Sea* (1966).

RICHARDSON, SAMUEL (1689–1761), printer and novelist, born in Derbyshire. He was the author of a letter-writing manual, *Letters Written to and for Particular Friends* (1741), and of three novels, *Pamela* (1740–1), *Clarissa* (1747–8), and *Sir Charles Grandison* (1753–4).

RITSON, JOSEPH (1752–1803), antiquarian, whose collection of the Robin Hood ballads was published in 1795.

RUSHDIE, SALMAN (1947–), novelist, born in India, educated and subsequently resident in England, whose works include *Midnight's Children* (1981), which won the Booker Prize, *Shame* (1983), *The Satanic Verses* (1988), *The Moor's Last Sigh* (1995), and a collection of essays, *Imaginary Homelands* (1991).

'RUTHERFORD, MARK' (William Hale White) (1831–1913), novelist, born in Bedford, author of *The Autobiography of Mark Rutherford* (1881), *Mark Rutherford's Deliverance* (1885), *The Revolution in Tanner's Lane* (1887), *Clara Hopgood* (1896), and other works. In 1852 he was expelled from theological college, thus abandoning his planned career in the Nonconformist ministry.

SALKEY, ANDREW (1928–95), Jamaican novelist and poet who studied in England. His novels include *Escape to an Autumn Pavement* (1960).

SCHREINER, OLIVE (1855–1920), South African novelist and social theorist, author of *The Story of an African Farm* (1883). She was resident in England from 1881 to 1889.

SCOTT, PAUL (1920–78), novelist, born in London, whose fiction includes *Johnny Sahib* (1952), the *Raj Quartet* (1966–75), and *Staying On* (1977), which won the Booker Prize. He served in the Army in India from 1943 to 1946.

SCOTT, WALTER (1771–1832), Scottish novelist and poet. *Waverley* (1814) was published anonymously. Its successors, known as the 'Waverley novels', include *Guy Mannering* (1815), *Old Mortality* (1816), *Rob Roy* (1817), *The Heart of Mid-Lothian* (1818), *Ivanhoe* (1819), *Kenilworth* (1821), *The Fortunes of Nigel* (1822), *Peveril of the Peak* (1823), *Redgauntlet* (1824), and *Woodstock* (1826). His *Lives of the Novelists* (1821–4) were prefixed to Ballantyne's Novelist's Library. He was knighted in 1818.

SEELEY, JOHN ROBERT (1834–95), historian, author of *The Expansion of England* (1883). He was knighted in 1894.

SELVON, SAMUEL (1923–94), Trinidadian novelist who lived in England from 1950 to 1975, author of *The Lonely Londoners* (1956), *Moses Ascending* (1975), *Moses Migrating* (1983), and other works.

SHAFTESBURY, ANTHONY ASHLEY COOPER, 3rd EARL OF (1671–1713), philosopher and author, whose *Characteristics* was first published in 1711.

SHELLEY, MARY (1797–1851), novelist and romancer, born in London, daughter of William Godwin and Mary Wollstonecraft. Her fiction includes *Frankenstein* (1818) and *The Last Man* (1826).

SHERIDAN, FRANCES (1724–66), Irish novelist and playwright, resident in London from 1754. She was the author of *Memoirs of Miss Sidney Bidulph* (1761).

SIDNEY, SIR PHILIP (1554–86), poet and courtier, born in Kent, whose prose romance *Arcadia* was published posthumously in 1590.

SMITH, ALEXANDER (fl.1714–26), criminal biographer, whose *History of the Lives of the Most Noted Highwaymen* was first published in 1714.

SMITH, CHARLOTTE (1749–1806), poet and novelist, born in London, author of *Emmeline, the Orphan of the Castle* (1788), *Desmond* (1792), *The Old Manor House* (1793), *Marchmont* (1796), and other works.

SMITH, ZADIE (1975–), novelist, born in London, author of *White Teeth* (2000), *The Autograph Man* (2002), and *On Beauty* (2005).

SMOLLETT, TOBIAS (1721–71), Scottish novelist, resident in England from 1744 to 1768, when he moved to Italy. He was the author of *Roderick Random* (1748), *Peregrine Pickle* (1751), *Ferdinand Count Fathom* (1753), *Sir Launcelot Greaves* (1760–2), and *Humphry Clinker* (1771). He translated Cervantes's *Don Quixote* (1755), and wrote a *Complete History of England* (1757).

SNOW, CHARLES PERCY, BARON (1905–80), novelist, scientist, and politician, author of the eleven-novel sequence *Strangers and Brothers* (1940–70). He was knighted in 1957 and made a life peer in 1964.

SOUEIF, AHDAF (1950–), novelist, born in Cairo, resident in England since 1981, author of *In the Eye of the Sun* (1992), *The Map of Love* (1999), and other novels.

SPARK, MURIEL (1918–), Scottish novelist, resident in Italy since 1966. Among her many novels are *The Comforters* (1957), *Memento Mori* (1959), *The Ballad of Peckham Rye* (1960), *The Prime of Miss Jean Brodie* (1961), *The Girls of Slender Means* (1963), and *Loitering with Intent* (1981). She became a DBE in 1993.

STEPHEN, LESLIE (1832–1904), biographer and critic, father of Virginia Woolf, founding editor of the *Dictionary of National Biography*. His literary essays were collected as *Hours in a Library* (1874–9). His later works included a study of George Eliot (1902).

STERNE, LAURENCE (1713–68), novelist and Church of England clergyman, born in Ireland, resident in England from 1724. He was the author of *Tristram Shandy* (1759–67) and *A Sentimental Journey through France and Italy* (1768).

STEVENSON, ROBERT LOUIS (1850–94), Scottish romancer and novelist, whose works include *Treasure Island* (1883), *The Strange Case of Dr Jekyll and Mr Hyde* (1886), *The Master of Ballantrae* (1889), *The Ebb-Tide* (1894), and *Weir of Hermiston* (1896). His unfinished romance *The Great North Road* was written in 1884–5. He lived in England for three years (1884–7), and made his home in Samoa in 1890.

STURT, GEORGE ('George Bourne') (1863–1927), rural writer, author of *Memoirs of a Surrey Labourer* (1927), *Change in the Village* (1912), and *The Wheelwright's Shop* (1923).

SWIFT, GRAHAM (1949–), novelist, born in London, author of *The Sweetshop Owner* (1980), *Shuttlecock* (1981), *Waterland* (1983), *Last Orders* (1996), *The Light of Day* (2003), and other works.

SWIFT, JONATHAN (1667–1745), Anglo-Irish satirist and clergyman, born in Dublin, frequently resident in England between 1689 and 1714. His works include *A Tale of a Tub* (1704) and *Gulliver's Travels* (1726).

SYAL, MEERA (1963–), novelist, actor, and screenwriter, born near Wolverhampton, author of *Anita and Me* (1996) and *Life Isn't All Ha Ha Hee Hee* (1999).

TAYLOR, PHILIP MEADOWS (1808–76), army officer and novelist, born in Liverpool, resident in India from 1823 to 1860. He was the author of *The Confessions of a Thug* (1839).

THACKERAY, WILLIAM MAKEPEACE (1811–63), novelist and satirist, born in India, resident in England from 1816. His fiction includes *The Tremendous Adventures of Major Gahagan* (1838), *The Luck of Barry Lyndon* (1844), *Vanity Fair* (1847–8), *Pendennis* (1848–50), *Rebecca and Rowena* (1850), *The History of Henry Esmond, Esq* (1852), *The Newcomes* (1853–5), *The Virginians* (1857–9), and many other works.

TOLKIEN, JOHN RICHARD REUEL (1892–1973), romancer and philologist, author of *The Hobbit* (1937) and *The Lord of the Rings* (1954–5). *The Silmarillion* (1977) was published posthumously.

TREVELYAN, GEORGE MACAULAY (1876–1962), historian, whose works include a *History of England* (1926) and *English Social History* (1944).

TROLLOPE, ANTHONY (1815–82), novelist, born in London. His fiction includes *The Warden* (1855), *Barchester Towers* (1857), *Doctor Thorne* (1858), *Framley Parsonage* (1861), *Phineas Finn* (1869), *The Way We Live Now* (1874–5), *The Prime Minister* (1876), *Is He Popenjoy?* (1878), and many other works. He also wrote *An Autobiography* (1875–6).

WALPOLE, HORACE, 4th EARL OF ORFORD (1717–97), author and politician, born in London. He wrote the first Gothic novel, *The Castle of Otranto* (1764), and was a Member of Parliament from 1741 to 1767.

WARD, MARY AUGUSTA (Mrs Humphry) (1851–1920), novelist and philanthropist, born in Tasmania, resident in England from 1856, author of *Robert Elsmere* (1888), *Marcella* (1894), and other works. She was a niece of Matthew Arnold.

WARNER, MARINA (1946–), novelist and cultural historian, author of *The Lost Father* (1988), *Indigo* (1992), and *The Leto Bundle* (2001).

WAUGH, EVELYN (1903–66), novelist, born in London. His fiction includes *Decline and Fall* (1928), *Vile Bodies* (1930), *Black Mischief* (1932), *A Handful of Dust* (1934), *Brideshead Revisited* (1945), the *Sword of Honour* trilogy (1952–61), and *The Ordeal of Gilbert Pinfold* (1957).

WELLS, HERBERT GEORGE (1866–1946), novelist and social prophet, born in Kent. His fiction includes *The Time Machine* (1895), *The Island of Doctor Moreau* (1896), *The War of the Worlds* (1898), *Love and Mr Lewisham* (1900), *Kipps* (1905), *Tono-Bungay* (1909), *The History of Mr Polly* (1910), and *The New Machiavelli* (1911). He also wrote *The Outline of History* (1920), *A Short History of the World* (1922), and *Experiment in Autobiography* (1934).

WHITE, TERENCE HANBURY (1906–64), novelist, born in India, resident in England from 1911, author of the Arthurian tetralogy *The Once and Future King* (1938–58).

WINTERSON, JEANETTE (1959–), novelist, born in Lancashire, author of *Oranges Are Not the Only Fruit* (1985), *Sexing the Cherry* (1989), *Written on the Body* (1992), and other works.

WODEHOUSE, PELHAM GRENVILLE (1881–1975), novelist, born in Surrey, author of *Mike* (1909), *Psmith in the City* (1910), *Something Fresh* (1915), and of fourteen novels featuring Jeeves and his master Bertie Wooster (1917–74). He was interned in Belgium and Germany in 1940–1, and lived in the United States after the war. He was knighted in 1975.

WOLLSTONECRAFT, MARY (1759–97), author and feminist, born in London, wife of William Godwin and mother of Mary Shelley. Her works include *A Vindication of the Rights of Woman* (1792), *A Short Residence in Sweden,*

Norway and Denmark (1796), and the novels *Mary: A Fiction* (1788) and the unfinished *The Wrongs of Woman, or Maria* (1798).

WOOLF, VIRGINIA (1882–1941), novelist and essayist, born in London, daughter of Leslie Stephen, author of *The Voyage Out* (1915), *Night and Day* (1919), *Jacob's Room* (1922), *Mrs Dalloway* (1925), *To the Lighthouse* (1927), *Orlando* (1928), *The Waves* (1931), *The Years* (1937), and *Between the Acts* (1941). Her literary essays were collected in *The Common Reader* (1925–32); many others have been published posthumously.

WYNDHAM, JOHN (John Wyndham Parkes Lucas Beynon Harris) (1903–69), science-fiction writer, born in Warwickshire, author of *The Day of the Triffids* (1951), *The Kraken Wakes* (1953), *The Midwich Cuckoos* (1957), and many other works.

YONGE, CHARLOTTE MARY (1823–1901), novelist, born in Hampshire, author of *The Heir of Redclyffe* (1853), *The Daisy Chain* (1856), and many other works.

ZANGWILL, ISRAEL (1864–1926), novelist and Zionist, born in London, whose works include *Children of the Ghetto* (1892), *Ghetto Tragedies* (1893), *The Master* (1895), and the play *The Melting Pot* (1908).

Further Reading

This guide to further reading focuses on modern scholarship on the English novel and its history, excluding original editions, earlier collections, and simple reprints such as the early twentieth-century volumes of Everyman's Library and World's Classics (invaluable as many of these still are). For the sake of simplicity, books are in general only listed once, without cross-referencing even though they may be relevant to more than one chapter. The place of publication given is the first place mentioned on the title-page.

INTRODUCTION AND CHAPTER 1: THE NOVEL AND THE NATION

No history of the English novel from its beginnings can ignore earlier accounts such as Ernest A. Baker's ten-volume *History of the English Novel* (London, 1924–39) and Walter Allen's *The English Novel* (London, 1954). Still worth consulting, though manifestly partial and polemical, are Ford Madox Ford's *The English Novel from the Earliest Days to the Death of Joseph Conrad* (London, 1930), Ralph Fox's *The Novel and the People* (London, 1937), and Arnold Kettle's *Introduction to the English Novel* (2 vols., London, 1951). V. S. Pritchett's fine essays on English and European novelists were collected in *The Living Novel* (London, 1946) and *The Working Novelist* (London, 1965). Margaret Anne Doody's *The True Story of the Novel* (London, 1997) attempts to assimilate the history of the novel to that of prose fiction in general. Among numerous accounts of the nature of modern fictional interpretation, the best to my mind is Peter Brooks's *Reading for the Plot: Design and Intention in Narrative* (Cambridge, Mass., 1992). The novel's relationship to other literary genres is explored in Georg Lukács, *The Historical Novel* (London, 1962), and M. M. Bakhtin, *The Dialogic Imagination: Four Essays* (Austin, Tex., 1981).

The quotations from Shakespeare in this chapter are from *The Complete Works*, ed. Peter Alexander (London, 1951). David Hume's 1748 essay 'Of National Character' is collected in his *Political Essays*, ed. Knud Haakanson (Cambridge, 1994). John Stuart Mill's *Considerations on Representative Government* (1861) exists in many editions, although Walter Bagehot's essay on national character, *Physics and Politics* (1872), remains comparatively little known; see, however, Bagehot's *Collected Works*, 15 vols. (London, 1965–86). Anthony D. Smith's *National Identity* (London, 1991) is an authoritative recent study of its subject. Edward W. Said contrasts 'filiation' and 'affiliation' in *The World, the Text, and the Critic* (London, 1984). Perry Anderson foregrounds the concepts of national character and national identity in his review-article on 'Nation-States and National Identity', *London Review of Books* 13: 9 (9 May 1991), 3–8. Almost all recent scholarly discussions of nationhood have been influenced by Benedict Anderson's *Imagined Communities: Reflections on the Origin and Spread of Nationalism* (London, 1983).

Of the many recent books on Englishness, the most stimulating, wide-ranging, and controversial academic study is Krishan Kumar's *The Making of English National Identity* (Cambridge, 2003). Anthony Easthope's *Englishness and National Culture* (London, 1999) and Roger Scruton's *England: An Elegy* (London, 2000) are challenging and polemical accounts from opposing political perspectives. They should be contrasted with such largely empirical studies as Paul Langford's *Englishness Identified: Manners and Character 1650–1850* (Oxford, 2000), Robert Colls's *Identity of England* (Oxford, 2002), and Peter Ackroyd's *Albion: The Origins of the English Imagination* (London, 2002), each of which has some of the virtues of a good anthology. For more traditional ideas of Englishness, the best sources remain Daniel Defoe's *The True-Born Englishman and Other Writings*, ed. P. N. Furbank and W. R. Owens (London, 1997), Edmund Burke's *Reflections on the Revolution in France*, ed. Conor Cruise O'Brien (Harmondsworth, 1968), Walter Bagehot's *The English Constitution*, with an introduction by R. H. S. Crossman (London, 1964), and George Orwell's essays (see below under Early Twentieth-Century Fiction). See also J. B. Priestley, *English Journey* (London, 1934) and *The English* (London, 1973), and Peter Vansittart, *In Memory of England* (London, 1998).

Relations between the nation, nationalism, and fiction are explored in a collection of essays edited by Homi K. Bhabha, *Nation and Narration* (London, 1990); see also Bhabha's *The Location of Culture* (London, 1994), and Pericles Lewis's *Modernism, Nationalism, and the Novel* (Cambridge, 2000). Fredric Jameson discusses the novel as 'national allegory' in his analysis of Wyndham Lewis's fiction, *Fables of Aggression* (Berkeley, 1979). Among the classic studies of other nations' fictional traditions are Leslie A. Fiedler, *Love and Death in the American Novel* (2nd edn., New York, 1966); Richard Chase, *The American Novel and its Tradition* (New York, 1957); and Margaret Atwood, *Survival: A Thematic Guide to Canadian Literature* (Toronto, 1972). More recently, I would especially recommend Gerry Smyth's *The Novel and the Nation: Studies in the New Irish Fiction* (London and Chicago, 1997). Paul Gilbert reflects on 'The Idea of a National Literature' in John Horton and Andrea T. Baumeister, eds., *Literature and the Political Imagination* (London, 1996).

There have been influential discussions of Englishness in relation to other art forms, notably Nikolaus Pevsner's *The Englishness of English Art* (London, 1956), and to other literary genres: poetry, for example, is the principal concern of John Lucas's *England and Englishness* (London, 1990) and of David Gervais's *Literary Englands* (Cambridge, 1993). For seminal insights into English poetry and fiction across the centuries see Raymond Williams's *The Country and the City* (London, 1973). Q. D. Leavis, however, is virtually alone along important twentieth-century critics in discussing 'The Englishness of the English Novel', *English Studies* 62: 2 (1981), 128–45. William Hazlitt's course of *Lectures on the*

English Comic Writers (1819) has been much reprinted, while the earlier version of his essay on the English novelists is 'Standard Novels and Romances', in *Complete Works*, ed. P. P. Howe (London, 1933), xvi. 5–24. Walter Scott's prefaces to Ballantyne's *Novelist's Library* (1821) were collected as *Lives of the Novelists* (London, 1910).

Studies of particular fictional forms include Claudio Guillén's 'Toward a Definition of the Picaresque' in *Literature as System* (Princeton, 1971), 71–106; Walter L. Reed's *An Exemplary History of the Novel: The Quixotic versus the Picaresque* (Chicago, 1981); and Franco Moretti's essay on the *Bildungsroman*, *The Way of the World* (London, 1987). English courtship fiction is the subject of Nancy Armstrong's *Desire and Domestic Fiction: A Political History of the Novel* (New York, 1987), Joseph Allen Boone's *Tradition Counter Tradition* (Chicago, 1987), and Ruth Bernard Yeazell's *Fictions of Modesty: Women and Courtship in the English Novel* (Chicago, 1991). Lionel Trilling's reflections on the 'young man from the provinces' are found in his essay on Henry James's *The Princess Casamassima* in *The Liberal Imagination* (London, 1951). Martin Green contrasts domestic fiction with the imperial adventure novel in his brilliant and provocative study *Dreams of Adventure, Deeds of Empire* (London, 1980).

CHAPTER 2: CAVALIERS, PURITANS, AND ROGUES

The history of English prose fiction before 1558 is the subject of an appendix to William A. Ringler, Jr., and Michael Flachmann's edition of *Beware the Cat: The First English Novel* (San Marino, Calif., 1988), 75–90. The standard edition of *The Works of Sir Thomas Malory* is edited by Eugene Vinaver (3 vols., Oxford, 1947). Stephen Knight's *Arthurian Literature and Society* (London, 1983) includes discussion of *Le Morte d'Arthur* as an allegory of the Wars of the Roses. All students of Elizabethan and seventeenth-century English fiction are indebted to the work of Paul Salzman, author of *English Prose Fiction 1558–1700: A Critical History* (Oxford, 1985) and editor of two World's Classics anthologies, *Elizabethan Prose Fiction* (Oxford, 1987) and *Seventeenth-Century Fiction* (Oxford, 1991). The most significant supplement to Salzman's work is to be found in the earlier chapters of Josephine Donovan's *Women and the Rise of the Novel, 1405–1726* (New York, 2000). For the Elizabethan period I have also drawn on Katherine Duncan-Jones's edition of Sidney's *Arcadia* (Oxford, 1994); David Margolies's *Novel and Society in Elizabethan England* (London, 1985); Robert Mayer's *History and the Early English Novel* (Cambridge, 1987); and Gamini Salgado's anthology of Elizabethan low life, *Cony-Catchers and Bawdy Baskets* (Harmondsworth, 1972). Spiro Peterson has edited an anthology of seventeenth-century criminal fiction, *The Counterfeit Lady Unveiled* (Garden City, New York, 1961).

Janet Todd has edited a valuable selection of Aphra Behn's *Oroonoko, The Rover and Other Works* (London, 1992), while the Virago reprint of *Love-Letters*

Between a Nobleman and His Sister (London, 1987) has an introduction by Maureen Duffy. S. J. Wiseman's *Aphra Behn* (Plymouth, 1996) is a useful introductory survey of Behn's writings. Bunyan's principal modern editor, Roger Sharrock, has published editions of *Grace Abounding* (Oxford, 1962), *The Pilgrim's Progress* (Harmondsworth, 1965), and, with James F. Forrest, of *The Holy War* (Oxford, 1980) and *The Life and Death of Mr Badman* (Oxford, 1988). A. A. Parker discusses Bunyan, Defoe, and Fielding in relation to the Spanish picaresque in *Literature and the Delinquent* (Edinburgh, 1977), while Leopold Damrosch, Jr., considers Bunyan's place in the fictional tradition in *God's Plot and Man's Stories: Studies in the Fictional Imagination from Milton to Fielding* (Chicago, 1985).

CHAPTERS 3, 4, 5, AND 6: EIGHTEENTH-CENTURY FICTION

Among recent histories of eighteenth-century England, those most concerned with national identities are Linda Colley's *Britons: Forging the Nation 1701–1837* (New Haven, 1992), H. T. Dickinson's *The Politics of the People in Eighteenth-Century Britain* (Basingstoke, 1995), and Gerald Newman's *The Rise of English Nationalism* (London, 1987). Raphael Samuel is editor of an important collection of essays, *Patriotism: The Making and Unmaking of British National Identity* (3 vols., London, 1989). Laird Okie surveys eighteenth-century histories of England in *Augustan Historical Writing* (Lanham, Md., 1991), while R. C. Richardson has summarized *The Debate on the English Revolution* (London, 1977).

Every modern scholar of eighteenth-century fiction is indebted to Ian Watt's classic study of Defoe, Richardson, and Fielding, *The Rise of the Novel* (London, 1957). Among the numerous revisions and rewritings of Watt's thesis are Michael McKeon's *The Origins of the English Novel, 1600–1740* (London, 1988), Lennard J. Davis's *Factual Fictions: The Origins of the English Novel* (New York, 1983), Marthe Robert's *Origins of the Novel* (Brighton, 1980), and Jane Spencer's *The Rise of the Woman Novelist* (Oxford, 1986). Other accounts of the novel's emergence as a distinct genre in the eighteenth century include Geoffrey Day, *From Fiction to the Novel* (London, 1987); J. Paul Hunter, *Before Novels* (New York, 1990); and John J. Richetti, *Popular Fiction Before Richardson* (Oxford, 1969). Aspects of the eighteenth-century novel as a 'social institution' are discussed in Deirdre Lynch and William B. Warner, eds., *Cultural Institutions of the Novel* (Durham, NC, 1996); Clifford Siskin, *The Work of Writing* (Baltimore, 1998); and Diana Spearman, *The Novel and Society* (London, 1966). A number of readers' guides to eighteenth-century fiction contain valuable essays: mention should be made of *The English Novel*, ed. Richard Kroll (2 vols., London, 1998), and *The Cambridge Companion to the Eighteenth-Century Novel*, ed. John Richetti (Cambridge, 1996). The journal *Eighteenth-Century Fiction* is indispensable reading if one wishes to keep up with recent scholarship on the novel in the 'long eighteenth century' (that is, including Austen and Scott). Among more general literary histories, John Barrell's *English Literature in*

History 1730–80 (London, 1983) and Laura Brown's *English Dramatic Form, 1660–1760* (New Haven, 1981) are particularly notable.

Studies of the eighteenth-century novel in relation to other contemporary genres include Martin C. Battestin, *The Providence of Wit* (Oxford, 1974); Terry Castle, *Masquerade and Civilization* (London, 1986); Paul J. Korshin, *Typologies in England 1650–1820* (Princeton, 1982); Ronald J. Paulson, *Satire and the Novel in Eighteenth-Century England* (New Haven, 1967); and, on fiction and auto-biography, Patricia Meyer Spacks's *Imagining a Self* (Cambridge, Mass., 1976). Jonathan Lamb surveys eighteenth-century readings of the Book of Job in *The Rhetoric of Suffering* (Oxford, 1995).

Modern editions of the political classics of the period include C. B. Macpherson's edition of Hobbes's *Leviathan* (Harmondsworth, 1968); Locke's *Two Treatises of Government*, ed. Peter Laslett (revised edn., New York, 1965); and Shaftesbury's *Characteristics*, ed. John M. Robertson (Indianapolis, 1964). Gordon J. Schochet discusses versions of the 'authoritarian family' in *Patriarchalism in Political Thought* (Oxford, 1975). Carol Kay's *Political Constructions* (Ithaca, NY, 1988) and Everett Zimmerman's *The Boundaries of Fiction* (Ithaca, NY, 1996) are studies of the novel in relation to political thought, while Richard Braverman's *Plots and Counterplots* (Cambridge, 1993) is concerned with 'sexual politics and the body politic' in the literature of the period 1660–1830. Other studies of literature in relation to politics are Miranda J. Burgess, *British Fiction and the Production of Social Order, 1740–1830* (Cambridge, 2000); W. Austin Flanders, *Structures of Experience* (Columbia, SC, 1984); Christine Gerrard, *The Patriot Opposition to Walpole* (Oxford, 1994); and Howard D. Weinbrot, *Britannia's Issue* (Cambridge, 1993).

On crime and society in the eighteenth century, two classic studies are Douglas Hay and others, *Albion's Fatal Tree* (London, 1975) and Peter Linebaugh, *The London Hanged* (London, 1991). Lincoln B. Faller discusses the criminal biographies in *Turned to Account* (London, 1987), while Ian A. Bell's *Literature and Crime in Augustan England* (London, 1991) includes a notable analysis of Fielding. More generally, Bertrand H. Bronson published a biography of *Joseph Ritson* (2 vols., Berkeley, 1938), while Graham Seal relates the English highwayman to American and Australian outlaws in *The Outlaw Legend* (Cambridge, 1996). Among the vast popular literature on Robin Hood and other outlaws, the only title that need be mentioned here is E. J. Hobsbawm's *Bandits* (London, 1958).

Modern editions of Defoe include *A Journal of the Plague Year*, ed. Anthony Burgess and Christopher Bristow (Harmondsworth, 1966); *Memoirs of a Cavalier*, ed. James T. Boulton (London, 1972); *Moll Flanders*, ed. G. A. Starr (Oxford, 1981); *Robinson Crusoe*, ed. Michael Shinagel (2nd edn., New York, 1994); *Roxana*, ed. Jane Jack (Oxford, 1981); and *A Tour through the Whole Island of Great Britain*, ed. Pat Rogers (Harmondsworth, 1971). Rogers has also edited *Daniel Defoe: The Critical Heritage* (London, 1972), while David Fausett gives an excellent account of *The Strange Surprizing Sources of Robinson Crusoe* (Amsterdam, 1994). The other critical books on Defoe that I have drawn on are Lincoln B. Faller, *Crime and Defoe* (Cambridge, 1993); Maximillian E. Novak, *Realism, Myth, and History in Defoe's Fiction* (Lincoln, Nebr., 1983); Manuel Schonhorn, *Defoe's Politics* (Cambridge, 1991); Lieve Spaas and Brian Stimpson, eds., *Robinson Crusoe: Myths and Metamorphoses* (Basingstoke, 1996); and David Trotter, *Circulation: Defoe, Dickens, and the Economies of the Novel* (Basingstoke, 1988).

Fielding's *Amelia* has been edited by Martin C. Battestin (Oxford, 1983); *An Enquiry into the Causes of the Late Increase of Robbers*, ed. Malvin R. Zirker (Oxford, 1988); *Joseph Andrews and Shamela*, ed. Arthur Humphreys (revised edn., London, 1993); *The Journal of a Voyage to Lisbon*, ed. Tom Keymer (London, 1996); *Tom Jones*, ed. R. P. C. Mutter (Harmondsworth, 1966); and *The True Patriot and Related Writings*, ed. W. B. Coley (Oxford, 1987). A classic article on Fielding and the politics of his time is Homer Obed Brown, '*Tom Jones*: The "Bastard" of History', *Boundary* 2, 7: 2 (1979), 201–33; see also Brian McCrea's *Henry Fielding and the Politics of Mid-Eighteenth-Century England* (Athens, G., 1981). The debate over Jacobitism in criticism of *Tom Jones* is reviewed in Peter J. Carlton, '*Tom Jones* and the '45 Once Again', *Studies in the Novel* 20: 4 (1988), 361–73. The standard modern biography is Martin C. Battestin with Ruthe R. Battestin, *Henry Fielding: A Life* (London, 1989). Two other general critical studies are Robert Alter's *Fielding and the Nature of the Novel* (Cambridge, Mass., 1968) and Jill Campbell's *Natural Masques: Gender and Identity in Fielding's Plays and Novels* (Stanford, 1995).

Recent editions of Richardson include *Clarissa*, ed. Angus Ross (Harmondsworth, 1985); *The History of Sir Charles Grandison*, ed. Jocelyn Harris (3 vols., London, 1972); *Pamela*, ed. Peter Sabor (Harmondsworth, 1980), and ed. Thomas Keymer and Alice Wakely (Oxford, 2001); and *Selected Letters*, ed. John Carroll (Oxford, 1964). Carroll has also edited *Samuel Richardson: A Collection of Critical Essays* (Englewood Cliffs, NJ, 1969); a more recent collection is *Samuel Richardson: Tercentenary Essays*, ed. Margaret Anne Doody and Peter Sabor (Cambridge, 1989). Other general studies of Richardson include Ewha Chung, *Samuel Richardson's New Nation* (New York, 1998); Jocelyn Harris, *Samuel Richardson* (Cambridge, 1987); and Cynthia Griffin Wolff, *Samuel Richardson and the Eighteenth-Century Puritan Character* (Hamden, Conn., 1972). For a classic discussion of *Clarissa*, see Christopher Hill's essay 'Clarissa Harlowe and her Times' in *Puritanism and Revolution* (London, 1958). Other studies of Richardson's masterpiece are Lois E. Bueler, *Clarissa's Plots* (Newark, Del., 1994); Terry Eagleton, *The Rape of Clarissa* (Oxford, 1982); and Tom Keymer, *Richardson's 'Clarissa' and the Eighteenth-Century Reader* (Cambridge, 1992).

Tobias Smollett's *The Expedition of Humphry Clinker* is edited by Louis M. Knapp and Paul-Gabriel Boucé (Oxford, 1984). Smollett criticism has been collected in *Tobias Smollett: The Critical Heritage*, ed. Lionel Kelly (London, 1987) and *Tobias Smollett: Bicentennial Essays*, ed. G. S. Rousseau and P.-G. Boucé (New York, 1971). Among modern editions of other eighteenth-century fiction, I have used the following: Joseph Addison, Sir Richard Steele and Eustace Budgell, *Sir Roger de Coverly*, ed. John Hampden (London, 1967); John Arbuthnot, *The History of John Bull*, ed. Alan W. Bower and Robert A. Erickson (Oxford, 1976); Fanny Burney, *Evelina*, ed. Edward A. Bloom and Lillian D. Bloom (Oxford, 1982); Sarah Fielding, *The Adventures of David Simple*, ed. Malcolm Kelsall (Oxford, 1994); William Godwin, *Things As They Are or the Adventures of Caleb Williams*, ed. Maurice Hindle (London, 1988); Oliver Goldsmith, *Collected Works*, ed. Arthur Friedman (Oxford, 1966); Eliza Haywood, *Three Novellas*, ed. Earla A. Wilputte (East Lansing, Mich., 1995); Henry Mackenzie, *The Man of Feeling*, ed. Brian Vickers (London, 1970); Charlotte Smith, *The Old Manor House*, ed. Anne Henry Ehrenpreis (London, 1969); Laurence Sterne, *The Life and Opinions of Tristram Shandy*, ed. Graham Petrie (Harmondsworth, 1967); Horace Walpole, *The Castle of Otranto*, ed. W. S. Lewis (Oxford, 1964); and Mary Wollstonecraft, *Mary, A Fiction and The Wrongs of Woman*, ed. Gary Kelly (London, 1976). Kelly is the author of *The English Jacobin Novel 1780–1805* (Oxford, 1976); other studies of Jacobin fiction are Pamela Clemit, *The Godwinian Novel* (Oxford, 1993) and Loraine Fletcher, 'Four Jacobin Women Novelists' in John Lucas, ed., *Writing and Radicalism* (London, 1996), 102–27.

CHAPTERS 7 AND 8 (i): SCOTT, JANE AUSTEN, AND THEIR CONTEMPORARIES

Some further examples of Jacobin fiction and other late eighteenth-century modes are referred to in these chapters, notably Thomas Holcroft, *Anna St. Ives*, ed. Peter Faulkner (London, 1970); Elizabeth Inchbald, *A Simple Story*, ed. J. M. S. Tompkins (London, 1967); Clara Reeve, *The Old English Baron*, ed. James Trainer (London, 1967); and Charlotte Smith, *Desmond*, ed. Antje Blank and Janet Todd (Peterborough, Ont., 2001), and *Emmeline*, ed. Anne Henry Ehrenpreis (London, 1971). See also Loraine Fletcher, *Charlotte Smith: A Critical Biography* (Basingstoke, 1998).

Novels contemporary with Austen and Scott include Frances Burney, *The Wanderer*, ed. Margaret Anne Doody, Robert L. Mack, and Peter Sabor (Oxford, 1991); Maria Edgeworth, *Castle Rackrent and Ennui*, ed. Marilyn Butler (London, 1992); and Susan Ferrier, *Marriage*, ed. Herbert Feltinek (London, 1971).

Two major general studies are Igor Webb, *From Custom to Capital* (Ithaca, NY, 1981), on English fiction and the industrial revolution, and Katie Trumpener, *Bardic Nationalism* (Princeton, 1997), on the Romantic novel and the British Empire. Daniel Cottam looks at Austen, Scott, and Gothic fiction in *The Civilized Imagination* (Cambridge, 1985), while Cannon Schmitt's *Alien Nation* (Philadelphia, 1997) is a study of the Gothic in relation to English nationality. Scott and the Gothic are the subject of two further studies, Ian

Duncan's *Modern Romance and the Transformations of the Novel* (Cambridge, 1992) and Fiona Robertson's *Legitimate Histories* (Oxford, 1994). David Kaufmann's *The Business of Common Life* (Baltimore, 1995) looks at the Romantic novelists in relation to classical economics. Scott's relationship to later historical fiction is discussed in Avrom Fleishman, *The English Historical Novel* (Baltimore, 1971) and Andrew Sanders, *The Victorian Historical Novel 1840–1880* (London, 1978). Criticism of Mary Russell Mitford and her successors is to be found in P. D. Edwards, *Idyllic Realism from Mary Russell Mitford to Hardy* (Basingstoke, 1988) and Elizabeth K. Helsinger, *Rural Scenes and National Representation* (Princeton, 1997). Washington Irving is one of the subjects of Malcolm Bradbury's account of Anglo-American literary relations, *Dangerous Pilgrimages* (London, 1995).

Among the innumerable editions of Scott, I am indebted to *The Heart of Mid-Lothian*, ed. Tony Inglis (London, 1994); *Ivanhoe*, ed. Graham Tulloch (Edinburgh, 1998); *Kenilworth*, ed. J. H. Alexander (London, 1999); *On Novelists and Fiction*, ed. Ioan Williams (London, 1968); and *Rob Roy*, ed. John Sutherland (London, 1995). Scott's 1830 'Introduction' to *Ivanhoe*, omitted from Tulloch's edition, is found in many other reprints of the novel. Critical responses to Scott's work are collected in John O. Hayden, ed., *Scott: The Critical Heritage* (London, 1970) and D. D. Devlin, ed., *Walter Scott: Modern Judgements* (Nashville, 1970). Alexander Welsh's *The Hero of the Waverley Novels* (New Haven, 1963) is a critical classic, and I am also indebted to Cairns Craig's *Out of History* (Edinburgh, 1996), James Kerr's *Fiction against History: Scott as Storyteller* (Cambridge, 1989), and Graham McMaster's *Scott and Society* (Cambridge, 1981).

Editions of Jane Austen include *Catharine and Other Writings*, ed. Margaret Anne Doody and Douglas Murray (Oxford, 1998); *Emma*, ed. Ronald Blythe (Harmondsworth, 1966); *Mansfield Park*, ed. Tony Tanner (Harmondsworth, 1966); *Northanger Abbey, Lady Susan, The Watsons, and Sanditon*, ed. John Davis (Oxford, 1990); and *Sense and Sensibility*, ed. Tony Tanner (Harmondsworth, 1969). Among collections of critical essays are *Jane Austen*, ed. Ian Watt (Englewood Cliffs, NJ, 1963), which reprints Donald J. Greene's important essay on 'Jane Austen and the Peerage', *Jane Austen: Bicentenary Essays*, ed. John Halperin (Cambridge, 1975), and *Jane Austen in a Social Context*, ed. David Monaghan (Basingstoke, 1981). An excellent recent introduction is Robert Miles's *Jane Austen* (Tavistock, 2003). For political readings of the novels see Marilyn Butler, *Jane Austen and the War of Ideas* (Oxford, 1975); Claudia L. Johnson, *Jane Austen: Women, Politics and the Novel* (Chicago, 1988); and Edward Neill, *The Politics of Jane Austen* (Basingstoke, 1999). Edward W. Said discusses slavery in *Mansfield Park* in his *Culture and Imperialism* (London, 1993). Other thematic studies include Frank W. Bradbrook, *Jane Austen and Her Predecessors* (Cambridge, 1966); Jocelyn Harris, *Jane Austen's Art of Memory* (Cambridge, 1989); and Margaret Kirkham, *Jane Austen, Feminism and Fiction* (Sussex, 1983). See also Shinobu Minma, 'Self-Deception and Superiority

Complex: Derangement of Hierarchy in Jane Austen's *Emma*', *Eighteenth-Century Fiction* 14: 1 (2001), 49–65.

CHAPTERS 7 AND 8 (ii), 9, 10, AND 11: VICTORIAN FICTION

Thomas Carlyle's *Selected Writings* are edited by Alan Shelston (Harmondsworth, 1971), while Bulwer-Lytton's *England and the English* has been edited by Standish Meacham (Chicago, 1970). J. W. Burrow's *A Liberal Descent* (Cambridge, 1981) is a major study of Victorian historiography; Martin J. Wiener's *English Culture and the Decline of the Industrial Spirit* (Cambridge, 1981) is a provocative and influential account of Victorian attitudes to class. See also the essays collected in Herbert F. Tucker, ed., *A Companion to Victorian Literature and Culture* (Oxford, 1999).

Like his earlier *The Way of the World*, Franco Moretti's *Atlas of the European Novel 1800–1900* (London, 1998) looks at English fiction in a European context. Two starting points for the study of Victorian political fiction are Kathleen Tillotson, *Novels of the Eighteen-Forties* (Oxford, 1954), and John Lucas, ed., *Literature and Politics in the Nineteenth Century* (London, 1971). More recent criticism includes Rosemarie Bodenheimer, *The Politics of Story in Victorian Social Fiction* (Ithaca, NY, 1988); Catherine Gallagher, *The Industrial Reformation of English Fiction* (Chicago, 1985); and, among gender studies, Patricia Ingham's *The Language of Gender and Class* (London, 1996), Mary Poovey's *Uneven Developments* (London, 1989), and Ruth Bernard Yeazell's 'Why Political Novels Have Heroines', *Novel* 18: 2 (1985), 126–44. English national identity is a specific concern of Michael Ragussis' study of the 'Jewish question' in Disraeli and others, *Figures of Conversion* (Durham, NC, 1995), and of Julian Wolfreys' *Being English* (Albany, NY, 1994). The novel's relation to empire is at the forefront of Patrick Brantlinger's *Rule of Darkness* (Ithaca, NY, 1988) and a number of more recent books such as Jonathan Arac and Harriet Ritvo, eds., *Macropolitics of Nineteenth-Century Literature* (Durham, NC, 1995); Daniel Bivona, *Desire and Contradiction: Imperial Visions and Domestic Debates in Victorian Literature* (Manchester, 1990); Terry Eagleton's essays on Irish culture, *Heathcliff and the Great Hunger* (London, 1995); Susan Meyer, *Imperialism at Home* (Ithaca, NY, 1996); and Jenny Sharpe's study of 'women in the colonial text', *Allegories of Empire* (Minneapolis, 1993). Joss Marsh's *Word Crimes* (Chicago, 1998) is an outstanding account of anticlericalism and Victorian literature. Among more formalistic approaches, particularly notable are Peter K. Garrett, *The Victorian Multiplot Novel* (New Haven, 1980) and John R. Reed, *Victorian Conventions* (Athens, Ohio, 1975). Peter Keating's *The Haunted Study* (London, 1989) is a social history of the novel at the turn of the twentieth century; this may be supplemented by Keating's earlier study of *The Working Classes in Victorian Fiction* (London, 1971), and by Sally Ledger's *The New Woman* (Manchester, 1997). Daniel Born's *The Birth of Liberal Guilt in the English Novel* (Chapel Hill, NC, 1995) looks at a series of novelists from Dickens to Wells.

Recent editions of Dickens's novels that I have consulted include *Bleak House*, ed. Norman Page (London, 1985) and ed. Nicola Bradbury (London, 1996); *Martin Chuzzlewit*, ed. P. N. Furbank (London, 1986) and ed. Patricia Ingham (London, 1999); *Oliver Twist*, ed. Peter Fairclough (London, 1985); *Our Mutual Friend*, ed. Adrian Poole (London, 1997); and *A Tale of Two Cities*, ed. Richard Maxwell (London, 2000). Among Dickens criticism, I particularly recommend James Buzard, ' "Anywhere's Nowhere": *Bleak House* as Autoethnography', *Yale Journal of Criticism* 12: 1 (1999), 7–39; J. Hillis Miller, *Charles Dickens: The World of his Novels* (Cambridge, Mass., 1958); John Kucich, *Excess and Restraint in the Novels of Charles Dickens* (Athens, Ga., 1981); John Lucas, *Charles Dickens: The Major Novels* (London, 1972); Richard Maxwell, *The Mysteries of Paris and London* (Charlottesville, Va., 1992); William J. Palmer, *Dickens and New Historicism* (Basingstoke, 1997); Anny Sadrin, *Parentage and Inheritance in the Novels of Charles Dickens* (Cambridge, 1994); and two books by Alexander Welsh, *The City of Dickens* (Oxford, 1971) and *From Copyright to Copperfield* (Cambridge, Mass., 1987).

Disraeli's *Sybil* is edited by Thom Braun (Harmondsworth, 1980). The standard biography is Robert Blake's *Disraeli* (London, 1966); to this may be added Charles Richmond and Paul Smith, eds., *The Self-Fashioning of Disraeli 1818–1851* (Cambridge, 1998).

Charlotte Brontë's *Jane Eyre* has been edited by Q. D. Leavis (Harmondsworth, 1966). Other modern Brontë editions are *Villette*, ed. Mark Lilly (Harmondsworth, 1979); Emily Brontë, *Wuthering Heights*, ed. Ian Jack (Oxford, 1995); and Anne Brontë, *The Tenant of Wildfell Hall*, ed. G. D. Hargreaves (Harmondsworth, 1979). Christine Alexander has edited two volumes of Charlotte Brontë's *Early Writings* (Oxford, 1987, 1991). Barbara Timm Gates, ed., *Critical Essays on Charlotte Brontë* (Boston, 1990) is highly recommended, as is Enid L. Duthie, *The Foreign Vision of Charlotte Brontë* (London, 1975). Terry Eagleton's *Myths of Power* (2nd edn., Basingstoke, 1988) is a Marxist study of the Brontës. See also the books by Bodenheimer, Meyer, Sharpe, and others listed above.

Editions of Elizabeth Gaskell's fiction include *Cousin Phillis and Other Tales*, ed. Angus Easson (Oxford, 1981); *My Lady Ludlow and Other Stories*, ed. Edgar Wright (Oxford, 1989); *North and South*, ed. Dorothy Collin (London, 1986); *Sylvia's Lovers*, ed. Andrew Sanders (Oxford, 1982); and *Wives and Daughters*, ed. Frank Gloversmith (Harmondsworth, 1969). Two critical studies are Deirdre d'Albertis, *Dissembling Fictions* (New York, 1997) and Coral Lansbury, *Elizabeth Gaskell: the Novel of Social Crisis* (London, 1975). Editions of Anthony Trollope include *An Autobiography*, ed. Michael Sadleir and Frederick Page (Oxford, 1992); *Doctor Thorne*, ed. David Skilton (Oxford, 1980); *The Warden*, ed. Robin Gilmour (London, 1986); and *The Way We Live Now*, ed. Sir Frank Kermode (London, 1994).

George Eliot's *Adam Bede* has been edited by Valentine Cunningham (Oxford, 1996); *Daniel Deronda*, ed. Barbara Hardy (Harmondsworth, 1967); *Felix Holt*, *the Radical*, ed. Fred C. Thomson (Oxford, 1988); *Middlemarch*, ed. David Carroll (Oxford, 1998); *The Mill on the Floss*, ed. Gordon S. Haight (Oxford, 1980); and *Scenes of Clerical Life*, ed. Thomas A. Noble (Oxford, 1988). Haight has also edited *A Century of George Eliot Criticism* (London, 1966), while Barbara Hardy is the editor of *Critical Essays on George Eliot* (London, 1970). More recent criticism includes Nancy Henry, *George Eliot and the British Empire* (Cambridge, 2002); Neil NcCaw, *George Eliot and Victorian Historiography* (Basingstoke, 2000); Bernard Semmel, *George Eliot and the Politics of National Inheritance* (New York, 1994); and Sally Shuttleworth, *George Eliot and Nineteenth-Century Science* (Cambridge, 1986).

Thackeray's novels have been comparatively neglected in recent years. Scholarly editions include *The Memoirs of Barry Lyndon*, ed. Andrew Sanders (Oxford, 1984) and *Vanity Fair*, ed. John Sutherland (Oxford, 1983). Geoffrey Tillotson and Donald Hawes edited *Thackeray: The Critical Heritage* (London, 1968), while John Carey's *Thackeray: Prodigal Genius* (London, 1977) is a stimulating critical study. The works of Henry James most relevant to the present book are *The Princess Casamassima*, ed. Derek Brewer (London, 1987) and *Selected Literary Criticism*, ed. Morris Shapira (London, 1963). *Clara Hopgood* by 'Mark Rutherford' is edited by Lorraine Davies (London, 1996), while Arthur Morrison's *A Child of the Jago* is edited by P. J. Keating (London, 1969). Pierre Coustillas and Colin Partridge edited *Gissing: The Critical Heritage* (London, 1972). Coustillas has also edited *Collected Articles on George Gissing* (London, 1968). Raymond Williams discusses Gissing's 'negative identification' in *Culture and Society 1780–1950* (London, 1958); see also Fredric Jameson, *The Political Unconscious* (London, 1981). Modern editions of Thomas Hardy's novels include *Jude the Obscure*, ed. P. N. Furbank (London, 1974); *A Pair of Blue Eyes*, ed. Alan Monford (Oxford, 1985); *The Return of the Native*, ed. Derwent May (London, 1974); and *The Woodlanders*, ed. David Lodge (London, 1974).

CHAPTERS 12, 13, AND 14 (i): EARLY TWENTIETH-CENTURY FICTION

The principal historical texts cited in these chapters are Sir J. R. Seeley, *The Expansion of England* (2nd edn., London, 1897); J. A. Hobson, *Imperialism* (3rd edn., London, 1938); C. R. L. Fletcher and Rudyard Kipling, *A School History of England* (Oxford, 1911); G. K. Chesterton, *A Short History of England* (London, 1917); G. M. Trevelyan, *History of England* (London, 1926); and, on the 'Whig interpretation', H. Butterfield, *The Englishman and his History* (Cambridge, 1944). Judy Giles and Tim Middleton, eds., *Writing Englishness 1900–1950* (London, 1995) is a wide-ranging 'introductory sourcebook on national identity'.

Among the numerous general studies of the English literature of the period, the following are particularly relevant: David Craig, *The Real Foundations: Literature and Social Change* (London, 1973); Jed Esty, *A Shrinking Island* (Princeton, 2004); Martin Green, *The English Novel in the Twentieth Century [The Doom of Empire]* (London, 1984); Jefferson Hunter, *Edwardian Fiction*

(Cambridge, Mass., 1982); Karen R. Lawrence, ed., *Decolonizing Tradition* (Urbana, Ill., 1992); and David Trotter, *The English Novel in History 1895–1920* (London, 1993). For a recent overview see Laura Marcus and Peter Nicholls, eds., *The Cambridge History of Twentieth-Century English Literature* (Cambridge, 2004).

Elaine Showalter discusses turn-of-the-century romances in *Sexual Anarchy* (London, 1991). Christopher Harvie's *The Centre of Things* (London, 1991) surveys political fiction from Disraeli to the present. Thomas Richards, *The Imperial Archive* (London, 1993) looks at imperialism in early twentieth-century fiction. Studies of literary representations of the aristocracy and the 'English gentleman' include Richard Gill, *Happy Rural Seat* (New Haven, 1972), on the country house; Mark Girouard, *The Return to Camelot* (New Haven, 1981); and Len Platt, *Aristocracies of Fiction* (Westport, Conn., 2001). For a background to twentieth-century uses of the Arthurian theme see Stephanie L. Barczewski, *Myth and National Identity in Nineteenth-Century Britain* (Oxford, 2000).

Ford Madox Ford's novel-sequences have been collected as *The Fifth Queen* (Oxford, 1984) and *Parade's End* (London, 1992). His biography has been written by Max Saunders as *Ford Madox Ford: A Dual Life* (2 vols., Oxford, 1996). Saunders and Richard Stang have edited Ford's *Critical Essays* (Manchester, 2002). Critical studies of Ford include Robert Green, *Ford Madox Ford: Prose and Politcs* (Cambridge, 1981); H. Robert Huntley, *The Alien Protagonist of Ford Madox Ford* (Chapel Hill, NC, 1970); and, on *Parade's End*, Andrzej Gasiorek, 'The Politics of Cultural Nostalgia', *Literature and History* 3rd series, 11: 2 (2002), 52–77. *Agenda* 27: 4–28: 1 (1989–90), a special issue on Ford, includes David Trotter on 'Hueffer's Englishness' (148–55).

Among E. M. Forster's works, *Abinger Harvest and England's Pleasant Land* have been edited by Elizabeth Heine (London, 1996) and *Where Angels Fear to Tread* by Oliver Stallybrass (London, 2001). A classic critical study is Lionel Trilling's *E. M. Forster* (2nd edn, London, 1967), while the novelist's life has been written by P. N. Furbank (2 vols., London, 1977). On Forster and the East see Mohammad Shaheen, *E. M. Forster and the Politics of Imperialism* (London, 2004).

John Galsworthy's *The Forsyte Saga* is edited by Geoffrey Harvey (Oxford, 1995).

Rudyard Kipling's *Kim* has been edited by Edward W. Said (London, 1987) and, with a copious selection of critical material, by Zohreh T. Sullivan (New York, 2002). See also Sullivan's *Narratives of Empire* (Cambridge, 1993), and Parama Roy's *Indian Traffic* (Berkeley, 1998). An earlier selection of criticism is Andrew Rutherford, ed., *Kipling's Mind and Art* (Edinburgh, 1964).

D. H. Lawrence's *Women in Love* is edited by Charles L. Ross (Harmondsworth, 1986), and by David Farmer, Lindeth Vasey, and John Worthen (Cambridge, 1987); *A Selection from Phoenix* is edited by A. A. H. Inglis (Harmondsworth, 1971). Lawrence criticism includes Colin Clarke, *River of Dissolution* (London, 1967) and Scott Sanders, *D. H. Lawrence: The World of the Major Novels* (London, 1973).

George Orwell's *Complete Works* have been edited by Peter Davison (20 vols., London, 1998). Davison has also edited a selection entitled *Orwell's England* (London, 2001), but Orwell's *Collected Essays, Journalism and Letters*, ed. Sonia Orwell and Ian Angus (4 vols., London, 1968) remains a valuable source for his essays. The fullest Orwell biography is still Bernard Crick's *George Orwell* (London, 1980). Criticism on Orwell includes Christopher Hitchens, *Orwell's Victory* (London, 2002) and Alex Zwerdling, *Orwell and the Left* (New Haven, 1974).

H. G. Wells's *Tono-Bungay* has been edited by Bryan Cheyette (New York, 1997) and by Patrick Parrinder (London, 2005). Critical works include Michael Draper's *H. G. Wells* (Basingstoke, 1987).

Virginia Woolf's *Between the Acts* has been edited by Frank Kermode (Oxford, 1992) and by Gillian Beer and Stella McNichol (London, 1992); *Jacob's Room*, ed. Sue Roe (London, 1992); *The Voyage Out*, ed. Lorna Sage (Oxford, 1992); *The Years*, ed. Hermione Lee (Oxford, 1992). Selections of Woolf's essays include *Women and Writing*, ed. Michèle Barrett (London, 1979) and *The Common Reader*, Vol. ii, ed. Andrew McNeillie (London, 2003). Her unpublished essays 'Anon' and 'The Reader' have been edited by Brenda R. Silver in *Twentieth-Century Literature* 25: 3–4 (1979), 356–441. See also Woolf's *Diary*, ed. Anne Olivier Bell and Andrew McNeillie (5 vols., London, 1984). A recent biography is Hermione Lee, *Virginia Woolf* (London, 1966). For criticism see Margaret Homans, ed., *Virginia Woolf: A Collection of Critical Essays* (Englewood Cliffs, NJ, 1993), and Robin Majumdar and Allen McLaurin, eds., *Virginia Woolf: The Critical Heritage* (London, 1975); also Gillian Beer, 'Virginia Woolf and Prehistory' in *Arguing with the Past* (London, 1989), and Rachel Bowlby, *Virginia Woolf: Feminist Destinations* (Oxford, 1988).

CHAPTERS 13 AND 14 (ii) , 15, AND EPILOGUE: ENGLISH FICTION SINCE 1950

Modern discussions of English national identity may be said to begin with Tom Nairn, *The Break-Up of Britain* (2nd edn., London, 1981); see also Patrick Wright's study of the 'national past' in contemporary Britain, *On Living in an Old Country* (London, 1985), and Declan Kiberd, 'Reinventing England', *Key Words 2* (1999), 47–57, as well as the works by Ackroyd, Colls, Easthope, Kumar, and Scruton listed in the first section of this bibliography. An influential work of contemporary national historiography is Norman Davies, *The Isles* (London, 1999).

Recent studies of contemporary English fiction include the following: Steven Connor, *The English Novel in History 1950–1985* (London, 1996); Andrzej Gasiorek, *Post-War British Fiction* (London, 1995); Dominic Head, *The Cambridge Introduction to Modern British Fiction, 1950–2000* (Cambridge, 2002); Richard J. Lane, Rod Mengham and Philip Tew, eds., *Contemporary British Fiction* (London, 2003); Zachary Leader, ed., *On Modern British Fiction* (Oxford, 2002); Alan Sinfield, *Literature, Politics and Culture in Postwar Britain* (Oxford, 1989); D. J. Taylor, *After the War: The Novel and English Society since 1945* (London, 1993); Philip Tew, *The Contemporary British Novel* (London,

2004); Patricia Waugh, *The Harvest of the Sixties* (Oxford, 1995); and James Wood, 'England', in John Sturrock, ed., *The Oxford Guide to Contemporary Writing* (Oxford, 1996), 113–41. The final two volumes of the *Oxford English Literary History* cover the later twentieth century: Randall Stevenson, *The Last of England?* (Oxford, 2004), and Bruce King, *The Internationalization of English Literature* (Oxford, 2004). Volumes of essays specifically concerned with national identity are Ian A. Bell, ed., *Peripheral Visions* (Cardiff, 1995), and Tracey Hill and William Hughes, eds., *Contemporary Writing and National Identity* (Bath, 1995). Two earlier books are still well worth consulting: Bernard Bergonzi, *The Situation of the Novel* (London, 1970) and Malcolm Bradbury and David Palmer, eds., *The Contemporary English Novel* (London, 1979). A. S. Byatt's critical essays have been collected as *On Histories and Stories* (London, 2000).

Studies of multicultural English fiction include Ian Baucom, *Out of Place* (Princeton, 1999); Simon Gikandi, *Maps of Englishness* (New York, 1996); A. Robert Lee, ed., *Other Britain, Other British* (London, 1995); John McLeod, *Postcolonial London* (London, 2004); Susheila Nasta, *Home Truths* (Basingstoke, 2002); James Procter, *Dwelling Places* (Manchester, 2003); and Lars Ole Sauerberg, *Intercultural Voices in Contemporary British Literature* (Basingstoke, 2001). See also Caryl Phillips's anthology *Extravagant Strangers* (London, 1998), Salman Rushdie's essays collected in *Imaginary Homelands* (London, 1991), and Bryan Cheyette, *Constructions of 'the Jew' in English Literature and Society* (Cambridge, 1993). Israel Zangwill's *Children of the Ghetto* has been edited by Mari-Jane Rochelson (Detroit, 1998).

Jean Rhys's pre-war fiction has been collected as *The Early Novels* (London, 1984). Anthony Burgess's 'Malayan Trilogy' was reprinted as *The Long Day Wanes* (London, 1984), and Evelyn Waugh's 'final version' of his trilogy has appeared in a critical edition as *Sword of Honour*, ed. Angus Calder (London, 1999). See also Carole Angier, *Jean Rhys: Life and Work* (London, 1990), and Christopher Sykes, *Evelyn Waugh: A Biography* (2nd edn., Harmondsworth, 1977). Isabelle Joyau is the author of *Investigating Powell's 'A Dance to the Music of Time'* (Basingstoke, 1994).

Critical introductions to V. S. Naipaul's work include Landeg White, *V. S. Naipaul* (London, 1975) and, more recently, Bruce King, *V. S. Naipaul* (Basingstoke, 1993) and Fawzia Mustafa, *V. S. Naipaul* (Cambridge, 1995). See also Selwyn R. Cudjoe, *V. S. Naipaul: A Materialist Reading* (Amherst, Mass., 1988); Rob Nixon, *London Calling* (New York, 1992); and Timothy F. Weiss, *On the Margins* (Amherst, Mass., 1992).

Index